SIGNS OF LIFE
IN THE U.S.A.

Readings on Popular Culture for Writers

SIGNS OF LIFE IN THE U.S.A.

Readings on Popular Culture for Writers

SONIA MAASIK
University of California, Los Angeles

JACK SOLOMON
California State University, Northridge

Bedford Books *of* St. Martin's Press
Boston

For Bedford Books

Publisher: Charles H. Christensen
Associate Publisher/General Manager: Joan E. Feinberg
Managing Editor: Elizabeth M. Schaaf
Developmental Editor: Steven A. Scipione
Production Editor: John Amburg
Copyeditor: Dan Otis
Text Design: Anna Post George
Cover Design: Hannus Design
Cover Art: Tom Wesselmann, *Still Life #31,* 1963. Copyright © Tom Wesselmann/ VAGA, New York, 1993.

Library of Congress Catalog Card Number: 92–75309

Manufactured in the United States of America.

8   7   6   5   4
f   e   d   c   b   a

For information, write: St. Martin's Press, Inc.
175 Fifth Avenue, New York, NY 10010

Editorial Offices: Bedford Books *of* St. Martin's Press
29 Winchester Street, Boston, MA 02116

ISBN: 0–312–09020-X

Acknowledgments

McCrea Adams, "Advertising Characters: The Pantheon of Advertising." Reprinted by permission of the author.

(Acknowledgments and copyrights are continued at the back of the book on pages 715–720, which constitute an extension of the copyright page.)

CONTENTS

Preface for Instructors   *xv*

Introduction:
   POPULAR SIGNS: *Or, Everything You've Always Known About American Culture (But Nobody Asked)* *1*

PART ONE

IMAGES   *15*

1.   CONSUMING PASSIONS: *The Culture of American Consumption* *17*

LAURENCE SHAMES: *The More Factor*   *25*

"Frontier: opportunity: more. This has been the American trinity from the very start."

PETER GIBIAN: *The Art of Being Off-Center: Shopping Center Spaces and Spectacles* *32*

"Malls probably have the most to learn from the *amusement park*, 'where most people spend more than they intend.'"

ELIZABETH WILSON: *Oppositional Dress*   45

"Subcultural styles reinterpret conflicts of the wider society."

SCOTT POULSON-BRYANT: *B-Boys*   56

"Black boys—regardless of who's censoring whom or which white cop is bulleting down which black cousin or uncle or bro—reconstruct themselves, and ultimately reconstruct the culture around them."

STUART EWEN: *Hard Bodies*   60

"'Soft flesh,' once a standard phrase in the American erotic lexicon, is now . . . a sign of failure and sloth. The hard shell is now a sign of achievement, visible proof of success in the 'rat race.'"

JOAN KRON: *The Semiotics of Home Decor*   66

"We use our possessions in the same way we use language—the quintessential symbol—to *communicate* with one another."

ANDREW WERNICK: *Vehicles for Myth: The Shifting Image of the Modern Car*   78

"The production of cars as symbols is a special case of the way in which, since the industrial revolution of the late eighteenth century, all mass commodities have come to intersect with the world of meaning."

ROLAND BARTHES: *Toys*   95

"Current toys are made of a graceless material, the product of chemistry, not nature."

2. **BROUGHT TO YOU B(U)Y:** *The Signs of Advertising*   101

ROLAND MARCHAND: *The Parable of the Democracy of Goods*   109

"'Body Odor plays no favorites,' warned Lifebuoy Soap. No one, 'banker, baker, or society woman,' could count himself safe from B.O."

JANE CAPUTI: *IBM's Charlie Chaplin: A Case Study*   117

"Stuck with a multinational, cold, colossus, remote, and even a totalitarian 'Big Brother' public image, IBM took the plunge and set out to manufacture some warmer and more sympathetic associations for itself and its 'personal' computer."

PATRICIA J. WILLIAMS: *The Fiction of Truth in Advertising*   122

"Ours is not the first generation to fall prey to false needs; but ours is the first generation of admakers to realize the complete fulfillment of the consumerist vision through the fine-tuning of sheer hucksterism."

DIANE BARTHEL: *A Gentleman and a Consumer*   128

"The masculine role of always being in charge is a tough one."

GLORIA STEINEM: *Sex, Lies, and Advertising*   139

"If *Time* and *Newsweek* had to lavish praise on cars in general and credit General Motors in particular to get GM ads, there would be a scandal. . . . When women's magazines from *Seventeen* to *Lear's* praise beauty products in general and credit Revlon in particular to get ads, it's just business as usual."

Portfolio of Advertisements   *156*

3.   M(ORE) TV: *The Television and Video Revolution*   167

HOLLY BRUBACH: *Rock-and-Roll Vaudeville*   175

"The vast majority of videos look as if they had been directed by the same two or three people, all of whom you would guess to be seventeen-year-old boys."

LISA A. LEWIS: *Male-Address Video*   182

"The male-address videos activated textual signs of patriarchal discourse, reproducing coded images of the female body, and positioning girls and women as the objects of male voyeurism."

BELL HOOKS: *Madonna: Plantation Mistress or Soul Sister?*   190

"If Madonna had to depend on masses of black women to maintain her status as cultural icon she would have been dethroned some time ago."

MINABERE IBELEMA: *Identity Crisis: The African Connection in African American Sitcom Characters*   198

"'If you think I'm gonna change the sign from Sanford and Son to Sanford and Kalunda, you're crazy.'"

JOSH OZERSKY: *TV's Anti-Families: Married . . . with Malaise*   209

"TV has absorbed the American family's increasing sense of defeat and estrangement and presented it as an ironic in-joke."

SUSAN FALUDI: *Teen Angels and Tart-Tongued Witches* 219

"Women's disappearance from prime-time television in the late eighties repeats a programming pattern from the last backlash when, in the late fifties and early sixties, single dads ruled the TV roosts and female characters were suddenly erased from the set."

WALTER KIRN: *Twentysomethings* 229

"Resigning one's self to living off the table scraps of the American century is what twentystuff culture is all about."

4. **THE HOLLYWOOD SIGN: *The Semiotics of American Film* 233**

ROBERT B. RAY: *The Thematic Paradigm* 241

"To the outlaw hero's insistence on private standards of right and wrong, the official hero offered the admonition, 'You cannot take the law into your own hands.'"

LINDA SEGER: *Creating the Myth* 250

"Whatever our culture, there are universal stories that form the basis for all our particular stories. . . . Many of the most successful films are based on these universal stories."

UMBERTO ECO: Casablanca, *or, the Clichés Are Having a Ball* 260

"Aesthetically speaking (or by any strict critical standards) *Casablanca* is a very mediocre film."

DIANE RAYMOND: *Not as Tough as It Looks* 264

"If one can truly achieve 'motherhood without stretch marks,' then there is nothing that women can do that men cannot."

TANIA MODLESKI: *Dead White Male Heterosexual Poets Society* 278

"The film lyricizes life in the closet."

MICHAEL PARENTI: *Class and Virtue* 283

"The entertainment media present working people not only as unlettered and uncouth but also as less desirable and less moral than other people."

SHELBY STEELE: *Malcolm X* 287

"How can a new generation of blacks—after pervasive civil rights legislation, Great Society programs, school busing, open housing, and

more than two decades of affirmative action—be drawn to a figure of
such seething racial alienation?"

VALERIE BOYD: *The Word on* Malcolm X   *296*

"What *Birth of a Nation* was to Southerners or *The Godfather* was to
Italian-Americans, *Malcolm X* will be to African-Americans—a defining
element of our culture."

5. LARGER THAN LIFE: *The Mythic Characters of American
Culture*   *301*

GARY ENGLE: *What Makes Superman So Damned American?*   *309*

"It is impossible to imagine Superman being as popular as he is and
speaking as deeply to the American character were he not an immigrant
and an orphan."

PETER RAINER: *Antihero Worship*   *318*

"Is it a coincidence that Superman died the same week the movie
Malcolm X opened?"

ANDY MEDHURST: *Batman, Deviance, and Camp*   *323*

"If I want Batman to be gay, then, for me, he is."

GEORGE H. LEWIS: *From Common Dullness to Fleeting Wonder:
The Manipulation of Cultural Meaning in the Teenage Mutant Ninja
Turtles Saga*   *340*

"This uniquely American wrinkle on the superhero, the smoothly
functioning team, is reflective of our faith in bureaucratic models—like
a football team or a military unit, we win when our plugged-in
specialist selves each play their part."

EMILY PRAGER: *Our Barbies, Ourselves*   *353*

"I used to look at Barbie and wonder, What's wrong with this picture?"

WANDA COLEMAN: *Say It Ain't Cool, Joe*   *356*

"At root, old Joe's shtick is plain-and-simple racist."

McCREA ADAMS: *Advertising Characters: The Pantheon of
Consumerism*   *359*

"How much difference is there really between the two Ronalds,
McDonald and Reagan?"

GERARD JONES, RON RANDALL, AND RANDY ELLIOTT:
Doomed by Deconstructo   *370*

"There is no meaning. In art. In life. In history. In heroes. We can only know what our minds choose to let us know."

PART TWO

ISSUES   *375*

6.   SPEAK NO EVIL: *The Politics of Free Speech*   *377*

NAT HENTOFF: *"Speech Codes" on the Campus and Problems of Free Speech*   *385*

"Universities cannot censor or suppress speech, no matter how obnoxious in content, without violating their justification for existence."

THOMAS C. GREY: *Responding to Abusive Speech on Campus: A Model Statute*   *392*

"Prohibited harassment includes discriminatory intimidation by threats of violence, and also includes personal vilification of students on the basis of their sex, race, color, handicap, religion, sexual orientation, or national and ethnic origin."

CORNEL WEST: *Diverse New World*   *400*

"We need to see history as in part the cross-fertilization of a variety of different cultures, usually under conditions of hierarchy."

TODD GITLIN: *On the Virtues of a Loose Canon*   *405*

"Academic conservatives who defend a canon . . . sometimes sound as if American universities were fully and finally canonized until the barbarians showed up to smash up the pantheon . . . the academic left has degenerated into a loose aggregation of margins—often cannibalistic, romancing the varieties of otherness, speaking in tongues."

RICHARD GOLDSTEIN: *Hate Speech, Free Speech, and the Unspoken*   *411*

"How can the law possibly regulate something as fundamentally subjective as symbolic expression? And yet, given the power of symbols to incite fear and loathing, not to mention violence, how can it not?"

BARBARA EHRENREICH: *Ice-T: Is the Issue Creative Freedom?*   *418*

"Just, please, don't dignify Ice-T's contribution with the word 'sedition.'"

ELAINE LAFFERTY AND TAMMY BRUCE: *Suddenly, They Hear the Words*   *422*

"If you want to criticize Ice-T for 'Cop Killer,' fine. But understand that women have been the targets of this kind of lyrical assault for years."

JAMES CRAWFORD: *Hold Your Tongue: The Question of Linguistic Self-Determination*   *424*

"Rights that individuals would otherwise enjoy, including free access to government, must not be limited on account of language ability."

GLORIA ANZALDÚA: *How to Tame a Wild Tongue*   *431*

"If you want to really hurt me, talk badly about my language."

7. A GATHERING OF TRIBES: *Multicultural Semiotics*   *441*

MICHAEL OMI: *In Living Color: Race and American Culture*   *449*

"Popular culture has been an important realm within which racial ideologies have been created, reproduced, and sustained."

SAM FULWOOD III: *The Rage of the Black Middle Class*   *462*

"I straddle two worlds and consider neither home."

RICHARD MAJORS: *Cool Pose: The Proud Signature of Black Survival*   *471*

"Being cool, illustrated in its various poses and postures, becomes a very powerful and necessary tool in the black man's constant fight for his soul."

DORINNE K. KONDO: *On Being a Conceptual Anomaly*   *477*

"How could someone who *looked* Japanese not *be* Japanese?"

FAN SHEN: *The Classroom and the Wider Culture: Identity as a Key to Learning English Composition*   *485*

"Learning the rules of English composition is, to a certain extent, learning the values of Anglo-American society."

LESLIE MARMON SILKO: *Language and Literature from a Pueblo Indian Perspective* *495*

"The stories are always bringing us together, keeping this whole together, keeping this family together, keeping this clan together."

ADA MARÍA ISASI-DIAZ: *Hispanic in America: Starting Points* *503*

"It is only within our own culture that Hispanics can acquire a sense of belonging, of security, of dignity, and of participation."

STUDS TERKEL: *Speaking About Race* *508*

"Show me a white community and a black community and I'll show you an adjoining community between both."

8. STREET SIGNS: *Gang Culture in the U.S.A.* *527*

CARL ROGERS: *Children in Gangs* *535*

"The average age of youth gang members continues to decline."

LÉON BING: *Faro* *540*

"'If you die, you die.'"

ANNE CAMPBELL: *The Praised and the Damned* *544*

"Despite the volumes written on male gang members, however, little is actually known about the girls."

SONIA MAASIK AND JACK SOLOMON: *Signs of the Street: A Conversation* *560*

"The point is, everybody just wants respect, okay? Sometimes being in the gangs gets you that respect or being a tagger gets you that respect from other taggers. You know, it depends on where you're coming from."

JAMES DIEGO VIGIL: *Gang Styles: Cholo Dress and Body Adornment, Speech, Demeanor, Partying, and Car Culture* *570*

"Gangs, like many youth groups, are notorious for encouraging their members to dress, talk, and act in a certain way to show that they belong and identify with peers."

SETH MYDANS: *Not Just the Inner City: Well-to-Do Join Gangs* 587

"'If you want to be able to walk the mall, you have to know you've got your boys behind you.'"

TEEN ANGELS MAGAZINE: *Summer Time* 592

9. YOU'VE COME A LONG WAY, MAYBE: *Gender Codes in American Culture* 595

HOLLY DEVOR: *Gender Role Behaviors and Attitudes* 603

"Persons who perform the activities considered appropriate for another gender will be expected to perform them poorly; if they succeed adequately, or even well, at their endeavors, they may be rewarded with ridicule or scorn for blurring the gender dividing line."

PETER LYMAN: *The Fraternal Bond as a Joking Relationship* 609

"We have a sense of crudeness you don't have. That's a cultural aspect of the difference between girls and guys."

ROBERT BLY: *Men's Initiation Rites* 617

"American men in general cannot achieve separation from the father because they have not achieved bonding with the father."

ROBIN TOLMACH LAKOFF: *Women's Language* 624

"Some form of women's language exists in every culture that has been investigated."

DEBORAH TANNEN: *Wears Jump Suit. Sensible Shoes. Uses Husband's Last Name.* 629

"Some days you just want to get dressed and go about your business. But if you're a woman, you can't, because there is no unmarked woman."

ELIZABETH CHISERI-STRATER: *Anna* 635

"For women, gaining access to the dominant discourse is often problematic, particularly in public settings."

RICHARD K. HERRELL: *The Symbolic Strategies of Chicago's Gay and Lesbian Pride Day Parade* 643

"'Ethnicity' has become a model for gays and lesbians."

10. **JOURNALS OF THE PLAGUE YEARS:** *The Social Mythology of AIDS*   *653*

PAUL MONETTE: *Borrowed Time: An AIDS Memoir*   *661*

"The world around me is defined now by its ending and its closures— the date on the grave that follows the hyphen."

SUSAN SONTAG: *AIDS and Its Metaphors*   *668*

"AIDS, like cancer, does not allow romanticizing or sentimentalizing, perhaps because its association with death is too powerful."

MICHAEL D. QUAM: *Stigma*   *679*

"The ascription of stigma to any condition arises out of the symbol system within a culture, and . . . follows a logic within which relationships are more emotional than rational."

KATE SCANNELL: *Skills and Pills*   *688*

"I have officially prescribed sunshine, a trip to Macy's, and massages for some patients who had no need for my traditional skills and pills."

EVELYNN HAMMONDS: *Race, Sex, AIDS: The Construction of "Other"*   *692*

"In this culture, how we think about disease determines who lives and who dies."

RANDY SHILTS: *AIDSpeak Spoken Here*   *703*

"The linguistic roots of AIDSpeak sprouted not so much from the truth as from what was politically facile and psychologically reassuring."

DOUGLAS CRIMP AND ADAM ROLSTON: *The Semiotics of AIDS Activism*   *708*

"SILENCE = DEATH declares that silence about the oppression and annihilation of gay people, *then and now,* must be broken as a matter of our survival."

Glossary   *711*

Index of Authors and Titles   *721*

PREFACE FOR INSTRUCTORS

Thirty years ago, Marshall McLuhan announced the beginning of a new era in the history of Western communication. The printing press, he argued in his classic study *The Gutenberg Galaxy* (1962), was yielding to a new set of media—to radio, television, and film—and a new consciousness was emerging in response to the change. The years that have passed since the publication of McLuhan's book have borne out many of his predictions, especially concerning the growth of video technologies. Today, ours is indeed a culture of the electronic media, centered on the visual image rather than the printed word, and the shape of our knowledge and experience has shifted accordingly.

This transformation from a text-centered to an image-centered culture presents a certain challenge to writing teachers. How can such a textually based enterprise as writing instruction respond to a video-driven world? How are reading and writing related to seeing and hearing? Can the habits of critical thinking that are so central to the analytical tasks of academic writing be adapted to McLuhan's brave new world?

We have written *Signs of Life in the U.S.A.* because we believe not only that such bridges can be built but that building them represents our best hope for training a new generation of students in critical thinking and writing. Thus, while the goal of our text remains the traditional one of helping students become strong writers of argument and analysis, our method departs from convention by using printed texts to guide students in the analysis and interpretation of an unwritten world: The world of

American popular culture, wherein images, often electronically conveyed, can be more important than words.

Readings on American Popular Culture

The 75 readings in this book address a broad cross-section of contemporary American popular culture. We have chosen popular culture as our field because we believe that students think and write best when they are in command of their subject matter. Too often, academic ways of thinking, reasoning, arguing, and even speaking and writing seem like a foreign language for students, especially those in their first year. As a result, students may find it difficult to develop ideas, risking either writer's block or the adoption of an awkward, pedantic style that hinders their own creativity and insights. Unfortunately, both within and outside academia, students' attempts to grapple with this foreign language are sometimes interpreted as proof of their apparent "illiteracy."

But we believe that today's students are not illiterate at all; they simply have a different kind of literacy, one that exists outside the boundaries of traditional academic knowledge. We also believe that there need not be a split between academic and "real world" knowledge in the first place; rather, the two should inform each other, with the most exciting inquiry combining the riches of everyday life with the discipline and depth of academic study. *Signs of Life in the U.S.A.* is thus designed to let students take advantage of their expertise in the culture around them, allowing them to build on their strengths as they sharpen their ability to write cogent analyses, insightful interpretations, and persuasive arguments. We have included, for example, materials ranging from analyses of shopping mall designs to interpretations of the film *Malcolm X,* from explorations of women's language to advertisements for jeans and backpacks. This is not to say that we assume students are all consumers of popular culture in the same way. Indeed, the book is structured to encourage students to bring to their writing class a variety of backgrounds, interests, and experiences, a variety that will generate lively class discussion and create a community of writers.

The Book's Organization

Reflecting the increasing academic interest in cultural studies, we've assumed an inclusive definition of popular culture. This definition can be seen in the book's organization, for it is divided into two broad sections—Images and Issues—to highlight the essential cultural connection between the things we do and the things we believe. The five chapters in the Images section focus on popular cultural behavior, especially as it is stimulated and mediated by the images projected through the objects we consume, the ads that sell us those objects, the entertainments we enjoy, and the heroes and popular characters we admire and emulate. The five Issues chapters may seem a bit more sobering, but they are inextricably linked to the text's first half. For in addressing the First Amendment controversy, multiculturalism, gangs, gender, and AIDS, they show that behind every image there is an issue, an ideology and belief system that shapes our behavior.

The Critical Method: Semiotics

Signs of Life departs from some textbook conventions in that it makes explicit an interpretive approach, semiotics, that can guide students' analyses of popular culture. We've made this approach explicit because it has struck us that while students enjoy assignments that ask them to look at popular cultural phenomena, they often have trouble distinguishing between an argued interpretive analysis and simple expression of an opinion. Some textbooks, for example, suggest assignments that involve analyzing a TV program or film, but they don't always tell a student how to do that. The semiotic method provides that guidance.

At the same time, semiotics reveals that there's no such thing as a pure, ideologically neutral analysis, even in freshman composition. Anthologies typically present analysis as a "pure" category: They present readings that students are asked to analyze, but articulate no conceptual framework and neither explore nor define theoretical assumptions and ideological positions. Being self-conscious about one's point of view, however, is an essential part of academic writing, and we can think of no better place for students to learn that lesson than in a writing class.

We've found through experience that a semiotic approach is especially well suited to this purpose. As a conceptual framework, semiotics teaches students to formulate cogent, well-supported interpretations. It emphasizes the examination of assumptions and how language shapes our apprehension of the world. Because it focuses on *how beliefs are formulated* within a social and political context (rather than just judging or evaluating those beliefs), it's ideal for discussing sensitive or politically charged issues. As an approach used in literature, media, anthropology, sociology, law, and business, to name only a few fields, semiotics has a cross-disciplinary appeal that makes it ideal for a writing class of students from a variety of majors and disciplines. We recognize that semiotics has a reputation for being highly technical or theoretical; rest assured that *Signs of Life* does not require students or instructors to have a technical knowledge of semiotics. In fact, we've provided clear and accessible introductions that explain what students need to know.

We also recognize that adopting a theoretical approach may be new to some instructors, so we've designed the book to allow instructors to be as semiotic with their students as they wish. The book does not obligate instructors or students to spend a lot of time with semiotics— although we do hope you'll find the approach intriguing and provocative.

The choice of semiotics is also based on classroom experience. In adopting the approach for classes ranging from freshmen to graduate students, we've found that students respond quickly and positively to this approach. Students have told us how much they appreciate learning something entirely new in our classes, and what they learn extends beyond the topics covered to a new way of looking at the world. But we haven't relied just on our own experience; a colleague, Patrick McCord, tested most of the book with his freshman writing students at California State University, Northridge, and found that his students were impressed not only with how semiotics opened their eyes but with the respect of their own activities that the approach conveyed.

The Editorial Apparatus

With its emphasis on popular culture, *Signs of Life* should generate lively class discussion and inspire many kinds of writing and thinking activities. The general introduction provides an overall framework for the book, acquainting students with the semiotic method they can use to interpret the topics raised in each chapter. The chapters start off with a frontispiece, a provocative visual image related to the chapter's topic, and an introduction, which suggests ways to "read" the topic, presents model interpretations, and links the issues raised by the reading selections. Every chapter introduction contains two types of boxed questions designed to stimulate student thinking on the topic. The Exploring the Signs questions invite students to explore an issue in a journal entry or other prewriting activity, whereas Discussing the Signs questions trigger class activities such as debates, discussions, or small-group work. Each reading selection is followed by two sorts of assignments. The Reading the Text questions help students comprehend the selections, asking them to identify important concepts and arguments, explain key terms, and relate main ideas to each other and to the evidence presented. The Reading the Signs questions are writing and activity prompts designed to produce clear analytical thinking and strong persuasive writing; they often make connections among reading selections from different chapters. Most assignments call for analytic essays, while some ask for journal responses, in-class debates, group work, or other creative activities. We've also added a Glossary of semiotic terms to serve as a ready reference for key terms and concepts used in the chapter introductions.

Finally, the *Instructor's Manual* provides suggestions for organizing your syllabus, encouraging student response to the readings, and using popular culture and semiotics in the writing class.

Acknowledgments

Books can't be made without publishers, but our gratitude to Bedford Books goes beyond the fundamental appreciation that authors feel for those who have enabled their work to see print. For Bedford doesn't simply publish books: It helps make them. From Chuck Christensen and Joan Feinberg, who shared our initial vision and involved themselves in the development of the text from start to finish, to Steve Scipione, our editor, whose expertise in textbook construction was absolutely indispensable to our work, the people at Bedford were part of our entire project. Elizabeth Schaaf, as managing editor, and John Amburg, Dan Otis, Jonathan Burns, Jane Betz, Laura McCready, Beth Chapman, Kim Chabot, and Martha Friedman completed our team at Bedford, contributing not only their editorial skills but their own creative vision of how the text would actually look in the end.

We would like to thank the reviewers of our manuscript—Mary Louise Bardas, University of Texas at El Paso; Bruce Beiderwell, University of California, Los Angeles; Kathleen Shine Cain, Merrimack College; Russel Durst, University of Cincinnati; and Irwin Weiser, Purdue University—whose constructive suggestions helped us shape our book to the needs of our readers.

Friends and colleagues who assisted us with suggestions and the occasional loan of a book include Teresa Gonzalez, Janette Lewis, Bonnie Lisle, Dennis Lynch, Susan Popkin, and Randy Woodland. We would like especially to thank Principal Henry Castillo and Susan Weiner of the West Valley Occupational Center for letting us speak with their students. Their cooperation added depth to our chapter on gangs that it would otherwise have lacked.

Finally, we would like to thank Patrick McCord, a teaching assistant at California State University, Northridge, for his enthusiastic field testing of an early draft of the manuscript in his composition class, and Kellie Koch Rymes, an undergraduate at CSUN, who provided both research assistance and advice on multicultural approaches.

SIGNS OF LIFE IN THE U.S.A.

Readings on Popular Culture for Writers

POPULAR SIGNS

*Or, Everything You've Always Known About
American Culture (But Nobody Asked)*

Every year it happens again. As December fades coldly into January and the New Year beyond, suddenly everything seems to become super-charged. Super sweepstakes invite us to peer into specially marked cans and bottles to find super prizes. Super sales brochures announce super savings on super products, which you can find in super shopping centers. Super travel agencies offer super rates for super holidays, while super-markets offer super snacks for super parties. What's all the super fuss about? Unless you've spent the last quarter century spelunking in Manchuria, it's impossible for you not to know the answer. Why, of course, it's Superbowl Sunday.

The Superbowl: It's more than just a football game. It's an Event, a ritual, a national celebration, and show-time for such corporate high rollers as Nike, Inc., for whom the game is but a stage to present the latest chapter in the Air Jordan saga, and Apple Computer, which waited to introduce the Macintosh to a waiting world one Superbowl Sunday. And then, of course, there's always Budweiser and the Bud Bowl.

In short, the Superbowl has become a major part of American popular and commercial culture. But despite its important place in American life, it is unlikely that you would find yourself being asked to write about it in a typical college class. Nor, for that matter, would you expect to be writing about the latest U2 tour, nor, on a more serious note, about that brochure on preventing AIDS that you picked up at the student health center. Such things are ordinarily regarded as being outside the traditional

1

academic curriculum. But in this class, things are going to be different. For by choosing this book, your teacher has chosen to take a stand. And that stand is, quite simply, that America's popular culture—a field that includes everything from the Superbowl to the movies to the way we define and express our sexuality—is worth writing about. This is a book designed to show you how to do it, how to write about pop culture as you would write about any other academic subject.

We have prepared *Signs of Life in the U.S.A.* because we believe that you are already a sophisticated student of American culture. Think of all you already know. Just list all of the rock bands you can name. And all the various categories they fall into (Is techno-pop still on the horizon? How's the grunge scene doing? Where's hip-hop these days?). Face it, you're an expert. So isn't that a good place to start learning how to write college essays, with what you know already? We all write best when we can write from our strengths, and this book is intended to let you strut your stuff as you learn to write college essays.

Signs of Life in the U.S.A., then, is designed to let you tap into your knowledge of popular culture so that you may grow into a better writer about any subject. You can interpret the Superbowl, for example, in the same manner you would interpret, say, a short story, because the Superbowl too is a kind of *sign*. A sign is something, *anything,* that carries a meaning. A stop sign, for instance, means exactly what it says: "Stop when you approach this intersection," while carrying the implied meaning, "or risk getting a ticket." Words, too, are signs: You read them to figure out what they mean. You had to be trained to read such signs, but that training began so long ago that you may well take your ability to read for granted. All of your life you have been encountering, and interpreting, other sorts of signs that you were never taught to read. You know what they mean anyway. Take the way you wear your hair. When you get your hair cut, you are not simply removing hair: You are making a statement, sending a message about yourself. Think of the different messages you'd send to your friends and to your parents if you got a crew cut, a Lady Di bob, or a fade. Why was your hair short last year and long this year (or long last year and short this year)? Aren't you saying something with the scissors? In this way, you make your hairstyle into a sign that sends a message about your identity. You are surrounded by such signs. Just look at your classmates.

The world of signs, which includes everything from the Superbowl to haircuts, could be called a kind of text, the text of America's popular culture. We want you to think of *Signs of Life in the U.S.A.* as a window onto that text. What you read in the essays and introductions included in this book, in other words, should lead you to study and analyze the world around you for yourself. Let the readings guide you to your own interpretations, your own readings, of the text of America.

We have chosen ten "windows" that look upon America's cultural scene. In some cases, we have put some of the scenery directly into this book, as when we include actual ads in our chapter on advertising. In other cases, where it is impossible to get something directly into a textbook, such as a TV show or a movie, we have included essays that help you think about specific programs and films and assignments that invite you to go out and interpret a TV show or movie of your own choosing.

Each chapter contains an introduction designed to alert you to the kinds of signs you will find there, as well as tips on how to go about interpreting them. The readings that follow offer positions and interpretations of their own, as well as texts and contexts for your further analysis. Shelby Steele's provocative essay on Malcolm X, for example, argues that Malcolm X was an essentially *conservative* figure and that Spike Lee's film about him presents us with a myth rather than a man. To make your own judgment on the matter, you might want to read a biography of Malcolm X and compare it to the movie. Then you could write an essay stating your position. Will you agree or disagree with Steele? Only by looking closely into the matter will you be able to decide.

Two Books in One

We have divided *Signs of Life in the U.S.A.* into two broad sections embracing, on the one hand, some of the dominant "images" in American popular culture, and on the other, some of the most prominent "issues" of our times. The images section explores the visible signs of America's popular culture, the icons of our media-dominated society. "Consuming Passions" is the lead chapter in this section because America is a consumer culture, so the environment within which the galaxy of popular signs functions will, more often than not, be a consumerist one (as you can see in the commercialization of the Superbowl). Next, "Brought to You B(u)y" explores the related world of advertising, for advertising provides the grease that lubricates the engine of America's consumer culture. Because television and the movies are the source of many of our most significant cultural images and icons, we include a chapter on each in this section. And we have also included a chapter on American pop culture "characters"—from comic book superheroes to Elvis—that America consumes along with all the other products of our consumer culture. In every chapter we have chosen topics that date from the last few years and that relate to topics in the other chapters through the connecting links of American consumption.

The second section of the book focuses on issues of contemporary importance, social and political issues that you may already be coping with: i.e., First Amendment rights, multiculturalism, street gangs, the politics of gender, and the AIDS epidemic. These chapters ask you to explore national issues and controversies that affect the quality of American life, both today and into the future. While our selections are not intended to be inclusive, we have tried to provide readings and topics on some of the most pressing of contemporary issues and controversies.

The twofold structure of *Signs of Life in the U.S.A.* is intended to provide two related but tonally different sets of readings and exercises. You may find that interpreting popular images can be amusing as well as informative, while looking at certain issues provokes profound soul-searching as you seek to unmask the implications of your beliefs and values. Throughout the book, however, you will find readings and assignments that invite you to go out and select your own "texts" for analysis (a video, an advertisement, a film, a fashion fad, a political opinion, and so on). Here's where your own experience is of particular value, for often you're a great deal more adept at choosing and decoding the signs around you than your teachers or parents are, not only because you are more familiar with popular signs but because you are also more familiar with their background, with the particular popular cultural *system* or environment to which they belong.

The Semiotic Method

To interpret and write effectively about the signs of popular culture, you need a method, and it is part of the purpose of this book to introduce such a method to you. Without a methodology for interpreting signs, writing about them could become little more than producing descriptive reviews or opinion pieces. There is nothing wrong with writing descriptions and opinions, but one of your tasks in your writing class is to learn how to write academic essays, that is, analytical essays that are well supported by evidence. The method we are drawing upon in this book—a method that is known as "semiotics"—is especially designed for the analysis of popular culture. Whether or not you're familiar with this word, you are already practicing sophisticated semiotic analyses every day of your life. Reading this page is an act of semiotic decoding (words and even letters are signs that must be interpreted), but so is figuring out just what your classmate *means* by wearing a particular shirt or dress. For a semiotician (one who practices semiotic analysis), a shirt, a haircut, a television image, anything at all, can be taken as a sign, as a message to be decoded and analyzed to discover its meaning. Every cultural activity for the semiotician leaves a trace of meaning, a kind of blip on the semiotic Richter scale, that remains for us to read, just as a geologist "reads" the earth for signs of earthquakes, volcanoes, and other geological phenomena.

|||||||||||||||||||||||||||||||||||||||||||||||||||||||||||||||||||||||||||||||||||||||||||||||||||||||||||||||||||||||||||||||||||||||||||||||||||||||||

Exploring the Signs of American Life

Throughout this text, you'll read essays that connect the signs of American life to consumer and commercial culture. In your journal, brainstorm a list of events and holidays, such as the Superbowl, Thanksgiving, and Christmas, that are central to American life, along with the signs and symbols associated with them (e.g., turkeys, Santa Claus). Then reflect on the significance of your list. How are the signs and symbols used as marketing tools? How does that affect your attitude toward the various events and holidays? Can you imagine what the events and holidays would be like if they were more abstract, without the signs and symbols?

Many who hear the word "semiotics" for the first time assume that it is the name of a new, and forbidding, subject. But in truth, the study of signs is neither very new nor forbidding. Its modern form took shape in the late nineteenth and early twentieth century through the writings and lectures of two men. Charles Sanders Peirce (1839–1914) was an American philosopher and physicist who first coined the word "semiotics," while Ferdinand de Saussure (1857–1913) was a Swiss linguist whose lectures became the foundation for what *he* called "semiology." Without knowing of each other's work, Peirce and Saussure established the fundamental principles that modern semioticians or semiologists—the terms are essentially interchangeable—have developed into the contemporary study of semiotics.

The application of semiotics to the interpretation of popular culture was pioneered in the 1950s by the French semiologist Roland Barthes (1915–1980) in a book entitled *Mythologies.* The basic principles of semiotics had already been explored by linguists and anthropologists, but Barthes took the matter to the heart of his own contemporary France, analyzing the cultural significance of everything from professional wrestling to striptease, from toys to plastics.

It was Barthes, too, who established the political dimensions of semiotic analysis. In our society (especially in the aftermath of the Watergate scandal), "politics" has become something of a dirty word, and to "politicize" something seems somehow to contaminate it. But Barthes's point—and the point of semiotics in general—is that all social behavior is political in the sense that it reflects some kind of personal or group interest. Such interests are encoded in what are called "ideologies," which are essentially world views that express the values and opinions of those who hold them. Politics, then, is just another name for the clash of ideologies that takes place in any complex society where the interests of all those who belong to it are constantly in competition with each other.

But often the ideological interests that guide our social behavior remain concealed behind images that don't look political at all. Consider, for example, the depiction of the "typical" American family in the classic TV sitcoms of the fifties and sixties, particularly all those images of happy, docile housewives. To most contemporary viewers, those images looked "normal" or natural at the time that they were first broadcast—the way families and women were supposed to be. The shows didn't seem at all ideological. To the contrary, they seemed a retreat from political rancor to domestic harmony. But to a feminist semiotician, the old sitcoms were in fact highly political, because the happy housewives they presented were really images designed to *convince* women that their place is in the home, not in the workplace competing with men. Such images—or signs—did not reflect reality; they reflected, rather, the interests of a patriarchal, male-centered society. If you think not, then ask yourself why there were shows called *Father Knows Best, Bachelor Father,* and *My Three Sons,* but no *My Three Daughters?* And why did few of the women in the shows have jobs or ever seem to leave the house? Of course, there was always *I Love Lucy,* but wasn't Lucy the screwball character that her husband Ricky had to rescue from one crisis after another?

These are the kinds of questions that semiotics invites us to ask. They may be put more generally. When analyzing any popular cultural phenomenon, always ask yourself questions like these: *Why does this thing look the way it does? Why are they saying this? Why am I doing this? What are they really saying? What am I really doing?* In short, take nothing for granted when analyzing any image or activity.

Take, for instance, the reason you may have joined a health club (or decided not to). Did you happen to respond to a photo ad that showed you a gorgeous girl or guy (with a nice-looking guy or girl in the background)? On the surface of the ad, you simply see an image showing—or denoting—a patron of the club. You may think: "I want to look like that." But there's probably another dimension to the ad's appeal. The ad may *show* you someone with a nice body, but what it is *suggesting*—or connoting—is that this club is a good place to pick up a hot date. That's why there's that other figure in the background. That's supposed to be *you.* The one in the foreground is the sort of person you're being promised you'll find at the club. The ad doesn't say this, of course, but that's what it wants you to think because that's a more effective way to get you to join. Suggestion, or connotation, is a much more powerful stimulant than denotation, but it is often deliberately masked in the signs you are presented with every day. Semiotics, one might say, reveals the denotative smokescreens around you.

Health club membership drives, you may be thinking, aren't especially political (though actually they are when you think of the kinds of bodies that they are telling you are desirable to have), but the powerful effect of a concealed suggestion is used all the time in actual political campaigns. The now infamous "Willie Horton" episode during the 1988 presidential campaign provides a classic instance. What happened was this: Some Republican supporters of George Bush's candidacy ran a series of TV ads featuring the photographic image of one Willie Horton, a convicted rapist from Massachusetts who murdered someone while on parole. On the surface, the ads simply showed, or denoted, this fact. But what they connoted was racial hatred and fear (Willie Horton is black), and they were very effective in prompting white voters to mistrust Massachusetts governor Michael Dukakis and to vote instead for George Bush.

Signs, in short, often conceal some interest or other, whether political, or commercial, or whatever. And the proliferation of signs and images in an era of electronic technology has simply made it all the more important that we learn to decode the interests behind them.

Semiotics, accordingly, is not just about signs and symbols: It is equally about ideology and power. This makes semiotics sound rather serious, and often the seriousness of a semiotic analysis is quite real. But reading the text of modern life can also be fun, for it is a text that is at once popular and accessible, a "book" that is intimately in touch with the pulse of American life. As such, it is constantly changing. The same sign can change meaning if something else comes along to change the environment in which it originally appeared. Take the way shoelaces have changed their meaning in recent years.

Image . . . Is Everything, or, the Semiotics of Shoelaces

A few years ago (fashion systems move quickly), American high school students began wearing hightop basketball sneakers (preferably Nike or Reebok) with the laces *unlaced*. At the time, our students explained why they did this: "Because it's more convenient," they told us, "keeping them unlaced makes it easier to put them on and take them off." A functional answer. One that appears "natural" and therefore politically neutral. But then, if mere function were behind it all, why were kids lacing their sneakers the year before and why are they lacing them again now? Or why weren't they wearing loafers? To answer such questions, we first must look at the *difference* between a laced and an unlaced sneaker.

In itself, the difference between lacing and unlacing a sneaker means nothing. But consider it as part of the teen fashion system of the late 1980s. That is, compare it to the other accessories and ways of wearing those accessories that were in fashion then among American teens. Consider baseball caps. If you were to wear one, would you put it on bill forward or bill backward? Or take overalls. Would you wear them with the straps hanging or buckled? Now, how would you interpret a young man wearing a baseball cap bill forward, with buckled overalls and laced Keds hightops? How would he differ from one wearing his cap backward, dangling both straps of his overalls, and wearing unlaced Nike Air Jordans? The differences are everything here, for in the last few years, an observer of fashion example number one who knew the code would interpret him as an unfashionable hick, while example number two would have registered as dressing in the height of teen fashion.

But why was it fashionable to wear one's baseball cap backward, shoelaces untied, and overall straps unbuckled? To answer these questions, we must take our fashion statement and associate it with related popular trends from the period, including music, television, and the movies. In short, we have to look at the whole spectrum of pop culture to see what was going on and whether any of it relates to our fashion sign.

So, what music was hot when unlaced Nikes came into fashion? Heavy metal? Yes, but metal fans wore motorcycle boots with chains on them. Black leather. Stuff like that. Meanwhile, the post-punk scene was getting into Doc Martens. So what else was important at the time? Rap, of course. "Straight outta Compton." And what did rap fans wear at the time? Baseball caps worn bill backward, unlaced hightops (preferably Nikes and Reeboks), and flapping overalls (or, perhaps, baggy trousers). Now, who else dressed this way? Who, in fact, started it in the first place?

If you answered that question "black street gangs and rap stars," you are on to the system through which we may interpret such things as shoelaces and baseball caps. In semiotic terms, a system is a kind of field of related things, and their meaning comes from how they relate to each other. Unlaced shoelaces may mean nothing when taken by themselves, for example, but when viewed within the system of teen fashion in the late eighties, a system that included the growing popularity of the imagery of the urban street gang, they may mean a lot, projecting an image that anyone who knew the system could quickly pick up. To those in the know, the system even had a name: hip-hop.

At this point in our analysis (which we have slowed down, so to speak, to show how it happens), we can ask some simple questions whose answers may be quite complex. Why, for example, was it so important to wear Nikes or Reeboks? Why did some kids literally kill for a certain brand of shoe? What images did these brand lines project that Keds did not? And why, finally, did a fashion sign once associated with street gangs, and thus with a racial and economic underclass, become such a popular fashion sign among middle- and upper-class kids?

To answer such questions, you must first make a distinction between what a fashion sign might mean to you personally and what it signifies to society at large. You may have some very private reasons for dressing as you do, for example, and many of the signs in your life may have deeply *personal* meanings (your favorite blue jeans, for instance, may remind you of your first date). But in a cultural interpretation, you want to focus on the *social* meaning of things, what they mean to others. To discover the social dimensions of the signs in your life, you will want to explore as much of the American cultural spectrum as you can. In the case of unlaced sneakers, you may want to look at what was popular at the time in teen television programming. Do you remember, for example, *The Fresh Prince of Bel Air,* a sitcom featuring a kid from Compton (a code word for the black ghetto) who moves to Bel Air (code for extreme white affluence)? Or *In Living Color,* a teen-audience variety show that featured, among other regulars, Homey the Clown, a white-middle-class-bashing street parody of Bozo the Clown (that icon of the lily-white suburban sixties) whose appeal crossed over (like the Fresh Prince) from Compton to Bel Air? Such popular shows belonged to the same system of teen fashion that shoes and caps belonged to and can help you to decode what was going on among America's teens at the time they appeared.

Rather than pursuing this interpretation, we will stop to let you draw your own conclusions. Try to recall what you yourself thought. Did you reverse your cap because everyone else was doing it, or because you wanted to identify with your favorite rapper? Did you feel that your way of dressing conveyed a political message, or were you just being fashionable? If fashion *was* all there was to it, ask yourself why the styles of an urban underclass became fashionable to suburban kids?

In practice, the interpretational process we are inviting you to begin may occur in the blink of an eye, as you quickly size up the meaning of the innumerable signs that present themselves to you in an average day. Some signs may even look rather "obvious" to you, but that's because you've already made the interpretation. Ordinarily, however, our interpretations stop at the threshold of the more probing questions—just as we have paused here—at the questions that ask not only whether something is fashionable but what it means that the thing is fashionable in the first place. That's what cultural semiotics is all about: going beyond what a sign *is* to explain what it *means.*

The Classroom Connection

That is also what analytic writing is about: going beyond the surface of a text or issue toward an interpretation. The skills you already have as an interpreter of the signs around you—of images, objects, and forms of behavior—are the same skills that you develop as a writer of critical essays that present a point of view and an argument to defend it. There is a difference, that is, between asserting an opinion and presenting evidence in a carefully constructed argument. All of us can make our opinions known, but analytic writing requires the marshaling of supporting evidence. A lawyer doesn't simply assert a client's innocence: Evidence is required. Similarly, when we conducted our analysis of unlaced Nikes, we brought together supporting evidence from the teen fashion system of the late 1980s to refute the claim that function alone was behind it all. By learning to write semiotic analyses of our culture, by searching for supporting evidence to underpin your interpretive take on modern life, then, you are also learning to write critical arguments.

"But how," you (and perhaps your teacher) may ask, "can I know that a semiotic interpretation is right?" Good question—it is commonly asked. But then, it can be asked of the writer of any interpretive essay, and the answer in each case is the same. That is, rarely can one absolutely *prove* the truth of any argument; what you do is *persuade* your audience through the use of pertinent evidence. In writing analyses about popular culture, that evidence comes from your knowledge of the system to which the object you are interpreting belongs. The more you know about the system, the more convincing your interpretations will be. And this is true whether you are writing about shoelaces or about more traditional academic subjects.

There are several essential principles to follow as you attempt to persuade your reader of the force of your interpretations. The most crucial is that the meaning of a sign is determined by *what that sign may be related to within a system*. We tested this principle by looking at unlaced sneakers—which, in themselves, may indeed mean nothing at all, or only that someone has forgotten to lace them up—and then by relating them to other signs within a fashion system. Similarly, an interpretation of the popularity of rap music might proceed by associating rap with the cultural signs (like teen fashions) that belong to a related system.

But often our interpretations of popular culture involve issues that are larger than the latest fad. How, for instance, are we to analyze fully the widespread belief—as reflected in the classic sitcoms mentioned earlier—that it is more natural for women to stay at home and take care of the kids than it is for men to do so? Why, in other words, is the concept of "housewife" so easy to accept while the idea of a "house-husband" may appear somewhat ridiculous? How, in short, can we interpret some of our most basic values semiotically? To see how, we need to look at those value systems that semioticians call "cultural mythologies."

Of Myths and Men

As we have seen, in a semiotic analysis we do not search for the meanings of things in the things themselves. Rather, we find meaning in the way we can relate things together. We've done this with shoelaces,

---

D i s c u s s i n g   t h e   S i g n s   o f   A m e r i c a n   L i f e

To start looking critically at the world around you, bring to class one object, and give a short (two-minute) semiotic interpretation of it to your class. Your object can be anything, ranging from clothing to food, a book to an album cover. What does your object say about modern American culture? Be sure to consider what system it belongs to (its relationship to similar objects) and what values and beliefs it reflects. And be sure to focus not on personal or private meanings but on social meanings.

After everyone in the class has spoken, stand back and reflect on the collection of objects discussed. What do they say about your class as a whole?

---

but what about with beliefs? This book asks you to explore the implications of social issues like gender norms and free speech that involve a great many personal beliefs and values that we do not always recognize as beliefs and values. Rather, we think of them as truths (one might think, "Of course it's odd for a man to stay home and take care of the house!"). But from a semiotic perspective, our values too belong to special systems from which they take their meaning. Semioticians call these systems of belief cultural "mythologies."

A cultural mythology, or "myth" for short, is not some fanciful story from the past; it is a kind of lens that governs the way we view our world. Think of it this way: Say you were born with rose-tinted eyeglasses permanently attached over your eyes, but you didn't know they were there. The world would look rose-colored to you and you would presume that it *was* rose-colored. You wouldn't wonder whether the world might look otherwise through different lenses. But there are other kinds of eyeglasses in the world with different lenses, and reality does look different to those who wear them. Those lenses are cultural mythologies, and no culture can claim to have the one set of glasses that sees things as they really are.

The profound effect our cultural mythologies have on the way we view reality, on our most basic values, is especially apparent today when the myths of European culture are being challenged by the world views of the many other cultures that have taken root in American soil. Where, for example, European-American culture upholds a profoundly individualistic social mythology, valuing individual rights before those of the group, traditional Chinese culture believes in the primacy of the family and the community over the individual. Maxine Hong Kingston's short story "No Name Woman" poignantly demonstrates how such opposing ideologies can collide with painful results in its tale of a Chinese woman who is more or less sacrificed to preserve the interests of her village. The story, from *The Woman Warrior,* tells of a young woman who gives birth to a baby too many months after her husband's departure to America with most of her village's other young men for it to be her husband's child. The men had left to earn the money in America that keeps the impoverished villagers from starving. They may be away for years and so need to be assured that their wives will remain faithful to them in their absence lest they refuse to go at all. The unfortunate heroine of the tale—who, to sharpen the agony, had probably been more the victim of rape than the instigator of adultery—is horribly punished by the entire village as an example to any other wives who might disturb the system and ends a tragic suicide.

That Kingston wrote "No Name Woman" as a self-consciously "hyphenated" Asian-American, as one whose identity fuses both Chinese and Euro-American values, reveals the fault lines between conflicting mythologies. On the one hand, as an Asian, Kingston understands the communal values behind the horrific sacrifice of her aunt, and her story makes sure that her Euro-American readers understand this too. But on the other hand, as an American and as a feminist, she is outraged by the violation of an individual woman's rights on behalf of the group (or mob, which is as the villagers behave in the story). Kingston's own sense of personal conflict in this clash of mythologies—Asian, American, and feminist—offers a striking example of the inevitable conflicts that America itself faces as it changes from a monocultural to a multicultural society.

To put this another way, from the semiotic perspective, *how* you interpret something is very much a product of *who* you are; for culture is just another name for the mythic frames that shape our values and perceptions. Traditionally, American education has presumed a mono-cultural perspective, a "melting pot" view that no matter what one's cultural background, truth is culture-blind. Langston Hughes took on this assumption many years ago in his classic poem "Theme for English B," where he writes, "I guess I'm what / I feel and see and hear," and wonders whether "my page will be colored" when he writes. "Being me, it will not be white," the poet suggests, but while he struggles to find what he holds in common with his white instructor, he can't suppress the differences. In essence, that is the challenge of multicultural education itself: to identify the different cultural codes that inform the mythic frameworks of the many cultures that share America while searching for what holds the whole thing together.

That meaning is not culture-blind, that it is conditioned by systems of ideology and belief that are codified differently by different cultures, is a foundational semiotic judgment. Human beings, in other words, construct their own social realities, so who gets to do the constructing becomes very important. Every contest over a cultural code is, accordingly, a contest for power, but the contest is usually masked because the winner generally defines its mythology as the "truth," as what is most "natural" or "reasonable." Losers in the contest become objects of scorn and are marginalized, declared "unnatural," or "deviant," or even "insane." The stakes are high as myth battles myth, with "truth" itself as the highest prize.

This does not mean that you must abandon your own beliefs when conducting a semiotic analysis, only that you cannot take them for granted and must be prepared to argue for them. We want to assure you that semiotics will not tell you what to think and believe. It *does* assume that what you believe reflects some cultural system or other and that no cultural system can claim absolute validity or superiority. This judgment may sound heretical precisely because human beings operate within mythological constructs whose very invisibility is guaranteed by the myth. No mythology, that is to say, begins by saying, "This is just a construct or interpretation." Every myth begins, "This is the truth." It is very difficult to imagine, from within the myth, any alternatives. Indeed, as you read this book, you may find it upsetting to see that some beliefs we take for granted—such as the "proper" roles of men and women in society—are socially constructed and not absolute. But the outlines of the myth, the bounding (and binding) frame, best appear when challenged by another myth, and this challenge is probably nowhere more insistent than in America, where so many of us are really "hyphenated" Americans, citizens combining in our own persons two (or more) cultural traditions.

Getting Started

Mythology, like culture, is not static, however, and so the semiotician must always keep his or her eye on the clock, so to speak. History, time itself, is a constant factor in an ever-changing world. Consider once again teen fashion. Since we began writing this introduction, a new street fashion has come to our attention, a kind of hip-hop/grunge fusion in which Seattle meets Compton. Do you recognize what we mean? Have you worn what we mean? What's it all about? Can you connect it to anything else in your life or in the life of America?

So it's your turn now. Start asking questions, pushing, probing. That's what critical writing is all about, but this time *you're* part of the question. Arriving at answers, conclusions, is the fun part here, but answers aren't the basis of analytic thinking: questions are. You always begin with a question, a query, an hypothesis, something to explore. If you already knew the answer, there would be no point in conducting the analysis. We leave you to it to explore the almost infinite variety of questions that the readings in this book will raise. Many of them come equipped with their own answers, but you may (indeed will and should) find such "answers" in need of further questions. To help you ask those questions, keep in mind the two elemental principles of semiotics that we have explored so far:

1. The meaning of a sign can be found not in itself but in its *relationships* (both differences and similarities) with other signs within a *system*. To interpret an individual sign, then, you must determine the general system in which it belongs.

2. What we call social "reality" is a human construct, the product of a cultural *mythology* that intervenes between our minds and the world we experience. Such cultural myths reflect the values and ideological interests of their builders, not the laws of nature or logic.

Perhaps our first principle could be more succinctly rephrased, "everything is connected," and our second simply says, "question authority." Think of them that way if it helps. Or just ask yourself whenever you are interpreting something, "what's going on here?" In short, question *everything*. And one more reminder: Signs are like weather vanes; they point in response to invisible historical winds. We invite you now to start looking at the weather.

PART ONE

IMAGES

1.   CONSUMING PASSIONS: THE CULTURE OF AMERICAN
     CONSUMPTION

2.   BROUGHT TO YOU B(U)Y: THE SIGNS OF ADVERTISING

3.   M(ORE)TV: THE TELEVISION AND VIDEO REVOLUTION

4.   THE HOLLYWOOD SIGN: THE SEMIOTICS OF AMERICAN FILM

5.   LARGER THAN LIFE: THE MYTHIC CHARACTERS OF
     AMERICAN CULTURE

CONSUMING PASSIONS

The Culture of American Consumption

Take a moment to think about your bedroom. It doesn't matter whether it's in a dorm, an apartment, your own house, or the home you grew up in, just so long as it's *your* space. How have you decorated it? Do you have a CD system? A poster of Megadeth on the wall? Teddy bears on the shelves? College football stuff? Michael Jordan stuff? Michael Jackson stuff? It doesn't matter what you've got there, just make an inventory.

Now, open your clothes closet. What do you see? A pair of Doc Martens? Or Nikes? Any sweat suits? Plaid flannel shirts? Jeans? Jeans cut off at the knees? Any oversized chinos? Oversized shorts? Dresses? For work? Play? Any leotards? Miniskirts? Any business suits? Boots? In short, what's on the program to wear today?

These questions aren't meant to be nosy; we're getting ready for some semiotic analyses. For every choice you make in the decoration of your room, and every choice you make in the decoration of yourself, is a sign, a signal you are sending to the world about yourself. Those aren't just a pair of shoes you're wearing: They're a statement about your identity. That's not just a CD player: It's a message about your world view. And, by the way, what CDs have you bought? Your music collection may say more about you than anything else you own.

To read the signs of American consumption, it is best to start with yourself, because you've already got an angle on the answers. But be careful and be honest: Remember, a cultural sign gets its meaning from the system in which it appears. Its significance does not lie in its usefulness but rather in its symbolism, in the image it projects, and that image is socially constructed. You didn't make it by yourself. To decode the stuff in your room and the stuff in your wardrobe, you've got to ask yourself what you are trying to say with it and what you want other people to think about you. And you've got to remember the difference between fashion and function.

To give you an idea of how to go about analyzing consumer objects, let's look at a very simple product that on the surface looks completely functional. Let's look at bottled water.

A Message in a Bottle

The message begins here: Sometime around the end of the 1980s, a good many of our students started to lug plastic bottles of Evian water around with them from class to class. They still do, but bottles of natural fruit juice seltzers and Snapple are beginning to join them. Asking our students why they're carrying liquids around tends to elicit the predictably functional explanation that Evian water (or fruit seltzer) is healthier than the chlorinated water that comes out of a tap. So it would seem that the trend simply signifies an increased sense of health consciousness in American society. And to a certain extent it does. But if that were all there is to it, why are the bottles (of whatever sort) so openly displayed? And why, in the case of bottled water, are they so often Evian water bottles rather than, say, Poland Spring of Maine, or some generic brand?

"OK," you may be thinking, "so people carry bottles of water around with them. So what?" Well, think about it. If you want to tote liquids about, would you carry them in a canteen? Or in a brown paper bag? Or a thermos? You could, but is it likely? But an Evian bottle: Now, that's different. What sort of image does *it* send?

You can interpret the Evian water phenomenon by doing exactly what we did when we interpreted unlaced basketball shoes in the introduction to this book. The first thing you need to do is to determine the fashion system to which the Evian bottles belong. Look at the way people who carry liquids around with them dress. Are the bottles in any way a fashion accessory to a certain style? Look also at who carries them and what images those people usually project. Any connections? How, too, has Evian water been marketed and advertised? What images do you find in the ads? How do they relate to the personal style of those who carry Evian water around?

Now ask yourself, does the fact that Evian water is bottled in France have any effect on your choice? Would you carry a generic bottle of distilled water? Would you carry a Perrier water bottle, and if not, why not? Be honest now. There are a number of possible interpretations you may come up with in your semiotic analysis of Evian water, but a purely functional answer cannot be among them because too many other choices are available if merely having a healthy drink was all there is to it.

Some of you, of course, may never carry bottled water around. How does the fad look to you? What's your take on your classmates who do? Do you believe that it's really Evian water in all those bottles? One of our students who was carrying a bottle of Crystal Geyser water around campus claimed she chose *that* brand "because it was cheaper and it wasn't as 'trendy' as Evian"—and she admitted that the bottle didn't really have Crystal Geyser in it anyway. She refilled it out of a water dispensing machine at the local supermarket. How do you interpret her actions?

If you find Evian water out of your line, think of any current consumer trend and question it. What messages are people sending when they buy the thing? What images do they project? How does the fad relate to other cultural trends? Such are the questions that you must ask as a reader of consuming images, probing everything that you may find in the marketplace of goods and services, and taking care never to be satisfied with the answer, "because this product is *better* than that," or, more simply, "just because. . . ."

Disposable Decades

When analyzing a consumer sign, you will often find yourself referring to particular decades in which certain popular fads and trends were prominent, for the decade in which a given style appears may be an essential key to the system that explains it. You can do that when looking at Evian water. Fancy French bottled water first became fashionable in the seventies, but the preferred drink then, Perrier, was associated with preppie cocktail parties, not health clubs. The *difference* between Perrier and Evian, then, partly reflects the difference between the preppie seventies and the yuppie, body-conscious eighties. As the nineties progress, Evian itself is giving way to new signs (fruit seltzers, Crystal Geyser, who knows what's next?), as the new decade does what all recent American decades have done: bring in a new set of trendy images and styles.

Have you ever wondered *why* American cultural trends seem to change with every decade, why it is so easy to speak of the "sixties," or the "seventies," or the "eighties" and immediately recognize the popular styles that dominated each decade? Have you ever looked at the style of a friend and thought "Oh, she's so sixties"? Can you place an Earth Shoe at the drop of a hat, or a Nehru jacket? A change in the calendar always seems to herald a change in style in a consuming culture. But why?

The decade-to-decade shift in America's pop cultural identity goes back a good number of years. It is still easy, for example, to distinguish

---

Discussing the Signs of Consumer Culture

On the board, list in categories the fashion styles worn by members of the class. Be sure to note details, such as styles of shoes, jewelry, watches, or sunglasses, as well as broader trends. Then discuss what the clothing choices say about individuals. What messages are people sending about their personal identity? Do individual students agree with the class's interpretations of their clothing choices? Can any distinctions be made by gender or ethnicity? Then discuss what the fashion styles worn by the whole class say: Is a group identity projected by class members?

F. Scott Fitzgerald's Jazz Age twenties from John Steinbeck's wrathful thirties. The fifties, an especially connotative decade, raise images of ducktail haircuts and poodle skirts, drive-in culture and Elvis, family sitcoms and white-bread innocence, while the sixties are remembered for acid rock, hippies, the student revolution, and back-to-the-land communes. We remember the seventies as a pop cultural era divided between disco, Nashville, and preppiedom, with John Travolta, truckers, and Skippy and Muffy as dominant pop icons. The boom-boom eighties gave us Wall Street glitz and the yuppie invasion. Indeed, each decade since the First World War—which, not accidentally, happens to coincide roughly with the rise of modern advertising and mass production—seems to carry its own consumerist style.

It's no accident that the decade-to-decade shift in consumer styles seems to coincide with the advent of modern advertising and mass production because it was mass production that created a need for constant consumer turnover in the first place. Mass production, that is, promotes stylistic change because with so many products being produced, a market must be created to consume all of them, and this means constantly consuming *more*. To get consumers to keep buying all the new stuff, you have to convince them that the stuff they already have has gone out of style. Why else, do you think, do fashion designers completely redesign their lines each year? Why else do car manufacturers annually change their color schemes and body shapes when the old model year seemed quite good enough? The new designs aren't simply functional improvements (though they are marketed as such); they are inducements to go out and replace what you already have lest you appear to be out of fashion. Just think: If you could afford to buy any car that you want, what would it be? Would your choice a few years ago have been the same?

And so, mass production creates consumer societies based on the constant production of new products that are intended to be disposed of with the next product year. But something happened along the way to the establishment of our consumer culture: We began to value consumption more than production. Listen to the economic news: Consumption, not production, is relied upon to carry America out of its economic downturns. When Americans stop buying, our economy sputters. Consumption lies at the center of our economic system now, and the result has been a transformation in the very way we view ourselves.

A Tale of Two Cities

It has not always been thus in America, however. Once, Americans prided themselves on their productivity. In 1914, for example, the poet Carl Sandburg boasted of a Chicago that was "Hog Butcher for the World, Tool Maker, Stacker of Wheat, Player with Railroads and the Nation's Freight Handler." One wonders what Sandburg would think of the place today. From the south shore east to the industrial suburb of Gary, Indiana, Chicago's once-proud mills and factories rust in the winter wind. The broken windows of countless tenements stare blindly at the Amtrak commuter lines that transport the white-collared brokers of the Chicago Mercantile Exchange to the city center, where trade today is in commodity futures, not commodities. Even Michael Jackson, Gary's most famous export, hesitates to go home.

Meanwhile, a few hundred miles to the northwest, Bloomington, Minnesota, buzzes with excitement. For there in 1992 the Mall of America opened, a colossus of consumption so large that it contains within its walls a seven-acre Knott's Camp Snoopy theme park, with lots of room to spare. You can find almost anything you want in the Mall of America, including all the latest Michael Jackson records, but most of what you will find won't have been manufactured in America. Jackson himself is under contract with Sony. The proud tag "Made in the USA" is an increasingly rare item.

It's a long way, in short, from Sandburg's Chicago to the Mall of America, a trip that traverses America's shift from a producer to a consumer economy. You are probably only too aware of this transformation. The uncertainties of finding work after graduation, a stubborn international trade deficit, and the substitution of low-paying service industry jobs for high-paying positions in the manufacturing sector are the all-too-familiar consequences of America's economic "restructuring." But what is less obvious is the cultural effect of our consumer economy, the way that it is shaping a new *mythology* within which we define ourselves, our hopes, and our desires.

Ask yourself right now what your own goals are in going to college. Do you envision a career in law, or medicine, or banking and finance? Do you want to be a teacher, an advertising executive, or a civil servant?

If you've considered any of these career examples, you are contemplating what are known as service jobs. While essential to a society, none of them actually produces anything. If you've given thought to going into some facet of manufacturing, on the other hand, you are unusual because America offers increasingly fewer opportunities in that area and little prestige. The prestige jobs are in law and medicine, by and large, a fact that it is easy to take for granted. But ask yourself: Does it have to be so?

Simply to ask such questions is to begin to reveal the outline of a cultural mythology based in consumption rather than production. For one thing, while law and medicine require specialized training available to only a few, doctors and lawyers also make a lot of money and so are higher up on the scale of consumption. Quite simply, they can buy more than others can. It is easy to presume that this would be the case anywhere, but in the former Soviet Union physicians—most of whom were women—were relatively low on the social scale. Male engineers, on the other hand, were highly valued for their role in facilitating military production. In what was a producer rather than a consumer culture, it was the producers who roosted high on the social ladder.

But to live in a consumer culture is not simply a matter of shopping; it is a matter of *being*. For in a consumer society, you are what you consume, and the entire social and economic order is maintained by the constant encouragement to buy. The ubiquity of television and advertising in America is a direct reflection of this system, for these media deliver the constant stimulus to consume in avalanches of consuming images. Consider how difficult it is to escape the arm of the advertiser. You may turn off your TV set, but a screen awaits you at the check-out counter of your supermarket, displaying incentives to buy. If you rush to the restroom to hide, you may find advertisements tacked to the stalls. And after all, weren't you planning to do some shopping this weekend anyway?

When the Going Gets Tough, the Tough Go Shopping

In a cultural system where our very identities are displayed in the things we buy, it accordingly behooves us to pay close attention to what we consume and why. From the cars we drive to the clothes we wear, we are enmeshed in a web of consuming images. Early in the 1990s, however, a particular consumer profile of the decade has yet to emerge. Yuppies are very much out of fashion, but the fashion styles featuring baggy, oversized clothing, the ongoing appeal of surfer wear, or of "Gothic" and punk studded leather, the street wear featuring pro sports team insignia caps and sweat suits—all these insignia of a youthful, distinctively anti-yuppie culture—still come to the nineties from the

‖‖

> ### Exploring the Signs of Consumer Culture
>
> "You are what you buy." In your journal, freewrite on the importance of consumer products in your life. How do you respond to being told your identity is equivalent to the products you buy? Do you resist the notion? Do you recall any instances when you have felt lost without a favorite object? How do you communicate your sense of self to others through objects, whether they be clothing, books, food, home decor, cars, or something else?

eighties. This is not at all unusual. In general, a particular decade's style really emerges a few years through the decade and then spills into the next one. Much of the sixties, for example, really unfolded in the early seventies, and the glitzy, go-for-the-gold and you-can-have-it-all tone of the eighties did not appear on January 1, 1980.

What *is* certain about the consumer style of the nineties is that it too will reflect economic and social conditions, and *you* will help shape it. Already the if-you've-got-it-flaunt-it style of the eighties has been much toned down in the context of a lingering recession. Consumers, for instance, who ran out to get BMWs in the eighties are now trading them in for more utilitarian Land Rovers and Jeep Cherokees. Meanwhile, the grunge look has become the nineties' version of inverse snobbery: The grungier your wardrobe, the hipper you are.

Note how things don't really change when it comes to status symbols, however, in a consumer culture. In each decade, affluent consumers search for status items to project public images of their superior social position. Take the Land Rover. While it is certainly less ostentatious a vehicle than a BMW or Mercedes—and thus more reflective of the toned-down nineties—the Land Rover's long history as the vehicle of choice among safari-bound aristocrats still sends a signal of social superiority. Or think of the way dress T-shirts are replacing the evening wear of the eighties among the Hollywood elite in the nineties. Sure, they're less glitzy in actual appearance, but the message they send is the same when seen in the context of the current fashion system. It isn't that affluent consumers are changing their habits of consumption in the nineties, in other words, only the images they may choose to buy.

For whatever the economic environment, people in a consumer society use products as *signs* of their public identities, indicators of what they want others to think of them and of what they think of themselves. The choice of a pair of Doc Martens rather than a pair of Reeboks or Birkenstocks, for example, says a good deal about your own sense of personal identity. Your decision to decorate your dorm room with teddy bears, or, conversely, with posters of Megadeth, sends another strong signal to your friends about how you want them to read *you*.

As students, you are probably freer to choose the images you wish to project through the products you consume than most other demographic groups in America. This may sound paradoxical: After all, don't working adults have more money than starving students? Yes, generally. But the working world places severe restrictions on the choices employees can make in their clothing and grooming styles, and even automobile choice may be restricted (real estate agents, for example, can't escort their clients around town in Suzuki Samurais). Corporate business wear, for all its variations, still revolves around a central core of necktied and dark-hued sobriety, regardless of the gender of the wearer. And even with the return of long hair for men into fashion in the early nineties, few professions allow it on the job. On the campus, however, you can be pretty much whatever you want to be, which is why your own daily lives provide you with a particularly rich field of consumer signs to read and decode.

So go to it. By the time you read this book, a lot will have changed. Grunge fashion and probably even hip-hop will be old hat and something else will have come along that you alone will be able to decode because your teacher will probably not be in on it. Look around your classroom now. Start reading.

The Readings

As this chapter's lead essay, Laurence Shames's "The More Factor" provides a mythological background for the discussions of America's consuming behavior that follow. Shames takes an historical approach to American consumerism, making a connection between our frontier history and our ever-expanding desire for more goods and services. Peter Gibian's survey of the types of American shopping malls shows how the places where we shop are themselves complex sign systems designed to stimulate consumption, while Elizabeth Wilson and Scott Poulson-Bryant shed light on some of the clothing styles that we look for when we hit the mall. Stuart Ewen analyzes the way cultural style affects personal style through his reading of the "hard body" trend of the 1980s, while Joan Kron studies the way we use home furnishings to reflect our sense of identity. Andrew Wernick surveys the history of the imagery of the American automobile, analyzing the shifting fantasies that our cars project, and Roland Barthes concludes the chapter with his pioneering semiotic analysis of the materials from which the French built children's toys in the 1950s—an analysis that is as timely today as when it was written.

LAURENCE SHAMES

The More Factor

‖‖

A bumper sticker popular in the 1980s read, "Whoever dies with the most toys wins." In this selection from The Hunger for More: Searching for Values in an Age of Greed *(1989), Laurence Shames shows how the great American hunger for more—more toys, more land, more opportunities—is an essential part of our history and character, stemming from the frontier era when the horizon alone seemed the only limit to American desire. In an era when the frontier has run out and even our consumer economy is sputtering, Shames warns that Americans will have to adjust their expectations and resign themselves to limited horizons. The author of* The Big Time: The Harvard Business School's Most Successful Class and How It Shaped America *(1986), and himself the holder of a Harvard MBA, Shames is a journalist who has contributed to such publications as* Playboy, Vanity Fair, Manhattan, inc., *and* Esquire.

1

Americans have always been optimists, and optimists have always liked to speculate. In Texas in the 1880s, the speculative instrument of choice was towns, and there is no tale more American than this.

What people would do was buy up enormous tracts of parched and vacant land, lay out a Main Street, nail together some wooden sidewalks, and start slapping up buildings. One of these buildings would be called the Grand Hotel and would have a saloon complete with swinging doors. Another might be dubbed the New Academy or the Opera House. The developers would erect a flagpole and name a church, and once the workmen had packed up and moved on, the towns would be as empty as the sky.

But no matter. The speculators, next, would hire people to pass out handbills in the Eastern and Midwestern cities, tracts limning the advantages of relocation to "the Athens of the South" or "the new plains Jerusalem." When persuasion failed, the builders might resort to bribery, paying people's moving costs and giving them houses, in exchange for nothing but a pledge to stay until a certain census was taken or a certain inspection made. Once the nose count was completed, people were free to move on, and there was in fact a contingent of folks who made their living by keeping a cabin on skids and dragging it for pay from one town to another.

The speculators' idea, of course, was to lure the railroad. If one could create a convincing semblance of a town, the railroad might come through it, and a real town would develop, making the speculators staggeringly rich. By these devices a man named Sanborn once owned Amarillo.[1]

But railroad tracks are narrow and the state of Texas is very, very   5
wide. For every Wichita Falls or Lubbock there were a dozen College Mounds or Belchervilles,[2] bleached, unpeopled burgs that receded quietly into the dust, taking with them large amounts of speculators' money.

Still, the speculators kept right on bucking the odds and depositing empty towns in the middle of nowhere. Why did they do it? Two reasons—reasons that might be said to summarize the central fact of American economic history and that go a fair way toward explaining what is perhaps the central strand of the national character.

The first reason was simply that the possible returns were so enormous as to partake of the surreal, to create a climate in which ordinary logic and prudence did not seem to apply. In a boom like that of real estate when the railroad barreled through, long shots that might pay one hundred thousand to one seemed worth a bet.

The second reason, more pertinent here, is that there was a presumption that America would *keep on* booming—if not forever, then at least longer than it made sense to worry about. There would always be another gold rush, another Homestead Act, another oil strike. The next generation would always ferret out opportunities that would be still more lavish than any that had gone before. America *was* those opportunities. This was an article not just of faith, but of strategy. You banked on the next windfall, you staked your hopes and even your self-esteem on it, and this led to a national turn of mind that might usefully be thought of as the habit of more.

A century, maybe two centuries, before anyone had heard the term *baby boomer,* much less *yuppie,* the habit of more had been installed as the operative truth among the economically ambitious. The habit of more seemed to suggest that there was no such thing as getting wiped out in America. A fortune lost in Texas might be recouped in Colorado. Funds frittered away on grazing land where nothing grew might flood back in as silver. There was always a second chance, or always seemed to be, in this land where growth was destiny and where expansion and purpose were the same.

---

1. For a fuller account of railroad-related land speculation in Texas, see F. Stanley, *Story of the Texas Panhandle Railroads* (Borger, Tex.: Hess Publishing Co., 1976).

2. T. Lindsay Baker, *Ghost Towns of Texas* (Norman, Okla.: University of Oklahoma Press, 1986).

The key was the frontier, not just as a matter of acreage, but as idea.   10
Vast, varied, rough as rocks, America was the place where one never
quite came to the end. Ben Franklin explained it to Europe even before
the Revolutionary War had finished: America offered new chances to
those "who, in their own Countries, where all the Lands [were] fully
occupied . . . could never [emerge] from the poor Condition wherein
they were born."[3]

So central was this awareness of vacant space and its link to economic
promise that Frederick Jackson Turner, the historian who set the tone
for much of the twentieth century's understanding of the American past,
would write that it was "not the constitution, but free land . . . [that]
made the democratic type of society in America."[4] good laws mattered;
an accountable government mattered; ingenuity and hard work mattered. But those things were, so to speak, an overlay on the natural,
geographic America that was simply *there,* and whose vast and beckoning
possibilities seemed to generate the ambition and the sometimes reckless
liberty that would fill it. First and foremost, it was open space that
provided "the freedom of the individual to rise under conditions of
social mobility."[5]

Open space generated not just ambition, but metaphor. As early as
1835, Tocqueville was extrapolating from the fact of America's emptiness
to the observation that "no natural boundary seems to be set to the
efforts of man."[6] Nor was any limit placed on what he might accomplish,
since, in that heyday of the Protestant ethic, a person's rewards were
taken to be quite strictly proportionate to his labors.

Frontier; opportunity; more. This has been the American trinity
from the very start. The frontier was the backdrop and also the raw
material for the streak of economic booms. The booms became the goad
and also the justification for the myriad gambles and for Americans'
famous optimism. The optimism, in turn, shaped the schemes and visions
that were sometimes noble, sometimes appalling, always bold. The frontier, as reality and as symbol, is what has shaped the American way of
doing things and the American sense of what's worth doing.

But there has been one further corollary to the legacy of the frontier,
with its promise of ever-expanding opportunities: given that the goal—
a realistic goal for most of our history—was *more,* Americans have been
somewhat backward in adopting values, hopes, ambitions that have to
do with things *other than* more. In America, a sense of quality has lagged

---

3. Benjamin Franklin, "Information to Those Who Would Remove to America,"
in *The Autobiography and Other Writings* (New York: Penguin Books, 1986), 242.

4. Frederick Jackson Turner, *The Frontier in American History* (Melbourne, Fla.:
Krieger, 1976 [reprint of 1920 edition]), 293.

5. Ibid., 266.

6. Tocqueville, *Democracy in America.*

far behind a sense of scale. An ideal of contentment has yet to take root in soil traditionally more hospitable to an ideal of restless striving. The ethic of decency has been upstaged by the ethic of success. The concept of growth has been applied almost exclusively to things that can be measured, counted, weighed. And the hunger for those things that are unmeasurable but fine—the sorts of accomplishment that cannot be undone by circumstance or a shift in social fashion, the kind of serenity that cannot be shattered by tomorrow's headline—has gone largely unfulfilled, and even unacknowledged.

2

If the supply of more went on forever, perhaps that wouldn't matter very much. Expansion could remain a goal unto itself, and would continue to generate a value system based on bulk rather than on nuance, on quantities of money rather than on quality of life, on "progress" itself rather than on a sense of what the progress was for. But what if, over time, there was less more to be had?

That is the essential situation of America today.

Let's keep things in proportion: the country is not running out of wealth, drive, savvy, or opportunities. We are not facing imminent ruin, and neither panic nor gloom is called for. But there have been ample indications over the past two decades that we are running out of more.

Consider productivity growth—according to many economists, the single most telling and least distortable gauge of changes in real wealth. From 1947 to 1965, productivity in the private sector (adjusted, as are all the following figures, for inflation) was advancing, on average, by an annual 3.3 percent. This means, simply, that each hour of work performed by a specimen American worker contributed 3.3 cents worth of more to every American dollar every year; whether we saved it or spent it, that increment went into a national kitty of ever-enlarging aggregate wealth. Between 1965 and 1972, however, the "more-factor" decreased to 2.4 percent a year, and from 1972 to 1977 it slipped further, to 1.6 percent. By the early 1980s, productivity growth was at a virtual standstill, crawling along at 0.2 percent for the five years ending in 1982.[7] Through the middle years of the 1980s, the numbers rebounded somewhat—but by then the gains were being neutralized by the gargantuan carrying costs on the national debt.[8]

---

7. These figures are taken from the Council of Economic Advisers, *Economic Report of the President,* February 1984, 267.

8. For a lucid and readable account of the meaning and implications of our reservoir of red ink, see Lawrence Malkin, *The National Debt* (New York: Henry Holt and Co., 1987). Through no fault of Malkin's, many of his numbers are already obsolete, but his explanation of who owes what to whom, and what it means, remains sound and even entertaining in a bleak sort of way.

Inevitably, this decline in the national stockpile of more held consequences for the individual wallet.[9] During the 1950s, Americans' average hourly earnings were humping ahead at a gratifying 2.5 percent each year. By the late seventies, that figure stood just where productivity growth had come to stand, at a dispiriting 0.2 cents on the dollar. By the first half of the eighties, the Reagan "recovery" notwithstanding, real hourly wages were actually moving backwards—declining at an average annual rate of 0.3 percent.

Compounding the shortage of more was an unfortunate but crucial demographic fact. Real wealth was nearly ceasing to expand just at the moment when the members of that unprecedented population bulge known as the baby boom were entering what should have been their peak years of income expansion. A working man or woman who was thirty years old in 1949 could expect to see his or her real earnings burgeon by 63 percent by age forty. In 1959, a thirty-year-old could still look forward to a gain of 49 percent by his or her fortieth birthday.

But what about the person who turned thirty in 1973? By the time that worker turned forty, his or her real earnings had shrunk by a percentage point. For all the blather about yuppies with their beach houses, BMWs, and radicchio salads, and even factoring in those isolated tens of thousands making ludicrous sums in consulting firms or on Wall Street, the fact is that between 1979 and 1983 real earnings of all Americans between the ages of twenty-five and thirty-four actually declined by 14 percent.[10] The *New York Times,* well before the stock market crash put the kibosh on eighties confidence, summed up the implications of this downturn by observing that "for millions of breadwinners, the American dream is becoming the impossible dream."[11]

Now, it is not our main purpose here to detail the ups and downs of the American economy. Our aim, rather, is to consider the effects of those ups and downs on people's goals, values, sense of their place in the world. What happens at that shadowy juncture where economic prospects meld with personal choice? What sorts of insights and adjustments are called for so that economic ups and downs can be dealt with gracefully?

Fact one in this connection is that, if America's supply of more is in fact diminishing, American values will have to shift and broaden to fill the gap where the expectation of almost automatic gains used to be. Something more durable will have to replace the fat but fragile bubble that had been getting frailer these past two decades and that finally popped—a tentative, partial pop—on October 19, 1987. A different sort

20

---

9. The figures in this paragraph and the next are from "The Average Guy Takes It on the Chin," *New York Times,* 13 July 1986, sec. 3.

10. See, for example, "The Year of the Yuppie," *Newsweek,* 31 December 1984, 16.

11. "The Average Guy," see above.

of growth—ultimately, a growth in responsibility and happiness—will have to fulfill our need to believe that our possibilities are still expanding.

The transition to that new view of progress will take some fancy stepping, because, at least since the end of World War II, simple economic growth has stood, in the American psyche, as the best available substitute for the literal frontier. The economy has *been* the frontier. Instead of more space, we have had more money. Rather than measuring progress in terms of geographical expansion, we have measured it by expansion in our standard of living. Economics has become the metaphor on which we pin our hopes of open space and second chances.

The poignant part is that the literal frontier did not pass yesterday: 25 it has not existed for a hundred years. But the frontier's promise has become so much a part of us that we have not been willing to let the concept die. We have kept the frontier mythology going by invocation, by allusion, by hype.

It is not a coincidence that John F. Kennedy dubbed his political program the New Frontier. It is not mere linguistic accident that makes us speak of Frontiers of Science or of psychedelic drugs as carrying one to Frontiers of Perception. We glorify fads and fashions by calling them Frontiers of Taste. Nuclear energy has been called the Last Frontier; solar energy has been called the Last Frontier. Outer space has been called the Last Frontier; the oceans have been called the Last Frontier. Even the suburbs, those blandest and least adventurous of places, have been wryly described as the crabgrass frontier.[12]

What made all these usages plausible was their being linked to the image of the American economy as an endlessly fertile continent whose boundaries never need be reached, a domain that could expand in perpetuity, a gigantic playing field that would never run out of room and on which the game would get forever bigger and more filled with action. This was the frontier that would not vanish.

It is worth noting that people in other countries (with the possible exception of that other America, Australia) do not talk about frontier this way. In Europe, and in most of Africa and Asia, "frontier" connotes, at worst, a place of barbed wire and men with rifles, and at best, a neutral junction where one changes currency while passing from one fixed system into another. Frontier, for most of the world's people, does not suggest growth, expanse, or opportunity.

For Americans, it does, and always has. This is one of the things that sets America apart from other places and makes American attitudes different from those of other people. It is why, from *Bonanza* to the Sierra Club, the notion or even the fantasy of empty horizons and untapped

---

12. With the suburbs again taking on a sort of fascination, this phrase was resurrected as the title of a 1985 book—*Crabgrass Frontier: The Suburbanization of America,* by Kenneth T. Jackson (Oxford University Press).

resources has always evoked in the American heart both passion and wistfulness. And it is why the fear that the economic frontier—our last, best version of the Wild West—may finally be passing creates in us not only money worries but also a crisis of morale and even of purpose.

3

It might seem strange to call the 1980s an era of nostalgia. The decade, after all, has been more usually described in terms of coolness, pragmatism, and a blithe innocence of history. But the eighties, unawares, were nostalgic for frontiers; and the disappointment of that nostalgia had much to do with the time's greed, narrowness, and strange want of joy. The fear that the world may not be a big enough playground for the full exercise of one's energies and yearnings, and worse, the fear that the playground is being fenced off and will no longer expand— these are real worries and they have had consequences. The eighties were an object lesson in how people play the game when there is an awful and unspoken suspicion that the game is winding down.

It was ironic that the yuppies came to be so reviled for their vaunting ambition and outsized expectations, as if they'd invented the habit of more, when in fact they'd only inherited it the way a fetus picks up an addiction in the womb. The craving was there in the national bloodstream, a remnant of the frontier, and the baby boomers, described in childhood as "the luckiest generation,"[13] found themselves, as young adults, in the melancholy position of wrestling with a two-hundred-year dependency on a drug that was now in short supply.

True, the 1980s raised the clamor for more to new heights of shrillness, insistence, and general obnoxiousness, but this, it can be argued, was in the nature of a final binge, the storm before the calm. America, though fighting the perception every inch of the way, was coming to realize that it was not a preordained part of the natural order that one should be richer every year. If it happened, that was nice. But who had started the flimsy and pernicious rumor that it was normal?

Reading the Text

1. Summarize in a paragraph how, according to Shames, the frontier functions as a symbol of American consciousness.
2. What connection does Shames make between America's frontier history and consumer behavior?
3. Why does Shames term the 1980s "an era of nostalgia"?

---

13. Thomas Hine, *Populuxe* (New York: Alfred A. Knopf, 1986), 15.

Reading the Signs

1. Shames asserts that Americans have been influenced by the frontier belief
   that "America would keep on booming." Do you feel that this belief
   continues to be influential in the 1990s? Write an essay arguing for your
   position.
2. Shames claims that, because of the desire for more, "the ethic of decency
   has been upstaged by the ethic of success" in America. In class, form teams
   that either agree or disagree with this position, and debate the validity of
   Shames's claim.
3. Read or review Joan Kron's "The Semiotics of Home Decor" (p. 66) and
   Stuart Ewen's "Hard Bodies" (p. 60). How are Martin J. Davidson and
   Raymond H—— influenced by the frontier myth that Shames describes?
4. In groups, discuss whether street gang members share the desire for "more"
   that Shames claims is a distinctly American trait. (You might read or review
   "Faro," p. 540, "Children in Gangs," p. 535, or "Gang Styles," p. 570.)
   Then write an essay in which you argue whether you believe gangs can be
   called "typically American."
5. Shames does not discuss ethnicity in his essay. Read Sam Fulwood III's
   "The Rage of the Black Middle Class" (p. 462) and discuss the extent to
   which the African-Americans in his essay share the desire for more. Are
   there any social factors affecting their outlook on life that Shames neglects
   to mention?

PETER GIBIAN

The Art of Being Off-Center:
Shopping Center Spaces and Spectacles

||||||||||||||||||||||||||||||||||||||||||||||||||

Shopping malls aren't just places where you can shop: They are archi-
tecturally designed to get you to spend your money. In this selection
published in Tabloid, *Peter Gibian (b. 1952) traces the history of the*
American shopping center, beginning with its inception in the California
car culture of the 1920s, when land was plentiful and cheap and shopping
centers sprawled around vast parking lots, and moving to today's atrium
malls, which hide the parking lots and imitate a car-free urban park. A
specialist in nineteenth-century American literature and twentieth-
century mass culture, Gibian has taught at Williams College and cur-
rently is assistant professor of English at McGill University.

"The commercial spirit has nurtured some of our most interesting
American design," writes historian Neil Harris, of the virtuosity of tech-

nical innovation in the service of spectacle that has formed the "architectural fantasy" of today's malls: "The last architectural form that serviced American dreams so effectively was the movie palace of the interwar years."[1] Of course, malls have now absorbed the movie-theater concept, offering their own multiscreen cinamettes, along with exhibits, lectures, concerts—at least one mall even has enclosed amusement park rides and a carnival-style midway. But the real spectacle is always the mall space itself: its escalator and elevator rides and ramps, its vistas and displays, its gardens and waterworks, graphics and glass, its recreated ambiences and "quartiers." This larger focus is what has sparked the technical virtuosity of these new designs in space and light, extensions of the metal-and-glass structural experiments of the mall ancestors: arcades, exhibition halls, and railroad stations.

Actually, the American shopping center itself has a surprisingly short history, but development has been rapid and design has become extremely self-conscious. These are now highly defined, highly designed environments.

But what do designers think about when they try to organize such a complex phenomenon? In the half-century history of American malls, there seem to have been five phases of design strategy.[2]

Phase one came out of the car culture of 1920s–1930s California, when people discovered the simple "one-stop" attraction of putting several small stores (with maybe a grocery store as base) near a single parking area. Through all suburban mall development, this basic structure has remained the same: a cluster of stores surrounded by seeming acres of barren parking lot. From outside, a mall is just cars and walls, as exciting as the solid brick exterior of a panorama building or a theater. But the only mall "show," of course, is directed inwards. And the paved lot can serve as a sort of transitional "moat," accenting the insular feel, the "otherness," of that self-enclosed "palace" at the core. (We think: "That must be someplace really different!")

Phase two is the gold-rush rise of the regional centers, produced by the addition of large "anchor" department stores to the grouping of smaller shops. Because of the boom of highway construction in the Eisenhower era and the huge migrations of people to the suburbs, the 1950s and 1960s were the golden years for shopping center development.

Centralized ownership was the radical innovation that really made things happen, that laid the foundations for these new giant centers. The department store anchor magnets, which provided the drawing power for these regional complexes, were also able to attract major financing from insurance companies, and so often singly owned and planned the

5

---

1. N. Harris, "Spaced Out at the Shopping Center," *New Republic,* Dec. 13, 1975: 26.

2. This schematic history is especially indebted to Harris.

entire operation. Controlled by one large-scale developer, the regional center could now begin to regulate both its economy and atmosphere: carefully choosing its tenants, avoiding internal economic competition, and working for a unity of architectural "effect."

Turning Backs . . . Wishing Away . . .

The movement toward "unity" in these phase-two centers only accented some crucial aspects latent in the phase-one designs: basic tendencies toward *self-containment* and *introversion*. Even before the 1920s, the trail-blazing J. C. Nichols was using the "Spanish mission" model with stores facing inward on a central pedestrian courtyard so that they could be set apart from cars and (in a move paradigmatic for later malls) *"turn their backs to the street."*[3] The large phase-two centers would simply expand on these principles. The influential design of Seattle's Northgate, for example, creates a central pedestrian mall between its two big straight-lined strips of stores (which "turn their backs to the highway"[4]) and relegates service activities to a hidden underground tunnel.

Harris notes that the earliest experiments in the separation of pedestrian customers from cars and from any service activities—creating a carefree inner circle distant from outside concerns (forget your car, forget the street, forget services, forget yourself)—were made at shopping centers and at Disneyland.[5] Both malls and Disney's Main Street derive from the townscape, but their closed, cleaned stage-set "streets" move in similar ways to keep practical services (deliveries, employee access, building supports, circuitry, etc.) behind or below the "scene." While one critic describes the Disney wonderland as "acres of fibreglass fantasy resting upon an unseen technological superstructure,"[6] mall designers combine an interest in this kind of fantasy entertainment with the more directed goals of selling. They have good reason to seek to wish away mall superstructure and let the for-sale merchandise take over center stage. The separation from cars and "the elimination of all service facilities from the public consciousness" become the "necessary ingredients" of a shopping center to a 1950s design theorist[7]; these are "necessary" because, as a 1950s planner sees it, the future center should be a fantasy-realm "kaleidoscope of movement . . . where *shoppers will not be conscious of the building but only of the displays.*"[8]

3. G. Baker and B. Furnaro, *Shopping Centers: Design and Operation* (N.Y.: Reinhold, 1951).

4. J. S. Hornbeck, ed., *Stores and Shopping Centers* (N.Y.: McGraw-Hill, 1962): 195.

5. Harris, 24.

6. C. Rowe, *Collage City* (Cambridge, MA.: MIT Press, 1978): 44.

7. Hornbeck, 188.

8. C. Darlow, *Enclosed Shopping Centers,* (London: Architectural Press, 1972).

So already in phases one and two the basic mall structure is set—or, rather, what is set is the *denial* of superstructure, the desire for an inner "open" domain freed from external necessities. In this, the earliest shopping centers join the most modern ones. For example, Victor Gruen, creator of the first modern enclosed mall (what he aptly calls the "introverted center") writes that he found his inspiration in many aspects of the nineteenth-century arcades: their self-enclosure around a central pedestrian plaza, their separation from external weather, from services, from traffic, and from the hostile city environment.[9] Like the 1950s suburban malls, Gruen says, the arcades were born in a *movement away from the city,* with architectural gestures of *introversion.*

Turning Inward

In the 1950s, even with the advent of large-scale single-developer centers, some regional malls continued to be built simply as giant extensions of the earliest plans—just your basic straight lines and big blocks on a monumental scale. But in the late 1950s and early 1960s, some developers began to place a great new emphasis on design planning and environmental control. Reacting against the early centers that simply rose up out of the demands of the road—growing uncontrolled, unstyled, on the "strip"—new mall designs would turn their focus ever more clearly inwards, strengthening the existing impulse to self-containment with further major shifts in the direction of the fully orchestrated mall.

A new self-consciousness in design centered on new problems: (1) the *choice* of an atmosphere, and (2) the question of *scale.* How should the plan reflect or deflect the fact of a mall's increasingly giant size, its self-enclosure, its clearly controlled environment? Responses to these problems took two general forms—in phases three and four. Both alternatives, though, are part of a general movement inward, towards enclosure, and concentration of effect—reacting to the imposing realities of mall superstructure with a new focus on special effects for the mall interior.

What we might call phase-three centers are the "market town" styles which deliberately underplayed their large size (they now often included several department stores), reacting against the straight lines of the earlier malls with meandering, informal patterns. Even in earlier phases, this approach had been very successful. The prototype "Town and Country Village" chain, for example, backed its name with designs accenting "the

9. V. Gruen, *Centers for the Urban Environment: Survival of the Cities* (N.Y.: Van Nostrand Reinhold, 1973).

charm of irregularity" and "picturesque congestion,"[10] adding old materials, heavy timber, and tile roofs for down-home informality. The
aptly named Old Orchard mall in Skokie, Illinois, the first of the extensively landscaped malls, is often seen as the classic example of the "country market" style in its late 1950s boom years. Streams, bridges, finely
gardened courtyards, and shop squares of varying dimensions were to
suggest the atmosphere of a country village. As in a diorama,[11] the goal
was to dissolve the static sense of the building frame, making it serve
simply as the site for perception of changes in visual effects: "changes of
pace, of scale, of direction, of shape, of surface."[12] Informal arrangements
divided the mall experience into a series of cozy limited views, with
meandering water and bridges to lead shoppers on to each new surprise;
as one planner comments, at Old Orchard "the lure of around-the-
corner urges the shopper on" so that "he sees more than he otherwise
would" and he "concentrates his attention upon the attractions most
nearly at hand."[13] Some other of these phase-three rustic malls have two
levels, a crucial innovation (begun by James Rouse) which halves the
distance shoppers have to walk, accents and insulates the courts, allows
more views and more people-watching, and increases the psychological
intimacy of the "rural" setting.

Love Story:
Mall as Movie: "Looking," "Buying"

Clearly, the design self-consciousness of the late 1950s brought a
great new emphasis on the psychological effects of mall environments;
the big new design buzzword is "the experience." With the new concentration on special effects for the mall's *"inner realm"* comes a new
concern with the emotional *"inner realm"* of the shopper. A seminal 1957
article by planner and pop psychologist Richard Bennett speaks for the
whole complex of emerging orthodoxies involving (1) the "village"
atmosphere with irregular lines, changing effects, the "lure of around-
the-corner"; (2) the focus on the "psychological needs" of shoppers; and
(3) the new stress on shopping as a nonutilitarian "visual experience," a
quasicinematic spectacle, an adventure.

"The 'looking at' becomes as important as 'the buying,'" writes Bennett, and so the mall is seen as a sort of "moving picture," with a coyly
erotic plot of Girl Meets Goods: "a piece of architecture—the building
—should be considered as a frame for the picture of the love affair

---

10. Baker and Furnaro, 85.
11. **diorama** A three-dimensional scene that depicts people, animals, or natural
settings, commonly used in museums.—EDS.
12. Hornbeck, 70.
13. Hornbeck, 75.

between a customer and a piece of merchandise."[14] If a mall is a successful movie, its shopper will lose herself (Bennett's 1950s customer is always female), forget that building frame, suspend disbelief, and consummate "the experience." Like a spectator at a Panorama, this customer should step inside the frame of the "moving pictures" and walk around immersed in illusion.

When the "buying act" becomes so deeply associated with this kind of illusionistic visual spectacle, a very special mode of shopping is involved: It enters an arena of entertainment in which the experience of looking is as important as the object found, in which customers are willing to "pay for the atmosphere," for "just looking," and their surplus money goes for emotional rather than physical necessities. At this turning point in the late 1950s, Bennett's excitement with the strategies of visual display is part of an effort to urge a basic mall reorientation to "the *impulse-buying* which comes after the essentials are bought."[15] (And the "radical shift" to what is now given the strange name of "nonmerchandise retailing" has indeed continued as a major "trendline" for malls from Bennett's time into the 1980s; with our current emphasis on "specialty" food-and-entertainment centers, it is the dominant mode.)[16]

Bennett details and reenacts the psychology of impulse-buying because, for him, the designer's goal is to help release these "impulses," to help free a shopper's "inner" desires from external concerns (with the "frames" of time, money, self, and so on). An interior atmosphere of fantasy and festivity can make shopping an adventure, a "quest," and so bring "more dollars out of women's purses."[17] (These fresh 1950s inventions have become our commonplaces, our ad copy, our household words.) So the changing, irregular views of an "English village" mall work to keep the buyer dazzled and nearsighted, to prevent a static overview of the whole, to close off awareness of the outside. And Bennett relates this to the *carnival* model of "high-powered merchandising," with its multiplicity of attractions and rides luring customers into continual movement while providing no focal point. In fact, malls probably have the most to learn from the *amusement park,* "where most people spend more than they intend." Bennett finally presents the curved lines of Coney Island as an ideal system for the "country village" mall. This is the vision of amusement-in-enclosure, of shoppers' losing themselves in involuntary repetition within the oneiric circles of fun visual attractions: "a meandering closed ring which returns on itself so that one starts a second circuit before one realizes it."[18]

14. Bennett in Hornbeck, 145.

15. Bennett in Hornbeck, 153.

16. G. Sternlieb and J. W. Hughes, eds., *Shopping Centers USA* (Center for Urban Policy Research, Rutgers State U. of New Jersey, 1981).

17. Redstone in Hornbeck, 75.

18. Bennett in Hornbeck, 158.

Closing the Ring:
Phase Four's "Introverted Center"

Many of these open, village-garden style centers of phrase three are still flourishing attractions, but it was the era's phase-four design alternative that set the pattern for most mall development in the next two decades. The Southdale Shopping Center near Minneapolis, a 1956 work by Victor Gruen and Associates, added a second major innovation to the new two-level concept: It was the first large, *fully enclosed,* air-conditioned mall design. Inspired by the Milan Galleria and nineteenth-century arcades, what Gruen called "the first introverted center" offered a series of arcade entrances opening into a large covered central "mall." With this move to overall enclosure, the center becomes a completely separate domain, sealed off, an economy in itself. As one observer writes, from this point on, "Malls aren't part of the community . . . they *are* the community."[19] Like the nineteenth-century arcades, the panoramas, and the exhibition halls, the enclosed mall can here be seen as a sort of city in itself. And in fact Southdale's interior sought not village serenity or old-style charm but a simulation of downtown activity and bustle.

In this enclosed-mall prototype, Gruen arranged his indoor sculpture and trees, and the closeness of his two levels, to recreate the effects of urban variety and energy. The interior model was a suburbanite's dream of an early 1800s unplanned city, offering substitutes for streets and an arena of concentration to those feeling the uniformity and isolation of suburban sprawl. In 1960, Gruen wrote that the new shopping spaces must "represent an essentially urban environment, be busy and colorful, exciting and stimulating, full of variety and interest."[20] And indeed the decade of the 1960s saw a mall boom with "increasing sophistication . . . in successfully repackaging an idealized urban form into the suburban milieu."[21]

In our day, two-level *verticality* and overall *enclosure* have become standard in the designs produced and reproduced by the large mall development companies. Since multiple levels create problems of access and shopper mobility, systems of undulating ramps, connecting bridges, broad staircases, escalators and other "rides" have become necessary features. And these can only add high-tech pizzazz to the color and activity of the desired urban "effect."

---

19. W. Kowinski, "The Malling of America," *New Times,* May 1, 1978: 33.
20. Gruen cited in Harris, 24.
21. Sternlieb, 2.

Utopia: No Place

But of course part of the mysterious attraction of a mall's city "feel"   20
is that it *is* an "effect"—a designer's virtuoso recreation. First of all, the
background fact of mall enclosure always works in an intriguing tension
with the surfaces of an urban ambience, reminding us of the differences
between such highly defined space and the organic chaos of a town. We
get a *frisson* in recognizing a sameness of mechanical reproduction behind
a mall's "downtown style" diversity: instead of a competition of unique
one-owner "specialty" shops, most malls offer outlets of the same widespread franchise chains; reproduced clones of an entirely standardized
mall design, in fact, often reappear throughout the continent—with the
same Muzak, fixtures, and controlled climate—denying regional differences or local color; the mall crowds, actually, are much more homog-
enous (housewives, older people, teenagers) than those on a city street
(or in the ghettos the urban malls have "renewed"); and those dizzying
mall traffic patterns, we soon recognize, are also clearly preplanned and
permanently fixed.

But too much of this sort of demystifying customer "recognition"
is the main threat to the phase-four designer. These urban-style malls,
though they imitate the city rather than the garden village, share basic
design goals with phase-three plans. Again the accent is on changing
views and variety of stimulation; the concern is still to break up the vast
distances and stark vistas, the increasingly monolithic financial and structural frames, of the new malls. At Southridge, for example, an urban
bustle of changing elevations, false walls, shifting angles, prismatic lighting, and dispersed niches is intended, the designer writes, to "minimize
the effect" of the mall's horizontal size, to "break up" and "distort the
measurements of space and distance." Here again, the basic point is to
"provide *no focal point* to distract from the visual attraction of the stores,"[22]
to keep shoppers dazzled by each display as it rises before their eyes—
and unaware of the enclosing frame.

The Bird-Cage Mall

With this late 1950s culmination of the mall tendency to introversion, as the phase-four mall becomes literally enclosed, comes a great
new designer concern with interior effects of "openness." It seems the

---

22. Redstone in Hornbeck, 71.

more indoor the reality, the more outdoor will be its desired effects. Gruen speaks for this fundamental ambiguity when he states that "The underlying purpose of the enclosed mall is to make people feel that they are outdoors."[23] To achieve this "psychological connection with nature,"[24] Gruen's 1960s mall plans involved skylighting, extensive waterworks, programs of kaleidoscopic light shows, an almost tropical density of plantings, sidewalk cafes (with umbrellas for an illusion of "weather"), and "a much more daring use of works of art than ever before undertaken."[25] In fact, as mall enclosure brought a strong demand for art works (to bring variety to uniform patterns), several early designs featured giant sculptural *birdcages*—a surprising indication of the appropriateness of Michael Snow's 1979 Eaton Centre sculpture to the base themes of "openness" in mall enclosure, of nature brought indoors. The live ancestors of Snow's flock of Canada geese (gliding through their glass galleria) flew in the courtyard birdcage at Southdale, the central symbol of Gruen's first enclosed mall. The later Southridge mall, too, used its central aviary as a natural attraction joining the vertical levels of the mall with their celebration of floating lightness and highlighting the surrounding vertical transportation system of elevators, escalators, and stairs. Like anything connected with malls, this germ idea has proliferated widely and rapidly. The motif continues in many present-day malls: a tall "aviary court" centers Tyson's Corner Mall, near Washington; a new birdcage mall opened just last year [1980] in California.

The Herd Instinct: Flocks and Schools

The enclosure of the mall now seems to be its essential feature and its main allure. Even in areas with mild climates, new developments are almost always covered and temperature-controlled. Revitalizing an old center usually involves adding an all-encompassing roof. Culture critics now focus their attacks on this move toward the self-contained environment; Romero's *Dawn of the Dead* turns a mall's closure to horror; *The Blues Brothers* betrays a similar pent-up aggression when its chase scene gets sidetracked and its slapstick turns unfunny, vicious—as rampaging cars try to escape a sealed mall.

But there still seems to be a hunger for large, enclosed spaces, where people can be a part of a collective movement while avoiding the "shocks" and dangers of actual city life. Many mall planners point to ancient origins in the oriental bazaar, the Arab souk, the marché: mar-

---

23. Gruen in Hornbeck, 165.
24. Gruen, 37.
25. Gruen.

keting has long been associated with enclosure; the Jerusalem bazaar shows that "the covered shopping center has existed for at least 2,000 years"[26] (though it certainly was not controlled by one developer). And Gruen appeals to even more primitive "natural" urges: His centers are erected in the faith that "the human animal's herd instinct which makes him gather in groups, tribes, and nations . . . will endure."[27] Certainly some such nexus of impulses is behind the incredible drawing power of today's advanced urban malls. Toronto's Eaton Centre (1979) attracts more visitors per year than nearby Niagara Falls, with its feature sculpture of migrating Canada geese mirroring the movements of those indoor flocks of tourists below. Baltimore's Harborplace brought in more customers than Disneyworld in its first year (1980–1981), with a festive "chaotic marketplace" atmosphere "blending commerce and showmanship." *Time* magazine was fascinated by this new sort of crowd movement in a glass galleria where people become the display: ". . . translucent pleasure domes where visitors can be seen from outside swarming in rhythmic schools like the angelfish at the nearby National Aquarium. . . ."[28]

In such a regulated environment, we come for the spectacle, the   25
playful imitations and virtuoso effects of the designers. The absence of weather is actually a selling point: Ironically, Snow's geese are moving through the sort of controlled climate and timeless space that one mall advertised with this mock weather report: "Forecast: consistently pleasant . . . Skies over . . . enclosed street continued irrelevant."[29] With controlled lighting, plantings, and music, we want to see what scenes *man* (one of the new Daguerres[30]) can create or recreate. Like the urban crowds which flocked to the circular Panorama buildings to see illusory cities, perhaps we come to the panoramic mall minicities to experience for ourselves one of the themes of Snow's optical illusion in *Flight Stop:* the paradox of *visionary freedom in enclosure.*

New Directions

The ambiguous status of the enclosed phase-four "city-style" malls is only compounded in the current phase five of mall design—with the advent of the urban or vertical mall. City planners have always criticized the suburban mentality of the inauthentic creations that were draining

---

26. Darlow, 38.
27. Gruen, 3.
28. "Cities Are Fun," *Time,* Sept. 24, 1981: 42.
29. Kowinski, 36.
30. **daguerre** Named for inventor Louis J. M. Daguerre (1789–1851), an early method of photography using chemically treated glass or metal plates.—EDS.

the downtown: "Of course, any real downtown is more interesting than
a single mall, just as Los Angeles is more interesting than Disneyland,"
said Dick Rosann, director of New York City's Office of Development,
in 1977.[31] But by now malls are opening in many city centers, and it
appears that downtowns may be rebuilt with the help of these thriving
city replicas in their midst: the Embarcadero Center in San Francisco,
Water Tower Place in Chicago, Citicenter in New York, Eaton Centre
in Toronto, Harborplace in Baltimore, etc., etc.

These urban supermalls are pushing the potentials in verticality and
enclosure to new extremes. Often, such expanded projects absorb many
new functions to increase their status as self-contained economies: They
can contain dances, lectures, exhibits, concerts, all high-school events.
Water Tower Place, for example, supports a twenty-two-story hotel and
forty floors of high-price condominiums, so that people can live, work,
eat, shop, tour, or mingle there—both earning money and spending it
—day and night. And this trend could continue: There seems to be an
omnivorousness inherent in the mall concept; this hardy form proliferates
by absorbing ever-new life functions. The enclosed mall does not want
to close itself off, but instead wants always to enclose more.

From early on, shopping centers have been linked to planned communities. J. C. Nichols's Country Club Plaza, perhaps America's first
center, was part of a planned Kansas housing development. In the 1930s
and 1940s, planned towns (such as Greenbelt, Maryland, Levittown,
Long Island, and Park Forest, Illinois) often had experimental "malls" at
their center. The James Rouse Company, behind one of the earliest
enclosed malls in 1958 and now one of the most prolific mall developers
on many fronts, owns several of today's model planned communities
(with Columbia, Maryland, as centerpiece).[32] And Victor Gruen, inventor of the enclosed mall, has built on his youthful excitement with the
"ville radieuse" of Le Corbusier in recent work on Paris's "new city" at
La Defense, and has written a book on the need to expand the mall
concept (as a way out of atomized closure) into the planning of minicities
or "multi-functional centers."[33]

"People Movers"

Since they are all several stories high (a dramatic escalation of the
earlier two-story idea), "vertical malls" make use of new possibilities for
large-scale construction in metal and glass. Glittering light-drenched

---

31. Rosann in *Horizon,* Sept. 1977: 48.
32. Kowinski, 51.
33. Gruen, 48.

courts are designed for dazzlement. But planners use displays, vistas, lights, and conveyances to accent a vertiginous sense of movement for a pragmatic reason: Extended verticality presents a great problem of shopper circulation. How do you draw people along, how do you stimulate them to explore all levels? The main spectacles in vertical malls, then, are often fun, fancy forms of *moving people:* Some modern mall courts have the playful amusement-park feel of a flamboyant Portman hotel (and Portman's Hyatts and multifunctional cities-within-the-city, with their structured chaos and whimsy, have certainly influenced mall plans); a few malls actually incorporate amusement park rides under their roofs; and some current experiments even replace that glass roof—with huge, light-permeable, billowing circus tents more suggestive of the desired shopping mood. Benjamin, we remember, described the "art of being off center" as a sort of Dodg'em Cars ride; urban mall planners must work to suggest just such an experience.

The elegant Water Tower Place, celebrated as "a system to move   30 and attract people,"[34] greets the shopper with a "cascading garden escalator" which combines a perspectival waterfall with automatic stairs. Called a "spectacular," this cascade suggests an analogy from nature for the mechanical movement of people; it invites crowds to "flow." Such organic analogies for traffic patterns are now basic to almost every design: When streams flow, we flow; when they change levels, we change levels; at a pool, we stop and collect ourselves. In a similar way, designers use trees to link mall levels visually, to encourage shoppers to "climb." Snow's geese—mirroring crowd circulation from the air, "joining" all levels of the central galleria by their position in the "landscape" of mall "earth" and "sky"—are successful in this way, almost too uncannily so. (Their movement, suspended animation, is also reified wax-model fixity; their freeflight is closing on the end of the corridor; their natural flow is also artificially "stopped." Like the *Time* writer at Harborplace, we see this group movement from outside, in display form, and this the "natural" "herd" analogy becomes unsettling.)

The mall designer's main goal is continual "flow." The cascade/ escalator at Water Tower Place leads directly to a second "spectacular" —a seven-story grand atrium traversed by three glass-windowed elevators, which glitter in spotlighting and can provide a panoramic ride. Such a moving spectacle is carefully planned to bring people in for what the designer (and we recall Bennett's views here) calls "the experience."

Even more than the suburban malls, these new projects link architecture and entertainment. The stress is on affective "experience," writes one critic praising "the new concept of architecture" in Water Tower Place, because a mall building is not "an object, a thing," but is "an

---

34. *Architectural Record,* April 1976: 136–40.

environmental phenomenon," a spectacle surrounding its perceivers: "The question of what it *is* . . . is less urgent than the question of how it *feels.*"[35] (Though this seems to beg the question: What *is* it?) So here a planner must aim for pizzazz, combining profit and pleasure, commerce and showmanship, in a site for the emotional encounters of adventuring shoppers. This can create a strange atmosphere for the "perceiver's" main activity—for buying. If the "feeling" is of amusement, distraction, and continual motion, we may be so involved in moving and looking that buying seems incidental; in fact, in malls we *do* mostly buy "incidentals."

As Bennett foresaw, "impulse-buying is one result of this combination of shopping and spectacle"—we just pick up what suddenly appears before our eyes, out of the continual flow of surrounding merchandise. (Is this like buying a still from a movie, or a souvenir from a tour?) The new concept in mall bookstores, for example, seems to be to maximize random table-top displays (the new arrivals) and to minimize old-style cataloguing by subject. It may be very difficult to find the specific book that we come for; instead of such goal-directed shopping, we are invited, almost forced, to *browse.* Buzzed with coffee, lulled by music, we find an endless series of colorful covers rising before us. In such off-center distraction, we will almost inevitably discover a surprise, an unexpected object of desire.[36]

Reading the Text

1. What are the five phases of shopping mall design that Peter Gibian describes?
2. According to Gibian, how does each of the five designs of shopping mall stimulate consumption?
3. In what ways do the most modern shopping malls link architecture and entertainment?

Reading the Signs

1. One sort of mall that Gibian does not discuss is the urban minimall. Do minimalls fit any of his five phases? If so, explain which one; if not, invent a sixth phase and describe its features, using Gibian's analysis as a model.
2. Interview at least three other students in your class, asking them about their behavior when visiting malls. Do they shop purposefully? Browse? Hang out? Then write an essay in which you explain their behavior, using Gibian's arguments about mall architecture as a critical framework.

---

35. *Architectural Record,* April 1976: 99–104.
36. *New Yorker,* Sept. 30, Oct. 6, Oct. 13, 1980.

3. Visit a local shopping mall, and write a semiotic analysis of its design. How does the mall's design encourage shoppers to consume?

4. Visit two different kinds of mall in your community (a birdcage mall, for instance, and an older one-stop mall). To what extent does your behavior as a consumer—your "looking" and your "buying"—differ in the two malls? Analyze these differences, using Gibian's article as a critical framework.

5. Visit a local department store and a warehouse-style retail outlet. Basing your argument on Gibian's analysis, compare and contrast the interior designs of each, paying attention to the way they stimulate impulse buying.

ELIZABETH WILSON

Oppositional Dress

IIIIIIIIIIIIIIIIIIIIIIIIIIIIIIIIIIIIIIIIIIIIIIIIIIIIIII

Every generation believes that it is the first to use clothing to annoy the preceding generation, but as Elizabeth Wilson (b. 1936) shows in this selection from Adorned in Dreams *(1985), the young have been dressing to shock and annoy for quite a long time. Ranging from hippies to American blacks and gays, Wilson surveys how clothing fashions have been deployed as a sign of rebellion against the status quo. In our own era, styles that postdate Wilson's essay, from hip-hop to grunge, provide clear signals both of their wearers' opposition to mainstream culture and to their sense of solidarity with those who dress as they do. You can be certain that new oppositional styles will be appearing even as you read this chapter. A senior lecturer in social studies at the Polytechnic Institute of North London, Wilson is also the author of, among several other books,* Through the Looking Glass: A History of Dress From 1860 to the Present Day *(1989) and* The Sphinx in the City: Urban Life, the Control of Disorder, and Women *(1991).*

The first American hippies adopted a naturalistic, flowing style, apparently in total opposition to the mainstream styles; yet, like the pre-Raphaelite style,[1] it turned out to be evolutionary rather than revolutionary, a prefiguration of the way all dress was evolving. Hippie fashion in the late 1960s swung the pendulum against the rectilinear and the

---

1. **Pre-Raphaelite** A nineteenth-century English art movement that imitated the realism and delicacy of design characteristics of early Renaissance Italian art.—EDS.

straight, for it was a walking adaptation of the fashionable art-nouveau[2] spirals. Hair, which had been short, lacquered, and straight, became long and curly, for both sexes. Sleeves which had been tight and shortish became long, gathered, flowing. Bell-bottomed trousers widened until they looked like skirts, and skirts which had been short and straight sank to the floor. Jackets were suddenly flowery, eighteenth-century, and brocade and velvet bloomed. Scarves . . . were festooned in twos, threes, fours around the throat, to sink floating to the knees. Collars got larger and longer, like rabbits' ears. Make-up became first naturalistic, then vampishly exaggerated. . . . Model girls—and Brigitte Bardot—took up the cause of cruelty to animals and refused to wear coats made from endangered species; and a demand for "natural" home remedies for skin and hair was catered to by commercial cosmetic firms which introduced new lines in which herbal and vegetable ingredients figured.

The word "hippie" came from the United States, where the hippies and their rock music originated in the student counterculture and the student campus rebellions of the anti–Vietnam war 1960s. In Britain the hippie style meant something different from its transatlantic counterpart, although both were related to student radicalism. The British variant bore a message that was anticapitalist in the sense that to create a unique appearance out of a bricolage of secondhand clothes, craft work, and army surplus was to protest sartorially against the wastefulness of the consumer society. You rejected the mass-produced road, and simultaneously wasteful luxury, and produced your own completely original look. Yet although this was undertaken in a spirit of anticonsumerism, it did involve the expenditure of much time if not money, and reintroduced the snobbery of uniqueness, since there was, necessarily, only *one* of the "frock" you had found—just as much as if you'd bought a Dior original.

British hippies were urban nomads; the Americans (as recorded, for example, in the film of *Woodstock*) were living a wholly other dream from the dream of little frocks and squats in the twilight zones of every British city. Chelsea hippies were the spiritual descendants of the Chelsea art students of earlier decades. The Americans were pioneers. To a 1980s audience the Woodstock rock fans of 1970 look like the settlers of the Old West and it's possible to see now with a clarity that couldn't be there at the time (when the eye was distracted by the paraphernalia of beads, nudity, and body make-up that went toward the flower-power style) how deeply conservative this image was—of women in long hair and long skirts, naturally lovely and winsome, and of men whose hair was long in a manly way that went with beards, Levi's, and wide-brimmed

---

2. **Art Nouveau**   A highly ornamental early twentieth-century architectural style characterized by sweeping lines, weaving spirals, and tight curves.—EDS.

Stetsons. Even nudity in the American hippie ethic meant a return to nature in the manner of Thoreau or Walt Whitman—no whiff of English decadence there. For the radical counterculture of the United States was infused more deeply than the British could ever be with a rejection of the world of the city, and took its inspiration from the existence of the enormous wide-open spaces of the American hinterland. In crowded Britain a commune meant just another urban squat, or at most a country farmhouse; in the States it could really mean a life in the wilds. The American hippie idiom had available to it a counterimagery of human unification with nature simply not present in British culture.

It is in the United States, too, more than in any Western European country that time has embalmed the hippie style, for it is still possible to find West Coast communities where the hippies live on. The growing of marijuana up in the empty California hills has in some cases become a business, but the growers are still hippies too; and with their long print dresses and big western hats, their long hair and sunburned faces and hordes of naked children, they now look less like campus radicals than like the Amish communities of Pennsylvania, where whole towns still wear the long dresses, suits, and sunbonnets of their nineteenth-century German immigrant forbears.

British hippiedom, by contrast, could mutate without too much   5
difficulty into punk. Punk took to the London streets in the long hot summer of 1976 and took modernism much further than the mods had done. This really was the fashion equivalent of modernism in art:

> Like [Marcel] Duchamp's[3] "ready mades"—manufactured objects which qualified as art because he chose to call them such—the most unremarkable and inappropriate items—a pin, a plastic clothes peg, a television component, a razor blade, a tampon—could be brought within the province of punk (un)fashion.[4]

This "confrontation dressing" aimed to shock—but also to "make strange," which is precisely what the modernist artists of the early twentieth century (the Russian formalists,[5] for example) had also tried to do —to look at the everyday world in a new way, and force others to do so:

> Objects borrowed from the most sordid of contexts found a place in the punks' ensembles: lavatory chains were draped in graceful arcs across chests encased in plastic bin-liners. Safety pins were taken out

---

3. **Marcel Duchamp** (1887–1968) French artist and champion of the Dada movement, which emphasized nonsensical, nihilistic themes.—EDS.

4. Hebdige, Dick (1979), *Subculture: The Meaning of Style,* London: Methuen, p. 107.

5. **Russian formalists** An early twentieth-century movement that proposed that the purpose of literature is to present ordinary experience in an unfamiliar and even bizarre manner.—EDS.

of their domestic "utility" context and worn as gruesome ornaments through the cheek, ear or lip. "Cheap" trashy fabrics (PVC, plastic, lurex, etc.) in vulgar designs (e.g., mock leopard skin) and "nasty" colours . . . were salvaged by the punks and turned into garments (flyboy drainpipes, "common" miniskirts) which offered self-conscious commentaries on the notions of modernity and taste.[6]

What was important was that nothing should look natural. In this sense punk was the opposite of mainstream fashion which always attempts to naturalize the strange rather than the other way about. This is the sophistication of punk, its surrealism and its modernism in the true sense: It radically questions its own terms of reference, questions what fashion *is,* what style *is,* making mincemeat of received notions of beauty and trashing the very idea of "charm" or "taste."

As a countercultural style punk soon lost its hard, working-class edge; in the early eighties a pink, yellow, or green flash in short, spiky hair was more likely to be the hallmark of a middle class radical feminist or post-neo-Marxist student. A lot of zips on a jumpsuit or two earrings in one ear became mainstream fashions. At the same time there remain those who do still identify as punks—just as there remain those of an earlier generation who have gone on being teds.[7]

Because of the doomy, freaked-out feel of punk—shaved heads, green hair, and slashed clothes are reminiscent of a band of medieval pilgrims on a penitential journey, or at least of a band of film extras done up to look like pilgrims—there's been a tendency to read it simplistically as an expression of angst about nuclear war and dread of the futility of postindustrial, postmodernist life, a general nihilism—and maybe the kids of the eighties are the secular equivalents of the witches and the dances of death of the later Middle Ages, another period when Armageddon was thought to be just around the corner. Yet to see punk in this light misses the possibility that to create one's identity in a shocking and deviant way that is none the less well supported within a subculture may actually contribute to the building of self-confidence, a sense of self, and even optimism, albeit within a generalized pessimism.

Punk was followed by a plethora of put-together styles and youth fashion crazes. So much did dressing up become the rage that even *Vogue* ran a feature on it (August 1983). Any and every style could be brought into play. Most were still hitched to a style of music or a single band or star, and some of them recycled previous youth styles. There were the neo-mods who surfaced in the wake of *Quadrophenia,* a film made by one of the original mod bands, The Who. Singers took androgyny even further than David Bowie in his Ziggy Stardust days. There have for years been audiences of fans whose aim has been to reproduce exactly

---

6. Hebdige.
7. **teds** English countercultural fashion movement of the 1950s.—EDS.

the appearance of "their" star, but Boy George, best known androgynous pop star yet, who contrived a style of dress from a mélange of sources —Hasidic Jewish black hat, plaited dreadlocks tied with curl rags, shapeless Japanese style tunic and trousers, and masses of make-up—had a following of *girls* who copied exactly this unmasculine male star.

Then there were the "new romantics" who created a style of big, floppy collars (also incorporated in the Princess Di style), black velvet, and exaggerated make-up. There were weird "horror movie" and "vampire" styles, all of which were essentially variants of romanticism-decadence, related ultimately to glam-rock, and using artifice of every kind, especially make-up. They are the theatrical, performance-orientated fashions.

Slightly different were the styles associated with football club followers, although Kevin Sampson and David Rimmer, writing in *The Face,* suggested that "high street fashion" of this kind started with a style based on a mixture of David Bowie and punk in 1977: "mohairs worn with straights and plastic sandals, complemented by duffel coats," and a "wedge" haircut from "the last great depression." At first another cult music club style, it was taken up by football fans, and fad followed fad culminating in a bizarre parody of classic antifashions with an emphasis on labels fashion. This look was "an incongruous mixture of Nike trainers, frayed Lois jeans and Lacoste shirts, worn with cashmere scarves and jumpers, topped with long Burberry raincoats."[8] This was "football chic." The school children and kids on the dole who longed for these expensive clothes would do anything to get hold of them; and Kevin Sampson recounts the desperation of Lacoste in the face of complaints from British retailers of an epidemic of shoplifting, smash-and-grab raids, and assaults on garments: "they even cut the crocodiles off with razor blades, tearing *great holes* in the shirts."

Dick Hebdige argues that the styles are neither arbitrary nor necessarily a substitute for politics or engagement with the "real world." Subcultural styles reinterpret conflicts of the wider society: In the case of punks and skinheads, it is racism. Punks really did aspire to be outsiders alongside blacks—"we're niggers"; while the racism of the skinheads who wear their heads almost shaved, and caricature traditional working-class clothes in the shape of old-fashioned shirts, braces with shrunken trousers, and heavy "bovver boots," seemed "to represent a conservative proletarian backlash to the radical 'working class' posturings of the new wave."

Blacks and other ethnic minorities have also developed their own oppositional styles, but these have usually had a conscious and deliberate message. With the expansion of Harlem in the early twentieth century

8. Sampson, Kevin and Rimmer, David (1983), "The Ins and Outs of High Street Fashion," *The Face,* July, pp. 20–22.

came many, often exaggerated versions of fashionable wear. By the 1940s the young urban blacks had evolved a highly distinctive style: the zoot suit. This had exaggerated, padded shoulders and peg-top trousers narrowing to the ankle, and both jacket and trousers were lavishly draped. The word "zoot" came from the urban jazz culture of the 1930s, but the origins of the style itself are uncertain, and several explanations have been suggested, but it seems possible that the style was first developed by the second-generation children of migrant Mexican workers.

During the war, in 1943, zoot suits led to serious riots, for gangs of predominantly Mexican and black youths in suits that flouted rationing regulations outraged the servicemen stationed in Pacific ports. What were essentially race riots flared first in Los Angeles and then spread along the West Coast. According to one interpretation—unsurprisingly, the most popular explanation at the time—the zoot suiters came from the underworld of petty criminals, evading the draft (although many turned out to have medical exemption) and indulging in a traditional machismo.

Yet not all zoot suiters were men. At least two female gangs, the Slick Chicks and the Black Widows, were reported, the latter so named on account of their black uniforms of zoot suit jackets, short skirts and fishnet stockings. The active and aggressive role that these young women played suggests that the riots expressed something potentially more radical than juvenile deviance: social rebellion against poverty, against the alienation of American city life, especially for the ethnic minorities. They were also bred of the disruptions of wartime and women's rapidly changing role.

The zoot suit is an especially clear example of a symbolic counter-cultural style that caused a moral panic and led to actual violence in the streets. The zoot suit was defiance, a statement of ethnic pride and a refusal of subservience.[9]

Malcolm X, himself a zoot suiter in his youth, when he did live by petty crime, pimping, and drugs, was later to reject any positive connotations of the style. His condemnation gestures to the ambivalence, perhaps, of any attempt to defy by stylistic means:

> I'd go through that Grand Central Station afternoon rush-hour crowd, and many white people simply stopped in their tracks to watch me pass. The drape and the cut of the zoot suit showed to the best advantage if you were tall—and I was over six feet. My conk was fire red. I was really a clown, but my ignorance made me think I was "sharp." My knob-toed orange coloured "kick up" shoes were nothing but Florsheim's, the ghetto's Cadillac of shoes in those days.

9. Cosgrove, Stuart (1984), "The Zoot Suit and Style Warfare," *History Workshop Journal,* Issue 18, Autumn.

The "conk" was hair straightened at home by a method of using lye, which burned the scalp:

> When Shorty let me stand up and see in the mirror, my hair hung down in limp, damp strings. My scalp still flamed . . . My first view in the mirror blotted out the hurting. I'd seen some pretty conks, but when it's the first time, on your *own* head, the transformation, after the lifetime of kinks, is staggering . . . on top of my head was this thick, smooth sheen of shining red hair—real red—as straight as any white man's . . .
>
> This was my first really big step towards self-degradation.[10]

Later, Malcolm X went to prison. There he became a Black Muslim, and, after his release, a black political leader until his assassination in 1965. Then, rebellion and a refusal of the dominant, white culture, took a more conscious and more explicit form. The natural, Afro hair and the slogan "Black is Beautiful" were a much more openly ideological reassertion of the distinctive nature of the black experience. Before the 1960s, the majority of black women and men in the West had had only white models of beauty on which to base their own looks. Music stars such as the Supremes and Shirley Bassey had straightened hair or wore wigs.

Yet although in the glass of fashion ethnic diversity was allowable, this was usually still—as in the 1920s—because it was "exotic." Indeed, Donyale Luna, who was the first internationally famous black fashion model, in the 1960s, was marketed not just as exotic, but even as freakish ("Is it a plane? No. Is it a bird? Yes . . . it's Donyale Luna") and she herself did not survive this objectification.[11]

Nevertheless, in the 1960s, 1970s, and 1980s a variety of distinctively black styles developed, some wholly oppositional, some combining styles adapted, for example, from Africa, with Western fashions. In Britain, Rastafarian men wear long, twisted dreadlocks beneath high-crowned hats or knitted caps of red, gold, and green. The style is an open and deliberate sign of affiliation and both friends and foes recognize it as such. It often leads to harassment on the streets and in prison, where dreadlocks may be forcibly cut off. Similarly Sikh men, who wear their hair long beneath a turban, are sometimes or have been until recently penalized, for example by being prosecuted for not wearing a safety helmet when riding a motorbike. (And of course white men with long hair have also been ritually punished: When two members of the editorial

---

10. Malcolm X (1965), *The Autobiography of Malcolm X,* Harmondsworth: Penguin, pp. 164, 137–8.

11. Keenan, Brigid (1977), *The Women We Wanted to Look Like,* New York: St. Martin's Press, p. 178.

group of *Oz* were sent to prison in the early 1970s in London, their shorn hair made the national news headlines.)

The symbolic significance of long hair on men—in contemporary Western culture at least—takes us beyond fashion and its use and subversion by black minority groups. In women's fashions, especially, fashion and dissidence may combine. The Afro-Caribbean fashion for beaded and plaited hairstyles originated in adaptations of African styles and asserted a pride in African descent; they may also reinterpret Western styles, for example when a head of narrow plaits is then pinned into a 1940s sideswept roll, or recreated as a twenties bob.

Perhaps what is distinctive about countercultural, oppositional dressing as opposed to the direct statement of black identity made by the original Afro style, or the adoption of politically or religiously committed groups of what becomes virtually a uniform, is the ambiguity of the former. In the early days of the Harlem expansion, ghetto fashions seem to have expressed the desire of a particularly oppressed urban multitude for some joy and glamour in their lives, and countercultural dressing is usually most distinctive when it expressed hedonism and rebellion simultaneously.

Yet outrage dressing, ambiguous as it is, may on occasion express simply—ambiguity. At first glance the androgyny of rock stars such as David Bowie shocks. New boundaries of boldness have surely been set when a man wears make-up, or a woman shaves her head. Not necessarily; these styles may turn out to be little more than new forms of dandyism. Dandyism expresses difference and disengagement as much as rebellion. The dandyism of the American ghettos of the 1950s, which was greatly to affect emergent music styles, suggested a sense of élitism rather than identification with a group:

> The hipster was [a] typical lower class dandy, dressed up like a pimp, affecting a very cool, cerebral tone—to distinguish him from the gross impulsive types that surrounded him in the ghetto—and aspiring to the finer things in life.[12]

Moreover there is nothing more secretive than dandyism, nothing more coy than androgyny. They are the opposite of open affiliation. So it was significant that none of the male androgynous stars of the early 1980s "came out" as gay. They played hard to get, hinted at bisexuality, oracularly suggested that "love takes many forms." During a big promotion in late 1983, Boy George, lead singer with the group Culture Club, played down or even refuted any idea of either a homosexual identity or a "gay life" at the social level. He admitted to having slept with men

12. Goldman, A. (1974), *Ladies and Gentlemen, Lenny Bruce,* London: Panther, quoted in Hebdige, Dick, op. cit.

in the past, but now: "I'd rather have a cup of tea."[13] He claimed—correctly—to be in the British grand eccentric tradition; and is also in the time-honored tradition of the British drag artist.

It's as if gender, on the surface so outraged, is for that very reason divorced from a sexuality that remains opaque, a carefully guarded arena of privacy. Yet perhaps the impenetrable ambiguity represents a fidelity to the most fashionable of all sexual "truths" of the seventies: that gender and desire are ultimately unstable. The rigid sexual identities we cultivate, and which are popularly experienced as "natural" and given at birth, are really fictions elaborated by the nineteenth-century sexologists; they merely imprison the waywardness of lust, constraining us in sexual and social roles.

In the 1970s there was, perhaps paradoxically, a proliferation of styles of dress linked to deviant sexualities. Gay Liberation (GLF) as a political movement began in Greenwich Village; brought to England it was the first political movement to elevate dress to the center of its political practice. The gay liberationists of 1970 had yet to abandon their belief in sexual identity; they still believed that they "were" homosexuals. The first and archetypal act for a member of GLF was therefore to "come out"—publicly to declare himself gay. One of the most dramatic ways of doing this was to subvert the traditional "drag" of the entertainment industry, and to wear—publicly—make-up and a frock. (The word "frock" had languished in an old-fashioned limbo since the 1940s. It was retrieved by the hippies when they started to wear their secondhand forties finds.)

The GLF ideology was that forms of cross-dressing broke down stereotyped gender roles; to wear a skirt and high heels was to give up "male privilege." But Gay Liberation went much further, even, than that. There was to be a general breaking down of all conventional divisions, and a revolutionary life-style in which individualism would be smashed:

> Long nights were spent talking, crying, confessing, barriers came down with painful crashes. Egos took an incredible battering . . . Because it was not always possible for us in the collective to be in one room all the time, we decided that if two or more of us got together and talked, then anything said should be repeated to whoever was missing. This helped us to fight couples and factions.
>
> In practical terms some beautiful things started to happen. It was fabulous to see Richard walking around in Lorna's cardigan; Jenny in Richard's underpants; and Julia in my shoes. Soon it was possible not to feel that a particular article belonged to anyone.[14]

---

13. *Woman,* October 8, 1983.
14. Walter, Aubrey (ed.) (1981), "Fuck the Family," *Come Together: The Years of Gay Liberation 1970–1973,* London: Gay Men's Press, pp. 156–7.

Because society had already made their sexuality into a problem, it was perhaps easier for young homosexuals to act out this attack on gender than it would have been for others. The problem with full-scale drag still remained: Although it caricatured traditional drag, it still often caricatured women as well, and could be offensively sexist.

Among gay men there was a movement toward the reassertion of   25
masculinity. The homosexuals of the midseventies wanted to make the statement that fags were not weeds, that manliness has no necessary connection with sexual orientation. Out of this came the "clone" look. In a way, the clone was a caricature of masculinity. The clone wore jeans, lumber shirts and jackets, distressed leather and heavy boots, and although clean-shaven sported a moustache.[15] This almost uniform style had a number of advantages. The clone was instantly recognizable to other gay men, yet did not invite violence from queer-bashers. The look would not offend at work for most colleagues would miss its significance; yet it gave the wearer the satisfaction of being able to feel that he was, in one sense, being openly gay even if most straights didn't realize it. The clone uniform emphasized the masculinity of gayness; it also had the advantage of aging well. A bald clone looked much better than a bald Ganymede, while the heavy belts and flying jackets could conceal a fair amount of paunch.

Leather freaks and s/m (sadomasochist) men and lesbians wore yet more daring styles. Some lesbians returned to the exaggerated "butch" and "femme" styles seen in the clubs and bars of the 1950s and 1960s but out of tune with the androgynous and feminist seventies. And, as is well known, American homosexuals even developed an elaborate sexual code based on the placing of handkerchiefs and bunches of keys. So while gender has been destabilized and—within avant-garde circles at least—it has become customary to downplay the permanency of sexual orientation, at the same time a more and more exquisitely specific scale of sexual desires is signaled with absolute precision.

Yet it would be a mistake to see this as more subversive than it really is. Suzy Menkes[16] wrote about the 1984 fashions for "androgynous undies" and masculinity in women's dress, suggesting that these were "the ultimate fashion statement about the sexual revolution." Suzy Menkes goes on to reveal, however, that this form of "cross dressing," which is opening up the way to "gender-bending" unisex departments in exclusive fashion stores, is simply a new fad and that—significantly— the market it is aimed at is the market of affluent heterosexual *couples* for whom androgynous dress symbolizes not an attack on gender but merely a reaffirmation of middle-class togetherness.

---

15. See Altman, Dennis (1982), *The Homosexualization of America,* Boston: Beacon Press.
16. *The Times,* May 1, 1984.

Why should oppositional dress have been so recurrent a feature of life in the industrial world? In a fluid society, that is nevertheless still grossly unequal, individuals and groups find new ways to distinguish themselves; moreover individualism is encouraged, and dissent, up to a point, tolerated. In this "democracy of wealth" in which everyone is free to make herself or himself unequal and in which society oscillates between the poles of public show and private self, a space opens up between the iron order of the body politic and the wayward lawlessness of the ego.

Reading the Text

1. Explain in your own words what "oppositional dress" means. How does such a style differ from mainstream fashion tastes?
2. Wilson focuses on hippie and punk styles. List the "oppositional" features of the fashions adopted by these groups. What do they have in common? How do they differ?
3. According to Wilson, how have blacks, other ethnic minorities, and gays expressed their difference from mainstream culture through fashion?

Reading the Signs

1. Write a semiotic analysis of your own taste in fashion. What messages do you send to your friends or to other groups by your choice of clothing? How do you want others to "read" you?
2. Drawing on Wilson's argument, analyze the popularity of grunge fashion in the 1990s. How does this fashion trend signify "opposition"?
3. In what ways does the meaning of oppositional styles differ for traditionally oppressed groups, such as blacks and gays, compared to that for hippies and punks? How can you account for any differences? Be sure to support your argument by referring to specific styles.
4. Compare the hippie fashions that Wilson describes with the 1960s fashion revival in the 1990s, perhaps by looking at fashion magazines from both eras (check your college library for 1960s editions of *Vogue* or *Glamour*). Is the meaning of such clothing the same? What does the choice of oppositional style say about each decade?
5. In class, analyze the clothing choices and hair styles of class members. What messages are your classmates sending about their identity? Does your class have a single group identity, or are there variations?
6. Read or review Anne Campbell's "The Praised and the Damned" (p. 544) and James Diego Vigil's "Gang Styles" (p. 570). Then write an essay in which you explain the extent to which gang styles work as signs of opposition to mainstream society.

SCOTT POULSON-BRYANT
B-Boys

||||||||||||||||||||||||||||||||||||||||||||||||||||||

By the late 1980s, B-boys (or black boys) had become the standard bearers of youth fashion in America. In this article published in Spin *magazine, Scott Poulson-Bryant tells us what middle-class B-boys were wearing in 1990—and it wasn't all hip-hop at all. Interestingly, as white boys were turning their caps backward, Poulson-Bryant's young relatives were going preppie, it seems, adopting some of the styles of the prep school seventies. Poulson-Bryant's freelance essays on hip-hop and alternative culture have appeared in the* New York Times, Rolling Stone, *the* Source, New York, Essence, *and the* Village Voice. *Currently he is a senior writer at* VIBE *magazine in New York.*

Overheard downtown, from a white girl who's sporting two pairs of doorknocker earrings that do not particularly complement her Betsey Johnson multiples: "Black boys have the hardest time. But they still manage to be the most fabulous-looking things on the street."

I. Some History

A couple of summers ago I escorted my sister and her friends to the Def Jam hip-hop extravaganza at Madison Square Garden. Tami and Carlos and William and Roberto poured into Penn Station with tons of other Long Island kids who had taken the Long Island Railroad into Manhattan for a night of music and adventure. They were in the City now: the dangerous, exploitative City, consumer and regurgitator of nice little black teenagers like themselves. They were looking at each other, at the numbers of teens who looked back at them, at me. I was expected to get them safely upstairs into Madison Square Garden, not knowing that these young fashion and culture sophisticates would teach me—the jaded old Ivy Leaguer who'd long ago escaped the suburbs for the City —a thing or two.

We got in, got seated, and the fun began. Teams of teenagers in gold chains and hightops roamed the aisles looking not so much, I suppose, for "violence," but for others looking just enough not like themselves—mirrors with cracks or blemishes, literal representations of their own insecurities—to provoke casual disgust, B-boy giggles, or blind terror. They were weirdly ritualistic about it all. One brother would step on a sneaker and fists would fly. A chain might be glimpsed—in envy, in admiration—and before you could say "Krugerrand," words would be exchanged: "Faggot," "Long Island Boy," "You mean Strong Island man," "Your Mama," "Yours." And they'd continue on in their baggy khakis and NBA T-shirts, which seemed to be the latest (and oddly conservative) dress code: preppie B-boy or academic hardrock. And smart jackets, not the bulbous, ballooning bomber jackets or tacky sheepskins of a few years ago.

A typical hip black boy in NYC and its surroundings that summer, then: a boxcut fade, a button-down oxford waving over widecut khakis, or denims almost hanging off the ass (so as to show off the beautiful boxers underneath), and the oddest feature of all, Docksider bluchers. What had prompted the shift from the black boy–style gangsterism of fat gold chains and designer sweats? What had motivated the trade-off: L. L. Cool J for L. L. Bean? Hoodlum conservatism for Ivy League buyout?

The change was most apparent when the artists paraded across stage.   5
KRS-ONE lamented the death of Scott La Rock—wearing hightops and Levi's. Eric B. and Rakim knew we got soul—in thick ropes of gold and Gucci paraphernalia. The same for the rest of the groups, culminating in L. L., the hardest-working hard rock in show biz, in his designer sweats and Kangols. Where were the Kangols in the audience?

"That's played out now," Carlos said, relegating it all to silly cliché. "That B-boy stuff is for gangsters—"

"Pseudogangsters," William shot in.

"—and criminals. That's not us."

Well, what's with the bank teller look? I wanted to scream at them, in my fatigues and Guatemalan shirt and Converse hightops—the clothes, I'd been told, that scream (WHITE) COLLEGE BOY!—"It's a cop-out. Where are the gold chains when we need them? Where are the Kangols? Where's our difference?"

Out of a job or in jail, Carlos informed me. Or dead.   10

Then I understood. Even the gangster had gone out of style.

The new uniform was that, though: a uniform. Everyone, even the drug dealers I knew, as sporting these preppy-looking duds, perhaps as a way of cleaning up the image, returning to the constantly evolving drawing board that is our culture and emerging with a model for the post–hip-hop nation: Good-by New Black Aesthetic, hello New Black Antiseptic.

II. Some Theory

I used the above situation to show how black boys—regardless of who's censoring whom or which white cop is bulleting down which black cousin or uncle or bro—reconstruct themselves, and ultimately reconstruct the culture around them. Black British theorist Paul Gilroy once wrote: "Black culture actively makes and remakes itself." Ah, yes.

The neo-Afrocentrism of the educated black left combined with the residue of black power that still resides in the bloodstreams of the urban and suburban post–Malcolm X young has filtered down fashionwise. Dreads are the rage—the little stylish hair-spokes have been added to the aforementioned big, preppy look. African beads are swinging in unison with the dreads and it's all getting topped off by a new wave of caps. Caps: The kids are wearing baseball caps with a vengeance; across class lines, sexuality lines, and team support lines, baseball caps have managed to make a fashionable return.

So, I went on a hunt to find out what this return to team-logo-bearing cap-wearing meant. Did the girlies go for a certain team? Did certain high schools divide along baseball cap lines? Or did the caps simply represent a new stage of the ever-changing style war that is the birthright of young black men everywhere?

A. THE ICON THEORY

At a party the other night, a brother was beautifully turned out in a   15
white denim cut-off, cuffed-over overall set with a white BVD T-shirt underneath. One strap fell casually over his left shoulder. A simple string of beads fell to the pocket of the bib. His parted fade was hidden beneath a Chicago Bulls cap, but he was wearing a pair of spanking-new Patrick Ewing Adidas. I asked him if he preferred one team to the other. "Nope. The sneakers are just dope." He thought for a second. "Actually, Jordan is bad. And he's fine."

Hmmmm. . . .

At my barbershop near my parents' house in Long Island, an eighteen-year-old in a Pistons cap says plainly, "I wear this 'cause Detroit is the shit. Period." He pulls at the blue boxers riding over the edge of his sweatshorts. "Actually, I'm wearing this because I needed a cut. I probably won't bother with it again until about a week or two," he says. "And yeah, it will be this one."

Which is what I call the Wig Theory. I wear my own Korean-stand Yankees cap like a wig. Meaning, when my almost-played-out fade needs a touchup or I just don't feel like running that comb through my naps before I go out, I throw on a cap—a baseball cap—to cover up what folks don't have to see. My cousin sports a Yankees one day and a Mets the next. It doesn't matter to him, he says. "I ain't getting paid like Strawberry. I ain't got no loyalty."

B. THE COLOR THEORY

Which has nothing to do with Frances Cress Welsing. Just the color scheme of the cap. Most of the brothers I spoke to said simply that they wear the caps they wear simply because of the color. The colors of the caps match the colors of their outfits. Rob has twelve caps. Not out of loyalty to twelve teams, but because his summer outfits may need additional accessories. Tim has a Yankees cap because most of his shorts and T-shirts are blue and/or white.

C. THE BANJY REALNESS THEORY

In the Ball culture of black gay folk, there's a category called Banjy   20
Realness. After the vogueing category, but before runway modeling, boys butch, queen, or anywhere in between don their hardest-looking ensemble and make like the toughest thing on the block. They pimp-roll; they crotch-grab; they lay it on thick, partly commenting on the street-warrior-posse poses of the B-boy oppressor, partly showing the straight world who the "real men" are. But it's all for the ironic sake of "realness": Who can be the fiercest, roughest trade? Baseball caps obviously play an important role here. Caps representing teams (like the Raiders) with aggressive reputations are often the caps of choice because if you're bad, your clothes must symbolize badness as well. Actually, that sounds a lot like how straight boys behave. . . .

D. THE BEST CAP THEORY

Perry is an anti-Mets fan. He wears the caps of the teams that beat the Mets. The Cubs were better than the Mets last season. And in three games in three days this season, the Reds beat the Shea Boys in all three. "I'm a Yankees fan. This is how I show it," he says.

In my barbershop, all the discussion that was started by my innocent question—"Why do you wear that cap?"—led to a discussion about sneakers and the deaths "caused" by them. Rev, the barber who's cut my hair and my friends' hair for years, broke out with the best cap theory of them all: "Choose righteousness. It's healthy for you."

Reading the Text

1. Who are B-boys and what is their style?
2. What is Bryant's attitude toward B-boy style? How does his perspective influence the tone of his essay?

Reading the Signs

1. Do you agree with Bryant's interpretation of baseball caps? To develop your argument, interview at least five students, preferably from various

ethnicities, whom you see on campus wearing caps, questioning them about their stylistic choices. Remember to be wary of functional responses.

2. Why do African-Americans have such an impact on fashion, according to Bryant? Do you agree with his explanation?

3. In class, discuss how fashions have changed among African-Americans since Bryant's essay was published. What do the new styles say about their wearers? What do they say about other ethnic groups that may have adopted such styles?

4. To what extent could be B-boy style be considered "oppositional dress," in Elizabeth Wilson's terms (see p. 45)?

5. Using Richard Majors's thesis in "Cool Pose" (p. 471) as your critical framework, write an essay in which you explain the motivation behind the choice of "B-boy" style.

STUART EWEN
Hard Bodies

||||||||||||||||||||||||||||||||||||||||||||||||||||||

In this selection from All-Consuming Images: The Politics of Style in Contemporary Culture *(1988), Stuart Ewen (b. 1945) analyzes the way our bodies themselves can be signs of cultural desire. Focusing on the body sculpting popular among urban professionals in recent years, Ewen argues that the "hard body" fad reflects a postindustrial transformation of the body into a kind of industrial product, something you "build" every day at the gym. Health clubs thus can be seen as factories that produce the sorts of bodily objects that America values, with Nautilus machines standing in as the tools of mass production. Ewen documents the pulse of American culture as a professor of media studies in the Department of Communications at Hunter College, and he also serves as professor in the Ph.D. program in sociology at the City University of New York Graduate Center. He is the author of numerous books and articles on American popular and consumer culture, including* Channels of Desire: Mass Images and the Shaping of American Consciousness *with Elizabeth Ewen (1982) and* Captains of Consciousness: Advertising and the Social Roots of the Consumer Culture *(1976).*

Writing in 1934, the sociologists George A. Lundberg, Mirra Komarovsky, and Mary Alice McInerny addressed the question of "leisure" in the context of an emerging consumer society. Understanding the symbiotic relationship between mass-production industries and a consumerized definition of leisure, they wrote of the need for society to achieve a compatibility between the worlds of work and daily life. "The ideal to be sought," they proposed, "is undoubtedly the gradual obliteration of the psychological barrier which today distinguishes work from leisure."[1]

That ideal has been realized in the daily routine of Raymond H——, a thirty-four-year-old middle-management employee of a large New York City investment firm. He is a living cog in what Felix Rohatyn has termed the new "money culture," one in which "making things" no longer counts; "making money," as an end in itself, is the driving force.[2] His days are spent at a computer terminal, monitoring an endless flow of numerical data.

When his workday is done, he heads toward a local health club for the relaxation of a "workout." Three times a week this means a visit to the Nautilus room, with its high, mirrored walls, and its imposing assembly line of large, specialized "machines." The workout consists of exercises for his lower body and for his upper body, twelve "stations" in all. As he moves from Nautilus machine to Nautilus machine, he works on his hips, buttocks, thighs, calves, back, shoulders, chest, upper arms, forearms, abdomen, and neck, body part by body part.

At the first station, Raymond lies on the "hip and back machine," making sure to align his hip joints with the large, polished, kidney-shaped cams which offer resistance as he extends each leg downward over the padded roller under each knee. Twelve repetitions of this, and he moves on to the "hip abduction machine," where he spreads his legs outward against the padded restraints that hold them closed. Then leg extensions on the "compound leg machine" are followed by leg curls on the "leg curl machine." From here, Raymond H—— proceeds to the "pullover/torso arm machine," where he begins to address each piece of his upper body. After a precise series of repetitions on the "double chest machine," he completes his workout on the "four-way neck machine."

While he alternates between different sequential workouts, and different machines, each session is pursued with deliberate precision, following exact instructions.   5

Raymond H—— has been working on his body for the past three years, ever since he got his last promotion. He is hoping to achieve the

---

1. George A. Lundberg et al., *Leisure: A Suburban Study* (1934), p. 3.
2. *New York Times,* 3 June 1987, p. A27.

body he always wanted. Perhaps it is fitting that this quintessential, single, young, urban professional—whose life has become a circle of work, money culture, and the cultivation of an image—has turned himself, literally, into a piece of work. If the body ideal he seeks is *lean,* devoid of fatty tissue, it is also *hard.* "Soft flesh," once a standard phrase in the American erotic lexicon, is now—within the competitive, upscale world he inhabits—a sign of failure and sloth. The hard shell is now a sign of achievement, visible proof of success in the "rat race." The goal he seeks is more about *looking* than *touching.*

To achieve his goal, he approaches his body piece by piece; with each machine he performs a discrete task. Along the way he also assumes the job of inspector, surveying the results of each task in the mirrors that surround him. The division of labor, the fragmentation of the work process, and the regulating function of continual measurement and observation—all fundamental to the principles of "scientific management"—are intrinsic to this form of recreation. Like any assembly line worker, H—— needs no overall knowledge of the process he is engaged in, only the specific tasks that comprise that process. "You don't have to understand *why* Nautilus equipment works," writes bodybuilder Mike Mentzer in the forward to one of the most widely read Nautilus manuals. "With a tape measure in hand," he promises, "you will see what happens."[3]

The body ideal Raymond H—— covets is, itself, an aestheticized tribute to the broken-down work processes of the assembly line. "I'm trying to get better definition," H—— says. "I'm into Nautilus because it lets me do the necessary touchup work. Free weights [barbells] are good for building up mass, but Nautilus is great for definition."[4] By "definition," H—— is employing the lingo of the gym, a reference to a body surface upon which each muscle, each muscle group, appears segmented and distinct. The perfect body is one that ratifies the fragmentary process of its construction, one that mimics—in flesh—the illustrative qualities of a schematic drawing, or an anatomy chart.

Surveying his work in the mirror, H—— admires the job he has done on his broad, high pectorals, but is quick to note that his quadriceps "could use some work." This ambivalence, this mix of emotions, pursues him each time he comes for a workout, and the times in between. He is never quite satisfied with the results. The excesses of the weekend-past invariably leave their blemish. An incorrectly struck pose reveals an overmeasure of loose skin, a sign of weakness in the shell. Despite all efforts, photogenic majesty is elusive.

---

3. Ellington Darden, *The Nautilus Bodybuilding Book* (1986), pp. viii–ix.
4. Style Project, interview I-13.

The power of the photographic idiom, in his mind's eye, is rein-   10
forced, again and again, by the advertisements and other media of style
visible everywhere. The ideal of the perfectly posed machine—the cold,
hard body in response—is paraded, perpetually, before his eyes and ours.
We see him, or her, at every glance.

An advertisement for home gym equipment promises a "Body By
Soloflex." Above is the silent, chiaroscuro portrait of a muscular youth,
his torso bare, his elbows reaching high, pulling a thin-ribbed undershirt
up over his head, which is faceless, covered by shadow. His identity is
situated below the neck, an instrumentally achieved study in brawn. The
powerful expanse of his chest and back is illuminated from the right side.
A carefully cast shadow accentuates the paired muscle formations of his
abdominal wall. The airbrush has done its work as well, effecting a
smooth, standardized, molded quality, what John Berger has termed "the
skin without a biography." A silent, brooding hulk of a man, he is the
unified product of pure engineering. His image is a product of expensive
photographic technology, and expensive technical expertise. His body
—so we are informed—is also a technical achievement. He has reached
this captured moment of perpetual perfection on a "machine that fits in
the corner" of his home. The machine, itself, resembles a stamping
machine, one used to shape standardized, industrial products. Upon this
machine, he has routinely followed instructions for "twenty-four traditional iron pumping exercises, each correct in form and balance." The
privileged guidance of industrial engineering, and the mindless obedience
of work discipline, have become legible upon his body; yet as it is
displayed, it is nothing less than a thing of beauty, a transcendent aspi-
ration.

This machine-man is one of a generation of desolate, finely tuned
loners who have cropped up as icons of American style. Their bodies,
often lightly oiled to accentuate definition, reveal their inner mechanisms
like costly, open-faced watches, where one can see the wheels and gears
moving inside, revealing—as it were—the magic of time itself. If this is
eroticism, it is one tuned more to the mysteries of technology than to
those of the flesh.

In another magazine advertisement, for Evian spring water from
France, six similarly anatomized figures stand across a black and white
two-page spread. From the look of things, each figure (three men and
three women) has just completed a grueling workout, and four of them
are partaking of Evian water as part of their recovery. The six are
displayed in a lineup, each one displaying a particularly well-developed
anatomical region. These are the new icons of beauty, precisely defined,
powerful machines. Below, on the left, is the simple caption: "Revival

of the Fittest." Though part of a group, each figure is conspicuously alone.

Once again, the modern contours of power, and the structures of work discipline, are imprinted upon the body. In a world of rampant careerism, self-absorption is a rule of thumb. If the division of labor sets each worker in competition with every other, here that fragmentation is aestheticized into the narcissism of mind and body.

Within this depiction, sexual equality is presented as the meeting point between the anorectic and the "nautilized." True to gender distinctions between evanescent value and industrial work discipline, the three women are defined primarily by contour, by the thin lines that their willowy bodies etch upon the page. Although their muscles are toned, they strike poses that suggest pure, disembodied form. Each of the men, situated alternately between the women, gives testimony on behalf of a particular fraction of segmented flesh: abdomen, shoulders and upper arms, upper back. In keeping with the assembly line approach to muscle building, each man's body symbolizes a particular station within the labor process.

Another ad, for a health and fitness magazine, contains an alarmingly discordant statement: "Today's women workers are back in the sweat shop." There is a basis to this claim. In today's world, powerful, transnational corporations search the globe looking for the cheapest labor they can find. Within this global economy, more and more women— from Chinatown to Taiwan—are employed at tedious, low-paying jobs, producing everything from designer jeans to computer parts.

Yet this is not the kind of sweatshop the ad has in mind. The photographic illustration makes this clear. Above the text, across the two-page color spread, is the glistening, heavily muscled back of a woman hoisting a chrome barbell. Her sweat is self-induced, part of a "new woman" life-style being promoted in *Sport* magazine, "the magazine of the new vitality." Although this woman bears the feminine trademark of blonde, braided hair, her body is decidedly masculine, a new body aesthetic in the making. Her muscles are not the cramped, biographically induced muscles of menial labor. Hers is the brawn of the purely symbolic, the guise of the middle-class "working woman."

While the text of the advertisement seems to allude to the real conditions of female labor, the image transforms that truth into beauty, rendering it meaningless. Real conditions are copywritten into catchy and humorous phrases. The harsh physical demands of women's work are reinterpreted as regimented, leisure-time workouts at a "health club." Real sweat is reborn as photogenic body oil.

The migration of women into the social structures of industrial discipline is similarly aestheticized in an ad for Jack LaLanne Fitness

Centers. A black and white close-up of a young woman wrestling with a fitness "machine" is complemented by the eroticized grimace on her face. Once again, the chiaroscuro technique accentuates the straining muscles of her arms. The high-contrast, black and white motif may also suggest the "night and day" metamorphosis that will occur when one commits to this particular brand of physical discipline.

In large white letters, superimposed across the shadowy bottom of the photograph, are the words: "Be taut by experts." With a clever play on words the goal of education moves from the mind to the body. Muscle power is offered as an equivalent substitute for brain power. No problem. In the search for the perfectly regulated self, it is implicit that others will do the thinking. This woman, like the Soloflex man, is the product of pure engineering, of technical expertise:

> We were building bodies back when you were building blocks. . . .
> We know how to perfectly balance your workout between swimming, jogging, aerobics and weight training on hundreds of the most advanced machines available. . . . Sure it may hurt a little. But remember. *You only hurt the one you love.* [Emphasis added.]

These advertisements, like Raymond H——'s regular visits to the Nautilus room, are part of the middle-class bodily rhetoric of the 1980s. Together they mark a culture in which self-absorbed careerism, conspicuous consumption, and a conception of *self* as an object of competitive display have fused to become the preponderant symbols of achievement. The regulated body is the nexus where a cynical ethos of social Darwinism, and the eroticism of raw power, meet.

Reading the Text

1. Write a one-paragraph description of the 1980s' "hard body" style.
2. How, according to Ewen, is the body treated like a machine in the "hard body" exercise regimen?
3. Why does Raymond H—— exercise so much?

Reading the Signs

1. Ewen accuses those who follow the hard body trend of conceiving the self as "an object of competitive display." To what extent do you find his accusation valid? To support your argument, draw on your own habits of exercising and those of your friends.

2. In class, discuss the tone Ewen adopts in his essay. How does that tone affect your response to his argument?

3. Break your class into two groups according to gender. In each group, brainstorm ideal body types for both men and women, then rank them according to the group's preferences. Compare the results of the two groups: How are they gender-related?

4. Read a current issue of a magazine devoted to fitness such as *Shape*. To what extent is the body "fashion" that Ewen describes still current? How do you explain any changes?

5. Interview three or four people who are working out in your school or local gym, asking them about the results they want to achieve through their exercising. Then using Ewen's argument about hard bodies as your model, analyze the results of your interviews.

JOAN KRON

The Semiotics of Home Decor

‖‖‖

Just when you thought it was safe to go back into your living room, here comes Joan Kron with a reminder that your home is a signaling system just as much as your clothing is. In Home-Psych: The Social Psychology of Home and Decoration *(1983), from which this selection is taken, Kron takes a broad look at the significance of interior decoration, showing how home design can reflect both an individual and a group identity. Ranging from a New York entrepreneur to Kwakiutl Indian chiefs, Kron further discusses how different cultures use possessions as a rich symbol system. The author of* High Tech: The Industrial Style and Source Book for the Home *(1978) and of some five hundred articles for American magazines, she is particularly interested in fashion, design, and the social psychology of consumption. Kron currently is an editor at* Allure *magazine.*

On June 7, 1979, Martin J. Davidson entered the materialism hall of fame. That morning the thirty-four-year-old New York graphic design entrepreneur went to his local newsstand and bought fifty copies of the *New York Times* expecting to read an article about himself in the Home section that would portray him as a man of taste and discrimination. Instead, his loft and his life-style, which he shared with singer Dawn Bennett, were given the tongue-in-cheek treatment under the headline: "When Nothing but the Best Will Do."[1]

Davidson, who spent no more money renovating his living quarters than many of the well-to-do folks whose homes are lionized in the *Times*'s Thursday and Sunday design pages—the running ethnographic record of contemporary upper-middle-class life-style—made the unpardonable error of telling reporter Jane Geniesse how much he had paid for his stereo system, among other things. Like many people who have not been on intimate terms with affluence for very long, Davidson is in the habit of price-tagging his possessions. His 69-cent-per-bottle bargain Perrier, his $700 Armani suits from Barney's, his $27,000 cooperative loft and its $150,000 renovation, his sixteen $350-per-section sectionals, and his $11,000 best-of-class stereo. Martin J. Davidson wants the world to know how well he's done. "I live the American dream," he told Mrs. Geniesse, which includes, "being known as one of Barney's best customers."[2]

Davidson even wants the U.S. Census Bureau's computer to know how well he has done. He is furious, in fact, that the 1980 census form did not have a box to check for people who live in cooperatives. "If someone looks at my census form they'll think I must be at the poverty level or lower."[3] No one who read the *Times* article about Martin Davidson would surmise that.

It is hard to remember when a "design" story provoked more outrage. Letters to the editor poured in. Andy Warhol once said that in our fast-paced media world no one could count on being a celebrity for more than fifteen minutes. Martin Davidson was notorious for weeks. "All the Martin Davidsons in New York," wrote one irate reader, "will sit home listening to their $11,000 stereos, while downtown, people go

---

1. Jane Geniesse, "When Nothing But the Best Will Do," *New York Times,* June 7, 1979, p. C1ff.
2. Ibid.
3. Author's interview with Martin Davidson.

to jail because they ate a meal they couldn't pay for."[4] "How can one man embody so many of the ills afflicting our society today?"[5] asked another offended reader. "Thank you for your clever spoof," wrote a third reader. "I was almost convinced that two people as crass as Martin Davidson and Dawn Bennett could exist."[6] Davidson's consumption largesse was even memorialized by Russell Baker, the *Times*'s Pulitzer Prize-winning humorist, who devoted a whole column to him: "While simultaneously consuming yesterday's newspaper," wrote Baker, "I consumed an article about one Martin Davidson, a veritable Ajax of consumption. A man who wants to consume nothing but the best and does."[7] Counting, as usual, Davidson would later tell people, "I was mentioned in the *Times* on three different days."

Davidson, a self-made man whose motto is "I'm not taking it with   5
me and while I'm here I'm going to spend every stinking penny I make," couldn't understand why the *Times* had chosen to make fun of him rather than to glorify his 4,000-square-foot loft complete with bidet, Jacuzzi, professional exercise gear, pool table, pinball machine, sauna, two black-tile bathrooms, circular white Formica cooking island, status-stuffed collections of Steiff animals, pop art (including eleven Warhols), a sound system that could weaken the building's foundations if turned up full blast, and an air-conditioning system that can turn cigarette smoke, which both Davidson and Bennett abhor, into mountain dew—a loft that has everything Martin Davidson ever wanted in a home except a swimming pool and a squash court.

"People were objecting to my life-style," said Davidson. "It's almost as if there were a correlation between the fact that we spend so much on ourselves and other people are starving. No one yells when someone spends $250,000 for a chest of drawers at an auction," he complained. "I just read in the paper that someone paid $650,000 for a stupid stamp. Now it'll be put away in a vault and no one will ever see it."[8]

But Dawn Bennett understood what made Davidson's consumption different. "It's not very fashionable to be an overt consumer and admit it,"[9] she said.

---

4. Richard Moseson, "Letters: Crossroads of Decadence and Destitution," *New York Times*, June 14, 1979, p. A28.

5. Letter to the Editor, *New York Times*, June 14, 1979, p. C9.

6. Letter to the Editor, ibid.

7. Russell Baker, "Observer: Incompleat Consumer," *New York Times*, June 9, 1979, p. 25.

8. Author's interview with Martin Davidson.

9. Author's interview with Dawn Bennett.

What Are Things For?

As anyone knows who has seen a house turned inside out at a yard sale, furnishing a home entails the acquisition of more objects than there are in a spring housewares catalog. With all the time, money, and space we devote to the acquisition, arrangement, and maintenance of these household possessions, it is curious that we know so little about our relationships to our possessions.

"It is extraordinary to discover that no one knows why people want goods," wrote British anthropologist Mary Douglas in *The World of Goods.*[10] Although no proven or agreed-upon theory of possessiveness in human beings has been arrived at, social scientists are coming up with new insights on our complicated relationships to things. Whether or not it is human nature to be acquisitive, it appears that our household goods have a more meaningful place in our lives than they have been given credit for. What comes across in a wide variety of research is that things matter enormously.

Our possessions give us a sense of security and stability. They make   10
us feel in control. And the more we control an object, the more it is a part of us. If it's *not mine,* it's *not me.*[11] It would probably make sense for everyone on the block to share a lawn mower, but then no one would have control of it. If people are reluctant to share lawn mowers, it should not surprise us that family members are not willing to share TV sets. They want their own sets so they can watch what they please. Apparently, that was why a Chicago woman, furious with her boyfriend for switching from *The Thorn Birds* to basketball, stabbed him to death with a paring knife.[12]

Besides control, we use things to compete. In the late nineteenth century the Kwakiutl Indian chiefs of the Pacific Northwest made war with possessions.[13] Their culture was built on an extravagant festival

---

10. Mary Douglas and Baron Isherwood, *The World of Goods* (New York: Basic Books, 1979), p. 15. A number of other social scientists have mentioned in recent works the lack of attention paid to the human relationship to possessions: See Coleman and Rainwater, *Social Standing,* p. 310. The authors observed that "the role of income in providing a wide range of rewards—consumption—has not received sufficient attention from sociologists." See Carl F. Graumann, "Psychology and the World of Things," *Journal of Phenomenological Psychology,* Vol. 4, 1974–75, pp. 389–404. Graumann accused the field of sociology of being thing-blind.

11. Lita Furby, "Possessions: Toward a Theory of Their Meaning and Function Throughout the Life Cycle," in Paul B. Baltes (ed.), *Life-Span Development and Behavior,* Vol. 1 (New York: Academic Press, 1978), pp. 297–336.

12. "'Touch That Dial and You're Dead,'" *New York Post,* March 30, 1983, p. 5.

13. Ruth Benedict, *Patterns of Culture* (Boston: Houghton Mifflin [1934], 1959); Frederick V. Grunfeld, "Homecoming: The Story of Cultural Outrage," *Connoisseur,* February 1983, pp. 100–106; and Lewis Hyde, *The Gift* (New York: Vintage Books, [1979, 1980], 1983), pp. 25–39.

called the "potlatch," a word that means, roughly, to flatten with gifts. It was not the possession of riches that brought prestige, it was the distribution and destruction of goods. At winter ceremonials that took years to prepare for, rival chiefs would strive to outdo one another with displays of conspicuous waste, heaping on their guests thousands of spoons and blankets, hundreds of gold and silver bracelets, their precious dance masks and coppers (large shields that were their most valuable medium of exchange), and almost impoverishing themselves in the process.

Today our means of competition is the accumulation and display of symbols of status. Perhaps in Utopia there will be no status, but in this world, every human being is a status seeker on one level or another—and a status reader. "Every member of society," said French anthropologist Claude Levi-Strauss, "must learn to distinguish his fellow men according to their mutual social status."[14] This discrimination satisfies human needs and has definite survival value. "Status symbols provide the cue that is used in order to discover the status of others, and, from this, the way in which others are to be treated," wrote Erving Goffman in his classic paper, "Symbols of Class Status."[15] Status affects who is invited to share "bed, board, and cult,"[16] said Mary Douglas. Whom we invite to dinner affects who marries whom, which then affects who inherits what, which affects whose children get a head start.

Today what counts is what you eat (gourmet is better than greasy spoon), what you fly (private jet is better than common carrier), what sports you play (sailing is better than bowling), where you matriculate, shop, and vacation, whom you associate with, how you eat (manners count), and most important, where you live. Blue Blood Estates or Hard Scrabble zip codes? as one wizard of demographics calls them. He has figured out that "people tend to roost on the same branch as birds of a feather."[17] People also use status symbols to play net worth hide-and-seek. When *Forbes* profiled the 400 richest Americans,[18] its own in-house millionaire Malcolm Forbes refused to disclose his net worth but was delighted to drop clues telling about his status entertainments—his ballooning, his Fabergé egg hunts, his châteaux, and his high life-style. It is up to others to translate those obviously costly perks into dollars.

---

14. Edmund Leach, *Claude Levi-Strauss* (New York: Penguin Books, 1980), p. 39.

15. Erving Goffman, "Symbols of Class Status," *British Journal of Sociology,* Vol. 2, December 1951, pp. 294–304.

16. Douglas and Isherwood, *World of Goods,* p. 88.

17. Michael J. Weiss, "By Their Numbers Ye Shall Know Them," *American Way,* February 1983, pp. 102–106 ff. "You tell me someone's zip code," said Jonathan Robbin, "and I can predict what they eat, drink, drive, buy, even think."

18. "The Forbes 400," *Forbes,* September 13, 1982, pp. 99–186.

A high price tag isn't the only attribute that endows an object with status. Status can accrue to something because it's scarce—a one-of-a-kind artwork or a limited edition object. The latest hard-to-get item is Steuben's $27,500 bowl etched with tulips that will be produced in an edition of five—one per year for five years. "Only one bowl will bloom this year,"[19] is the headline on the ad for it. Status is also found in objects made from naturally scarce materials: Hawaii's rare koa wood, lapis lazuli, or moon rock. And even if an object is neither expensive nor rare, status can rub off on something if it is favored by the right people, which explains why celebrities are used to promote coffee, cars, casinos, and credit cards.

If you've been associated with an object long enough you don't even have to retain ownership. Its glory will shine on you retroactively. Perhaps that is why a member of Swiss nobility is having two copies made of each of the Old Master paintings in his collection. This way, when he turns his castle into a museum, both his children can still have, so to speak, the complete collection, mnemonics of the pictures that have been in the family for centuries. And the most potent status symbol of all is not the object per se, but the *expertise* that is cultivated over time, such as the appreciation of food, wine, design, or art.

If an object reflects a person *accurately*, it's an index of status. But *symbols* of status are not always good indices of status. They are not official proof of rank in the same way a general's stars are. So clusters of symbols are better than isolated ones. Anyone with $525 to spare can buy one yard of the tiger-patterned silk velvet that Lee Radziwill used to cover her dining chair seats.[20] But one status yard does not a princess make. A taxi driver in Los Angeles gets a superior feeling from owning the same status-initialed luggage that many of her Beverly Hills fares own. "I have the same luggage you have," she tells them. "It blows their minds," she brags. But two status valises do not a glitterati make. Misrepresenting your social status isn't a crime, just "a presumption," said Goffman. Like wearing a $69 copy of a $1,000 watch that the mail-order catalog promises will make you "look like a count or countess on a commoner's salary."[21]

"Signs of status are important ingredients of self. But they do not exhaust all the meanings of objects for people," wrote sociologists Mihaly Csikszentmihalyi and Eugene Rochberg-Halton in *The Meaning of*

15

19. Steuben Glass advertisement, *The New Yorker*, April 4, 1983, p. 3.

20. Paige Rense, "Lee Radziwill," *Celebrity Homes* (New York: Penguin Books, 1979), pp. 172–81.

21. *Synchronics* catalog, Hanover, Pennsylvania, Fall 1982.

Things: Domestic Symbols of the Self.[22] The study on which the book was based found that people cherished household objects not for their status-giving properties but especially because they were symbols of the self and one's connections to others.

The idea that possessions are symbols of self is not new. Many people have noticed that *having* is intricately tied up with *being.* "It is clear that between what a man calls *me* and what he simply calls *mine,* the line is difficult to draw," wrote William James in 1890.[23] "Every possession is an extension of the self," said Georg Simmel in 1900.[24] "Humans tend to integrate their selves with objects," observed psychologist Ernest Beaglehole some thirty years later.[25] Eskimos used to *lick* new acquisitions to cement the person/object relationship.[26] We stamp our visual taste on our things making the totality resemble us. Indeed, theatrical scenic designers would be out of work if Blanche DuBois's boudoir could be furnished with the same props as Hedda Gabler's.

Csikszentmihalyi and Rochberg-Halton discovered that "things are cherished not because of the material comfort they provide but for the information they convey about the owner and his or her ties to others."[27] People didn't value things for their monetary worth, either. A battered toy, a musical instrument, a homemade quilt, they said, provide more meaning than expensive appliances which the respondents had plenty of. "What's amazing is how few of these things really make a difference when you get to the level of what is important in life,"[28] said Csikszentmihalyi. All those expensive furnishings "are required just to keep up with the neighbors or to keep up with what you expect your standard of living should be."

"How else should one relate to the Joneses if not by keeping up 20 with them," asked Mary Douglas provocatively.[29] The principle of rec-

---

22. Mihaly Csikszentmihalyi and Eugene Rochberg-Halton, *The Meaning of Things: Domestic Symbols and the Self* (New York: Cambridge University Press, 1981), p. 18.

23. William James, *Principles of Psychology,* Vol. 1 (New York: Macmillan, 1890), p. 291.

24. Georg Simmel, *The Philosophy of Money,* trans. Tom Bottomore and David Frisby (Boston: Routledge & Kegan Paul, 1978), p. 331.

25. Ernest Beaglehole, *Property: A Study in Social Psychology* (New York: Macmillan, 1932).

26. Ibid., p. 134.

27. Csikszentmihalyi and Rochberg-Halton, p. 239.

28. Author's interview with Mihaly Csikszentmihalyi.

29. Douglas and Isherwood, *World of Goods,* p. 125. Also see Jean Baudrillard, *For a Critique of the Political Economy of the Sign,* trans. Charles Levin (St. Louis, MO: Telos Press, 1981), p. 81. Said Baudrillard: "No one is free to live on raw roots and fresh water. . . . The vital minimum today . . . is the standard package. Beneath this level, you are an outcast." Two classic novels on consumption are (1). Georges Perec, *Les Choses* (New

iprocity requires people to consume at the same level as one's friends.[30] If we accept hospitality, we have to offer it in return. And that takes the right equipment and the right setting. But we need things for more than "keeping level" with our friends. We human beings are not only tool-makers but symbol makers as well, and we use our possessions in the same way we use language—the quintessential symbol—to *communicate* with one another. According to Douglas, goods make the universe "more intelligible." They are more than messages to ourselves and others, they are "the hardware and the software . . . of an information system."[31] Possessions speak a language we all understand, and we pay close attention to the inflections, vernacular, and exclamations.

The young husband in the film *Diner* takes his things very seriously. How could his wife be so stupid as to file the Charlie Parker records with his rock 'n' roll records, he wants to know. What's the difference, she wants to know. What's the difference? How will he find them otherwise? Every record is sacred. Different ones remind him of different times in his life. His things *take* him back. Things can also *hold* you back. Perhaps that's why Bing Crosby's widow auctioned off 14,000 of her husband's possessions—including his bed. "'I think my father's belongings have somehow affected her progress in life,'" said one of Bing's sons.[32] And things can tell you where you stand. Different goods are used to rank occasions and our guests. Costly sets of goods, especially china and porcelain, are "pure rank markers. . . . There will always be luxuries because rank must be marked," said Douglas.[33]

One of the pleasures of goods is "sharing names."[34] We size up people by their expertise in names—sports buffs can converse endlessly about hitters' batting averages, and design buffs want to know whether you speak spongeware, Palladio, Dansk, or Poggenpohl. All names are not equal. We use our special knowledge of them to show solidarity and exclude people.

In fact, the social function of possessions is like the social function of food. Variations in the quality of goods define situations as well as different times of day and seasons. We could survive on a minimum daily allotment of powdered protein mix or grains and berries. But we much prefer going marketing, making choices, learning new recipes. "Next to actually eating food, what devout gastronomes seem to enjoy

---

York: Grove Press, [1965], 1967). (2). J. K. Huysmans, *Against the Grain (A Rebours)* (New York: Dover Publications, [1931], 1969).

30. Douglas and Isherwood, *World of Goods,* p. 124.

31. Ibid., p. 72.

32. Maria Wilhelm, "Things Aren't Rosy in the Crosby Clan as Kathryn Sells Bing's Things (and not for a Song)," *People,* May 31, 1982, pp. 31–33.

33. Douglas and Isherwood, *World of Goods,* p. 118.

34. Ibid., p. 75.

most is talking about it, planning menus, and remembering meals past," observed food critic Mimi Sheraton.[35] But it's not only experts who thrive on variety. Menu monotony recently drove a Carlsbad, New Mexico, man to shoot the woman he was living with. She served him green beans once too often. "Wouldn't you be mad if you had to eat green beans all the time?" he said.[36] If every meal were the same, and if everyone dressed alike and furnished alike all meanings in the culture would be wiped out.[37]

The furnishings of a home, the style of a house, and its landscape are all part of a system—a system of symbols. And every item in the system has meaning. Some objects have personal meanings, some have social meanings which change over time. People understand this instinctively and they desire things, not from some mindless greed, but because things are necessary to communicate with. They are the vocabulary of a sign language. To be without things is to be left out of the conversation. When we are "listening" to others we may not necessarily agree with what this person or that "says" with his or her decor, or we may misunderstand what is being said; and when we are doing the "talking" we may not be able to express ourselves as eloquently as we would like. But where there are possessions, there is always a discourse.

And what is truly remarkable is that we are able to comprehend and manipulate all the elements in this rich symbol system as well as we do —for surely the language of the home and its decor is one of the most complex languages in the world. But because of that it is also one of the richest and most expressive means of communication.

Decor as Symbol of Self

One aspect of personalization is the big I—Identity. Making distinctions between ourselves and others. "The self can only be known by the signs it gives off in communication," said Eugene Rochberg-Halton.[38] And the language of ornament and decoration communicates particularly well. Perhaps in the future we will be known by our computer communiqués or exotic brainwaves, but until then our rock gardens, tabletop compositions, refrigerator door collages, and other design language will have to do. The Nubian family in Africa with a steamship

---

35. Mimi Sheraton, "More on Joys of Dining Past," *New York Times,* April 9, 1983, p. 48.

36. "Green Beans Stir Bad Blood," *New York Times,* March 26, 1983, p. 6.

37. Douglas and Isherwood, *World of Goods,* p. 66.

38. Eugene Rochberg-Halton, "Where Is the Self: A Semiotic and Pragmatic Theory of Self and the Environment." Paper presented at the 1980 American Sociological Meeting, New York City, 1980, p. 3.

painted over the front door to indicate that someone in the house works in shipbuilding, and the Shotte family on Long Island who make a visual pun on their name with a rifle for a nameplate, are both decorating their homes to communicate "this is where our territory begins and this is who we are."

Even the most selfless people need a minimum package of identity equipment. One of Pope John Paul I's first acts as pontiff was to send for his own bed. "He didn't like sleeping in strange beds," explained a friend.[39] It hadn't arrived from Venice when he died suddenly.

Without familiar things we feel disoriented. Our identities flicker and fade like ailing light bulbs. "Returning each night to my silent, pictureless apartment, I would look in the bathroom mirror and wonder who I was," wrote D. M. Thomas, author of *The White Hotel,* recalling the sense of detachment he felt while living in a furnished apartment during a stint as author-in-residence at a Washington, D.C., university. "I missed familiar things, familiar ground that would have confirmed my identity."[40]

Wallpaper dealers wouldn't need fifty or sixty sample books filled with assorted geometrics, supergraphics, and peach clamshells on foil backgrounds if everyone were content to have the same roses climbing their walls. Chintz wouldn't come in forty flavors from strawberry to licorice, and Robert Kennedy, Jr.'s, bride Emily wouldn't have trotted him around from store to store "for ten hours" looking for a china pattern[41] if the home wasn't an elaborate symbol system—as important for the messages it sends to residents and outsiders as for the functions it serves.

In the five-year-long University of Chicago study[42] into how modern Americans relate to their things, investigators Mihaly Csikszentmihalyi and Rochberg-Halton found that we all use possessions to stand for ourselves. "I learned that things can embody self," said Rochberg-Halton. "We create environments that are extensions of ourselves, that serve to tell us who we are, and act as role models for what we can become."[43] But what we cherish and what we use to stand for ourselves,

30

39. Dora Jane Hamblin, "Brief Record of a Gentle Pope," *Life,* November 1978, p. 103.

40. D. M. Thomas, "On Literary Celebrity," *New York Times Magazine,* June 13, 1982, pp. 24–38, citation p. 27.

41. "Back Home Again in Indiana Emily Black Picks Up a Freighted Name: Mrs. Robert F. Kennedy, Jr.," *People,* April 12, 1982, pp. 121–23, citation p. 123.

42. Eugene Rochberg-Halton, "Cultural Signs and Urban Adaptation: The Meaning of Cherished Household Possessions." Ph.D. dissertation, Department of Behavioral Science, Committee on Human Development, University of Chicago, August 1979; and Mihaly Csikszentmihalyi and Eugene Rochberg-Halton, *The Meaning of Things: Domestic Symbols of the Self* (New York: Cambridge University Press, 1981).

43. Author's interview with Eugene Rochberg-Halton.

the researchers admitted, seemed to be "scripted by the culture."[44] Even though the roles of men and women are no longer so tightly circumscribed, "it is remarkable how influential sex-stereotyped goals still remain."[45] Men and women "pay attention to different things in the same environment and value the same things for different reasons," said the authors.[46] Men and children cared for action things and tools; women and grandparents cared for objects of contemplation and things that reminded them of family. It was also found that meaning systems are passed down in families from mothers to daughters—not to sons.

Only children and old people cared for a piece of furniture because it was useful. For adults, a specific piece of furniture embodied experiences and memories, or was a symbol of self or family. Photographs which had the power to arouse emotions and preserve memories meant the most to grandparents and the least to children. Stereos were most important to the younger generation, because they provide for the most human and emotional of our needs—release, escape, and venting of emotion. And since music "seems to act as a modulator of emotions," it is particularly important in adolescence "when daily swings of mood are significantly greater than in the middle years and . . . later life."[47] Television sets were cherished more by men than women, more by children than grandparents, more by grandparents than parents. Plants had greater meaning for the lower-middle class, and for women, standing for values, especially nurturance and "ecological consciousness."[48] "Plateware," the term used in the study to cover all eating and drinking utensils, was mentioned mostly by women. Of course, "plates" are the tools of the housewife's trade. In many cultures they are the legal possession of the women of the house.

The home is such an important vehicle for the expression of identity that one anthropologist believes "built environments"—houses and settlements—were originally developed to "*identify a group*—rather than to provide shelter."[49] But in contemporary Western society, the house more often identifies a person or a family instead of a group. To put no personal stamp on a home is almost pathological in our culture. Fear of attracting attention to themselves constrains people in crime-ridden areas from personalizing, lack of commitment restrains others, and insecurity

44. Csikszentmihalyi and Rochberg-Halton, *Meaning of Things,* p. 105.
45. Ibid., p. 112.
46. Ibid., p. 106.
47. Ibid., p. 72.
48. Ibid., p. 79.
49. Amos Rapoport, "Identity and Environment," in James S. Duncan (ed.), *Housing and Identity: Cross-Cultural Perspectives* (London: Croom Helm, 1981), pp. 6–35, citation p. 18.

about decorating skill inhibits still others. But for most people, painting some sort of self-portrait, decoratively, is doing what comes naturally.

All communications, of course, are transactions. The identity we express is subject to interpretation by others. Will it be positive or negative? David Berkowitz, the "Son of Sam" murderer, didn't win any points when it was discovered he had drawn a circle around a hole in the wall in his apartment and written "This is where I live."[50] A person who fails to keep up appearances is stigmatized.

Reading the Text

1. Summarize how, according to Kron, our possessions act as signs of our identity.
2. How do our living places work to create *group* identity?
3. Why did *New York Times* readers object to the consumption habits of Martin J. Davidson?

Reading the Signs

1. In a small group, discuss the brand names of possessions that each of you own. Then interpret the significance of each brand: What do they say about each of you? About the group?
2. With your class, brainstorm factors other than possessions that can communicate a person's identity. Then write your own essay in which you compare the relative value of possessions to your own sense of identity with the additional factors your class brainstormed.
3. Write an essay in which you argue for or against Kron's claim that "To put no personal stamp on a home is almost pathological in our culture."
4. Analyze semiotically your own apartment or a room in your house, using Kron's essay as a critical framework. How do your possessions and furnishings act as signs of your identity?
5. With Roland Barthes's comments on the meaning of materials in mind (see "Toys," p. 95), write an essay interpreting the *materials* with which you have decorated your home environment.
6. How would Joan Kron explain the "body culture" as described by Stuart Ewen ("Hard Bodies," p. 60)?

---

50. Leonard Buder, "Berkowitz Is Described as 'Quiet' and as a Loner," *New York Times,* August 12, 1977, p. 10.

ANDREW   WERNICK

Vehicles for Myth:
The Shifting Image of the Modern Car

||||||||||||||||||||||||||||||||||||||||||||||||||||||

> *Since the invention of the automobile roughly a century ago, cars have*
> *been among the most important of American signs, signaling from gen-*
> *eration to generation not only the social status of their owners but the*
> *general mood of American culture as well. In "Vehicles for Myth,"*
> *Andrew Wernick (b. 1945) shows just how complex and changeable*
> *those moods can be by tracing the transformation of the American car*
> *from a symbol of technological progress to a sign of an emerging synthesis*
> *between technology and nostalgia. A professor of cultural studies and*
> *sociology at Trent University, Ontario, Wernick currently is researching*
> *contemporary symbols of death and the semiotics of popular music. He*
> *is the author of* Promotional Culture: Advertising Ideology and
> Symbolic Expression *(1991) and coeditor of* Shadow of Spirit:
> Religion and Postmodernism *(1992) and the forthcoming* Images
> of Aging.

> *He doesn't design cars, he designs missiles.*
> — ENZO FERRARI, *referring to*
> *Ferdinand Porsche*

Cars as Signs

The production of cars as symbols is a special case of the way in
which, since the industrial revolution of the late eighteenth century, all
mass commodities have come to intersect with the world of meaning.
Of course, human artifacts, down to the most mundane, have always
had symbolic as well as functional significance. But the inception—with
pottery, furniture, clothes, and guns—of commercial mass production
marked a watershed by introducing and making systematic the producer's
need, prior to consumption, to be strictly instrumental and market-
oriented in shaping the meaning products are designed to have.

Attention to image was necessary because of the need to promote
—an activity that became important both because of the general need
to increase the market's absorptive capacity, and because of the competitive need to give such otherwise hard-to-distinguish items as soap,
cigarettes, and beer their own brand identity. The result was the rise of
advertising (made increasingly prominent through the media growth it
stimulated); and an ever more sophisticated concern with how products,

via packaging, decoration, and design, are made to appear.[1] That these developments have long been linked is illustrated by the case of Wedgwood pottery.[2] The celebrated neoclassical and pseudo-Ming designs which for centuries have been its hallmark, were originally supplied, with a keen eye for late Georgian[3] middle-class taste, by Josiah Wedgwood's partner, Thomas Bentley, whose role in the company was to handle promotion and sales.[4]

Whether in ads or design the promotional point has been the same: to deck products out as signs endowed with maximum cultural appeal. And, for this, not just any codings would do. Values invoked had to be positive, identifiable, consensual; and it was also necessary to take account of the product's existing insertion into the culture, together with the value associations this would automatically bring. When for example Proctor launched Ivory (the name itself evoking the virtues of the white empire), soap was already linked, through a germ-based medical model and the propertied classes' fear of urban/industrial disorder, to the Protestant obsession with hygiene. But, as Listerine's later invention of "halitosis" suggests, the values stamped onto products can also have an independent effect, here by heightening hygiene anxiety and giving it a new physiological site.

As a mass-promoted product, the peculiarity of cars, in all this regard, has been twofold: First, besides their function as transport, for users themselves cars have always had a promotional role. Parked at home, like furniture, like the domicile itself, they project a sense of their owner's relative social standing. Out on the road they carry that same sense of class/cultural identification into the wider cultural domain. Cars, in this respect, are similar to clothes, constituting indeed a kind of third skin for ambient industrial man. Like clothes, too, as markers of identity with an anonymously circulating public they readily become subject to the fashion dynamics of competitive display, which manufacturers themselves have naturally encouraged to accelerate obsolescence and sales.

Despite there being fewer and fewer corporate players, the proliferation and turnover of styles has thus kept far ahead of strictly engineering innovation. Ford, the first American auto giant, was at first slow to change lines. But declining sales for its Model T brought home the

5

---

1. For a critical account of this historical process see, for example, Stuart Ewen, *Captains of Consciousness* (New York: McGraw-Hill, 1976); and Dallas Smythe, *Dependency Road* (Norwood, N.J.: Ablex, 1980).

2. **Wedgwood pottery**   English pottery with delicately designed neoclassical figures that appear in white relief on a colored background.—EDS.

3. **Georgian**   Period of English history from 1714 to 1830, characterized by aristocratic tastes.—EDS.

4. Q.v. Adrian Forty, *Objects of Desire: Design and Society from Wedgwood to IBM* (New York: Pantheon, 1986), pp. 22–24.

lesson of fashion. Thus the Model A of 1927 was followed by the V8 in 1932—after which came a complete change of look with the introduction of streamlining, pioneered by the Chrysler "Airflow" in 1934. After the Second World War, with the establishment of GM's Styling Division[5] the fashion mode became institutionalized, complete with traveling Motoramas and the still surviving ritual of "this year's new model." The overall effect has been that car design (especially at the level of feel and look) has become a predominant element of car promotion. Overwhelmingly, from billboards to showrooms, cars have been advertised by being shown, giving pseudoauratic texture to that endless parade of vehicles on the actual highway, which itself has served as one vast ad.

Secondly, unlike pottery, furniture, and clothes, the automobile was a new product, one that never existed outside the framework of industrialized mass production. The history of its received meaning has always been bound up, then, with that of its manufactured meaning as a promotionally designed product; so tightly, indeed, that for consumers as well as producers cars have been taken, from the start, as veritable emblems of the technical and organizational transformation which made them possible. By the mid-1920s, cars meant mass affluence[6] and Ford(ism) had become an international byword for the whole assembly-line system pioneered in its Michigan plant.[7] In that same period, for Futurist[8] poets like Mario de Leone and Auro d'Alba and visual artists like Francis Picabia, the combustion engine itself became a stock image for industrialism, a machine that linked the precise interlocking of parts with the reverie of male sexual power.

More than this, however, like other unprecedented products—e.g., refrigerators, typewriters, phonographs, cameras, radios, etc.—cars became construed and constructed as embodiments of that entire new world—a world of the new—that industry and science were sensed as ushering in. They became, in short, a sign of modernity itself. And quintessentially: for the spread of cars began at once to transform the

---

5. Under the direction of Harley Earl, it was first called "Art and Color," then renamed in 1955. For a vivid description of Earl and his pivotal place in the history of postwar car design see Stephen Bayley's *Sex, Drink and Fast Cars: The Creation and Consumption of Images* (London: Faber and Faber, 1986), pp. 9–20 and ff.

6. In President Hoover's memorable 1924 election phrase: "a chicken in every pot; two cars in every garage."

7. The American painter Charles Sheeler, who developed a whole purist aesthetic on the basis of such industrial landscapes, transformed the Ford plant at Dearborn into a quintessential icon of the new era. Patronized by Ford himself, several of his paintings, including Criss-Crossed Conveyors (the name says it all) hung in the Henry Ford Museum. See Gerald Silk, "The Automobile in Art." Gerald Silk, Angelo Anselmi, Henry Robert, Jr., and Strother MacMinn, *Automobile and Culture* (New York: Abrams, 1984).

8. **Futurists** Artists and writers in the early twentieth century who believed that artistic design should be inspired by modern industry.—EDS.

whole ecology of life, both at the individual level (affecting private and occupational mobility, indeed our whole sense of time and space) and socially (creating massive dependent industries, road systems and transformed cities). Promoting cars as symbols of Modernity, Technology, and Progress, then, has never been entirely arbitrary. For cars really became, for better or worse, a powerful element in that civilizational change to which these mythicized terms ultimately refer.

The Evolving Code

Up to this point I have focused on cars-in-general, but their constructed symbolism has been complicated by divisions within their market. Since the earliest Fords and Oldsmobiles, there have, in fact, been three cultural reference points for car imagery, each broadly corresponding to a different market segment for which different kinds of cars have been designed.

First, and closest to the technology complex itself, is the imagistic set associated with the roadsters, sports cars, and Porsches, Trans-Ams, etc., that are now their "muscle-car" equivalent. Inspiring them all, for over eighty years, has been the spectator sport of car racing, a powerful ritual of male competitive prowess that has conveniently enabled companies to promote themselves while testing research and development. From which, not surprisingly, the racing car (and the road models derived from it) has emerged as an almost perfect symbol for the masculinist technology values racing itself celebrates: a male-identified machine, shaped like a bullet, and experienced from within as an exhilarating rush towards orgasm, death, and the future.[9]

In complete contrast has been the styling characteristic of the luxury   10
car: a vehicle which has continued to trail associations of the genteel upper-class carriage that immediately came before. Such archaism, marked even today by the use of wood and the relative "boxiness" of limousines, has functioned not just as a salve against future shock, but as a sign of that abstract Tradition that industrialism itself has converted into a token of status. Hence, too, the wider diffusion of this complex,

---

9. This sense of the car has perhaps never been more passionately expressed than in Marinetti's 1905 encomium (also called "To Pegasus") "To the Automobile":

> I finally unleash your metallic bridle . . . You launch yourself,/intoxicatingly into the liberating Infinite! . . . Hurrah! No longer contact with the impure earth! . . ./Finally, I am unleashed and I supplely fly/on the intoxicating plenitude/of the streaming stars in the great bed of the sky!

Cited in Silk et al., *Automobile and Culture*, p. 67.

whether in the persistence of "tonneau"[10] types until the mid-1920s, or in the use of coachwork language ("Bodies by Fisher") in mainstream ads since then.

Finally, and occupying a kind of symbolic midpoint, we have the family sedan. Designed for mixed use by the whole family (at first: one car per household), its imagery has likewise been mixed. As a commuter/leisure vehicle for the chief breadwinner, it has invited sportiness; as an index of social status, indications that the household is up-to-date, tasteful, or rich. But an element of symbolism has also attached to it as a vehicle for the family as such.

Generally, as a kind of moving home, it has been built to appear respectable, functional, and safe. More specifically, it has been given design features which materially represent "the family" as a particular (yet seemingly universal) type of group. Thus, transposing from the Victorian landau,[11] the two-row sedan—throughout this century the family car's instantly recognizable form—not only assumes that the family is nuclear. It also sets up a seating grid within which, by custom, the father/husband drives, the wife sits at his side, and the children form a row at the back. More latterly, as this hierarchical, role-divided model has softened and car ownership by youth and women has increased, the mass car has continued to reflect the prevailing family form, though in a way that is correspondingly more unisex, age-neutral, and varied in size.

This, then, is the matrix within which the history of car imagery has had to unfold. Evidently, like the matrix itself, that history has been multileveled and does not reduce to any single thread. Its main features, though, can readily be discerned.

To be noted, first, is a dynamic constant: that, while no type has been symbolically pure, the family car (still the industry's backbone) has peculiarly come to serve as a condensation point for all the image clusters cars can attract. As a mass vehicle it was, and is, designed to appeal to all but the wealthiest households, as well as to all in them. For that reason, too, since artisanal traditionalism, technofuturism, and the values surrounding "the family" (not to mention their class/ethnic variants) do not exactly cohere, its imagery has tended toward ambiguity and compromise. Hence, whatever the idiom of the day, its characteristically "average" look, in which potentially clashing elements are softened at the edges or even made to cancel one another out. Within the mix, it should immediately be added, modernist/masculinist technology values have always been prominently expressed. But by the same token their

---

10. **tonneau**   The enclosed rear passenger compartment in early automobiles.—EDS.

11. **landau**   A type of covered carriage.—EDS.

influence has also been checked; and by considerations no less related to the logic of market appeal.

With respect to the coding of status, secondly, there has been a steady tendency, despite its anachronistic persistence, for Quality Street references to horse-and-carriage to recede gradually from view. A major change came when modernized styling (introduced in the early 1930s in such models as the 1933 Ford V8) began to connect engine to cab in one steady line.[12] Therewith, pre-car imagery migrated from the car's actual body to the once-removed rhetoric contained in its ads. In the 1940s and 1950s, through such devices as depicting cars as paintings, the Victorian "craft" cluster was still further attenuated: blurring into an image of timeless preindustrialism ("Buick: a classic") wherein, having separated from the car's material form, it lost contact with that form's history as well.

Besides the present-oriented push of fashion, the boom and bust of capitalism have, as a countertrend, increasingly made "modernity" itself an essential aspect of the car's capacity to convey esteem. For post-1945 working- and middle-class householders, new-looking cars were a visible way to put the Depression and poverty behind. More generally, in the anxious and dispersed culture of twentieth-century consumerism, being up to date and "modern" became a crucial badge of social membership. The import of this for the imaged car's incorporation of technology values has again been ambiguous. With midmarket cars, as with fashion, if it became important to be contemporary it also became risky to seem too far in front.

Thirdly, and against the background of these dynamics, the technological element of car imagery has itself significantly changed. Most importantly, the car as a symbol of driven speed, and thence of "progress," became outmoded by faster forms of transport, especially ones moving through air. In pace with this, the mass-produced car was successively redesigned—from the "airflows" of the 1930s and the fins-and-tails of postwar Detroit to the "aero" models of today—with each new style mimicking the transport form currently closest to the speed/progress ideal.

On one level, of course, the airplane-influenced trend toward streamlining has been a practical move, reducing not only wind resistance but the attendant costs of fuel. But it has also had a purely symbolic aspect.[13] In such baroque, rocketlike machines as the 1955 Cadillac "Eldorado" aerodynamic efficiency was actually sacrificed in the interest of an aerodynamic look. If the symbolic result was that cars became

---

12. Q.v. John Heskett, *Industrial Design* (New York and Toronto: Oxford University Press, 1980), pp. 72–74.

13. The streamlining idea, replete with futurist enthusiasm, was popularized by the publication of Norman Bel Geddes's *Horizons* in 1932.

15

planes, missiles, and spaceships, driving, in fantasy, became flight: a potent metaphor which, as postwar "depth" promoters well understood, alluded at once to a technicist (and space age) notion of progress and to the promptings of sexual desire.

In its guise as a machine, the car has also been made to seem alive. This has by no means been merely a matter of consumer transference, though the ease with which popular speech has absorbed the metaphor ("she handles really well") shows how culturally resonant it is. Through promotion and design, rather, such animism has been given tangible shape. In a first step, the engine radiator, mounted at the front, was given a grille (mouth). Then two separated headlights (eyes) were added, and a pointed hood (nose)—compensating, presumably, for the vanished face of the horse. The high point came with the customizing craze of the 1940s and 50s, together with the (almost equally) flamboyant monster types it inspired in the industry.[14] Figuration in so blatant a form, however, declined after the Ford Edsel—a car whose spectacular marketing failure (in 1958) was perhaps best explained by customer comments that its grille looked like a vagina (replete, we may add, with teeth). Since then, the beast theme has been domesticated and made the stuff of advertising copy and brand names (Mustangs, Colts, Foxes, Rabbits, etc.); while cars, physically, have been contoured more as cyborglike extensions of their own drivers. On the darker side, this robotic trend has triggered horror film images of riderless vehicles (Stephen King's *Christine,* Stephen Spielberg's *Duel*), out to destroy their human creators for giving them no soul.

The car's imaging as alive has also implied its presentation as sexed. 20 In the first instance, and from the side of the male driver, it has been projected as Woman: whether a flashy possession, boy-toy (as in E. E. Cumming's car-as-virgin poem, "XIX"),[15] or wife. But in this (variously nuanced) scene of the male-led couple the car has also figured as rocket, bullet, or gun, i.e., as a sexual extension of the male; while for both sexes, as an enclosed place in which to escape, it has at the same time played the part of a womb. This is, in fact, one of the car's most striking

---

14. A wonderful extension of such imagery is to be seen in the classic Australian underground film, *The Cars That Ate Paris.*

15. The poem begins

> she being Brand
> -new; and you
> know consequently a
> little stiff i was
> careful of her and (having
> thoroughly oiled the universal
> joint tested my gas felt of
> her radiator made sure her springs were O.
> K . . .

symbolic features: its gender ambiguity. If promotion and use have tied it, like Adam's rib, to the cosmos of phallic technology, they have also given it the character of an androgyne.

Until recently, in the car's symbolization of technology, these intertwined tendencies (toward flight and animation) have constituted the main line of development. But over the past decade the story has been complicated by the rise of two additional symbolic clusters: First, advances in transport (with missiles and space the new frontier) have increasingly come to rely on improvements not so much in propulsion as in guidance systems and their finger-tip control. In turn, with the rise of computers and informatics, this has made communications, rather than transport, the exemplar of technological progress as such. While there are parallels between the accelerated movement of things/persons and of information/thought, they are not the same. A shift in attention from one to the other has implied as well, then, a shift in the register of "technology" as a cultural idea. Marshall McLuhan,[16] who was beguiled by this, saw an "explosive"/atomistic world of mechanization giving way to an "implosive"/holistic one of electronics.[17] For imaged cars, more narrowly, it has been reflected in the way that looking "modern" has come to mean not just looking fast and airborne, but being linked to computers and all that they connote.

Secondly, and cutting across symbolism of any kind, car design and promotion have been nagged at by a functionalist conscience. Until the late 1960s, the Bauhaus[18] maxim of "form follows function" was, to be sure, more prevalent among European than American manufacturers, both as a creed and as an aesthetic stick with which to beat their transatlantic rivals. But in the wake of the 1960s cultural upheaval and in the shape of energy-crisis "econoboxes," such antidecorative purism began to exert a strong pull on this continent too. Like streamlining, to which it has been related, the functionalist *revanche*[19] has had a partly economic motive—reflecting, during the post-Vietnam downturn, the renewed importance of efficiency and price. But the preeminence of function is also a value; and as such (despite itself) it is always liable to become a coded element in the rhetoric and styling of the artifacts made over in its name. For progressive designers in the 1920s[20] functionalist principles

---

16. **Marshall McLuhan** (1911–1980)   Cultural historian who invented modern media studies.—EDS.

17. Q.v. Marshall McLuhan, *Understanding Media* (New York: Signet, 1963).

18. **Bauhaus**   Architectural school developed in 1920s Germany that considered buildings an expression of the machine age.—EDS.

19. **revanche**   Revenge, retaliation.—EDS.

20. And also architects, of whom the most influential in this regard was Le Corbusier, both through his actual buildings and through his own manifesto, *Vers Une Architecture*.

provided a utopian definition of modernity itself. In the North American car market, more prosaically, they have come to provide a saleable counterimage to set against the self-congratulatory Frontierism which, at least in the United States, has been that idea's predominant form.

With all these various forces and tendencies in mind let us now turn directly to our original question: the meaning of the car's post-1950s imagistic shift.

The Rise and Fall of the Rocket

The 1950s-style American car, today an object of veneration, is an instantly recognizable type. Through all its variants, from the 1948–1949 GM models that initiated it to the fins-and-tails cult classics that came to epitomize the whole Eisenhower period, it was marked by a combination of animism and streamlining taken to almost self-parodying heights of excess. In such a form, serving at once as a commuter vehicle for the suburban family and as a freedom-endowing one for the restless young[21] it became an internationally recognizable symbol of the postwar boom, indeed of free-enterprising America itself. Soaked in Buck Rogers[22] images of space and the future, it signified, above all, that new romance with technology which gave Cold War ideology its heady, expansive edge.[23]

In popular form, a 1953 ad for Oldsmobile [Figure 1] shows clearly   25 the value complex such a vehicle was designed to evoke. The ad is a two-pager, with the car itself, inclined slightly upward, triumphantly occupying the horizontal plane. Its sleek, forward-thrusting design, emphasized by decorative chrome, repeats the same theme, which is echoed again in the miniature spaceship jetting away in the top left. In case the point is missed we also get a caption: The car's "rocket engine" (what else?) gives you "sm-o-o-o-th" driving. Beyond this, the identified ensemble of car, rocket, and phallus is also framed by a social context, indicated by the respectable young couple ranged alongside. In fact they appear twice. In the main picture he, clean-cut, bejacketed, is smoothly at the wheel while the brunette beside him—decorously apart—looks

---

21. It was no accident that several of Chuck Berry's rock and roll songs were about or set in cars, and that Jack Kerouac's beat classic was called *On the Road*.

22. **Buck Rogers** Fictional star of space-hero films.—EDS.

23. This did not pass critical commentators by, and there were masterful dissections of the car's stylistic embodiment of the technology complex on both sides of the Atlantic. See, for example, Marshall McLuhan's *The Mechanical Bride: Folklore of Industrial Man* (Boston: Beacon, 1951), pp. 82–84; and Roland Barthes's essay in *Mythologies* on the 1955 Citroen DS.

FIGURE 1

confidently ahead. At the top left, in the rocket's literal reprise, the machine actually lifts off. And here they straddle it like bikers, with hubby waving from the front and wifey lovingly hanging on. In this moment, we are led to suppose, the car becomes theirs: a dream-come-true of upward mobility, growing affluence, and technological progress, all fused together in the happily consummated marriage at the center of the scene.

The arrival of computers aside, there is clearly some discontinuity between this ideological universe and our own. And not surprisingly, for between the two lies a cultural shakeup whose origins (in the story of cars) can be traced back at least as far as the Edsel. The failure of that exaggerated vehicle, as we can now see, signaled not just the end of a design era but the onset of a crisis for the whole nexus of values such styling bespoke.

Most fundamentally, techno-worship itself came under attack. A succession of international crises (Suez, Cuba, Berlin, Vietnam)[24] made the nightmare of the nuclear arms race frighteningly alive. And to this problematizing of blind technology ("a riderless vehicle," as Northrop Frye[25] put it) was added dampened economic expectations that set in after the fifteen-year boom plateaued out and, then, in the financial turmoil of 1971–1972, came to an end. The result, aided by the antiurban side of late 1960s counterculture[26] and carried forward into middle-class life-styles ever since, was a wholescale resuscitation of Nature as the repressed Other of all-conquering Industry. In keeping with such changed sensibilities, car design became less blatantly wasteful; fins and chrome were shed; and cars in ads were depicted in fields, identified with free-ranging animals (especially horses) and tied to leisure-related reveries of rural escape.

Reinforcing this, the oil crisis of the mid-1970s, growing traffic congestion, and unease with rampant road construction[27] changed mass attitudes to the car itself. On the one hand, the car's identification with individual freedom was undermined. On the other, this value came into collision with the car's master value as exemplar of techno-industrial advance. With respect to the latter, cars materially became a bad sign of what they had earlier celebrated. Just as cigarette promoters had to exorcise the cancer scare (hence cigarettes as symbols of Life), car promoters found themselves having to deflect the negative associations with which their own product had become endowed. Reversing the sign (making car into Nature) was one common tactic. Occasionally, though (as with a 1979 Datsun ad that cited George Orwell,[28] or with a recent Toyota campaign about fighting "road monotony"), the car's dystopic associations have been taken head on. As a further response, the decline of the "gas guzzler" paved the way for more functional (and functional-looking) designs. And this was mirrored in the greater stress ads began to place on the product's performative side. (An irony of modern business is that American manufacturers, so attached to their own vision of "technology," were slow to make this turn; leaving a market weakness ex-

---

24. **Suez, Cuba, Berlin, Vietnam**   International political crises during the Cold War marked by confrontation between the Soviet Union and the United States and its allies.—EDS.

25. **Northrop Frye** (1912–1992)   Canadian literary theorist who pioneered study of archetypes in literature.—EDS.

26. A good account of this is provided in Theodor Rosak's *The Making of a Counter-culture* (Garden City, NY: Doubleday, 1969).

27. For the relation between expressway construction and the modernity crisis see Marshall Berman's account of Robert Moses and the South Bronx expressway in *All That Is Solid Melts into Air* (New York: Simon and Schuster, 1982), pp. 290–312.

28. **George Orwell** (1903–1950)   British writer whose works include *1984* and *Animal Farm*.—EDS.

ploited first by the North Europeans and then by the Japanese with the aid of Italian design.)[29]

With the rise of the women's movement, the emergence of a gay subculture, and the sex/gender *frisson* of the 1970s, the sexual values exemplified by the "Rocket" also came unstuck. The dominance of males and the cowboy complex were not wholly eliminated, but they were pushed on the defensive by the rise of a more egalitarian code. Increased participation by women in work and public life coincided, too, with a proportionate increase in the number of women on the road. In market as well as ideological terms, then, the straightforward insertion of the car into the masculinity complex identified with heroic techno-industrial progress simply ceased to work. In the imaging of cars, correspondingly, assumptions about family structure, the gender of the driver, and the sexual valency of the car itself became more blurred; combined with which, the Nature/Technology categories to which the car was also tied became loosened, as well, from their patriarchal frame.[30]

The Imagery of "High Tech"

All these developments created real difficulties for the imaging of cars. Just as the North American market was becoming tougher, the symbolic resources available to manufacturer/promoters became unstable and difficult to use. To some degree the European-inspired return to functionality has plugged this anomic gap. But in the heartlands of consumerism the appeal of such semantic restraint (which made its appearance with the VW, system-designed European cars, and Detroit compacts) has been safe rather than charged—raising the specter, indeed, of entropy and meaning's final collapse. Additional ways have had to be found, then, for infusing the duller-looking vehicles the functionalist reaction has led to with new symbolic life.

It is in just that context, from the early 1980s on, that the car's symbolism as "technology" has begun to be revised. In effect, after a long hiatus, the car's linkage to the romance of rockets has been replaced by a newly generated enthusiasm for the "communications revolution" centered on the microchip. But what, we may wonder, is the broader value import of this new sign? Does it connote anything more than just a differently dressed version of the same old myth?

---

29. See Bayley, *Sex, Drink and Fast Cars,* pp. 63–67, 101–110.

30. I have explored this point with respect to the overall development of recent advertising in "From voyeur to narcissist: the changing imagery of men, 1950–80," in Michael Kaufmann, ed., *Beyond Patriarchy: Essays by Men on Pleasure and Power* (Toronto: Oxford University Press, 1987).

Again, let us take our cues from ads. Two from *Time* in the winter of 1982, published during the initial burst of mass computer excitement, will at least show the kind of values brought into play. The first, for Volkswagen Rabbit [Figure 2], is constructed around the caption "High tech. Who gives a heck?" each phrase heading a differently designed page. Both are text heavy with various performance-related claims; but the graphics and layout of the "high tech" panel on the left recall a computer screen, while the writing on the right is in hard print. The immediate implication is that with the aid of computers this car is ultraintelligently designed. But the caption in the lower right (by a picture of the car itself) shows that the computer's supposed qualities of benign intelligence are also (and with disarmingly pet-oriented cuteness) transferred on to the car: "If you thought about Rabbit as much as Rabbit thinks about you you'd think about Rabbit."

The second, for Toyota [Figure 3], plays with a similar theme. Again there are two panels, topped by a visually bifurcated phrase: "The Toyota/Edge." Foregrounded in each is a front-on picture of the car: on the left, as it actually appears; on the right, to the same scale, as a skeletal (X-ray-like) engineering drawing, drafted on a screen. Again, one notes the computer's deployment as a sign of embodied intelligence, with that meaning similarly relayed on to the car. In both cases, likewise, the wonders of the computer mediated by its god/man operator as medic and bioengineer, give us magical access to the car's hidden essence. And in both cases, finally, this focus on the car's inside emphasizes the car's fantasy role as a womb, a role that is immediately qualified by its doubling as the center of designer (and driver) control. In the Toyota case, this whole interiorizing movement is given a further twist by the campaign slogan (from the dance movie *Flashdance*) which appears at the foot of the computer-oriented panel on the right: "Oh what a feeling!"[31]

In other respects, too, the car's entry into the world of high tech has been accompanied by a movement of interiorization. On the material side, we have seen growing design attention to seating and driver ergonomics, to dashboard setups (now digitalized, and with voice controls), and to car sound systems (quadraphonic speakers, tape decks, CDs, etc.). In promotion more generally (whether computer-referenced or not) the car has been projected as a king of wraparound experience, or even as a mystical inner trip. A current TV ad for Honda shows a woman stealing from her husband/lover's bed at dawn. She descends to the garage and the car, followed by a dreamy drive along a deserted coastal road. Have you ever wondered, goes the voice-over, where your wife is . . .? Here,

---

31. On another level, Toyota's reference to *Flashdance* was a tactic for Americanizing its product in the face of protectionist (and, to a degree, xenophobic) resistance to "foreign competition." In the present phase of its assimilationist campaign Toyota has reached back to Gershwin: "Who could ask for anything more?"

then, is a real difference: In moving from the technology complex that
came to a head in the 1950s to the one more recently linked to computers
there has been a change in emphasis from outer to inner space.

It is tempting to treat the linkage between computer images and   35
interiorization as intrinsic, reflecting, for example, a real technological
bias.[32] We might further speculate that this bias, reinforced by pressures
towards cultural feminization, has also led to a change in Technology's
imputed sex. But in a crucial sense the linkage permitting such recoding
is also historically contingent. A renewed emphasis on subjectivity, experience, and the personal world extends beyond advertising and has
independent roots in the whole sociocultural crisis of the past twenty
years. In ads, as in movies and popular songs, it registers an exhaustion
with the growth complex of industrial society and anxieties about its
future: a mood which has combined with the ongoing effects of consumerized privatism to deflect attention away from the whole public
realm. And here, we may note, the contemporary imaged car is caught
in a deep contradiction: It is part of the problem it cannot (for market
reasons) name and from which it is posited as an escape.

For that reason, too, paradoxically, the 1950s car and its related
insignia (diners, milkbars, ducktails, golden-age rock and roll) has made
something of a comeback. In films, music, and the general symbology
of contemporary youth it has been recycled; so that what first made its
appearance as futurist euphoria has returned, in the context of newer
fears, as a symbol of a better past. With respect to cars themselves, the
impact of such revivalism has been more evident in ads (through *Grease*
and *American Graffiti*[33]-type references) than in actual design. Still, in the
play of fashion, and throughout our culture, a stylized past is the obverse
of novelty as a source for new trends. So we may conjecture that here,
too—perhaps building on the recently revived craze for rodding and
customizing—nostalgic references to earlier models will make their way
into the manufactured appearance of current ones.

Cars, Today

Overall, then, it would be one-sided to suppose that car imagery, in
its adoption of computer references, has simply moved to install an
updated version of progress-based technological myth. This is certainly
one trend, but it has been interwoven with others, including the resurgence of functionalism, the unsettling of patriarchy, a personalist

---

32. See McLuhan, *Understanding Media*, pp. 346–369.
33. *Grease* and *American Graffiti*   1970s movies about American teenagers living
in the 1950s and 1960s.—EDS.

FIGURE 2

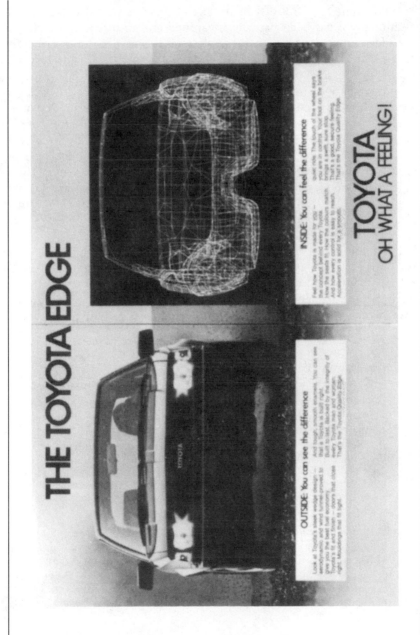

FIGURE 3

withdrawal from the adventures of industrialism, and indications that cars are beginning to be caught up in what Fredric Jameson calls the "nostalgia mode."[34] All of which, taken together, would suggest that if techno-myth has been partially revamped and restored, it has also, in broader compass, ceased to be symbolically central or even coherent. Indeed, an alternative hypothesis can be advanced: that car imagery, like other sign-bearing material in the cultural vortex of advanced capitalism, is evolving towards a decorative electicism whose signifying gestures refer us only to the universe of symbols from which they are drawn.

In fact, with the public circulation of signs severed from life by commerce, media, and reactive privatism there are grounds for arguing that it is not our technology but our culture that is imploding, parallel with a further disintegration of society in the old organic sense.[35] In its costly, computer-linked, postmodern guise, the contemporary car certainly bears all the marks of such a process. But its witness is blind since, as a promotional construct, its imagery can scarcely acknowledge what has happened, let alone its own—doubly—mystifying role. What the decorative play on the car's functionalized surface ultimately hides, that is, is not just the negativity of the product but the relation between that negativity and the kind of gloss it is given. Simply put: that the car's own disruptive dominance as a transport form is part of the disaffected reality from which our culture, as written into the car's very body, has recoiled.

Reading the Text

1. According to Wernick, how does a car function as a sign of its owner's identity? In this respect, how are cars similar to other consumer products?
2. Summarize the cultural symbolism that Wernick attributes to three categories of automobiles: the muscle car, the luxury car, and the family car.
3. What does Wernick mean when he says that promotion and advertising make cars "seem alive"?

Reading the Signs

1. Wernick claims that the identification of the car with male heroism and sexual prowess became more complicated by the late 1970s. Do you agree or disagree with his claim?
2. In the last section of his essay, Wernick only suggests how cars today

---

34. See Fredric Jameson's essay "Post-modernism: The Cultural Logic of Capitalism," *New Left Review*, No. 146 (July–August 1984).

35. For this now familiar neo-Marxist inversion of McLuhan see Jean Baudrillard's *In the Shadow of the Silent Majority* (New York: Semiotext(e), 1983).

function as signs. In groups, brainstorm current car designs, and do a
semiotic reading of automobiles in the early to middle 1990s.
3. Compare and contrast the automotive styles of the 1950s with those of the
   1990s, using your comparison to formulate your own argument about the
   significance of design changes.
4. Write a journal entry in which you interpret how your own car (or that
   of a friend or relative) acts as a sign. What messages does it send about your
   identity?
5. Collect advertising brochures from local new car dealers and bring them
   to class. In groups, discuss what today's car designs say about our values and
   desires in the 1990s.
6. Using Wernick's approach as a model, interpret an automotive category
   not discussed in the essay: pickup trucks and four-wheel-drive vehicles such
   as the Chevy Blazer.
7. Cull automobile advertisements from a collection of popular magazines,
   and analyze how the cars are promoted as signs. What slogans are used to
   catch your interest? What values and ideologies are attributed to particular
   makes and models?

ROLAND BARTHES
Toys

‖‖

*The founder of modern semiology and its application to popular culture,
Roland Barthes (1915–1980) is a major figure in literary as well as
cultural criticism, whose interests ranged from the French dramatist Ra-
cine to the fashion magazine* Elle. *In this selection from his ground-
breaking book* Mythologies *(1957, trans. 1972), Barthes analyzes
the cultural significance of French toys and the materials they are made
of, hinting at a personal nostalgic preference for traditional materials like
wood over the plastics that have taken over the toy world. Elsewhere in*
Mythologies, *Barthes analyzes professional wrestling spectacles, striptease, plastic, Greta Garbo, cookery, and a host of other cultural signs.
Without his pioneering studies, texts like the one you are reading
probably would not have been possible.*

The author of over twenty books, of which Mythologies *is one of
the earliest, Barthes was a professor at the College de France at his death
in 1980.*

French toys: One could not find a better illustration of the fact that
the adult Frenchman sees the child as another self. All the toys one

commonly sees are essentially a microcosm of the adult world; they are all reduced copies of human objects, as if in the eyes of the public the child was, all told, nothing but a smaller man, a homunculus to whom must be supplied objects of his own size.

Invented forms are very rare: a few sets of blocks, which appeal to the spirit of do–it–yourself, are the only ones which offer dynamic forms. As for the others, French toys *always mean something,* and this something is always entirely socialized, constituted by the myths or the techniques of modern adult life: the army, broadcasting, the post office, medicine (miniature instrument-cases, operating theaters for dolls), school, hair styling (driers for permanent-waving), the air force (parachutists), transport (trains, Citroëns, Vedettes, Vespas,[1] petrol stations), science (Martian toys).

The fact that French toys *literally* prefigure the world of adult functions obviously cannot but prepare the child to accept them all, by constituting for him, even before he can think about it, the alibi of a Nature which has at all times created soldiers, postmen and Vespas. Toys here reveal the list of all the things the adult does not find unusual: war, bureaucracy, ugliness, Martians, etc. It is not so much, in fact, the imitation which is the sign of an abdication, as its literalness: French toys are like a Jivaro head, in which one recognizes, shrunken to the size of an apple, the wrinkles and hair of an adult. There exist, for instance, dolls which urinate; they have an esophagus, one gives them a bottle, they wet their nappies; soon, no doubt, milk will turn to water in their stomachs. This is meant to prepare the little girl for the causality of housekeeping, to "condition" her to her future role as mother. However, faced with this world of faithful and complicated objects, the child can only identify himself as owner, as user, never as creator; he does not invent the world, he uses it: There are, prepared for him, actions without adventure, without wonder, without joy. He is turned into a little stay-at-home householder who does not even have to invent the mainsprings of adult causality; they are supplied to him ready-made: He has only to help himself, he is never allowed to discover anything from start to finish. The merest set of blocks, provided it is not too refined, implies a very different learning of the world: Then, the child does not in any way create meaningful objects, it matters little to him whether they have an adult name; the actions he performs are not those of a user but those of a demiurge. He creates forms which walk, which roll, he creates life, not property: Objects now act by themselves, they are no longer an inert and complicated material in the palm of his hand. But such toys are rather rare: French toys are usually based on imitation, they are meant to produce children who are users, not creators.

---

1. **Vespa**   Italian motor scooter.—EDS.

The bourgeois status of toys can be recognized not only in their forms, which are all functional, but also in their substances. Current toys are made of a graceless material, the product of chemistry, not of nature. Many are now molded from complicated mixtures; the plastic material of which they are made has an appearance at once gross and hygienic, it destroys all the pleasure, the sweetness, the humanity of touch. A sign which fills one with consternation is the gradual disappearance of wood, in spite of its being an ideal material because of its firmness and its softness, and the natural warmth of its touch. Wood removes, from all the forms which it supports, the wounding quality of angles which are too sharp, the chemical coldness of metal. When the child handles it and knocks it, it neither vibrates nor grates, it has a sound at once muffled and sharp. It is a familiar and poetic substance, which does not sever the child from close contact with the tree, the table, the floor. Wood does not wound or break down; it does not shatter, it wears out, it can last a long time, live with the child, alter little by little the relations between the object and the hand. If it dies, it is in dwindling, not in swelling out like those mechanical toys which disappear behind the hernia of a broken spring. Wood makes essential objects, objects for all time. Yet there hardly remain any of these wooden toys from the Vosges, these fretwork farms with their animals, which were only possible, it is true, in the days of the craftsman. Henceforth, toys are chemical in substance and color; their very material introduces one to a coenaesthesis[2] of use, not pleasure. These toys die in fact very quickly, and once dead, they have no post-humous life for the child.

Reading the Text

1. What does Barthes mean by saying that "French toys literally prefigure the world of adult functions"?
2. What, according to Barthes, is the significance of the *materials* with which toys are made? What is the difference between the meaning of plastic and wood?

Reading the Signs

1. Barthes assumes that children are passive users of toys. Discuss whether you agree with his assumption, basing your argument on your own experience as a child and your observations of young children.
2. In small groups, brainstorm American toys, then classify them according to areas of adult life as Barthes does in his second paragraph. How do your

---

2. **coenaesthesis**   One's general awareness of the body and its condition.—EDS.

categories compare with Barthes's? What is the significance of any differences you may find?

3. Bring a toy to class and, in a brief oral presentation, interpret its significance. Then, after the entire class has presented, look at the *range* of toys brought in. What does the range say about the values and culture of your class?

4. Barthes claims that French toys are small versions of the adult world. Visit a local toy store, and survey the products to see if this claim applies to American toys in the 1990s. What do the results of your survey reveal about American culture?

5. Read or review Emily Prager's "Our Barbies, Ourselves" (p. 353). Writing as Roland Barthes, interpret Barbie semiotically, being sure to relate Barbie to other dolls in the toy system.

CHAPTER TWO

BROUGHT TO YOU
B(U)Y

The Signs of Advertising

Are you wearing jeans? What brand? Lee? Levi's? Cross Colours? Jordache? (Does anyone still wear Jordache?) The brand matters, doesn't it? Because those aren't just jeans you're wearing, they're a statement. They project an image. In the last chapter we looked at the many ways in which the products you buy make statements, but there is another part of the story to tell. You often have an assistant on hand to help you choose the images that you want your belongings to project, an assistant whose primary interest is that you buy a particular product. He or she goes by another name, however: This assistant is an advertiser.

Advertising: It's not just show and tell. Just think of the many ways jeans alone are pitched in America. Take Levi's as an example. How are they packaged for the marketplace? What sorts of images are associated with them today? Take care to be up to date, because those images change rapidly, as the trends of popular culture change. In the early 1980s, for example, Levi's were promoted as hip urban wear in TV spots set on city streets, where they were associated with the blues as "Levi's 501 Blues." If you watched the 1984 Olympics on television, you saw a number of these commercials. They were notable for the way they took a fashion that had been associated with rural and wilderness settings in the 1960s, with the "back-to-the-land" movement, and redefined them as a part of the "back-to-the-city" trends of the early eighties. The significance of this shift, once more, lay in a *difference,* in the vast gap between Walden Pond and Wall Street. But that was then and this is

101

now. Look at a Levi's display in your local department store. With what
are they associated today? Do these associations make you want to go
out and buy a pair?

Or how about Guess? jeans? What image do *they* project? Is it
different from the image of Levi's? Would you wear both brands, or only
one of them? Why?

Chances are that the image you associate with Guess? jeans was
created by advertising. To see how ads can shape a product image, look
at the Guess? ad on page 161. Does it leave you wondering whether
they are hawking sportswear or brassieres? Ask yourself some of those
essential semiotic questions: Why are they showing us *this?* What are
they really doing? How am I responding to the ad? Why am I responding
the way I am? If you get the impression that the ad intends to connote
the stimulating suggestion that buying Guess? jeans will lead to plenty
of entertaining opportunities to take them off, then you are on your way
to decoding the semiotic significance of it all.

But your interpretation will not stop there. That's only the beginning. Let's keep going for a moment. Let's look at the story the ad tells.
It seems to tell a story in two parts. What is that story? Reconstruct it
for yourself. Does the story fit your sense of ordinary reality, of how
people typically behave? Is there anything dangerous about it? What?
Consider too the appearance of the story's "heroine." All clothing advertisers use attractive models, but think of the sorts of models you usually
see in *Glamour* or *Vogue.* Aren't they usually less voluptuous? Now look
at Claudia Schiffer, the model in the Guess? ad. How does she compare
with the models who appear in magazines where clothing is not what is
on display but rather the bodies of the models themselves?

In interpreting the Guess? ad (or any ad), you may want to do a
little outside research to see if the advertisers themselves had anything to
say about their campaign. In this case, they did. Guess?, Inc., deliberately
chose models for their 1990s ad campaigns to resemble 1950s sex goddesses, such as Brigitte Bardot and Marilyn Monroe. They claim that
they want to bring back the particular sensuality of that period and to
appeal to the nostalgia of their market for a more innocent era in American history. That's what they claim. But look again at the ad. Does it
appear innocent? Does the fact that Claudia Schiffer's successor in the
Guess? campaign, Anna Nicole Smith, was *Playboy*'s 1993 Playmate of
the Year say anything about what is really going on in the Guess? ads?

In short, when interpreting advertising you have to be suspicious of
what advertisers say about their intentions. What an advertiser may claim
to be doing is usually different from what is really happening. Think of
all those beer commercials that tell you to be careful not to drink too
much at parties (yeah, right!), or those pickup truck ads that advise you
not to attempt these driving stunts yourself (oh, yeah?). All that is a
smokescreen. To interpret an ad, you have to look not only at what it

|||||||||||||||||||||||||||||||||||||||||||||||||||||||||||||||||||||||||||||||||||||||||||||||||||||||||||||||||||

Discussing the Signs of Advertising

Bring to class a print ad from a newspaper or magazine, and in small groups discuss your semiotic reading of it. Be sure to ask, "Why am I being shown this or being told that?" How do the characters in the ad function as signs? What sort of people don't appear as characters? What cultural myths are invoked in this ad? What relationship do you see between those myths and the intended audience of the publication? Which ads do your group members respond to positively, and why? Which ads doesn't your group like?

---

shows and says but what it *does* as well. And in the case of the beer and truck ads, what they *tell* you is belied by what they *suggest:* That all of the real fun of the product lies exactly in doing what they say you shouldn't do.

To be alert for the suggestiveness of an ad, however, doesn't mean that you need to look for some truly subliminal signal like the letters "sex" inscribed faintly on the ice cubes in a beverage commercial. Subliminal advertising of this type may or may not exist, but in a semiotic analysis you needn't worry about it, because what you are looking for is what the ad *visibly* accomplishes. When the imagery of an ad, for example, suggests that if you buy this car you will be more popular, have more dates, or be envied by your neighbors, all that is on the screen for you to see. Everything you need to know for a semiotic analysis of advertising should be right there before you in images that you can rationally analyze, even when sex *is* part of the come-on, as in the Guess? ad.

The Semiotic Foundation

There is perhaps no better field for semiotic analysis than advertising, for ads work characteristically by substituting signs for things, and by reading those signs you can discover the values and desires that advertisers seek to exploit.

It has long been recognized that advertisements substitute images of desire for the actual products, that Coca-Cola ads, for example, don't really sell soda: They sell images of fun, or popularity, or of sheer celebrity, promising a gratifying association with the likes of Paula Abdul or Whitney Houston if you'll only drink "The Real Thing." Automobile commercials, for their part, are notorious for selling not transportation but fantasies of power, prestige, or sexual potency.

By substituting desirable images for concrete needs, modern advertising seeks to transform desire into necessity. You *need* food, for example, but it takes an ad campaign to convince you through attractive images that you need a Big Mac. Your job may require you to have a car, but it's an ad that persuades you that a Dodge Shadow is necessary for your happiness. If advertising worked otherwise, it would simply present you with a functional profile of a product and let you decide whether it will do the job.

From the early twentieth century, advertisers have seen their task as the transformation of desire into necessity. In the twenties and thirties, for example, voluminously printed advertisements created elaborate story lines designed to convince readers that they needed this mouthwash to attract a spouse or that caffeine-free breakfast drink to avoid trouble on the job or in the home. In such ads, products were made to appear not only desirable but absolutely necessary. Without them, your very survival as a socially competent being would be in question.

Many ads still work this way, particularly "guilt" ads that prey on your insecurities and fears. Classic examples from the 1960s include the Ice Blue Secret deodorant campaign that promised that your body odor would be your own little secret if you just bought the product, and the Wisk "ring-around-the-collar" ads that transformed a liquid laundry detergent into an elixir of social salvation. Stop a moment and think of an ad that works this way now. Is anyone out there trying to get you to buy a product out of a feeling of guilt or shame?

The Commodification of Desire

Associating a logically unrelated desire with an actual product (as in pitching beer through sexual come-ons) can be called the "commodification" of desire. In other words, desire itself becomes the product that the advertiser is selling. This marketing of desire was recognized as early as the 1950s in Vance Packard's *The Hidden Persuaders*. In that book, Packard points out how by the 1950s America was well along in its historic shift from a producing to a consuming economy. The implications for advertisers were enormous. Since the American economy was increasingly dependent on the constant growth of consumption, as the introduction to Chapter 1 of this text discusses, manufacturers had to find ways to convince people to consume ever more goods. So they turned to the advertising mavens on Madison Avenue, who produced advertisements that persuaded consumers to replace perfectly serviceable products with "new and improved" substitutions within an overall economy of planned design obsolescence.

America's transformation from a producer to a consumer economy also explains that while advertising is a worldwide phenomenon, it is nowhere so prevalent as it is here. Open a copy of the popular French picture magazine *Paris Match*. You'll find plenty of paparazzi photos of international celebrities, but almost no advertisements. Then open a copy of *Vogue*. It is essentially a catalog, where scarcely a page is without its ad. Indeed, advertisers themselves call this plethora of advertising "clutter" that they must creatively "cut through" each time they design a new ad campaign. The ubiquity of advertising in our lives points to a society in which people are constantly pushed to buy, as opposed to economies like Japan's that emphasize constant increases in production. And desire is what loosens the pocketbook strings.

While the basic logic of advertising may be similar from era to era, the content of an ad, and hence its significance, differs as popular culture changes. Looking at ads from different eras tells the tale. Advertising in the 1920s, for example, focused especially on its market's desires for improved social status. Ads for elocution and vocabulary lessons, for example, appealed to working- and lower-middle-class consumers, who were invited to fantasize that buying the product or service could help them enter the middle class. Meanwhile, middle-class consumers were invited to compare their enjoyment of the sponsor's product with that of the upper-class models shown happily slurping this coffee or purchasing that vacuum cleaner in the ad. Of course, things haven't changed *that* much since the twenties. Can you think of any ads that use this strategy today? How often are glamorous celebrities called in to make you identify with his or her "enjoyment" of a product? Have you heard ads for vocabulary-building programs that promise you a "verbal advantage" in the corporate struggle?

One particularly amusing ad from the twenties played upon America's fear of communism in the wake of the Bolshevik Revolution in Russia. "Is your washroom breeding Bolsheviks?" asks a print ad from the Scot paper towel company. The ad's lengthy copy explains how it might be doing so: If your company restroom is stocked with inferior paper towels, it says, discontent will proliferate among your employees and lead to subversive action. R.C.A. Victor and Campbell's Soup, we are assured, are no such breeding grounds of subversion, thanks to their contracts with Scot. You, too, can fight the good fight against communism by buying Scot Towels, the ad suggests. To whom do you think this ad was directed? What did they fear?

Populism vs. Elitism

American advertising tends to swing in a pendulum motion between the status-conscious ads that dominated the twenties and the more populist approach of decades like the seventies, when country music and truck-driving cowboys lent their popular appeal to Madison Avenue.

ll

Exploring the Signs of Advertising

Select one of the products advertised in the "Portfolio of Advertisements" (pp. 156–65), and design in your journal an alternative ad for that product. Consider what different images or cast of characters you could include. What different myths—and thus different values—could you use to pitch this product?

Then freewrite on the significance of your alternative ad. If you have any difficulty imagining an alternative image for the product, what does that say about the power of advertising to control our view of the world? What does your choice of imagery and cultural myths say about you?

This swing between elitist and populist approaches in advertising reflects a basic division within the American Dream itself, a mythic promise that at once celebrates democratic equality *and* encourages you to rise above the crowd, to be better than anyone else. Sometimes Americans are more attracted to the one side than to the other, but there is bound to be a shift back to the other side when the thrill wears off. Thus, the populist appeal of the seventies (even disco music had a distinct working-class flavor: Recall John Travolta's character in *Saturday Night Fever*) gave way to the elitist eighties, and advertising followed. Products such as Gallo's varietal wines, once considered barely a step up from jug wine, courted an upscale market through ads that featured classy yuppies serving it along with their salmon and asparagus, while Michelob light beer promised its fans that they "could have it all." Status advertising was all the rage in that glitzy, go-for-the-gold decade. Do ads work this way today? Or has the pendulum shifted back to populism, to democratic equality? Can you think of any ads that might be a sign of such a shift?

Determining whether the dominant tone of advertising at any given time is populist or elitist is one way of using advertisements as a kind of weather vane of shifting cultural trends. They help you know which way the wind blows. But a lot of other things in an ad can help you get a sense of the cultural environment in which they appeared. Let's look now at a famous ad campaign from the early 1990s to see what else may have been going on at the beginning of our current decade.

Pink Rabbits

Consider the Energizer battery ad series that features a pink mechanical bunny who beats his drum as he storms through a sequence of mock advertisements to show how he "keeps going and going and going" on an Energizer battery. The ad's apparent point is to tell you how long an Energizer battery lasts, but it could have done that by simply presenting battery test statistics (a dull though still usable advertising strategy). So what is the ad really doing?

First, it helps to know that when the pink bunny commercials initially appeared, a chief competitor, Duracell, had for some time been running ads that featured contests between battery-operated toys which "demonstrated" the long-lasting superiority of Duracell products. That's part of the system in which the Energizer ad functions. So, here comes that bunny. How does his appearance relate to the Duracell ads? Does it suggest that the Energizer people have come up with a better *battery* or a better *ad?*

Now let's expand the system. When that bunny suddenly interrupts a startlingly realistic "commercial" for "Chateau Marmoset" wine, for instance, it reminds us of the rather pretentious campaign that Gallo had pitched to the yuppie market. In spoof after spoof, the Energizer ads invite us to relate them to the commercial system as a whole, to the entire terrain of American advertising. So what effects do *these* comparisons have?

Think about it. When you're sick of something, don't you like to see a good parody of it? It appears, then, that the Energizer spoofs are appealing to a certain disgust in its intended audience, a weariness with Madison Avenue gimmicks. Isn't that what the ads are doing, playing to your skepticism of advertising?

In short, in a skeptical climate, the Energizer bunny tells us, really clever advertisers (like the creators of the Joe Isuzu campaign that played upon consumer skepticism of extravagant claims in automotive advertising) come up with new ways of making us identify with their product. Gladly recognizing spoof ads as reflections of their own frustrations with silly and manipulative advertising, viewers find themselves identifying with the creators and sponsors of spoof commercials. And thus they buy a product not because it is better but because they feel good about the way it was presented to them (so good that, in the case of the Energizer bunny, they went out in large numbers to buy pink bunny toys and other spin-off paraphernalia). So nothing has really changed: Once again a sign has been substituted for a thing, commodifying the consumer desire to be free of commodified desire.

We can go further. The Energizer bunny campaign can be referred to a larger system beyond the advertising world, to a social complex where citizen-consumers are becoming increasingly exasperated with the cynicism of the powerful in America, whether they be politicians or advertisers. As such, our bunny serves as a kind of cultural barometer, pointing toward the same social forces that produced Ross Perot's campaign for the presidency in 1992. But the fact that our barometric reading comes from an *ad* is itself a sign of just how entrenched the current system is. For as the bunny tells us, the powerful are always one step ahead. In response to voter frustration, political incumbents run their campaigns as if they were political "outsiders," while advertisers, detecting a growing consumer immunity to advertising, run anticommercial commercials. The system remains the same; only the strategies change.

So in reading an ad, you must always ask yourself, "Why am I being shown *that,* or being told *this*?" Cast yourself as the director of an ad, asking yourself what you would do to pitch a product, then look at what the advertiser has done. Pay attention to the way an ad's imagery is organized. Every detail counts. Why are these colors used (or lack of color, as in most of the Guess? ads)? Why are cute stuffed animals chosen to pitch toilet paper? What are those people *doing* in that perfume commercial? Why the cowboy hat in an ad for jeans? How does the slogan "Just Do It" sell Nikes? Look too for what the ad *doesn't* include: Is it missing a clear view of the product itself or an ethnically diverse cast of characters? In short, when interpreting an ad, transform it into a text and read it as you would a poem or an editorial or any piece of rhetoric, for in its mandate to persuade, advertising constitutes the most potent rhetoric of our times.

The Readings

Our selections in this chapter include interpretations and analyses of the world of advertising, as well as advertisements for you to interpret yourselves. The chapter begins with an historical perspective: Roland Marchand's "The Parable of the Democracy of Goods" shows how advertisers in the 1920s played upon the unconscious desires of their market by exploiting the fundamental myths of American culture. Jane Caputi provides an in-depth semiotic analysis of a single ad campaign, IBM's "Charlie Chaplin" series, while Patricia J. Williams examines both the elusiveness of truth in advertising imagery and the resulting legal implications. A pair of readings address gender issues: Diane Barthel's analysis of the images of men in advertising complements Gloria Steinem's insider's view of what goes on behind the scenes at women's magazines. And finally, we include a portfolio of print ads for you to decode for yourselves.

ROLAND MARCHAND
The Parable of the Democracy of Goods

<hr>

IIIIIIIIIIIIIIIIIIIIIIIIIIIIIIIIIIIIIIIIIIIIIIIIIIIIIIIIII

Advertisements do not simply reflect American myths, they create them, as Roland Marchand shows in this selection from Advertising the American Dream *(1985). Focusing on elaborate advertising narratives, he describes "The Parable of the Democracy of Goods," which pitches a product by convincing middle-class consumers that, by buying this toilet seat or that brand of coffee, they can share an experience with the very richest Americans. The advertising strategies Marchand analyzes date from the 1920s to 1940s, and new "parables" have since appeared that reflect more modern times, but even the oldest are still in use today. A professor of history at the University of California, Davis, Marchand is also the author of* The American Peace Movement and Social Reform, 1898–1918 *(1973). A specialist in the history of advertising and of American culture, Marchand currently is writing a book on the history of corporate public relations.*

As they opened their September 1929 issue, readers of the *Ladies' Home Journal* were treated to an account of the care and feeding of young Livingston Ludlow Biddle III, scion of the wealthy Biddles of Philadelphia, whose family coat-of-arms graced the upper right-hand corner of the page. Young Master Biddle, mounted on his tricycle, fixed a serious, slightly pouting gaze upon the reader, while the Cream of Wheat Corporation rapturously explained his constant care, his carefully regulated play and exercise, and the diet prescribed for him by "famous specialists." As master of Sunny Ridge Farm, the Biddles's winter estate in North Carolina, young Livingston III had "enjoyed every luxury of social position and wealth, since the day he was born." Yet, by the grace of a modern providence, it happened that Livingston's health was protected by a "simple plan every mother can use." Mrs. Biddle gave Cream of Wheat to the young heir for both breakfast and supper. The world's foremost child experts knew of no better diet; great wealth could procure no finer nourishment. As Cream of Wheat's advertising agency summarized the central point of the campaign that young Master Biddle initiated, "every mother can give her youngsters the fun and benefits of a Cream of Wheat breakfast just as do the parents of these boys and girls who have the best that wealth can command."[1]

<hr>

1. *Ladies' Home Journal*, Sept. 1929, second cover; *JWT News Letter*, Oct. 1, 1929, p. 1, J. Walter Thompson Company (JWT) Archives, New York City.

While enjoying this glimpse of childrearing among the socially distinguished, *Ladies' Home Journal* readers found themselves schooled in
one of the most pervasive of all advertising tableaux of the 1920s—the
parable of the Democracy of Goods. According to this parable, the
wonders of modern mass production and distribution enabled every
person to enjoy the society's most significant pleasure, convenience, or
benefit. The definition of the particular benefit fluctuated, of course,
with each client who employed the parable. But the cumulative effect
of the constant reminders that "any woman can" and "every home can
afford" was to publicize an image of American society in which concentrated wealth at the top of a hierarchy of social classes restricted no
family's opportunity to acquire the most significant products.[2] By implicitly defining "democracy" in terms of equal access to consumer
products, and then by depicting the everyday functioning of that "democracy" with regard to one product at a time, these tableaux offered
Americans an inviting vision of their society as one of incontestable
equality.

In its most common advertising formula, the concept of the Democracy of Goods asserted that although the rich enjoyed a great variety
of luxuries, the acquisition of their *one* most significant luxury would
provide anyone with the ultimate in satisfaction. For instance, a Chase
and Sanborn's Coffee tableau, with an elegant butler serving a family in
a dining room with a sixteen-foot ceiling, reminded Chicago families
that although "compared with the riches of the more fortunate, your
way of life may seem modest indeed," yet no one—"king, prince, statesman, or capitalist"—could enjoy better coffee.[3] The Association of Soap
and Glycerine Producers proclaimed that the charm of cleanliness was
as readily available to the poor as to the rich, and Ivory Soap reassuringly
related how one young housewife, who couldn't afford a $780-a-year
maid like her neighbor, still maintained a significant equality in "nice
hands" by using Ivory.[4] The C. F. Church Manufacturing Company
epitomized this version of the parable of the Democracy of Goods in an
ad entitled "a bathroom luxury everyone can afford": "If you lived in
one of those palatial apartments on Park Avenue, in New York City,
where you have to pay $2,000 to $7,500 a year rent, you still couldn't
have a better toilet seat in your bathroom than they have—the Church
Sani-white Toilet Seat which you can afford to have right now."[5]

2. *Saturday Evening Post,* Apr. 3, 1926, pp. 182–83; Nov. 6, 1926, p. 104; Apr. 16,
1927, p. 199; Scrapbook 54 (Brunswick-Balke-Collender), Lord and Thomas Archives,
at Foote, Cone and Belding Communications, Inc., Chicago.

3. *Chicago Tribune,* Nov. 21, 1926, picture section, p. 2.

4. *Los Angeles Times,* July 14, 1929, part VI, p. 3; *Tide,* July 1928, p. 10; *Photoplay
Magazine,* Mar. 1930, p. 1.

5. *American Magazine,* Mar. 1926, p. 112.

Thus, according to the parable, no discrepancies in wealth could prevent the humblest citizens, provided they chose their purchases wisely, from retiring to a setting in which they could contemplate their essential equality, through possession of an identical product, with the nation's millionaires. In 1929, Howard Dickinson, a contributor to *Printers' Ink,* concisely expressed the social psychology behind Democracy of Goods advertisements: "'With whom do the mass of people think they want to foregather?' asks the psychologist in advertising. 'Why, with the wealthy and socially distinguished, of course!' If we can't get an invitation to tea for our millions of customers, we can at least present the fellowship of using the same brand of merchandise. And it works."[6]

Some advertisers found it more efficacious to employ the parable's   5
negative counterpart—the Democracy of Afflictions. Listerine contributed significantly to this approach. Most of the unsuspecting victims of halitosis in the mid-1920s possessed wealth and high social position. Other discoverers of new social afflictions soon took up the battle cry of "nobody's immune." "Body Odor plays no favorites," warned Lifebuoy Soap. No one, "banker, baker, or society woman," could count himself safe from B.O.[7] The boss, as well as the employees, might find himself "caught off guard" with dirty hands or cuffs, the Soap and Glycerine Producers assured readers of *True Story.* By 1930, Absorbine Jr. was beginning to document the democratic advance of "athlete's foot" into those rarefied social circles occupied by the "daintiest member of the junior set" and the noted yachtsman who owned "a railroad or two" (Figure 1).[8]

The central purpose of the Democracy of Afflictions tableaux was to remind careless or unsuspecting readers of the universality of the threat from which the product offered protection or relief. Only occasionally did such ads address those of the upper classes who might think that their status and "fastidious" attention to personal care made them immune from common social offenses. In 1929 Listerine provided newspaper readers an opportunity to listen while a doctor, whose clientele included those of "the better class," confided "what I know about *nice* women."[9] One might have thought that Listerine was warning complacent, upper-class women that they were not immune from halitosis— except that the ad appeared in the *Los Angeles Times,* not *Harper's Bazaar.* Similarly, Forhan's toothpaste and the Soap Producers did not place their

---

6. *Printers' Ink,* Oct. 10, 1929, p. 138.

7. *Tide,* Sept. 15, 1927, p. 5; *American Magazine,* Aug. 1929, p. 93; *True Story,* June 1929, p. 133; *Chicago Tribune,* Jan. 11, 1928, p. 16; Jan. 18, 1928, p. 15; Jan. 28, 1928, p. 7; *Photoplay Magazine,* Feb. 1929, p. 111.

8. *True Story,* May 1928, p. 83; June 1929, p. 133; *American Magazine,* Feb. 1930, p. 110; *Saturday Evening Post,* Aug. 23, 1930, p. 124.

9. *Los Angeles Times,* July 6, 1929, p. 3.

FIGURE 1   A negative appeal transformed the Democracy of Goods into the Democracy of Afflictions. Common folk learned from this parable that they could inexpensively avoid afflictions that beset even the yachting set.

Democracy of Afflictions ads in *True Story* in order to reach the social elite. Rather, these tableaux provided enticing glimpses into the lives of the wealthy while suggesting an equalizing "fellowship" in shared susceptibilities to debilitating ailments. The parable of the Democracy of Goods always remained implicit in its negative counterpart. It assured readers that they could be as healthy, as charming, as free from social offense as the very "nicest" (richest) people, simply by using a product that anyone could afford.

Another variation of the parable of the Democracy of Goods employed historical comparisons to celebrate even the humblest of contemporary Americans as "kings in cottages." "No monarch in all history ever saw the day he could have half as much as you," proclaimed Paramount Pictures. Even reigning sovereigns of the present, Paramount continued, would envy readers for their "luxurious freedom and opportunity" to enter a magnificent, bedazzling "palace for a night," be greeted with fawning bows by liveried attendants, and enjoy modern entertainment for a modest price (Fig. 2). The Fisher Body Corporation coined the phrase "For Kings in Cottages" to compliment ordinary Americans on their freedom from "hardships" that even kings had been forced to endure in the past. Because of a lack of technology, monarchs who traveled in the past had "never enjoyed luxury which even approached that of the present-day automobile." The "American idea," epitomized by the Fisher Body Corporation, was destined to carry the comforts and luxuries conducive to human happiness into "the life of even the humblest cottager."[10]

Even so, many copywriters perceived that equality with past monarchs might not rival the vision of joining the fabled "Four Hundred" that Ward McAllister had marked as America's social elite at the end of the nineteenth century. Americans, in an ostensibly conformist age, hungered for exclusivity. So advertising tableaux celebrated their ascension into this fabled and exclusive American elite. Through mass production and the resulting lower prices, the tableaux explained, the readers could purchase goods formerly available only to the rich—and thus gain admission to a "400" that now numbered millions.

The Simmons Company confessed that inner-coil mattresses had once been a luxury possessed only by the very wealthy. But now (in 1930) they were "priced so everybody in the United States can have one at $19.95." Woodbury's Soap advised the "working girl" readers of *True Story* of their arrival within a select circle. "Yesterday," it recalled, "the skin you love to touch" had been "the privilege of one woman in 65," but today it had become "the beauty right of every woman."[11] If the Democracy of Goods could establish an equal consumer right to beauty, then perhaps even the ancient religious promise of equality in death might be realized, at least to the extent that material provisions sufficed. In 1927 the Clark Grave Vault Company defined this unique promise: "Not so many years ago the use of a burial vault was confined largely to the rich. . . . Now every family, regardless of its means, may provide absolute protection against the elements of the ground."[12] If it seemed that the residents of Clark vaults had gained equality with the "400" too belatedly for maximum satisfaction, still their loving survivors could now share the same sense of comfort in the "absolute protection" of former loved ones as did the most privileged elites.

---

10. *Saturday Evening Post,* May 8, 1926, p. 59; *American Magazine,* May 1932, pp. 76–77. See also *Saturday Evening Post,* July 18, 1931, pp. 36–37; Aug. 1, 1931, pp. 30–31; *Better Homes and Gardens,* Mar. 1930, p. 77.

11. *Saturday Evening Post,* Nov. 10, 1928, p. 90; *True Story,* Aug. 1934, p. 57. See also *Chicago Tribune,* Oct. 8, 1930, p. 17; *American Magazine,* Aug. 1930, p. 77; *Woman's Home Companion,* May 1927, p. 96.

12. *American Magazine,* Feb. 1927, p. 130

FIGURE 2   Of course, real kings had never shared their status with crowds of other "kings." But the parable of the Democracy of Goods offered a brief, "packaged experience" of luxury and preference.

The social message of the parable of the Democracy of Goods was   10
clear. Antagonistic envy of the rich was unseemly; programs to redistribute wealth were unnecessary. The best things in life were already available to all at reasonable prices. But the prevalence of the parable of the Democracy of Goods in advertising tableaux did not necessarily betray a concerted conspiracy on the part of advertisers and their agencies to impose a social ideology on the American people. Most advertisers employed the parable of the Democracy of Goods primarily as a narrow, nonideological merchandising tactic. Listerine and Lifebuoy found the parable an obvious, attention-getting strategy for persuading readers that if even society women and bankers were unconsciously guilty of social offenses, the readers themselves were not immune. Simmons Mattresses, Chevrolet, and Clark Grave Vaults chose the parable in an at-

tempt to broaden their market to include lower-income groups. The parable emphasized the affordability of the product to families of modest income while attempting to maintain a "class" image of the product as the preferred choice of their social betters.

Most advertisers found the social message of the parable of the Democracy of Goods a congenial and unexceptionable truism. They also saw it, like the other parables prevalent in advertising tableaux, as an epigrammatic statement of a conventional popular belief. Real income was rising for nearly all Americans during the 1920s, except for some farmers and farm workers and those in a few depressed industries. Citizens seemed eager for confirmation that they were now driving the same make of car as the wealthy elites and serving their children the same cereal enjoyed by Livingston Ludlow Biddle III. Advertisers did not have to impose the parable of the Democracy of Goods on a contrary-minded public. Theirs was the easier task of subtly substituting this vision of equality, which was certainly satisfying *as a vision,* for broader and more traditional hopes and expectations of an equality of self-sufficiency, personal independence, and social interaction.

Perhaps the most attractive aspect of this parable to advertisers was that it preached the coming of an equalizing democracy without sacrificing those fascinating contrasts of social condition that had long been the touchstone of high drama. Henry James, writing of Hawthorne, had once lamented the obstacles facing the novelist who wrote of an America that lacked such tradition-laden institutions as a sovereign, a court, an aristocracy, or even a class of country gentlemen. Without castles, manors, and thatched cottages, America lacked those stark juxtapositions of pomp and squalor, nobility and peasantry, wealth and poverty that made Europe so rich a source of social drama.[13] But many versions of the parable of the Democracy of Goods sought to offset that disadvantage without gaining James's desired "complexity of manners." They dressed up America's wealthy as dazzling aristocrats, and then reassured readers that they could easily enjoy an essential equality with such elites in the things that really mattered. The rich were decorative and fun to look at, but in their access to those products most important to comfort and satisfaction, as the magazine *Delineator* put it, "The Four Hundred" had become "the four million."[14] Advertisers left readers to assume that they could gain the same satisfactions of exclusiveness from belonging to the four million as had once been savored by the four hundred.

While parables of consumer democracy frequently used terms like "everyone," "anyone," "any home," or "every woman," these categories were mainly intended to comprise the audience of "consumer-citizens"

---

13. Henry James, *Hawthorne,* rev. ed. (New York, 1967 [c. 1879]), p. 55.
14. *Printers' Ink,* Nov. 24, 1927, p. 52.

envisioned by the advertising trade, or families economically among the nation's top 50 percent. Thus the *Delineator* had more in mind than mere alliteration when it chose to contrast the old "400" with the new "four million" rather than a new "one hundred and twenty million." The standard antitheses of the Democracy of Goods parables were "mansion" and "bungalow." Advertising writers rarely took notice of the many millions of Americans whose standard of living fell below that of the cozy bungalow of the advertising tableaux. These millions might over-hear the promises of consumer democracy in the newspapers or maga-zines, but advertising leaders felt no obligation to show how their prom-ises to "everyone" would bring equality to those who lived in the nation's apartment houses and farmhouses without plumbing, let alone those who lived in rural shacks and urban tenements.

In the broadest sense, the parable of the Democracy of Goods may be interpreted as a secularized version of the traditional Christian assur-ances of ultimate human equality. "Body Odor plays no favorites" might be considered a secular translation of the idea that God "sends rain on the just and on the unjust" (Matt. 5:45). Promises of the essential equality of those possessing the advertised brand recalled the promise of equality of access to God's mercy. Thus the parable recapitulated a familiar, cher-ished expectation. Far more significant, however, was the parable's in-sinuation of the capacity of a Democracy of Goods to redeem the already secularized American promise of political equality.

Incessantly and enticingly repeated, advertising visions of fellowship in a Democracy of Goods encouraged Americans to look to similarities in consumption styles rather than to political power or control of wealth for evidence of significant equality. Francesco Nicosia and Robert Mayer describe the result as a "deflection of the success ethic from the sphere of production to that of consumption." Freedom of choice came to be perceived as a freedom more significantly exercised in the marketplace than in the political arena. This process gained momentum in the 1920s; it gained maturity during the 1950s as a sense of class differences was nearly eclipsed by a fascination with the equalities suggested by shared consumption patterns and "freely chosen" consumer "lifestyles."[15]

Reading the Text

1. Summarize in your own words what Marchand means by the "parable of the democracy of goods."

---

15. Francesco M. Nicosia and Robert N. Mayer, "Toward a Sociology of Con-sumption," *The Journal of Consumer Research* 3(1976): 73; Roland Marchand, "Visions of Classlessness; Quests for Dominion: American Popular Culture, 1945–1960," in *Reshaping America: Society and Institutions, 1945–1960,* ed. Robert H. Bremner and Gary W. Rei-chard (Columbus, Ohio, 1982), pp. 165–70.

2. What is the "democracy of afflictions," in your own words?
3. In class, brainstorm examples of current ads that illustrate the parable of the democracy of goods and the democracy of afflictions.

Reading the Signs

1. Does the parable of the democracy of goods work to make society more egalitarian or does it reinforce existing power structures? Write an essay arguing for one position or the other, focusing on particular ads for your support.
2. Bring to class a popular magazine of your own choosing. In groups, study your selections. In which magazines is the myth of the democracy of goods most common? Do you find any relationship between the use of this myth and the intended audience of the magazines?
3. Look through a "women's" magazine such as *Vogue* or *Glamour*. Which myth do you find more prevalent, the democracy of goods or the democracy of affliction? How would Diane Barthel (p. 128) explain your finding?
4. Study a "home" magazine such as *Better Homes and Gardens* and find one or more ads that use the democracy of goods as strategies. Then write a semiotic interpretation of the ads you have selected.
5. Obtain from your college library an issue of *Time* magazine dating from the 1920s, and compare it with a current issue. In what ways, if any, have the social messages communicated in the advertising changed? Try to account for any changes you identify.
6. Compare and contrast the myth of the democracy of goods to the frontier myth that Laurence Shames describes in "The More Factor" (p. 25). Consider how the two myths shape our consuming behavior and the advertising designed to trigger such behavior; you may also want to show how the myths appear in some current ads.

JANE CAPUTI

IBM's Charlie Chaplin: A Case Study

꙳꙳

The early 1980s marked a new era in the computer industry: the introduction of the personal computer designed to create a new mass market. Apple, Inc., accomplished this task by dubbing its flagship product a "Macintosh" and creating for it a nonthreatening, rainbow-colored logo. In this selection, Jane Caputi (b. 1953) reveals how corporate giant IBM transformed the forbidding technology of its PC line by associating it with the beloved icon of Charlie Chaplin's Tramp. In advertising, Caputi shows, image is everything. A professor in the

Department of American Studies at the University of New Mexico, Caputi has written voluminously on American popular culture. Her works, which take a feminist perspective, include The Age of Sex Crime *(1978) and* Gossips, Gorgons, and Crones: The Fates of the Earth *(1993)*.

Remembering and Forgetting

Chiefly, we wanted something that people would remember. Using the Chaplin character was one way to create ads with stopping power.
　　　　　　　　　　　　　　　 – P. DAVID MCGOVERN, *ad director at IBM*

The Tramp campaign has been so successful that it has created a new image for IBM. The firm has always been seen as efficient and reliable, but it has also been regarded as somewhat cold and aloof. The Tramp, with his ever present red rose, has given IBM a human face.
　　　　　　　　　　　　　　　　　　　　 – Time, 11 July 1983

Soldiers! Don't give yourselves to these brutes. . . . Don't give yourselves to these unnatural men—machine men with machine minds and machine hearts.
　　　　　　　　　　　 – CHARLIE CHAPLIN, *The Great Dictator (1939)*

Stuck with a multinational, cold, colossus, remote, and even a totalitarian "Big Brother" public image, IBM took the plunge and set out to manufacture some warmer and more sympathetic associations for itself and its "personal" computer. Investing a quick 36 million, it mounted one of the largest ad campaigns ever for a computer, producing ads calling the PC "a tool for modern times" and using Charlie Chaplin's internationally recognized and beloved character, the Little Tramp. These ads proved to be both extraordinarily memorable and successful, winning not only business gains but also acclaim and awards from the advertising world.[1]

The method of these spots, as with so many others, was to set up a metaphor—to link a particular product with some positive symbol or association already held by the viewers, to induce "resonance." Literal absurdity is by no means a disqualifier for such metaphors. Consider cigarette advertising whereby cigarettes are said to be "only natural," to taste "like Springtime," or are consistently linked with fresh, outdoor, and highly physical activities. Such ads use nature the way the military uses camouflage. And although they may seem merely ridiculous, met-

---

1. Kathy Root, "Kudos for a Tramp and a Motor Mouth," *Nation's Business,* April 1984, 44–45; "Softening a Starchy Image," *Time,* 11 July 1983, 54.

aphors such as these further the pollution and destruction of both environments—the body and the ecosystem—by bridging our feelings about each with, of all things, a cigarette.

The absurdity of the smoking ads, however, is more than matched by the contradictions inherent in the IBM campaign. In these, the Little Tramp, "perhaps the most famous creation in any art medium of the 20th century,"[2] provides the positive associations, for Charlie the Tramp was a clown whose "appeal was virtually universal."[3] His very image came to immediately signify humanity, survival, innocence, the beauty of the commonplace, and, above all, the soul or spirit. James Agee has written that "the Tramp is as centrally representative of humanity, as many-sided and as mysterious as Hamlet, and it seems unlikely that any dancer or actor can ever have excelled him in eloquence, variety, or poignancy of motion."[4] Thus does IBM acquire a human face and graft a soul onto its new machine. The method is virtually indistinguishable from the way that Salem bonds itself to Springtime or Marlboro to the western landscape. All are highly *memorable* ads, ones with "stopping power."

But of course the IBM ads are as much about forgetting as remembering for, although they evoke those positive memories of Charlie, they simultaneously arrest and reverse the recollection that Chaplin himself was expressly opposed to big business, mechanization, and those technological goals and/or gods of timekeeping, speed, and efficiency. Those views, evident throughout much of his work, are nowhere more clearly expressed than in the 1936 *Modern Times,* Chaplin's last film to feature the Tramp, a character he had then played for over twenty years. It was in *Modern Times,* as Parker Tyler has observed, that, "the Machine was the thoroughly identified enemy, the robber of art and poetry."[5] Now, however, in perfect accord with double-think, the home computer is plugged as "a tool for modern times," and the image of the Tramp is made to perform as the thoroughly identified advocate, indeed *tool,* of the Machine—International Business Machines to be precise.

In *Modern Times,* Chaplin as the Tramp is a worker in some colossal factory, his job to tighten the nuts on some unidentifiable product as it comes down an assembly line. The line becomes a synchronized mechanical dance, and each time Charlie takes a break his shoulders and

2. R.A.E. Pickard, *Dictionary of 1,000 Best Films* (New York: Association Press, 1971), 296.

3. Louis Giannetti, *Masters of the American Cinema* (Englewood Cliffs, N.J.: Prentice-Hall, 1981), 83.

4. James Agee, "Comedy's Greatest Era," in *Film Theory and Criticism,* 2d ed., edited by Gerald Mast and Marshall Cohen (New York: Oxford University Press, 1979), 535–58.

5. Parker Tyler, *Chaplin: Last of the Clowns* (New York: Horizon Press, 1972), 158.

arms twitch in helpless repetition of the nut-tightening gesture. In one of the most celebrated scenes from the film, the Big Brother–like boss of the factory orders a speedup on the line and Charlie snaps. Jumping onto the assembly line, he plunges headfirst into the machine and is swallowed though finally disgorged by the gigantic gears. Emerging from the machine, he frolics and spins out his own outrageous ballet in response to the monotone of the line, spreading sheer chaos throughout the factory. The sequence closes with him being taken off to a mental hospital.

Thus, in Chaplin's own account, the Machine might swallow him, temporarily, but it could not digest him and had to spit him out. Now, however, IBM figuratively swallows him whole, thoroughly assimilates and converts him, effectively erasing his original message by producing a doppelgänger who now befriends and promotes the Machine and its order—and all accompanied by studied references to *Modern Times*.

For example, one of the print ads in this series features the Chaplin figure dashing madly by on a bicycle; his hat flies off and tie swings back to register the velocity. A computer is strapped to the back of his bike. The copy reads: "How to move with modern times and take your PC with you." A television spot portrays the Tramp straddling the intersection of two assembly lines in a bakery. He is placing decorated cakes from one line into boxes from the other. But the cakes don't match the boxes, the machinery starts going haywire, and chaos results. The scene then changes by means of a wipe taking the form of a hand sweeping round a clock's face, and next we see the Tramp seated in front of a personal computer. His problems, we know, will soon be techno-magically solved. And indeed, next he is back at the factory, but this time a baker has taken his place on the line. The Tramp is there only to put the decoration on a cake and present it to a purely decorative female. The moral of this thirty-second parable is clear. The Tramp, backed by the Machine, has *restored* Order; he is now the Owner, the Boss; he gets kissed by the Girl; the End.

These very specific and specifically reversed references to *Modern Times* indicate something of a willful effort to undercut the integrity of that film and indeed of Chaplin himself. Although the question was raised early in the campaign as to whether the Tramp and this film actually represented an "antitechnology sentiment," both IBM and the ad agency concluded, in the words of an IBM director, that the character actually "stands fear of technology on its head."[6] Of course, it is really the Chaplin character who is being stood on his head and shaken until the original content and message have been expunged, leaving only an empty if still appealing image to be infused with new meaning by IBM.

---

6. "Softening a Starchy Image," 54.

Or, as O'Brien said to Winston in *1984,* "You will be hollow. We shall squeeze you empty, and then we shall fill you with ourselves."[7] The final punch or stopping power of these ads thus lies in their subtle suggestion that the dissident has been assimilated and converted. Just as Winston finally loves Big Brother, "Charlie" now loves the Machine.

Reading the Text

1. What are the contradictions that Caputi finds in IBM's use of the Little Tramp?
2. Why, according to Caputi, was it so important for IBM to pick a character like the Little Tramp to represent its computers?
3. Why does Caputi say the IBM ads are as much about "forgetting as remembering"?

Reading the Signs

1. Rent a videotape of *Modern Times* and view it. Then write an essay describing how Chaplin attacks industrial culture.
2. Read a magazine such as *Business Week* and write a semiotic analysis of the computer advertisements. How do the ads reflect American attitudes toward computers in the 1990s?
3. Compare the Little Tramp to the advertising characters that McCrea Adams studies in "Advertising Characters: The Pantheon of Consumerism" (p. 359): Is the Little Tramp just another example of the blurring of fiction and reality?
4. Both Caputi and Stuart Ewen ("Hard Bodies," p. 60) lambaste the image of industrialism in advertising. Do you agree with their critique? If so, write a defense of their position, using ads you select yourself as further support; if not, refute them, basing your argument on an alternative analysis of the ads they discuss.

PATRICIA J. WILLIAMS

The Fiction of Truth in Advertising

<hr>

|||||||||||||||||||||||||||||||||||||||||||||||||||

In The Alchemy of Race and Rights *(1991), from which this selection is taken, Patricia J. Williams (b. 1951) explores the relationship between the law and everyday life, focusing particularly on the ways that race and gender can complicate American social relations. In this passage, Williams brings her legal training to bear on advertising: Notions of "truth" are increasingly absent from modern advertising, she finds, as she reflects on the dehumanizing and disenfranchising effect of media fictions. Educated at Harvard Law School, she currently is professor of law at Columbia Law School and has written widely on civil rights issues and legal ethics.*

When I first started teaching consumer protection a decade ago, the mathematics of false advertising was simple. If the box or brochure said "100% cotton," you merely took the item in question and subtracted it from the words: Any difference was the measure of your legal remedy. Sometimes you had to add in buyer's expertise or multiply the whole by seller's bad faith, but generally the whole reason people even took a class in consumer protection was that you didn't have to learn logarithms. Today, however, advertisers almost never represent anything remotely related to the reality of the product—or the politician—they are trying to sell; misrepresentation, the heart of false-advertising statutes, is very hard to prove. Increasingly, television ads are characterized by scenarios that neither mention the product nor contain a description of any sort. What fills the sixty seconds are "concepts" and diffuse images—images that used to be discursive, floating in the background, creating a mellow consumerist backdrop—which now dominate and direct content. Nothing is promised, everything evoked: warm fuzzy camera angles; "peak" experiences; happy pictures, mood-shaping music; almost always a smarmy, soft-peddling overvoice purring "This magic moment has been brought to you by . . ."

An example, in the form of an anecdote: About a year ago, I was sitting at home, installed before the television set. I was preparing for a class in consumer protection. The next day's assignment was false advertising, and I was shopping for an advertisement whose structure I could use as a starting point for discussion. An ad for Georges Marciano clothing flashed on the screen and dragged me in, first with the music, South African music of haunting urgency, the echoing simultaneity of nonlinear music, the syncopation of quickening-heartbeat percussive music, dragging the ear. In the picture, a woman with long blond hair in sunglasses ran from a crowd of photographers and an admiring public. The film was black and white, a series of frames jaggedly succeeding each other, like a patchwork of secretly taken stills. Sliced into the sequence of her running away were shots of the blond and her manager/bodyguard/ boyfriend packing. He packed the passports and the handgun, she packed the Georges Marciano jeans. The climax came when she burst into a room of exploding flashbulbs—a blazing bath of white light.

The effect of this particular visual and aural juxtaposition was the appearance of the music as being inside the woman's head or her heart. The music was primal, dangerous, desperate. The woman's crisis of adoration framed the burning necessity of this profound music, and the soaring universality of sound became white, female, privatized. The pulsing movement of the music elevated this event of narcissistic voyeurism to elemental importance. The music overflowed boundaries. Voices merged and surged; mood drifted and soared in the listening. African voices swelled and rose in the intricate music of knowledge, the wisdom of rhythm, the physics of echoing chasms bounded in intervals, the harmonic bells of voices striking each other in excitement and the wind, black African voices making music of the trees, of groundhogs, of whistling birds and pure chortling streams. It was generous shared music, open and eternal.

The pictures presented sought privacy. The chase was an invasion; the photographers pursued her private moments; she resisted even as her glamour consented. The viewer was drawn into desire to see her never-quite-revealed face, swept along by the urgency of her running to privacy, even as we never quite acknowledged her right to it. Thus the moment of climax, the flashing of cameras in her face (and ours, so completely have we identified with her), was one of release and relief. The music acted against the pictures. The mind resolved it queerly. The positive magnetic boundlessness of the music was turned into negative exposure. The run for privacy became an orgasmic peep show, the moment of negative exposure almost joyful.

In my lap, my textbook lay heavy, unattended pages drifting open to the Lanham Act:[1]   5

> *False designations of origin and false descriptions forbidden:*
>   . . . any person who shall affix, apply, or annex, or use in connection with any goods or services . . . a false designation of origin, or any false description or representation, including words or other symbols tending falsely to describe or represent the same, and shall cause such goods or services to enter into commerce, and any person

---

1. **Lanham Act**   U.S. statute enacted in 1947 that revised trademark laws.— EDS.

who shall with knowledge of the falsity of such . . . description or representation cause or procure the same to be transported or used in commerce . . . or used, shall be liable to a civil action . . . by any person who believes that he is or is likely to be damaged by the use of any such false description or representation.[2]

I have recounted this story at some length, not just for its illustrative contrast between the sight and the sound of an advertisement, but also because the relationship between the music and the pictures can serve as a metaphor for the tension between the political and marketplace dynamic that is my larger subject. I think that the invisible corruption of one by the other has consequences that are, ultimately, dehumanizing.

Ours is not the first generation to fall prey to false needs; but ours is the first generation of admakers to realize the complete fulfillment of the consumerist vision through the fine-tuning of sheer hucksterism. Surfaces, fantasies, appearances, and vague associations are the order of the day. So completely have substance, reality, and utility been subverted that products are purified into mere wisps of labels, floating signifiers of their former selves. "Coke" can as easily add life plastered on clothing as poured in a cup. Calculating a remedy for this new-age consumptive pandering is problematic. If people like—and buy—the enigmatic emptiness used to push products, then describing a harm becomes elusive. But it is elusive precisely because the imagery and vocabulary of advertising have shifted the focus from need to disguise. With this shift has come—either manipulated or galloping gladly behind—a greater public appetite for illusion and disguise. And in the wake of that has come an enormous shift of national industry, national resources, and national consciousness.

Some years ago, when I first started teaching, most of my students agreed that a nice L. L. Bean Baxter State Parka delivered without a label saying "L. L. Bean" was minor default indeed. Today I have to work to convince them that the absence of the label is not a major breach of contract; I have to make them think about what makes the parka "an L. L. Bean": its utility or its image? Its service to the wearer or its impact on those around the wearer? If masque becomes the basis of our bargains, I worry that we will forget the jazzy, primal King Lear-ish essence of ourselves from which wisdom springs and insight grows. I worry that we will create new standards of irrelevance in our lives, reordering social relations in favor of the luxurious—and since few of us can afford real luxury, blind greed becomes the necessary companion.

On a yet more complicated level, I worry that in accustoming ourselves to the emptiness of media fictions, we will have reconstructed our very notion of property. If property is literally the word or the

2. §243 (a), Lanham Act, 15 U.S.C.S. §21125 (a) (1988).

concept used to describe it, then we have empowered the self-willed speaker not just as market actor but as ultimate Creator. If property is nothing more than what it evokes on the most intimate and subjective levels, then the inherence of its object is denied; the separateness of the thing that is property must be actively obliterated in order to maintain the privately sensational pleasantry of the mirror image. A habituated, acculturated blindness to the inherent quality of the people and things around us grows up, based on our safety from having to see. Our inter-relationships with these things is not seen; their reasons for being are rendered invisible.

At the simplest level of market economics, the modern algebra of advertising deprives society of a concept of commodities as enduring. Sales of goods are no longer the subject of express or long-term prom-issory relationships—there is at best an implied warranty of merchant-ability at the fleeting moment of contract and delivery. Contract law's historic expectation interest[3] becomes even more thoroughly touch and go, in the most virulent tradition of caveat emptor. It is an unconscious narrowing of expectation to the extent that we lose our expectations. Thus, in some way, Coke and Pepsi lead us to obliterate the future, not just with empty calories but with empty promises. The illusion of a perky, sexy self is meaningless as to the reality of a can of corn syrup: But this substitution, this exchange of images, is a harm going beyond wasted money, tooth decay, or defeated notions of utility. The greater harm is that it is hypnotic, and culturally addictive.

In theory, contract doctrine is the currency of law used to impose economic order on human beings for certain purposes; defenses to con-tract formation such as fraud, duress, and undue influence are, I think, a theoretical attempt to impose an ordered humanity on economics. Increasingly, however, the day-to-day consumer purchases that form most of what is governed by contract have been characterized by a shift in popular as well as legal discourse: Contract is no longer a three-party transliterative code, in which law mediates between profit and relation-ship, and in which property therefore remains linked to notions of shared humanity. Instead, consumerism is locked into a two-party, bipolar code that is little more mediative than a mirror. Money reflects law and law reflects money, unattached to notions of humanity. The neat jurispru-dence of interpretive transposition renders the whole into a system of equations in which money = money, words = words (or law = law). The worst sort of mindless materialism arises. The worst sort of punitive literalism puts down roots.

---

3. The "expectation interest" in contract law is the promisee's "interest in having the benefit of his bargain by being put in as good a position as he would have been in had the contract been performed." §344 (a), *Restatement of the Law, Contracts (2d)*.

Some time ago, my friend and colleague Dinesh Khosla traveled to Costa Rica for a conference. On his way back to the United States, he found himself in the airport behind throngs of Costa Ricans pushing five or six huge suitcases apiece. Dinesh stopped often to assist several different people; each time he was surprised by how light the suitcases felt. After this much of the story, I already imagined its end, filling the suitcases with media images of feathery coca leaves and dusty white powders. But I was wrong; it turned out that these travelers were all wealthy Costa Ricans going to Miami for the sole purpose of shopping. They planned to load up the suitcases with designer clothes and fancy consumables and cart them back home. I was reminded of the Sufi tale of the customs official who for years scrutinized the comings and goings of a man famed as a smuggler. For years he subjected each parcel to thorough searches, but all he ever found was straw. Many years later when they were both retired, he asked the smuggler where he had hidden the contraband all that time. The man replied: "I was smuggling straw." Dinesh's account made the conspicuous luxury of North American commodities into a similar form of invisible contraband, a sinfully expensive and indulgent drug.

One last anecdote: A little way down Broadway from the 14th Street subway station in Manhattan, there is a store called the Unique Boutique. Yards from the campus of New York University, it is a place where stylish coeds shop for the slightly frumpy, punky, slummy clothes that go so well with bright red lipstick and ankle-high black bootlets. One winter day I saw a large, bright, fun-colored sign hanging in the window: "Sale! Two-dollar overcoats. No bums, no booze." Offended, and not wanting to feel how offended I was, I turned my head away toward the street. There, in the middle of the intersection of Broadway and Washington Place, stood a black man dressed in the ancient remains of a Harris Tweed overcoat. His arms were spread-eagled as if to fly, though he was actually begging from cars in both directions. He was also drunk and crying and trying to keep his balance. Drivers were offended, terrified of disease or of being robbed. Traffic slowed as cars described wide avoiding arcs around him and his broad-winged pleading.

So the sign was disenfranchising the very people who most needed two-dollar overcoats, the so-called bums. Moreover, it was selling the image of the disenfranchised themselves. The store is a trendy boutique aimed at NYU's undergraduate population. It was selling an image of genteel poverty, of casual dispossession. It attracted those who can afford to slum in style: yet it simultaneously exploited the slum itself. It was segregationist in the same way that "whites only" signs are. And it was not just segregationist along race and class lines; it also stole the images of those who had nothing and styled it as a commodity (slumminess) to be sold to those who have much. It was the ultimate in short-term consumerist redundance: Clothes do not just make the man, they would admit him into the clothing store itself.

In discussing the tension between liberty and authority, John Stuart 15 Mill observed that self-government means "not the government of each by himself but of each by all the rest." Mill feared what he called the "tyranny of the majority" and cautioned,

> Protection . . . against the tyranny of the magistrate is not enough; there needs protection also against the tyranny of prevailing opinion and feeling; against the tendency of society to impose, by other means than civil penalties, its own ideas and practices as rules of conduct on those who dissent from them . . . how to make the fitting adjustment between individual independence and social control—is a subject on which nearly everything remains to be done.[4]

The tyranny of the majority has survived in liberal political theory as a justification for all manner of legislative restraint, particularly economic restraint. But what Mill did not anticipate was that the persuasive power of the forum itself would subvert the polis, as well as the law, to the extent that there is today precious little "public" left, just the tyranny of what we call the private. In this nation there is, it is true, relatively little force in the public domain compared to other nations, relatively little intrusive governmental interference. But we risk instead the life-crushing disenfranchisement of an entirely owned world. Permission must be sought to walk upon the face of the earth. Freedom becomes contractual and therefore obligated; freedom is framed by obligation; and obligation is paired not with duty but with debt.

Reading the Text

1. What relationship does Williams see between products and their advertising images?
2. Why does Williams find the legal designation of "false advertising" almost irrelevant in today's marketing world?
3. How, according to Williams, has our notion of "property" been altered by modern advertising?

Reading the Signs

1. Williams assumes that the fleeting relationship between product and image in advertising is a recent phenomenon. Visit your college library, and survey

---

4. John Stuart Mill, *On Liberty,* ed. David Spitz (New York: Norton, 1975), p. 6.

some popular magazines published at the beginning of this century. What sort of relationship between product and image do you see in advertising? What does the relationship you find say about social values?

2. Compare the "image of the disenfranchised" Williams mentions on p. 126 to grunge fashion in the 1990s. Is grunge similarly "segregationist"?

3. Read or review Gloria Steinem's "Sex, Lies, and Advertising" (p. 139), and write an essay in which you explain how the business practices of the magazine industry illustrate Williams's concluding point: "Freedom becomes contractual and therefore obligated; freedom is framed by obligation; and obligation is paired not with duty but with debt."

4. Read or review Diane Barthel's "A Gentleman and a Consumer" (p. 128) and bell hooks's "Madonna: Plantation Mistress or Soul Sister?" (p. 190). Using their essays as models, analyze the roles of gender and ethnicity in the Georges Marciano commercial that Williams describes.

DIANE BARTHEL

A Gentleman and a Consumer

||||||||||||||||||||||||||||||||||||||||||||||||||

It's not only women who are pressured to conform to unattainable standards of physical appearance: Men are victims, too. Diane Barthel (b. 1949), in this selection from Putting on Appearances: Gender and Advertising *(1988), surveys the various images men are expected to live up to as presented in advertisements in men's magazines. From the cowboy to the corporate jungle fighter, from the playboy to the polo player, men are urged to adopt traditionally aggressive male gender roles. At the same time, Barthel points out, they are to become obsessed with their appearance—a role that, ironically, is traditionally considered feminine. Barthel is also the author of* Amana: From Pietist Sect to American Community *(1984).*

There are no men's beauty and glamour magazines with circulations even approaching those of the women's magazines. The very idea of men's beauty magazines may strike one as odd. In our society men traditionally were supposed to make the right appearance, to be well groomed and neatly tailored. What they were *not* supposed to do was to be overly concerned with their appearance, much less vain about their beauty. That was to be effeminate, and not a "real man." Male beauty was associated with homosexuals, and "real men" had to show how red-blooded they were by maintaining a certain distance from fashion.

Perhaps the best-known male fashion magazine is *GQ* founded in 1957 and with a circulation of 446,000 in 1986. More recently, we have seen the launching of *YMF* and *Young Black Male,* which in 1987 still [had] few advertising pages. *M* magazine, founded in 1983, attracts an audience "a cut above" that of *GQ*.[1]

Esquire magazine, more venerable (founded in 1933), is classified as a general interest magazine. Although it does attract many women readers, many of the columns and features and much of the advertising are definitely directed toward attracting the attention of the male readers, who still make up the overwhelming majority of the readership.

The highest circulations for men's magazines are for magazines specializing either in sex (*Playboy,* circulation 4.1 million; *Penthouse,* circulation nearly 3.8 million; and *Hustler,* circulation 1.5 million) or sports (*Sports Illustrated,* circulation 2.7 million).[2] That these magazines share an emphasis on power—either power over women or over other men on the playing field—should not surprise. In fact, sociologist John Gagnon would argue that sex and sports now represent the major fields in which the male role, as defined by power, is played out, with physical power in work, and even in warfare, being less important than it was before industrialization and technological advance.[3]

If we are looking for comparative evidence as to how advertisements   5
define gender roles for men and women, we should not then see the male role as defined primarily through beauty and fashion. This seems an obvious point, but it is important to emphasize how different cultural attitudes toward both the social person and the physical body shape the gender roles of men and women. These cultural attitudes are changing, and advertisements are helping to legitimate the use of beauty products and an interest in fashion for men, as we shall see. As advertisements directed toward women are beginning to use male imagery, so too advertisements for men occasionally use imagery resembling that found in advertisements directed toward women. We are speaking of two *modes,* then. As Baudrillard[4] writes, these modes "do not result from the differentiated nature of the two sexes, but from the differential logic of the system. The relationship of the Masculine and the Feminine to real men and women is relatively arbitrary."[5] Increasingly today, men and women use both modes. The two great terms of opposition (Masculine and

---

1. Katz and Katz, *Magazines,* pp. 703–5.

2. Ibid.

3. John Gagnon, "Physical Strength: Once of Significance," in Joseph H. Pleck and Jack Sawyer, eds., *Men and Masculinity* (Englewood Cliffs, N.J.: Prentice-Hall, 1974), pp. 139–49.

4. **Jean Baudrillard** French semiologist.—EDS.

5. Baudrillard, *La société de consommation,* pp. 144–47.

Feminine) still, however, structure the forms that consumption takes; they provide identities for products and consumers.

Baudrillard agrees that the feminine model encourages a woman to please herself, to encourage a certain complacency and even narcissistic solicitude. But by pleasing herself, it is understood that she will also please others, and that she will be chosen. "She never enters into direct competition. . . . If she is beautiful, that is to say, if this woman is a woman, she will be chosen. If the man is a man, he will choose his woman as he would other objects/signs (HIS car, HIS woman, HIS eau de toilette)."[6]

Whereas the feminine model is based on passivity, complacency, and narcissism, the masculine model is based on exactingness and choice.

> All of masculine advertising insists on rule, on choice, in terms of rigor and inflexible minutiae. He does not neglect a detail . . . It is not a question of just letting things go, or of taking pleasure in something, but rather of distinguishing himself. To know how to choose, and not to fail at it, is here the equivalent of the military and puritanical virtues: intransigence, decision, "virtus."[7]

This masculine model, these masculine virtues, are best reflected in the many car advertisements. There, the keywords are masculine terms: *power, performance, precision*. Sometimes the car is a woman, responding to the touch and will of her male driver, after attracting him with her sexy body. "Pure shape, pure power, pure Z. It turns you on." But, as the juxtaposition of shape and power in this advertisement suggests, the car is not simply other; it is also an extension of the owner. As he turns it on, he turns himself on. Its power is his power; through it, he will be able to overpower other men and impress and seduce women.

> How well does it perform?
> How well can you drive? (Merkur XR4Ti)
>
> The 1987 Celica GT-S has the sweeping lines and aggressive stance that promise performance. And Celica keeps its word.
>
> Renault GTA:
> Zero to sixty to zero in 13.9 sec.
> It's the result of a performance philosophy where acceleration and braking are equally important.
> There's a new Renault sports sedan called GTA. Under its slick monochromatic skin is a road car with a total performance attitude. . . . It's our hot new pocket rocket.

In this last example, the car, like the driver, has a total performance attitude. That is what works. The slick monochromatic skin, like the

---

6. Ibid.
7. Ibid.

Bond Street suit, makes a good first impression. But car, like owner, must have what it takes, must be able to go the distance faster and better than the competition. This point is explicitly made in advertisements in which the car becomes a means through which this masculine competition at work is extended in leisure. Some refer directly to the manly sport of auto-racing: "The Mitsubishi Starion ESI-R. Patiently crafted to ignite your imagination. Leaving little else to say except . . . gentlemen, start your engines." Others refer to competition in the business world: "To move ahead fast in this world, you've got to have connections. The totally new Corolla FX 16 GT-S has the right ones." Or in life in general. "It doesn't take any [Japanese characters] from anyone. It won't stand for any guff from 300ZX. Or RX-7. Introducing Conquest Tsi, the new turbo sport coupe designed and built by Mitsubishi in Japan." Or Ferrari, which says simply, "We are the competition." In this competition between products, the owners become almost superfluous. But the advertisements, of course, suggest that the qualities of the car will reflect the qualities of the owner, as opposed to the purely abstract, apersonal quality of money needed for purchase. Thus, like the would-be owner, the BMW also demonstrates a "relentless refusal to compromise." It is for "those who thrive on a maximum daily requirement of high performance." While the BMW has the business attitude of the old school ("aggression has never been expressed with such dignity"), a Beretta suggests what it takes to survive today in the shark-infested waters of Wall Street. In a glossy three-page cover foldout, a photograph of a shark's fin cutting through indigo waters is accompanied by the legend "Discover a new species from today's Chevrolet." The following two pages show a sleek black Beretta similarly cutting through water and, presumably, through the competition: "Not just a new car, but a new species . . . with a natural instinct for the road . . . Aggressive stance. And a bold tail lamp. See it on the road and you won't soon forget. Drive it, and you never will."

And as with men, so with cars. "Power corrupts. Absolute power corrupts absolutely" (Maserati). Not having the money to pay for a Maserati, to corrupt and be corrupted, is a source of embarrassment. Advertisements reassure the consumer that he need not lose face in this manly battle. Hyundai promises, "It's affordable. (But you'd never know it.)"

> On first impression, the new Hyundai Excel GLS Sedan might seem a trifle beyond most people's means. But that's entirely by design. Sleek European design, to be exact.

Many advertisements suggest sexual pleasure and escape, as in "Pure   10
shape, pure power, pure Z. It turns you on." Or "The all-new Chrysler Le Baron. Beauty . . . with a passion for driving." The Le Baron may initially suggest a beautiful female, with its "image of arresting beauty"

and its passion "to drive. And drive it does!" But it *is* "Le Baron," not "La Baronness." And the advertisement continues to emphasize how it "*attacks* [emphasis mine] the road with a high torque, 2.5 fuel-injected engine. And its turbo option can blur the surface of any passing lane." Thus the object of the pleasure hardly has to be female if it is beautiful or sleek. The car is an extension of the male that conquers and tames the (female) road: "Positive-response suspension will calm the most demanding roads." The car becomes the ultimate lover when, like the Honda Prelude, it promises to combine power, "muscle," with finesse. Automobile advertisements thus play with androgyny and sexuality; the pleasure is in the union and confusion of form and movement, sex and speed. As in any sexual union, there is ultimately a merging of identities, rather than rigid maintenance of their separation. Polymorphous perverse? Perhaps. But it sells.

Though power, performance, precision as a complex of traits find their strongest emphasis in automobile advertisements, they also appear as selling points for products as diverse as shoes, stereos, and sunglasses. The car performs on the road, the driver performs for women, even in the parking lot, as Michelin suggests in its two-page spread showing a male from waist down resting on his car and chatting up a curvaceous female: "It performs great. And looks great. So, it not only stands out on the road. But in the parking lot. Which is one more place you're likely to discover how beautifully it can handle the curves" (!).

As media analyst Todd Gitlin points out, most of the drivers shown in advertisements are young white males, loners who become empowered by the car that makes possible their escape from the everyday. Gitlin stresses the advertisements' "emphasis on surface, the blankness of the protagonist; his striving toward self-sufficiency, to the point of displacement from the recognizable world."[8] Even the Chrysler advertisements that coopt Bruce Springsteen's "Born in the USA" for their "Born in America" campaign lose in the process the original political message, "ripping off Springsteen's angry anthem, smoothing it into a Chamber of Commerce ditty as shots of just plain productive-looking folks, black and white . . . whiz by in a montage-made community." As Gitlin comments, "None of Springsteen's losers need apply—or rather, if only they would roll up their sleeves and see what good company they're in, they wouldn't feel like losers any longer."[9]

This is a world of patriarchal order in which the individual male can and must challenge the father. He achieves identity by breaking loose of the structure and breaking free of the pack. In the process he recreates

---

8. Todd Gitlin, "We Build Excitement," in Todd Gitlin, ed., *Watching Television* (New York: Pantheon, 1986), pp. 139–40.
    9. Ibid.

the order and reaffirms the myth of masculine independence. Above all, he demonstrates that he knows what he wants; he is critical, demanding, and free from the constraints of others. What he definitely does not want, and goes to some measure to avoid, is to appear less than masculine, in any way weak, frilly, feminine.

Avoiding the Feminine

Advertisers trying to develop male markets for products previously associated primarily with women must overcome the taboo that only women wear moisturizer, face cream, hair spray, or perfume. They do this by overt reference to masculine symbols, language, and imagery, and sometimes by confronting the problem head-on.

There is not so much of a problem in selling products to counteract balding—that traditionally has been recognized as a male problem (a bald woman is a sexual joke that is not particularly amusing to the elderly). But other hair products are another story, as the March 1987 *GQ* cover asks, "Are you man enough for mousse?" So the advertisements must make their products seem manly, as with S-Curl's "wave and curl kit" offering "The Manly Look" on its manly model dressed in business suit and carrying a hard hat (a nifty social class compromise), and as in college basketball sportscaster Al McGuire's testimonial for consort hair spray:

> "Years ago, if someone had said to me, 'Hey Al, do you use hair spray?' I would have said, 'No way, baby!'"
>
> "That was before I tried Consort Pump."
>
> "Consort adds extra control to my hair without looking stiff or phony. Control that lasts clean into overtime and post-game interviews . . ."
>
> Grooming Gear for Real Guys. *Consort.*

Besides such "grooming gear" as perms and hair sprays, Real Guys use "skin supplies" and "shaving resources." They adopt a "survival strategy" to fight balding, and the "Fila philosophy"—"products with a singular purpose: performance"—for effective "bodycare." If they wear scent, it smells of anything *but* flowers: musk, woods, spices, citrus, and surf are all acceptable. And the names must be manly, whether symbolizing physical power ("Brut") or financial power ("Giorgio VIP Special Reserve," "The Baron. A distinctive fragrance for men," "Halston—For the privileged few").

As power/precision/performance runs as a theme throughout advertising to men, so too do references to the business world. Cars, as we have seen, promise to share their owner's professional attitude and aggressive drive to beat out the competition. Other products similarly reflect the centrality of business competition to the male gender role. And at the center of this competition itself, the business suit.

> At the onset of your business day, you choose the suit or sportcoat that will position you front and center . . .
> The Right Suit can't guarantee he'll see it your way. The wrong suit could mean not seeing him at all.

Along with the Right Suit, the right shirt. "You want it every time you reach across the conference table, or trade on the floor, or just move about. You want a shirt that truly fits, that is long enough to stay put through the most active day, even for the taller gentleman." The businessman chooses the right cologne—Grey Flannel, or perhaps Quorum. He wears a Gucci "timepiece" as he conducts business on a cordless telephone from his poolside—or prefers the "dignity in styling" promised by Raymond Weil watches, "a beautiful way to dress for success."

Men's products connect status and success; the right products show that you have the right stuff, that you're one of them. In the 1950s C. Wright Mills[10] described what it took to get ahead, to become part of the "power elite":

> The fit survive, and fitness means, not formal competence . . . but conformity with the criteria of those who have already succeeded. To be compatible with the top men is to act like them, to look like them, to think like them: to be of and for them—or at least to display oneself to them in such a way as to create that impression. This, in fact, is what is meant by "creating"—a well-chosen word—"a good impression." This is what is meant—and nothing else—by being a "sound man," as sound as a dollar.[11]

Today, having what it takes includes knowing "the difference between dressed, and well dressed" (Bally shoes). It is knowing that "what you carry says as much about you as what you put inside it" (Hartmann luggage). It is knowing enough to imitate Doug Fout, "member of one of the foremost equestrian families in the country."

> Because of our adherence to quality and the natural shoulder tradition, Southwick clothing was adopted by the Fout family years ago. Clearly, they have as much appreciation for good lines in a jacket as they do in a thoroughbred.

There it is, old money. There is no substitute for it, really, in business or in advertising, where appeals to tradition form one of the mainstays guaranteeing men that their choices are not overly fashionable or feminine, not working class or cheap, but, rather, correct, in good form,

---

10. **C. Wright Mills** (1916–1962)   American sociologist.—EDS.
11. C. Wright Mills, *The Power Elite* (New York: Oxford University Press, 1956), p. 141.

above criticism. If, when, they achieve this status of gentlemanly perfection, then, the advertisement suggests, they may be invited to join the club.

> When only the best of associations will do
>
> Recognizing style as the requisite for membership, discerning men prefer the natural shoulder styling of Racquet Club. Meticulously tailored in pure wool, each suit and sportcoat is the ultimate expression of the clubman's classic good taste.

Ralph Lauren has his Polo University Club, and Rolex picks up on the polo theme by sponsoring the Rolex Gold Cup held at the Palm Beach Polo and Country Club, where sixteen teams and sixty-four players competed for "the pure honor of winning, the true glory of victory":

> It has added new lustre to a game so ancient, its history is lost in legend. Tamerlane is said to have been its patriarch. Darius's Persian cavalry, we're told, played it. It was the national sport of 16th-century India, Egypt, China, and Japan. The British rediscovered and named it in 1857.
>
> The linking of polo and Rolex is uniquely appropriate. Both sponsor and sport personify rugged grace. Each is an arbiter of the art of timing.

In the spring of 1987, there was another interesting club event—or nonevent. The prestigious New York University Club was ordered to open its doors to women. This brought the expected protests about freedom of association—and of sanctuary. For that has been one of the points of the men's club. It wasn't open to women. Members knew women had their place, and everyone knew it was not there. In the advertisements, as in the world of reality, there is a place for women in men's lives, one that revolves around:

20

Sex and Seduction

The growing fascination with appearances, encouraged by advertising, has led to a "feminization" of culture. We are all put in the classic role of the female: manipulable, submissive, seeing ourselves as objects. This "feminization of sexuality" is clearly seen in men's advertisements, where many of the promises made to women are now made to men. If women's advertisements cry, "Buy (this product) and he will notice you," men's advertisements similarly promise that female attention will follow immediately upon purchase, or shortly thereafter. "They can't stay away from Mr. J." "Master the Art of Attracting Attention." She says, "He's wearing my favorite Corbin again." Much as in the advertisements directed at women, the advertisements of men's products promise that they will do the talking for you. "For the look that says come closer." "All the French you'll ever need to know."

Although many advertisements show an admiring and/or dependent female, others depict women in a more active role. "I love him—but life in the fast lane starts at 6 A.M.," says the attractive blonde tying on her jogging shoes, with the "him" in question very handsome and very asleep on the bed in the background. (Does this mean he's in the slow lane?) In another, the man slouches silhouetted against a wall; the woman leans aggressively toward him. He: "Do you always serve Tia Maria . . . or am I special?" She: "Darling, if you weren't special . . . you wouldn't be here."

The masculine role of always being in charge is a tough one. The blunt new honesty about sexually transmitted diseases such as AIDS appears in men's magazines as in women's, in the same "I enjoy sex, but I'm not ready to die for it" condom advertisement. But this new fear is accompanied by old fears of sexual embarrassment and/or rejection. The cartoon shows a man cringing with embarrassment in a pharmacy as the pharmacist yells out, "Hey, there's a guy here wants some information on Trojans." ("Most men would like to know more about Trojan brand condoms. But they're seriously afraid of suffering a spectacular and ter-minal attack of embarrassment right in the middle of a well-lighted drugstore.") Compared with such agony and responsibility, advertise-ments promising that women will *want* whatever is on offer, and will even meet the male halfway, must come as blessed relief. Men can finally relax, leaving the courting to the product and seduction to the beguiled woman, which, surely, must seem nice for a change.

Masculine Homilies

A homily is a short sermon, discourse, or informal lecture, often on a moral topic and suggesting a course of conduct. Some of the most intriguing advertisements offer just that, short statements and bits of advice on what masculinity is and on how real men should conduct themselves. As with many short sermons, many of the advertising hom-ilies have a self-congratulatory air about them; after all, you do not want the consumer to feel bad about himself.

What is it, then, to be a man? It is to be *independent*. "There are   25
some things a man will not relinquish." Among them, says the adver-tisement, his Tretorn tennis shoes.

It is to *savor freedom*. "Dress easy, get away from it all and let Tom Sawyer paint the fence," advises Alexander Julian, the men's designer. "Because man was meant to fly, we gave him wings" (even if only on his sunglasses).

It is to live a life of *adventure*. KL Homme cologne is "for the man who lives on the edge." Prudential Life Insurance preaches, "If you can dream it, you can do it." New Man sportswear tells the reader, "Life is more adventurous when you feel like a New Man."

It is to *keep one's cool*. "J. B. Scotch. A few individuals know how to keep their heads, even when their necks are on the line."

And it is to stay one step *ahead of the competition*. "Altec Lansing. Hear what others only imagine." Alexander Julian again: "Dress up a bit when you dress down. They'll think you know something they don't."

What is it, then, to be a woman? It is to be *dependent*. "A woman   30 needs a man," reads the copy in the Rigolletto advertisement showing a young man changing a tire for a grateful young woman.

The American cowboy as cultural model was not supposed to care for or about appearances. He was what he was, hard-working, straight-forward, and honest. He was authentic. Men who cared "too much" about how they looked did not fit this model; the dandy was effete, a European invention, insufficient in masculinity and not red-blooded enough to be a real American. The other cultural model, imported from England, was the gentleman. A gentleman did care about his appearance, in the proper measure and manifestation, attention to tailoring and to quality, understatement rather than exaggeration.[12]

From the gray flannel suit of the 1950s to the "power look" of the 1980s, clothes made the man fit in with his company's image. Sex appeal and corporate correctness merged in a look that spelled success, that exuded confidence.

Whether or not a man presumed to care about his appearance, he did care about having "the right stuff," as Tom Wolfe and *Esquire* call it, or "men's toys," as in a recent special issue of *M* magazine. Cars, motor-cycles, stereos, sports equipment: These are part of the masculine appearance. They allow the man to demonstrate his taste, his special knowl-edge, his affluence: to extend his control. He can be and is demanding, for only the best will do.

He also wants to be loved, but he does not want to appear needy. Advertisements suggest the magic ability of products ranging from cars to hair creams to attract female attention. With the right products a man can have it all, with no strings attached: no boring marital ties, hefty mortgages, corporate compromises.

According to sociologist Barbara Ehrenreich, *Playboy* magazine did   35 much to legitimate this image of male freedom. The old male ethos, up to the postwar period, required exchanging bachelor irresponsibility for

12. See Diane Barthel, "A Gentleman and a Consumer: A Sociological Look at Man at His Best," paper presented at the annual meeting of the Eastern Sociological Society, March 1983, Baltimore.

married responsibility, which also symbolized entrance into social adulthood.[13] The perennial bachelor, with his flashy cars and interchangeable
women, was the object of both envy and derision; he had fun, but . . .
he was not fully grown up. There was something frivolous in his lack of
purpose and application.

　　This old ethos has lost much of its legitimacy. Today's male can, as
Baudrillard suggests, operate in both modes: the feminine mode of indulging oneself and being indulged and the masculine mode of exigency
and competition. With the right look and the right stuff, he can feel
confident and manly in boardroom or suburban backyard. Consumer
society thus invites both men and women to live in a world of appearances and to devote ever more attention to them.

Reading the Text

1. Define in your own words what Barthel means by the "masculine" and
   "feminine" modes.
2. Why, according to Barthel, are men's magazines less popular than women's
   magazines?
3. Summarize what Barthel claims "being a man" means in magazine advertising.
4. How are women typically portrayed in men's magazine ads, according to
   Barthel?

Reading the Signs

1. Buy a copy of one of the men's magazines that Barthel mentions in her
   essay, and study the advertising. Do the ads corroborate Barthel's claim that
   men today are allowed to demonstrate both their "masculine" and "feminine" sides?
2. Write an essay in which you apply Barthel's analysis of car advertising to
   the examples in Andrew Wernick's "Vehicles for Myth" (p. 78). To what
   extent have the key words "power," "performance," and "precision" influenced automotive advertising throughout its history?
3. Have each class member bring a copy of a men's or women's magazine to
   class. Form same-sex groups, and give each group a few magazines designed
   for the opposite sex. Analyze the gender roles depicted in the magazines,
   and report to the class the group's findings.
4. Barthel claims that "the growing fascination with appearances" has led to
   a "feminization" of our culture. Read or review Holly Devor's "Gender

-----

　　13. Barbara Ehrenreich, *The Hearts of Men: American Dreams and the Flight from
Commitment* (New York: Anchor Books, 1983).

Role Behaviors and Attitudes" (p. 605), and use her essay as a critical framework to critique Barthel's claim.

5. In class, brainstorm images of "masculinity" and "femininity" and write your results on the board. Then compare the class's list to the gender traits that Barthel claims are common in advertising. Discuss with your class the possible origins of your brainstormed images.

GLORIA STEINEM

Sex, Lies, and Advertising

|||||||||||||||||||||||||||||||||||||||||||||||||||||||||||||||||||||

One of the best-known icons of the women's movement, Gloria Steinem (b. 1934) has been a leader in transforming the image of women in America. As a cofounder of Ms. *magazine, in which this selection first appeared, Steinem has provided a forum for women's voices for more than twenty years, but as her article explains, it has not been easy to keep this forum going. For a commercial publication requires commercials, and the needs of advertisers do not always mesh nicely with the goals of a magazine like* Ms. *Steinem ruefully reveals the compromises* Ms. *magazine had to make over the years to satisfy its advertising clients, compromises that came to an end only when* Ms. *ceased to take ads. Steinem's most recent book is* Revolution from Within *(1992), a personal exploration of the power of self-esteem. Currently the president of Voters for Choice and a consulting editor for* Ms., *Steinem continues to combine her passion for writing and activism as an unflagging voice in American feminism.*

About three years ago, as *glasnost* was beginning and *Ms.* seemed to be ending, I was invited to a press lunch for a Soviet official. He entertained us with anecdotes about new problems of democracy in his country. Local Communist leaders were being criticized in their media for the first time, he explained, and they were angry.

"So I'll have to ask my American friends," he finished pointedly, "how more *subtly* to control the press." In the silence that followed, I said, "Advertising."

The reporters laughed, but later, one of them took me aside: How *dare* I suggest that freedom of the press was limited? How dare I imply that his newsweekly could be influenced by ads?

I explained that I was thinking of advertising's media-wide influence on most of what we read. Even newsmagazines use "soft" cover stories to sell ads, confuse readers with "advertorials,"[1] and occasionally self-censor on subjects known to be a problem with big advertisers.

But, I also explained, I was thinking especially of women's maga-   5
zines. There, it isn't just a little content that's devoted to attracting ads, it's almost all of it. That's why advertisers—not readers—have always been the problem for *Ms.* As the only women's magazine that didn't supply what the ad world euphemistically describes as "supportive editorial atmosphere" or "complementary copy" (for instance, articles that praise food/fashion/beauty subjects to "support" and "complement" food/fashion/beauty ads), *Ms.* could never attract enough advertising to break even.

"Oh, *women's* magazines," the journalist said with contempt. "Everybody knows they're catalogs—but who cares? They have nothing to do with journalism."

I can't tell you how many times I've had this argument in 25 years of working for many kinds of publications. Except as moneymaking machines—"cash cows" as they are so elegantly called in the trade—women's magazines are rarely taken seriously. Though changes being made by women have been called more far-reaching than the industrial revolution—and though many editors try hard to reflect some of them in the few pages left to them after all the ad-related subjects have been covered—the magazines serving the female half of this country are still far below the journalistic and ethical standards of news and general interest publications. Most depressing of all, this doesn't even rate an exposé.

If *Time* and *Newsweek* had to lavish praise on cars in general and credit General Motors in particular to get GM ads, there would be a scandal—maybe a criminal investigation. When women's magazines from *Seventeen* to *Lear's* praise beauty products in general and credit Revlon in particular to get ads, it's just business as usual.

1

When *Ms.* began, we didn't consider *not* taking ads. The most important reason was keeping the price of a feminist magazine low enough for most women to afford. But the second and almost equal reason was providing a forum where women and advertisers could talk to each other and improve advertising itself. After all, it was (and still is) as potent a source of information in this country as news or TV and movie dramas.

---

1. **advertorial**   Advertisement designed to mimic the appearance of a feature article.—EDS.

We decided to proceed in two stages. First, we would convince   10
makers of "people products" used by both men and women but advertised mostly to men—cars, credit cards, insurance, sound equipment,
financial services, and the like—that their ads should be placed in a
women's magazine. Since they were accustomed to the division between
editorial[2] and advertising in news and general interest magazines, this
would allow our editorial content to be free and diverse. Second, we
would add the best ads for whatever traditional "women's products"
(clothes, shampoo, fragrance, food, and so on) that surveys showed *Ms.*
readers used. But we would ask them to come in *without* the usual quid
pro quo of "complementary copy."

We knew the second step might be harder. Food advertisers have
always demanded that women's magazines publish recipes and articles on
entertaining (preferably ones that name their products) in return for their
ads; clothing advertisers expect to be surrounded by fashion spreads
(especially ones that credit their designers); and shampoo, fragrance, and
beauty products in general usually insist on positive editorial coverage
of beauty subjects, plus photo credits besides. That's why women's magazines look the way they do. But if we could break this link between
ads and editorial content, then we wanted good ads for "women's products," too.

By playing their part in this unprecedented mix of *all* the things our
readers need and use, advertisers also would be rewarded: Ads for products like cars and mutual funds would find a new growth market; the
best ads for women's products would no longer be lost in oceans of ads
for the same category; and both would have access to a laboratory of
smart and caring readers whose response would help create effective ads
for other media as well.

I thought then that our main problem would be the imagery in ads
themselves. Car makers were still draping blondes in evening gowns over
the hoods like ornaments. Authority figures were almost always male,
even in ads for products that only women used. Sadistic, he-man campaigns even won industry praise. (For instance, *Advertising Age* had hailed
the infamous Silva Thin cigarette theme, "How to Get a Woman's
Attention: Ignore Her," as "brilliant.") Even in medical journals, tran-
quilizer ads showed depressed housewives standing beside piles of dirty
dishes and promised to get them back to work.

Obviously, *Ms.* would have to avoid such ads and seek out the best
ones—but this didn't seem impossible. *The New Yorker* had been selecting
ads for aesthetic reasons for years, a practice that only seemed to make
advertisers more eager to be in its pages. *Ebony* and *Essence* were asking

---

2. **editorial** In the magazine industry, all nonadvertising content in a magazine,
including regular columns and feature articles.—EDS.

for ads with positive black images, and though their struggle was hard, they weren't being called unreasonable.

Clearly, what *Ms.* needed was a very special publisher and ad sales   15
staff. I could think of only one woman with experience on the business side of magazines—Patricia Carbine, who recently had become a vice president of *McCall's* as well as its editor in chief—and the reason I knew her name was a good omen. She had been managing editor at *Look* (really *the* editor, but its owner refused to put a female name at the top of his masthead) when I was writing a column there. After I did an early interview with Cesar Chavez, then just emerging as a leader of migrant labor, and the publisher turned it down because he was worried about ads from Sunkist, Pat was the one who intervened. As I learned later, she had told the publisher she would resign if the interview wasn't published. Mainly because *Look* couldn't afford to lose Pat, it *was* published (and the ads from Sunkist never arrived).

Though I barely knew this woman, she had done two things I always remembered: put her job on the line in a way that editors often talk about but rarely do, and been so loyal to her colleagues that she never told me or anyone outside *Look* that she had done so.

Fortunately, Pat did agree to leave *McCall's* and take a huge cut in salary to become publisher of *Ms.* She became responsible for training and inspiring generations of young women who joined the *Ms.* ad sales force, many of whom went on to become "firsts" at the top of publishing. When *Ms.* first started, however, there were so few women with experience selling space that Pat and I made the rounds of ad agencies ourselves. Later, the fact that *Ms.* was asking companies to do business in a different way meant our saleswomen had to make many times the usual number of calls—first to convince agencies and then client companies besides—and to present endless amounts of research. I was often asked to do a final ad presentation, or see some higher decision-maker, or speak to women employees so executives could see the interest of women they worked with. That's why I spent more time persuading advertisers than editing or writing for *Ms.* and why I ended up with an unsentimental education in the seamy underside of publishing that few writers see (and even fewer magazines can publish).

Let me take you with us through some experiences, just as they happened:

■ Cheered on by early support from Volkswagen and one or two other car companies, we scrape together time and money to put on a major reception in Detroit. We know U.S. car-makers firmly believe that women choose the upholstery, not the car, but we are armed with statistics and reader mail to prove the contrary: A car is an important purchase for women, one that symbolizes mobility and freedom.

But almost nobody comes. We are left with many pounds of shrimp

on the table, and quite a lot of egg on our face. We blame ourselves for
not guessing that there would be a baseball pennant play-off on the same
day, but executives go out of their way to explain they wouldn't have
come anyway. Thus begins ten years of knocking on hostile doors,
presenting endless documentation, and hiring a full-time saleswoman in
Detroit; all necessary before *Ms.* gets any real results.

This long saga has a semihappy ending: foreign and, later, domestic   20
car-makers eventually provided *Ms.* with enough advertising to make
cars one of our top sources of ad revenue. Slowly, Detroit began to take
the women's market seriously enough to put car ads in other women's
magazines, too, thus freeing a few pages from the hothouse of fashion-
beauty-food ads.

But long after figures showed a third, even a half, of many car models
being bought by women, U.S. makers continued to be uncomfortable
addressing women. Unlike foreign car-makers, Detroit never quite
learned the secret of creating intelligent ads that exclude no one, and
then placing them in women's magazines to overcome past exclusion.
(*Ms.* readers were so grateful for a routine Honda ad featuring rack and
pinion steering, for instance, that they sent fan mail.) Even now, Detroit
continues to ask, "Should we make special ads for women?" Perhaps
that's why some foreign cars still have a disproportionate share of the
U.S. women's market.

■ In the *Ms.* Gazette, we do a brief report on a congressional hearing
into chemicals used in hair dyes that are absorbed through the skin and
may be carcinogenic. Newspapers report this too, but Clairol, a Bristol-
Myers subsidiary that makes dozens of products—a few of which have
just begun to advertise in *Ms.*—is outraged. Not at newspapers or news
magazines, just at us. It's bad enough that *Ms.* is the only women's
magazine refusing to provide the usual "complementary" articles and
beauty photos, but to criticize one of their categories—*that* is going too
far.

We offer to publish a letter from Clairol telling its side of the story.
In an excess of solicitousness, we even put this letter in the Gazette, not
in Letters to the Editors where it belongs. Nonetheless—and in spite of
surveys that show *Ms.* readers are active women who use more of almost
everything Clairol makes than do the readers of any other women's
magazine—*Ms.* gets almost none of these ads for the rest of its natural
life.

Meanwhile, Clairol changes its hair-coloring formula, apparently in
response to the hearings we reported.

■ Our saleswomen set out early to attract ads for consumer electronics: 25
sound equipment, calculators, computers, VCRs, and the like. We know
that our readers are determined to be included in the technological
revolution. We know from reader surveys that *Ms.* readers are buying

this stuff in numbers as high as those of magazines like *Playboy,* or "men 18 to 34," the prime targets of the consumer electronics industry. More-over, unlike traditional women's products that our readers buy but don't need to read articles about, these are subjects they want covered in our pages. There actually *is* a supportive editorial atmosphere.

"But women don't understand technology," say executives at the end of ad presentations. "Maybe not," we respond, "but neither do men—and we all buy it."

"If women *do* buy it," say the decision-makers, "they're asking their husbands and boyfriends what to buy first." We produce letters from *Ms.* readers saying how turned off they are when salesmen say things like "Let me know when your husband can come in."

After several years of this, we get a few ads for compact sound systems. Some of them come from JVC, whose vice president, Harry Elias, is trying to convince his Japanese bosses that there is something called a women's market. At his invitation, I find myself speaking at huge trade shows in Chicago and Las Vegas, trying to persuade JVC dealers that showrooms don't have to be locker rooms where women are made to feel unwelcome. But as it turns out, the shows themselves are part of the problem. In Las Vegas, the only women around the technology displays are seminude models serving champagne. In Chi-cago, the big attraction is Marilyn Chambers, who followed Linda Love-lace of *Deep Throat* fame as Chuck Traynor's captive and/or employee. VCRs are being demonstrated with her porn videos.

In the end, we get ads for a car stereo now and then, but no VCRs; some IBM personal computers, but no Apple or Japanese ones. We notice that office magazines like *Working Woman* and *Savvy* don't benefit as much as they should from office equipment ads either. In the elec-tronics world, women and technology seem mutually exclusive. It re-mains a decade behind even Detroit.

■ Because we get letters from little girls who love toy trains, and who   30 ask our help in changing ads and box-top photos that feature little boys only, we try to get toy-train ads from Lionel. It turns out that Lionel executives *have* been concerned about little girls. They made a pink train, and were surprised when it didn't sell.

Lionel bows to consumer pressure with a photograph of a boy *and* a girl—but only on some of their boxes. They fear that, if trains are associated with girls, they will be devalued in the minds of boys. Needless to say, *Ms.* gets no train ads, and little girls remain a mostly unexplored market. By 1986, Lionel is put up for sale.

But for different reasons, we haven't had much luck with other kinds of toys either. In spite of many articles on child-rearing; an annual listing of nonsexist, multiracial toys by Letty Cottin Pogrebin; Stories for Free Children, a regular feature also edited by Letty; and other prizewinning features for or about children, we get virtually no toy ads. Generations of *Ms.* saleswomen explain to toy manufacturers that a larger proportion of *Ms.* readers have preschool children than do the readers of other women's magazines, but this industry can't believe feminists have or care about children.

■ When *Ms.* begins, the staff decides not to accept ads for feminine hygiene sprays or cigarettes: they are damaging and carry no appropriate health warnings. Though we don't think we should tell our readers what to do, we do think we should provide facts so they can decide for themselves. Since the antismoking lobby has been pressing for health warnings on cigarette ads, we decide to take them only as they comply.

Philip Morris is among the first to do so. One of its brands, Virginia Slims, is also sponsoring women's tennis and the first national polls of women's opinions. On the other hand, the Virginia Slims theme, "You've come a long way, baby," has more than a "baby" problem. It makes smoking a symbol of progress for women.

We explain to Philip Morris that this slogan won't do well in our   35
pages, but they are convinced its success with some women means it will work with *all* women. Finally, we agree to publish an ad for a Virginia Slims calendar as a test. The letters from readers are critical— and smart. For instance: Would you show a black man picking cotton, the same man in a Cardin suit, and symbolize the antislavery and civil rights movements by smoking? Of course not. But instead of honoring the test results, the Philip Morris people seem angry to be proven wrong. They take away ads for *all* their many brands.

This costs *Ms.* about $250,000 the first year. After five years, we can no longer keep track. Occasionally, a new set of executives listens to *Ms.* saleswomen, but because we won't take Virginia Slims, not one Philip Morris product returns to our pages for the next 16 years.

Gradually, we also realize our naiveté in thinking we *could* decide against taking cigarette ads. They became a disproportionate support of magazines the moment they were banned on television, and few magazines could compete and survive without them; certainly not *Ms.*, which lacks so many other categories. By the time statistics in the 1980s showed that women's rate of lung cancer was approaching men's, the necessity of taking cigarette ads has become a kind of prison.

■ General Mills, Pillsbury, Carnation, DelMonte, Dole, Kraft, Stouffer, Hormel, Nabisco: You name the food giant, we try it. But no matter how desirable the *Ms.* readership, our lack of recipes is lethal.

We explain to them that placing food ads *only* next to recipes associates food with work. For many women, it is a negative that works *against* the ads. Why not place food ads in diverse media without recipes (thus reaching more men, who are now a third of the shoppers in supermarkets anyway), and leave the recipes to specialty magazines like *Gourmet* (a third of whose readers are also men)?

These arguments elicit interest, but except for an occasional ad for   40 a convenience food, instant coffee, diet drinks, yogurt, or such extras as avocados and almonds, this mainstay of the publishing industry stays closed to us. Period.

- Traditionally, wines and liquors didn't advertise to women: Men were thought to make the brand decisions, even if women did the buying. But after endless presentations, we begin to make a dent in this category. Thanks to the unconventional Michel Roux of Carillon Importers (distributors of Grand Marnier, Absolut Vodka, and others), who assumes that food and drink have no gender, some ads are leaving their men's club.

Beermakers are still selling masculinity. It takes *Ms.* fully eight years to get its first beer ad (Michelob). In general, however, liquor ads are less stereotyped in their imagery—and far less controlling of the editorial content around them—than are women's products. But given the underrepresentation of other categories, these very facts tend to create a disproportionate number of alcohol ads in the pages of *Ms.* This in turn dismays readers worried about women and alcoholism.

- We hear in 1980 that women in the Soviet Union have been producing feminist *samizdat* (underground, self-published books) and circulating them throughout the country. As punishment, four of the leaders have been exiled. Though we are operating on our usual shoestring, we solicit individual contributions to send Robin Morgan to interview these women in Vienna.

The result is an exclusive cover story that includes the first news of a populist peace movement against the Afghanistan occupation, a prediction of *glasnost* to come, and a grassroots, intimate view of Soviet women's lives. From the popular press to women's studies courses, the response is great. The story wins a Front Page award.

Nonetheless, this journalistic coup undoes years of efforts to get an ad schedule from Revlon. Why? Because the Soviet women on our cover *are not wearing make-up.* 45

- Four years of research and presentations go into convincing airlines that women now make travel choices and business trips. United, the first airline to advertise in *Ms.,* is so impressed with the response from our readers that one of its executives appears in a film for our ad presentations. As usual, good ads get great results.

But we have problems unrelated to such results. For instance: Because American Airlines flight attendants include among their labor demands the stipulation that they could choose to have their last names preceded by "Ms." on their name tags—in a long-delayed revolt against the standard, "I am your pilot, Captain Rothgart, and this is your flight attendant, Cindy Sue"—American officials seem to hold the magazine responsible. We get no ads.

There is still a different problem at Eastern. A vice president cancels subscriptions for thousands of copies on Eastern flights. Why? Because he is offended by ads for lesbian poetry journals in the *Ms.* Classified. A "family airline," as he explains to me coldly on the phone, has to "draw the line somewhere."

It's obvious that *Ms.* can't exclude lesbians and serve women. We've been trying to make that point ever since our first issue included an article by and about lesbians, and both Suzanne Levine, our managing editor, and I were lectured by such heavy hitters as Ed Kosner, then editor of *Newsweek* (and now of *New York Magazine*), who insisted that *Ms.* should "position" itself *against* lesbians. But our advertisers have paid to reach a guaranteed number of readers, and soliciting new subscriptions to compensate for Eastern would cost $150,000, plus rebating money in the meantime.

Like almost everything ad-related, this presents an elaborate orga- 50 nizing problem. After days of searching for sympathetic members of the Eastern board, Frank Thomas, president of the Ford Foundation, kindly offers to call Roswell Gilpatrick, a director of Eastern. I talk with Mr. Gilpatrick, who calls Frank Borman, then the president of Eastern. Frank Borman calls me to say that his airline is not in the business of censoring magazines: *Ms.* will be returned to Eastern flights.

■ Women's access to insurance and credit is vital, but with the exception of Equitable and a few other ad pioneers, such financial services address men. For almost a decade after the Equal Credit Opportunity Act passes in 1974, we try to convince American Express that women are a growth market—but nothing works.

Finally, a former professor of Russian named Jerry Welsh becomes head of marketing. He assumes that women should be cardholders, and persuades his colleagues to feature women in a campaign. Thanks to this 1980s series, the growth rate for female cardholders surpasses that for men.

For this article, I asked Jerry Welsh if he would explain why American Express waited so long. "Sure," he said, "they were afraid of having a 'pink' card."

■ Women of color read *Ms.* in disproportionate numbers. This is a source of pride to *Ms.* staffers, who are also more racially representative that the editors of other women's magazines. But this reality is obscured by ads filled with enough white women to make a reader snowblind.

Pat Carbine remembers mostly "astonishment" when she requested 55 African American, Hispanic, Asian, and other diverse images. Marcia Ann Gillespie, a *Ms.* editor who was previously the editor in chief of *Essence,* witnesses ad bias a second time: Having tried for *Essence* to get white advertisers to use black images (Revlon did so eventually, but L'Oréal, Lauder, Chanel, and other companies never did), she sees similar problems getting integrated ads for an integrated magazine. Indeed, the ad world often creates black and Hispanic ads only for black and Hispanic media. In an exact parallel of the fear that marketing a product to women will endanger its appeal to men, the response is usually, "But your [white] readers won't identify."

In fact, those we are able to get—for instance, a Max Factor ad made for *Essence* that Linda Wachner gives us after she becomes president—are praised by white readers, too. But there are pathetically few such images.

■ By the end of 1986, production and mailing costs have risen astronomically, ad income is flat, and competition for ads is stiffer than ever. The 60/40 preponderance of edit over ads that we promised to readers becomes 50/50; children's stories, most poetry, and some fiction are casualties of less space; in order to get variety into limited pages, the length (and sometimes the depth) of articles suffers; and, though we do refuse most of the ads that would look like a parody in our pages, we get so worn down that some slip through. Still, readers perform miracles. Though we haven't been able to afford a subscription mailing in two years, they maintain our guaranteed circulation of 450,000.

Nonetheless, media reports on *Ms.* often insist that our unprofitability must be due to reader disinterest. The myth that advertisers simply follow readers is very strong. Not one reporter notes that other comparable magazines our size (say, *Vanity Fair* or *The Atlantic*) have been losing more money in one year than *Ms.* has lost in 16 years. No matter how much never-to-be-recovered cash is poured into starting a magazine or keeping one going, appearances seem to be all that matter. (Which is why we haven't been able to explain our fragile state in public. Nothing causes ad flight like the smell of nonsuccess.)

My healthy response is anger. My not-so-healthy response is constant worry. Also an obsession with finding one more rescue. There is hardly a night when I don't wake up with sweaty palms and pounding heart, scared that we won't be able to pay the printer or the post office; scared most of all that closing our doors will hurt the women's movement.

Out of chutzpah and desperation, I arrange a lunch with Leonard 60 Lauder, president of Estée Lauder. With the exception of Clinique (the brainchild of Carol Phillips), none of Lauder's hundreds of products has been advertised in *Ms.* A year's schedule of ads for just three or four of them could save us. Indeed, as the scion of a family-owned company whose ad practices are followed by the beauty industry, he is one of the few men who could liberate many pages in all women's magazines just by changing his mind about "complementary copy."

Over a lunch that costs more than we can pay for some articles, I explain the need for his leadership. I also lay out the record of *Ms.*: more literary and journalistic prizes won, more new issues introduced into the mainstream, new writers discovered, and impact on society than any other magazine; more articles that became books, stories that became movies, ideas that became television series, and newly advertised products that became profitable; and, most important for him, a place for his ads to reach women who aren't reachable through any other women's magazine. Indeed, if there is one constant characteristic of the ever-changing *Ms.* readership, it is their impact as leaders. Whether it's waiting until later to have first babies, or pioneering PABA as sun protection in cosmetics, *whatever* they are doing today, a third to a half of American women will be doing three to five years from now. It's never failed.

But, he says, *Ms.* readers are not *our* women. They're not interested in things like fragrance and blush-on. If they were, *Ms.* would write articles about them.

On the contrary, I explain, surveys show they are more likely to buy such things than the readers of, say, *Cosmopolitan* or *Vogue*. They're good customers because they're out in the world enough to need several sets of everything: home, work, purse, travel, gym, and so on. They just don't need to read articles about these things. Would he ask a men's magazine to publish monthly columns on how to shave before he advertised Aramis products (his line for men)?

He concedes that beauty features are often concocted more for advertisers than readers. But *Ms.* isn't appropriate for his ads anyway, he explains. Why? Because Estée Lauder is selling "a kept-woman mentality."

I can't quite believe this. Sixty percent of the users of his products   65
are salaried, and generally resemble *Ms.* readers. Besides, his company has the appeal of having been started by a creative and hardworking woman, his mother, Estée Lauder.

That doesn't matter, he says. He knows his customers, and they would *like* to be kept women. That's why he will never advertise in *Ms.*

In November 1987, by vote of the Ms. Foundation for Education and Communication (*Ms.*'s owner and publisher, the media subsidiary of the Ms. Foundation for Women), *Ms.* was sold to a company whose officers, Australian feminists Sandra Yates and Anne Summers, raised the investment money in their country that *Ms.* couldn't find in its own. They also started *Sassy* for teenage women.

In their two-year tenure, circulation was raised to 550,000 by investment in circulation mailings, and, to the dismay of some readers, editorial features on clothes and new products made a more traditional bid for ads. Nonetheless, ad pages fell below previous levels. In addition, *Sassy,* whose fresh voice and sexual frankness were an unprecedented success with young readers, was targeted by two mothers from Indiana who began, as one of them put it, "calling every Christian organization I could think of." In response to this controversy, several crucial advertisers pulled out.

Such links between ads and editorial content was a problem in Australia, too, but to a lesser degree. "Our readers pay two times more for their magazines," Anne explained, "so advertisers have less power to threaten a magazine's viability."

"I was shocked," said Sandra Yates with characteristic directness. "In   70
Australia, we think you have freedom of the press—but you don't."

Since Anne and Sandra had not met their budget's projections for ad revenue, their investors forced a sale. In October 1989, *Ms.* and *Sassy* were bought by Dale Lang, owner of *Working Mother, Working Woman,* and one of the few independent publishing companies left among the conglomerates. In response to a request from the original *Ms.* staff—as well as to reader letters urging that *Ms.* continue, plus his own belief that *Ms.* would benefit his other magazines by blazing a trail—he agreed to try the ad-free, reader-supported *Ms.* . . . and to give us complete editorial control.

2

In response to the workplace revolution of the 1970s, traditional women's magazines—that is, "trade books" for women working at home—were joined by *Savvy, Working Woman,* and other trade books for women working in offices. But by keeping the fashion/beauty/ entertaining articles necessary to get traditional ads and then adding career articles besides, they inadvertently produced the antifeminist stereotype of Super Woman. The male-imitative, dress-for-success woman carrying a briefcase became the media image of a woman worker, even though a blue-collar woman's salary was often higher than her glorified secretarial sister's, and though women at a real briefcase level are statistically rare. Needless to say, these dress-for-success women were also thin, white, and beautiful.

In recent years, advertisers' control over the editorial content of women's magazines has become so institutionalized that it is written into "insertion orders" or dictated to ad salespeople as official policy. The following are recent typical orders to women's magazines:

■ Dow's Cleaning Products stipulates that ads for its Vivid and Spray 'n Wash products should be adjacent to "children or fashion editorial"; ads for Bathroom Cleaner should be next to "home furnishing/family" features; and so on for other brands. "If a magazine fails for the brands or more," the Dow order warns, "it will be omitted from further consideration."

■ Bristol-Myers, the parent of Clairol, Windex, Drano, Bufferin, and   75
much more, stipulates that ads be placed next to "a full page of compatible editorial."

■ S.C. Johnson & Son, makers of Johnson Wax, lawn and laundry products, insect sprays, hair sprays, and so on, orders that its ads "*should not be opposite extremely controversial features or material antithetical to the nature/copy of the advertised product."* (Italics theirs.)

- Maidenform, manufacturer of bras and other apparel, leaves a blank for the particular product and states: "The creative concept of the ＿＿＿＿ campaign, and the very nature of the product itself appeal to the positive emotions of the reader/consumer. Therefore, it is imperative that all editorial adjacencies reflect that same positive tone. The editorial must not be negative in content or lend itself contrary to the ＿＿＿＿ product imagery/message (e.g., *editorial relating to illness, disillusionment, large size fashion, etc.*)." (Italics mine.)

- The De Beers diamond company, a big seller of engagement rings, prohibits magazines from placing its ads with "adjacencies to hard news or anti/love-romance themed editorial."

- Procter & Gamble, one of this country's most powerful and diversified advertisers, stands out in the memory of Anne Summers and Sandra Yates (no mean feat in this context): Its products were not to be placed in *any* issue that included *any* material on gun control, abortion, the occult, cults, or the disparagement of religion. Caution was also demanded in any issue covering sex or drugs, even for educational purposes.

Those are the most obvious chains around women's magazines. There are also rules so clear they needn't be written down: for instance, an overall "look" compatible with beauty and fashion ads. Even "real" nonmodel women photographed for a woman's magazine are usually made up, dressed in credited clothes, and retouched out of all reality. When editors do include articles on less-than-cheerful subjects (for instance, domestic violence), they tend to keep them short and unillustrated. The point is to be "upbeat." Just as women in the street are asked, "Why don't you smile, honey?" women's magazines acquire an institutional smile.

Within the text itself, praise for advertisers' products has become so ritualized that fields like "beauty writing" have been invented. One of its frequent practitioners explained seriously that "It's a difficult art. How many new adjectives can you find? How much greater can you make a lipstick sound? The FDA restricts what companies can say on labels, but we create illusion. And ad agencies are on the phone all the time pushing you to get their product in. A lot of them keep the business based on how many editorial clippings they produce every month. The worst are products," like Lauder's as the writer confirmed, "with their own name involved. It's all ego."

Often, editorial becomes one giant ad. Last November, for instance, *Lear's* featured an elegant woman executive on the cover. On the contents page, we learned she was wearing Guerlain makeup and Samsara, a new fragrance by Guerlain. Inside were full-page ads for Samsara and Guerlain antiwrinkle cream. In the cover profile, we learned that this executive was responsible for launching Samsara and is Guerlain's director

80

of public relations. When the *Columbia Journalism Review* did one of the few articles to include women's magazines in coverage of the influence of ads, editor Frances Lear was quoted as defending her magazine because "this kind of thing is done all the time."

Often, advertisers also plunge odd-shaped ads into the text, no matter what the cost to the readers. At *Woman's Day,* a magazine originally founded by a supermarket chain, editor in chief Ellen Levine said, "The day the copy had to rag around a chicken leg was not a happy one."

Advertisers are also adamant about where in a magazine their ads appear. When Revlon was not placed as the first beauty ad in one Hearst magazine, for instance, Revlon pulled its ads from *all* Hearst magazines. Ruth Whitney, editor in chief of *Glamour,* attributes some of these demands to "ad agencies wanting to prove to a client that they've squeezed the last drop of blood out of a magazine." She also is, she says, "sick and tired of hearing that women's magazines are controlled by cigarette ads." Relatively speaking, she's right. To be as censoring as are many advertisers for women's products, tobacco companies would have to demand articles in praise of smoking and expect glamorous photos of beautiful women smoking their brands.

I don't mean to imply that the editors I quote here share my objec- [85] tions to ads: Most assume that women's magazines have to be the way they are. But it's also true that only former editors can be completely honest. "Most of the pressure came in the form of direct product mentions," explains Sey Chassler, who was editor in chief of *Redbook* from the sixties to the eighties. "We got threats from the big guys, the Revlons, blackmail threats. They wouldn't run ads unless we credited them.

"But it's not fair to single out the beauty advertisers because these pressures came from everybody. Advertisers want to know two things: What are you going to charge me? What *else* are you going to do for me? It's a holdup. For instance, management felt that fiction took up too much space. They couldn't put any advertising in that. For the last ten years, the number of fiction entries into the National Magazine Awards has declined.

"And pressures are getting worse. More magazines are more bottom-line oriented because they have been taken over by companies with no interest in publishing.

"I also think advertisers do this to women's magazines especially," he concluded, "because of the general disrespect they have for women."

Even media experts who don't give a damn about women's magazines are alarmed by the spread of this ad–edit linkage. In a climate *The Wall Street Journal* describes as an unacknowledged Depression for media, women's products are increasingly able to take their low standards wherever they go. For instance: Newsweeklies publish uncritical stories on fashion and fitness. *The New York Times Magazine* recently ran an article on "firming creams," complete with mentions of advertisers. *Vanity Fair* published a profile of one major advertiser, Ralph Lauren, illustrated by the same photographer who does his ads, and turned the lifestyle of another, Calvin Klein, into a cover story. Even the outrageous *Spy* has toned down since it began to go after fashion ads.

And just to make us really worry, films and books, the last media   90 that go directly to the public without having to attract ads first, are in danger, too. Producers are beginning to depend on payments for displaying products in movies, and books are now being commissioned by companies like Federal Express.

But the truth is that women's products—like women's magazines—have never been the subjects of much serious reporting anyway. News and general interest publications, including the "style" or "living" sections of newspapers, write about food and clothing as cooking and fashion, and almost never evaluate such products by brand name. Though chemical additives, pesticides, and animal fats are major health risks in the United States, and clothes, shoddy or not, absorb more consumer dollars than cars, this lack of information is serious. So is ignoring the contents of beauty products that are absorbed into our bodies through our skins, and that have profit margins so big they would make a loan shark blush.

3

What could women's magazines be like if they were as free as books? as realistic as newspapers? as creative as films? as diverse as women's lives? We don't know.

But we'll only find out if we take women's magazines seriously. If readers were to act in a concerted way to change traditional practices of *all* women's magazines and the marketing of *all* women's products, we could do it. After all, they are operating on our consumer dollars; money that we now control. You and I could:

■ write to editors and publishers (with copies to advertisers) that we're willing to pay *more* for magazines with editorial independence, but will *not* continue to pay for those that are just editorial extensions of ads;

■ write to advertisers (with copies to editors and publishers) that we want fiction, political reporting, consumer reporting—whatever is, or is not, supported by their ads;

■ put as much energy into breaking advertising's control over content as into changing the images in ads, or protesting ads for harmful products like cigarettes;

■ support only those women's magazines and products that take *us* seriously as readers and consumers.

■ Those of us in the magazine world can also use the carrot-and-stick technique. For instance: Pointing out that, if magazines were a regulated medium like television, the demands of advertisers would be against

FCC rules. Payola and extortion could be punished. As it is, there are probably illegalities. A magazine's postal rates are determined by the ratio of ad to edit pages, and the former costs more than the latter. So much for the stick.

The carrot means appealing to enlightened self-interest. For instance: There are many studies showing that the greatest factor in determining an ad's effectiveness is the credibility of its surroundings. The "higher the rating of editorial believability," concluded a 1987 survey by the *Journal of Advertising Research,* "the higher the rating of the advertising." Thus, an impenetrable wall between edit and ads would also be in the best interest of advertisers.

Unfortunately, few agencies or clients hear such arguments. Editors   95 often maintain the false purity of refusing to talk to them at all. Instead, they see ad salespeople who know little about editorial, are trained in business as usual, and are usually paid by commission. Editors might also band together to take on controversy. That happened once when all the major women's magazines did articles in the same month on the Equal Rights Amendment. It could happen again.

It's almost three years away from life between the grindstones of advertising pressures and readers' needs. I'm just beginning to realize how edges got smoothed down—in spite of all our resistance.

I remember feeling put upon when I changed "Porsche" to "car" in a piece about Nazi imagery in German pornography by Andrea Dworkin—feeling sure Andrea would understand that Volkswagen, the distributor of Porsche and one of our few supportive advertisers, asked only to be far away from Nazi subjects. It's taken me all this time to realize that Andrea was the one with a right to feel put upon.

Even as I write this, I get a call from a writer for *Elle,* who is doing a whole article on where women part their hair. Why, she wants to know, do I part mine in the middle?

It's all so familiar. A writer trying to make something of a nothing assignment; an editor laboring to think of new ways to attract ads; readers assuming that other women must want this ridiculous stuff; more women suffering for lack of information, insight, creativity, and laughter that could be on these same pages.

I ask you: Can't we do better than this?   100

Reading the Text

1. What does Steinem mean by "complementary copy"?
2. Summarize the relationship that Steinem sees between editorial content and advertising in women's magazines.

3. According to Steinem, what messages about gender roles does complementary copy send readers of women's magazines?

Reading the Signs

1. Steinem asserts that virtually all content in women's magazines is a disguised form of advertising. Test her hypothesis by writing a detailed analysis of a single issue of a magazine such as *Cosmopolitan, Glamour,* or *Elle.* Do you find instances of complementary copy? How do you react as a potential reader of such a magazine?
2. Explore whether Steinem's argument holds for men's magazines such as *GQ.* If you identify differences, how might they be based on different assumptions about gender roles?
3. Steinem ends her essays by claiming that the *Ms.* published without advertising will exhibit greater journalistic freedom than the *Ms.* supported by advertising. Compare a current issue of *Ms.* with an earlier, advertising-laden issue (check your college library), and test Steinem's claim.
4. Have each member of the class bring in a favorite magazine. In small groups, study the relationship between ads and articles. Which magazines have the most complementary copy? How can you account for your findings?
5. How do you feel about the claim that Estée Lauder can't advertise in *Ms.* because it is selling a "kept-woman mentality"? If you are disturbed by this statement, write a letter to Estée Lauder's president, arguing against this characterization of women; if you're not bothered by it, write a letter to Gloria Steinem, trying to persuade her that an outraged response is not necessary.
6. Do advertisers infringe upon the freedom of the press, as the publisher of *Sassy* believes? Write a journal entry in which you explore this issue.

The Subaru Legacy

Weld a peace sign to the hood and make believe you're driving a Mercedes that gets really great gas mileage.

THE BRAZEN audacity. To compare a Subaru® Legacy™ to one of Germany's finest and most-revered automobiles.

Hey, why not. They both are designed to do the same thing. Transport people and their stuff from point A to point B. And they both perform that basic automotive function effectively and comfortably.

For example, the Legacy LSi Sedan, which costs many thousands less than the cheapest Mercedes, offers most of the amenities you'd only expect from a fine, absurdly priced luxury car:

Soft grain leather seats. All-Wheel Drive. Compact disc player. Moonroof. Driver's-side air bag. The 4-Channel Anti-Lock Braking System which monitors each wheel to help prevent the car from locking up during emergency stops. And the Legacy is also blessed

with numerous other engineering features which translate into the type of durability Subaru is famous for.

(Important selling point — 93% of all Subaru cars registered in the last 10 years are still on the road and running today.[1])

Now, if you've read this far, you'd probably like a second opinion about the Legacy. Alright, here's one from *Car and Driver:* "The Subaru Legacy is the nicest driving, least expensive, and best equipped 4-wheel drive sedan on the market."[2]

We repeat — nicest driving, least expensive, best equipped.

So if you're into haughty status symbols, go into the closet and grab that medallion off that ancient Nehru jacket and affix it to the hood. Or, then again, with all the money you'll be saving on your new Legacy you could just imagine you're driving the world's peppiest, most elegantly styled Brink's truck.

Subaru Legacy LSi

Subaru. What to drive.™

[1] Based on R.L. Polk & Co., registration statistics. [2] May, 1990. For additional information, 1-800-284-8584. © Subaru of America, 1991.

ask people
to judge me by my
ability
not my
disability

cindy bolas, colorado

tell us what you'd do. write to esprit, p.o. box 77903, san francisco, ca 94107.
for more information on rights for the disabled, contact the Disability Rights Education
and Defense Fund, 2212 6th street, berkeley, ca 97710, 800-466-4232.

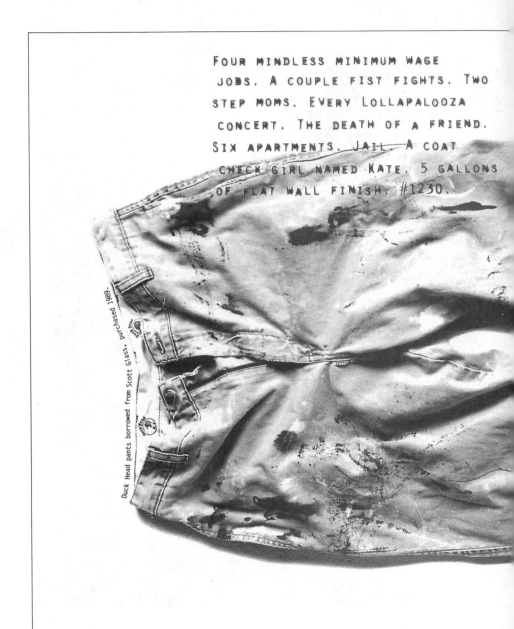

FOUR MINDLESS MINIMUM WAGE
JOBS. A COUPLE FIST FIGHTS. TWO
STEP MOMS. EVERY LOLLAPALOOZA
CONCERT. THE DEATH OF A FRIEND.
SIX APARTMENTS. JAIL. A COAT
CHECK GIRL NAMED KATE. 5 GALLONS
OF FLAT WALL FINISH. #1230.

Duck Head pants borrowed from Scott Glass, purchased 1989.

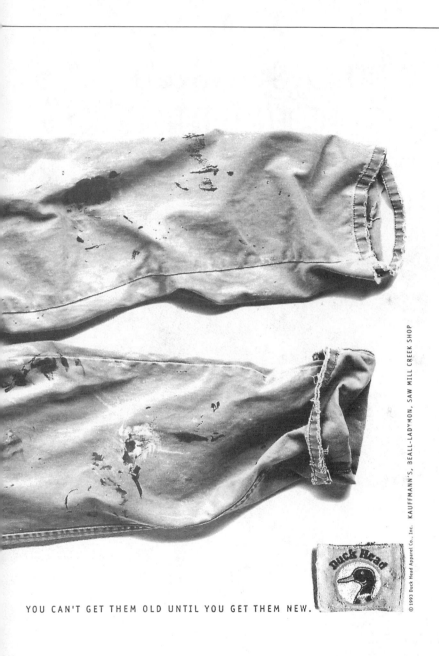

YOU CAN'T GET THEM OLD UNTIL YOU GET THEM NEW.

Who says guys are afraid of commitment? He's had the same backpack for years.

When it comes to choosing a lifelong companion, lots of guys pick one of our backpacks. Each one comes with a lifetime guarantee not to rip, tear, break, or ask for a ring.

Reading the Signs

1. Have the class vote for the ads contained in the Portfolio that are most effective and least effective in persuading the target audience to purchase the products. Then discuss the significance of the results. What strategies does the class consider more persuasive? Do you see any gender-related patterns in the class's votes?

2. Together, the text and imagery of the Eastpak ad tell a story about the male figure who owns the backpack. What is that story? Do you think the ad is intended to appeal to men, women, or both? Why the same food displayed in each photograph? Use your observations to formulate an argument about the strategies this ad uses to appeal to consumers.

3. Write a semiotic interpretation of the Duck Head ad. Be sure to analyze details such as the copy, the typeface, and the condition of the pants. How do those details relate to the ad's probable audience and to the fashion system to which the pants belong?

4. Advertisers call the Esprit ad a "message" ad. Discuss that message and why you think the advertiser found it a useful strategy to sell clothing.

5. The Subaru ad deliberately uses signs, both visual and verbal, to target consumers of a particular social class and age group. In class, discuss the significance of details such as the peace sign and the Nehru jacket and how they appeal to the ad's audience. In addition, why is the model car black? What are the connotations of the cartoon image?

6. The Honda ad appeared in *Hispanic* magazine. Write an essay in which you explain the ad's appeal to its intended audience. To develop your argument, you might consult Ada María Isasi-Díaz's "Hispanic in America: Starting Points" (p. 503).

MUSIC TELEVISION®

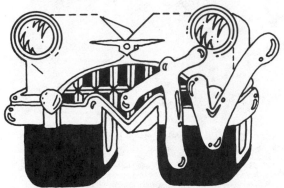

MUSIC TELEVISION®

MUSIC TELEVISION®

CHAPTER THREE

M (O R E) T V

The Television and Video Revolution

They're all in college now or living on Melrose Place. It's hard to keep track, what with the ratings system the way it is. But just a few years ago they were the most famous high school students in America, with the most famous love affairs and the most famous zip code, because millions of kids tuned in every week to watch them grow up in the everlasting sunshine of Southern California. Do you remember their address? Does Beverly Hills 90210 ring a bell?

It should, because only a few years ago *Beverly Hills, 90210* became America's most popular teen television drama. Its popularity leads us to our prime semiotic question: Why? Why, that is, was *Beverly Hills, 90210* the smash hit among teenagers that it was?

Don't say "Because it was a hip program." When analyzing the significance of a TV show or video, you have to go beyond its surface appeal to probe what may be going on behind the scenes. Would *Beverly Hills, 90210* have been as popular if it were called *Van Nuys, 91405*—a working- and middle-class neighborhood in the San Fernando Valley several miles from Beverly Hills? What if the characters attended a predominantly black and Latino school, or rode the bus, or couldn't afford five changes of clothing per day? What if they had bad hair days, or bad skin outbreaks? What if they lived with their parents in crowded apartments? What if there were no blonds? How would these differences have affected the show? Why was it set in Beverly Hills?

|||||||||||||||||||||||||||||||||||||||||||||||||||||||||||||||||||||||||||||||||||||||||||||||||||||||||||||||||||||||||||||||||||||||

Exploring the Signs of Music Videos

In your journal, explore the impact music videos have had on you. How have videos shaped your desires and expectations about life? How were your actions and behavior influenced by MTV? What videos were especially meaningful to you? What did you think about them when you were younger, and how do you see them now? (If you didn't watch MTV, you might focus instead on television programs.)

Such questions can lead you to examine the social class issues that a show like *Beverly Hills, 90210* raises. You might compare it to another series with teenaged characters, the even more popular *Roseanne*. What is the difference between the two shows? Which did you (or do you) prefer? Why?

As you consider why a given TV show appeals to you, be careful of the temptation to explain things in terms of the *explicit* "message" that the show may try to send. Usually, such messages are at odds with what is really going on in the more powerful realm of semiotic suggestion. Take an early episode of *Beverly Hills, 90210,* wherein Brandon Walsh's old girlfriend from Minneapolis shows up for a visit. Eventually we learn that this is no simple visit between young lovers but that Brandon's old girlfriend has run away from home because of her unhappiness with her stepfather, with whom she quarrels, and her father, who does not communicate with her anymore. The explicit message of the episode, as it turns out, concerns the pain felt by teens from all over America whose parents have divorced.

Such messages as this may be a part of what the fans of *Beverly Hills, 90210* respond to at the conscious level (and the show has lots of such messages), but a semiotic analysis can reveal a deeper appeal—the sort of appeal that makes for a hit series. To find that appeal, we have to look behind the message toward the more subtle signals that the episode communicates. Let's look at it again now, but this time wearing our semiotic eyeglasses.

First, it's important to note just how gorgeous Brandon and his girlfriend are. Consider the teenage fantasies involved in such good looks (and the fact that both parts are played by actors well beyond the awkward stage of adolescence). Next, look at the general plot. In this episode, all the characters seem to have complete freedom to do what they want. Not only are they free to go out and party at L.A.'s trendiest nightclub without being carded (on a school night, no less), but at one point Brandon and his girl climb into bed together even as Brandon's parents down the hall wonder whether they should check up on him. Mom's worried, but Dad's cool: He'll talk to Brandon in the morning about "responsibility." But come morning, Brandon is running out the door, no time to talk, and that's the pattern of the episode: The kids literally and figuratively run circles around their parents. Indeed, this is shown openly in the episode's final scene, as Brandon, who with Dylan's help has sorted out his problems with his girlfriend, plays a little one-on-one basketball with his old man. Dad tries to start his little chat about responsibility, but Brandon cuts him off. "Are we talking about sex, Dad?" he asks. Dad stutters. Brandon smirks. "We were careful, Dad," he assures the old guy, and then grabs the ball from his hands and heads for the hoop for a slam dunk. End of conversation. End of episode.

Now aside from the fact that Brandon is probably too short to be able to slam dunk a basketball (someone lowered the net), what is peculiar about all these details? What is really going on? These are the questions we've got to ask, not what was the message of this episode.

Think about it. These kids, who are much more attractive than their parents (how, one wonders, do such stodgy-looking people produce such gorgeous children?), hold all the cards. The Walshes, senior, don't have a chance against these kids, who, though still in high school, don't seem to have to ask permission to go out or explain when they return home in the wee hours of the morning. So what are we really seeing? What's the fantasy and to whom does it belong? As you ponder these questions, consider one of the commercials broadcast during this episode. It pitched a home pregnancy testing device, which produced a little message that read "not pregnant." This brief signal might be the most significant sign of all, for in its juxtaposition with a story line that features a steamy sex scene between Brandon and his girl, it more or less told its audience to just go out and say "yes," like Brandon's girlfriend. "Go ahead," the ad said in effect, "you won't get pregnant if you just buy our product."

The producers of the program, and many of its viewers, would probably object to this reading by pointing out that when Brandon sleeps with his girlfriend, she asks him if he has "protection." "Sure," he says to her. In such a way, TV writers cover their tracks. The surface "message" to teens, the one the producers of the show can sell to critical parents, is that it encourages "responsibility." But the superficial, "pro-social" message of a program is rarely the same as its real significance. A few words vaguely uttered about "protection" (which, of course, we never see actually being used) haven't a fraction of the power of the image of two sexy young people together in bed. The power of the medium lies in what it shows, not in what it says (after all, we call TV programs "shows," not "tells"), and what we see is a fantasy of teenaged freedom—both sexual and economic—beyond anything most of the show's viewers could ever experience.

Such are the sorts of issues you need to consider when interpreting a TV show. Maybe *Beverly Hills, 90210* never did much for you and you'd prefer to think about a different show. Fine, go to it. But the rules

|||||||||||||||||||||||||||||||||||||||||||||||||||||||||||||||||||||||||||||||||||||||||||||||||||||||||||||||||||||||||||||||

Discussing the Signs of Television

In class, choose a current television program and have the entire class watch one episode (either watch the episode as "homework" or ask someone to tape it and then watch it in class). Interpret the episode semiotically. What values and cultural myths does the show project? What do the commercials broadcast during the show say about the presumed audience for it? Go beyond the episode's surface appeal or "message" to look at the particular images it uses to tell its story, always asking, "What is this program *really* saying?"

are the same: Don't let the surface appeal of the program lead you away from the deeper issues involved. Be sure to relate the show to other cultural phenomena—like social class relations—and take nothing for granted. After all, even *Roseanne,* a more grittily realistic show than *Beverly Hills, 90210,* contains plenty of myths and fantasies.

Altered States

Interpreting TV is especially important at a time when television is blurring the line between fantasy and reality in an ever more profound manner. Just think of the presidential election of 1992 when Dan Quayle made Murphy Brown a campaign issue because she chose to become a single mother. For months the fictional protagonist of the show, played by Candice Bergen, sparred with the real vice president over the rights of single mothers in a public battle whose most interesting significance was that everyone acted as if Murphy Brown was as real as Dan Quayle.

Such blurring of the line between fiction and reality (a process recently accelerated by the advent of "docudrama" style "news" shows like *Inside Edition*) reflects television's profound effect upon the very way that we perceive our world. If television were to vanish today—no more shows, no more prime time—its effects would live on in the way it has altered our sense of reality. We expect instant visual access to every corner of the earth because of TV, and we want to get to the point quickly. It is often claimed that our attention spans have been shortened in a universe of televised sound bites, but at the same time our desire for information has been expanded (inquiring minds want to know). Indeed, the television age has equally been an information age.

In semiotic terms, the ubiquity of television and video in our lives represents a shift from one kind of sign system to another. As Marshall McLuhan pointed out thirty years ago in *The Gutenberg Galaxy,* Western culture since the fifteenth century has defined itself around the printed word, the linear text that reads from left to right and top to bottom. The printed word, in the terminology of the American founder of semiotics, Charles Sanders Peirce, is a *symbolic* sign, one whose meaning is entirely arbitrary or conventional. A symbolic sign means what it does because those who use it have decided so. Words don't look like what they mean. Their significance is entirely abstract.

Not so with a visual image like a photograph (or TV picture), which does resemble its object and is not entirely arbitrary. Though a photograph is not literally the thing it depicts and often reflects a good deal of "staging" and manipulation on the part of the photographer, we often respond to it as if it were an innocent reflection of the world. Peirce called such signs *icons,* referring by this term to any sign that resembles what it means. The way you interpret an icon, then, differs from the way you interpret a symbol or word. The interpretation of words involves your cognitive capabilities; the interpretation and reception of icons are far more sensuous, more a matter of vision than cognition. The shift from a civilization governed by the paradigm of the book to one dominated by television accordingly involves a shift in the way we "read" our world, as the symbolic field of the printed page yields to the iconic field of the video screen.

The shift from a symbolic, or word-centered, world to an iconic universe filled with visual images carries profound cultural implications. Such implications are not necessarily negative ones. The relative accessibility of video technology, for example, has created opportunities for personal expression that have never existed before. It is very difficult to publish a book, but anyone can create a widely reproducible video simply by possessing a video camera. The rapid transmissibility of video images speeds up communication and can bond groups of linguistically and culturally diverse people together, as MTV speaks to millions of people around the nation and world at once in the language of dance and music.

At the same time, video images may be used to change consciousness and stimulate political action. Feminist rappers like Salt-n-Pepa, for example, stage their music videos as calls to action, prodding their audiences to duplicate in reality the fantasies they see on the screen. Indeed, while many critics of TV deplore the passivity of its viewers, there is nothing inherently passive about the medium. Look at it this way: TV has a visceral power that print does not. Words abstractly describe things; television can show you concrete images. The world pretty much ignored the famine in sub-Saharan Africa in the early eighties, for example, until the TV cameras arrived to broadcast its images of starvation. Television, in short, bears the potential to awake the apathetic as written texts often do not.

But there is a price to be paid for the new modes of perception that the iconic world of TV has stimulated. For while one *can* read the signs of TV and video actively and creatively, and one can be moved to action by a video image, the sheer visibility of icons tempts one to receive them uncritically. Icons look so much like the realities they refer to that it is easy to forget that icons, too, are signs: images people construct that carry ideological meanings.

Just think of all those iconic images of the classic fifties-era sitcoms. *Leave It to Beaver, Father Knows Best, The Ozzie and Harriet Show,* and so on have established an American mythology of an idyllic era by the sheer persuasiveness of their images. In fact, the fifties were not such idyllic years. Along with the McCarthyite hysteria of the Cold War and the looming specter of nuclear war and contamination from open-air nuclear testing, there were economic downturns, the Korean War, and a growing sense that American life was becoming sterile, conformist, and materialistic—though it wasn't until the sixties that this uneasiness broke into the open. Few fathers in the fifties had the kind of leisure that the sitcom dads had, and the feminist resurgence in the late sixties demonstrated that not all women were satisfied with the housewifely roles assigned them in every screenplay. And yet, those constructed images of white middle-class contentment and security have become so real in the American imagination that they can be called upon in quite concrete ways. *Leave It to Beaver* is not simply the sort of thing that shows up in Trivial Pursuit games: The image of the show has become a potent political tool. Conservative campaigners point to the classic sitcoms as exemplars of the "family values" that America is losing, apparently forgetting that many a modern sitcom, from *The Cosby Show* to *Roseanne,* reflect strikingly similar images of family solidarity. After all, the whole point of *Leave It to Beaver* was to show every week how "the Beav" might mess something up, create a family crisis, and then have the whole matter resolved in time for the closing commercials. While it may take several episodes to do the trick, how is *Roseanne* different?

The Audience Is the Authority

One thing has changed in the relatively brief history of television, however: the emergence of cable TV. The proliferation of cable companies and channels has fostered a more finely targeted programming schedule by which producers can focus on narrowly defined audiences, from nature lovers to home shoppers. In one respect, the fine-tuning of audiences simply reflects a fine-tuning of marketing: Specially defined audiences can be targeted for specially defined marketing campaigns. In this sense, the advent of cable repeats the same history as that of traditional commercial television, which became a medium primarily for the pitching of goods and services. But the proliferation of channels bears the potential, at least, to upset television's commercial monopoly. When NBC, CBS, ABC, and their affiliates ruled the airways, programming decisions for an entire nation were made by a tiny group of executives. Aside from the Nielsen ratings, viewers had little chance to let programmers know what they wanted to see. While certainly no revolution has occurred in the wake of cable, there has at least been some movement toward audience participation in viewing.

The phenomenal success of MTV provides a good example of the increasing power of the television audience. In its early years, rock music appeared on TV in such programs as *American Bandstand* and *The Monkees.* In each case, a rock act had to be toned down considerably before it could be televised (Elvis was ordered not to bump and grind lest he be banned from the TV screens of the fifties). What amounted to censorship worked because the venues for televising rock were often adult-oriented (consider how the Beatles and the Rolling Stones first appeared to American audiences on the adult variety program *The Ed Sullivan Show*). MTV, on the other hand, is an entirely youth-oriented station. Though it too exists to promote products—through both the videos it displays and the commercials it runs—MTV has to conform to the tastes of its audience to succeed. This means that it has to appeal to adolescent fantasies and frustrations in a way that *The Monkees,* for instance, never did. *The Monkees* was a sanitized adventure sitcom whose scripts were written by anonymous professionals. The "scripts" of MTV videos are largely determined by the performers whose popularity among adolescents brought them to the screen in the first place. In other words, while MTV serves establishment corporate sponsors like any other commercial program, it nevertheless derives its authority from its audience more than the three networks do.

No one has received more attention in this vein than Madonna, who has created something of an industry among academic critics eager to interpret her. Some see her as a postmodern feminist heroine, others as an irresponsible promoter of teenaged sexuality. Whatever one thinks of her, her preeminent place in American pop culture fairly screams for analysis. And it is likely that you have more authority to conduct such an analysis than many an academic commentator.

Given the emphasis on sexuality that Madonna's videos are so famous for, you might think that that's all there is to their interpretation. But we'd like you to consider another angle for a moment. Look at "Papa Don't Preach," for example. Oh yeah, it's about teenage pregnancy, but look at that sentimental conclusion, where father and daughter are reunited. Or look at "Open Your Heart," where the peepshow star in the end runs away into an innocent sunset with the kid, like a female Charlie Chaplin. Such fantasies go beyond sex, reflecting a deep-seated sentimentality, a desire for innocence, that runs at the heart of American culture. Rather than being subversive, these videos can actually be seen to reinforce the cultural status quo. Can the same be said of Madonna's current videos?

Maybe you always preferred videos like "Borderline," however, where Madonna plays a character who lives in two worlds, frolicking at once with handsome, sultry street boys and handsome, glitzy photographers. Beyond the sexual fantasies here is a social fantasy, a teen desire to identify with both the underclass and the ruling class. In some ways, this may be the most significant element in the Madonna phenomenon —the way she appeals to her audience's sense of identification with both the very rich and the urban poor. This identification may well be related to the white middle-class embrace of rap music and gang culture, on the one hand, and shows like *Beverly Hills, 90210,* on the other. For when analyzing the culture of American video and TV, everything ties together.

The Readings

We begin the readings in this chapter with Holly Brubach's overview of MTV, written when the now-ubiquitous channel was only three years old but had already evolved many of its current conventions, from Michael Jackson's dance routines to surrealistic, dreamy landscapes. Lisa A. Lewis's analysis of the male coding in MTV videos develops a point implicit in Brubach's essay: MTV's preferred audience is male adolescents who see their own social and sexual fantasies played out in the videos they see on the screen. Next, bell hooks takes on Madonna, whose embrace of the imagery of black culture is sometimes seen as a sign of her revolutionary intentions; hooks views it as a successful white woman's appropriation of black life in ways that reflect enduring racial—and even racist—stereotypes. Minabere Ibelema turns his gaze upon the representation of the African heritage of black America on television, concluding that when that heritage is not ignored it is portrayed in an assimilationist manner that eventually reinforces the values and traditions of mainstream—that is, non-African—America. Josh Ozersky follows with a critique of the "new realism" in American sitcoms, showing how programs like *The Simpsons, Married . . . with Children,* and *Roseanne* aren't nearly as realistic as the critics say they are; instead, they seduce their viewers with a reality effect that keeps them glued to their screens, safely in the grasp of corporate sponsors who have found that portraying dysfunctional family life is a good way to keep America's dysfunctional families in the field of docile consumers. Susan Faludi's scathing indictment of television's portrayal of women in the 1980s looks at the gender wars that take place behind the scenes in Hollywood, showing how what we watch on TV reflects the political will of those who control the medium. And finally, Walter Kirn's opinion piece on "twentysomething" TV and culture presents a critical view of a "lost generation" whose "slacker rebellion" is, he believes, just another form of consumerism.

Rock-and-Roll Vaudeville

|||||||||||||||||||||||||||||||||||||||||||||||||||||||||||||

In the beginning were the Buggles and their now quaintly obsolete rock video "Video Killed the Radio Star." In this critical survey of the early years of MTV, Holly Brubach (b. 1953) shows how it all began and the crucial intervention of such dance-video stars as Michael Jackson, who changed the look of MTV forever. Though something of a Michael Jackson fan, Brubach criticizes the monotony that has overtaken MTV—the same baby-faced women, the same surrealistic scenes—and suggests that many of pop music's most talented acts look rather silly as video performers. Brubach, who received her B.A. in English and History from Duke University, writes on fashion and dance. A member of the Dance Critics Association, she is a fashion editor at the New Yorker *and has written for publications such as* Mademoiselle, Atlantic, Ballet Review, *and the* New York Times Book Review.

The first video shown on MTV, or Music Television . . . was a song called "Video Killed the Radio Star," by the Buggles. The title was wishful thinking, a prophecy that rock-and-roll singers who couldn't hold the camera's attention would go the way of silent-movie actors with cartoon-character voices. Anyone who took the lyrics at their word and assumed that this new form posed a threat to pure music had only to look at the video itself, which showed the Buggles in an airless, all-white TV studio, surrounded by a lot of futuristic-looking synthesizers and state-of-the-art equipment, lip-synching their hearts out. Every now and again a girl in a tight skirt and spike heels (all the women in music videos wear spike heels) wandered across the screen. That was it. Radio stars had nothing to fear here.

Since then music videos have come a long way, though not nearly far enough. Videos now play a large part in selling records, and singers are under pressure from their record companies to make videos, just as fifteen years ago they were obliged to go on tour. Even Dean Martin has gotten into the act, sitting poolside in his tuxedo and singing "Since I Met You Baby."

"Beat It," made in 1983, wasn't the first good video, but it may have been the first great one. Michael Jackson epitomizes the form at its best—intense and brief. "Beat It" is one of the few videos that actually improve on their songs, which is what a video ought to do, and the song is pretty good to begin with. But the music alone lacks the breakneck momentum that the video has. Where the song is merely agitated, the video is all worked up. The lyrics are about macho pride and territorial rights, and Jackson grunts and whoops between the lines, accompanying himself. We watch members of two rival gangs leave their hangouts, a sleazy luncheonette and a pool hall, and head for the scene of a fight, a warehouse loading dock. The video cuts back and forth from one gang to the other to Jackson. He stops by the luncheonette, slams the doors open—empty—does a little dance at the counter, a preview of what's to come, and then heads on out. The camera cuts pick up speed and the suspense builds until we finally arrive at the big number. When Jackson comes bouncing down a flight of stairs, snapping his fingers double time, breaking up a knife fight like an agent of divine intervention through dance, we feel like cheering. He parts the gangs, steps to the front, and bursts out dancing, and the tough guys fall in behind, in a finale that goes to show how much better a place the world would be if everybody danced.

"Beat It" was a breakthrough. Slick and well made, dramatic, concise, it showed everybody how good music videos could be and inspired a long line of imitations. Suddenly all the people on MTV were dancing, whether they could or not. There was "Uptown Girl," with Billy Joel and the Lockers, set in a garage. Stevie Nicks galumphed her way through "If Anyone Falls." A big finale was part of the formula. Donna Summer belted "She Works Hard for the Money" from a fire escape overlooking the street, where a squadron of waitresses, nurses, cleaning ladies, and lady cops rolled their hips and churned a dance routine in unison. Bob Giraldi, who directed "Beat It," went on to make Pat Benatar's "Love Is a Battlefield," another video with a miniature plot that culminates in a big dance finish. Benatar leaves home, in what looks like a small town in New Jersey, and rides the bus into Manhattan, where she walks 42nd Street and winds up a hooker—though you would think that she had joined a sorority: the other girls look on indulgently as she writes a letter to her little brother. The finale takes place in a bar, where a sinister-looking Latin type (Gary Chryst, formerly of the Joffrey Ballet) stares Benatar down and provokes her into dancing with him, to no real avail. Benatar is not what you would call a natural dancer. She's concentrating so hard that you can read the choreography as it crosses her mind: shimmy two three four, walk, walk, turn . . . .

Even Michael Jackson went on to plagiarize his own performance in "Beat It" with "Thriller," in which he leads a phalanx of dancing ghouls. Weird Al Yankovic has done a "Beat It" parody, called "Eat It," in which the tough guys wear Happy Face T-shirts and he reproduces Michael Jackson's moves, verbatim.

Aside from "Beat It" and its sequels, there is a certain sameness to music videos. Most are set in a new-wave never-never land, where logic and the law of gravity don't apply. Now that acid rock has given way to coke rock, the corresponding images have gone from psychedelic to surrealistic. A sequence of pictures or events that makes no apparent sense teases the viewer, who keeps watching, waiting for the piece that will explain the entire puzzle; the piece is usually missing. Rooms furnished with a single chair, long billowing curtains, corridors with no exit, empty swimming pools, forests of old gas pumps in the middle of the desert—these are standard features of the landscape, typically lit by a single bare bulb, or a full moon, or the sun's flat brightness.

The women are long-stemmed, with sexy bodies and baby faces. They wear lots of lipstick, leather clothes, and, when their clothes are off, lingerie that makes them look vaguely sadistic. The men are less attractive, but then they're the ones who write the songs.

The vast majority of videos look as if they had been directed by the same two or three people, all of whom you would guess to be seventeen-year-old boys. The screen is overrun with fantasies of wide-open spaces and wicked girls. Parents get their comeuppance. Everyone drives sexy cars—stretch limos, Chevy convertibles, and Thunderbirds. "I'm in love with a working girl," the Members sing, wearing sleeveless black leather jackets and jeans, as they guzzle champagne paid for by gorgeous, expensively dressed career women. In Huey Lewis and the News's "I Want a New Drug" Lewis falls for a pretty fan in the front row, thereby staging his fantasy of what it's like to be a rock-and-roll star and every groupie's fantasy of what could happen at a concert.

Compare these predominantly male notions of a good time with Cyndi Lauper's "Girls Just Want to Have Fun," a *Bye Bye Birdie*–style romp in which she dances up and down the street, sings on the phone to her friends, and throws a party in her room, and men begin to look like an awfully self-important, dull bunch. Whether or not girls just want to have fun, they appear to be the only ones who know how.

Videos divide fairly neatly into two broad categories. The first is   10
performances—either in a studio, where the director has more control and can devise some fancy effects with lights and cameras, or in concert, where the band is seen in its full glory, at the height of an adrenalin rush, in front of a sellout audience going wild. These are some of the dullest, most gratuitous videos on the screen, and they all tend to look alike, even when the monotonous frenzy of the performance is alleviated by intermittent glimpses of beautiful girls or exotic landscapes. Unfortunately, good singers are not necessarily interesting performers, and music videos consistently expose this in a way that concerts, which get by on being events, almost never do. Furthermore, there is probably nothing to redeem a concert video if you don't like the song in the first place. While Def Leppard, a heavy-metal band I am not fitted to appreciate, beats its music to a pulp, there is not much to look at, unless it's the drummer dressed in briefs made out of a Union Jack. The Scorpions

sing "Rock You Like a Hurricane," a song that isn't bad, behind bars, surrounded by an audience. This scene, with the fans getting carried away and shaking the bars in time to the music, is intercut with images of girls in cages. The video ends with the girls and the band members lying down in glass boxes and the lids slamming shut. Despite its use of such loaded images, this video does not purport to mean anything.

Prince and David Bowie are better in concert situations. In "Little Red Corvette" Prince curls his upper lip and half-closes his eyes, coming on to the camera in closeup. This is the kind of shot that a lot of singers attempt but few carry off, and the ones who don't look ludicrous. (David Lee Roth, the lead singer for Van Halen, flexing his pelvis and crawling on all fours toward the camera, should have been saved from himself.) David Bowie, in "Modern Love," doesn't even acknowledge the camera, but he's riveting to watch and sexy without trying to be. With his hollow-cheeked, hungry look and his loose-jointed restlessness he captures the song's nervous energy.

Videos that aren't performances are referred to as "concept" videos, which may be giving a lot of directors the benefit of the doubt. Nearly all concept videos include shots of the singer singing, but they differ from performance videos in that there's something else going on and the goings-on dominate the video. Some concepts are better than others, and some are pretty obscure. You wonder, for instance, why there is a gymnast vaulting over and around video monitors on which Asia is seen singing "Only Time Will Tell." A lot of the weakest videos on MTV seem to be the work of so-called visual people who are careful not to let their minds get in the way of their creativity.

The more successful concept videos are those that are based, however loosely, on a plot: There are characters, a situation is established, and something happens. Bowie's "China Girl," a fairly straightforward love story, is a good example. One of the most common devices is to follow two parallel plots simultaneously, cutting from one to the other, until they come together in the final scene. Elton John's "That's Why They Call It the Blues" does this, keeping track of a boy in boot camp and his girl back home; in the end the sweethearts are reunited. In the Rolling Stones' "Undercover" the action alternates between a suburban rec room, where a teenage couple sits watching TV, and some Central American-looking country in the throes of violent revolution, where a truck drives into a cathedral and a man is marched onto a bridge and shot. These two stories converge in the rec room when the girl's parents walk in on her and her boyfriend making out: The father is wearing an army general's uniform. In the alternative version of this two-track plot the camera cuts from a story or a dramatic situation to the band playing and in the end the band steps into the plot. Even when there's a story to be told, it seems, rock bands insist on being the stars of their own videos.

The few exceptions are notable. Bruce Springsteen's "Atlantic City" serves as the soundtrack for a series of desolate black-and-white scenes in which no one, not even Springsteen, appears. One of the most inventive music videos to date is Barnes and Barnes's "Fish Heads," an offbeat, amusing, unpretentious sequence of events that dignifies a silly song ("You can ask fish heads anything you want to; They won't answer, they can't talk"). No description of these scenes of real fish heads dressed in miniature turtleneck sweaters, propped up in plush theater seats or gathered around a table at a birthday party, can do this bizarre gem justice. "Fish Heads" proves that imagination can take a video a long way, further than closeup shots of celebrity singers or an elaborate, high-budget production can.

Some videos are up to nothing more than entertainment, song-and-dance sales pitches to the camera. ABC, a band with a reputation for inventive video productions, is mastering this form: In "Look of Love" its members roam around a bright-colored fantasyland version of Central Park—steep rolling hills, bridges, and lampposts squeezed onto a tiny sound stage—with such ingenuous conviction that you expect Danny Kaye to turn up and join in. 15

After watching a lot of music videos, it's hard to escape the conclusions that no one has the nerve to say no to a rock-and-roll star and that most videos would be better if someone did. A lot of these people ought to be told that they're not irresistible, or that they can't dance, or that their concept is dumb. Culture Club, for instance, makes dopey videos that do its music, which is pleasant and intelligent, a disservice.

Good videos work for various reasons. Despite the conventions that exist already, there is no surefire formula, but the fact remains that dancing can make a video take off. This happens when the choreography is decent and well shot, the performance is good, and the images are edited according to the rhythm of the song. But it doesn't happen often enough. Judging from most music videos, you would think that dance on television hadn't come very far. Toni Basil is considered one of the best rock-and-roll choreographers. But her cheerleading routine in "Mickey" doesn't look any better than my memories of *Shindig* and *Hullabaloo.*

The mystery is why music videos aren't enlisting the best talents in dance today. We know that more interesting possibilities for choreography to rock music exist and that they are surprisingly varied, because we've seen them on stage, in works by Twyla Tharp, William Forsythe, Marta Renzi, Karole Armitage, and others. Twyla Tharp's choreography for *The Golden Section,* set to the marked rhythms of David Byrne's music, has a jittery lyricism. In *Love Songs,* at the Joffrey Ballet, William Forsythe lays bare the obsession and violence inherent in love relations, with highly dramatic choreography that alternates between tender gestures and brutal attacks, set to a score of songs by Aretha Franklin and Dionne Warwick. By comparison the choreography in music videos looks tame and stale.

If this new form is going to justify itself, it might well be by giving us dance performances that we can't see anywhere else. Though it looks to me as if there is more dancing in recent music videos, it's astonishing how slow directors have been to catch on to the thrill of watching somebody like Mick Jagger or Michael Jackson cut loose to a good song.

In "Going to a Go-Go" Mick Jagger makes a spectacle of himself,   20 and it's the spectacle that is impossible to turn away from. You marvel at how he manages to look so magnificently peculiar and ridiculous. He slithers along, sticking his neck out, jerking his knees in a hyperactive, Egyptian-looking style of movement. It's hard to believe that anyone can be so completely uninhibited in front of an audience. Jagger furthers his songs by losing himself in his music.

Michael Jackson never lets go the way Mick Jagger does, but watching him is a more kinesthetic experience. The audience gets keyed up, waiting for the dancing that is his release. Unlike Fred Astaire or Peter Martins, Michael Jackson doesn't feign effortlessness. He has taken the concertgoer's urge to tap his foot in response to good music and the willpower it takes to keep that urge in check and magnified the tug-of-war between them, so that you can see it all over his body: This is the basis of his performance. When he can't contain the music inside him any longer, he blurts out the steps that have been building up for the past eight or sixteen bars.

It looks as if Michael Jackson has only ten or twelve steps in his repertory and the rest are variations on those. Even so, his ten steps are better than most dancers' whole vocabularies. One is a staccato kick, a chest-high punch with his foot. Another is a special way of snapping his fingers, with a sideways flick of the wrist, as if he were dealing cards. Another is a high-speed spin: He crosses his knees, wraps one foot around the other, and turns to unwind his legs. His dancing owes something to break dancing, robotics, and mime, but his style is more sophisticated than any of these.

Performances like his are all too rare. You tune in to MTV for a few minutes and you're still there two hours later, seduced by the rapid turnover into hoping that the next video will be a good one. It isn't long before you've grown weary of the innumerable scenes that feature a rock-and-roll singer lying on a psychiatrist's couch, intended as an excuse for the fantasies that follow. On the evidence of music videos, most people's wildest dreams come down to the same few basic themes— vanity, greed, debauchery, retaliation, and sex—and the forms they take are disappointingly similar.

Reading the Text

1. Why does Brubach say that "the vast majority of videos look as if they had been directed by the same two or three people"?
2. What are the two categories of video that Brubach describes, and what are the characteristics of each?
3. What, according to Brubach, are the qualities of a "good" video?

Reading the Signs

1. Brubach wrote her essay in 1984. Does her claim that "there is a certain sameness to music videos" apply to videos being produced today? Write an essay in which you argue for or against the applicability of this statement to today's videos, basing your argument on an analysis of specific videos you have seen.
2. In class, brainstorm current videos that fit Brubach's two categories of performance and concept video. Then study your lists to see if her criticisms of these two categories are still valid. If they are, what does that say about evolution of music videos in the last few years? If they aren't, how have videos changed?
3. Brubach asserts that "it's hard to escape the conclusions that no one has the nerve to say no to a rock-and-roll star and that most videos would be better if someone did." Do you think that this statement applies to Madonna and her videos? Write an essay in which you argue whether someone should "just say no" to some of Madonna's videos, basing your essay on specific examples. To develop your essay, you may want to read or review bell hooks's "Madonna: Plantation Mistress or Soul Sister?" (p. 190).
4. Brubach notes that women in most videos exist only as passive sex objects. Write an essay in which you explore the role of women in videos today. What roles do women tend to play? What is their typical physical appearance? What differences, if any, do you see in videos produced by male and female artists? To focus your analysis, you may want to consult Lisa A. Lewis, "Male-Address Video" (p. 182), and Susan Faludi, "Teen Angels and Tart-Tongued Witches" (p. 219).

L I S A   A .   L E W I S
Male-Address Video

*If you've ever gotten the impression that MTV is a veritable fantasy
land for adolescent male desires, then Lisa A. Lewis's "Male-Address
Video" is for you. Analyzing four representative video performances,
Lewis decodes the signs in each, showing how they appeal to teenage
boys, who are invited to identify with the males they see on the screen.
Teenage girls who watch the same videos can only hope to grow up to
be as sexy and desirable as the girls dangled before the guys—or they
can turn off the TV set. A producer as well as media critic, Lisa Lewis
currently is writing screenplays in Los Angeles and has lectured on media
and modern culture at colleges across the nation. She is the author of*
The Adoring Audience: Fan Culture and Popular Media *(1992)
and* Gender Politics and MTV *(1990), from which this selection is
taken.*

MTV's preferred address to male adolescents was executed in individual music videos by making the image of "the street" an overarching
sign system for male-adolescent discourse. To invoke this attachment of
young males to the street, male musicians were shown loitering on
sidewalks, strolling along avenues, and riding in cars. These representations of street-corner activities served to valorize leisure, the arena in
which adolescent boys carve out their own domain. Even when the
physical image of the street was absent from a video, it remained an
implied presence, for as a sign system it summarized perfectly the male-
adolescent quest for adventure, rebellion, sexual encounter, peer relationships, and male privilege. The videos evoked male-adolescent discourse by representing boys' privileged position with respect to their
female peers. Drawing on the connection between male-adolescent license and adult-male rule, the male-address videos activated textual signs
of patriarchal discourse, reproducing coded images of the female body,
and positioning girls and women as the objects of male voyeurism. Both
the image of the female peer (the adolescent girl) and the more mythical
(for boys) image of the adult woman were prominently featured. When
girls appeared, they were not represented as equal participants in the
symbolic system of the street, but functioned as devices to delineate the
male-adolescent discourse. Male-address videos empowered male-adolescent viewers by providing them with a symbolic equation between
the representations of the street and the female body, and their own
privileged access to public space and patriarchal prerogatives.

Four videos from 1983 serve as specific examples of MTV's preferred male-adolescent discourse. As a group, the videos execute male address in distinct and particular ways, with differing levels of implied self-consciousness about the discourse they construct. They contain a limited range of approaches to female representation, and none can be said to present a female point of view on adolescence. The year 1983 is significant because during this year male-address appeared to be on a strong footing as the preferred textual practice, but . . . female-address video was on the verge of coalescence.

"Tender Is the Night"

In Jackson Browne's "Tender Is the Night," the world of the street is developed as a boy's physical and spiritual haven. The video opens with Browne, who plays the protagonist, walking alone at night down a long urban alley. A lengthy photographic shot builds suspense and gives viewers time to contemplate the direction of the narrative line, the video's unfolding point of view. The boy is at ease, self-absorbed. The late hour and the secluded location are not threatening to him. As a male, he commands the street; as an adolescent, he revels in it. Unlike a woman or girl, he is unafraid; unlike a female adolescent, he is not excluded from the aura of the night streets. The corner of an X-rated movie marquee becomes visible in the frame. Its presence in no way alters the boy's route, nor does it make him wary, as it might a girl or woman. This is where the protagonist wants to be, where he feels he belongs.

The boy arrives at the section of street designated visually as "the strip." The production's design and photography add to the street's overall allure, refracting and blurring the neon lights on its wet surface. Colored light washes over cars that cruise the street with deliberate slowness. Lovers are out in full force. The scene glorifies the strip as a symbol of male adolescence, representing the ritualized activities of "stepping out" and "cruising" and the privileges of sexual pursuit and leisure. The video depicts the world of the street as organized by pleasure, spontaneity, free agency, and male desire. The vision is further developed in scenes that oppose the image of street life with images of domestic life. The camera peers in the protagonist's kitchen window to witness him quarreling with his live-in girlfriend (played by Browne's [then] girlfriend, Darryl Hannah). The girl functions as a sign of the adult roles and responsibilities against which adolescence is posed—commitment to a monogamous relationship and a work routine. The couple's quarrel represents not merely an interpersonal conflict, but an enactment of the boy's adolescent rebellion. While he appreciates the "tender" lovemaking that lies at the core of his sentiment for the girl (presented visually in a sensual montage sequence), he balks at the socially prescribed outcome of sexual intimacy—the expectation of exclusivity and the restrictions of marriage. When his relationship with the girl moves toward this "adult" configuration, he wants out. It is the whole culture of the street (of adolescence), the freedom and sexual exploration it affords, that the protagonist finds ultimately more "tender," more physically and spiritually rewarding.

Out on the street, as the video illustrates, girls are easily available,   5
and on less demanding terms. Spontaneous associations spring from car cruising, and even the girls who appear with other boys are not committed to exclusive relationships (as the flirtatious face of one female passenger in a car driven by a boy suggests). The protagonist's castoff girlfriend is forced to resume her position within the male-adolescent discourse. Leaving home after the quarrel, her possessions in hand, she ends up on the street and immediately comes to the attention of a boy who is out cruising in his car. She becomes the object of another male adolescent's spontaneous, commanding, yet fleeting desire. The exchange between the boy in the car and the girl on the street recalls the transaction between a trick and a prostitute; he stops and calls out to her, she approaches the car, they talk, and she gets in.

"Sharp Dressed Man"

An expanded version of the prostitute motif is elaborated in ZZ Top's video "Sharp Dressed Man," in which sexual experimentation in adolescence is linked symbolically to the assumption of adult-male power. The band's members, who wear beards and are themselves too old to play male-adolescent protagonists, assume the collective role of adviser to the male lead. They direct the boy in male-adolescent discourse, guiding him from an innocent and impotent childhood toward a sophisticated and powerful adult-male image.

The boy's innocence and ineffectuality are represented by his service job as a car attendant at an exclusive nightclub, a representation that concurrently emasculates working-class males. He observes male privilege from afar, symbolized by the cars and women of club members. His desire to have what they have, to be what they are, is manifested in his expression of desire for a woman who arrives with one of the members. Magically, the band appears on the scene, rock-and-roll shamans, to lead him to the fulfillment of his desire. They produce the keys to a ruby-red car (the band's trademark), dangling them enticingly before the boy like a symbol of male-adolescent license. Out of the car, step three scantily dressed, "hot" women, their erect nipples visible through their blouses. A photographer immediately takes their picture, affirming their status as objects of the male gaze. As fantastic creations of ZZ Top, the three direct their attentions to the boy. The band members recreate the mythical avuncular role, initiating the boy into manhood by leading him to experienced prostitutes. Sexual experimentation is not only sanctioned but is presented as a fundamental step toward the boy's maturation into manhood.

Only by living out the male-adolescent discourse, by shirking his responsibilities as an employee, going off into the night with a flashy car and lusty women, does he qualify for the previously unattainable woman, and for life as a potent male. Interestingly, the woman who is the boy's object of desire is presented in a visual mode that was developed by female-address videos to reveal female sexual exploitation.[1] Inside the club, she appears bored by and disinterested in her date, is subjected to his roving hands and accelerating harassment, until finally she pours a drink in his lap and leaves. But this is not the woman's story, and the details of her character only serve to further the narrative of the boy's transition to manhood. From the moment the woman makes eye contact with the boy in the parking lot, she is destined by the narrative line and ZZ Top's omnipotent direction to become increasingly dissatisfied with her date and more desirous of the boy. Her rejection of her date is required by the discourse of male adolescence, which asserts the boy's privileged position by showing him attracting a woman who "belongs" to another man.

"Sexy and 17"

Stray Cats' video "Sexy and 17" establishes male-adolescent authority by making the band's members into juvenile delinquents who disrupt the site of social authority most salient for adolescents—the school. The sign system of the street remains an implied presence. The boys challenge their teacher by wearing street attire in the classroom—black leather, T-shirts, sunglasses—nostalgic emblems of male-teen culture from the fifties. The school boys use rock and roll to promote a disreputable image, playing instruments in the hallway and singing, "Hey man, I don't feel like going to school no more!" The prestige the display wins among their peers is demonstrated as the song provokes their classmates to a dancing frenzy.

The central enactment of male-adolescent discourse involves the boys' perceptions of female adolescents. The video reveals the fundamental confusion over who girls are, what they do, what they think

10

---

1. Similar representations occur in Pat Benatar's "Love Is a Battlefield" and Tina Turner's "Private Dancer."

about, and what they want that tacitly permeates the male-adolescent experience. Friendships among girls form a strong social network during their school years, with some friendships even lasting into adulthood. Boys often see girls in groups, and this configuration becomes the subject of speculation and a sphere of conflict within male culture. Male-address videos filter girl friendships through the ideology of male adolescence by including images of girls in groups but then visually suggesting that the configuration is intended to facilitate male sexual experimentation. In both "Sharp Dressed Man" and "Sexy and 17" groups of girls are treated in this way.

Girls' involvement with their looks and make-up is also given the status of a fetish in "Sexy and 17." Female beauty culture is presented as male-inspired and lacks the resonance it attains in female-address videos. "Little Marie," the main object of the protagonist's affections according to the lyrics ("my little rock-and-roll queen"), is photographed in pornographic style as she showers, puts on make-up, and paints her toenails in the "privacy" of her bathroom and dressing room. A close-up shot of her face turned toward the (male) spectator emphasizes her painted lips and eyes. The camera tilts up the length of her legs to reveal her provocative costume—high heels, one fishnet stocking, and bikini panties. The lyric lines, "It's a little bit obscene, got to let off a little steam," attempt to reposition the blatant objectification of the girl within the parameters of normal male adolescence. The song's refrain, "She's sexy and 17," claims the video's voyeuristic stance for all men, not just boys, while at the same time privileging male adolescence as a time of unbounded sexual exploits.

Part of what imbues the boys in "Sexy and 17" with authority is their ability to play rock and roll on stage and make girls dance and feel sexual desire for them. The boys play as a band after school in a scene that allows Stray Cats to perform while maintaining a narrative presence. The fictional band's popularity with the girls at the nightclub comments on Stray Cats' own motivations for playing music—their desire for a cadre of female fans. "Little Marie" jumps up boldly to dance, in a narrative moment that offers female audiences the possibility of exploring female-adolescent pleasures. But as is typical in male-address videos, male pleasure and power take priority, and "Little Marie" is reduced to the role of a groupie, with her pleasure defined in terms of the male point of view. While modes of female adolescence are manifested in her defiant dress and expressions, and in the intensity of her involvement with music and dance, all of these elements are finally made subservient to male discourse. Her independent absorption in dancing alone to rock music is undermined as the protagonist steps in and establishes a firm male lead, throwing her into twirls and twisting dance moves while he remains controlled and essentially motionless.

"Beat It"

Michael Jackson's video "Beat It" presents a contradictory and conflicted portrait of male-adolescent discourse and addresses boys' own doubts about destructive and violent behavior, the discourse's most extreme manifestation. Its representation of an ethnic-male point of view threatens to expose the discourse's racial prejudice, perhaps even open it up to a female sensibility. However, the video is designed to appropriate (white) male-adolescent discourse for black males and leaves the discourse's gender bias intact. By exploring the contradictory recesses of male discourse, "Beat It" approaches a female point of view; but because this is not its main concern, the address to girls is largely mitigated.

In the video, two street gangs (whose numbers include members of real Los Angeles gangs) converge on a warehouse for a stylized fight scene. The textual system of the street, a sign of male-adolescent unity, has broken down under the scrutiny of an "authentic" ethnic environment. Instead, Jackson's street is the site of territorial disputes and male competition. Danger is present, and the potential destruction of the fictional gang members is a clear possibility. The gang members themselves are studies in (and provide lessons in) black-male affectation. Expertly they control their body language, attitude, and overall appearance; their faces are drawn and intensely serious. Their every gesture is calculated and aggressive—a flipped cigarette, snapped fingers, slaps on the back, exaggerated gaits. Each boy dresses "thickly," in leather: hats, headbands, chains, insignias, jeans; as a group they are individually, yet cohesively, styled. Together, they create tremendous presence, an air of indomitable power. The song's lyrical content, in the context of the narrative, is addressed to viewers who feel that they are outside the gangs' powerful community: whites, boys who have been unable to command gang membership or who are the objects of torment by gangs, and all girls and women.

> They told you don't you ever come around here,
> Don't want to see your face,
> You better disappear,
> The fire's in their eyes,
> Their voice is really clear,
> So beat it, just beat it.

Jackson does not play a gang member, but has a complex and contradictory role in the video. His words to the audience invoke the many issues of power and powerlessness, authority and lack of authority, blackness and whiteness, and maleness and femaleness. As the video's narrator, he tells viewers how to feel about the gangs and their slow convergence on one another for a violent showdown. As a character, his intervention in the action determines its crucial resolution. Yet at the video's start his character is presented visually as weak and ineffectual. He lies on a bed in his bedroom. His thin, nearly scrawny physique is in marked contrast to the gang members' size and weight. Appearing within domestic space, lying across his bed, Jackson has none of the street presence of the gang members, and is linked visually to the feminine. Lying on the bed, "speaking" about the gangs' threats, the boy appears to be a victim. But as he rises from the bed, his anger swells, and he begins to assume a position of strength and superiority. The lyrics he speaks to the camera begin to analyze the gangs' psychological and social motivations, relating their terrorism to the discourse of masculinity and adolescence, and to the social reality of black urban existence.

> Don't want to be a boy,
> You want to be a man,
> You want to stay alive,
> Better do what you can,
> You have to show them
> —that you're really not scared.

The transition to manhood, the lyrics imply, is bound up with the necessity to display courage, force, and an ability to dominate. The lyrics, juxtaposed with the intensely male affectation of the gang members, serve to create a context for their actions. The line "You have to show them that you're really not scared" creates an ambiguous address. The "you" addresses those who are afraid—according to the narrative, those who fear gang violence. But because fear is an emotion that defines female existence, it may be easily appropriated by female audiences. The "you" also refers to the gang members who fight and allows the video to explain their violent behavior within the context of (black) male ideology, even to suggest that despite appearances and dictates, they too live in fear. Such ambiguity opens the video to a number of viewer perspectives and creates a critical space for evaluating the male-adolescence discourse as represented in the gang members' rule of the street.

Yet as the video unfolds, male-adolescent discourse is upheld through Jackson's actions, costuming, and attitude as the protagonist. He goes to the gangs' "hangouts," the pool hall and the diner, to head off the confrontation. He knows their turf and is not afraid to enter. Once inside, his anger, which remained contained in the bedroom scene, is unleashed. He begins to dance aggressively with clenched fists and kicks, the implied violence that the gangs themselves practice. His own style statement functions to give him an air of command and charisma, thus aligning him with the gang members and particularly with their leaders. Although the color of his red leather jacket can be seen as a sign of his association with the feminine (blood, menstruation), its fabric and styling are the same as the gang members' jackets. He goes to the warehouse ostensibly to stop the gangs from fighting, to intercede in the male-adolescent discourse; but once there, he becomes their new leader. Both gangs begin to move to his dance, the new rhythm he establishes, just as previously they had followed the rhythm of their respective gang leaders. He succeeds in interrupting the fight, but in the process forms an even larger, more unified gang. He effectively eliminates the violent male competition that had threatened to undo the male-adolescent discourse, and thus preserves the discourse itself. The black-male adolescent fantasy of rising above the threat of the gang, even of joining their ranks, is also satisfied.

For girls who identify with Jackson's articulation of fear, there is greater ambiguity. Aside from Jackson's own androgynous nod to female viewers, the only female representation in the video is of one gang member's adoring girlfriend, whose head is yanked back by the hair so that he may kiss her before leaving for the fight. Compared to *West Side Story,* from which the video's visual motif of gang warfare appears to have been lifted, "Beat It"'s portrayal of female participation in and around male-adolescent discourse is practically nonexistent.

The four videos described move from the uncritical, naturalized male-adolescent discourse of "Tender Is the Night" to the overtly symbolic treatment of male adolescence in "Sharp Dressed Man" to the nostalgic, comic portrayal of juvenile delinquency and the confused, somewhat vicious representation of female adolescence in "Sexy and 17" to the more serious, fractured vision of male adolescence in "Beat It." Other male-address videos on MTV in 1983 executed the address differently, selecting other "workable" representations, but in the end all were united by a central focus on articulating adolescence within the context of male-adolescent experience and sexual desire.

Reading the Text

1. What does Lewis mean by "male-address video"?
2. How, according to Lewis, does the "street" function as a sign for adolescent males?
3. In the four videos that Lewis describes, what roles do women play?
4. Summarize the range of male-adolescent discourse as seen in the four videos that Lewis analyzes.

Reading the Signs

1. Lewis assumes that music videos predominantly address male adolescents as their audience. To what extent is this assumption valid for videos today?

Write an essay in which you explore the implied audience of current videos, basing your argument on specific examples of videos you have seen.

2. Read or review Holly Devor's "Gender Role Behaviors and Attitudes" (p. 605). Using her selection as your critical framework, write an essay in which you explain to what extent the four videos that Lewis analyzes illustrate traditional gender roles.

3. If your school has the necessary equipment, have a class member tape some current videos and replay them in class. Divide the class into small same-sex groups, and discuss whether the videos are "male-address" and what gender roles you see in them. Then share your conclusions with the whole class. What differences, if any, are there in the conclusions drawn by male and female groups?

4. Compare Lewis's analysis of Michael Jackson's "Beat It" with Holly Brubach's comments on the same video (p. 175). Which do you find more persuasive?

5. Lewis suggests that a minority of videos are "female-address." What would such videos be like? In your journal, first freewrite on the probable characteristics of female-address videos, then write an essay in which you apply your definition of female-address videos to videos you have seen. If you have trouble thinking of any female-address videos, write about why that may be the case.

b e l l   h o o k s

Madonna: Plantation Mistress or Soul Sister?

||||||||||||||||||||||||||||||||||||||||||||||||||||

Through such videos as "Like a Prayer," Madonna has established a reputation for being a friend to black America. bell hooks isn't so sure. In this critique of Madonna's career she shows how often the material girl has exploited racial stereotypes in her rebellion against middle-class sexual codes. Using "the black female body as a sign of sexual experience," hooks argues, Madonna at once insults and exploits black women and men. And like a contemporary Shirley Temple, hooks continues, Madonna domineers over the black dancers she employs in her videos, keeping them in their place and making sure that she is never upstaged by them. bell hooks (the pen name of Gloria Watkins; b. 1952) is the author of Black Looks: Race and Representation *(1992), from which this selection is taken, and numerous other books, including* Talking Back: Thinking Feminist, Thinking Black *(1989). She is a professor in the departments of English and Women's Studies at Oberlin College.*

Subversion is contextual, historical, and above all social. No matter how exciting the "destabilizing" potential of texts, bodily or otherwise, whether those texts are subversive or recuperative or both or neither cannot be determined by abstraction from actual social practice.
— SUSAN BORDO

White women "stars" like Madonna, Sandra Bernhard, and many others publicly name their interest in, and appropriation of, black culture as yet another sign of their radical chic. Intimacy with that "nasty" blackness good white girls stay away from is what they seek. To white and other nonblack consumers, this gives them a special flavor, an added spice. After all it is a very recent historical phenomenon for any white girl to be able to get some mileage out of flaunting her fascination and envy of blackness. The thing about envy is that it is always ready to destroy, erase, take over, and consume the desired object. That's exactly what Madonna attempts to do when she appropriates and commodifies aspects of black culture. Needless to say this kind of fascination is a threat. It endangers. Perhaps that is why so many of the grown black women I spoke with about Madonna had no interest in her as a cultural icon and said things like, "The bitch can't even sing." It was only among young black females that I could find die-hard Madonna fans. Though I often admire and, yes at times, even envy Madonna because she has created a cultural space where she can invent and reinvent herself and receive public affirmation and material reward, I do not consider myself a Madonna fan.

Once I read an interview with Madonna where she talked about her envy of black culture, where she stated that she wanted to be black as a child. It is a sign of white privilege to be able to "see" blackness and black culture from a standpoint where only the rich culture of opposition black people have created in resistance marks and defines us. Such a perspective enables one to ignore white supremacist domination and the hurt it inflicts via oppression, exploitation, and everyday wounds and pains. White folks who do not see black pain never really understand the complexity of black pleasure. And it is no wonder then that when they attempt to imitate the joy in living which they see as the "essence" of soul and blackness, their cultural productions may have an air of sham and falseness that may titillate and even move white audiences yet leave many black folks cold.

Needless to say, if Madonna had to depend on masses of black women to maintain her status as cultural icon she would have been dethroned some time ago. Many of the black women I spoke with expressed intense disgust and hatred of Madonna. Most did not respond to my cautious attempts to suggest that underlying those negative feelings might lurk feelings of envy, and dare I say it, desire. No black woman I talked to declared that she wanted to "be Madonna." Yet we have only to look at the number of black women entertainers/stars (Tina Turner, Aretha Franklin, Donna Summer, Vanessa Williams, Yo-Yo, etc.) who gain greater crossover recognition when they demonstrate that, like Madonna, they too, have a healthy dose of "blonde ambition." Clearly their careers have been influenced by Madonna's choices and strategies.

For masses of black women, the political reality that underlies Madonna's and our recognition that this is a society where "blondes" not only "have more fun" but where they are more likely to succeed in any endeavor is white supremacy and racism. We cannot see Madonna's change in hair color as being merely a question of aesthetic choice. I agree with Julie Burchill in her critical work *Girls on Film,* when she reminds us: "What does it say about racial purity that the best blondes have all been brunettes (Harlow, Monroe, Bardot)? I think it says that we are not as white as we think. I think it says that Pure is a Bore." I also know that it is the expressed desire of the nonblonde Other for those characteristics that are seen as the quintessential markers of racial aesthetic superiority that perpetuate and uphold white supremacy. In this sense Madonna has much in common with the masses of black women who suffer from internalized racism and are forever terrorized by a standard of beauty they feel they can never truly embody.

Like many black women who have stood outside the culture's fascination with the blonde beauty and who have only been able to reach it through imitation and artifice, Madonna often recalls that she was a working-class white girl who saw herself as ugly, as outside the mainstream beauty standard. And indeed what some of us like about her is the way she deconstructs the myth of "natural" white girl beauty by exposing the extent to which it can be and is usually artificially constructed and maintained. She mocks the conventional racist-defined beauty ideal even as she rigorously strives to embody it. Given her obsession with exposing the reality that the ideal female beauty in this society can be attained by artifice and social construction, it should come as no surprise that many of her fans are gay men, and that the majority of nonwhite men, particularly black men, are among that group. Jennie Livingston's film *Paris Is Burning* suggests that many black gay men, especially queens/divas, are as equally driven as Madonna by "blonde ambition." Madonna never lets her audience forget that whatever "look" she acquires is attained by hard work—"it ain't natural." And as Burchill comments in her chapter "Homosexual Girls":

> I have a friend who drives a cab and looks like a Marlboro Man but at night is the second best Jean Harlow I have ever seen. He summed up the kind of film star he adores, brutally and brilliantly, when he said, "I like actresses who look as if they've spent hours putting themselves together—and even then they don't look right."

Certainly no one, not even die-hard Madonna fans, ever insists that her beauty is not attained by skillful artifice. And indeed, a major point of the documentary film *Truth or Dare: In Bed With Madonna* was to demonstrate the amount of work that goes into the construction of her image. Yet when the chips are down, the image Madonna most exploits is that of the quintessential "white girl." To maintain that image she must always position herself as an outsider in relation to black culture. It is that position of outsider that enables her to colonize and appropriate black experience for her own opportunistic ends even as she attempts to mask her acts of racist aggression as affirmation. And no other group sees that as clearly as black females in this society. For we have always known that the socially constructed image of innocent white womanhood relies on the continued production of the racist/sexist sexual myth that black women are not innocent and never can be. Since we are coded always as "fallen" women in the racist cultural iconography we can never, as can Madonna, publicly "work" the image of ourselves as innocent female daring to be bad. Mainstream culture always reads the black female body as sign of sexual experience. In part, many black women who are disgusted by Madonna's flaunting of sexual experience are enraged because the very image of sexual agency that she is able to project and affirm with material gain has been the stick this society has used to justify its continued beating and assault on the black female body. The vast majority of black women in the United States, more concerned with projecting images of respectability than with the idea of female sexual agency and transgression, do not often feel we have the "freedom" to act in rebellious ways in regards to sexuality without being punished. We have only to contrast the life story of Tina Turner with that of Madonna to see the different connotations "wild" sexual agency has when it is asserted by a black female. Being represented publicly as an active sexual being has only recently enabled Turner to gain control over her life and career. For years the public image of aggressive sexual agency Turner projected belied the degree to which she was sexually abused and exploited privately. She was also materially exploited. Madonna's career could not be all that it is if there were no Tina Turner and yet, unlike her cohort Sandra Bernhard, Madonna never articulates the cultural debt she owes black females.

In her most recent appropriations of blackness, Madonna almost always imitates phallic black masculinity. Although I read many articles which talked about her appropriating male codes, no critic seems to have noticed her emphasis on black male experience. In his *Playboy* profile, "Playgirl of the Western World," Michael Kelly describes Madonna's crotch grabbing as "an eloquent visual put-down of male phallic pride." He points out that she worked with choreographer Vince Paterson to perfect the gesture. Even though Kelly tells readers that Madonna was consciously imitating Michael Jackson, he does not contextualize his interpretation of the gesture to include this act of appropriation from black male culture. And in that specific context the groin grabbing gesture is an assertion of pride and phallic domination that usually takes place in an all-male context. Madonna's imitation of this gesture could just as easily be read as an expression of envy.

Throughout [many] of her autobiographical interviews runs a thread of expressed desire to possess the power she perceives men have. Madonna may hate the phallus, but she longs to possess its power. She is always first and foremost in competition with men to see who has the biggest penis. She longs to assert phallic power, and like every other group in this white supremacist society, she clearly sees black men as embodying a quality of maleness that eludes white men. Hence they are often the group of men she most seeks to imitate, taunting white males with her own version of "black masculinity." When it comes to entertainment rivals, Madonna clearly perceives black male stars like Prince and Michael Jackson to be the standard against which she must measure herself and that she ultimately hopes to transcend.

Fascinated yet envious of black style, Madonna appropriates black culture in ways that mock and undermine, making her presentation one that upstages. This is most evident in the video "Like a Prayer." Though I read numerous articles that discussed public outrage at this video, none focused on the issue of race. No article called attention to the fact that Madonna flaunts her sexual agency by suggesting that she is breaking the ties that bind her as a white girl to white patriarchy, and establishing ties with black men. She, however, and not black men, does the choosing. The message is directed at white men. It suggests that they only labeled black men rapists for fear that white girls would choose black partners over them. Cultural critics commenting on the video did not seem at all interested in exploring the reasons Madonna chooses a black cultural backdrop for this video, i.e., black church and religious experience. Clearly, it was this backdrop that added to the video's controversy.

In her commentary in the *Washington Post,* "Madonna: Yuppie Goddess," Brooke Masters writes: "Most descriptions of the controversial video focus on its Catholic imagery: Madonna kisses a black saint, and develops Christ-like markings on her hands. However, the video is also a feminist fairy tale. Sleeping Beauty and Snow White waited for their princes to come along, Madonna finds her own man and wakes him up." Notice that this writer completely overlooks the issue of race and gender. That Madonna's chosen prince was a black man is in part what made the representation potentially shocking and provocative to a white supremacist audience. Yet her attempt to exploit and transgress traditional racial taboos was rarely commented on. Instead critics concentrated on whether or not she was violating taboos regarding religion and representation.

In the United States, Catholicism is most often seen as a religion that has [few] or no black followers and Madonna's video certainly perpetuates this stereotype with its juxtaposition of images of black non-Catholic representations with the image of the black saint. Given the

10

importance of religious experience and liberation theology in black life, Madonna's use of this imagery seemed particularly offensive. For she made black characters act in complicity with her as she aggressively flaunted her critique of Catholic manners, her attack on organized religion. Yet, no black voices that I know of came forward in print calling attention to the fact that the realm of the sacred that is mocked in this film is black religious experience, or that this appropriative "use" of that experience was offensive to many black folk. Looking at the video with a group of students in my class on the politics of sexuality where we critically analyze the way race and representations of blackness are used to sell products, we discussed the way in which black people in the video are caricatures reflecting stereotypes. They appear grotesque. The only role black females have in this video is to catch (i.e., rescue) the "angelic" Madonna when she is "falling." This is just a contemporary casting of the black female as Mammy. Made to serve as supportive backdrop for Madonna's drama, black characters in "Like a Prayer" remind one of those early Hollywood depictions of singing black slaves in the great plantation movies or those Shirley Temple films where Bojangles was trotted out to dance with Miss Shirley and spice up her act. Audiences were not supposed to be enamored of Bojangles, they were supposed to see just what a special little old white girl Shirley really was. In her own way Madonna is a modern day Shirley Temple. Certainly her expressed affinity with black culture enhances her value.

Eager to see the documentary *Truth or Dare* because it promised to focus on Madonna's transgressive sexual persona, which I find interesting, I was angered by her visual representations of her domination over not white men (certainly not over Warren Beatty or Alek Keshishian), but people of color and white working-class women. I was too angered by this to appreciate other aspects of the film I might have enjoyed. In *Truth or Dare* Madonna clearly revealed that she can only think of exerting power along very traditional, white supremacist, capitalistic, patriarchal lines. That she made people who were dependent on her for their immediate livelihood submit to her will was neither charming nor seductive to me or the other black folks that I spoke with who saw the film. We thought it tragically ironic that Madonna would choose as her dance partner a black male with dyed blonde hair. Perhaps had he appeared less like a white-identified black male consumed by "blonde ambition" he might have upstaged her. Instead he was positioned as a mirror, into which Madonna and her audience could look and see only a reflection of herself and the worship of "whiteness" she embodies— that white supremacist culture wants everyone to embody. Madonna used her power to ensure that he and the other nonwhite women and men who worked for her, as well as some of the white subordinates, would all serve as the backdrop to her white-girl-makes-good-drama. Joking about the film with other black folks, we commented that

Madonna must have searched long and hard to find a black female that was not a good dancer, one who would not deflect attention away from her. And it is telling that when the film directly reflects something other than a positive image of Madonna, the camera highlights the rage this black female dancer was suppressing. It surfaces when the "subordinates" have time off and are "relaxing."

As with most Madonna videos, when critics talk about this film they tend to ignore race. Yet no viewer can look at this film and not think about race and representation without engaging in forms of denial. After choosing a cast of characters from marginalized groups—nonwhite folks, heterosexual and gay, and gay white folks—Madonna publicly describes them as "emotional cripples." And of course in the context of the film this description seems borne out by the way they allow her to dominate, exploit, and humiliate them. Those Madonna fans who are determined to see her as politically progressive might ask themselves why it is she completely endorses those racist/sexist/classist stereotypes that almost always attempt to portray marginalized groups as "defective." Let's face it, by doing this, Madonna is not breaking with any white supremacist, patriarchal status quo; she is endorsing and perpetuating it.

Some of us do not find it hip or cute for Madonna to brag that she has a "fascistic side," a side well documented in the film. Well, we did not see any of her cute little fascism in action when it was Warren Beatty calling her out in the film. No, there the image of Madonna was the little woman who grins and bears it. No, her "somebody's got to be in charge side," as she names it, was most expressed in her interaction with those representatives from marginalized groups who are most often victimized by the powerful. Why is it there is little or no discussion of Madonna as racist or sexist in her relation to other women? Would audiences be charmed by some rich white male entertainer telling us he must "play father" and oversee the actions of the less powerful, especially women and men of color? So why did so many people find it cute when Madonna asserted that she dominates the interracial casts of gay and heterosexual folks in her film because they are crippled and she "like[s] to play mother." No, this was not a display of feminist power, this was the same old phallic nonsense with white pussy at the center. And many of us watching were not simply unmoved—we were outraged.

Perhaps it is a sign of a collective feeling of powerlessness that many   15
black, nonwhite, and white viewers of this film who were disturbed by the display of racism, sexism, and heterosexism (yes, it's possible to hire gay people, support AIDS projects, and still be biased in the direction of phallic patriarchal heterosexuality) in *Truth or Dare* have said so little. Sometimes it is difficult to find words to make a critique when we find ourselves attracted by some aspect of a performer's act and disturbed by others, or when a performer shows more interest in promoting progressive social causes than is customary. We may see that performer as above

critique. Or we may feel our critique will in no way intervene on the worship of them as a cultural icon.

To say nothing, however, is to be complicit with the very forces of domination that make "blonde ambition" necessary to Madonna's success. Tragically, all that is transgressive and potentially empowering to feminist women and men about Madonna's work may be undermined by all that it contains that is reactionary and in no way unconventional or new. It is often the conservative elements in her work converging with the status quo that have the most powerful impact. For example: Given the rampant homophobia in this society and the concomitant heterosexist voyeuristic obsession with gay life-styles, to what extent does Madonna progressively seek to challenge this if she insists on primarily representing gays as in some way emotionally handicapped or defective? Or when Madonna responds to the critique that she exploits gay men by cavalierly stating: "What does exploitation mean? . . . In a revolution, some people have to get hurt. To get people to change, you have to turn the table over. Some dishes get broken."

I can only say this doesn't sound like liberation to me. Perhaps when Madonna explores those memories of her white working-class childhood in a troubled family in a way that enables her to understand intimately the politics of exploitation, domination, and submission, she will have a deeper connection with oppositional black culture. If and when this radical critical self-interrogation takes place, she will have the power to create new and different cultural productions, work that will be truly transgressive—acts of resistance that transform rather than simply seduce.

Reading the Text

1. Why does hooks call Madonna's claim that she wanted to be black as a child a "sign of white privilege"?
2. Why does hooks believe that Madonna mocks and thereby denigrates black style and culture?
3. How, according to hooks, does "blondeness" function as a sign in American culture?

Reading the Signs

1. While Madonna has a reputation for being revolutionary, hooks asserts that Madonna often endorses and perpetuates a "white supremacist, patriarchal status quo." Write an essay in which you support, challenge, or modify hooks's position, being sure to base your essay on *Truth or Dare* or on specific Madonna videos you have seen.

2. Rent Madonna's *Immaculate Collection* videotape, and watch "Like a Prayer."
   Do you agree or disagree with hooks's analysis of it?
3. In class, brainstorm other examples of white artists who have appropriated
   black culture as signs of their "radical chic." Then discuss whether these
   other artists have thus mocked and undermined black culture, as hooks says
   Madonna has done. To shape your discussion, read first Sam Fulwood III's
   "The Rage of the Black Middle Class" (p. 462).
4. In your journal, explore an answer to hooks's question "Why is it there is
   little or no discussion of Madonna as racist or sexist in her relation to other
   women?"
5. Read or review Seth Mydans's "Not Just the Inner City: Well-to-Do Join
   Gangs" (p. 587). How might hooks explain suburban kids' imitation of
   gang culture?

MINABERE IBELEMA

Identity Crisis: The African Connection in African American Sitcom Characters

||||||||||||||||||||||||||||||||||||||||||||||||||||||||

*In recent years, American television has included more and more positive
images of black Americans—especially in such megahits as* The Cosby
Show—*but how well has it represented the African heritage of African-
Americans? In this essay, Minabere Ibelema (b. 1952) studies some
episodes from such sitcoms as* Sanford and Son *and* Diff'rent Strokes
*and concludes that TV has not simply done a poor job of it but has
actively downplayed the African-ness of black Americans to encourage
blacks to adopt Euro-American values. Cultural assimilation, not cultural exploration, seems to be television's agenda, Minabere suggests in
this semiotic reading of black sitcoms. Minabere Ibelema is an associate
professor of journalism at Eastern Illinois University.*

Besides concerns with representation and coverage, studies and critical appraisal of African Americans in the media have focused on their
portrayal from the early years of film at the turn of the century, through
radio a few decades later, to television in the 1980s. The thrust of these
studies is that their portrayal has been negative and stereotypical.[1] Among

---

1. Among the studies and reports on stereotypical portrayals are: Thomas Cripps,
Slow Fade to Black: The Negro in American Film (1900–1942) (New York: Oxford Uni-

the stereotypes identified by critics and researchers are the shiftless Negro, the happy-go-lucky singer/dancer, the street-smart hustler, the buffoon, the fat, docile mammy, the matriarch, and the lecherous black man.[2]

These stereotypes have evolved through the various media and apparently reflect deep-rooted societal attitudes towards African Americans. Some scholars have traced some of the stereotypes to Euro-American perception of Africans and African culture. Anthropologist Elliot P. Skinner, for instance, sees a link between the negative portrayal of Africa and the views held of black Americans by white Americans. "This portrayal has meaning for American society in that the presence of blacks in America serves to underscore the supportive myths about Africa," Skinner has been quoted as saying. If this is the case, then the portrayal of African Americans in relation to their African cultural identity may be revealing of the nature and impetus of media stereotyping.

But in spite of the potential insight, little has been done to examine the overt portrayal of blacks in the media with regard to their expression or projection of identity with African culture. Even studies and critical appraisals of the television program *Roots* glossed over this element apparently because, as a miniseries, it could not have established a pattern from which to draw larger conclusions.[3] This study explores the African connection in the characterization of African Americans by examining how the theme of African cultural identity is dealt with in television situation comedies.

Three specific questions are examined: (1) How frequently is identity with African culture an episodic theme in situation comedies featuring major African American characters? (2) Is development of that theme, taken as a whole, supportive or dissuasive of such identity? And (3) What

versity Press, 1977); United States Civil Rights Commission, "Window Dressing: Women and Minorities in Television" (Washington, D.C.: United States Government Printing Office, 1977); Marilyn Diane Fife, "Black Image in American TV: The First Two Decades," *The Black Scholar* (Nov. 1974), pp. 7–15. Even empirical research that finds that negative black characters are proportionately not greater than negative white characters still conclude that the net effect of portrayal is more negative for blacks. See, for instance, J. L. Hinton et al., "Tokenism and Improving Imagery for Blacks in TV Drama and Comedy: 1973," *Journal of Broadcasting,* 18 (Fall 1974), pp. 423–432.

2. Some of these stereotypes are mentioned in the works cited above and also in Robert Toll, *Black Up: The Minstrel Show in 19th Century America* (New York: Oxford University Press, 1974); H. L. Gates, Jr., "Portraits in Black: From Amos 'n' Andy to Coonskin," *Harper's* (June 1976), pp. 16–19; and Melbourne S. Cummings, "The Changing Image of the Black Family on Television," *Journal of Popular Culture,* 22 (Fall 1988), pp. 75–85.

3. See, for instance, "Forum: Symposium on 'Roots,'" *The Black Scholar* (May 1977), pp. 36–42 and Philip Vandor, "On the Meaning of 'Roots'," *Journal of Communication,* 4 (Fall 1977), pp. 64–69.

theoretical perspectives best explain the supportive or dissuasive portrayal?

Research Methods and Rationale

Situation comedies or "sitcoms" were chosen for this study for several reasons. First, they are the most popular form of programming (*World Almanac,* 357). Second, of all dramatic programs (night and daytime soaps, cop shows, adventure series, mysteries) sitcoms have the highest African American representation (Reid). For instance, compared to other dramatic forms, there have been more sitcom programs that revolve around African American characters. Third, contrary to popular belief, as David Marc notes, sitcoms tend to be more reflective of societal tendencies than any other dramatic form. Given these considerations then, an examination of sitcoms is as good a beginning as any for the study of the subject of this paper.

The programs examined are *Sanford and Son, What's Happening, The Jeffersons, Diff'rent Strokes, Facts of Life,* and *Gimme a Break.* All but one of these programs feature blacks as the main characters. The exception, *Facts of Life,* has one major black character.

Data for this paper were gathered first by perusing the synopses of every episode of the programs. Episodes dealing with racial or ethnic identity were selected and viewed for the critique. Scripts for episodes that for logistical or contractual reasons could not be viewed were obtained and perused. Thus, the research data do not represent casual references to issues of identity; they represent only treatment of the topic as an episodic theme.

Frequency of Identity as Episodic Theme

Very few episodes of the programs explore African American identity with Africa as a primary or secondary storyline. No episode of *Gimme a Break* deals with racial or ethnic identity. Only one episode of *What's Happening* deals with a racial theme[4] and none deals with cultural identity with Africa. *The Jeffersons* has one episode that deals with African ancestry and *Facts of Life* has one on African identity. Another episode of *Facts of Life* explores interracial dating. *Diff'rent Strokes* has one episode dealing directly with African identity and *Sanford and Son* has two.

---

4. That episode was about a case of reverse-reverse discrimination: Dee is denied a place on her school's cheerleading squad in favor of a less deserving white rival, who is chosen to meet racial quotas.

Nature of Portrayal

There is a definite pattern in all the episodes on African or racial identity. First, concern with African identity results from a personal crisis. The African American character does not project his African cultural identity in normal times. Overt awareness and projection are triggered by an event or in moments of self-doubt. Secondly, the character begins to engage in uncharacteristic behavior, rejects most social norms, and acts in exaggeratedly strange ways. In other words, overt awareness and expression of African identity is portrayed as a form of personal revolution and social rebellion. Thirdly, the character is confronted with "evidence" that convinces him that assertion of African identity is not necessary. Fourthly and finally, the character reverts to his old ways, and the identity crisis is over.

One of the two episodes of *Sanford and Son* dealing with African   10
identity is the most illustrative of this pattern of portrayal. In that episode, entitled "Lamont goes African," Lamont Sanford's meeting with a princessly Nigerian woman precipitates a fanatical embrace of his African heritage. He drops the name Lamont in favor of an African name, replaces his Western shirts with "dashiki" and insists that his father, Fred Sanford, not eat sausage because it contains "pig poison." When Lamont comes home for the first time following his cultural conversion and tries to persuade Fred to accept his new identity, the following dialogue ensues:

LAMONT: I'm a black man, right?

FRED: You can say that again. (Laughter)

LAMONT: So I should have a name and a language and clothes that let everybody know I am a black man.

FRED: Listen, people will know you are a black man if your name was Spiro D. Agnew. (Heavy laughter)

LAMONT: We shouldn't even have these names. Do you know any white people with names like Lumumba, or Kasavubu or De Shaka?

FRED: I don't even know no black people with names like that.

LAMONT: That's the point, pop. Black people in America have been cut off from their homeland for so long they don't even know the names of their ancestors.

FRED: My father's name was Sanford, his father's name was Sanford. And their fathers'. We've all been Sanford. Now I've been cut off from my homeland a little over 30 years. (Laughter)

LAMONT: And I suppose that's when your ancestors left Africa, ha?

FRED: No, that's when I left St. Louis. (Heavy laughter)

LAMONT: I'm talking about before that.

FRED: Before that, well, that was ancient history. Don't even bring that up.

LAMONT: Pop, what we called ourselves before we called ourselves Sanford is what is important to black people, because that reflects where we originally came from. And that's why I have chosen a name that leaves no doubt about my origin.

FRED: And what's your original new name?

LAMONT: Kalunda. (Scattered laughter)

FRED: Kaa what? (Laughter)

LAMONT: Kalunda.

FRED: If you think I'm gonna change the sign from Sanford and Son to Sanford and Kalunda, you're crazy. (Laughter) (*Sanford and Son*, "Lamont Goes African," Tandem Productions, 1972.)

After some jesting with the name, Fred said, "It just doesn't sound right for a junk dealer. With a name like that you should be driving an elephant, not a truck" (Heavy laughter).

Fred was unsuccessful in convincing Lamont to shed his new identity, but a subsequent development in the plot did. During a visit by the Nigerian woman, Olaiya, Lamont is irked by Fred's continued skepticism about the "African thing," as Fred calls it, and they both go into a spirited argument. Olaiya is stunned by Lamont's conduct and chastises him for disrespecting his father, a behavior she says is not tolerated in Africa. Before departing, to underscore her disapproval of Lamont's behavior, Olaiya counsels Lamont:

> Brother Kalunda, you have far to go along this path you have chosen for yourself before you reach your destination. Do not mistake Dashiki and sculpture and hairstyle for Africa, because they aren't. Nor can you expect merely to put on that cloth and become such a man as your ancestors were. The clothes you can put on and take off; it is the heart you must change—the heart.

This counsel apparently convinced Lamont that African identity, at least in the forms he was expressing it, was not for him. Soon after Olaiya's departure, Lamont shed his dashiki, and when Fred referred to him as Kalunda, he responded: "The name is Lamont." There was no explicit or implicit commitment by Lamont to "change the heart," and subsequent episodes of the program reflected neither an outward expression that Lamont engaged in nor the inward transformation that Olaiya prescribed.

An episode of *Diff'rent Strokes* entitled "Roots" explores the issue of identity with the same pattern of crisis, resolution, and normalcy. The two black boys living with a benevolent white millionaire take steps to assert their African cultural identity after being told by their Harlem mate that they were getting indoctrinated into white American culture. They suddenly became aware that their adoptive father takes them to ballets and similar elite cultural events, but not to black ones. The boys adopt African names, insist on eating only ethnic dishes, obtain African cultural artifacts, including decorative masks and drums, mount them all over their rooms, and begin to beat their drums to a deafening frenzy, screaming in the tradition of Tarzan movies. After trying in vain to get the boys to moderate their nascent cultural expressiveness, their adoptive father, Mr. Drummond, turns to a black psychologist for help. The psychologist gets Mr. Drummond to admit that he has done little to expose the boys to black culture and influences and to promise to redress that. And he counsels the boys that "blackness isn't just a matter of what you eat or the way you walk or talk. It's the way you think, feel and conduct your life." (Tandem Productions, 1981, *Diff'rent Strokes,* "Roots"). With the family crisis thus resolved, the boys return to normalcy, the masks and drums all gone.

Another example is an episode of *Facts of Life.* Tootie, the black 15 character among a group of white students, has an identity crisis when her segregationist new boyfriend implied that she may be becoming too "white." In the episode entitled "Who Am I?" Tootie begins to assert her cultural differences with her white mates in every way possible. She even refuses to go to a dance contest with a white dance partner with whom she won the contest the previous year and opts instead for her black boyfriend. But during the dance she realizes that the boyfriend is not nearly as good a dancer as her white partner. An ensuing dialogue with the boyfriend convinces Tootie that her nascent concern with her cultural identity is unwarranted. Accordingly, she turns again to her white dance partner and they win the contest again.

The pattern of thematic development in these three episodes is typical of all the episodes dealing with African Americans' identity with their ethnic origin.[5] That is, African American identity with African culture is depicted as a passing fancy that surfaces only in times of cultural identity crisis, rather than as an enduring element of the black psyche. In no episode is the new awareness sustained to the end. In "Lamont Goes African," it is not clear why Olaiya's well-meaning advice to Lamont causes him to abandon his new cultural views. In "Roots," the *Diff'rent Strokes* episode, the adoptive father makes promises to the boys to appease them and so they give up their new cultural commitment— entirely. And in "Who Am I?" Tootie returns to her "normal" ways for very tenuous reasons. The moral of each story seems to be that nascent identity with African culture is an abnormality, and, like most abnormalities, it can be rectified with appropriate measures or in due course.

It is important to emphasize that in no episode is African (or African-American) culture denigrated. In "Lamont Goes African," for instance,

---

5. Participants at a panel of the 1989 Popular Culture Association Conference commented after the presentation of this paper that the sitcoms *Fish* and *Good Times* also have episodes on identity crisis that follow the pattern here.

the Nigerian woman is portrayed as beautiful, intelligent, cultured, and dignified. Even the skeptical Fred ends up trying on the dashiki and owning that there is substance to the "African thing." Nothing in the portrayal could make a strong case of racism, per se. Yet the portrayal of African Americans' cultural identity with Africa as a transient abnormality begs for explanation.

Theoretical Perspectives on Portrayal

The pattern of portrayal identified here bears some resemblance to a theory of identity evolution first postulated by William E. Cross, Jr. Cross posited that African Americans come to terms with their identity through a process involving five stages: The preencounter (or prediscovery) stage, the encounter (or discovery) stage, the immersion-emersion stage, the internalization stage, and the commitment stage. The programs under analysis imply the first stage, specify the second stage, deal rapidly with the third, and reverse the process before it reaches the fourth and fifth stages in which permanent transformation is attained.[6] While Cross states that progression to the final stage is not automatic and, in fact, that some people revert to preencounter characteristics, there is no suggestion that reversion is the dominant or usual tendency. And while there are no figures on the rate at which African Americans come to terms with their identity (internalization-commitment) and it is probably impossible to quantify, studies of groups such as black Moslems suggest that those who have the encounter and immersion experience do not typically revert to their preencounter outlook (see, e.g. Essien-Udom; Porter and Washington). Thus the portrayal of identity with Africa as a transient phenomenon does not seem to have a basis in reality.

There is probably no one theory that exclusively explains the pattern of portrayal identified here, but two theories seem to be the most plausible, namely, media determinism and cultural assimilation. The dictates of the medium and media producers' inherent belief in the soundness and vitality of the American sociopolitical and cultural system seem to be the most plausible explanations for the portrayal.

Marshall McLuhan's notorious aphorism that "The medium is the message" provides a general basis for understanding the constraints of the medium on the message. McLuhan's point, in essence, is that every medium places some parameters within which the messenger must work.

---

6. This writer does not assume that the program producers were aware of Gross's model and actually intended to reflect it in the plots.

For this study, the parameters are those of the medium of the situation comedy.

The format of the sitcom is quite rigid. As Sholle notes, "A look at its structure . . . reveals a fixed form that limits not only possible narratives but possible solutions." Unlike straight dramas, which thrive on what Hollywood calls "cliffhangers," sitcoms have self-contained episodes. Few episodes have storylines that are "To be continued." Therefore, the plot for each episode has to be developed and resolved within the 23 or so minutes of actual body time. That forces a quick resolution to every storyline. And since the episodes are self-contained, writers avoid leaving "unfinished businesses" which will affect the storylines of other episodes. They are especially careful not to introduce a new situation to the situation comedy. That explains, for instance, why Rebecca never goes to bed with Sam (in *Cheers*), and Fred and Lamont always lose whatever wealth comes their way. If Lamont had not abandoned his nascent Africanness, for instance, the "situation" of *Sanford and Son* would have changed in a way that would have affected future storylines.

In regular drama there is continuity in story line. For that reason, a theme introduced in one episode is likely to remain with the show indefinitely or for several episodes. In contrast, sitcom episodes tend to be independent of each other. The characters and their situation are the elements of continuity. The storylines are not. The sitcom medium, thus, limits the options for ending its episodes.

Also, since sitcoms thrive on exaggeration, the exaggerated behavior of the transformed characters may be attributed to the medium. In this case, the exaggeration provides a justification for treating the new identity as a passing crisis. Thus the medium not only prescribes the nature of characterization but also justifies a particular resolution.

However, though exaggeration is a common element of comedy, it is not an essential one. As Mel Watkins has noted, for instance, traditional African-American comedy derives more from nuances of delivery than [from] punchlines. Producers and writers in the programs here did not have to resort to exaggeration. Also, though the medium limits options for ending episodes, it does not specify them. Thus, producers who have reason to modify characters or situations still do so. Therefore, neither the whimsical element of comedy nor the constraint of sitcom plots satisfactorily explains the portrayal of African identity as transient.

A more cogent explanation of the depiction is the media's tendency 25 to portray mainstream American values and tradition as all-serving and self-redeeming. Lee Loevinger's "reflective-projective theory" of mass communication explains this tendency. Loevinger "postulates that mass communications are best understood as mirrors of society that reflect an ambiguous image in which each observer projects or sees his own version of himself and society" (252). Loevinger supports his characterization of the nature of mass communication by arguing that:

> A nation or community is formed by common interest and culture—
> by a common image and vision of itself. But to have a common image
> or vision, there must be one that is seen, understood, and accepted by
> most people, not merely by a minority or by an elite. This requires
> that the social image reflected in the media mirrors be one that truly
> reflect the masses. (p. 256)

While Loevinger's argument is aimed at those who wonder why television is not dominated by elite programming, his point does also explain
why African-American expression of African identity is portrayed as
rebellious and transient. To let the characters' new identity become
permanent would be to suggest that American mainstream values [are]
not good enough for all Americans. That would be a deviation from the
collective image in Loevinger's theory. Moreover, as Gans has noted,
the media rarely blame American mainstream political and social values
for American problems (in the sense that they blame communism for
the problems of the Soviet Union, Cuba, or Nicaragua, for instance).
Rather the media treat them as rectifiable conditions or "as deviant cases,
with the implication that American ideals, at least, remain viable" (Gans,
42). Thus, the African American characters' reversion to their old identity serves to reinforce the viability of mainstream values and to uphold
the collective mirror. That is, all problems can be redressed in the context
of mainstream values, not outside them.

The portrayal of African Americans is also consistent with Milton
Myron Gordon's theory of assimilation in America. Gordon posits that
the concept of assimilation, rather than that of "the melting pot" or
"cultural pluralism," is the dominant tendency in race interaction in the
United States. Gordon writes that assimilation is characterized by Anglo-
conformity, which has "as a central assumption the desirability of maintaining English institutions (as modified by the American Revolution),
the English language, and English-oriented cultural patterns as dominant
and standard in American life" (88). That contrasts with the melting pot
(in which all cultures contribute to a shared new standard) and cultural
pluralism (in which each culture maintains its separate identity in co-
existence with others.) The programs seem to encourage Anglo-con-
formity, with minor tradeoffs as necessary.

That minority portrayal is consistent with the goals of assimilation is
further supported by stages in minority presence in the media. Cedric
Clark has identified four stages in the portrayal of minorities as: (1)
nonrecognition (when the minority is hardly present in the media), (2)
ridicule, (3) regulation (when the group is portrayed in roles that convey
adherence to law and order), and (4) respect. These stages may be
explained as follows: A minority group is initially ignored in the media
because it is not considered a part of the culture. But when that minority
can no longer be ignored (for social or political reasons), it is ridiculed
to discredit its culture and values. Discrediting of the group's culture
induces self-doubt within the group and thus a willingness to be assim-

ilated into the dominant culture.[7] Regulation then would have the effect of conditioning the dominant culture for acceptance of the minority. Having been assimilated, at least to a satisfactory degree, the minority is then respected. This granted, one may add "maintenance" as a fifth level of portrayal by which assimilation is reinforced. Thus, projection of African identity as a transitory frame of mind may serve to remind African Americans that they have no reason to look beyond their American identity.

It is important to distinguish between this argument and the one that attributes black characterization to the stereotypical images held of blacks. Crediting the idea to Tony Brown, Melbourne S. Cummings writes, for instance, that the characters in most black sitcoms are "appealing precisely because (their) images do not disturb or dispute the overall view of black people generally held in the minds of the viewing American audience." However, the unprecedented popularity of The (unstereotypical) Cosby Show defies this theory. Granted one can dismiss The Cosby Show as an exception. Still, the larger idea that mainstream values, not stereotypes, per se, are the dominant force in program creation and acceptance provides a more compelling explanation of black portrayal on television. Certainly, stereotypes are inherent aspects of cultural values. But as The Cosby Show demonstrates, consistency with other aspects of the values can override stereotypes in determining program acceptance and popularity.

The Cosby Show epitomizes family wholesomeness, fun, and comfortable living, in easy combination with individuality, adolescent misadventures, and adult wisdom. These are aspects of the American cultural vision which, without going into a detailed analysis of the factors of program popularity, must be elements of the popularity of The Cosby Show. Moreover, while the program is nonracial in tone and theme, it seems to convey a sense that the American ideal has no regard for race, and perhaps that African Americans are at last an integral part of that ideal. In short, The Cosby Show seems a perfect exemplification of the reflective—projective—mirror theory.

Conclusion

The foregoing findings and analysis suggest two predictions on media 30
portrayal of African Americans. One is that, even if society's stereotypical

---

7. One support for this conjecture is a finding that blacks who watch a lot of entertainment programs tend to have lower self-esteem while whites who watch at comparable levels do not: Alexis S. Tan and Gerdean Tan, "Television Use and Self-Esteem: Ethnic Studies in Black and White," *Journal of Communication,* 29 (Winter 1979), pp. 129–135.

views of African Americans continue, African Americans increasingly
will be portrayed positively—successfully—in the media, if the programs
tap into aspects of the American collective self-image that can override
the stereotypical views. Conversely, and for the same reasons, African
American assertion of African cultural identity is less likely to be endorsed
in mainstream entertainment programs. Certainly, it will not be a recurrent theme in such programming.

WORKS CITED

Artis, William Jr. "The Tribal Fixation," *Columbia Journalism Review* (Fall 1970): 48–49.
Clark, Cedric. "Television and Social Controls: Some Observations on the Portrayal of
  Ethnic Minorities," *Television Quarterly* (Spring, 1969): 18–22.
Cross, William E. Jr. "The Negro-to-Black Conversion Experience: Toward a Psychol-
  ogy of Black Liberation," *Black World* (July 1971): 13–27.
Cummings, Melbourne S. "The Changing Image of the Black Family on Television,"
  Journal of Popular Culture 22 (Fall 1988): 75–85.
Essien-Udom, Essien-Udosien. *Black Nationalism: A Search for an Identity in America.*
  Chicago: University of Chicago Press, 1962.
Gans, Herbert J. *Deciding What's News: A Study of CBS Evening News, NBC Nightly News,
  Newsweek and Time.* New York: Vintage, 1979.
Gordon, Milton Myron. *Assimilation in American Life: The Role of Race, Religion and
  National Origins.* New York: Oxford University Press, 1964.
Loevinger, Lee. "The Ambiguous Mirror: The Reflective-Projective Theory of Broad-
  casting and Mass Communication," Gary Gumpert and Robert Cathcart, eds., *Inter/
  Media: Interpersonal Communication in a Media World.* New York: Oxford University
  Press, 1979, pp. 243–260.
Marc, David. *Comic Visions: Television Comedy and American Culture.* Winchester, MA:
  Unwin Hyman, 1989.
McLuhan, Marshall. *Understanding Media: The Extensions of Man.* New York: McGraw-
  Hill, 1964.
Porter, Judith R. and Robert E. Washington, "Black Identity and Self-Esteem: A Review
  of Studies of Black Self-Concept, 1968–1978," *Annual Review of Sociology* 5 (1979):
  53–74.
Reid, Pamela Trotman. "Racial Stereotyping on Television: A Comparison of the Be-
  havior of Both Black and White Television Characters," *Journal of Applied Psychology*
  64 (October 1979): 465–471.
Sholle, David J. "Critical Studies: From the Theory of Ideology to Power/Knowledge,"
  Critical Studies in Mass Communication 5 (1988): 16–41.
Watkins, Mel. "Beyond the Pale," *Channels* (April/May 1982): 56–60.
World Almanac and Book of Facts, 1989. New York: World Almanac, 1989.

Reading the Text

1. What pattern does Ibelema find in sitcoms' portrayal of African identity?
2. Explain what Ibelema means by "media determinism" and "cultural assimilation."

3. What constraints on writers and producers are imposed by the sitcom as a genre?

Reading the Signs

1. Ibelema only briefly discusses *The Cosby Show* in his essay. Watch an episode of *The Cosby Show* (it's broadcast in reruns in most parts of the country). To what extent does the episode you watch demonstrate Ibelema's general claim that African-American expression of African identity tends to be transient or crisis-driven in sitcoms?
2. Watch a current sitcom that features African-American characters (such as *The Fresh Prince of Bel Air*). Using Ibelema's argument as your critical framework, write an essay in which you analyze the portrayal of African-Americans in the episode. How much do the characters identify with African identity? If they do, what is the nature of that identification? If they don't, how would you explain the absence of such identification?
3. Read or review bell hooks's "Madonna: Plantation Mistress or Soul Sister?" (p. 190). How would hooks interpret the episodes of *Sanford and Son*, *Diff'rent Strokes*, and *Facts of Life* that Ibelema describes?
4. Ibelema focuses exclusively on television sitcoms, but the issues of racial identity that he discusses can be applied to movies as well. Write an essay in which you explore the treatment of African identity in Spike Lee's film *Malcolm X*, taking care to recognize the differences between television and film. To develop your essay, you may want to consult Shelby Steele's "Malcolm X" (p. 287) and Peter Rainer's "Antihero Worship" (p. 318).
5. Ibelema ends his essay with two predictions: that African-Americans increasingly will be portrayed positively in the media, and that such characters will be less likely to assert African cultural identity. In class, discuss whether you see any evidence in current television programming that his predictions are accurate.

JOSH   OZERSKY

TV's Anti-Families: Married . . . with Malaise

||||||||||||||||||||||||||||||||||||||||||||||||||||||||||

In this critique of the modern antifamily sitcom, Josh Ozersky argues that one of TV's shrewdest ploys is to make fun of itself in shows like The Simpsons *to "ingratiate itself with Americans, who in an age marked by pervasive irony want to . . . feel superior to TV and yet keep watching it." Finding in such hit series as* Married . . . with Children *a bleak exaggeration of America's real family problems, Ozersky sees, at best, trivialization of dysfunctional families and, at*

worst, a kind of "counsel of despair." Josh Ozersky obtained his B.A.
in English literature from Rutgers University and is doing graduate work
in cultural history at Notre Dame University. A specialist in American
popular culture of the past forty years, Ozersky has published in Seventeen, Tikkun, The Washington Times, Chronicles, *and other*
magazines.

It's an odd thing when a cartoon series is praised as one of the most
trenchant and "realistic" programs on TV, but there you are. Never
mind the Cosby-size ratings: If merchandising says anything about American culture, and it does, then America was utterly infatuated with *The*
Simpsons in 1990. "Utterly," because unlike other big winners in the
industry such as the Teenage Mutant Ninja Turtles and the New Kids
on the Block, the Simpsons graced not only T-shirts for the clamoring
young, but T-shirts (and sweatshirts and posters and mugs) that went out
in droves to parents, who rivaled kids for viewer loyalty.

The animated series chronicles the life of the Simpson family: father
Homer, who works in a nuclear power plant and reads bowling-ball
catalogs; mother Marge, with her blue beehive hairdo and raspy voice;
misunderstood-Bohemian daughter Lisa; baby Maggie; and bratty son
Bart, the anti-everything star of the series. Bart appeals to kids, who see
a flattering image of themselves, and to their parents, who, even as they
identify with Bart against his lumpkin parents, enjoy Bart's caricature of
their own children, with his incomprehensible sloganeering ("Don't have
a cow, man!") and bad manners. Nor, tellingly, has the popularity of the
show stopped with the white mainstream: a black Bart soon began to
turn up in unlicensed street paraphernalia.

In the first of the unauthorized shirts, Bart was himself, only darkened. The novelty soon wore off, however, and in successive generations
Bart found himself ethnicized further: "Air Bart" had him flying toward
a basketball hoop exclaiming "In your face, home boy." Another shirt
had Bart leering at zaftig black women, loutishly yelling "Big Ole Butt!"
at their retreating figures. And in later versions, Bart has a gold tooth, a
razor cut, and an angry snarl—the slogan "I got the power!" juts over-
head in an oversized balloon.

The "I got the power!" Bart is barely recognizable, disfigured by
rancor. But even more jarring than his appearance is his vitriol, so out
of keeping with the real Bart's laid-back, ironic demeanor—an endemic
condition among TV characters. The naked discontent on that shirt is
jarring, disturbing. It lacks the light touch. TV does not—but then the
playful suppression of unhappiness has always been one of TV's great
strengths; and in its latest, ugliest form, it subtly discourages alarm at the

decline of the family, its own complicity in that decline, and the resulting effects on a disintegrating society.

The success in the last few seasons of new, "antifamily" sitcoms,   5
such as Fox's *Married . . . with Children* and *The Simpsons* and ABC's
Roseanne, began a trend that has made waves in television. "Whether it's
the influence of Bart Simpson and those cheeky sitcoms from Fox,"
wrote *TV Guide* in September [1990] "or ABC's artsy anti-soap *Twin
Peaks,* unconventionality is in; slick and safe are out." The "cheeky
sitcoms" began that trend. *Roseanne,* about an obese and abrasive proletarian mom, and *Married . . . with Children,* a half hour of pure viciousness, represented along with *The Simpsons* a new development of the
situation comedy, TV's definitive genre. Each program (as well as its
inevitable imitators) focuses on a family marked by visual styles and
characterization as bleak and miserable as those of former TV families
had been handsome or cheerful.

The innovation received a lot of attention in the mass media, most
of it favorable. Richard Zoglin in *Time* hailed the "real-world grit these
shows provide," produced psychological authorities, and quoted Barbara
Ehrenreich's wide-eyed "Zeitgeist Goddess" piece in the *New Republic.*
The *New York Times's* Caryl Rivers wrote approvingly of the new realism, although she noted perfunctorily that gays, minorities, and women
were less visible than they should have been. What all sides had in
common, however, was a willingness to point out the improvement over
other forms of TV. "The anti-family shows aren't against the family,
exactly, just scornful of the romantic picture TV has often painted of it,"
Zoglin pointed out. "We're like a mutant Ozzie and Harriet," Simpsons
creator Matt Groening boasted in *Newsweek,* which went on to point
out that the show was "hardly the stuff of Saturday-morning children's
programming." "Thankfully, we are past the days of perfect Mom and
all-wise Dad and their twin beds," wrote the *New York Times's* Rivers,
speaking for reviewers and feature writers everywhere. And this was
prior to the advent of the "unconventional" mystery serial *Twin Peaks,*
which still has feature writers striving for superlatives to describe its
"innovations" and "departures."

This unanimous juxtaposition of the "antifamilies" to the stern TV
households of yesteryear is a specious comparison designed to amuse and
flatter. Not as the result of any conspiracy—writers in the commercial
mass media generally write to please, and what they say is true enough
if you have as your entire frame of reference the past and present of TV.
But far from the "authenticity" it pretends to, the "grit" for the new
shows is merely an improved artifice, a challenge only to the verisimi-
litude of art directors and casting companies. By pretending to realism,
TV only extends its own hegemony, in which every standard of com-

parison points back to another sham. "Gosh," gushed *TV Guide* of Bart, "can you imagine Bud Anderson being so . . . *disrespectful* to Dad?" As if the lead of *Father Knows Best* had only recently become a figure of fun.

It is through this sort of pseudo–self-deprecation that TV tries to ingratiate itself with Americans, who in an age marked by pervasive irony want to run with the hare and hunt with the hound—to feel superior to TV and yet keep watching it. TV offers this target audience an abundance of self-images that will permit them this trick. The target viewers may be enlightened, making the "choice of a new generation" by seeing through *My Little Margie,* or avant-garde, on the cutting edge, for watching *Twin Peaks,* which, like *Hill Street Blues* before it, supposedly "breaks all the rules." They are in utter harmony with the very mechanics of TV production, which has no secrets from us, as we know from David Letterman's insider gags, such as the "Late Night Danger Cam."

As for discrediting paternalistic authority figures, Mark Crispin Miller has pointed out that the imperious Dads of fifties TV, now such a rich source of burlesque, were overturned by a maturing medium very early on. The "grim old abstinence" of the Puritan patriarch stood in the way of the "grim new self-indulgence" of consumer culture and was hence banished. Dads turned into "pleasant nullities," like Dick York in *Bewitched* and Timothy Busfield in *thirtysomething,* or unenlightened butts of knowing and self-flattering jokes, like Archie Bunker and Homer Simpson.

The downfall of Dad, however, saw no concomitant rise of Mom   10 or the kids. Rather, it was advertisers and corporations that benefited from the free-spending self-indulgence of all parties, liberated from patriarchal discipline. And the networks, of course, cashed in and sold advertisers airtime. In the world beyond the screen, the family has disintegrated into epidemic divorces and deteriorating marriages, latchkey children, and working parents reduced to spending "quality time" with their children, as though they were hospital visitors or the lovelorn spouses of soldiers on leave. Meanwhile, the TV world—not only in sitcoms but in endless "special reports" and talk shows and (particularly) commercials—insists again and again that we are hipper, more "open," more enlightened, and facing changing "relationships" in a new and better way. Mom, often divorced and underpaid, has her new "independence," a standard theme of programming, and Dad and the kids, faced with other losses and hardships, are offered the bold new "grittiness" of prime-time entertainment. TV has absorbed the American family's increasing sense of defeat and estrangement and presented it as an ironic in-joke.

This dynamic is seldom noted, although the mere *fact* of watching is noted by critics and commentators everywhere, and nowhere more visibly than on TV itself. The opening credits of *The Simpsons* end with the family, assembled at the end of the day, jumping mutely into fixed position on the sofa and clicking on the TV set. This absorption of criticism is and has been, except for sheer distraction, TV's greatest weapon against criticism. The transformation of the hearth into an engine of negation, after all, should have caused *some* stir. And so it would have, if TV were no more than the yammering salesman it has caricatured itself as in satirical moments. But, as Miller demonstrates, TV has never shown us TV; rather, it shows itself to us as a laughable, absurd, and harmless entity, much like the characters on its shows.

When not played for background noise—whooping Indians in older shows, unctuous game-show hosts or newsmen in newer ones—depictions of the TV set on TV itself render it invisible and omnipresent. TV itself, its conventions and production, may be the crucial point of reference for the sophisticated appeal it enjoys today, but the set as household centerpiece is seldom seen, and then only as a joke, as on *The Simpsons*. Instead, the set most often poses as a portal to the outer world: hence its constant stream of images that tease us with alluring beaches, blue waters, busy city streets. Even in its living rooms, where we know its presence to be inescapable, the TV is often missing. This effect is accomplished by a simple trick of photography when the family watches TV in *All in the Family*, in *Good Times*, in *Married . . . with Children*, etc., the scene is shot from behind the TV set. As the family sits facing us, with the screen nowhere in sight, the illusion exists for a moment that the TV really is, if not a portal, then a mirror or reflection of us. A close look at these families, and at our own, soon banishes this impression. We are not like these TV families at all; and the TV set is obtrusive, ideological, and tendentious.

When speaking of the "anti-family" sitcoms, most of the commentators seem to have in mind *Married . . . with Children*. No other show so luridly plays up the sheer negativity of the current "authenticity" trend, nor does any other show do so with such predictable regularity. The series portrays the Bundys, a lower-middle-class family with two children and a dog. Father Al (Ed O'Neill) only has "knotted bowels" to show for his life supporting the family. Peg (Katey Sagal) is Al's castrating wife. There is also the inevitable sharp-tongued teenage son, who singles out for special heckling his brainless and sleazy sister. The relentlessly ironic quality of a happy family turned thoroughly upside-down flatters the audience for their enlightenment (no *Donna Reed*, this) even as it invites them to enjoy the ongoing frenzy of spite in which the show indulges. And frenzy is indeed the word. Every member of the family despises everyone else, and any given program consists of little more than continuous insults, interspersed with snide loathing or occasional expressions of despair.

FATHER (to son): Did I ever tell you not to get married?
SON: Yeah, Dad.
FATHER: Did I ever tell you not to become a shoe salesman?
SON: Yeah, Dad.
FATHER: Well, then I've told you everything I know.

This sort of resigned and paralytic discontent dominates the tone of *Married . . . with Children;* it lacks even the dim rays of hope that occasionally lifted Ralph Kramden's or Riley's gloomy existence. Every show is devoted to a new kind of humiliation: to earn extra money, Al becomes a burger-flipper; when son Bud falls victim to a practical joke perpetrated by an old flame his slutty sister Kelly comes to his defense by crucifying the girl against a locker; wife Peg belittles Al's manhood in front of strangers. Again and again, the unrelenting negativity of the show finds new ways to expand, purifying itself of any nonironic, positive content. Lovebird neighbors intended for contrast in the first season soon divorce, adding to the show's already vast reserve of bitterness. Christina Applegate, the young actress who plays Kelly, filled out during the first two years, adding a missing element of nasty prurience to the show.

The result of this hermetic exclusion of all warmth, say a number of apologists for the show, is positive: "With these new programs," says Barbara Cadow, a psychologist at USC, "we see we're doing all right by comparison." Yet at the same time, it is the very "realism" of these shows that won them praise again and again. This "realism" appeals to a cynical element in us—no one would ever admit to resembling Roseanne Barr or her family, but they are eminently "realistic" portraits of the losers next door. Roseanne Barr is shrewish and miserable to the point of self-parody, and this is seen as the great strength of her series. "Mom" (who Roseanne, it is assumed, represents) "is no longer interested in being a human sacrifice on the altar of 'pro-family' values," says Barbara Ehrenreich in the *New Republic.* 15

The praise of the same style of TV both for its realism and for its horrific exaggeration, while apparently contradictory, is based on a common assumption. In each case, the pervasive unhappiness and derision on TV sitcoms is assumed to be a reflection, albeit a negative one, of the unhappiness of real families. Cadow assumes that it is caricature, and Ehrenreich that it is a manifesto, but neither woman doubts that both shows offer some kind of corrective to real life for their viewers, and that this explains their popularity. This congratulatory view of hit TV shows contains a fundamental error: the old network executive's rationale that TV "gives people what they want," in response to their Nielsen-measured "choice."

The concentration of mass media into a few corporate hands invalidates that idea even more today than in the past. Given TV's entirely corporate nature, it is unreasonable to assume that the channels are referenda, since almost every channel, at least until recently, offered almost identical options. What succeeds with the public makes it, yes. But that "success" is determined by TV's agenda—which now, as always, is more than selling dog biscuits. Consumption must be encouraged psychologically; sectors and tendencies in American society have to be identified and exploited. "Since the major broadcasters are no longer winning the big numbers," observes *TV Guide,* "they're now fighting for the youthful demographics that bring in the highest revenues. That's why everyone is hyping bold, hip shows."

Of course, the success of a culture based on mass consumption depends on the creation of boundless needs; boundless needs presuppose boundless discontent. Boundless discontent must begin with the family, where social patterns are first internalized. If, latchkey in hand, TV can flatter a kinless and dispossessed child into adulthood and at the same time kid his or her parents about it, perfect consumers are thereby made. The family becomes a breeding ground for easygoing and independent citizens of the marketplace, transported beyond the inner struggle and deep feeling of family life, and bound in their place by the laws of supply and demand, consumer "choices," and a continual negation of their truest selves.

By presenting unhappy families to viewers, TV achieves many gains. First, as Cadow rightly points out, mocking the traditional family does flatter the distorted family of our times. However, this does not necessarily lift spirits. On the contrary, it lowers expectations; it stupefies discontent instead of healing it. *Married . . . with Children* is the prototype of this strategy. The petty or profound resentments of real families do not rival those of the Bundys, but then neither does their ability to punish and humiliate each other. By making our problems "seem all right by comparison," the series trivializes them rather than taking them seriously. It in fact worsens them by its counsel of despair.

Secondly, the dysfunctional TV family aids advertisers in their perennial quest for credibility by creating a supersaturated atmosphere of irony, which atrophies our ability to believe in anything. Commercials themselves work on a principle of pseudorebelliousness. Burger King—now officially touted by the Simpsons—proudly sports the "radical" motto, "Sometimes you've gotta break the rules." Swallowing these giant absurdities relies not on credulity, but on an ironic, self-assured disbelief. *Roseanne,* with its trademark sarcasm, and *Twin Peaks,* with its tongue-in-cheek grotesqueries, are good examples.

Third, and most insidious, is the stability of TV's dysfunctional families, and their passive acceptance of their fate. A successful cast is the source of "ensemble acting," which has been the formula for success for some time now on TV. Since TV characters now move in herds, they do not get divorced, move out, have devastating affairs, or anything else

20

that would disrupt the fabric of the show's format. Implicitly, these shows assure us that family life is largely a nightmare, but one that is self-perpetuating and only requires handling with a deft, protective irony. This irony, the antithesis of deep feeling, is the essential assault on the family and on all human relationships, reducing them to problems of managerial acumen. Thus, while remaining intact in their own impoverished world, sitcom families undermine the stability of real families, discrediting the embarrassingly earnest, often abject bonds of kin while hermetically sealing themselves off from the possibility of familial collapse. And this while they consume the increasingly rare time in which American families are actually together.

The Simpsons, the most popular of the group and certainly the least ironic and "antifamily," is TV's most effective reinforcer. This paradox begins with the fact that the show is a cartoon: With their yellow skin, bulging eyes, and comical motions, the Simpsons are funny just to look at, and hence relieve the audience of the need to continually jeer at them. The Bundy family of Married . . . with Children, like all sitcom characters, aspire to the televisual purity of cartoon characters, but are stuck in rubbery bags of protoplasm with nothing but one-liners and a laugh track to hide behind. The Simpsons, oddly, are freer than other TV families to act human.

And so they do. There is an element of family loyalty and principle to be found in the Simpsons, often combined with witty and valid social criticism. Brother Bart and sister Lisa petulantly demand of baby Maggie to "come to the one you love most," to which the infant responds by crawling lovingly to the TV. Or again, when father Homer's sinister boss inquires disbelievingly, "You'd give up a job and a raise for your principles?" Homer responds (with almost none of the usual sitcom character's irony), "When you put it that way, it does sound farfetched—but that's the lunk you're lookin' at!" "Hmm," the boss replies. "You're not as dumb as you look. Or sound. Or as our best testing indicates."

With pointed jokes such as these, The Simpsons might prompt us to conclude the same about its vast audience. The harmlessness of these jokes can be taken for granted; no one who watches TV is going to stop because they see TV criticized. We criticize it ourselves as a matter of course. On the contrary, we feel flattered, and less inclined to stop watching.

And we are that much less inclined to object to the continuing   25
presence of unsafe workplaces, vast corporations, the therapy racket, and all the other deserving targets of the Simpsons' harmless barbs. The genial knowingness of shows like The Simpsons subverts criticism through an innocuous pseudocriticism, just as the familial discontents of TV shows subvert alarm at graver discontents in real life. Criticism is further weakened by the show's irony, which although less than some other programs is still pervasive and fundamental to its humor. No one in an ironic show

can get too far out of line. For example, in one episode, misunderstood Lisa meets that well-worn figure of Caucasian lore, the wise and virtuous old colored bluesman, ever ready to act as mentor to young white people in their search for self-knowledge. *The Simpsons* is far too hip to hand us such a hackneyed cliché. The Virtuous Old Blues Man is as empty a conceit as the Perfect Family—so on the show, he is named "Bleeding Gums Murphy" (Why? "I haven't brushed my teeth in thirty years, that's why.") In place of the usual soulful laments, he sings the "I Don't Have an Italian Suit Blues."

Such undercutting is typical of TV as a whole; attempts to transcend the flattened-out emotional landscape of TV are almost invariably punished by some droll comeuppance. But since as bizarre cartoons there is little need to belittle them, the Simpsons get a little more than most, and are occasionally allowed moments of earnestness unmitigated by the selfishness of *thirtysomething,* the weirdness of *Twin Peaks,* or the inevitable "comic relief"—the stock entrances of deadpan tots and witty oldsters, etc.—used to terminate the maudlin embraces of nonanimated sitcomites. None of this is to be had on *The Simpsons,* but the picture it presents is still fundamentally hopeless. The Simpsons are basically boobs, and their occasional bursts of tenderness or insight are buried under biting irony and superior, if affectionate, mockery. More than any of the other "antifamily" shows, *The Simpsons* seems to come close to our lives; more than any of the other shows, as a result, it commits us to a shared vision of pessimism and self-deprecation.

Because the TV screen is neither a mirror, reflecting ourselves paralyzed in chairs in front of it, nor a window, through which we observe the antics of distant players, it is an implicit invitation to participate in a vision of "society" largely designed to flatter us in sinister ways, manipulate our attention, and commit us to the status quo. In discrediting "yesterday's" family values in its various "breakthrough" shows (ostensibly defining *A Different World* for us, as the title of one series has it), TV seeks only to impose its own values—which is to say, the values of the marketplace. Bart Simpson, master sneerer, is the prototype of the modern series character who—by the social scripts of TV—reflects us. Small, ridiculous, and at the same time admirable for his sarcasm and enlightened self-interest, Bart is the child of the culture of TV, his parents mere intermediaries.

Paradoxically, that is why the most powerless sector of American society has adopted him, fitting him with their own wishful slogan—"I got the power!" Though black Bart's anger may be incongruous with TV, his proclamation is not, since TV is so successful an invitation to impotent posturing. At the moment, the rage of the underclass cannot be appropriated by TV, yet in black Bart, in the fatal joining of ironic hipness and earnest wrath, we see perhaps a glimpse of the future (and in fact there are already a spate of new black shows—e.g., *Fresh Prince of Bel Air, In Living Color*). "I got the power!" says black Bart. But in the world of the TV family, no one has power. Empty fantasies of might, like cynical, knowing giggles, are terminal symptoms of our capitulation to TV's vision.

Life outside of that vision *is* ugly and is becoming uglier as ties, familial and societal, dissolve and decay. But the only power we do have is the power of our own real selves to reject the defensive posture of materialist or ironist or cynic, and the soullessness of TV's "hip, bold," antilife world. Bart and his aspirants exist in that world, and their example serves only to impoverish us.

Reading the Text

1. What does Ozersky mean by "antifamilies"?
2. How, according to Ozersky, are the antifamily sitcoms a sign of the state of American families today?
3. What is Ozersky's view of the realism of today's sitcoms?
4. How does Ozersky see television as turning today's children into "perfect consumers"?

Reading the Signs

1. Do you agree with Ozersky's argument that "by presenting unhappy families to viewers, TV achieves many gains"? Write an essay in which you defend or refute Ozersky's thesis, supporting your position with specific examples of television shows you have seen.
2. Read or review Susan Faludi's "Teen Angels and Tart-Tongued Witches" (p. 219). Using her analysis as your critical framework, analyze an episode of *The Simpsons*, focusing on the character of Marge and her relationship with her family.
3. Ozersky claims that antifamily shows encourage consumer behavior. In an essay, explore the validity of his position. To develop your argument, consult Laurence Shames's "The More Factor" (p. 25).
4. In class, brainstorm television programs that depict "profamilies," shows that feature traditional, idealized families. Then compare the "profamily" shows with the antifamily programs that Ozersky discusses. Which do you prefer to watch? What do the class's preferences say about its values and views on life?
5. While focusing on different subjects, both Josh Ozersky and bell hooks ("Madonna: Plantation Mistress or Soul Sister?" p. 190) argue that supposedly "revolutionary" media icons in fact support the prevailing ideologies that they pretend to subvert. Write an essay in which you explore this contention by examining their subjects or other media examples that seem

to be "breakthroughs"; you might consider films such as *Basic Instinct* or artists such as Michael Jackson or Vanilla Ice.

SUSAN FALUDI

Teen Angels and Tart-Tongued Witches

|||||||||||||||||||||||||||||||||||||||||||||||||||||||||||

Already the holder of a Pulitzer Prize in journalism, Susan Faludi (b. 1958) leaped onto the center stage of American social controversy with the publication of Backlash: The Undeclared War Against Women *in 1991. Arguing that the 1980s constituted a decade of nationwide cultural backlash against the advances of the women's movement, Faludi chronicles the many ways in which women were put back in their place. This backlash ranged from the wildly publicized claim that unmarried women over thirty stood little chance of ever marrying, to the "traditional values" trend that urged working women to return home and have children by threatening them with stories of ticking biological clocks. The media were especially culpable in this regard, Faludi argues, and in this selection from her book she reveals television's role in the eighties' treatment of women. Focusing on the relative absence of female leads in late eighties programming, Faludi examines what the men who call the shots in Hollywood think about the women they chose to include and exclude. Currently Faludi is a reporter with the San Francisco bureau of* The Wall Street Journal.

"Under no circumstances is this going to be the return of 'jiggle.' These aren't just girls who look good; they have actual personalities."[1] Tony Shepherd, vice president of talent for Aaron Spelling Productions, puts his full weight behind each word, as if careful enunciation might finally convince the remaining skeptics in the Hollywood press corps. Thankfully, most of the reporters assembled at the Fox Television Center for the announcement of the network's new television series, *Angels '88,* see things Shepherd's way; they reach across the buffet table's mountain of pastries to shake his hand. "Great work, Tony," says one of the guys from the tabloids, his mouth full of croissant. "Great work selecting the girls."

---

1. Personal interview with Tony Shepherd, 1988; personal observations at the Fox press conference for *Angels '88,* May 5, 1988.

This May morning in 1988 is the grand finale of Fox's two-month quarter-million-dollar nationwide search for the four angels—a quest the company publicists liken to "the great search for Scarlett O'Hara" and "the glamour days of Old Hollywood."[2] Shepherd has crossed the country four times ("I had to watch *Three Men and a Baby* five times on the plane"), personally conducted open casting calls in twelve of the forty-four cities, and eyeballed at least six thousand of the sixteen thousand women who stood in half-mile-long lines all day for one-and-a-half-minute interviews. Secretaries and housewives, he says, weathered 25-degree temperatures just to see him; one woman even passed out from hypothermia.

But a few journalists at this event can't resist asking: Isn't *Angels '88* just a reprise of Spelling's *Charlie's Angels,* where three jiggle-prone private eyes took orders from invisible boss Charlie and bounced around in bikinis? "No, no, no!" Shepherd, the chain-smoking great-grandson of Louis B. Mayer, exhales a fierce stream of smoke. "*They* didn't have distinct characters. They were just beauties." The characters in *Angels '88,* he says, are more "advanced," independent women who won't even necessarily be fashion plates. That's why the network interviewed so many real women for the leading roles. These new angels "might not have perfect hair and be the perfect model types," he says. "In *Angels '88,* you're going to find these girls sometimes wearing no makeup at all. Particularly, you know, when they are running around on the beach."

Just then, a Fox publicist takes the stage to announce the angels' imminent debut. No interviews, he warns the media, until the photographers finish their "beauty shots." The angels file on stage and the cameramen begin shouting, "Girls, over here, over here!" "Oh, young ladies, right here!" The angels turn this way and that, well-coiffed hair swinging around flawlessly made-up faces. The idle reporters leaf through their press kits, which offer large photographs and brief biographies of each star—Tea Leoni, "the 5'7" blonde beauty"; Karen Kopins, "the 5'8" brunette beauty"; and so on. Of the four, only Leoni was actually picked from the nationwide casting call. The others are models with minor acting backgrounds.

The angels spend a carefully timed five minutes with the press before they are whisked off for a lengthy photo session for *Time.* The stage mike is turned over to Aaron Spelling, creator of some of the most lucrative programs in television history, a list ranging from *Love Boat* to *Fantasy Island.* "How's this show going to be different from *Charlie's*

———————
2. D. Keith Mano, "So You Want to Be an Angel," *Life,* May 1988, p. 145; Lisa Wren, "Hundreds Wing It for a Chance to Be Angels," *Fort Worth Star Telegram,* March 5, 1988, p. 1; Zay N. Smith, "Angels Tryout Not So Divine," *Chicago Sun-Times,* March 5, 1988, p. 3; Bill Givens, "Fox Hunt for Charlie's Angels of the Eighties," *Star,* March 22, 1988, p. 2.

Angels?" a reporter asks. "These young ladies are on their own; they do not report to any men," Spelling says. "It's an entire ladies' show without guidance. It's a young ladies' buddy-buddy show is what it is." He turns a beseeching face on his audience. "Why, why," he wants to know, would anyone think that he wants to bring back "the beautiful bimbos"? He shakes his head. "It's going to be a show of today's young ladies of today [sic], and we'll go into their personal lives, we'll treat today's issues, we'll treat the problems of their dating and sex and safe sex and sex of our time. It's going to be a very attractive show."

Later that same day in Santa Monica, screenwriter Brad Markowitz rolls his eyes as he hears the details of the press conference. A few months earlier, Spelling had hired Markowitz and his writing partner to script the series pilot. "Spelling made all these fine speeches to us about how 'the girls' would be more real," Markowitz recalls. "He talked a good game about how the show would be more representative of how women really are, as opposed to that idealized, frosted look." But when it came down to drafting a script, Markowitz says, Spelling instructed the screenwriters to open the episode with scantily clad angels wriggling to a rock video. Spelling was unhappy with their first draft, Markowitz recalls, because "we didn't have enough girls in bikinis"; he ordered them to add more bathing-beauty scenes.[3] Spelling also insisted that the thirty-two-year-old police academy–trained detectives (their original status in *Charlie's Angels*) be demoted to unemployed actresses in their early twenties who just fall into police work and bungle the job. Spelling, who later denies demanding these changes—"the script just wasn't good enough is all I know"—defended the alterations this way: "That's what makes the show funny—that they are supposed to be doing it by themselves and they can't! They are incompetent!"[4]

After various delays and script battles, *Angels '88* was put on hold, then reformatted as a "telefilm," in which, Spelling says, the women will be even younger college "coeds." Meanwhile, for the 1988–89 season, Spelling applied his "young ladies' buddy-buddy show" concept to *Nightingales,* an NBC prime-time series about five jiggly student nurses who prance around the locker room in their underwear. While they aren't independent, their boss is a woman, Spelling says proudly—as if a female head nurse represents nontraditional casting.

Anyway, as Spelling pointed out at the *Angels* press conference, at least his shows have women in lead roles. "Go and look at television today. Tell me how many shows outside of a few comedies are dominated by women. You'll find the answer is very few."

3. Personal interview with Brad Markowitz, May 5, 1988.
4. Personal interviews with Aaron Spelling, May 1988, August 1990.

True enough. In the 1987–88 season, the backlash's high watermark on TV, only three of twenty-two new prime-time dramas featured female leads—and only two of them were adults.[5] One was a sorority girl and another a nubile private eye who spent much of her time posing and complaining about the dating scene. (The title of that show, *Leg Work,* speaks for itself.) In a sharp dropoff from previous seasons, 60 percent of the shows launched as series in this season had either no regular female characters or included women only as minor background figures; 20 percent had no women at all.[6] And women over the age of consent were especially hard to find.

Women were also losing ground in the one television genre they had always called their own: situation comedy. In a resurgence of the old *Odd Couple* format, bachelor buddies took up house together without adult women in one out of five new sitcoms, a list that included *Everything's Relative, My Two Dads, Trial and Error,* and *Full House.*[7] In the single-parent household sitcoms that took over prime time that year, two-thirds of the children lived with dad or a male guardian—compared with 11 percent in the real world.[8] "This season it's especially clear that TV writers are uncomfortable with the concept of working mothers," *New York Woman* observed. The magazine offered a quiz that starkly documented this discomfort; the "Moms at Work" puzzle invited readers to match each new prime-time show with the current status of the working-mother character. The correct answers: *A Year in the Life*—dead. *Full House*—dead. *I Married Dora*—dead. *My Two Dads*—dead. *Valerie's Family*—dead. *Thirtysomething*—quits work to become a housewife. *Everything's Relative*—show canceled. *Mama's Boy*—show canceled.[9]

Women's disappearance from prime-time television in the late eighties repeats a programming pattern from the last backlash when, in the late fifties and early sixties, single dads ruled the TV roosts and female characters were suddenly erased from the set.[10] By the 1960 season, only two of the top ten rated shows had regular female characters—*Gunsmoke* and *Real McCoys*—and by 1962 the one woman on *Real McCoys* had been killed off, too. The vanishing act eventually spread to domestic

5. Joanmarie Kalter, "What Working Women Want from TV," *TV Guide,* Jan. 30, 1988, p. 3.

6. Sally Steenland, *Women Out of View: An Analysis of Female Characters on 1987–88 TV Programs,* Washington, D.C.: report by National Commission on Working Women, Nov. 1987, pp. 2–4.

7. Jay Martel, "On Your Mark, Get Set, Forget It," *TV Guide,* Feb. 4, 1988, p. 28.

8. Steenland, *Women out of View,* p. 6.

9. "Moms at Work," *New York Woman,* Feb. 1988, p. 93.

10. Diana M. Meehan, *Ladies of the Evening: Women Characters of Prime-Time Television* (Metuchen, N.J.: The Scarecrow Press, 1983) pp. 42, 109–110.

dramas, where the single father took charge of the household on *Bachelor Father, My Three Sons, Family Affair,* and *The Andy Griffith Show.*

In the eighties, women began to shrink and dwindle in the 1985–86 season, as a new breed of action-adventure series that included women only as victimized girls began crowding out more balanced fare. In this new crop of programs, as uneasy critics commented at the time, the viciousness of the assaults on the young female characters rivaled slasher films. On *Lady Blue,* for example, teenage boys armed with scalpels eviscerate their female prey; on *Our Family Honor,* a seventeen-year-old girl is slashed to death with a coat hanger.[11] And that season, female characters who weren't under attack were likely to be muzzled or missing from action: An analysis of prime-time TV in 1987 found 66 percent of the 882 speaking characters were male—about the same proportion as in the fifties.[12]

While the new male villains were busy pulverizing women, male heroes on continuing series were toughening their act. The "return of the hard-boiled male," *New York Times* television writer Peter Boyer dubbed it in an article on the phenomenon.[13] In *St. Elsewhere,* the affable Dr. Caldwell was recast as an unapologetic womanizer. In *Moonlighting,* the immature hireling of the elegantly confident Maddie Hayes now overshadowed his boss lady—and cut her down to size. Network executives even instructed Tom Selleck to get more masculine on *Magnum, P.I.* And the networks continued to boost their macho output; of the ten new dramas unveiled in the fall of 1989, five were about male cops or cowboys, with such self-explanatory titles as *Nasty Boys* and *Hardball.*[14] The latter show's premier made it clear who would be on the receiving—and losing—end of this game. In the debut episode, a homicidal and evil female cop is beaten into submission by the male hero—a scene that reenacts the climactic confrontation in *Fatal Attraction.* (He holds her head under water in the bathroom and tries to drown her.)

If TV programmers had their reasons for bringing on the he-men, popular demand wasn't among them. In audience surveys, TV viewers show the *least* interest in police dramas and Westerns.[15] Nonetheless, Brandon Tartikoff, president of entertainment at NBC, asserted in the

---

11. Sally Steenland, "Trouble on the Set, An Analysis of Female Characters on 1985 Television Programs," report by National Commission on Working Women, Washington, D.C., 1985, p. 9.

12. Donald M. Davis, "Portrayals of Women in Prime-Time Network Television: Some Demographic Characteristics," *Sex Roles,* 23, no. 5–6 (1990): 325–30.

13. Peter J. Boyer, "Television Returns to the Hard Boiled Male," *New York Times,* Feb. 16, 1986, II, p. 1.

14. John Carman, "Networks Playing It Bland," *San Francisco Chronicle,* TV Week, Sept. 17–23, 1989, p. 3.

15. Michael A. Lipton, "What You Want to See in the New Decade," *TV Guide,* Jan. 20, 1990, p. 11.

New York Times that the TV men were turning brutish because "the audience" was sick of male "wimps" and "Alan Alda-esque heroes who wore their sensitivity on their shirtsleeves"; as proof, he pointed not to real people but to the outpouring of macho movies—yet another case of the makers of one cultural medium invoking another's handiwork to reinforce the backlash.[16] Glenn Gordon Caron, producer of *Moonlighting,* admitted to more personal motives in an interview in the *New York Times:* "I very much wanted to see a *man* on television." He complained that the last decade of social change has elbowed his sex off the screen. "[For] a long time, men just sort of went away," he grumbled; one could only tell the gender of these ineffectual guys "because their voices were lower and their chests were flatter."[17] Glen Charles, coproducer of *Cheers,* was even blunter: He turned his show's bartender Sam into a chauvinistic womanizer because "he's a spokesman for a large group of people who thought that [the women's movement] was a bunch of bull and look with disdain upon people who don't think it was."[18]

The backlash on television would to a degree follow the film in- 15 dustry's lead. *Fatal Attraction* became ABC's *Obsessive Love* a year later; *Baby Boom* became a television series of the same name; *Working Girl, Parenthood,* and *Look Who's Talking* all resurfaced as TV series; the Western returned to the big screen and the small set. (And in keeping with the single-dad theme, bachelor cowboy Ethan Allan, the hero of TV's *Paradise,* gets saddled with four orphans.) The same backlash trends were recycled: Single women panicked by the man shortage dashed into the arms of a maniac on *Addicted to His Love.* (The ABC TV movie even cited the Harvard-Yale marriage study's 20 percent odds for college-educated single women over thirty.) Career women swooned with baby fever and infertility on shows like *Babies.* ("My biological clock is beginning to sound like Big Ben!" cries one of the empty-vessel heroines.) Even the "epidemic" of sex abuse at day care centers was turned into ratings fodder: In *Do You Know the Muffin Man?* a divorced working mother discovers her four-year-old son has been raped and contracted gonorrhea at nursery school.

But TV's counterassault on women's liberation would be, by necessity, more restrained than Hollywood's. Women have more influence in front of their sets than they do at the movies; women represent not only the majority of viewers but, more important, they represent the viewers that advertisers most want to reach. When the TV programmers tried to force-feed its cast of overweening guys and wilting gals in the 1987–88 season, a devastating proportion of the female audience simply shut

---

16. Boyer, "Hard Boiled Male," p. 1.
17. *Ibid.*
18. *Ibid.*

off their sets.[19] None of the twenty-five new prime-time shows made it into the top twenty except for *A Different World,* which was a spinoff of the *Cosby* show (and one of the rare new shows with a female lead).[20] By December, the networks' prime-time ratings had plunged a spectacular nine points from a year earlier, an average loss of 3.5 million households a night and the lowest rated TV season ever. While the dropoff can be partly attributed to the phasing in of the "people meter," a more finely tuned measure of viewership, that technological change doesn't explain why the audience flight was so disproportionately female. Nor does it explain why, in subsequent backlash seasons, when the people meter was no longer at issue, a lopsidedly female exodus kept recurring. Moreover, the people meters were reputed to favor younger viewers more than the old "diary" methods of audience measurement had. But while younger men increased their weekly viewing time by more than two hours in the fall of 1987 over the previous year, the younger women *decreased* their viewing time by almost an hour in the same period.[21]

By the following season, the programmers backed off a bit to admit a couple of strong female leads to the prime-time scene. *Roseanne* and *Murphy Brown,* both featuring outspoken women—and both, not coincidentally, created by women—became instant and massive hits: *Roseanne* was one of the most successful series launched in television history and held the number-one ratings slot season after season. But two strong women were seen as two too many. Independent women were "seizing control of prime time," *Newsweek* griped in a 1989 cover story.[22] "The video pendulum has swung too far from the blissfully domestic supermoms who once warmed the electronic hearth." Behind the scenes, the network tried to make changes that amounted to "taking all the stuffing out of Murphy," the show's creator Diane English observed.[23] The tart-tongued Roseanne Barr especially became a lightning rod for that rancor. While her penchant for mooning crowds and singing the national anthem off-key clearly warrants no Miss Congeniality prizes, the level of bile and hysteria directed at this comic seemed peculiarly out of proportion with her offenses. The media declared her, just like the *Fatal Attraction* temptress, "the most hated woman in America"; television executives savaged her in print; her former executive producer even took out a full-page ad in *Daily Variety* to deride the comedian; and,

19. Peggy Ziegler, "Where Have All the Viewers Gone?" *Los Angeles Times,* May 1, 1988, p. 6; data from Nielsen Media Research.

20. Ziegler, "Where Have All," p. 6.

21. Nielsen Media Research, Nielsen Report on Television, "Weekly Viewing Activity," 1980–1989.

22. Harry F. Waters, "Networking Women," *Newsweek,* March 13, 1989, p. 48.

23. Michael E. Hill, "Murphy Brown: F.Y.I., We Like Your Show, Sort of," *Washington Post,* TV Week, Feb. 26, 1989, p. 8.

despite critical acclaim and spectacular ratings, *Roseanne* was shut out of the Emmys year after year after year.[24] Outside the network suites, a chorus of male voices joined the Barr-bashing crusade. Sportswriters, baseball players, and news columnists damned her in print as a "bitch" and a "dog." Even George Bush felt compelled to issue a condemnatory statement; he called her "disgraceful." (And later he told the troops in the Middle East that he would like to make her a secret weapon against Iraq.) Businessman James Rees, the son of the former congressman, launched a nationwide "Bar Roseanne Club," soliciting members in the classifieds section of *Rolling Stone* and *The National.* ("Hate Roseanne Barr?" the ad copy inquired. "Join the club.") In a few weeks, he had more than six hundred responses, almost all from men who thoroughly agreed with Rees's assessment of "old lard butt." She's "a nasty filthy ugly Jell-O-Bodied tasteless monster from the black lagoon," wrote one man. Another proposed, "Let's shish-Kebab [her]."

By the following season, prime time reverted to traditional feminine icons, as the new series filled the screen with teenage models, home-makers, a nun and—that peculiar prototype of the last TV backlash—the good suburban housekeeper witch. An updated version of the tamed genie of *Bewitched* reappeared in the ironically named *Free Spirit.* By the next season, women were shut out of so many new shows that even comic Jay Leno joked about it at the Emmys. TV critic Joyce Millman, observing that the new offerings were "overloaded with adolescent boys and motherless households," asked, "Whatever happened to TV's 'Year of the Woman'? . . . [I]t's back to 'Boys' Night Out' for the upcoming fall season."[25] Only two of thirty-three new shows were about women with jobs; on the rest they were housewives, little girls, or invisible.[26]

The lurching quality of television's backlash against independent women is the product of the industry's own deeply ambivalent affair with its female audience. TV prime-time programmers are both more dependent on women's approval than filmmakers and, because of their dependence, more resentful. To serve a female master is not why the TV men came west to Hollywood. (And most are men; more than 90 percent of television writers, for example, are white males.)[27] They say they want shows that draw a large audience, but when those shows

24. "People," *Orange County Register,* March 29, 1990, p. A2; Michael McWilliams, "Pauley and Barr: Two Notions of Womanhood," Gannett News Service, Aug. 8, 1990; Dennis Duggan, "What, Me Judge a Man on Looks Alone? Guilty!" *Newsday, Newsday Magazine,* Feb. 17, 1991, p. 6; Jeffrey Zaslow, "Roseanne Ban Would Be as Bad as Barr's Own Antics," *Chicago Sun-Times,* Nov. 19, 1990, II, p. 65; Michele Stanush, "Anti-War Sentiments," *Austin-American Statesman,* Dec. 16, 1990, p. E1.

25. Joyce Millman, "Prime Time: Where the Boys Are," *San Francisco Examiner,* Sept. 9, 1990, p. F1.

26. *Ibid.*

27. Davis, "Portrayals of Women," p. 330.

feature autonomous women, they try to cancel them. *Designing Women* and *Kate and Allie,* both tremendously popular series, have fought back repeated network attempts to chase them off the set.

The modern network programmers find themselves in a situation   20 roughly analogous to that of the late Victorian clergymen. Like those leaders of the last century's backlash, TV executives watch anxiously as their female congregation abandons the pews—in the daytime for work and in the evening for other forms of electronic entertainment that offer more control and real choices. Women are turning to VCRs and cable offerings. In 1987, as the networks took their free fall in the ratings, prime-time cable viewership increased 35 percent and the proportion of TV households that owned VCRs rose from 19 to 60 percent in one year. The networks' audience shrank by more than 25 percent in the decade—and women contributed most to that shrinkage.[28] By 1990, Nielsen was reporting that the percentage of decline in female prime-time viewers was two to three times steeper than male's.[29] Women's desertion was more than an insult; it represented a massive financial loss. (A mere one-point drop in prime-time ratings equals a loss of more than $90 million in the network's revenue in one season.)[30]

Not only do some programming executives personally want to expel the independent women from the American set; their advertisers, who still view the housewife as the ideal shopper, demand it. This puts TV programmers in an impossible bind: The message advertisers want the networks to promote appeals least to modern women. Female viewers consistently give their highest ratings to nontraditional female characters such as leaders, heroines, and comedians.[31] But TV's biggest advertisers, packaged-foods and household-goods manufacturers, want traditional "family" shows that fit a sales pitch virtually unchanged in two decades. Advertisers prefer to reflect the housewife viewer because she is perceived as a more passive and willing consumer, because she is likely to have more children, and because they are simply used to this arrangement. Since its inception, television has been marketed as a family-gathering experience—the modern-day flickering hearth—where merchandisers' commercial messages can hit the whole clan at once.

As the eighties television backlash against independent women proceeded in fits and starts from season to season, a few shows managed to

28. "VCRs Reach Working Women," *Marketing to Women,* 1, no. 3 (Dec. 1987): 11.

29. Dennis Kneale, "TV's Nielsen Ratings, Long Unquestioned, Face Tough Challenges," *The Wall Street Journal,* July 19, 1990, p. A1.

30. Paul Richter, "Eyes Focus on People Meter As It Gauges TV Viewing," *Los Angeles Times,* May 10, 1987, section IV, p. 1.

31. Jean Gaddy Wilson, "Newsroom Management Commission Report," Sept. 15–18, 1987, p. 7.

survive its periodic surges—*L.A. Law, Designing Women,* and *The Golden Girls* are some examples. But overall, it succeeded in depopulating TV of its healthy independent women and replacing them with nostalgia-glazed portraits of apolitical "family" women. This process worked its way through television entertainment in two stages. First in the early eighties it banished feminist issues. Then, in the mid-eighties it reconstructed a "traditional" female hierarchy, placing suburban homemakers on the top, career women on the lower rungs, and single women at the very bottom.

Reading the Text

1. What significance does Faludi see in the casting for *Angels '88*?
2. Why, according to Faludi, did healthy, independent women "disappear" from television programs in the late 1980s?
3. How is the character Roseanne a sign of America's backlash against women, in Faludi's view?

Reading the Signs

1. Apply Faludi's notion of "backlash" to the movies Diane Raymond discusses in "Not as Tough as It Looks: Images of Mothering in Popular Culture" (p. 264). To what extent are the images that Raymond describes symptomatic of an antifeminist backlash?
2. Watch one of the shows that Walter Kirn analyzes in "Twentysomethings" (p. 229), and write an essay in which you explore the role of women in the show. Do you see evidence of the backlash against healthy, independent women that Faludi describes? What does the treatment of female characters say about the show's presumed "twentysomething" audience?
3. At the end of her essay, Faludi describes two stages of television programming in the last decade: first, the abolition of feminist issues in the early eighties, and second, the resurrection of traditional female roles in the late eighties. Add a third stage to her list for the 1990s: What roles do women occupy in the 1990s? Be sure to explain your third stage by referring to specific examples from television programs.
4. Do you see any evidence of the backlash against independent women in advertising? Write an essay in which you explore the depiction of women in advertising, focusing perhaps on ads in a women's magazine such as *Glamour* or *Vogue*. To develop your argument, consult Gloria Steinem's "Sex, Lies, and Advertising" (p. 139).
5. Read or review Michael Parenti's "Class and Virtue" (p. 283). How would Faludi analyze *Pretty Woman,* and how would her reading compare with Parenti's?

W A L T E R   K I R N
Twentysomethings

‖‖

*They've been called "slackers," "generation X," and "the first generation
in American history that expects to do worse than its parents." And
"they" may be you. In this wicked look at "twentysomething" culture
— "a sluggish mainstream underground that sold out even before it could
drop out"—Walter Kirn (b. 1962) rips apart the movies, TV shows,
fashions, and attitudes of what may be your generation, accusing it of
being made up of "mopey" consumers whose greatest contribution to
culture is "the glum 'Seattle Sound.'" Kirn pulls no punches in this
media and cultural review; in fact, he practically begs you to respond.
A contributing writer for* Elle *magazine, Kirn has also published a novel*
She Needed Me *(1992), and a collection of short stories,* My Hard
Bargain *(1990).*

The pathology of the new kids is familiar: impatience, distrust of
authority, malaise, and a wistful, ironic sense of longing for defunct ideals
and lost horizons. Minus the rebelliousness and hedonism that lent punch
to earlier youth movements, this is almost the same set of traits shared
by Hemingway's post–World War I "lost generation," Kerouac's Beats
and Hoffman's hippies. What distinguishes the most recent brood of
disaffected youth—variously identified as "twentysomethings," "slackers" and "the first generation in American history that expects to do
worse than its parents"—is not its desolation but the curiously lame,
detached self-consciousness of its popular culture. Examples include TV
shows such as *Melrose Place* and *The Heights,* magazines from *Details* to
Pulse, bands such as R.E.M. and its countless psychedelic-lite imitators,
and all movies starring Bridget Fonda that use the word "single" in their
titles. The merits of the individual works vary widely, but taken together
they evoke an oddly soulless counterculture, a sluggish mainstream underground that sold out even before it could drop out.

The mopey inertia of twentystuff culture is, in a way, no surprise.
A generation whose defining collective experience is its lack of defining
collective experiences, whose Woodstock was watching *The Partridge
Family* with a couple of friends and whose great moral dilemma is "paper
or plastic?" is unlikely to produce a crop of quick-witted passionate
radicals. That would require adversaries; but the twentysomethings' one
true nemesis—the media monster that babysat them through their loveless youths—has managed to convince them that it's their buddy, a
partner in self-realization.

Consider *Melrose Place,* a show about a group of mildly disillusioned, urban young people, manufactured by Aaron Spelling, the same man who, with *The Love Boat* and *Dynasty,* did much of the initial illusioning. The program has all the twentystuff hallmarks, from a mailing address for a premise (in twentystuff narratives, zip code is destiny) to therapy-speak dialogue ("I think it's really good that you're feeling these things that you're talking about"). It's basically an ensemble coping drama, with stressors-of-the-week—career troubles, problem pregnancies—replacing storylines. The show ends when everyone has aired their issues, exchanged supportive hugs. Conflicts are not resolved, they're extinguished, flash fires of emotion brought under control by pouring words on them.

The same goes for the recent movie *Singles,* a cut above *Melrose* in craftsmanship and acting but identical in its tone of plucky pathos. Once again, the lazy organizing principle is physical location, a grungy, Seattle apartment building populated by pure-hearted young folks saddled with dead-end jobs and ingrown dreams. Jaded and wary, with uncertain prospects, these white-kid nouvelle losers struggle for intimacy, fail, and then try again and provisionally succeed. In this twentystuff soap opera, public causes exist to be gestured at ("Think Globally, Act Locally," reads a bumper sticker), but private life is all the life there is, the world's having shrunk to the cramped dimensions of one's wacky, sad, starter apartment with its sardonic, cheap, recycled furnishings. Indeed, it is this notion of recycling—both of material and cultural goods—that's the essence of the twentystuff esthetic. In *Singles,* casual friends are recycled into pseudo-family members, then into lovers, then back into friends. Portentous seventies rock 'n' roll is recycled into the glum "Seattle sound." Last night's takeout is this morning's breakfast and yesterday's philosophical fads (in this case, a paperback copy of *The Fountainhead* toted around by Bridget Fonda) are today's amusements. Resigning one's self to living off the table scraps of the American century is what twentystuff culture is all about. It's about recycling anger into irony, pain into poses.

Just check out an issue of *Details* magazine, a monthly lifestyle guide   5 for wannabe desolation angels. In a recent issue that also happens to feature an interview with recycled guru Allen Ginsberg—adopted bard of all postwar youthquakes—the bedrooms of arty young single males are inspected for hidden fashion statements ("What your crib says about you"). Paolo, described as a "sound engineer/motorcycle racer," takes obvious pride in his wacky scavenging, in the fragments he has shored against his ruin: "I found the dentist's chair on the street; the sofa is the back seat of a van." Then there's Craig, a "graphic designer/DJ" (the cute juxtapositions never end), who boasts: "The trunk's from a thrift shop, the cowhide rug was a gift." The implication, of course, is that one can never be too aware of the ironic signals one is sending, even while alone, in private. According to the twentystuff credo, one's life is a self-directed TV series (*Wayne's World! Wayne's World!*), and one is always spiritually on-camera.

That's sad, I think. Not funny-sad, just sad. Consumers tricked into thinking they're producers, entombed in their own bemused self-consciousness, acting at life instead of taking action, the devotees of twentystuff may be a lost generation, indeed.

Reading the Text

1. What, according to Kirn, are the characteristics of "twentysomethings" in television programs today?
2. What does Kirn mean by saying "resigning one's self to living off the table scraps of the American century is what twentystuff culture is all about"?
3. How does Kirn explain the "pathology" that he attributes to the "twentysomething" generation?

Reading the Signs

1. Kirn neglects to mention that many of the shows he criticizes are written and produced by people who are far from "twentysomething." How does this omission affect the credibility of his argument?
2. Take Kirn up on his challenge: Check out an issue of *Details* magazine. Is it, as Kirn claims, "a monthly lifestyle guide for wannabe desolation angels"? Write an essay in which you support, refute, or modify his characterization of this magazine and its readership.
3. Watch an episode of one of the TV shows that Kirn discusses, and write your own analysis of it. How does it function as a sign of the "twentysomething" generation, in your view?
4. In class, discuss Kirn's tone. How does it affect your response to his essay?
5. Kirn can be accused of stereotyping a generation. In a journal entry, explore the implications of such stereotyping. Is it based in reality? What difference does it make if a generation—as opposed to, say, an ethnic group—is stereotyped? If you are part of the generation Kirn attacks, how does his article make you feel? How does his stereotyping compare with images of "baby boomers"?

CHAPTER FOUR

THE HOLLYWOOD
SIGN

The Semiotics of American Film

Let's play Jeopardy. Category: Hollywood Movies for $100. Ready? "Based upon the adventures of a well-known comic book hero, it was the biggest grossing movie of 1989." Your response? And now a daily double for $500: "Another comics-based film released in 1990, its cast included a popular music star." Your response?

Time's up. Have you got them yet? The correct responses are "What is *Batman*?" and "What is *Dick Tracy*?" Did you get them both? Nice work.

We presume that you didn't have much difficulty with the first question. Who *didn't* see *Batman*? Or at least see an ad for it? Or a product tie-in: a T-shirt, cap, mug, cereal box? The bonus question, on the other hand, might have been a bit trickier, because *Dick Tracy,* in spite of its attempts to repeat *Batman's* magic box office formula, didn't do as well. No legends grew up around the film. Worse yet, no sequel. Not that *Dick Tracy* didn't try, with all of the hype and product tie-ins, but there it is: two rather similar films, similarly promoted and marketed, yet with two rather different popular outcomes. These two films can lead us to another semiotic question, another "Why?" Why *Batman* and not *Dick Tracy*?

You may be thinking: "That's easy; *Dick Tracy* was a lousy film. And Jack Nicholson was awesome!" This may be true, but such explanations involve judgments of value, and semiotic analysis doesn't call for value judgments. Besides, even *Batman's* fans thought its plot was poorly constructed and that the love interest between Bruce Wayne and Vickie Vale was a major blunder. They even agreed that Michael Keaton wasn't especially compelling in his role and that Kim Basinger was an outright disaster. And yet back they came, eager to watch once more this dark film about a millionaire crime fighter and his battle to the death against a savvy psychopath. To put this another way, if it *was* Jack Nicholson's Joker who did the trick for *Batman,* there had to be something about this character that especially appealed to his fans, something that can be explained not only in terms of the film's aesthetics but through an analysis of the popular cultural system into which it fit as well.

We must ask, then, not which film was better but what popular cultural mythologies did they reflect (or fail to reflect)? What was the *system* behind the screen?

The Postmodern Mythology

First, of course, *Batman* related to all those *other* cartoon-based feature films. Did you ever see *Popeye,* or the *Superman* films with Christopher Reeve? If you did, how did they differ from earlier movies based on comic book heroes? Did you detect any sense of parody in the films, a campy humor that let you know that you weren't supposed to take them seriously? For example, what about the seduction of Lois Lane in *Superman II,* which caused viewers to wonder, with a wicked chuckle, just what a genuinely super lover would be like in bed? Or what was the effect of casting Robin Williams as Popeye? Did you consider Williams a "serious" character? Or did you have fun watching what this zany comedian would do with such a corny part, how he'd play both Popeye *and* Robin Williams at the same time?

If you have ever detected an air of self-parody in a recent Hollywood film—any film, it doesn't have to be *Popeye* or *Superman*—then you are on to one of the prime strategies of *postmodern* movie making. The postmodern style, in brief, represents the world view that it is no longer possible or desirable to create new characters or images in movies; rather, one surveys the vast range of available images that old movies (and the electronic media in general) offer and repeats them, but with a difference. Consider what Madonna does with the image of Marilyn Monroe in her video "Material Girl," a half-serious, half-parodic remake of Monroe's film *Gentlemen Prefer Blondes.* In the video, Madonna both resembles Marilyn Monroe and doesn't. Her image recycles an older popular cultural icon—Marilyn—but with a new spin. It's the same, and not the same, simultaneously.

The sense of parody, of repetition with a difference, is crucial here, for many films repeat old images but are not at all postmodern. Disney's *Beauty and the Beast,* for instance, is a cartoon movie that repeats an old

|||||||||||||||||||||||||||||||||||||||||||||||||||||||||||||||||||||||||||||||||||||||||||||||||||||||||||||||||||||||||||||||||||||

Discussing the Signs of Film

In class, discuss why *Jurassic Park* was such a blockbuster in 1993. What popular cultural myths does *Jurassic Park* reflect? Does the film share any similarities with other Steven Spielberg hits, such as *E. T.*? What is the appeal of the visual imagery? Who is the audience for this film? Use the questions to guide your class discussion of why *this* film became such a success.

story, but the film is a romantic fantasy, not a postmodern parody. Monty Python's *Monty Python and the Holy Grail,* in contrast, is a purely postmodern spoof of the ancient tales of King Arthur and his court. The movie retells the old story of the quest for the Holy Grail, but oh what a difference! It's that zany difference, that repetition of what we've already seen somewhere but with a comic edge that mocks even as it retells, that sets off the truly postmodern flick.

Batman fully qualifies as a postmodern movie in this regard. For not only did it consciously recycle and parody existing pop cultural images and poses (as in its amusing send-ups of television news anchors), it appropriated images from earlier films. This strategy is particularly apparent in the movie's climactic scene, which contains visual references that range from Alfred Hitchcock's *Vertigo* to Ridley Scott's *Blade Runner* (all that falling off tall buildings in dark and sinister surroundings). Parts of the movie deliberately resemble classic detective movies from the thirties and forties, while others resemble science fiction film scenarios. And finally, there's the Joker, a postmodern villain if there ever was one, with his acute sensitivity to popular culture and the media (one of his first acts is to take over the airwaves) and his epic raid on an art museum, where he trashes the cherished images of traditional culture with a zeal that could make the most radical postmodern artist envious.

Dick Tracy similarly tried to be a postmodern film, but in the end it remained too faithful to Chester Gould's comic book values to qualify. Though, like *Batman, Dick Tracy* cultivated a "retro" look that recycled the classic settings of the old detective films and also featured a quasi-comic, philosophical archvillain, neither the set nor the characters broadcast the postmodern signal that the whole thing is a send-up. Madonna's Breathless Mahoney, for example, was too straight a portrayal, looking too much like a serious remake of a classic femme fatale, while Warren Beatty's Tracy, with his Tess Trueheart and Boy Scout imperviousness to sexual temptation, is far too corny to work in a postmodern context. And Al Pacino, hard as he tried to make Big Boy Caprice measure up to Nicholson's Joker, just wasn't given the proper postmodern material.

He's interested in the *stage,* in nightclub floor shows and torch singers, not TV or the movies. Quite simply, the old boy has no media savvy. He was outdated from the start.

Thus, in failing to make the postmodern scene, *Dick Tracy* failed to capture the imagination of a growing audience of postmodern viewers, of moviegoers whose own sensibilities have been shaped by the media and who know all the images and how they may be parodied or trashed. You are a part of that audience, and while you may not have been consciously aware of the postmodern appeal of *Batman* when you saw it, you were probably affected by it. Why not rent the video and have another look? See all those sly references to the media and the parodies? How does the Joker's museum-wrecking spree strike you now?

Official Heroes and Outlaw Heroes

We don't want to suggest, however, that the postmodern climate of *Batman's* appearance alone accounted for its monumental success. One reason for this success was the sheer number of Batman fans whose allegiance to the caped crusader had created a cottage industry in Bat lore long before the film's release. Graphic novels such as *Batman: The Dark Knight Returns* (1986) and *Arkham Asylum* (1989) had taken the story of the Batman well beyond the superhero format in which he appears in DC Comics, establishing him as a crime fighter of a wholly different kind than the sunnier Superman. Thus, like the trekkies (or trekkers) for whom *Star Trek: The Motion Picture* was a cinematic second coming, the Batfans were intrigued by this new entry into the Batfiles. All the trailers had hinted that this wasn't going to be jolly old Adam West. Instead, a dark, psychologically troubling Batman was in the works, and the Batfans came out in droves to see him.

But this doesn't explain *why* the Batman figure inspired such a de-voted following in the first place. Why were so many people waiting with such anticipation for a new film about him? To help you answer this question in semiotic terms, we suggest that you turn to Robert Ray's discussion of outlaw heroes and official heroes on page 241. There you will find an analysis of two types of hero that have traditionally appealed to Americans, both in the movies and in history. In Ray's terms, what sort of a hero is Batman? What sort is Dick Tracy? Which kind of hero do you prefer? Does this affect your opinion of the two films?

Race, Gender, and Just Plain Outlaws

Perhaps neither sort of hero particularly appeals to you, however. Perhaps another kind of hero captures your fancy these days, a hero who isn't a crime fighter at all but a pure outlaw. Deep down, did you find yourself *rooting* for the Joker, for example? Was Hannibal Lector your favorite character in *The Silence of the Lambs*? Were you on Sharon Stone's side in *Basic Instinct*? In short, do you find yourself drawn to clever outlaws who know how to manipulate the system against the system?

There are signs that many Americans, especially the young, are increasingly attracted to movie characters who are outside the law, pure and simple. Such characters may be seen to embody their viewers' own frustration with an increasingly dysfunctional society, with an official America that may be perceived as letting them down or even as being the cause of their troubles in the first place. Consequently, when official society itself is viewed as the enemy, only the pure outlaw can be a hero.

Such feelings of alienation from official society can be especially strong if you belong to a group that has been historically excluded from the mainstream culture. Do you belong to such a group? How do you respond to the official heroes you see on the silver screen? Does it make you long for some heroes who won't have anything to do with official America, heroes, for example, like Malcolm X?

The appearance in 1992 of Spike Lee's epic film *Malcolm X* was a sign of just such a desire for many Americans. For Malcolm X was a real-life outlaw, a man who refused to compromise with the racial status quo in America even to the extent of opposing Martin Luther King, Jr.'s, integrationist approach to the civil rights struggle. Martin Luther King has gone on to become one of America's official heroes, but Malcolm X is reemerging today as a hero of another sort, a mythic figure whose significance varies depending upon who is interpreting him. Thus, the meaning of a movie like *Malcolm X* is relative to its audience. The film may make some white viewers uncomfortable, whereas some black viewers may feel that the movie's portrait of the man isn't radical enough, that Lee toned down the image of Malcolm X to make him more acceptable to whites. What do you think? Does Lee turn Malcolm X into a would-be official hero? Does he let him be an outlaw? What sort of hero would you prefer Malcolm X to be?

About a year before *Malcolm X* appeared in the theaters, a feminist revenge fable called *Thelma and Louise* indicated that many white women were also looking for new heroes of their own. The surprise hit of the 1991 season, *Thelma and Louise* appealed to its viewers largely according to their gender. For millions of women, Thelma and Louise were heroes precisely because they broke the rules, because they preferred to die as outlaws rather than allow themselves to be captured by official America. Male viewers, on the other hand, were a lot less likely to identify with them. One can read the growing uneasiness of American men with the image of the female outlaw in movies like *Basic Instinct,* wherein a female bisexual murderer stalks Northern California in a gruesome depiction of men's greatest fears of female sexuality and power. Though she is sup- posedly exonerated of the crimes at the end, the final image of the film, a shot of the ice pick used to commit all the murders, sends the chilling

---

Exploring the Signs of Film

In your journal, list your favorite movies. Then consider your list: What does it say about you? What cultural myths do the movies tend to reflect, and why do you think those myths appeal to you? What signs particularly appeal to your emotions? What sort of stories about human life do you most respond to?

---

signal that she will kill again. Why, we can ask, have we been shown such a woman? Why does she get away with her crimes? What does *Basic Instinct* (which was written and directed by men) say about male attitudes toward women's liberation?

Reading the Hollywood Sign: The Poetics of Cinema

So far we have looked at the semiotics of film from a cultural perspective. In our analyses, we have focused on the plots and the characters of films, but a semiotic analysis can also consider the special language of film, the particular way that words and images combine in a cinematic text that is at once heard and seen. For movies have the power to transform visual images into metaphors and symbols, which may carry as much significance as the broad outline of a story.

Consider the Godzilla films of the 1950s. If we study only their plots, we would see nothing more than horror stories featuring a reptilian monster rather like the dragons of medieval literature. But Godzilla was no mere dragon transported to the modern world. The dragons that populate the world of medieval storytelling were often metaphors for Satan, or for the serpent in the Garden of Eden, but Godzilla was a wholly different sort of metaphor. Created by Japanese filmmakers, Godzilla arose from a biological mutation caused by nuclear contamination. He represented nuclear war itself, the overwhelming power of the bomb, which the Japanese alone have experienced. Similarly, all those "blob" movies, all the B horror films featuring laboratory experiments run amok, functioned as metaphors, as signifiers of a cultural fear that science—especially nuclear science—was leading not to progress but to annihilation.

Filmmakers work with smaller metaphors as well, using visual cues to clue their viewers in on the meaning of their films. At the end of the 1950s classic *Giant,* for example, we are shown a tableau of a white baby goat standing next to a black baby goat, and then of a white baby standing in a crib side by side with a brown baby. The human babies are the grandchildren of the film's hero, played by Rock Hudson, one of whose sons has married a woman of Mexican extraction. By the end of the film, racial harmony has been established through these first cousins, whose partial racial difference symbolizes the film's hopes for a future of harmonious relations between Texans of Anglo and Mexican heritage. The film's director added the goats to make sure we got the point.

While it is a director's job to use signs in a creative way, there are also mythic signs to be found in films that their directors may not be conscious of. Mythological structures—the heroic types, for example, that appear in American cinema as official and outlaw heroes—can tell you about the culture of a film, the unspoken presuppositions held by directors and viewers alike. Interpreting a film seriously, then, includes the analysis both of its director's intentions and of the culture to which the director belongs. The one type of analysis tends to be more aesthetically oriented, the other more sociological or anthropological. Which type you choose (of course, both may be pursued simultaneously) depends upon your purposes. If you are writing an analysis of the films of a particular director, you may want to concentrate on decoding his or her own visual metaphors and semiotic cues; if you are searching for the pulse of American society, you may prefer to look for myths that directors themselves may not be aware of *as myths*. In analyses of this type, one needn't be too concerned with the director's intentions. Often a film's cultural significance is invisible to its creator.

Reading a film, then, is much like reading a poem or a novel. Both are texts filled with intentional and unintentional signs. The major difference is in the medium of expression. Literary texts are entirely cast in written words; films combine verbal language, visual imagery, and sound effects. We perceive literary and cinematic texts differently, of course, for the written sign is perceived in a linear fashion that relies upon one's cognitive and imaginative powers, while a film primarily targets the senses: One sees and hears (and sometimes even smells!). The fact that film is such a sensory experience often conceals its textuality. One is tempted to lie back and enjoy the show, to say that it's only entertainment and doesn't have to "mean" anything at all. But as cinematic forms of storytelling overtake written forms of expression, the study of movies as complex texts bearing cultural messages and values is becoming increasingly important. Musician Paul Simon once wrote that "the words of the prophets are written on the subway walls," but now they are also on the screen, and our "libraries" are increasingly to be found in minimalls, where the texts of Hollywood can be had for two dollars a night.

The Readings

The readings in this chapter address the various kinds of myths that pervade Hollywood films, starting with Robert Ray's analysis of how America's official and outlaw heroes appear both in the cinema and in history. From a Hollywood insider's perspective, Linda Seger, addressing herself to aspiring screenwriters, explains which heroic archetypes work best in American movies. The remaining readings focus on what specific films reveal about the myths cherished by the cultures in which they were created. Umberto Eco's semiotic analysis of *Casablanca* argues that this old classic's enduring popularity can be attributed to its exploitation of just about every cultural myth in the book. Diane Raymond and Tania Modleski each take on the Hollywood patriarchy, providing feminist readings of *Three Men and a Baby* and *Dead Poets Society,* respectively. Michael Parenti provides a social class–based approach to the codes of American cinema, while Shelby Steele tackles Malcolm X, the man and the movie. Finally, some comments by African-American viewers of *Malcolm X* suggest what the film meant to members of the moviegoing public.

ROBERT B. RAY
The Thematic Paradigm

||||||||||||||||||||||||||||||||||||||||||||||||||||||

Usually we consider movies to be merely entertainment, but as Robert Ray (b. 1943) demonstrates in this selection from his book A Certain Tendency of the Hollywood Cinema *(1985), American films have long reflected fundamental patterns and contradictions in our society's myths and values. Whether in real life or on the silver screen, Ray explains, Americans have always been ambivalent about the value of civilization, celebrating it through official heroes like George Washington and Jimmy Stewart, while at the same time questioning it through outlaw heroes like Davy Crockett and Jesse James. Especially when presented together in the same film, these two hero types help mediate America's ambivalence, providing a mythic solution. Ray's analyses show how the movies are rich sources for cultural interpretation; they provide a framework for decoding movies as different as* Lethal Weapon *and* Malcolm X. *Robert Ray is a professor of English at the University of Florida, Gainesville.*

The dominant tradition of American cinema consistently found ways to overcome dichotomies. Often, the movies' reconciliatory pattern concentrated on a single character magically embodying diametrically opposite traits. A sensitive violinist was also a tough boxer (*Golden Boy*); a boxer was a gentle man who cared for pigeons (*On the Waterfront*). A gangster became a coward because he was brave (*Angels with Dirty Faces*); a soldier became brave because he was a coward (*Lives of a Bengal Lancer*). A war hero was a former pacifist (*Sergeant York*); a pacifist was a former war hero (*Billy Jack*). The ideal was a kind of inclusiveness that would permit all decisions to be undertaken with the knowledge that the alternative was equally available. The attractiveness of Destry's refusal to use guns (*Destry Rides Again*) depended on the tacit understanding that he could shoot with the best of them, Katharine Hepburn's and Claudette Colbert's revolts against conventionality (*Holiday, It Happened One Night*) on their status as aristocrats.

Such two-sided characters seemed particularly designed to appeal to a collective American imagination steeped in myths of inclusiveness. Indeed, in creating such characters, classic Hollywood had connected with what Erik Erikson has described as the fundamental American psychological pattern:

> The functioning American, as the heir of a history of extreme contrasts and abrupt changes, bases his final ego identity on some tentative combination of dynamic polarities such as migratory and

sedentary, individualistic and standardized, competitive and co-oper-
ative, pious and free-thinking, responsible and cynical, etc. . . . .
    To leave his choices open, the American, on the whole, lives with
two sets of "truths."[1]

The movies traded on one opposition in particular, American culture's traditional dichotomy of individual and community that had generated the most significant pair of competing myths: the outlaw hero
and the official hero.[2] Embodied in the adventurer, explorer, gunfighter,
wanderer, and loner, the outlaw hero stood for that part of the American
imagination valuing self-determination and freedom from entanglements. By contrast, the official hero, normally portrayed as a teacher,
lawyer, politician, farmer, or family man, represented the American belief
in collective action, and the objective legal process that superseded private notions of right and wrong. While the outlaw hero found incar-
nations in the mythic figures of Davy Crockett, Jesse James, Huck Finn,
and all of Leslie Fiedler's "Good Bad Boys" and Daniel Boorstin's "ring-
tailed roarers," the official hero developed around legends associated with
Washington, Jefferson, Lincoln, Lee, and other "Good Good Boys."
    An extraordinary amount of the traditional American mythology
adopted by Classic Hollywood derived from the variations worked by
American ideology around this opposition of natural man versus civilized
man. To the extent that these variations constituted the main tendency
of American literature and legends, Hollywood, in relying on this mythology, committed itself to becoming what Robert Bresson has called
"the Cinema."[3] A brief description of the competing values associated
with this outlaw hero-official hero opposition will begin to suggest its
pervasiveness in traditional American culture.
    1. *Aging:* The attractiveness of the outlaw hero's childishness and   5
propensity to whims, tantrums, and emotional decisions derived from
America's cult of childhood. Fiedler observed that American literature
celebrated "the notion that a mere falling short of adulthood is a guarantee of insight and even innocence." From Huck to Holden Caulfield,
children in American literature were privileged, existing beyond society's
confining rules. Often, they set the plot in motion (e.g., *Intruder in the
Dust, To Kill a Mockingbird*), acting for the adults encumbered by daily

---

    1. Erik H. Erikson, *Childhood and Society* (New York: Norton, 1963), p. 286.
    2. Leading discussions of the individual-community polarity in American culture
can be found in *The Contrapuntal Civilization: Essays Toward a New Understanding of the
American Experience,* ed. Michael Kammen (New York: Crowell, 1971). The most prom-
inent analyses of American literature's use of this opposition remain Leslie A. Fiedler's
Love and Death in the American Novel (New York: Stein and Day, 1966) and A. N. Kaul's
The American Vision (New Haven: Yale University Press, 1963).
    3. Robert Bresson, *Notes on Cinematography,* trans. Jonathan Griffin (New York:
Urizen Books, 1977), p. 12.

affairs. As Fiedler also pointed out, this image of childhood "has impinged upon adult life itself, has become a 'career' like everything else in America,"[4] generating stories like *On the Road* or *Easy Rider* in which adults try desperately to postpone responsibilities by clinging to adolescent lifestyles.

While the outlaw heroes represented a flight from maturity, the official heroes embodied the best attributes of adulthood: sound reasoning and judgment, wisdom and sympathy based on experience. Franklin's *Autobiography* and *Poor Richard's Almanack* constituted this opposing tradition's basic texts, persuasive enough to appeal even to outsiders (*The Great Gatsby*). Despite the legends surrounding Franklin and the other Founding Fathers, however, the scarcity of mature heroes in American literature and mythology indicated American ideology's fundamental preference for youth, a quality that came to be associated with the country itself. Indeed, American stories often distorted the stock figure of the Wise Old Man, portraying him as mad (Ahab), useless (Rip Van Winkle), or evil (the Godfather).

2. *Society and Women:* The outlaw hero's distrust of civilization, typically represented by women and marriage, constituted a stock motif in American mythology. In his *Studies in Classic American Literature,* D. H. Lawrence detected the recurring pattern of flight, observing that the Founding Fathers had come to America "largely to get *away. . . .* Away from what? In the long run, away from themselves. Away from everything."[5] Sometimes, these heroes undertook this flight alone (Thoreau, *Catcher in the Rye*); more often, they joined ranks with other men: Huck with Jim, Ishmael with Queequeg, Jake Barnes with Bill Gorton. Women were avoided as representing the very entanglements this tradition sought to escape: society, the "settled life," confining responsibilities. The outlaw hero sought only uncompromising relationships, involving either a "bad" woman (whose morals deprived her of all rights to entangling domesticity) or other males (who themselves remained independent). Even the "bad" woman posed a threat, since marriage often uncovered the clinging "good" girl underneath. Typically, therefore, American stories avoided this problem by killing off the "bad" woman before the marriage could transpire (*Destry Rides Again, The Big Heat, The Far Country*). Subsequently, within the all-male group, women became taboo, except as the objects of lust.

---

4. Leslie A. Fiedler, *No! In Thunder* (New York: Stein and Day, 1972), pp. 253, 275.

5. D. H. Lawrence, *Studies in Classic American Literature* (New York: Viking/Compass, 1961), p. 3. See also Fiedler's *Love and Death in the American Novel* and Sam Bluefarb's *The Escape Motif in the American Novel: Mark Twain to Richard Wright* (Columbus: Ohio State University Press, 1972).

The exceptional extent of American outlaw legends suggests an ideological anxiety about civilized life. Often, that anxiety took shape as a romanticizing of the dispossessed, as in the Beat Generation's cult of the bum, or the characters of Huck and "Thoreau," who worked to remain idle, unemployed, and unattached. A passage from Jerzy Kosinski's *Steps* demonstrated the extreme modern version of this romanticizing:

> I envied those [the poor and the criminals] who lived here and seemed so free, having nothing to regret and nothing to look forward to. In the world of birth certificates, medical examinations, punch cards, and computers, in the world of telephone books, passports, bank accounts, insurance plans, wills, credit cards, pensions, mortgages and loans, they lived unattached.[6]

In contrast to the outlaw heroes, the official heroes were preeminently worldly, comfortable in society, and willing to undertake even those public duties demanding personal sacrifice. Political figures, particularly Washington and Lincoln, provided the principal examples of this tradition, but images of family also persisted in popular literature from *Little Women* to *Life with Father* and *Cheaper by the Dozen*. The most crucial figure in this tradition, however, was Horatio Alger, whose heroes' ambition provided the complement to Huck's disinterest. Alger's characters subscribed fully to the codes of civilization, devoting themselves to proper dress, manners, and behavior, and the attainment of the very things despised by the opposing tradition: the settled life and respectability.[7]

3. *Politics and the Law:* Writing about "The Philosophical Approach of the Americans," Tocqueville noted "a general distaste for accepting any man's word as proof of anything." That distaste took shape as a traditional distrust of politics as collective activity, and of ideology as that activity's rationale. Such a disavowal of ideology was, of course, itself ideological, a tactic for discouraging systematic political intervention in a nineteenth-century America whose political and economic power remained in the hands of a privileged few. Tocqueville himself noted the results of this mythology of individualism which "disposes each citizen to isolate himself from the mass of his fellows and withdraw into the circle of family and friends; with this little society formed to his taste, he gladly leaves the greater society to look after itself."[8]

10

---

6. Jerzy Kosinski, *Steps* (New York: Random House, 1968), p. 133.

7. See John G. Cawelti, *Apostles of the Self-Made Man: Changing Concepts of Success in America* (Chicago: University of Chicago Press, 1965), pp. 101–123.

8. Alexis de Tocqueville, *Democracy in America,* ed. J. P. Mayer, trans. George Lawrence (Garden City, N.Y.: Anchor/Doubleday, 1969), pp. 430, 506. Irving Howe has confirmed Tocqueville's point, observing that Americans "make the suspicion of

This hostility toward political solutions manifested itself further in an ambivalence about the law. The outlaw mythology portrayed the law, the sum of society's standards, as a collective, impersonal ideology imposed on the individual from without. Thus, the law represented the very thing this mythology sought to avoid. In its place, this tradition offered a natural law discovered intuitively by each man. As Tocqueville observed, Americans wanted "To escape from imposed systems . . . to seek by themselves and in themselves for the only reason for things . . . in most mental operations each American relies on individual effort and judgment" (p. 429). This sense of the law's inadequacy to needs detectable only by the heart generated a rich tradition of legends celebrating legal defiance in the name of some "natural" standard: Thoreau went to jail rather than pay taxes, Huck helped Jim (legally a slave) to escape, Billy the Kid murdered the sheriff's posse that had ambushed his boss, Hester Prynne resisted the community's sexual mores. This mythology transformed all outlaws into Robin Hoods, who "correct" socially unjust laws (Jesse James, Bonnie and Clyde, John Wesley Hardin). Furthermore, by customarily portraying the law as the tool of villains (who used it to revoke mining claims, foreclose on mortgages, and disallow election results—all on legal technicalities), this mythology betrayed a profound pessimism about the individual's access to the legal system.

If the outlaw hero's motto was "I don't know what the law says, but I do know what's right and wrong," the official hero's was "We are a nation of laws, not of men," or "No man can place himself above the law." To the outlaw hero's insistence on private standards of right and wrong, the official hero offered the admonition, "You cannot take the law into your own hands." Often, these official heroes were lawyers or politicians, at times (as with Washington and Lincoln), even the executors of the legal system itself. The values accompanying such heroes modified the assurance of Crockett's advice, "Be sure you're right, then go ahead."

In sum, the values associated with these two different sets of heroes contrasted markedly. Clearly, too, each tradition had its good and bad points. If the extreme individualism of the outlaw hero always verged on selfishness, the respectability of the official hero always threatened to involve either blandness or repression. If the outlaw tradition promised adventure and freedom, it also offered danger and loneliness. If the official tradition promised safety and comfort, it also offered entanglements and boredom.

The evident contradiction between these heroes provoked Daniel Boorstin's observation that "Never did a more incongruous pair than Davy Crockett and George Washington live together in a national Val-

---

ideology into something approaching a national creed." *Politics and the Novel* (New York: Avon, 1970), p. 337.

halla." And yet, as Boorstin admits, "both Crockett and Washington were popular heroes, and both emerged into legendary fame during the first half of the 19th century."[9]

The parallel existence of these two contradictory traditions evinced   15 the general pattern of American mythology: the denial of the necessity for choice. In fact, this mythology often portrayed situations requiring decision as temporary aberrations from American life's normal course. By discouraging commitment to any single set of values, this mythology fostered an ideology of improvisation, individualism, and ad hoc solutions for problems depicted as crises. American writers have repeatedly attempted to justify this mythology in terms of material sources. Hence, Irving Howe's "explanation":

> It is when men no longer feel that they have adequate choices in their styles of life, when they conclude that there are no longer possibilities of honorable maneuver and compromise, when they decide that the time has come for "ultimate" social loyalties and political decisions— it is then that ideology begins to flourish. Ideology reflects a hardening of commitment, the freezing of opinion into system. . . . The uniqueness of our history, the freshness of our land, the plenitude of our resources—all these have made possible, and rendered plausible, a style of political improvisation and intellectual free-wheeling.[10]

Despite such an account's pretext of objectivity, its language betrays an acceptance of the mythology it purports to describe: "honorable maneuver and compromise," "hardening," "freezing," "uniqueness," "freshness," and "plenitude" are all assumptive words from an ideology that denies its own status. Furthermore, even granting the legitimacy of the historians' authenticating causes, we are left with a persisting mythology increasingly discredited by historical developments. (In fact, such invalidation began in the early nineteenth century, and perhaps even before.)

The American mythology's refusal to choose between its two heroes went beyond the normal reconciliatory function attributed to myth by Lévi-Strauss. For the American tradition not only overcame binary oppositions; it systematically mythologized the certainty of being able to do so. Part of this process involved blurring the lines between the two sets of heroes. First, legends often brought the solemn official heroes back down to earth, providing the sober Washington with the cherry tree, the prudent Franklin with illegitimate children, and even the upright Jefferson with a slave mistress. On the other side, stories modified the outlaw hero's most potentially damaging quality, his tendency to selfish isolationism, by demonstrating that, however reluctantly, he

---

9. Daniel J. Boorstin, *The Americans: The National Experience* (New York: Random House, 1965), p. 337.

10. *Politics and the Novel*, p. 164.

would act for causes beyond himself. Thus, Huck grudgingly helped Jim escape, and Davy Crockett left the woods for three terms in Congress before dying in the Alamo for Texas independence. In this blurring process, Lincoln, a composite of opposing traits, emerged as the great American figure. His status as president made him an ex officio official hero. But his Western origins, melancholy solitude, and unaided decision-making all qualified him as a member of the other side. Finally, his ambivalent attitude toward the law played the most crucial role in his complex legend. As the chief executive, he inevitably stood for the principle that "we are a nation of laws and not men"; as the Great Emancipator, on the other hand, he provided the prime example of taking the law into one's own hands in the name of some higher standard.

Classic Hollywood's gallery of composite heroes (boxing musicians, rebellious aristocrats, pacifist soldiers) clearly derived from this mythology's rejection of final choices, a tendency whose traces Erikson detected in American psychology:

> The process of American identity formation seems to support an individual's ego identity as long as he can preserve a certain element of deliberate tentativeness of autonomous choice. The individual must be able to convince himself that the next step is up to him and that no matter where he is staying or going he always had the choice of leaving or turning in the opposite direction if he chooses to do so. In this country the migrant does not want to be told to move on, nor the sedentary man to stay where he is; for the life style (and the family history) of each contains the opposite element as a potential alternative which he wishes to consider his most private and individual decision.[11]

The reconciliatory pattern found its most typical incarnation, however, in one particular narrative: the story of the private man attempting to keep from being drawn into action on any but his own terms. In this story, the reluctant hero's ultimate willingness to help the community satisfied the official values. But by portraying this aid as demanding only a temporary involvement, the story preserved the values of individualism as well.

Like the contrasting heroes' epitomization of basic American dichotomies, the reluctant hero story provided a locus for displacement. Its most famous version, for example, *The Adventures of Huckleberry Finn,* offered a typically individualistic solution to the nation's unresolved racial and sectional anxieties, thereby helping to forestall more systematic governmental measures. In adopting this story, Classic Hollywood retained its censoring power, using it, for example, in *Casablanca* to conceal the realistic threats to American self-determination posed by World War II.

---

11. *Childhood and Society,* p. 286.

Because the reluctant hero story was clearly the basis of the Western, American literature's repeated use of it prompted Leslie Fiedler to call the classic American novels "disguised westerns."[12] In the movies, too, this story appeared in every genre: in Westerns, of course (with *Shane* its most schematic articulation), but also in gangster movies (*Angels with Dirty Faces, Key Largo*), musicals (*Swing Time*), detective stories (*The Thin Man*), war films (*Air Force*), screwball comedy (*The Philadelphia Story*), "problem pictures" (*On the Waterfront*), and even science fiction (the Han Solo character in *Star Wars*). *Gone with the Wind,* in fact, had two selfish heroes who came around at the last moment, Scarlett (taking care of Melanie) and Rhett (running the Union blockade), incompatible only because they were so much alike. The natural culmination of this pattern, perfected by Hollywood in the 1930s and early 1940s, was *Casablanca.* Its version of the outlaw hero–official hero struggle (Rick versus Laszlo) proved stunningly effective, its resolution (their collaboration on the war effort) the prototypical Hollywood ending.

The reluctant hero story's tendency to minimize the official hero's role (by making him dependent on the outsider's intervention) suggested an imbalance basic to the American mythology: Despite the existence of both heroes, the national ideology clearly preferred the outlaw. This ideology strove to make that figure's origins seem spontaneous, concealing the calculated, commercial efforts behind the mythologizing of typical examples like Billy the Kid and Davy Crockett. Its willingness, on the other hand, to allow the official hero's traces to show enables Daniel Boorstin to observe of one such myth, "There were elements of spontaneity, of course, in the Washington legend, too, but it was, for the most part, a self-conscious product."[13]

The apparent spontaneity of the outlaw heroes assured their popularity. By contrast, the official values had to rely on a rational allegiance that often wavered. These heroes' different statuses accounted for a structure fundamental to American literature, and assumed by Classic Hollywood: a split between the moral center and the interest center of a story. Thus, while the typical Western contained warnings against violence as a solution, taking the law into one's own hands, and moral isolationism, it simultaneously glamorized the outlaw hero's intense self-possession and willingness to use force to settle what the law could not. In other circumstances, Ishmael's evenhanded philosophy paled beside Ahab's moral vehemence, consciously recognizable as destructive.

D. H. Lawrence called this split the profound "duplicity" at the heart of nineteenth-century American fiction, charging that the classic novels evinced "a tight mental allegiance to a morality which all [the author's]

---

12. *Love and Death in the American Novel,* p. 355.
13. *The Americans: The National Experience,* p. 337.

passion goes to destroy." Certainly, too, this "duplicity" involved the mythology's pattern of obscuring the necessity for choosing between contrasting values. Richard Chase has put the matter less pejoratively in an account that applies equally to the American cinema:

> The American novel tends to rest in contradictions and among extreme ranges of experience. When it attempts to resolve contradictions, it does so in oblique, morally equivocal ways. As a general rule it does so either in melodramatic actions or in pastoral idylls, although inter-mixed with both one may find the stirring instabilities of "American humor."[14]

Or, in other words, when faced with a difficult choice, American stories resolved it either simplistically (by refusing to acknowledge that a choice is necessary), sentimentally (by blurring the differences between the two sides), or by laughing the whole thing off.

Reading the Text

1. What are the two basic hero types that Ray describes in American cinema?
2. How do these two hero types relate to America's "psychological pattern"?
3. Explain why, according to Ray, the outlaw hero typically mistrusts women.

Reading the Signs

1. In "Malcolm X" (p. 287), Shelby Steele offers his reading of Malcolm X as a cinematic hero. Review Steele's selection and compare his analysis with Ray's discussion of heroes. To what extent does Ray's essay shed light on Malcolm's status as a hero?
2. Read Gary Engle's "What Makes Superman So Darned American?" (p. 309) and Andy Medhurst's "Batman, Deviance, and Camp" (p. 323), and write an essay in which you explain which type of heroes Superman and Batman are to their audiences.
3. What sort of hero is Arnold Schwarzenegger in the *Terminator* films? Write an essay in which you apply Ray's categories of hero to the Schwarzenegger character, supporting your argument with specific reference to one or more films.
4. In class, note on the blackboard official and outlaw heroes you've seen in movies. Then categorize these heroes according to characteristics they have in common (such as race, gender, profession, or social class). What patterns emerge in your categories, and what is the significance of those patterns?

---

14. Richard Chase, *The American Novel and Its Tradition* (Garden City, N.Y.: Anchor/Doubleday, 1957), p. 1.

5. Rent one of the *Alien* films, and discuss whether Sigourney Weaver fits either of Ray's two categories of hero.
6. Cartoon characters such as Bart Simpson and Ren of *Ren and Stimpy* don't readily fit Ray's two types of hero. Invent a third type of hero to accommodate such characters.

LINDA SEGER

Creating the Myth

To be a successful screenwriter, Linda Seger suggests in this selection from Making a Good Script Great *(1987), you've got to know your archetypes. Seger reveals the secret behind the success of such Hollywood creations as* Star Wars's *Luke Skywalker and tells you how you can create such heroes yourself. In this "how to" approach to the cinema, Seger echoes the more academic judgments of such semioticians of film as Umberto Eco—the road to popular success in mass culture is paved with cultural myths and clichés. A script consultant and author who has given professional seminars on filmmaking around the world, Seger also writes on drama, theology, and women's studies.*

All of us have similar experiences. We share in the life journey of growth, development, and transformation. We live the same stories, whether they involve the search for a perfect mate, coming home, the search for fulfillment, going after an ideal, achieving the dream, or hunting for a precious treasure. Whatever our culture, there are universal stories that form the basis for all our particular stories. The trappings might be different, the twists and turns that create suspense might change from culture to culture, the particular characters may take different forms, but underneath it all, it's the same story, drawn from the same experiences.

Many of the most successful films are based on these universal stories. They deal with the basic journey we take in life. We identify with the heroes because we were once heroic (descriptive) or because we wish we could do what the hero does (prescriptive). When Joan Wilder finds the jewel and saves her sister, or James Bond saves the world, or Shane saves the family from the evil ranchers, we identify with the character, and subconsciously recognize the story as having some connection with our own lives. It's the same story as the fairy tales about getting the three golden hairs from the devil, or finding the treasure and winning the princess. And it's not all that different a story from the caveman killing the woolly beast or the Roman slave gaining his freedom through skill and courage. These are our stories—personally and collectively—and the most successful films contain these universal experiences.

Some of these stories are "search" stories. They address our desire to find some kind of rare and wonderful treasure. This might include the search for outer values such as job, relationship, or success; or for inner values such as respect, security, self-expression, love, or home. But it's all a similar search.

Some of these stories are "hero" stories. They come from our own experiences of overcoming adversity, as well as our desire to do great and special acts. We root for the hero and celebrate when he or she achieves the goal because we know that the hero's journey is in many ways similar to our own.

We call these stories *myths.* Myths are the common stories at the   5 root of our universal existence. They're found in all cultures and in all literature, ranging from the Greek myths to fairy tales, legends, and stories drawn from all of the world's religions.

A myth is a story that is "more than true." Many stories are true because one person, somewhere, at some time, lived it. It is based on fact. But a myth is more than true because it is lived by all of us, at some level. It's a story that connects and speaks to us all.

Some myths are true stories that attain mythic significance because the people involved seem larger than life, and seem to live their lives more intensely than common folk. Martin Luther King, Jr., Gandhi, Sir Edmund Hillary, and Lord Mountbatten personify the types of journeys we identify with, because we've taken similar journeys—even if only in a very small way.

Other myths revolve around make-believe characters who might capsulize for us the sum total of many of our journeys. Some of these make-believe characters might seem similar to the characters we meet in our dreams. Or they might be a composite of types of characters we've met.

In both cases, the myth is the "story beneath the story." It's the universal pattern that shows us that Gandhi's journey toward independence and Sir Edmund Hillary's journey to the top of Mount Everest contain many of the same dramatic beats. And these beats are the same beats that Rambo takes to set free the MIAs, that Indiana Jones takes to find the Lost Ark, and that Luke Skywalker takes to defeat the Evil Empire.

In *Hero with a Thousand Faces,* Joseph Campbell traces the elements   10 that form the hero myth. "In their own work with myth, writer Chris Vogler and seminar leader Thomas Schlesinger have applied this criteria to *Star Wars.* The myth within the story helps explain why millions went to see this film again and again."

The hero myth has specific story beats that occur in all hero stories. They show who the hero is, what the hero needs, and how the story and character interact in order to create a transformation. The journey toward heroism is a process. This universal process forms the spine of all the particular stories, such as the *Star Wars* trilogy.

The Hero Myth

1. In most hero stories, the hero is introduced in ordinary surroundings, in a mundane world, doing mundane things. Generally, the hero begins as a nonhero; innocent, young, simple, or humble. In *Star Wars,* the first time we see Luke Skywalker, he's unhappy about having to do his chores, which consists of picking out some new droids for work. He wants to go out and have fun. He wants to leave his planet and go to the Academy, but he's stuck. This is the setup of most myths. This is how we meet the hero before the call to adventure.

2. Then something new enters the hero's life. It's a catalyst that sets the story into motion. It might be a telephone call, as in *Romancing the Stone,* or the German attack in *The African Queen,* or the holograph of Princess Leia in *Star Wars.* Whatever form it takes, it's a new ingredient that pushes the hero into an extraordinary adventure. With this call, the stakes are established, and a problem is introduced that demands a solution.

3. Many times, however, the hero doesn't want to leave. He or she is a reluctant hero, afraid of the unknown, uncertain, perhaps, if he or she is up to the challenge. In *Star Wars,* Luke receives a double call to adventure. First, from Princess Leia in the holograph, and then through Obi-Wan Kenobi, who says he needs Luke's help. But Luke is not ready to go. He returns home, only to find that the Imperial Stormtroopers have burned his farmhouse and slaughtered his family. Now he is personally motivated, ready to enter into the adventure.

4. In any journey, the hero usually receives help, and the help often comes from unusual sources. In many fairy tales, an old woman, a dwarf, a witch, or a wizard helps the hero. The hero achieves the goal because of this help, and because the hero is receptive to what this person has to give.

There are a number of fairy tales where the first and second son are sent to complete a task, but they ignore the helpers, often scorning them. Many times they are severely punished for their lack of humility and unwillingness to accept help. Then the third son, the hero, comes along. He receives the help, accomplishes the task, and often wins the princess.

In *Star Wars,* Obi-Wan Kenobi is a perfect example of the "helper" character. He is a kind of mentor to Luke, one who teaches him the

Way of the Force and whose teachings continue even after his death. This mentor character appears in most hero stories. He is the person who has special knowledge, special information, and special skills. This might be the prospector in *The Treasure of the Sierra Madre,* or the psychiatrist in *Ordinary People,* or Quint in *Jaws,* who knows all about sharks, or the Good Witch of the North who gives Dorothy the ruby slippers in *The Wizard of Oz.* In *Star Wars,* Obi-Wan gives Luke the light saber that was the special weapon of the Jedi Knight. With this, Luke is ready to move forward and do his training and meet adventure.

5. The hero is now ready to move into the special world where he or she will change from the ordinary into the extraordinary. This starts the hero's transformation, and sets up the obstacles that must be surmounted to reach the goal. Usually, this happens at the first Turning Point of the story, and leads into Act Two development. In *Star Wars,* Obi-Wan and Luke search for a pilot to take them to the planet of Alderan, so that Obi-Wan can deliver the plans to Princess Leia's father. These plans are essential to the survival of the Rebel Forces. With this action, the adventure is ready to begin.

6. Now begin all the tests and obstacles necessary to overcome the enemy and accomplish the hero's goals. In fairy tales, this often means getting past witches, outwitting the devil, avoiding robbers, or confronting evil. In Homer's *Odyssey,* it means blinding the Cyclops, escaping from the island of the Lotus-Eaters, resisting the temptation of the singing Sirens, and surviving a shipwreck. In *Star Wars,* innumerable adventures confront Luke. He and his cohorts must run to the *Millennium Falcon,* narrowly escaping the Stormtroopers before jumping into hyperspace. They must make it through the meteor shower after Alderan has been destroyed. They must evade capture on the Death Star, rescue the Princess, and even survive a garbage crusher.

7. At some point in the story, the hero often hits rock bottom. He often has a "death experience," leading to a type of rebirth. In *Star Wars,* Luke seems to have died when the serpent in the garbage-masher pulls him under, but he's saved just in time to ask R2D2 to stop the masher before they're crushed. This is often the "black moment" at the second turning point, the point when the worst is confronted, and the action now moves toward the exciting conclusion.

8. Now, the hero seizes the sword and takes possession of the treasure. He is now in charge, but he still has not completed the journey. Here Luke has the Princess and the plans, but the final confrontation is yet to begin. This starts the third-act escape scene, leading to the final climax.

9. The road back is often the chase scene. In many fairy tales, this is the point where the devil chases the hero and the hero has the last obstacles to overcome before really being free and safe. His challenge is

20

to take what he has learned and integrate it into his daily life. He *must* return to renew the mundane world. In *Star Wars,* Darth Vader is in hot pursuit, planning to blow up the Rebel Planet.

10. Since every hero story is essentially a transformation story, we need to see the hero changed at the end, resurrected into a new type of life. He must face the final ordeal before being "reborn" as the hero, proving his courage and becoming transformed. This is the point, in many fairy tales, where the Miller's Son becomes the Prince or the King and marries the Princess. In *Star Wars,* Luke has survived, becoming quite a different person from the innocent young man he was in Act One.

At this point, the hero returns and is reintegrated into his society. In *Star Wars,* Luke has destroyed the Death Star, and he receives his great reward.

This is the classic "Hero Story." We might call this example a *mission*   25
or *task myth,* where the person has to complete a task, but the task itself is not the real treasure. The real reward for Luke is the love of the Princess and the safe, new world he had helped create.

A myth can have many variations. We see variations on this myth in James Bond films (although they lack much of the depth because the hero is not transformed), and in *The African Queen,* where Rose and Allnutt must blow up the *Louisa,* or in *Places in the Heart,* where Edna overcomes obstacles to achieve family stability.

The *treasure myth* is another variation on this theme, as seen in *Romancing the Stone.* In this story, Joan receives a map and a phone call which forces her into the adventure. She is helped by an American bird catcher and a Mexican pickup truck driver. She overcomes the obstacles of snakes, the jungle, waterfalls, shootouts, and finally receives the treasure, along with the "prince."

Whether the hero's journey is for a treasure or to complete a task, the elements remain the same. The humble, reluctant hero is called to an adventure. The hero is helped by a variety of unique characters. S/he must overcome a series of obstacles that transform him or her in the process, and then faces the final challenge that draws on inner and outer resources.

The Healing Myth

Although the hero myth is the most popular story, many myths involve healing. In these stories, some character is "broken" and must leave home to become whole again.

The universal experience behind these healing stories is our psycho-   30
logical need for rejuvenation, for balance. The journey of the hero into

exile is not all that different from the weekend in Palm Springs, or the trip to Hawaii to get away from it all, or lying still in a hospital bed for some weeks to heal. In all cases, something is out of balance and the mythic journey moves toward wholeness.

Being broken can take several forms. It can be physical, emotional, or psychological. Usually, it's all three. In the process of being exiled or hiding out in the forest, the desert, or even the Amish farm in *Witness,* the person becomes whole, balanced, and receptive to love. Love in these stories is both a healing force and a reward.

Think of John Book in *Witness.* In Act One, we see a frenetic, insensitive man, afraid of commitment, critical and unreceptive to the feminine influences in his life. John is suffering from an "inner wound" which he doesn't know about. When he receives an "outer wound" from a gunshot, it forces him into exile, which begins his process of transformation.

At the beginning of Act Two, we see John delirious and close to death. This is a movement into the unconscious, a movement from the rational, active police life of Act One into a mysterious, feminine, more intuitive world. Since John's "inner problem" is the lack of balance with his feminine side, this delirium begins the process of transformation.

Later in Act Two, we see John beginning to change. He moves from his highly independent life-style toward the collective, communal life of his Amish hosts. John now gets up early to milk the cows and to assist with the chores. He uses his carpentry skills to help with the barn building and to complete the birdhouse. Gradually, he begins to develop relationships with Rachel and her son, Samuel. John's life slows down and he becomes more receptive, learning important lessons about love. In Act Three, John finally sees that the feminine is worth saving, and throws down his gun to save Rachel's life. A few beats later, when he has the opportunity to kill Paul, he chooses a nonviolent response instead. Although John doesn't "win" the Princess, he has nevertheless "won" love and wholeness. By the end of the film, we can see that the John Book of Act Three is a different kind of person from the John Book of Act One. He has a different kind of comradeship with his fellow police officers, he's more relaxed, and we can sense that somehow, this experience has formed a more integrated John Book.

Combination Myths

Many stories are combinations of several different myths. Think of   35
Ghostbusters, a simple and rather outrageous comedy about three men saving the city of New York from ghosts. Now think of the story of "Pandora's Box." It's about the woman who let loose all manner of evil upon the earth by opening a box she was told not to touch. In *Ghost-*

busters, the EPA man is a Pandora figure. By shutting off the power to the containment center, he inadvertently unleashes all the ghosts upon New York City. Combine the story of "Pandora's Box" with a hero story, and notice that we have our three heroes battling the Marshmallow Man. One of them also "gets the Princess" when Dr. Peter Venkman finally receives the affections of Dana Barrett. By looking at these combinations, it is apparent that even *Ghostbusters* is more than "just a comedy."

Tootsie is a type of reworking of many Shakespearean stories where a woman has to dress as a man in order to accomplish a certain task. These Shakespearean stories are reminiscent of many fairy tales where the hero becomes invisible or takes on another persona, or wears a specific disguise to hide his or her real qualities. In the stories of "The Twelve Dancing Princesses" or "The Man in the Bearskin," disguise is necessary to achieve a goal. Combine these elements with the transformation themes of the hero myth where a hero (such as Michael) must overcome many obstacles to his success as an actor and a human being. It's not difficult to understand why the *Tootsie* story hooks us.

Archetypes

A myth includes certain characters that we see in many stories. These characters are called *archetypes.* They can be thought of as the original "pattern" or "character type" that will be found on the hero's journey. Archetypes take many forms, but they tend to fall within specific categories.

Earlier, we discussed some of the helpers who give advice to help the hero—such as the *wise old man* who possesses special knowledge and often serves as a mentor to the hero.

The female counterpart of the wise old man is the *good mother.* Whereas the wise old man has superior knowledge, the good mother is known for her nurturing qualities, and for her intuition. This figure often gives the hero particular objects to help on the journey. It might be a protective amulet, or the ruby slippers that Dorothy receives in *The Wizard of Oz* from the Good Witch of the North. Sometimes in fairy tales it's a cloak to make the person invisible, or ordinary objects that become extraordinary, as in "The Girl of Courage," an Afghan fairy tale about a maiden who receives a comb, a whetstone, and a mirror to help defeat the devil.

Many myths contain a *shadow figure.* This is a character who is the 40 opposite of the hero. Sometimes this figure helps the hero on the journey; other times this figure opposes the hero. The shadow figure can be the negative side of the hero which could be the dark and hostile brother in "Cain and Abel," the stepsisters in "Cinderella," or the Robber Girl in "The Snow Queen." The shadow figure can also help the hero, as the whore with the heart of gold who saves the hero's life, or provides balance to his idealization of woman.

Many myths contain *animal archetypes* that can be positive or negative figures. In "St. George and the Dragon," the dragon is the negative force which is a violent and ravaging animal, not unlike the shark in *Jaws.* But in many stories, animals help the hero. Sometimes there are talking donkeys, or a dolphin which saves the hero, or magical horses or dogs.

The *trickster* is a mischievous archetypical figure who is always causing chaos, disturbing the peace, and generally being an anarchist. The trickster uses wit and cunning to achieve his or her ends. Sometimes the trickster is a harmless prankster or a "bad boy" who is funny and enjoyable. More often, the trickster is a con man, as in *The Sting,* or the devil, as in *The Exorcist,* who demanded all the skills of the priest to outwit him. The "Till Eulenspiegel" stories revolve around the trickster, as do the Spanish picaresque novels. Even the tales of Tom Sawyer have a trickster motif. In all countries, there are stories that revolve around this figure, whose job it is to outwit.

"Mythic" Problems and Solutions

We all grew up with myths. Most of us heard or read fairy tales when we were young. Some of us may have read Bible stories, or stories from other religions or other cultures. These stories are part of us. And the best way to work with them is to let them come out naturally as you write the script.

Of course, some filmmakers are better at this than others. George Lucas and Steven Spielberg have a strong sense of myth, and incorporate it into their films. They both have spoken about their love of the stories from childhood, and of their desire to bring these types of stories to audiences. Their stories create some of the same sense of wonder and excitement as myths. Many of the necessary psychological beats are part of their stories, deepening the story beyond the ordinary action-adventure.

Myths bring depth to a hero story. If a filmmaker is only thinking   45
about the action and excitement of a story, audiences might fail to connect with the hero's journey. But if the basic beats of the hero's journey are evident, a film will often inexplicably draw audiences, in spite of critics' responses to the film.

Take *Rambo* for instance. Why was this violent, simple story so popular with audiences? I don't think it was because everyone agreed with its politics. I do think Sylvester Stallone is a master at incorporating the American myth into his filmmaking. That doesn't mean it's done consciously. Somehow he is naturally in sync with the myth, and the myth becomes integrated into his stories.

Clint Eastwood also does hero stories, and gives us the adventure of the myth and the transformation of the myth. Recently Eastwood's films have given more attention to the transformation of the hero, and have been receiving more serious critical attention as a result.

All of these filmmakers—Lucas, Spielberg, Stallone, and Eastwood —dramatize the hero myth in their own particular ways. And all of them prove that myths are marketable.

Application

It is an important part of the writer's or producer's work to continually find opportunities for deepening the themes within a script. Finding the myth beneath the modern story is part of that process.

To find these myths, it's not a bad idea to reread some of Grimm's fairy tales or fairy tales from around the world to begin to get acquainted with various myths. You'll start to see patterns and elements that connect with our own human experience.

Also, read Joseph Campbell and Greek mythology. If you're interested in Jungian psychology, you'll find many rich resources within a number of books on the subject. Since Jungian psychology deals with archetypes, you'll find many new characters to draw on for your own work.

With all of these resources to incorporate, it's important to remember that the myth is not a story to force upon a script. It's more a pattern which you can bring out in your own stories when they seem to be heading in the direction of a myth.

As you work, ask yourself:

Do I have a myth working in my script? If so, what beats am I using of the hero's journey? Which ones seem to be missing?

Am I missing characters? Do I need a mentor type? A wise old man? A wizard? Would one of these characters help dimensionalize the hero's journey?

Could I create new emotional dimensions to the myth by starting my character as reluctant, naive, simple, or decidedly "unheroic"?

Does my character get transformed in the process of the journey?

Have I used a strong three-act structure to support the myth, using the first turning point to move into the adventure and the second turning point to create a dark moment, or a reversal, or even a "near-death" experience?

Don't be afraid to create variations on the myth, but don't start with the myth itself. Let the myth grow naturally from your story. Developing myths are part of the rewriting process. If you begin with the myth, you'll find your writing becomes rigid, uncreative, and predictable. Working with the myth in the rewriting process will deepen your script, giving it new life as you find the story within the story.

Reading the Text

1. How does Seger define the "hero myth"?
2. In your own words, explain what Seger means by "the healing myth."
3. What is an "archetypal" figure in film?

Reading the Signs

1. Linda Seger is writing to aspiring screenwriters. How does her status as an industry insider affect her description of heroic archetypes?
2. Compare Seger's formulation of heroes with Robert Ray's in "The Thematic Paradigm" (p. 241). To what extent do Seger and Ray adequately explain the role of women in movies?
3. Review Michael Parenti's "Class and Virtue" (p. 283), and then write an essay identifying the myths behind the modern stories *Pretty Woman* and *Indecent Proposal*.
4. Rent a videotape of *Super Mario Bros.,* and write an essay in which you explain how it functions as a "search" movie, in Seger's terms. What myths and archetypal characters does it include?
5. Seger recommends that aspiring screenwriters read Grimm's fairy tales for inspiration. Read some Grimm's tales, and then write an argument for or against the suitability of such tales as inspiration for films in the 1990s.
6. What myths about American history, race, and gender do you see in *Gone with the Wind*? Brainstorm these myths in class, then use your list of myths to write an essay in which you explain why the film has become an American classic.

UMBERTO ECO

Casablanca, or, the Clichés Are Having a Ball

|||||||||||||||||||||||||||||||||||||||||||||||||||||

Next to Roland Barthes, Umberto Eco (b. 1932) has probably been the most influential figure in semiotics in the postwar era. Best known for his acclaimed novels The Name of the Rose *(trans. 1983) and* Foucault's Pendulum *(trans. 1989), Eco has been a leading figure in the revival of the semiotic theories of Charles Sanders Peirce, which he has explored in numerous books and essays, most notably in his magisterial study* A Theory of Semiotics *(1976). An avid student of popular culture as well as technical semiotics, Eco turns his gaze in this selection upon one of the most beloved movies in American history to show how and why it succeeds. For Eco, the secret to the success of* Casablanca *lies in its articulation of just about every cultural myth and cliché in the book. From its archetypal opposition between official hero Victor Laszlo and outlaw hero Rick, to its presentation of a struggle between good and evil,* Casablanca *satisfies every mythological expectation. A professor of semiotics at the University of Bologna, Italy, Eco has also lectured on semiotics and popular culture at universities around the world.*

When people in their fifties sit down before their television sets for a rerun of *Casablanca,* it is an ordinary matter of nostalgia. However, when the film is shown in American universities, the boys and girls greet each scene and canonical line of dialogue ("Round up the usual suspects," "Was that cannon fire, or is it my heart pounding?"—or even every time that Bogey says "kid") with ovations usually reserved for football games. And I have seen the youthful audience in an Italian art cinema react in the same way. What then is the fascination of *Casablanca?*

The question is a legitimate one, for aesthetically speaking (or by any strict critical standards) *Casablanca* is a very mediocre film. It is a comic strip, a hotch-potch, low on psychological credibility, and with little continuity in its dramatic effects. And we know the reason for this: The film was made up as the shooting went along, and it was not until the last moment that the director and scriptwriters knew whether Ilse would leave with Victor or with Rick. So all those moments of inspired direction that wring bursts of applause for their unexpected boldness actually represent decisions taken out of desperation. What then accounts for the success of this chain of accidents, a film that even today, seen for a second, third, or fourth time, draws forth the applause reserved for the operatic aria we love to hear repeated, or the enthusiasm we accord to an exciting discovery? There is a cast of formidable hams. But that is not enough.

Here are the romantic lovers—he bitter, she tender—but both have been seen to better advantage. And *Casablanca* is not *Stagecoach,* another film periodically revived. *Stagecoach* is a masterpiece in every respect. Every element is in its proper place, the characters are consistent from one moment to the next, and the plot (this too is important) comes from Maupassant—at least the first part of it. And so? So one is tempted to read *Casablanca* the way T. S. Eliot reread *Hamlet.* He attributed its fascination not to its being a successful work (actually he considered it one of Shakespeare's less fortunate plays) but to something quite the opposite: *Hamlet* was the result of an unsuccessful fusion of several earlier Hamlets, one in which the theme was revenge (with madness as only a stratagem), and another whose theme was the crisis brought on by the mother's sin, with the consequent discrepancy between Hamlet's nervous excitation and the vagueness and implausibility of Gertrude's crime. So critics and public alike find *Hamlet* beautiful because it is interesting, and believe it to be interesting because it is beautiful.

On a smaller scale, the same thing happened to *Casablanca.* Forced to improvise a plot, the authors mixed in a little of everything, and everything they chose came from a repertoire of the tried and true. When the choice of the tried and true is limited, the result is a trite or mass-produced film, or simply kitsch. But when the tried and true repertoire is used wholesale, the result is an architecture like Gaudi's Sagrada Familia in Barcelona. There is a sense of dizziness, a stroke of brilliance.

But now let us forget how the film was made and see what it has to 5
show us. It opens in a place already magical in itself—Morocco, the Exotic—and begins with a hint of Arab music that fades into "La Marseillaise." Then as we enter Rick's Place we hear Gershwin. Africa, France, America. At once a tangle of Eternal Archetypes comes into play. These are situations that have presided over stories throughout the ages. But usually to make a good story a single archetypal situation is enough. More than enough. Unhappy Love, for example, or Flight. But *Casablanca* is not satisfied with that: It uses them all. The city is the setting for a Passage, the passage to the Promised Land (or a Northwest Passage, if you like). But to make the passage one must submit to a test, the Wait ("they wait and wait and wait," says the off-screen voice at the beginning). The passage from the waiting room to the Promised Land requires a Magic Key, the visa. It is around the winning of this Key that passions are unleashed. Money (which appears at various points, usually in the form of the Fatal Game, roulette) would seem to be the means for obtaining the Key. But eventually we discover that the Key can be obtained only through a Gift—the gift of the visa, but also the gift Rick makes of his Desire by sacrificing himself. For this is also the story of a

round of Desires, only two of which are satisfied: that of Victor Laszlo, the purest of heroes, and that of the Bulgarian couple. All those whose passions are impure fail.

Thus, we have another archetype: the Triumph of Purity. The impure do not reach the Promised Land; we lose sight of them before that. But they do achieve purity through sacrifice—and this means Redemption. Rick is redeemed and so is the French police captain. We come to realize that underneath it all there are two Promised Lands: One is America (though for many it is a false goal), and the other is the Resistance—the Holy War. That is where Victor has come from, and that is where Rick and the captain are going, to join de Gaulle. And if the recurring symbol of the airplane seems every so often to emphasize the flight to America, the Cross of Lorraine, which appears only once, anticipates the other symbolic gesture of the captain, when at the end he throws away the bottle of Vichy water as the plane is leaving. On the other hand the myth of sacrifice runs through the whole film: Ilse's sacrifice in Paris when she abandons the man she loves to return to the wounded hero, the Bulgarian bride's sacrifice when she is ready to yield herself to help her husband, Victor's sacrifice when he is prepared to let Ilse go with Rick so long as she is saved.

Into this orgy of sacrificial archetypes (accompanied by the Faithful Servant theme in the relationship of Bogey and the black man Dooley Wilson) is inserted the theme of Unhappy Love: unhappy for Rick, who loves Ilse and cannot have her; unhappy for Ilse, who loves Rick and cannot leave with him; unhappy for Victor, who understands that he has not really kept Ilse. The interplay of unhappy loves produces various twists and turns: In the beginning Rick is unhappy because he does not understand why Ilse leaves him; then Victor is unhappy because he does not understand why Ilse is attracted to Rick; finally Ilse is unhappy because she does not understand why Rick makes her leave with her husband. These three unhappy (or Impossible) loves take the form of a Triangle. But in the archetypal love-triangle there is a Betrayed Husband and a Victorious Lover. Here instead both men are betrayed and suffer a loss, but, in this defeat (and over and above it) an additional element plays a part, so subtly that one is hardly aware of it. It is that, quite subliminally, a hint of male or Socratic love is established. Rick admires Victor, Victor is ambiguously attracted to Rick, and it almost seems at a certain point as if each of the two were playing out the duel of sacrifice in order to please the other. In any case, as in Rousseau's *Confessions,* the woman places herself as Intermediary between the two men. She herself is not a bearer of positive values; only the men are.

Against the background of these intertwined ambiguities, the characters are stock figures, either all good or all bad. Victor plays a double role, as an agent of ambiguity in the love story, and an agent of clarity in the political intrigue—he is Beauty against the Nazi Beast. This theme of Civilization against Barbarism becomes entangled with the others, and to the melancholy of an Odyssean Return is added the warlike daring of an *Iliad* on open ground.

Surrounding this dance of eternal myths, we see the historical myths, or rather the myths of the movies, duly served up again. Bogart himself embodies at least three: the Ambiguous Adventurer, compounded of cynicism and generosity; the Lovelorn Ascetic; and at the same time the Redeemed Drunkard (he has to be made a drunkard so that all of a sudden he can be redeemed, while he was already an ascetic, disappointed in love). Ingrid Bergman is the Enigmatic Woman, or *Femme Fatale.* Then such myths as: They're Playing Our Song; the Last Day in Paris; America, Africa, Lisbon as a Free Port; and the Border Station or Last Outpost on the Edge of the Desert. There is the Foreign Legion (each character has a different nationality and a different story to tell), and finally there is the Grand Hotel (people coming and going). Rick's Place is a magic circle where everything can (and does) happen: love, death, pursuit, espionage, games of chance, seductions, music, patriotism. (The theatrical origin of the plot, and its poverty of means, led to an admirable condensation of events in a single setting.) This place is *Hong Kong, Macao, l'Enfer du Jeu,* an anticipation of *Lisbon,* and even *Showboat.*

But precisely because *all* the archetypes are here, precisely because   10
Casablanca cites countless other films, and each actor repeats a part played on other occasions, the resonance of intertextuality plays upon the spectator. *Casablanca* brings with it, like a trail of perfume, other situations that the viewer brings to bear on it quite readily, taking them without realizing it from films that only appeared later, such as *To Have and Have Not,* where Bogart actually plays a Hemingway hero, while here in *Casablanca* he already attracts Hemingwayesque connotations by the simple fact that Rick, so we are told, fought in Spain (and, like Malraux, helped the Chinese Revolution). Peter Lorre drags in reminiscences of Fritz Lang; Conrad Veidt envelops his German officer in a faint aroma of *The Cabinet of Dr. Caligari*—he is not a ruthless, technological Nazi, but a nocturnal and diabolical Caesar.

Thus *Casablanca* is not just one film. It is many films, an anthology. Made haphazardly, it probably made itself, if not actually against the will of its authors and actors, then at least beyond their control. And this is the reason it works, in spite of aesthetic theories and theories of filmmaking. For in it there unfolds with almost telluric[1] force the power of Narrative in its natural state, without Art intervening to discipline it. And so we can accept it when characters change mood, morality, and psychology from one moment to the next, when conspirators cough to interrupt the conversation if a spy is approaching, when whores weep at

---

1. **telluric**   Arising from the earth or soil.—EDS.

the sound of "La Marseillaise." When all the archetypes burst in shamelessly, we reach Homeric depths. Two clichés make us laugh. A hundred clichés move us. For we sense dimly that the clichés are talking *among themselves,* and celebrating a reunion. Just as the height of pain may encounter sensual pleasure, and the height of perversion border on mystical energy, so too the height of banality allows us to catch a glimpse of the sublime. Something has spoken in place of the director. If nothing else, it is a phenomenon worthy of awe.

Reading the Text

1. Why, according to Eco, was *Casablanca* so successful?
2. What does Eco mean by calling *Casablanca* an "anthology"?
3. Prepare a list of the clichés Eco finds in *Casablanca.*

Reading the Signs

1. Rent a videotape of *Casablanca.* Do you agree with Eco's judgment that this movie was a "very mediocre" film? Write an essay in which you support, refute, or modify his claim.
2. Review Linda Seger's "Creating the Myth" (p. 250). How can her discussion of archetypes and "search" films extend and complicate Eco's analysis of *Casablanca?*
3. Eco claims that *Stagecoach* is a "masterpiece." Rent the film, and write a critique of it supporting, refuting, or complicating Eco's claim.
4. Read Robert Ray's "The Thematic Paradigm" (p. 241), and write an essay in which you argue that Rick is either an outlaw or an official hero.

DIANE RAYMOND
Not as Tough as It Looks

||||||||||||||||||||||||||||||||||||||||||||||||||||

The 1980s were not a good decade for the women's movement in America. As Diane Raymond (b. 1949) demonstrates in this analysis of two of the more popular films from that era, even the traditional gender roles women occupy in American culture came under attack. At a time when women were being urged to return to their traditional roles as homemakers and mothers, movies like Three Men and a Baby *were implying that men make better mothers than women after all. Thus, women are not only subordinated but practically discarded as unnecessary.*

Diane Raymond points here to a phenomenon also recognized by Susan Faludi: the relative disappearance of women in Hollywood cinema as male leads come to dominate the marquees. A professor of philosophy at Simmons College, Diane Raymond has also published Existentialism and the Philosophical Tradition *(1989),* Popular Culture and the Politics of Sexuality *(ed., 1990), and, with Warren Blumenfeld,* Looking at Gay and Lesbian Life *(1991).*

Somehow the questions raised here did not take on a problem-solving or strategy-laden dimension but rather concerned mothers, mothering, motherhood. As we found them inside of us. No feminist theory of motherhood? Well, we will start to invent one. We start with our hands on our pulses.

— RACHEL BLAU DUPLESSIS

My children cause me the most exquisite suffering of which I have any experience.

— ADRIENNE RICH

In *The Dialectic of Sex,* radical feminist Shulamith Firestone argued that women's oppression is rooted in biology. Like conservatives who maintain that there are undeniable biological differences between men and women, she maintains that these differences—more specifically, women's biological capacity to bear and give birth to children—account for the inequalities between men and women. Unlike the conservative, however, Firestone rejects the notion that "biology is destiny" and defends the use of technology to free women from reproduction. Firestone found it unbelievable that anyone would want to *bear* children. The "joy of giving birth" is a patriarchal myth, more akin to "shitting a pumpkin" (198).

When Firestone wrote, only contraception, abortion, and sterilization were widely used. Today, however, embryo transfers, in vitro fertilization, embryo freezing, and surrogacy are realities. A woman who begets a child need not bear it, and a woman who bears a child need not rear it. Cloning and artificial placentas may be options in the not-too-distant future, making it possible for women's role in the reproductive process to be as limited as men's. Further, once born, a child would be able to have any number of either-sex parent(s), offering virtually limitless alternative family constellations.

Most feminists, however, now reject Firestone's technooptimism. For some, since it is men who control technology, it will be men who control reproductive technology; "through the years, with widespread use of the technologies, social institutions will be restructured to reflect a new reality—tightened male control over female reproductive processes" (Corea 38). It has become obvious, particularly since the litigations involved in the Baby M case and the more recent decision over "ownership" of frozen embryos, that one cannot assume that new reproductive technologies represent greater freedom for women; "in a system characterized by power imbalance, the greater the asymmetry, the greater the potential abuse of the less powerful group" (Hanmer 444–445). Critics of the new reproductive technologies maintain that these technologies may take from women the one source of power they possess—childbearing—and put it in the hands of men.

Radical feminist Adrienne Rich has distinguished the institution of mothering from the physical and emotional experiences of mothering particular women have. In her now classic work, *Of Woman Born,* she weaves theory and personal experience to construct a view of mothering which removes it from the realm of the ahistorical and asocial. Motherhood ceases to be a private, biological act divorced from a social system. Rather, motherhood

> has a history, it has an ideology, it is more fundamental than tribalism or nationalism. My individual private pains as a mother, the individual and seemingly private pains of the mothers around me and before me, whatever our class or colour, the regulation of women's reproductive power by men in every totalitarian system and every socialist revolution, the legal and technical control by men of contraception, fertility, abortion, obstetrics and extrauterine experiments—are all essential to the patriarchal system, as is the negative or suspect status of women who are not mothers. (15)

The debate over mothering continues to rage inside and outside the feminist community. After all, much of the energy of the women's movement has been taken up with the demand that the "private sphere" (of which mothering is an enormous part) be given the full recognition it deserves. At the same time, however, feminists have rejected patriarchal demands to reproduce—"compulsory motherhood"—along with the socialization that accompanies it. Thus, just as feminists must validate what women do and have historically done, they must also condemn the patriarchal co-optation which has sought to appropriate those experiences.

Mothering is central to the lives of all women, whether or not they bear their own children. Thus, an understanding of mothering is essential to feminist theory. Yet there is no unified feminist position on these issues. Some feminist theorists, for example, have gone even further than Firestone to argue that women should refuse to give birth at all. Jeffner Allen argues that birthing children buttresses the patriarchy, saps women's energy, and is evolutionarily unsound. She urges women to "evacuate" mothering.

Others (see, for example, Irigaray) have valorized women's childbearing as one of the few expressions of power women under patriarchy possess. These feminists "embrace motherhood" (Maroney) and decry the loss of female control over the spiritual and physical dimensions of childbirth. French feminist theory in particular has tended to focus on the power of the mother; but this power is not the patriarchal power of dominance and control, but of nurturance and creation. In fact, this sect of feminist theory has maintained that it is men's jealousy of women's power of creation which has led them to devalue women's experience and to seek the power to control reproduction in particular and women in general. Emancipation from the father (patriarchy), they claim, requires the liberation of the mother and the revaluing of women's bodily experiences of creation and of women's relationships with women.

Finally, a third strand (e.g., Held) defends the normative thesis that child *rearing* (if not child *bearing*) must be shared by men and women. According to this view, a biological connection between parent and child is neither necessary nor sufficient to make one a "mother." Rather, the role of mothering is one of nurturing and of caretaking; in this sense, almost anyone can mother. Further, neither biology nor technology per se is oppressive in this view; rather, it is how a community interprets those biological factors and uses its technological resources that makes the decisive difference. Mary O'Brien, for example, has argued from a Marxist perspective that women must be integrated into the productive realm and men must be integrated into the realm of reproduction and the care of the next generation. This view has received support from the psychoanalytic community in the writings of feminists like, for example, Nancy Chodorow and Dorothy Dinnerstein who, in *The Mermaid and the Minotaur,* links misogyny to the prevalence of single-sex parenting in Western societies.[1]

Even more recently, some feminists have attempted to explore maternal practice as a vehicle to re-vision ethical theory. Sara Ruddick, for example, has coined the phrase "maternal thinking" to refer to certain kinds of activities like protecting, nurturing, preserving, loving, and helping to grow—in short, to those activities historically and culturally tied to mothering. Her analysis follows from the empirical research of Carol Gilligan and others who have observed differences in men's and women's relational modes. Where men, Gilligan claims, tend to operate from a "rights" perspective, women are most comfortable in what Gilligan calls a "caring" mode, which focuses on responsibilities to others. The traditional family perhaps best exemplifies these "different voices";

---

1. More specifically, Dinnerstein argues that asymmetry in parenting arrangements leads to a matriphobia which is rooted in the infant's need to separate from its primary caretaker, i.e., its mother. In separating, the infant/child must devalue the mother (who is also familiar and easily accessible) and attach to the mysterious, powerful father. It is the mother, Dinnerstein maintains, who represents the infant's dependence needs and must hence be rejected; for these same reasons, the mother also represents death itself.

while the father works outside the home, teaches rules and fairness, and is the source of disciplinary measure, the mother is the one who comforts and cares, who may bend the rules at times in the interests of compassion and understanding. Though generalizations of the crudest sort, these styles of interaction have traditionally tended to be gender-linked. Ruddick argues, though, that anyone *can* and, from a normative perspective, everyone *should,* mother, even if one never has a biological child. Maternal practice has been undervalued in most societies; not only does it need to be valued fully, but its virtual monopolization by women must also end.

In this paper I shall follow the practice of the majority of feminist theorists and not assume that the notion of "mothering" depends on biology. Instead, I want to explore the ways in which images of mothering appear in popular culture, especially in film. These popular images not only reveal glimpses of our deeply mythic thinking about mothers and mothering; but they also create a popular mythology with new, and possibly, dissonant messages. It is to those messages that I wish to attend. Though I shall reference a number of examples from film and television, my focus here is on [two] recent popular films: *Baby Boom* and *Three Men and a Baby.*

Baby Boom

As *Baby Boom*'s opening credits roll, we catch scenes of New York City with its anxious residents struggling to get to work. Waiting for buses, taxis, and subways; carrying briefcases and cups of coffee; wearing sneakers and three-piece suits—all are daily consigned to this demanding rat race. Gradually, as we realize that we are observing more and more women in these throngs of workers, a voice-over announces: "53% of the American workforce is female. . . . As little girls, they were told to marry doctors and lawyers. When they grew up, they became doctors and lawyers."

The music picks up and soon Wall Street is our backdrop. We see Diane Keaton as J.C. Wyatt who is, we are told by our narrator, a woman on the move. She makes six figures a year and lives with an investment banker who, like her, is married to his job. With the last of the credits, the narrator warns us: "One must take it for granted that J.C. has it all. One must never take anything for granted." This notion of "having it all" continues thematically to haunt the film.

At work, J.C., known as "tiger lady" to her co-workers, reels off instructions to her subordinates and is crisply efficient. Later that day, she is offered a partnership in the firm, which she gratefully accepts. But, for the first time, we see her falter. As she is offered the partnership, her legs begin to shake uncontrollably under the table in a nervous reaction.

Is this her happiness at accomplishing her long-dreamed-of goal or is this a visible sign of her ambivalence? Regardless of its meaning, this reaction humanizes (and *feminizes*) J.C. for the viewer; we now realize that she is not "all business," and we cannot help but like her.

Her now-partner paternalistically urges her to think long and hard about the demands on her a partnership will make. It is his wife, he informs J.C., who makes it possible for him to do all he needs to do. Interestingly, he is in the dark about what goes on in the private world of home and family; but he is clear that, whatever *it* is, it provides a measure of stability for him. "A man can be a success and have a personal life . . . I can have it all," he says with some embarrassment. Rather than question his premise, J.C. demurs, "I don't want it all."

That evening, in the luxurious condominium she shares with Steven, her live-in boyfriend, J.C. and he finish up some work in bed; later she circles ads for Vermont estates. He quips: "You in Vermont without a speaker phone would not be a pretty sight." They make love, with before- and after-shots of the digital clock to let us know how quick it actually was (two minutes) and the camera shows us the longing on her face as he falls immediately off to sleep.

When J.C. later inherits the daughter of a distant relative, her life falls apart. Despite her "six figures," she is unable to find competent childcare. Steven demands that she put Elizabeth, the baby, up for adoption, and J.C. initially has the same desire. But she begins to bond with Elizabeth when the baby comes down with the flu, and she is unable (at the decisive moment) to give up Elizabeth to the provincial, Midwestern couple who want her ("Suddenly I saw her in frosted lipstick wearing a Dairy Queen uniform," she explains). Steven, who has made clear his feelings about parenthood, ends the relationship when she returns with Elizabeth, and J.C. moves out.

As Linda Singer points out . . . Hollywood filmmakers seem most interested in the aberrant and the exotic. So in *Baby Boom* we see a woman who is, at least initially, a thoroughly inept mother. Though a graduate of Yale and Harvard (and apparently without any of the usual babysitting experience), she is unable to diaper the baby, holds her slung under one arm, and shows none of the tenderness we have come to associate with maternal care.

But what *Baby Boom* makes clear is that one does not need biology to be a mother; one can *learn* mothering. Indeed, J.C. goes from an inept, uncaring woman to a *real* mother. Beginning with her care of Elizabeth and her decision not to abandon her to new parents (would she have done so, we wonder, if the prospective parents had not been so obviously and absurdly wrong for a child?), J.C. becomes Yuppie Supermom, bringing Elizabeth to classes, to the park, and even occasionally to work. But, consistent with our narrator's foreshadowing, J.C. is soon to realize that she cannot have it all.

15

J.C.'s behavior at work is erratic, and the Tiger Lady has lost her claws. Her office is now full of baby bottles and nursery toys, and co-worker Ken slowly eases her out of her favored position in the firm. After she loses an account to him, he explains: "You've changed. You've lost your concentration. You've gone soft." How can a woman—no, a *mother*—compete in such a cutthroat enterprise? It would seem that the moment that J.C. made the "soft" decision not to give up Elizabeth, every aspect of her life followed suit. It is almost as though J.C. has herself gone through a birthing experience; she has indeed, like the typical postpartum woman, "gone soft." Rather than accept a humiliating demotion, she quits the company, buys a home in Vermont, and begins to build a new life for Elizabeth.

The country, it seems, is the place for those who "go soft." For J.C., 20 the boredom and the expense of the constant repairs on her old home drive her to think about trying to market the baby food she has over-zealously made for Elizabeth. After some time, with her knowledge of marketing strategy (she is even able to make use of the town library), her line—Country Baby Applesauce—becomes a huge success. Her old company offers her a deal, and she travels back to New York to negotiate with them. In the meantime, though, she had gotten involved with the local veterinarian, played by Sam Shepard.

Back in New York, facing her old building in a pose reminiscent of *Rocky,* J.C. finally decides not to sell her trademark even though the deal would, in the words of one of the negotiators, "make you richer than you've ever dreamed." In an impassioned speech to the board, she an-nounces, "I'm not the tiger lady any more. Now I have a mobile over my desk and a crib in my office. . . . I'm doing very well on my own. . . . The rat race is going to have to survive with one less rat." In concluding from her own experience, she says "the bottom line is: Nobody should have to make those sacrifices" between family and work. Finally, she loses her ardor and begins to talk dreamily about her new relationship: "There's this veterinarian I'm seeing. . . ." She even rolls her eyes at the thought of him. This shift in tone and content serves to "feminize" the rest of her speech, to depoliticize it. This discourse is clearly outside the language of the boardroom; it is woman's language, the discourse of the mother, which is so private that it is unintelligible. Indeed, one man says, "What did she say? She's become a vegetarian?" This solipsism in the boardroom serves two purposes: It makes clear that the mother, contrary to popular views about women returning to the work force, cannot go back, for she has lost her access to the language of the public domain; but it also inverts this very real dynamic of exclu-sion by suggesting that J.C. is happier (and, let us not forget, richer and more sexually fulfilled) than she ever was. She has *chosen* to opt out.

The final scene of *Baby Boom* is of J.C. and Elizabeth together in a rocking chair. All of the energy of her visit to New York has been defused and J.C. is placid and content. Does she "have it all"? She has a man to love her, a baby, incredible wealth (she has informed the assembled members of the meeting that she can make the money off the line of baby food independently), a "career" that allows her to stay home and be with her child, and has wrecked revenge on the company that let her go. The final word of the movie is Elizabeth's: "Mama." Though we hear J.C. murmuring to Elizabeth, her words are undecipherable. That "Mama" makes it clear that mothering must be a priority and that the sacrifices it entails are not only worthwhile, but they also actually *pay off.*

Three Men and a Baby

Three Men and a Baby is a remake of the French film *Trois Hommes et Un Couffin* (1986) and stars three very popular actors: Tom Selleck (Peter), Steve Guttenberg (Michael), and Ted Danson (Jack). They live together in a very upscale apartment in New York City. Peter is an architect, Michael a cartoonist, and Jack an actor, and their apartment is the "bachelor pad" par excellence. In fact, during the opening credits we see each of the roommates entering and exiting in frenetic (and deliberately sped up) pace with a number of different, very attractive women. A party for Peter's birthday includes hundreds of the "beautiful people," lots of champagne, all the latest technology, and much bed-hopping. Whether all this womanizing is merely to make clear how ill-suited these three bachelors are for the baby soon to arrive; or whether it is to reassure us that, strange as this arrangement is, these men are *not* gay—the very definite message is that Peter, Michael, and Jack are to be envied.

Only Peter has a girlfriend, and their relationship is not a monogamous one. It is doubtful that any movie would ever feature three female roommates who do the kind of bed-hopping these men do. It is even more doubtful whether bed-hopping women would ever be as likeable and sympathetic as are Peter, Michael, and Jack. At the same birthday party, for example, Jack is searching for a bottle of wine to share with his most recently acquired female conquest. "What's a good year for pronging chicks?" he asks his roommates, and, interestingly, receives an immediate answer. But, it is worth noting that, once their sexual prowess is established, the pace slows and the film takes us in a different direction.

Due to a misunderstanding, Peter and Michael assume that a baby 25 left for Jack on their doorstep is the "package" he informs them will be delivered that day. The note which appears with the baby is from the biological mother: "I can't handle this now. Maybe some day you'll both forgive me." Jack is alleged to be the biological father and his roommates never question this claim. Jack is away filming a new movie, and they are unable to reach him.

Like *Baby Boom, Three Men and a Baby* entices us by taking us through the stages of the men's growing attachment to Mary, Jack's daughter. They find that they have no idea what size diapers to buy, what sort of baby food is appropriate, even whether Mary has teeth. They are horrified by their first diaper change. They seem to work out an arrangement for shared child care so that each can fulfill his work responsibilities (indeed, at times their roles seem to mimic those of a married couple). Gradually their lives adjust to having her there, and, despite obvious exhaustion, they seem to be enjoying her presence.

There is, however, another "package" which actually contains drugs left by a friend of Jack's to be picked up by two thugs. After a series of miscommunications, Michael and Peter realize what has occurred, but by then the police are involved and it is too late to set things right. Finally, Peter, Michael, and Jack end up employing some of their fancy camera equipment to amass evidence against the criminals and turn them over to the police.

This drug subplot gives *Three Men and a Baby* an odd, almost schizophrenic feeling. Is this a movie about "three men and a baby" or is it a movie about "three men, a baby, two bad guys, and some misplaced drugs"? It is almost as though a movie about men and a baby could not simply be about men and a baby. Rather, there must be some dramatic tension, which involves the real *action* of police and thugs. So this film forces us to move between the domestic world of home and children and the public world of crime and danger. Domesticity, it appears, would not be enough.

In *Maternal Thinking* Sara Ruddick maintains, like Dinnerstein and Chodorow, that men should participate in childrearing. The ability to mother is not related, she argues, to gender. Further, she claims that mothering by men has transformative power. "To be sure, by becoming a mother, [a man] will, in many social groups, challenge the ideology of masculinity" (45). *Three Men and a Baby* shows just how naive is Ruddick's claim. These three men only seem *more* masculine in the course of this film. Their devotion to Mary does not "emasculate" or "feminize" in any way; perhaps audiences would not even tolerate such a transformation. But Michael, Peter, and Jack offer no challenge to patriarchy or to the ideology of masculinity. Indeed, they epitomize the "new" man: Tough yet tender, made irresistible to women in their attachment to Mary. What better reassurance could we have of masculinity intact than the scene in which Peter lulls Mary to sleep by reading to her from a *Sports Illustrated* description of a boxing match?

Women in *Three Men and a Baby* seem either incapable of or not 30 interested in mothering. First, there is the unseen but felt presence of Sylvia, the baby's biological mother, who has abandoned her child to strangers. Jack's mother is quite taken with Mary, but she refuses to help him care for her: "You were a screw-up," she tells him. "Now you're a father." Peter's occasional lover is indignant that he would assume that, because she is a woman, she'd want to be involved in Mary's care. Finally, their landlady ends up bound and gagged when criminals break into the apartment while she is baby-sitting for Mary.

Hoffnung has discussed the "limiting effects" of mothering on women's public participation. But while women with children are often isolated from public life, the men in this film seem to suffer no such ill effects. In fact, their attractiveness to women only increases as we, for example, see them playing in the park with Mary while women crowd around them. They bring Mary with them to work; Peter even has a little hard hat for her when he brings her to construction sites.

When Sylvia returns at the end of this film, we cannot help but resent her intrusion. She wants her baby back, and very obviously loves the child. Yet our sympathies are with the men who learned to love this child and accommodated to her needs. We observe their anguish as they pack up Mary's belongings, and we cannot help but note that they know more about Mary's needs and habits than does her own mother.

How does the patriarchy resolve this dilemma? We cannot simply disregard the imperative of biological motherhood. Yet what about "fathers' rights"? Further, how can we deprive Mary of the material comforts she will obviously enjoy in her present home? Sylvia provides the key to the solution: "I have to work. And I can't take care of Mary alone. I need help. I need someone to help me." Realizing that they do not want to be occasional baby-sitters, Peter, Michael, and Jack propose that Sylvia move in with them.

The last scene of *Three Men and a Baby* is of Peter, Michael, Jack, and Sylvia all wheeling Mary in her stroller. Michael has even painted Sylvia's image on the wall with the three of them. In some ways this ending resembles the union of J.C. and her veterinarian in *Baby Boom*. There is, however, a relevant difference. J.C. needs a man, and to conclude *Baby Boom* with her still unattached would leave us (and her) frustrated and less able to care for Elizabeth. But men do not need women in this same way, and it is clear in *Three Men* that it is Sylvia who needs a roof over her head and help with Mary. Though on some level we recognize that there are three of them and only one mother, we cannot help but think "she can't do it alone." And it is their charity, their *noblesse oblige,* that allows her to stay; Mary seems to have suffered no ill effects from her mother's absence. With such power, men do not need to fear women's reproductive capabilities.

Conclusion

It is noteworthy that biological motherhood is not a central theme 35
in most of the recent Hollywood films that feature family/parenting

arrangements. . . . *Baby Boom* and *Three Men and a Baby* introduce us to individuals who seem the unlikeliest candidates imaginable for parenthood. Indeed, from our superior vantage point, we can laugh at their inept early attempts to parent: the pathetic try at diapering; the confusion over the source of a baby's discomfort; the chaos in which traditionally "child-free" households are thrown with the appearance of a child.

Further, the attachment to the child (because it is not rooted in the biological?) is never taken for granted in these films and so must be developed over time; Diane Keaton in *Baby Boom,* for example, is willing to leave newly acquired Elizabeth with the coat checker in a restaurant, and the men in *Three Men* search frantically for a way to unload "their" baby. The viewer, though, trusts that bonding will occur at some point and that there is no real threat—which would create excess anxiety— to the baby's welfare; what keeps us interested is that we do not know precisely when or how the bonding will occur. Those moments like, for example, when Elizabeth becomes ill or when Peter believes Mary could have been harmed by intruders, unite viewer, novice parent, and new child in a relationship which now ensures the safety of the infant. And for these adult characters—once materialistic and egocentric—the process which leads to their becoming competent, nonbiological parents also matures them in other aspects of their lives.

Where are the other biological mothers in films today? At times they are teenagers who become pregnant and give birth like Darcy (Molly Ringwald) in *For Keeps.* Occasionally, as in *Cry in the Dark,* biological mothers are of interest to filmmakers because their children have died. Other films (perhaps following in the wake of the popularity of *Three Men and a Baby*) focus on the masculine view of child-rearing. In *She's Having a Baby,* for example, Jefferson (Jake) Briggs (Kevin Bacon) is a dissatisfied, trapped husband who resents his loss of innocence and blames his wife for it. He narrates the film, which is full of his fantasies and complaints. The birth of their first child provides the basis for his own rebirth. Though the title tells us that *she's* having a baby, it is *he* who experiences the birth as a vehicle for his realization that "what I was looking for was not to be found but to be made."

For the most part, though, recent films which feature mothering (or parenting)—think, for example, of *Raising Arizona, Housekeeping,* and even *Aliens*—work hard to create bonds where there's no biological attachment. In *Aliens,* for example, Newt's own parents could not protect her, whereas Ripley (Sigourney Weaver) remains true to her promise (despite unbelievable obstacles) that she will never abandon the child (who rewards Ripley by calling her "mommy" at their climactic reunion). This phenomenon has been termed by Molly Haskell "motherhood without stretchmarks," and its popularity may result from its difference. Hollywood, as I have argued above, seems to mystify the atypical and the exotic. Today, though most single parents are women and women are the heads of 16% of all households, though more than a third of such households live in poverty, there has been almost no attention to these kinds of living arrangements. If one can truly achieve "motherhood without stretchmarks," then there is nothing that women can do that men cannot. In one scene in *Three Men and a Baby,* Jack stuffs a pillow under his sweater to simulate pregnancy and stands in front of a mirror admiring his new appearance. But he need feel no jealousy of the biological powers of women, since it is ultimately he (and his two companions) who are more suited to raise and nurture Mary.

In reality, women who are mothers actually *lose* power. Unless, like J.C. in *Baby Boom,* they find a man (and her veterinarian happens to be the *only* man in the town "within twenty years of her age"), mothers are likely to be underpaid and overworked. Statistics suggest that even women with husbands continue to put in a "double day" with housework and childcare. In contrast, the men in *Three Men* enhance their social position when they become mothers, never having difficulty meeting women or fulfilling their professional obligations. Women with children, however, encounter a number of obstacles which tend to increase their isolation from the public domain. "Taking care of children, therefore, does not provide women with any real power base. Men can afford to leave childrearing *responsibility* to women, because, given their superior power resources, they are still assured of substantial childrearing authority" (Polatnick 33).

Webster's Dictionary defines mothering as "caring for another with maternal affection or tenderness." Similarly, Sara Ruddick defines a mother as any person who "takes on responsibility for children's lives and from whom providing child care is a significant part of her or his working life" (40). Regardless of whether women are innately better suited to mothering (a question I do not consider here), it seems obvious that a person of either sex is capable of mothering in these senses. Furthermore, most feminists have struggled to reject theories which either explicitly or implicitly entail a biological determinism. Why, then, should we not applaud films which have the potential to subvert traditional norms? 40

Patriarchy has a knack for incorporating potentially destabilizing modes of behavior and neutralizing their subversive power in the process. Where it might be destabilizing for a woman to be successful *and* be a mother, films like *Baby Boom* trivialize the experience and end by repositioning the mother and child in a nonsubversive nuclear family. A nontraditional arrangement like the one we see in *Three Men and a Baby* has the potential to serve as an alternative to the mainstream family. But this film grounds its appeal precisely in its unreality—we know this model is not one we can seek to emulate. Virtually all these films revolve around upper-class families so that nasty issues like making ends meet need never interfere with plot. Films like these exploit the aberrant.

What really goes on in everyday domestic life is not of interest to Hollywood moviemakers. This is not to suggest that every Hollywood film ought to provide us with a blueprint for undermining patriarchy. But it is to suggest that these films have failed to provide any vision at all: They remove women from the sphere of mothering by turning children over to men; and they push biological mothers even further back into the privatized (i.e., invisible) domestic world. Unless the mother is pathological like Bette Davis's mother in the classic *Now, Voyager* or Faye Dunaway's portrayal of Joan Crawford in the more recent *Mommie, Dearest,* mothers' lives are not the "stuff of which dreams are made."

There is a pervasive popular ideology that all women want to be mothers and that all women make good mothers. Yet, coexisting with this ideology exist obstacles which prevent truly autonomous forms of mothering from occurring. Whether in the form of single mothering, lesbian mothering, or some other alternative arrangement which might be truly destabilizing—autonomous mothering is neglected, just as is biological mothering. Indeed, women seem entirely secondary to the plot and character development. It is no fluke that J.C. Wyatt finds a "real" man at the end of *Baby Boom* and that not one of the roommates in *Three Men* ends up in a committed relationship.

Further, the ideology of mothering minimizes the drudgery and the monotony of childrearing and magnifies the joys and compensations. The result is an illusion "whereby motherhood will appear to consist of compensations only, and thus come to be desired by those for whom the illusion is intended" (Hollingsworth 27). Most films about mothering make mothering tempting. Few films deal with working-class mothers or mothers of color or women who consciously opt out of having children (and don't later regret the decision!). Ironically, films cannot resist this ideology of mothering even when it comes to teenage mothers like Molly Ringwald in *For Keeps,* who, after great hardship, finds herself, finishes school, and saves her marriage. Abortion is taboo, as are women who choose not to have children.

Sara Ruddick has convincingly argued that we cannot "at will transcend a gender division of labor that has shaped our minds and lives" (41). Certainly, given the fact that women have disproportionately cared for children in most societies, we cannot expect an overnight transformation of these entrenched practices. But Ruddick then asks: "Where are the fathers? Where are the caretaking women who are not mothers?" The answer, as this paper has tried to show, is that they are disproportionately present in popular film.[2]

2. As a woman and a feminist, I have long eschewed the dualisms of traditional philosophy. In particular, I have sought not to ignore links between the "personal" and

WORKS CITED

Allen, Jeffner, "Mothering: The Annihilation of Women," in *Trebilcot,* pp. 315–330.

Chodorow, Nancy, *The Reproduction of Mothering.* Berkeley: University of California Press, 1978.

Corea, Gena, "The Reproductive Brothel," in *Man-Made Women,* ed. Gena Corea et al. Bloomington: Indiana University Press, 1987, pp. 38–51.

Dinnerstein, Dorothy, *The Mermaid and the Minotaur.* NY: Harper and Row, 1976.

Duplessis, Rachel Blau, "Washing Blood." *Feminist Studies* 4,2 (1978).

Firestone, Shulamith, *The Dialect of Sex* (Rev. ed.). New York: Bantam Books, 1971.

Gilligan, Carol, *In A Different Voice.* Cambridge: Harvard University Press, 1982.

Gimenez, Martha E., "Feminism, Pronatalism, and Motherhood," in *Trebilcot,* pp. 287–314.

Hanmer, Jalna, "A Womb of One's Own," in *Test-Tube Women,* ed. Rita Arditti, Duelli Klein, and Shelley Minden. Boston: Pandora Press, 1984.

Haskell, Molly, "Hollywood Madonnas." *MS. Magazine,* May 1988, pp. 84–87.

Held, Virginia, "The Equal Responsibilities of Fathers and Mothers," in *Trebilcot,* pp. 40–56.

Hoffnung, Michele, "Motherhood: Contemporary Conflict for Women," in Jo Freeman, ed., *Women: A Feminist Perspective.* Mountain View, CA: Mayfield Publishing, 1989, 157–175.

Hollingsworth, Leta S., "Social Devices for Impelling Women to Bear and Rear Children." *American Journal of Sociology* 22 (1916), pp. 20–27.

Irigaray, Luce, "And the One Doesn't Stir Without the Other," trans. Helen Vivienne Wenzel. *Signs* 7 (Autumn 1981), pp. 60–67.

Kuykendall, Eleanor H., "Toward an Ethic of Nurturance: Luce Irigaray on Mothering and Power," in *Trebilcot,* pp. 263–274.

Maroney, Heather Jon, "Embracing Motherhood: New Feminist Theory," in *The Politics of Diversity,* ed. Roberta Hamilton and Michele Barrett. London: Verso, 1986, pp. 398–423.

O'Brien, Mary, *The Politics of Reproduction.* London: Routledge and Kegan Paul, 1981.

Polatnick, M. Rivka, "Why Men Don't Rear Children: A Power Analysis," in *Trebilcot,* pp. 21–40.

Rich, Adrienne, *Of Woman Born.* New York: Bantam Books, 1976.

Ruddick, Sara, *Maternal Thinking.* Boston: Beacon Press, 1989.

Singer, Linda, "Just Say No: Repression, Anti-Sex, and the New Film," in *Sexual Politics and Popular Culture,* ed. Diane Raymond, Bowling Green, OH: Bowling Green State Univ. Popular Press, 1990.

Trebilcot, Joyce, ed., *Mothering, Essays in Feminist Theory.* Totowa, NJ: Rowman and Allanheld, 1984.

Reading the Text

1. Summarize in your own words the three views of motherhood that characterize recent feminist theory.

---

the "theoretical." Thus, I want to acknowledge here my debts to two members of my family, my daughter Katherine Raymond and my mother Rose Barsoum, with whom I have learned firsthand about these issues. I thank them here for the lessons they have taught me and for the inspiration for this paper.

2. Why does Raymond reject the notion that a woman's biology is her destiny?
3. What, according to Raymond, are the "images of mothering" that appear in *Baby Boom* and *Three Men and a Baby*? Why did men assume the role of "mother" in these films?
4. Raymond argues that "patriarchy has a knack for incorporating potentially destabilizing modes of behavior and neutralizing their subversive power in the process." What does she mean by this statement?

Reading the Signs

1. Test Raymond's claims about the images of mothering against examples of "family"-centered films you have seen. Are her claims accurate and complete? Have images of mothering changed since she wrote her essay?
2. Read Holly Devor's "Gender Role Behaviors and Attitudes" (p. 605). How are the images of mothering shaped by the traditional gender roles that Devor describes?
3. At the end of her essay, Raymond laments that fathers are "disproportionately present in popular film." How might Robert Bly (p. 619) respond to Raymond's lament? What view might Bly have of the images of mothering—and of fathering—in movies?
4. In class, brainstorm "images of mothering" from a variety of popular media (including film, television, and advertising). Then compare your class's brainstormed list with the images of mothering that Raymond sees in popular film. To what extent does your class's list correspond with Raymond's images? How can you account for any differences?
5. Watch a family-centered television show such as *Roseanne*. How might Raymond interpret the images of mothering in the program that you watch?
6. How would Linda Seger ("Creating the Myth," p. 250) explain the myths of mothering in the films that Diane Raymond interprets?

TANIA MODLESKI

Dead White Male Heterosexual Poets Society

||||||||||||||||||||||||||||||||||||||||||||||||

Often the significance of a movie is concealed behind an elaborate smoke screen—especially when the true object of the film violates a cultural taboo. As Tania Modleski (b. 1949) argues in this probing analysis of the popular film Dead Poets Society, *the taboo behind the scenes is Hollywood's prohibition on making openly gay films. To get around the taboos, filmmakers resort to carefully constructed codes—such as making Walt Whitman, America's great gay (as well as gray) poet, the poetic muse of* Dead Poets Society—*to pursue forbidden themes. For Modleski, however, there is a certain complicity by moviemakers with cultural censors when a film conceals its homoerotic material. This concealment also leads to flawed movies, in which certain parts of the action don't make any sense until you can decode them properly—as in the case of* Dead Poets Society. *Tania Modleski is a professor at the University of Southern California, where she teaches courses in film and women's studies; her books include* Loving with a Vengeance *(1982),* Studies in Entertainment *(1986),* The Woman Who Knew Too Much *(1987), and* Feminism Without Women *(1991), from which this selection is taken.*

Contemporary films are preoccupied with various *kinds* of male regression—physical, psychological, and historical—connecting nostalgia for the past and for childhood with male fears of the body and with a search for literalness in language. Nowhere are these fears and this quest more evident than in the hit film *Dead Poets Society,* which is set in a boys' boarding school in 1959. Here the insistence on boyhood sexual innocence is so extreme that the film may be said to mark the return of the "hysterical" text, in which the weight of the not-said, that which is again rapidly becoming "unspeakable," threatens to capsize the work's literal meaning. According to Geoffrey Nowell-Smith, who uses the term in discussing the family melodramas of the 1950s, the "hysterical text" is one in which the repressed sexual content of a film, banished from the film's narrative, returns to manifest itself in various ways in the *mise-en-scène* and through textual incoherences.[1] In *Dead Poets,* the repressed content is related to homoeroticism and gay sexuality. It is interesting to speculate on how the film's meaning would have changed were it to have introduced one literary figure in particular—Oscar Wilde, whose writing is judged by some critics to be the first in which "it was generally recognized that a literary work had a meaning other than its face value," whose work, then, posed a threat to the transparency and innocence of language, seeming to contaminate it with duplicitous double meanings.[2] In Wilde's case, of course, as a result of the trials, this doubleness has been lost to us and it has become impossible not to perceive the "gay" meanings of the texts.

So it is not surprising that the film turns to Walt Whitman as a more sexually ambiguous figure through whom to work out its ideologically

---

1. Geoffrey Nowell-Smith, "Minnelli and Melodrama," in *Home Is Where the Heart Is: Studies in Melodrama and the Woman's Film,* ed. Christine Gledhill (London: BFI, 1987), pp. 70–74.

2. Michael Bronski, *Culture Clash: The Making of a Gay Sensibility* (Boston: South End Press, 1984), p. 53.

conservative projects: first, not only to deny the homosexuality of Whitman but more generally to evade its own relation to homoeroticism;
second, to appear, in true post–gay rights fashion, to be endorsing rebellious antiauthoritarian modes of behavior, but, third, to be actually
evoking a longing for a closeted world in which such behavior would
only serve to perpetuate a power structure that would ceaselessly punish
it. Thus, despite the fact that Whitman's sexuality has been contested
throughout many decades of literary criticism, the film makes no references to the debates over Whitman's homosexuality, focusing only on
Whitman as the good gray poet: the free-thinking English teacher Mr.
Keating, played by Robin Williams, insists on being called "Captain" or
"Oh Captain, My Captain," singling out the one poem that exhibits
pious deference to male authority—the very authority the film pretends
to be challenging. It is not, incidentally, without relevance and certainly
not without irony that Whitman's "corporeal utopianism" has recently
been seen by one gay critic as existing in opposition to the moral-purity
writers of the nineteenth century who were especially alarmed by the
possible depravity of such homosocial environments as the male boarding
school.[3] Welton, the setting of *Dead Poets,* would have given these writers
no cause for concern.

Although the film exists in a genre of boys' boarding school films,
some of which (like *The Devil's Playground*) brilliantly explore the homoerotic tensions of such an environment, and although it is directed by
Peter Weir, whose previous work (e.g., *Gallipoli, Picnic at Hanging Rock*)
is suffused with a lyrical homoeroticism, *Dead Poets* denies this dimension
of boarding school life so resolutely that its repression can be systematically traced, the duplicitous meanings emerging after all. For example,
one of the characters is a kind of misfit and a loner, unable to articulate
his feelings and hence marginal to the group forming around Keating:
In fact, the character reveals many of the signs of a sexual identity crisis,
and in a more honest version of the film might have been shown struggling to come to terms with being gay in a heterosexual, homosocial
environment. That the possible "latent" homosexual theme is overde-
termined is suggested in one rather amazing scene in which Keating
instructs the boy to come to the front of the room and, since he has
been unable to complete the poetry writing assignment, to stare at a
picture of Walt Whitman and spew out poetic phrases, while Keating
spins him round and round, violently extracting the speech the boy has
been withholding.

---

3. Michael Moon, "Disseminating Whitman," special issue, "Displacing Homophobia," ed. Ronald R. Butters, John M. Clum, and Michael Moon, *The South Atlantic
Quarterly* 88, no. 1 (Winter 1989): 255.

As for Keating, whose presence spawns the boys' secret society, lest anyone suspect his motives in returning to the repressive boys' school in which he had been a student, we see him in a carefully staged scene writing a letter to his fiancée whose picture is conspicuously propped on the desk. (Performing similar roles as "disclaimers" are the girls whom the boys entertain at one point in their cave, reciting poems that one of them claims to be original compositions.[4]) Asked by a student why he stays in such a stifling place, Keating responds that he loves teaching more than anything in the world; he gives no explanation of why he left the school in England, where his fiancée still lives, or why he has ruled out teaching in the public schools—clearly a more congenial place for his democratic, free-thinking sympathies. Such "disclaimers" as the photo (as well as a banal subplot in which a boy falls in love with a cheerleader and becomes rivals with a football hero in one of the public schools) and such narrative incoherences might be taken as indicators of the film's repressed homoerotic content—the symptoms in the "hysterical text."

At the end of the film one boy, whose father has forbidden him to act in a play, defies his father by playing the role of Puck in a student production of *A Midsummer Night's Dream,* and then ends up killing himself because his father forbids him to continue in the role. Of all the roles to have chosen, this one seems most filled with latent—and because latent, homophobic—meaning, as if the struggle between a boy and his father were over the boy's right to "pose as a fairy." In the investigation that follows the suicide, John Keating becomes the scapegoat and is forced to leave the school, and the boys are called individually up to the principal, who orders them to "assume the position," and then paddles them. Implausibly, Keating comes to collect his things in the middle of an English class, which the principal has taken over, and as he leaves, one boy stands up to voice his support of his former teacher and then climbs up on his desk, repeating an act Keating had earlier urged the students to perform in order to encourage nonconformity. The other class members, conforming, as it were, to the boy's gesture of nonconformity, follow suit. In the final shot of the film, the camera frames the student as he stands looking at John Keating, the legs of another student straddling the image in the shape of an inverted V—the sexualized body which has been so systematically denied throughout the narrative emerging here, in hysterical fashion, in the body of the film itself, its *mise-en-scène.*

5

---

4. "Disclaimer" is a term used by Robin Wood to denote aspects of plot or the existence of characters whose sole purpose is to assure us of the protagonists' heterosexuality. See his *Hollywood from Vietnam to Reagan* (New York: Columbia University Press, 1985), p. 229.

. . . *Dead Poets Society* is a profoundly regressive film, fixated on adolescence and a mythical moment in the past that it appears to repudiate but really longs for: a moment of repression and discipline and stable authority, represented by fathers, high school principals, and dead poets. By no means does the film anticipate the real rebellions that were shortly to erupt, even though it presupposes an audience that has lived through them. Thus the film challenges the literary canon and the orthodoxies of the "discipline" of literary studies (represented, for Keating, by the "realists" and by the textbook's editor whose introduction Keating instructs the boys to tear out), but returns us to this canon via a sanitized image of one of our most heterodox and sexually explicit authors; pays lip service to feminist demands for an end to exclusionary male societies, but on the grounds that male sexual needs will be better served (i.e., as one of them jokes, so the boys won't have to masturbate); and encourages such marginalized people as gay youths to speak, but only in unintelligible language. Far from anticipating the specific struggles of the 1960s and 1970s, the film lyricizes life in the closet, yearning for the time just before these rebellions—a time when, for example, there were no dead women poets (not even Emily Dickinson) and live females apparently could not tell the difference between Shakespeare and a schoolboy's poetry, a time before gay men would aid in problematizing the very notion of adolescent sexual innocence and Whitman would be brought further out of the closet. Like Keating and despite its disclaimers, its bad-faith mockery of "tradition," the film chooses the particular chronotope of the 1950s boys' school because it *wants* to be there: at a time and place in which tradition seemed entirely a white male heterosexual affair and could itself appear innocent, devoid of substance and body.

Reading the Text

1. How, according to Modleski, does *Dead Poets Society* suppress its homoerotic meanings?
2. How is *Dead Poets Society* an "hysterical" text?
3. What does Modleski mean by claiming that *Dead Poets Society* "lyricizes life in the closet"?

Reading the Signs

1. Rent a videotape of *Dead Poets Society* and watch it with your class. Do you agree or disagree with Modleski's interpretation of the film? Discuss the issue in class, and then write an essay or journal entry supporting your position.
2. *Dead Poets Society* takes place at a boys' boarding school. Read or review

Peter Lyman's "The Fraternal Bond as a Joking Relationship" (p. 611). How might Lyman interpret the relationship among the boys and their teacher?
3. Read or review Linda Seger's "Creating the Myth" (p. 250). What myths about homosexuality might she find in *Dead Poets Society*?
4. Rent a videotape of *Scent of a Woman*. Using Modleski's arguments as your critical framework, interpret the relationships among the film's major characters. To what extent is this film another example of repressed homoeroticism?
5. Read or review Andy Medhurst's "Batman, Deviance, and Camp" (p. 323). How might Modleski interpret the homoeroticism implicit in the Batman-Robin relationship?

MICHAEL PARENTI
Class and Virtue

In 1993, a movie called Indecent Proposal *presented a story in which a billionaire offers a newly poor middle-class woman a million dollars if she'll sleep with him for one night. In Michael Parenti's terms, what was really indecent about the movie was the way it showed the woman falling in love with the billionaire, thus making a romance out of a class outrage. But the movie could get away with it, partly because Hollywood has always conditioned audiences to root for the ruling classes and to ignore the inequities of class privilege. In this selection from* Make-Believe Media: The Politics of Entertainment *(1992), Parenti (b. 1933) argues that Hollywood has long been in the business of representing the interests of the ruling classes. Whether it is forgiving the classist behavior in* Pretty Woman *or glamorizing the lives of the wealthy, Hollywood makes sure its audiences leave the theater thinking you can't be too rich. Michael Parenti is a writer who lectures widely at university campuses around the country. His publications include* Power and the Powerless *(1978),* Inventing Reality: The Politics of the News Media *(1986), and* Democracy for the Few *(1988).*

Class and Virtue

The entertainment media present working people not only as unlettered and uncouth but also as less desirable and less moral than other people. Conversely, virtue is more likely to be ascribed to those characters whose speech and appearance are soundly middle- or upper-middle class.

Even a simple adventure story like *Treasure Island* (1934, 1950, 1972) manifests this implicit class perspective. There are two groups of acquisitive persons searching for a lost treasure. One, headed by a squire, has money enough to hire a ship and crew. The other, led by the rascal Long John Silver, has no money—so they sign up as part of the crew. The narrative implicitly assumes from the beginning that the squire has a moral claim to the treasure, while Long John Silver's gang does not. After all, it is the squire who puts up the venture capital for the ship. Having no investment in the undertaking other than their labor, Long John and his men, by definition, will be "stealing" the treasure, while the squire will be "discovering" it.

To be sure, there are other differences. Long John's men are cut-throats. The squire is not. Yet, one wonders if the difference between a bad pirate and a good squire is itself not preeminently a matter of having the right amount of disposable income. The squire is no less acquisitive than the conspirators. He just does with money what they must achieve with cutlasses. The squire and his associates dress in fine clothes, speak an educated diction, and drink brandy. Long John and his men dress slovenly, speak in guttural accents, and drink rum. From these indications alone, the viewer knows who are the good guys and who are the bad. Virtue is visually measured by one's approximation to proper class appearances.

Sometimes class contrasts are juxtaposed within one person, as in *The Three Faces of Eve* (1957), a movie about a woman who suffers from multiple personalities. When we first meet Eve (Joanne Woodward), she is a disturbed, strongly repressed, puritanically religious person, who speaks with a rural, poor-Southern accent. Her second personality is that of a wild, flirtatious woman who also speaks with a rural, poor-Southern accent. After much treatment by her psychiatrist, she is cured of these schizoid personalities and emerges with a healthy third one, the real Eve, a poised, self-possessed, pleasant woman. What is intriguing is that she now speaks with a cultivated, affluent, Smith College accent, free of any low-income regionalism or ruralism, much like Joanne Woodward herself. This transformation in class style and speech is used to indicate mental health without any awareness of the class bias thusly expressed.

Mental health is also the question in *A Woman Under the Influence* (1974), the story of a disturbed woman who is married to a hard-hat husband. He cannot handle—and inadvertently contributes to—her emotional deterioration. She is victimized by a spouse who is nothing more than an insensitive, working-class bull in a china shop. One comes away convinced that every unstable woman needs a kinder, gentler, and above all, more *middle-class* hubby if she wishes to avoid a mental crack-up.

Class prototypes abound in the 1980s television series *The A-Team*. In each episode, a Vietnam-era commando unit helps an underdog, be it a Latino immigrant or a disabled veteran, by vanquishing some menacing force such as organized crime, a business competitor, or corrupt government officials. As always with the make-believe media, the A-Team does good work on an individualized rather than collectively organized basis, helping particular victims by thwarting particular villains. The A-Team's leaders are two white males of privileged background. The lowest ranking members of the team, who do none of the thinking nor the leading, are working-class palookas. They show they are good with their hands, both by punching out the bad guys and by doing the maintenance work on the team's flying vehicles and cars. One of them, "B.A." (bad ass), played by the African-American Mr. T., is visceral, tough, and purposely bad-mannered toward those he doesn't like. He projects an image of crudeness and ignorance and is associated with the physical side of things. In sum, the team has a brain (the intelligent white leaders) and a body with its simpler physical functions (the working-class characters), a hierarchy that corresponds to the social structure itself.[1]

Sometimes class bigotry is interwoven with gender bigotry, as in *Pretty Woman* (1990). A dreamboat millionaire corporate raider finds himself all alone for an extended stay in Hollywood (his girlfriend is unwilling to join him), so he quickly recruits a beautiful prostitute as his playmate of the month. She is paid three thousand dollars a week to wait around his superposh hotel penthouse ready to perform the usual services and accompany him to business dinners at top restaurants. As prostitution goes, it is a dream gig. But there is one cloud on the horizon. She is low-class. She doesn't know which fork to use at those CEO power feasts, and she's bothersomely fidgety, wears tacky clothes, chews gum, and, y'know, doesn't talk so good. But with some tips from the hotel manager, she proves to be a veritable Eliza Doolittle in her class metamorphosis. She dresses in proper attire, sticks the gum away forever, and starts picking the right utensils at dinner. She also figures out how to speak a little more like Joanne Woodward without the benefit of a multiple personality syndrome, and she develops the capacity to sit in a poised, wordless, empty-headed fashion, every inch the expensive female ornament.

She is still a prostitute but a classy one. It is enough of a distinction for the handsome young corporate raider. Having liked her because she was charmingly cheap, he now loves her all the more because she has real polish and is a more suitable companion. So suitable that he decides to do the right thing by her: set her up in an apartment so he can make

---

1. Gina Marchetti, "Class, Ideology and Commercial Television: An Analysis of 'The A-Team'," *Journal of Film and Video*, 39, Spring 1987, pp. 19–28.

regular visits at regular prices. But now she wants the better things in life, like marriage, a nice house, and, above all, a different occupation, one that would allow her to use less of herself. She is furious at him for treating her like, well, a prostitute. She decides to give up her profession and get a high-school diploma so that she might make a better life for herself—perhaps as a filing clerk or receptionist or some other of the entry-level jobs awaiting young women with high school diplomas.[2]

After the usual girl-breaks-off-with-boy scenes, the millionaire prince returns. It seems he can't concentrate on making money without her. He even abandons his cutthroat schemes and enters into a less lucrative but supposedly more productive, caring business venture with a struggling old-time entrepreneur. The bad capitalist is transformed into a good capitalist. He then carries off his ex-prostitute for a lifetime of bliss. The moral is a familiar one, updated for post-Reagan yuppiedom: A woman can escape from economic and gender exploitation by winning the love and career advantages offered by a rich male. Sexual allure goes only so far unless it develops a material base and becomes a class act.[3]

Reading the Text

1. What characteristics are attributed to working-class and upper-class film characters, according to Parenti?
2. How does Parenti see the relationship between class bigotry and gender bigotry in *Pretty Woman*?
3. What relationship does Parenti see between mental health and class values in films?

Reading the Signs

1. Rent a videotape of *Wall Street,* and analyze the class issues that the movie raises.
2. Using Parenti's argument as a critical framework, interpret the class values implicit in a television show such as *Beverly Hills, 90210* or *Roseanne.* Is the show that you've selected guilty of what Parenti calls "class bigotry"?
3. Do you agree with Parenti's interpretation of *Pretty Woman*? Write an argumentative essay in which you defend, challenge, or complicate his claims.
4. Read or review Holly Devor's "Gender Role Behaviors and Attitudes" (p. 605). How would Devor explain the gender bigotry that Parenti finds in *Pretty Woman*?

---

2. See the excellent review by Lydia Sargent, *Z Magazine,* April 1990, pp. 43–45.
3. Ibid.

5. Rent the 1954 film *On the Waterfront* and watch it with your class. How are labor unions and working-class characters portrayed in that film? Does the film display the "class bigotry" that Parenti describes?

6. Read or review Michael Omi's "In Living Color" (p. 449). Then write a journal entry in which you create a category of cinematic "racial bigotry" that corresponds to Parenti's two categories of class and gender bigotry. What films that you have seen illustrate your new category?

SHELBY STEELE
Malcolm X

⁣⁣

One of the most independent-minded and widely read of America's writers on racial relations, Shelby Steele (b. 1946) has never been afraid to take a controversial position. In this reading of Spike Lee's Malcolm X, *Steele goes beyond a critique of the film, which he feels oversimplifies the life and meaning of Malcolm X, to take on the myth of Malcolm X itself. At a time when Malcolm X is being celebrated as an icon of radical black nationalism, Steele argues that Malcolm was a profoundly conservative man whose appeal lies precisely in his cultural conservatism. From his beliefs in the family-building responsibilities of black women to his abhorrence of tobacco and alcohol, Malcolm X actually endorsed many of America's most traditional values—a side to his character that is often ignored. For Steele, who wishes to understand Malcolm X, not debunk him, all the mythmaking about the man does little to help us interpret his full cultural significance—a task that Steele begins here. Shelby Steele is currently professor of English at San Jose State University and the author of* The Content of Our Character: A New Vision of Race in America *(1990), which won a National Book Critics Circle Award.*

When asked recently what he thought of Malcolm X, Thurgood Marshall is reported to have said, "All he did was talk." And yet there is a kind of talk that constitutes action, a catalytic speech that changes things as irrevocably as do events or great movements. Malcolm X was an event, and his talk transformed American culture as surely, if not as thoroughly, as the civil rights movement, which might not have found the moderation necessary for its success had Malcolm not planted in the American consciousness so uncompromised a vision of the underdog's rage.

Malcolm staked out this territory against his great contemporary and foil, Martin Luther King, Jr. Sneering at King's turn-the-other-cheek Christianity, he told blacks, "Don't ask God to have mercy on him [the white man]; ask God to judge him. Ask God to do onto him what he did onto you. Ask God that he suffer as you suffered." To use the old Christian categories, Malcolm was the Old Testament to King's New Testament. Against the moral nobility of the civil rights movement, he wanted whites to know that he was not different from them; that he, too, would kill or die for freedom. "The price of freedom is death," he often said.

Like all true revolutionaries, Malcolm had an intimate relationship with his own death. By being less afraid of it than other men, he took on power. And this was not so much a death wish as it was the refusal of a compromised life. These seemed to be his terms, and for many blacks like myself who came of age during his era, there was nothing to do but love him, since he, foolishly or not, seemed to love us more than we loved ourselves.

It is always context that makes a revolutionary figure like Malcolm X a hero or a destroyer. Even when he first emerged in the late fifties and early sixties, the real debate was not so much about him (he was clear enough) as about whether or not the context of black oppression was severe enough to justify him. And now that Malcolm has explosively reemerged on the American scene, those old questions about context are with us once again.

Spike Lee has brought Malcolm's autobiography to the screen in one   5
of the most thoroughly hyped films in American history. Malcolm's life is available in airport bookstalls. Compact discs and videotapes of his "blue-eyed devil" speeches can be picked up at Tower Records. His "X" is ubiquitous to the point of gracing automobile air fresheners. Twenty-seven years after his death, in sum, he is more visible to Americans than he was during his life. Of course Americans will commercialize anything; but that is a slightly redundant point. The really pressing matter is what this says about the context of race relations in America today. How can a new generation of blacks—after pervasive civil rights legislation, Great Society programs, school busing, open housing, and more than two decades of affirmative action—be drawn to a figure of such seething racial alienation?

The life of Malcolm X touched so many human archetypes that his story itself seems to supersede any racial context, which is to say that it meshes with virtually every context. Malcolm X is a story. And so he meets people, particularly young people, in a deeply personal way. To assess whether or not he is a good story for these times, I think we have to consider first the nature of his appeal.

Let me say—without, I hope, too many violins—that when I was growing up in the 1950s, I was very often the victim of old-fashioned racism and discrimination. These experiences were very much like the literal experience of being burned. Not only did they hurt, they also caused me to doubt myself in some fundamental way. There was shame in these experiences as well, the suspicion that by some measure of human worth I deserved them. This, of course, is precisely what they were designed to make me feel. So right away there was an odd necessity to fight and to struggle for both personal and racial dignity.

Those were the experiences that enabled me to hear Malcolm. The very soul of his legend was the heroic struggle that he was waging against racial doubt and shame. After a tortuous childhood and an early life of crime that left him shattered, he reconstructed himself—against the injuries of racial oppression—by embracing an ideology of black nationalism. Black nationalism offered something very important to Malcolm, and this quickly became his magnificently articulated offering to other blacks. What it offered was a perfectly cathartic distribution of love and hate. Blacks were innocent victims, whites were evil oppressors, and blacks had to distribute their love and hate accordingly. But if one focuses on the called-for hatred of whites, the point of Malcolm's redistribution of emotion will be missed. If Malcolm was screaming his hatred of whites, his deeper purpose was to grant blacks a license to give themselves what they needed most: self-love.

This license to love and to hate in a way that soothed my unconscious doubts was nothing less than compelling by the time I reached college. Late at night in the dorm, my black friends and I would turn off the lights for effect and listen to his album of speeches, *The Ballot or the Bullet,* over and over again. He couldn't have all that anger and all that hate unless he really loved black people, and, therefore, us. And so he massaged the injured part of ourselves with an utterly self-gratifying and unconditional love.

With Martin Luther King, by contrast, there were conditions. King   10
asked blacks—despised and unloved—to spread their meager stock of love to all people, even to those who despised us. What a lot to ask, and of a victim. With King, we were once again in second place, loving others before ourselves. But Malcolm told us to love ourselves first and to project all of our hurt into a hatred of the "blue-eyed devil" who had hurt us in the first place.

In Malcolm's deployment of love and hate there was an intrinsic logic of dignity that was very different from King's. For King, racial dignity was established by enlarging the self into a love of others. For Malcolm, dignity came from constriction, from shrinking to the enemy's size, and showing him not that you could be higher than he was, but that you could go as low. If King rose up, Malcolm dropped down. And here is where he used the hatred side of his formula to lay down his two essential principles of black dignity: the dehumanization of the white man and the threat of violence.

What made those principles essential to the dignity of blacks for Malcolm was that they followed a tit-for-tat logic—the logic by which, in his mind, any collective established its dignity against another collective. And both these principles could be powerfully articulated by Malcolm because they were precisely the same principles by which whites had oppressed blacks for centuries. Malcolm dehumanized whites by playing back, in whiteface, the stereotypes that blacks had endured. He made them animals—if they like their meat rare, "that's the dog in 'em." In the iconography of his Black Muslim period, whites were heathen, violent, drooling beasts who lynched and raped. But he often let his humor get the best of him in this, and most blacks took it with a grain of salt.

What made Malcolm one of the most controversial Americans of this century was the second principle in his logic of dignity: the threat of violence. "If we have a funeral in Harlem, make sure they have one downtown, too." "If he puts his hand on you, send him to the cemetery." Tit-for-tat logic taken to its logical conclusion. In fact, Malcolm's focus on violence against whites was essentially rhetorical. Like today's black street gangs, his Black Muslims were far more likely to kill each other than go after whites. Yet no one has ever played the white hysteria over black violence better than Malcolm.

He played this card very effectively to achieve two things. The first was to breach the horrible invisibility that blacks have endured in America. White racism has always been sustained by the white refusal or reluctance to see blacks, to think about them as people, to grant them the kind of place in the imagination that one would grant, say, to the English or even the Russians. Blacks might be servile or troublesome, but never worthy of serious, competitive consideration. Against this Malcolm sent a concrete message: We are human enough to want to kill you for what you have done to us. How does it feel to have people you have never paid much attention to want to kill you? (This was the terror Richard Wright captured so powerfully in *Native Son:* Your humble chauffeur may kill your daughter. And that novel, too, got attention.) Violence was a means to black visibility for Malcolm, and later for many other militants.

Today this idea of violence as black visibility means that part of   15
Malcolm's renewed popularity comes from his power as an attention-getting figure. If today's "X" is an assertion of self-love, it is also a demand to be seen. This points to the second purpose of Malcolm's violent rhetoric: to restore dignity to blacks in an almost Hegelian sense. Those unwilling to kill and to die for dignity would forever be a slave class. Here he used whites as the model. They would go to war to meet any threat, even when it was far removed. Many times he told his black audiences that whites would not respect them unless they used "any means necessary" to seize freedom. For a minority outnumbered ten to

one, this was not rational. But it was a point that needed to be made in the name of dignity. It was something that many blacks needed to feel about themselves, that there was a line that no one could cross.

Yet this logic of dignity only partly explains Malcolm's return as an icon in our own day. I believe that the larger reason for his perdurability and popularity is one that is almost never mentioned: that Malcolm X was a deeply conservative man. In times when the collective identity is besieged and confused, groups usually turn to their conservatives, not to their liberals; to their extreme partisans, not to their open-minded representatives. The last twenty-five years have seen huge class and cultural differences open up in black America. The current bromide is that we are not a monolith, and this is profoundly true. We now have a black governor and a black woman senator and millions of black college graduates and so on, but also hundreds of thousands of young blacks in prison. Black identity no longer has a centrifugal force in a racial sense. And in the accompanying confusion we look to the most conservative identity figure.

Malcolm was conservative through and through. As a black nationalist, he was a hard-line militarist who believed in the principle of self-mastery through force. His language and thinking in this regard were oddly in line with Henry Kissinger's description of the world as a brutal place in which safety and a balance of power is maintained through realpolitik. He was Reaganesque in his insistence on negotiating with whites from a position of strength—meaning the threat of violence. And his commitment (until the last year of his life) to racial purity and separatism would have made him the natural ally of David Duke.

In his personal life, moreover, Malcolm scrupulously followed all the Islamic strictures against alcohol, tobacco, drugs, fornication, and adultery, and his attitude toward women was decidedly patriarchal: As a Black Muslim minister he counseled that women could never be completely trusted because of their vanity, and he forbade dancing in his mosque. In his speeches he reserved a special contempt for white liberals, and he once praised Barry Goldwater as a racial realist. Believing entirely in black self-help, he had no use for government programs to uplift blacks, and sneered at the 1964 Civil Rights Bill as nothing more than white expedience.

Malcolm X was one of the most unabashed and unqualified conservatives of his time. And yet today he is forgiven his sexism by black feminists, his political conservatism by black and white liberals, his Islamic faith by black Christians, his violent rhetoric by nonviolent veterans of the civil rights struggle, his anti-Semitism by blacks and whites who are repulsed by it, his separatism by blacks who live integrated lives, and even the apparent fabrication of events in his childhood by those who would bring his story to the screen. Malcolm enjoys one of the best Teflon coatings of all time.

I think one of the reasons for this is that he was such an extreme 20 conservative, that is, such an extreme partisan of his group. All we really ask of such people is that they love the group more than anything else, even themselves. If this is evident, all else is secondary. In fact, we demand conservatism from such people, because it is a testament of their love. Malcolm sneered at government programs because he believed so much in black people: They could do it on their own. He gave up all his vices to intensify his love. He was a father figure who distributed love and hate in our favor. Reagan did something like this when he called the Soviet Union an "evil empire," and he, too, was rewarded with Teflon.

The point is that all groups take their extreme partisans more figuratively than literally. Their offer of unconditional love bribes us into loving them back rather unconditionally, so that our will to be literal with them weakens. We will not see other important black leaders of the 1960s—James Farmer, Whitney Young, Andrew Young, Medgar Evers (a genuine martyr), Roy Wilkins, John Lewis—gracing the T-shirts of young blacks who are today benefiting more from their efforts than from Malcolm's. They were too literal, too much of the actual world, for iconography, for the needs of an unsure psyche. But Malcolm, the hater and the lover, the father figure of romantic blackness, is the perfect icon.

It helps, too, that he is dead, and therefore unable to be literal in our own time. We can't know, for example, if he would now be supporting affirmative action as the reparation that is due to blacks, or condemning it as more white patronization and black dependency. In a way, the revival of Malcolm X is one of the best arguments I know of for the validity of the deconstructionist view of things: Malcolm is now a text. Today we *read* Malcolm. And this—dare I say—is one quality he shares with Christ, who also died young and became a text. He was also an Odyssean figure who journeyed toward self-knowledge. He was a priest and a heretic. For many whites he was a devil and for many blacks a martyr. Even those of my generation who grew up with him really came to know him through the autobiography that he wrote with Alex Haley. Even in his time, then, he was a text, and it is reasonable to wonder if he would have the prominence he has today without that book.

How will the new epic movie of his life—yet another refracting text—add to his prominence? Clearly it will add rather than subtract. It is a film that enhances the legend, that tries to solidify Malcolm's standing as a symbol of identity. To this end, the film marches uncritically through the well-known episodes of the life. It is beautifully shot and superbly acted by a cast that seemed especially inspired by the significance of the project. And yet it is still, finally, a march. Spike Lee, normally filled with bravado, works here like a TV docudramatist with a big budget, for whom loyalty to a received version of events is more important than insight, irony, or vision. Bruce Perry's recent study of Malcolm's life, *Malcolm: A Life of the Man Who Changed Black America,* which contradicts much of the autobiography, is completely and indefensibly ignored.

Against Lee's portrayal of Malcolm's father as a stalwart Garveyite killed by the Klan, Perry reveals a man with a reputation for skirt-chasing who moved from job to job and was often violent with his children. Lee shows the Klan burning down Malcolm's childhood home, while Perry offers considerable evidence to indicate that Malcolm's father likely burned it down himself after he received an eviction notice. Lee offers a dramatic scene of the Klan running Earl Little and his family out of Nebraska, yet Malcolm's mother told Perry that the event never happened. The rather heroic cast that Malcolm (and Lee) gave to his childhood is contradicted by Perry's extensive interviews with childhood friends, who portray Malcolm as rather fearful and erratic. Lee's only response to Perry's work was simply, "I don't believe it."

It was Spike Lee's unthinking loyalty to the going racial orthodoxy,   25
I believe, that led him to miss more than he saw, and to produce a film that is finally part fact, part fiction, and entirely middlebrow. That racial orthodoxy is a problem for many black artists working today, since its goal is to make the individual artist responsible for the collective political vision. This orthodoxy arbitrates the artist's standing within the group: The artist can be as individual as he or she likes as long as the group view of things is upheld. The problem here for black artists is that their racial identity will be held hostage to the practice of their art. The effect of this is to pressure the work of art, no matter what inspired it, into a gesture of identification that reunites the artist and the group.

In this sense Lee's *Malcolm X* might be called a reunion film, or a gesture of identification on his part toward the group. Thus his loyalist, unquestioning march through Malcolm's mythology. It is certainly ironic, given the debate over whether a white man could direct this film, that Spike Lee sees his hero as only a black man with no more than black motivations. Human motivations like doubt, fear, insecurity, jealousy, and love, or human themes like the search for the father, betrayal, and tragedy, are present in the film because they were present in Malcolm's story, but Lee seems unaware of them as the real stuff of his subject's life. The film expresses its identification with much racial drama, but in a human monotone.

Thus many of the obvious ironies of Malcolm's life are left hanging. If black nationalism resurrected Malcolm in prison, it also killed him in the end. This was a man who put all his faith in the concept of a black nation, in the idea that blackness, in itself, carried moral significance, and yet it was black nationalist fingers pulling the triggers that killed him. Even on its surface this glaring irony points to the futility of cultish racial ideologies, to the collective insecurities that inspire them, and to the frightened personalities that adhere to them as single-mindedly as Malcolm did. But doesn't this irony also underscore the much more common human experience of falling when we grip our illusions too tightly, when we need them too much? It should not embarrass Lee to draw out the irony of Malcolm being killed by blacks. He was. And there is a lesson in it for everyone, since we are all hurt by our illusions. To make his gesture of identification, however, Lee prefers to sacrifice the deeper identification that his entire audience might have with his subject.

He also fails to perform the biographer's critical function. Clearly Malcolm had something of the true believer's compulsion to believe blindly and singularly, to eradicate all complexity as hypocrisy. All his life he seemed to have no solid internal compass of his own to rely on in the place of ideology—which is not to say that he didn't have brilliance once centered by a faith. But in this important way he was very unlike King, who, lacking Malcolm's wounds, was so well centered that he projected serenity and composure even as storms raged around him. Out of some underlying agitation Malcolm searched for authorities, for systems of belief, for father figures, for revelations: West Indian Archie, Elijah Muhammad, the Black Muslim faith, Pan Africanism, and finally the humanism of traditional Islam. All this in thirty-nine years! What else might have followed? How many more fathers? How many more isms?

Moreover, once Malcolm learned from these people, faiths, and ideologies—or had taken what he could from them—he betrayed them all, one after another. There was always this pattern of complete, true-believing submission to authority and then ,the abrupt betrayal of it. There was something a little narcissistic in this, as though his submissions were really setups for the victories that he would later seize. And with each betrayal-victory there was something of a gloat—his visit to West Indian Archie when he was broken, his telling Mike Wallace on national television about Elijah Muhammad's infidelities. Betrayal was triumph for Malcolm, a moving beyond some smallness, some corruption, some realm that was beneath him.

The corruption at the heart of Malcolm's legend is that he looked bigger than life because he always lived in small, cultish worlds, and always stood next to small people. He screamed at whites, but he had no idea of how to work with them to get things done. King was the man who had to get things done. I don't think that it is farfetched to suggest that finally Malcolm was afraid of white people. While King stared down every white from Bull Connor to the Kennedys, Malcolm made a big deal out of facing off with Elijah Muhammad, whom he had likely propped up for the purpose. His proclivity for little people who made him look big suggests that his black nationalism covered his fear of hard, ordinary work in the American crucible. Up against larger realities and bigger people, he might have felt inadequate.

Lee's film, as beautifully executed as it is, refuses to ask questions about Malcolm's legend. A quick look behind the legend, however, shows that Malcolm's real story was, in truth, tragedy. And the understanding of this grim truth would have helped the film better achieve the racial protest it is obviously after. Malcolm was hurt badly by oppression early in his childhood. If his family was not shattered in the way he claimed, it was shattered nevertheless. And this shattering had much to do with America's brutal racial history. He was, in his pain, a product of America. But his compensations for the hurt only extended the hurt. And the tragedy was the life that this extraordinary man felt that he needed to live, that Malcolm Little had to become Malcolm X, had to be a criminal, then a racial ideologue, and finally a martyr for an indefinable cause. Black nationalism is a tragedy of white racism, and can sometimes be as ruinous as the racism itself.

And so it is saddening to witness the reemergence of this hyped-up, legendary Mr. X, this seller of wolf tickets and excuses not to engage American society. This Malcolm is back to conceal rather than to reveal. He is here to hide our fears as he once hid his own, to keep us separated from any helpful illumination. Had the real Malcolm, the tragic Malcolm, returned, however, it would have represented a remarkable racial advancement. That Malcolm might have given both blacks and whites a way to comprehend our racial past and present. In him we all could have seen the damage done, the frustrations borne, and the fruitless heroism of the American insistence on race.

Reading the Text

1. How has the image of Malcolm X evolved since the 1950s, according to Steele?
2. Summarize in a paragraph Steele's opinion of the film *Malcolm X*.
3. Why does Steele see Malcolm X as a fundamentally conservative figure? What evidence does he offer in support of his thesis?
4. What does Steele mean by saying that "This Malcolm is back to conceal rather than to reveal"?

Reading the Signs

1. Rent a videotape of *Malcolm X* and write your own critique of it.
2. Do you agree with Steele's assertion that Malcolm X is a popular figure because of his conservatism? Write an essay in which you provide your own explanation of the popularity of Malcolm X (the movie and the character). Why were the 1990s the decade in which he made a comeback in American popular consciousness?
3. How would Richard Majors ("Cool Pose: The Proud Signature of Black Survival," p. 471) and Sam Fulwood III ("The Rage of the Black Middle Class," p. 462) explain the popularity of Malcolm X? In what ways would their perspectives on race in America contradict or extend Steele's analysis?
4. Read *The Autobiography of Malcolm X* and write an essay in which you compare the book's vision of Malcolm X with his portrayal in the film.
5. Drawing upon Robert Ray's "The Thematic Paradigm" (p. 241), write an essay in which you analyze Malcolm X as a hero for America in the 1990s.
6. Steele says that "the life of Malcolm X touched so many human archetypes that his story seems to supersede any racial context." How would Michael Omi ("In Living Color," p. 449) respond to this assertion?
7. Would Linda Seger (p. 250) say that Spike Lee was "creating a myth" in *Malcolm X*? If so, what would that myth be?

VALERIE BOYD

The Word on Malcolm X

꜏꜏

Some movies are just movies; others are cultural events. In 1992, Spike Lee's cinematic biography of Malcolm X hit the theaters with an impact that reverberated from coast to coast. Having already put race relations at the center stage of American film in such movies as Do the Right Thing *and* Jungle Fever, *Lee set out in* Malcolm X *to reestablish the place in American history of the man who became a symbol of black nationalism in the 1960s. In this collection of responses by black moviegoers collected by Valerie Boyd, a staff writer for the* Atlanta Journal and Constitution, *you can find signs of the power Malcolm X still has in America—and the grief African-Americans still feel about race relations in the United States.*

Director Spike Lee wants black professionals to discuss *Malcolm X* in water-cooler conversations at their offices. He envisions sisters in book clubs examining the film's portrayals of women; black nationalists analyzing it in fireside chats at bookstores; whites of good will grappling with its explosive indictment of racism.

Citing Hollywood studios' practice of quickly pulling films that don't perform well at the box office in their opening days, Mr. Lee wants folks to see *Malcolm X* fast—then spread the word.

We invited several Atlantans to an advance screening of *Malcolm X* and asked them to write their impressions. Here's what they had to say:

Robert Thompson, 43, *media specialist at Emory University*

Pain, joy, love, shame, pride. Spike Lee's *Malcolm X* makes you feel this entire range of emotions. If art is about feelings, and I believe it is, then this film is the highest form of art. What *Birth of a Nation* was to Southerners or *The Godfather* was to Italian Americans, *Malcolm X* will be to African-Americans—a defining element of our culture. I'm sure if you look hard enough, you can find something you don't like in a three-hour movie. I did. However, the flaws are insignificant compared with what is good about the film. Spike Lee and Denzel Washington have developed a creative force that has brought Malcolm's story to the large screen with sensitivity and power. The making of the film itself is a living example of the type of self-determination that Malcolm preached.

Sara M. Lomax, 26, *free-lance writer and publisher of* HealthQuest: The Publication of Black Wellness

At first I thought it was a simple case of hunger. After viewing *Malcolm X* on an empty stomach, I was drained, bleary-eyed, and famished. But after I ate, I still couldn't shake this overwhelming sense of fatigue. Forced to examine racial wounds that extend across decades and across continents, I was caught in a debilitating whirl of emotions that ranged from anger to frustration to sadness.

In essence, *Malcolm X* is an awesome reality check showing just how far we haven't come in this country. A powerful drama, it is likely to leave many burned-out and starving. Unafraid, *Malcolm X*—the man and the film—begins to nourish our minds and spirits with a direct, uncompromising assault on America's racist system. From Rodney King to Nelson Mandela, Spike Lee puts *Malcolm X*'s message into a context that defies time.

Shawn L. Williams, 26, *teacher at Price Middle School*

Aesthetically speaking, Spike Lee's *Malcolm X* is well-crafted and brilliantly performed. However, the story has several gaps that might seem conspicuous to Malcolm X scholars and would keep viewers of this film from gaining a full awareness of Malcolm's political impact on the African-American freedom struggle.

What I had hoped to see was Malcolm's eagerness to get involved with the civil rights struggle while a member of the Nation of Islam, his efforts to build a united front among civil rights leaders, and his lobbying of African and other so-called Third World nations to support the cause of African-American human rights. (This was only cursorily mentioned in the film.)

I hope this movie will inspire people to read and learn more about Malcolm X. A film about Malcolm is no substitute for personal research. And this film alone will not give anyone a real appreciation of his legacy.

Debbie Fraker, 35, *free-lance writer*

Malcolm X was sometimes racist, often sexist, and probably homophobic. But don't let that stop you from seeing this film. Spike Lee has produced a powerful film about a heroic life, clarifying Malcolm X's teachings, which have often been misunderstood, feared, or just lost in the hype.

Malcolm X taught African-Americans that change in the societal structure could only come about after they proudly claimed their difference and their heritage. The film gives him the historical place of honor that he deserves. Anyone engaged in a struggle for their own civil rights should see this film and take away its message of pride and strength to create change.

Reading the Text

1. Summarize in a sentence or two the opinions of each of the four Atlantans interviewed in the *Atlanta Journal and Constitution*.
2. To what extent do the Atlantans distinguish between Malcolm X the movie and the man?

Reading the Signs

1. Interview five classmates or friends who have seen *Malcolm X*, asking them their opinion of the film. How do their responses compare with those published in the *Atlanta Journal and Constitution*? To what extent do the age and racial identity of your interviewees shape their responses?
2. Do the *Atlanta Journal and Constitution* interviews work to support or disprove Shelby Steele's claim that Malcolm X is popular because of his conservative nature?
3. Read or review Sam Fulwood III's "The Rage of the Black Middle Class" (p. 462). How would Fulwood explain the responses of the Atlantans interviewed, all of whom are black and middle class?
4. Watch Francis Ford Coppola's *The Godfather,* and write an essay in which you support or refute the analogy that Atlantan Robert Thompson makes between that film and *Malcolm X*.

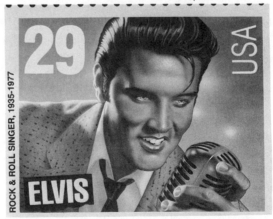

LARGER THAN LIFE

The Mythic Characters of American Culture

Did you vote for Elvis in '92? If so, for which one: the young Elvis or the aging King? Or maybe you didn't vote at all and wondered instead what all the fuss was about. Why, you may have thought, was the U.S. Postal Service holding an election to decide which Elvis would appear on a postage stamp? Or, more significantly, why was this long-dead pop star getting his own stamp in the first place?

If you have ever wondered about Elvis (note how we presume you know which Elvis we mean), if you've ever been puzzled by the almost sacred stature this former trucker from Nashville has assumed in American popular culture, then here's your chance to figure it all out. Because Elvis, too, is a sign, one among many that appear in the form of famous American characters, some real and some fictional, but all reflecting some cross section of America's cultural mythology. Thus, to interpret the significance of these characters is to learn something about ourselves, our hopes, and our dreams. And Elvis is a very good place to begin.

So let's get to it. Consider again the contest between the two Elvis stamps held in '92. Do you recall which stamp won? It was the young Elvis. Don't take his election for granted, for here is our first "Why?" As you ask why the young Elvis rather than the old was chosen for postal immortality, consider whether that would have been your choice. Then ask yourself, if you were given a choice between a stamp featuring Jim Morrison of the Doors slim and clean-shaven at twenty and chubby and bearded at twenty-five, which would you choose? Does the choice seem obvious? Do you see a pattern emerging, the outline of a myth?

A real mythology is at work here: America's mythic worship of youth. America almost inevitably went for the young Elvis in 1992, because no other culture has so valued youthfulness and has been so ambivalent about old age as ours has. Maturity brings power in America, but also a desperate struggle to maintain the body of youth. The old Elvis's failure to remain forever young had made him something of a laughingstock before his death, and it is accordingly significant that this is not the Elvis whom America chose to immortalize on a stamp.

But, of course, a lot of young pop stars have aged (look at the Grateful Dead), but no one is suggesting they belong on a stamp. Somehow Elvis is special, and his significance goes beyond his embodiment of America's adoration of youth. So we now have another question: Why Elvis, old or young? Let's look at the Elvis legend, at this obscure Southern kid who rose to become the most popular entertainer of his generation. In what ways does it exemplify that great mythic promise that we call the American Dream? How is Elvis's story like that of so many Americans, from Ben Franklin on, who started poor and ended on top? Can you relate Elvis's popularity in this regard to that of any other American star with humble origins who also went on to fame, fortune, and a mythic stature? What about "the Boss"? How is his mythic significance similar to that of the King's? How is it different?

And yet, even with the American Dream going for him, Elvis towers above the crowd. The Boss himself can't really touch Elvis when it comes to mass cultural appeal. So there must be even more to the matter. Don't let this worry you; in fact, that is the essence of semiotic interpretation: finding the multiplicity of forces at work in the construction of a popular sign. For most signs usually have more than one explanation. Certainly Elvis does. So let's keep digging.

It's useful to recall that Elvis was considered racy stuff in the sexually repressed 1950s, so racy that he was ordered to tone down his act if he wanted to appear on TV. But it was that act, his outrageously suggestive bumping and grinding, that helped make him a superstar in the first place. His legions of teen fans loved him for it. Why?

Here we need to look at the tone and style of American popular music in the fifties. It was rather white-bread stuff: With the exception of a few black rockers like Chuck Berry who were reluctantly allowed into the mainstream pop world, the top forty was a list of carefully controlled, sexually sanitized teen tunes. Think of the young Ricky Nelson. And then came Elvis, bringing the sexual energy of rhythm and blues to white audiences starved for a way to release their own repressed sexuality. Like a pagan deity, Elvis invited them to just let go.

In such a way, the Elvis cult hooks up with a far more ancient cult that helps explain his enduring and ecstatic appeal. More than two

II

Discussing the Signs of American Characters

In class, propose a list of American characters who could be candidates for stamps to be printed next year by the U.S. Postal Service. Have class members "campaign" for their favorite characters; students might give brief presentations arguing why their candidate's mythological significance warrants the status of an official American "sign." Then have the class vote for their favorite candidate.

thousand years ago, the cult of a beautiful young god named Dionysus swept through Greece, a cult whose rituals included the release of sexual energies that ordinary Greek life repressed. Dionysus has since become an enduring symbol of sexual expression, an archetypal figure whose popular appeal has been reflected in such male sex symbols as Rudolph Valentino and Elvis Presley, men who are not simply good looking or sexy but who seem to embody sexuality itself.

Dionysus offers us another clue into the mythic stature of Elvis. Part of the cult of Dionysus included his ritual murder, but he always came back to life, refusing to die. Now think of Elvis's death, and all those funny denials, the rumors: that he did not really die, that he is working as a grocery checkout clerk in Minneapolis, that he was just spotted at the 7 Eleven down the street. Refusing to stay dead, Elvis completes his mythic circuit. A sign of America's youth culture and an exemplar of the American Dream, Elvis becomes archetypal through the never-dying, ever-potent figure of Dionysus. Such a man can never die.

Like a Candle in the Wind

If all this sounds like a lot for one man to symbolize, don't worry, Elvis isn't alone in the mythic pantheon of American popular culture. For one thing, there's Marilyn. You know the one we mean.

In many ways, the mythological significance of Marilyn Monroe resembles that of Elvis. The rise of Norma Jean to superstardom, too, exemplifies the American Dream in its gaudiest aspects. Also like Elvis, Marilyn functions as a potent sex symbol in a society ever on the lookout for sex symbols. And again like Elvis, Marilyn died young and thus enjoys the legendary status of popular American characters who have also died young (have you seen her with Elvis and James Dean in that poster where they are all sitting together at a fifties-style coffee-shop counter?). But still Marilyn Monroe is different. She's no female Dionysus, for example. Her appeal is more subtle than that, less violent and ecstatic. But it has proven just as enduring.

What, for example, does Marilyn Monroe mean to you? Is she just another sex symbol? But then, why do some women still identify with her today, women who can hardly be said to be sexists in their response to her? And men too: Is the enduring popularity of Marilyn Monroe among American men simply a sexual thing? Is there more to it than that?

As you ponder such questions, you might consider the system of American sex symbols to which Marilyn Monroe belongs. Each decade seems to have its dominant figure. In the 1930s, for example, there was Jean Harlow, a platinum blonde sex goddess best remembered through a photograph in which she is posed lying seductively on a bearskin rug. In the 1940s, there was Rita Hayworth, whose most famous image shows her posed crouching in her lingerie on a bed. But then there's Monroe in *The Seven Year Itch,* playing a gentle if airheaded sex toy who displays her sexuality without being aware of it. Probably her most famous image comes from that film, when an updraft of air blows her skirts around her waist as she walks over a subway vent. She laughs as she tries to hold her skirts down. And that's how she's most often remembered.

Now consider the difference among these three images: Harlow's and Hayworth's, seductive, challenging poses, and Monroe's childlike laughter and innocence. It's that laughter and that innocence that sets Monroe apart, the vulnerability that distinguishes her from the other sex goddesses of American popular culture. Marilyn is remembered, in song, "like a candle in the wind." Why has fascination with her endured?

America in Whiteface

Focusing on Elvis Presley and Marilyn Monroe can show how two real people can be transformed into mythic symbols, American characters whose enduring appeal says a lot about American values and what sort of people we are. There are many such characters in our lives—from the fictional heroes who inhabit our folklore, films, and cartoon books to the real men and women who have come to symbolize our history. But when we survey the field of such characters, something else appears or, rather, doesn't appear: Just about all of the faces are white. And there is a semiotic lesson to be read here as well.

Think of the heroes of American folklore. There's Davy Crockett and Paul Bunyan, Pecos Bill and Daniel Boone, with only John Henry (significantly, a laborer) offering a different hue. Our cartoon books are filled with superheroes—Batman, Superman, Spiderman, the list is endless—but how many aren't white? Meanwhile Hollywood gives us the likes of Sylvester Stallone, Arnold Schwarzenegger, and Chuck Norris as larger-than-life cinema heroes. Indeed, there's something especially significant about Chuck Norris, for along with David Carradine and Jean-Claude Van Damme, Norris has appropriated what was originally an Asian role pioneered by Bruce Lee. Though the Asian origins of the martial arts tradition that such white actors have appropriated has not been concealed (Carradine's character was half white, half Chinese), it's instructive to note that whites often get the starring roles in such movies—as they usually do in the history of American characters.

Such a monochromatic set of characters sends a distinct signal. The message establishes a norm, a standard of Americanness from which a good proportion of nonwhite America is excluded. Toni Morrison dramatizes the potential consequences of this exclusion in her novel *The Bluest Eye,* in which a young African-American girl is driven crazy by her desire to be as lovable as the blonde-ringleted Shirley Temple, one of the most popular American characters in the 1930s.

If the effect of a popular character is to establish a norm, those who do not—and who in fact cannot—fit the norm are relegated to the status of the abnormal or deviant. The great American myth of the melting pot—the belief that all have the opportunity to assimilate into one vast American identity—is thus belied by the faces, the characters, that are seen as representing us. Non-Anglo-Saxon European immigrants can, if they wish, choose to identify with the homogeneous facade of Anglo-Saxon America, but African-Americans, Hispanics, Native Americans, and Asian-Americans are not genuinely offered that opportunity even if they desire it. Among popular culture characters, the American image is pictured in monochromatic portraits. All of the coloring of a Marvel comic book can't hide the prevailing whiteness of its heroes.

Still, there are signs that this is changing. New faces, new heroes, are appearing among America's characters, some real, such as Malcolm X, and others fictional. Can you name some of the new heroes? Are they widely known? What ethnicities do they represent? What new cartoon heroes have appeared who depart from the tradition of all-white super-heroes? What's new on TV or in the movies? In the 1990s, the face of America's characters is rapidly changing. If you were to rewrite this chapter, who would you add?

Pitching the Product

America's characters function in another way as well. Think of Joe Camel or Betty Crocker. Both characters were invented to sell something. In each case, they were designed to appeal to the values and sense of identity of their markets. Betty Crocker, for example, was invented to sell cake mix (a product that at first was a sign of an imperfect homemaker) to women who could identify with her unsullied image of

---

Exploring the Signs of American Characters

Children's television is filled with characters, ranging from Mr. Rogers to Miss Piggy, from G.I. Joe to Pee-wee Herman. Choose a character whom you grew up with and explore in your journal what role that character played in your life. Did you simply watch the character on TV, or did you playact games with it? Did you ever buy—or want to buy—any products related to that character? Why? Does that character mean anything to you today?

---

middle-class domesticity. More recent marketers, like the Sprint long distance telephone service, have chosen a more contemporary figure, Candice Bergen's Murphy Brown character, to sell its product. The distance between Betty Crocker and Murphy Brown measures the gap between the prefeminist myth of the happy housewife and the postfeminist image of the scrappy professional. But as different as the two characters are, both are designed to move the goods by embodying our culture's sense of a norm.

Then there are the athletes. On the one hand, they're real people, but on the other hand . . . well, consider Michael Jordan. A real-life sports hero, he is also the star of his own Saturday morning cartoon series (along with Bo Jackson and Wayne Gretzky), while at the same time he has become the central cog in the great Nike, Inc., advertising machine. In a recent version of the Jordan chronicles, for example, he appeared along with Bugs Bunny in a cartoon commercial extravaganza witnessed by millions during Superbowl XXVII. Michael Jordan's transformation from hoopster to hypester demonstrates that, when it comes to athletes, America's commercial culture has room for more than one race—but can you think of any athletic heroes who don't come in black or white?

Whatizit

Recently, a new sort of character has appeared on the American scene whose job also is to sell something, but that something is a good deal larger than any particular product or service. This character is the Olympic mascot, and the most recent version of this type—the Atlanta Games's Whatizit—offers us a particularly complex image for semiotic analysis. Let's look at it.

Whatizit first appeared during the closing ceremonies of the 1992 Olympic Games as the mascot for the succeeding Summer Olympiad in

Atlanta. The adoption of cute, cuddly animal mascots had become routine since the successful appearance of L.A.'s Sam the eagle, but Atlanta's new entry in the Olympic sweepstakes was both familiar and unfamiliar. It was familiar because Whatizit was, after all, a species of cartoon character like the others, but unfamiliar because no one could tell just what it was supposed to be. "What is it?" bewildered viewers asked of the blue, vaguely humanoid image with the big smile and oversized tennis shoes. "Neither man nor beast," its creators answered. Rather, the mascot for the twenty-sixth Olympic Games is a cybernetic concoction whose form depends on the operator of a computer screen. Hit one key and it's a sprinter; hit another, a gymnast; another, a basketball player; and so on through the whole range of Olympic events.

It's not too difficult to determine what Whatizit's designers are getting at with their little computer morph. Designed to showcase Atlanta's burgeoning high-tech industries, Whatizit reflects a certain democratic and technocratic optimism. If Sam the eagle echoed the old-fashioned symbolism of Uncle Sam, Whatizit heralds the democracy of the computer age, giving anyone with access to a properly equipped computer a shot at turning Atlanta's Olympic mascot into whatever one pleases. But that's what Whatizit's designers want us to think. The question is, why does he look the way he does? What's going on beneath the surface?

The first message to be read in the amorphous figure of Whatizit lies in the necessity for its creation in the first place. For this is not only a mascot, a mere emblem for the games. Rather, Whatizit is a marketable trademark, a product logo that Atlanta's Olympic committee can license to private corporations. The "product" Atlanta has to offer, of course, is the Olympic contest itself, which has been effectively transformed from its original purpose of providing a forum for international cooperation-through-amateur-competition into one of the world's leading money-making extravaganzas. Indeed, with the nationalistic side of the games much diminished since the collapse of the Soviet Union, moneymaking is practically all there is left in the new mythology of the Olympics, as professional athletes compete for endorsement opportunities and corporations strive to make their products the "Official (*fill in the blank*) of the Olympic Games."

The commodification of the Olympic mascot, then, reflects the commodification of the games themselves. Endorsed by countless producers of consumer goods and services, the Olympiad is now a gigantic product in an increasingly internationalized consumer economy. The true mascot for the games should be an animated dollar sign, or mark, or franc, or yen. But of course, that is one mascot no city will ever choose, because the purpose of a cute mascot, recognizable or not, is precisely to mask what is really going on, to present a cuddly, saleable image whose job is to distract everyone from all those salespeople hustling in the background.

But the semiotic story of Whatizit doesn't stop with its commodified profile. Fundamentally genderless, raceless, and devoid of nationalistic associations, Whatizit also functions as a sign of a certain hesitancy on the part of the Atlanta Olympic Committee. While Sam the Olympic eagle was obviously based on the image of good ol' Anglo-Saxon Uncle Sam, Whatizit seems to bend over backward not to refer to any particular race, class, or even gender. Why would Atlanta want to choose such a neutral symbol? Why, for instance, do you think it's blue, rather than white or black or brown or red or yellow? Why is it essentially genderless? How, in short, is Whatizit a political symbol as much as a mascot?

For even neutrality involves a political stance. Remember this as you consider the vast array of American characters who are out there for you to decode. Let nothing slip past you unquestioned. Why, for instance, did Tim Burton's *Batman* movie exclude Robin? Why was Superman killed off (in a specially printed, enormously hyped edition)? Would you tell the story of Davy Crockett and the Alamo differently if you had the chance? Or of Custer's last stand? And if you were to put a pop culture character on a postage stamp, would you choose Elvis Presley? If not, who?

The Readings

The readings in this chapter analyze a range of American characters, some of whom have been used for marketing purposes and others who function as American heroes, real and fictional. Gary Engle starts things off with an analysis of how a cartoon character, Superman, reflects and preaches mainstream American values, while Peter Rainer shows how a real person, Malcolm X, represents a new kind of American hero who is diametrically opposed to that mainstream. Andy Medhurst's interpretation of Batman from a gay perspective provides some clues as to why Robin was excluded from the *Batman* movie, illuminating how Batman and Robin have been read by gay fans over the years. George Lewis takes on the Teenage Mutant Ninja Turtles to show how they reflect archetypal heroic sagas, while Emily Prager takes a feminist stab at one of America's most famous toys, Barbie, skewering the image that this doll has presented to American girls for more than thirty years. Wanda Coleman's journalistic feature on Joe Camel and McCrea Adams's analytic survey of the characters that have been used in American advertising show just how entrenched fictional characters are in our consumer economy. And finally, our selection from DC Comics offers a new outlaw hero for a postmodern age: Deconstructo!

GARY ENGLE

What Makes Superman So Darned American?

||||||||||||||||||||||||||||||||||||||||||||||||||||

In 1992 Superman died—at least for a while. In bookstores and supermarkets across the nation, a special edition of DC Comics appeared, complete with a tableau of a dying Superman bleeding in Lois Lane's arms. In this semiotic analysis of the enduring appeal of Superman, Gary Engle (b. 1947) argues why the Man of Steel—whom Engle views as the ultimate immigrant—has dominated the pantheon of American characters for so many years. Of all our heroes, Engle claims, Superman alone "achieves truly mythic stature, interweaving a pattern of beliefs, literary conventions, and cultural traditions of the American people more powerfully and more accessibly than any other cultural symbol of the twentieth century, perhaps of any period in our history." A specialist in popular culture, Engle is an associate professor of English at Cleveland State University. In addition to over two hundred magazine and journal articles, he has written The Grotesque Essence: Plays from American Minstrel Style *(1978).*

When I was young I spent a lot of time arguing with myself about who would win in a fight between John Wayne and Superman. On days when I wore my cowboy hat and cap guns, I knew the Duke would win because of his pronounced superiority in the all-important matter of swagger. There were days, though, when a frayed army blanket tied cape-fashion around my neck signalled a young man's need to believe there could be no end to the potency of his being. Then the Man of Steel was the odds-on favorite to knock the Duke for a cosmic loop. My greatest childhood problem was that the question could never be resolved because no such battle could ever take place. I mean, how would a fight start between the only two Americans who never started anything, who always fought only to defend their rights and the American way?

Now that I'm older and able to look with reason on the mysteries of childhood, I've finally resolved the dilemma. John Wayne was the best older brother any kid could ever hope to have, but he was no Superman.

Superman is *the* great American hero. We are a nation rich with legendary figures. But among the Davy Crocketts and Paul Bunyans and Mike Finks and Pecos Bills and all the rest who speak for various regional identities in the pantheon of American folklore, only Superman achieves truly mythic stature, interweaving a pattern of beliefs, literary conventions, and cultural traditions of the American people more powerfully and more accessibly than any other cultural symbol of the twentieth century, perhaps of any period in our history.

The core of the American myth in *Superman* consists of a few basic facts that remain unchanged throughout the infinitely varied ways in which the myth is told—facts with which everyone is familiar, however marginal their knowledge of the story. Superman is an orphan rocketed to Earth when his native planet Krypton explodes; he lands near Small-ville and is adopted by Jonathan and Martha Kent, who inculcate in him their American middle-class ethic; as an adult he migrates to Metropolis where he defends America—no, the world! no, the Universe!—from all evil and harm while playing a romantic game in which, as Clark Kent, he hopelessly pursues Lois Lane, who hopelessly pursues Superman, who remains aloof until such time as Lois proves worthy of him by falling in love with his feigned identity as a weakling. That's it. Every narrative thread in the mythology, each one of the thousands of plots in the fifty-year stream of comics and films and TV shows, all the tales involving the demigods of the Superman pantheon—Superboy, Supergirl, even Krypto the superdog—every single one reinforces by never contradict-ing this basic set of facts. That's the myth, and that's where one looks to understand America.

It is impossible to imagine Superman being as popular as he is and speaking as deeply to the American character were he not an immigrant and an orphan. Immigration, of course, is the overwhelming fact in American history. Except for the Indians, all Americans have an imme-diate sense of their origins elsewhere. No nation on Earth has so deeply embedded in its social consciousness the imagery of passage from one social identity to another: the Mayflower of the New England separatists, the slave ships from Africa and the subsequent underground railroads toward freedom in the North, the sailing ships and steamers running shuttles across two oceans in the nineteenth century, the freedom airlifts in the twentieth. Somehow the picture just isn't complete without Superman's rocketship.

Like the peoples of the nation whose values he defends, Superman is an alien, but not just any alien. He's the consummate and totally uncompromised alien, an immigrant whose visible difference from the norm is underscored by his decision to wear a costume of bold primary colors so tight as to be his very skin. Moreover, Superman the alien is real. He stands out among the hosts of comic book characters (Batman is a good example) for whom the superhero role is like a mask assumed when needed, a costume worn over their real identities as normal Amer-icans. Superman's powers—strength, mobility, x-ray vision and the like —are the comic-book equivalents of ethnic characteristics, and they protect and preserve the vitality of the foster community in which he lives in the same way that immigrant ethnicity has sustained American culture linguistically, artistically, economically, politically, and spiritually.

The myth of Superman asserts with total confidence and a childlike innocence the value of the immigrant in American culture.

From this nation's beginnings Americans have looked for ways of coming to terms with the immigrant experience. This is why, for example, so much of American literature and popular culture deals with the theme of dislocation, generally focused in characters devoted or doomed to constant physical movement. Daniel Boone became an American legend in part as a result of apocryphal stories that he moved every time his neighbors got close enough for him to see the smoke of their cabin fires. James Fenimore Cooper's Natty Bumppo spent the five long novels of the Leatherstocking saga drifting ever westward, like the pioneers who were his spiritual offspring, from the Mohawk valley of upstate New York to the Great Plains where he died. Huck Finn sailed through the moral heart of America on a raft. Melville's Ishmael, Wister's Virginian, Shane, Gatsby, the entire Lost Generation, Steinbeck's Okies, Little Orphan Annie, a thousand fiddlefooted cowboy heroes of dime novels and films and television—all in motion, searching for the American dream or stubbornly refusing to give up their innocence by growing old, all symptomatic of a national sense of rootlessness stemming from an identity founded on the experience of immigration.

Individual mobility is an integral part of America's dreamwork. Is it any wonder, then, that our greatest hero can take to the air at will? Superman's ability to fly does more than place him in a tradition of mythic figures going back to the Greek messenger god Hermes or Zetes the flying Argonaut. It makes him an exemplar in the American dream. Take away a young man's wheels and you take away his manhood. Jack Kerouac and Charles Kurault go on the road; William Least Heat Moon looks for himself in a van exploring the veins of America in its system of blue highways; legions of gray-haired retirees turn Air Stream trailers and Winnebagos into proof positive that you can, in the end, take it with you. On a human scale, the American need to keep moving suggests a neurotic aimlessness under the surface of adventure. But take the human restraints off, let Superman fly unencumbered when and wherever he will, and the meaning of mobility in the American consciousness begins to reveal itself. Superman's incredible speed allows him to be as close to everywhere at once as it is physically possible to be. Displacement is, therefore, impossible. His sense of self is not dispersed by his life's migration but rather enhanced by all the universe that he is able to occupy. What American, whether an immigrant in spirit or in fact, could resist the appeal of one with such an ironclad immunity to the anxiety of dislocation?

In America, physical dislocation serves as a symbol of social and psychological movement. When our immigrant ancestors arrived on America's shores they hit the ground running, some to homestead on the Great Plains, others to claw their way up the socioeconomic ladder in coastal ghettos. Upward mobility, westward migration, Sunbelt relocation—the wisdom in America is that people don't, can't, mustn't end up where they begin. This belief has the moral force of religious doctrine. Thus the American identity is ordered around the psychological experience of forsaking or losing the past for the opportunity of reinventing oneself in the future. This makes the orphan a potent symbol of the American character. Orphans aren't merely free to reinvent themselves. They are obliged to do so.

When Superman reinvents himself, he becomes the bumbling Clark   10
Kent, a figure as immobile as Superman is mobile, as weak as his alter ego is strong. Over the years commentators have been fond of stressing how Clark Kent provides an illusory image of wimpiness onto which children can project their insecurities about their own potential (and, hopefully, equally illusory) weaknesses. But I think the role of Clark Kent is far more complex than that.

During my childhood, Kent contributed nothing to my love for the Man of Steel. If left to contemplate him for too long, I found myself changing from cape back into cowboy hat and guns. John Wayne, at least, was no sissy that I could ever see. Of course, in all the Westerns that the Duke came to stand for in my mind, there were elements that left me as confused as the paradox between Kent and Superman. For example, I could never seem to figure out why cowboys so often fell in love when there were obviously better options: horses to ride, guns to shoot, outlaws to chase, and savages to kill. Even on the days when I became John Wayne, I could fall victim to a never-articulated anxiety about the potential for poor judgment in my cowboy heroes. Then, I generally drifted back into a worship of Superman. With him, at least, the mysterious communion of opposites was honest and on the surface of things.

What disturbed me as a child is what I now think makes the myth of Superman so appealing to an immigrant sensibility. The shape-shifting between Clark Kent and Superman is the means by which this mid-twentieth-century, urban story—like the pastoral, nineteenth-century Western before it—addresses in dramatic terms the theme of cultural assimilation.

At its most basic level, the Western was an imaginative record of the American experience of westward migration and settlement. By bringing the forces of civilization and savagery together on a mythical frontier, the Western addressed the problem of conflict between apparently mutually exclusive identities and explored options for negotiating between them. In terms that a boy could comprehend, the myth explored the dilemma of assimilation—marry the school marm and start wearing Eastern clothes or saddle up and drift further westward with the boys.

The Western was never a myth of stark moral simplicity. Pioneers fled civilization by migrating west, but their purpose in the wilderness was to rebuild civilization. So civilization was both good and bad, what Americans fled from and journeyed toward. A similar moral ambiguity rested at the heart of the wilderness. It was an Eden in which innocence could be achieved through spiritual rebirth, but it was also the anarchic force that most directly threatened the civilized values America wanted to impose on the frontier. So the dilemma arose: In negotiating between civilization and the wilderness, between the old order and the new, between the identity the pioneers carried with them from wherever they came and the identity they sought to invent, Americans faced an impossible choice. Either they pushed into the New World wilderness and forsook the ideals that motivated them or they clung to their origins and polluted Eden.

The myth of the Western responded to this dilemma by inventing   15 the idea of the frontier in which civilized ideals embodied in the institutions of family, church, law, and education are revitalized by the virtues of savagery: independence, self-reliance, personal honor, sympathy with nature, and ethical uses of violence. In effect, the mythical frontier represented an attempt to embody the perfect degree of assimilation in which both the old and new identities came together, if not in a single self-image, then at least in idealized relationships, like the symbolic marriage of reformed cowboy and displaced school marm that ended Owen Wister's prototypical *The Virginian,* or the mystical masculine bonding between representatives of an ascendant and a vanishing America—Natty Bumppo and Chingachgook, the Lone Ranger and Tonto. On the Western frontier, both the old and new identities equally mattered.

As powerful a myth as the Western was, however, there were certain limits to its ability to speak directly to an increasingly common twentieth-century immigrant sensibility. First, it was pastoral. Its imagery of dusty frontier towns and breathtaking mountainous desolation spoke most affectingly to those who conceived of the American dream in terms of the nineteenth-century immigrant experience of rural settlement. As the twentieth century wore on, more immigrants were, like Superman, moving from rural or small-town backgrounds to metropolitan environments. Moreover, the Western was historical, often elegiacally so. Underlying the air of celebration in even the most epic and romantic of Westerns—the films of John Ford, say, in which John Wayne stood tall for all that any good American boy could ever want to be—was an awareness that the frontier was less a place than a state of mind represented in historic terms by a fleeting moment glimpsed imperfectly in the rapid wave of westward migration and settlement. Implicitly, then, whatever balance of past and future identities the frontier could offer was itself tenuous or illusory.

Twentieth-century immigrants, particularly the Eastern European Jews who came to America after 1880 and who settled in the industrial and mercantile centers of the Northeast—cities like Cleveland where

Jerry Siegel and Joe Shuster grew up and created Superman—could be entertained by the Western, but they developed a separate literary tradition that addressed the theme of assimilation in terms closer to their personal experience. In this tradition issues were clear-cut: Clinging to an Old World identity meant isolation in ghettos, confrontation with a prejudiced mainstream culture, second-class social status, and impoverishment. On the other hand, forsaking the past in favor of total absorption into the mainstream, while it could result in socioeconomic progress, meant a loss of the religious, linguistic, even culinary traditions that provided a foundation for psychological well-being. Such loss was particularly tragic for the Jews because of the fundamental role played by history in Jewish culture.

Writers who worked in this tradition—Abraham Cahan, Daniel Fuchs, Henry Roth, and Delmore Schwarz, among others—generally found little reason to view the experience of assimilation with joy or optimism. Typical of the tradition was Cahan's early novel *Yekl,* on which Joan Micklin Silver's film *Hester Street* was based. A young married couple, Jake and Gitl, clash over his need to be absorbed as quickly as possible into the American mainstream and her obsessive preservation of their Russian-Jewish heritage. In symbolic terms, their confrontation is as simple as their choice of headgear—a derby for him, a babushka for her. That the story ends with their divorce, even in the context of their gradual movement toward mutual understanding of one another's point of view, suggests the divisive nature of the pressures at work in the immigrant communities.

Where the pressures were perhaps most keenly felt was in the schools. Educational theory of the period stressed the benefits of rapid assimilation. In the first decades of this century, for example, New York schools flatly rejected bilingual education—a common response to the plight of non-English-speaking immigrants even today—and there were conscientious efforts to indoctrinate the children of immigrants with American values, often at the expense of traditions within the ethnic community. What resulted was a generational rift in which children were openly embarrassed by and even contemptuous of their parents' values, setting a pattern in American life in which second-generation immigrants migrate psychologically if not physically from their parents, leaving it up to the third generation and beyond to rediscover their ethnic roots.

Under such circumstances, finding a believable and inspiring balance   20 between the old identity and the new, like that implicit in the myth of the frontier, was next to impossible. The images and characters that did emerge from the immigrant communities were often comic. Seen over and over in the fiction and popular theater of the day was the figure of the *yiddische Yankee,* a jingoistic optimist who spoke heavily accented American slang, talked baseball like an addict without understanding the game, and dressed like a Broadway dandy on a budget—in short, one who didn't understand America well enough to distinguish between image and substance and who paid for the mistake by becoming the butt of a style of comedy bordering on pathos. So engrained was this stereotype in popular culture that it echoes today in TV situation comedy.

Throughout American popular culture between 1880 and the Second World War the story was the same. Oxlike Swedish farmers, German brewers, Jewish merchants, corrupt Irish ward healers, Italian gangsters —there was a parade of images that reflected in terms often comic, sometimes tragic, the humiliation, pain, and cultural insecurity of people in a state of transition. Even in the comics, a medium intimately connected with immigrant culture, there simply was no image that presented a blending of identities in the assimilation process in a way that stressed pride, self-confidence, integrity, and psychological well-being. None, that is, until Superman.

The brilliant stroke in the conception of Superman—the sine qua non that makes the whole myth work—is the fact that he has two identities. The myth simply wouldn't work without Clark Kent, mild-mannered newspaper reporter and later, as the myth evolved, bland TV newsman. Adopting the white-bread image of a wimp is first and foremost a moral act for the Man of Steel. He does it to protect his parents from nefarious sorts who might use them to gain an edge over the powerful alien. Moreover, Kent adds to Superman's powers the moral guidance of a Smallville upbringing. It is Jonathan Kent, fans remember, who instructs the alien that his powers must always be used for good. Thus does the myth add a mainstream white Anglo-Saxon Protestant ingredient to the American stew. Clark Kent is the clearest stereotype of a self-effacing, hesitant, doubting, middle-class weakling ever invented. He is the epitome of visible invisibility, someone whose extraordinary ordinariness makes him disappear in a crowd. In a phrase, he is the consummate figure of total cultural assimilation, and significantly, he is not real. Implicit in this is the notion that mainstream cultural norms, however useful, are illusions.

Though a disguise, Kent is necessary for the myth to work. This uniquely American hero has two identities, one based on where he comes from in life's journey, one on where he is going. One is real, one an illusion, and both are necessary for the myth of balance in the assimilation process to be complete. Superman's powers make the hero capable of saving humanity; Kent's total immersion in the American heartland makes him want to do it. The result is an improvement on the Western: an optimistic myth of assimilation but with an urban, technocratic setting.

One must never underestimate the importance to a myth of the most minute elements which do not change over time and by which we recognize the story. Take Superman's cape, for example. When Joe

Shuster inked the first Superman stories, in the early thirties when he was still a student at Cleveland's Glenville High School, Superman was strictly beefcake in tights, looking more like a circus acrobat than the ultimate Man of Steel. By June of 1938 when *Action Comics* no. 1 was issued, the image had been altered to include a cape, ostensibly to make flight easier to render in the pictures. But it wasn't the cape of Victorian melodrama and adventure fiction, the kind worn with a clasp around the neck. In fact, one is hard-pressed to find any precedent in popular culture for the kind of cape Superman wears. His emerges in a seamless line from either side of the front yoke of his tunic. It is a veritable growth from behind his pectorals and hangs, when he stands at ease, in a line that doesn't so much drape his shoulders as stand apart from them and echo their curve, like an angel's wings.

In light of this graphic detail, it seems hardly coincidental that Super- 25 man's real, Kryptonic name is Kal-El, an apparent neologism by George Lowther, the author who novelized the comic strip in 1942. In Hebrew, *el* can be both root and affix. As a root, it is the masculine singular word for God. Angels in Hebrew mythology are called *benei Elohim* (literally, sons of the Gods), or *Elyonim* (higher beings). As an affix, *el* is most often translated as "of God," as in the plenitude of Old Testament given names: Ishma-el, Dani-el, Ezeki-el, Samu-el, etc. It is also a common form for named angels in most Semitic mythologies: Israf-el, Aza-el, Uri-el, Yo-el, Rapha-el, Gabri-el and—the one perhaps most like Superman— Micha-el, the warrior angel and Satan's principal adversary.

The morpheme *Kal* bears a linguistic relation to two Hebrew roots. The first, *kal,* means "with lightness" or "swiftness" (faster than a speeding bullet in Hebrew?). It also bears a connection to the root *hal,* where *h* is the guttural *ch* of *chutzpah. Hal* translates roughly as "everything" or "all." *Kal-el,* then, can be read as "all that is God," or perhaps more in the spirit of the myth of Superman, "all that God is." And while we're at it, *Kent* is a form of the Hebrew *kana.* In its *k-n-t* form, the word appears in the Bible, meaning "I have found a son."

I'm suggesting that Superman raises the American immigrant experience to the level of religious myth. And why not? He's not just some immigrant from across the waters like all our ancestors, but a real alien, an extraterrestrial, a visitor from heaven if you will, which fact lends an element of the supernatural to the myth. America has no national religious icons nor any pilgrimage shrines. The idea of a patron saint is ludicrous in a nation whose Founding Fathers wrote into the founding documents the fundamental if not eternal separation of church and state. America, though, is pretty much as religious as other industrialized countries. It's just that our tradition of religious diversity precludes the nation's religious character from being embodied in objects or persons recognizably religious, for such are immediately identified by their attachment to specific sectarian traditions and thus contradict the eclecticism of the American religious spirit.

In America, cultural icons that manage to tap the national religious spirit are of necessity secular on the surface and sufficiently generalized to incorporate the diversity of American religious traditions. Superman doesn't have to be seen as an angel to be appreciated, but in the absence of a tradition of national religious iconography, he can serve as a safe, nonsectarian focus for essentially religious sentiments, particularly among the young.

In the last analysis, Superman is like nothing so much as an American boy's fantasy of a messiah. He is the male, heroic match for the Statue of Liberty, come like an immigrant from heaven to deliver humankind by sacrificing himself in the service of others. He protects the weak and defends truth and justice and all the other moral virtues inherent in the Judeo-Christian tradition, remaining ever vigilant and ever chaste. What purer or stronger vision could there possibly be for a child? Now that I put my mind to it, I see that John Wayne never had a chance.

Reading the Text

1. Why does Superman's status as an immigrant and orphan make him deeply American, according to Engle?
2. What is the significance of Superman's ability to fly?
3. Why does Engle see physical dislocation as being so typically American?
4. What is the significance of Superman's two identities, according to Engle?

Reading the Signs

1. Interview three classmates or friends whose families are immigrants to this country. Then compare their experience with that of the mythological character, Superman. To what extent does the Superman character reflect real-life immigrant experience? What does his story leave out? Try to account for any differences you may find.
2. Do you agree with Engle's suggestion that Superman "raises the American immigrant experience to the level of religious myth"?
3. How would Superman fit the definitions of hero that Robert Ray ("The Thematic Paradigm," p. 241) outlines?
4. Engle claims that Superman is a more authentically American hero than is John Wayne. Write an argument supporting or refuting this claim, basing your argument on specific roles that Wayne has played in film.
5. How would Linda Seger (p. 250) explain Superman's mythological status? How would her notions of myth and archetype complicate Engle's reading of this character?

6. Engle only briefly discusses the fact that Superman happens to be both male and Caucasian. What is the significance of his gender and race? How do you think they may have influenced his status as an American mythological hero? You might read or review Michael Omi's "In Living Color" (p. 449) for a discussion of the impact of race on American popular culture and Holly Devor's "Gender Role Behaviors and Attitudes" (p. 603) for her explanation of the significance of gender roles.

7. Rent a videotape of one of the *Superman* movies, and write an essay in which you explore whether the cinematic depiction of this character either perpetuates or alters his mythological status.

PETER RAINER
Antihero Worship

||||||||||||||||||||||||||||||||||||||||||||||||||

"Is it a coincidence that Superman died the same week the movie Malcolm X *opened?" Peter Rainer (b. 1951) asks in this probing analysis of the resurgence of Malcolm X as an American hero. An America weary of the goody-two-shoes style of heroism is turning to antiheroes like Malcolm X, but it is not America that is being transformed, Rainer suggests: It is Malcolm X. Locating the heroic figure of Malcolm X in the system of American heroes, Rainer argues that even he has not been immune from the sanctifying and commercializing effects of American hero worship. In a transformation that says more about America than it does about Malcolm, the complex voice of black nationalism has become "a kind of storybook hero," Rainer writes. A film critic for the* Los Angeles Times, *Rainer is chair of the National Society of Film Critics. His essays have also appeared in* The New York Times Magazine, Vogue, GQ, Newsday, American Film, *and* Mademoiselle.

Is it a coincidence that Superman died the same week the movie Malcolm X opened? In popular culture, styles of heroism have their cycles, and the square-jawed righter-of-wrongs, the lily-white goody-two-shoes suprahuman is currently out of the loop of fashion.

But Malcolm X has survived the gantlet of historical reassessment. A new generation responds to his principled rage precisely because he *isn't* lily white and goody-two-shoes. He's an antihero—a subverter of the white racist status quo—who, in the Spike Lee movie and in popular culture in general right now, has been sanctified with the legend-toned

look of the traditional hero. American culture is essentially transforma-
tional: Yesterday's firebrand is today's voice of reason.

Malcolm X comes out at a time when the movies are starved for
heroes—which is another way of saying that the country is starved for
them. One of the explicit themes of the recent presidential campaign
was the question of "character." Who could you trust to act properly
"heroic" when the chips were down? George Bush's old-guard war-
hero WASP Republicanism clashed with Bill Clinton's baby-boomer
New Covenant. Leaving aside the matter of political truth or untruth in
these poses, both were nevertheless presented as styles of heroism, and
Clinton's proved the more marketable.

Heroism—a display of courage and transcendence that appeals to
the finest in us—has been a sometime thing in our movies in part because
the country has had no unifying vision. We tend to import our heroes
nowadays: Lech Walesa, Nelson Mandela, Vaclav Havel, even Gor-
bachev. These men are linked with emergent and righteous national
movements. (And they're far enough away from us to avoid our home-
grown media scrutiny.) They testify to the force of national consciousness
in creating popular heroes.

Our most iconic movie heroes, whatever one thinks of their per-   5
sonas, have always been linked to a four-square concept of what America
was all about. John Wayne was two-fisted and rode hard and was never
without a gun; Jimmy Stewart had his drawling, homespun rootedness;
so did Henry Fonda and Gary Cooper. Humphrey Bogart was never so
American as when he was an expatriate, in *Casablanca.* The rebels without a cause, like James Dean or the young Brando, defined themselves
by their opposition to a society they felt excluded from.

American movies have often been better—livelier and more fun—
when they featured antiheroes. The rebels undercut the homiletics of
standard-issue heroism; they spoke to our discontent and our cynicism,
our sense of how things really were, to a far greater extent than the role-
model types. But their discontent was, in itself, an act of heroism—they
challenged the suffocating fitness of things.

Heroism and antiheroism both thrive on a national sense of identity,
a comprehensible core, a vision. Lacking these qualities in our national
life, our movies have been bereft of the sorts of heroes who might
connect up with us, even in opposition. We've been treated instead to
a spate of antihero heroes, ranging from RoboCop to the Terminator
to Batman, who operate out of a techno-pop-comic never-never-land.

There have been other movie hero sandwiches lately. In *Under Siege,*
Steven Seagal's aikido[1] moves have gone big-time patriotic. *JFK,* the
most hero-worshiping American movie in years, offered up a deliriously

---

1. **aikido** Japanese martial art.—EDS.

idealized version of President Kennedy and a countermyth about his assassination. We've been treated this year to musty neo-Capracorn,[2] like *Hero,* and the dumb-dumb revisionism of the Columbus movies. We've retreated safely to a quasimythic past, as in *Robin Hood* or *The Last of the Mohicans.* Heroism in our movies—as opposed to our TV shows, which often deal with the less action-oriented, "mundane" heroics of ordinary people, and which therefore provide virtually the only screen opportunities for female heroism—is almost exclusively the province of an idealized past or a cartoon present.

When the idealization works, as in Daniel Day-Lewis's full-out embodiment of Hawkeye in *Mohicans,* the results can be exhilarating. The film is strictly ersatz but Day-Lewis is a marvelous romantic image: He whips through the forest as if he were a rampaging revenant. There are other modern actors who have a heroic dimension: Nick Nolte, Mel Gibson, Morgan Freeman, for example. Unlike, say, Tom Cruise, who is often a hero in his films by virtue of casting rather than presence, these actors express the kinds of tensions and contradictions that give heroism in the movies a human face.

We can, if we choose, scan the faces of an older generation of movie-star heroes, like Robert Redford and Paul Newman and Clint Eastwood. But the effect they provide is not satisfying in the same old ways. They evoke a more complicated response now: Age has melancholized their features. The power with which Eastwood's *Unforgiven* moved audiences had its source in our response to Eastwood's deep-creased Westerner's face: a road map of time's passage—his and ours.

In the aftermath of the Vietnam war, the standard do-gooder action hero could no longer be taken straight in our movies; his heroics, fairly or not, took on a sinister, villainous cast. The cynical, tragic, hopeless tone that crept into our movies in the wake of Vietnam was responsible for some of the greatest movies of the era: *The Godfather* films, *Taxi Driver,* and many others. But it created a vacuum for the kind of traditional heroism that is one of the prime enjoyments of moviegoing.

It's no accident that this was the period in film history—the Toy Store Epoch—when George Lucas and Co., toting their well-thumbed copies of Joseph Campbell's *The Hero with a Thousand Faces,* began bombarding us with superhero jamborees; they provided us with heroes who were literally (and conveniently) out of this world. If heroism is what appeals to the best in us, then the subsequent Reagan-Bush reign, with its appeals to the mercenary in us, did not exalt the cause of heroism either. (In a mercenary culture, fame makes you a commodity.) It has left us with a yearning for the possibility of heroism cross-wired with a

10

---

2. **neo-Capracorn**   A punning reference to Frank Capra, American director of such legendary films as *It's a Wonderful Life.*—Eds.

cynicism and a self-consciousness that will not fully allow for such a possibility.

No doubt the problem is compounded by the ways in which celebrity, as first recognized by Daniel Boorstin in the early sixties in his book *The Image: A Guide to Pseudo-Events in America,* has replaced heroism as the modern archetype of greatness. But celebrity is fleeting. Our idea of the movie star—in Boorstin's terms the new celebrity hero—is an agglomeration not only of that star's screen appearances but also of everything else we are made to know through the media about his off-screen life. It's a system designed to sabotage specialness: We require a bit more mystery in our heroes.

This media climate, as Boorstin sees it, has made it difficult to recognize the "true" hero. (Fundamental to that recognition is a sense of history—something in scant supply in the short-attention-span generation.) Even when the heroes are acknowledged, the acknowledgment is in the same old celebrity-mongering terms. Gorbymania anyone?

This is conspicuously the case with Malcolm X. The full force of   15
media marketeering has been brought to bear on his life until its meaning is befogged in a welter of insignias and paraphernalia. The Spike Lee movie plays into this commercialization by making Malcolm a kind of storybook hero: He's sanctified by his martyrdom. *Malcolm X* is a significant sociological event: It's the coronation of a "new" black folk hero. There has hardly ever been a big biographical film about a black hero who was not a sports or entertainment star. But the most startling thing about the movie—once one gets past the opening credits with the burning American flag forming the letter "X" and the Rodney King footage—is how purposefully unstartling it is. It is being compared to *Gandhi,* as if that were high praise indeed. Has everyone forgotten what a high-minded, Oscarized long sit that film was?

Malcolm X has rhetorical power. Denzel Washington captures Malcolm's cool ferocity as an orator, his fierce, scary sense of entitlement. But the film, except for its opening, doesn't really have an in-your-face immediacy. It's part of an older, softer, more conventional tradition of biographical enshrinement. Lee doesn't draw on any psychological dimension for Malcolm. Perhaps he feels that a psychoanalytic view would demean black experience by separating it from its historical context. (Or more likely he's just better at creating characters who are mouthpieces.) He draws on the *Autobiography of Malcolm X,* the inspirational, "authorized" version of Malcolm's life, almost exclusively, barring from his film any controversial material from texts like the unsettling and not conventionally flattering 1991 Bruce Perry biography.

Except for childhood flashbacks, Malcolm's siblings, who were major influences throughout his life, have been eliminated. Lee doesn't really situate Malcolm's struggle in any larger framework: We don't get much sense of how his struggles were a part of the total home-front scene of

the fifties and sixties. We are shown Malcolm's progression from two-
bit hustler and convict to the man he became, but the episodes are like
a series of illuminated pages in a holy text. They are demonstrations, not
explications, of his spiritual journey.

This approach might have gotten by in the Golden Age of the
Biopic—the thirties and forties. (Except, of course, Hollywood would
never have dreamed of making a movie about someone like Malcolm X
back then.) But we require a fuller approach now, one which does justice
both to our yearnings and our cynicism.

Would a movie that dealt with Malcolm's racial and sexual fears, that
got more deeply into his white-devil preachings within the Nation of
Islam, that pointed up his anti-Semitism and his detestation of the black
civil rights movement and the bourgeois middle class—would such a
movie have upended his heroism? Or, more likely, would it have dra-
matized his final dilemma, when he felt caught in a trap between the
moderate and militant? Would it have humanized him and defined his
struggle so that we could feel the full resounding force of his evolution?
The challenge in this tell-all age of celebrity heroism is to create a hero
not only in spite of but *because of* the hero's failings—what he had to
overcome.

If Malcolm X, almost alone among "contemporary" American he-   20
roes now, seems aligned with the likes of Walesa and Mandela, it is
because he, too, is linked with an emergent and righteous national
movement—a movement of black pride. That's why his presence, as
contourless and spiritualized as it is in the film, still fills the screen. This
is a lot to get from a movie and yet it's not enough. *Malcolm X* is much
closer to political hagiography than political art.

Is the civics-lesson worshipfulness of *Malcolm X* justifiable because
so few films about black heroes are made? Is this what we can look
forward to if movies are produced about the lives of, say, Martin Luther
King or Paul Robeson? In light of the way his film has turned out, Spike
Lee's contention that only a black director, namely himself, could do
justice to Malcolm's life takes on an unexpected meaning. *Malcolm X*
suggests that movies about black heroes are entitled to partake of the
same big-picture piety and impersonality as the standard biopics about
white heroes. Hasn't the previously provocative work of filmmakers like
Lee rightly accustomed us to a more challenging standard?

Reading the Text

1. Summarize in your own words what Rainer means by "hero."
2. What does Rainer mean by calling the cinematic Malcolm X a "smoothed-
   out storybook hero"?
3. Why does Rainer see Malcolm X as a hero for the 1990s?

Reading the Signs

1. Watch a videotape of *Malcolm X* and write an essay in which you explain which assessment of the film you find more persuasive: Peter Rainer's or Shelby Steele's ("Malcolm X," p. 287)?
2. Rainer compares *Malcolm X* with *JFK* as two movies that turn historical figures into cultural icons. Watch the two films, and write an essay in which you argue for or against Rainer's thesis that the movies' directors have idealized their subjects.
3. Read or review Robert Ray's "The Thematic Paradigm" (p. 241). Is Malcolm X a typical outlaw hero, in Ray's terms, or would his character redefine the category described by Ray?
4. Rainer claims that Malcolm X succeeds as a hero for the 1990s because he subverts "the white racist status quo." Another such historical figure is Cesar Chavez. Go to the library and research Chavez's life; then write a narrative that would outline the parts of Chavez's life that would make for an effective cinematic story line.
5. In class, brainstorm modern heroes that influence your lives today. Then discuss Rainer's explanation of the qualities heroes must have to make it to the screen. Would heroes from the class's list qualify for a cinematic rendering, according to Rainer's analysis? If so, which ones? Why? If not, what does that say about the heroes of our time? About the role of film in our lives today?

ANDY MEDHURST

Batman, Deviance, and Camp

||||||||||||||||||||||||||||||||||||||||||||||||||||||||||

Have you ever wondered what happened to Robin in the recent Batman movies? In this analysis of the history of the Batman, excerpted from The Many Lives of the Batman *(1991), Andy Medhurst (b. 1959) explains why Robin had to disappear. Arguing that Batman has been "reheterosexualized" in the wake of the insinuatingly homoerotic TV series of the 1960s, Medhurst indicts the homophobia of Batfans whose "Bat-Platonic Ideal of how Batman should really be" holds no place for the "camped crusader." Andy Medhurst teaches media studies at the University of Sussex, England, and writes regularly for* Sight and Sound *and* Screen. *His current research interests include popular film and television and lesbian and gay studies.*

> *Only someone ignorant of the fundamentals of psychiatry and of the*
> *psychopathology of sex can fail to realize a subtle atmosphere of*
> *homoeroticism which pervades the adventure of the mature "Batman" and his*
> *young friend "Robin."*
>
> — FREDRIC WERTHAM[1]

> *It's embarrassing to be solemn and treatise-like about Camp. One runs the*
> *risk of having, oneself, produced a very inferior piece of Camp.*
>
> — SUSAN SONTAG[2]

I'm not sure how qualified I am to write this essay. Batman hasn't been particularly important in my life since I was seven years old. Back then he was crucial, paramount, unmissable as I sat twice weekly to watch the latest episode on TV. Pure pleasure, except for the annoying fact that my parents didn't seem to appreciate the thrills on offer. Worse than that, they actually laughed. How could anyone laugh when the Dynamic Duo were about to be turned into Frostie Freezies (pineapple for the Caped Crusader, lime for his chum) by the evil Mr. Freeze?

Batman and I drifted apart after those early days. Every now and then I'd see a repeated episode and I soon began to understand and share that once infuriating parental hilarity, but this aside I hardly thought about the man in the cape at all. I knew about the subculture of comic freaks, and the new and alarmingly pretentious phrase "graphic novel" made itself known to me, but I still regarded (with the confidence of distant ignorance) such texts as violent, macho, adolescent and, well, silly.

That's when the warning bells rang. The word "silly" reeks of the complacent condescension that has at various times been bestowed on all the cultural forms that matter most to me (Hollywood musicals, British melodramas, pop music, soap operas), so what right had I to apply it to someone else's part of the popular cultural playground? I had to rethink my disdain, and 1989 has been a very good year in which to do so, because in terms of popular culture 1989 has been the Year of the Bat.

This essay, then, is not written by a devotee of Batman, someone steeped in every last twist of the mythology. I come to these texts as an interested outsider, armed with a particular perspective. That perspective is homosexuality, and what I want to try and do here is to offer a gay reading of the whole Bat-business. It has no pretension to definitiveness, I don't presume to speak for all gay people everywhere. I'm male, white, British, thirty years old (at the time of writing) and all of those factors

---

1. Fredric Wertham, *Seduction of the Innocent* (London: Museum Press, 1955), p. 190.
2. Susan Sontag, "Notes on Camp," in *A Susan Sontag Reader* (Harmondsworth: Penguin Books), p. 106.

need to be taken into account. Nonetheless, I'd argue that Batman is especially interesting to gay audiences for three reasons.

Firstly, he was one of the first fictional characters to be attacked on   5
the grounds of presumed homosexuality, by Fredric Wertham in his book *Seduction of the Innocent*. Secondly, the 1960s TV series was and remains a touchstone of camp (a banal attempt to define the meaning of camp might well start with "like the sixties' *Batman* series"). Thirdly, as a recurring hero figure for the last fifty years, Batman merits analysis as a notably successful construction of masculinity.

Nightmare on Psychiatry Street: Freddy's Obsession

Seduction of the Innocent is an extraordinary book. It is a gripping, flamboyant melodrama masquerading as social psychology. Fredric Wertham is, like Senator McCarthy,[3] like Batman, a crusader, a man with a mission, an evangelist. He wants to save the youth of America from its own worst impulses, from its id, from comic books. His attack on comic books is founded on an astonishingly crude stimulus–and–response model of reading, in which the child (the child, for Wertham, seems an un-usually innocent, blank slate waiting to be written on) reads, absorbs, and feels compelled to copy, if only in fantasy terms, the content of the comics. It is a model, in other words, which takes for granted extreme audience passivity.

This is not the place to go into a detailed refutation of Wertham's work, besides which such a refutation has already been done in Martin Barker's excellent *A Haunt of Fears*.[4] The central point of audience pas-sivity needs stressing, however, because it is crucial to the celebrated passage where Wertham points his shrill, witch–hunting finger at the Dynamic Duo and cries "queer."

Such language is not present on the page, of course, but in some ways *Seduction of the Innocent* (a film title crying out for either D. W. Griffith or Cecil B. DeMille) would be easier to stomach if it were. Instead, Wertham writes with anguished concern about the potential harm that Batman might do to vulnerable children, innocents who might be turned into deviants. He employs what was then conventional psy-chiatric wisdom about the idea of homosexuality as a "phase":

> Many pre-adolescent boys pass through a phase of disdain for girls.
> Some comic books tend to fix that attitude and instill the idea that
> girls are only good for being banged around or used as decoys. A

---

3. **Senator McCarthy** United States Senator Joseph R. McCarthy (1908–1957), who in the 1950s hunted and persecuted suspected Communists and Communist sympathizers.—EDS.

4. Martin Barker, *A Haunt of Fears* (London: Pluto Press, 1984).

homoerotic attitude is also suggested by the presentation of masculine, bad, witch-like or violent women. In such comics women are depicted in a definitely anti-erotic light, while the young male heroes have pronounced erotic overtones. The muscular male supertype, whose primary sex characteristics are usually well emphasized, is in the setting of certain stories the object of homoerotic sexual curiosity and stimulation.[5]

The implications of this are breathtaking. Homosexuality, for Wertham, is synonymous with misogyny. Men love other men because they hate women. The sight of women being "banged around" is liable to appeal to repressed homoerotic desires (this, I think, would be news to the thousands of women who are systematically physically abused by heterosexual men). Women who do not conform to existing stereotypes of femininity are another incitement to homosexuality.

Having mapped out his terms of reference, Wertham goes on to peel   10
the lid from Wayne Manor:

> Sometimes Batman ends up in bed injured and young Robin is shown sitting next to him. At home they lead an idyllic life. They are Bruce Wayne and "Dick" Grayson. Bruce Wayne is described as a "socialite" and the official relationship is that Dick is Bruce's ward. They live in sumptuous quarters, with beautiful flowers in large vases, and have a butler, Alfred. Batman is sometimes shown in a dressing gown. . . . It is like a wish dream of two homosexuals living together. Sometimes they are shown on a couch, Bruce reclining and Dick sitting next to him, jacket off, collar open, and his hand on his friend's arm.[6]

So, Wertham's assumptions of homosexuality are fabricated out of his interpretation of certain visual signs. To avoid being thought queer by Wertham, Bruce and Dick should have done the following: Never show concern if the other is hurt, live in a shack, only have ugly flowers in small vases, call the butler "Chip" or "Joe" if you have to have one at all, never share a couch, keep your collar buttoned up, keep your jacket on, and never, ever wear a dressing gown. After all, didn't Noel Coward[7] wear a dressing gown?

Wertham is easy to mock, but the identification of homosexuals through dress codes has a long history.[8] Moreover, such codes originate as semiotic systems adopted by gay people themselves, as a way of signalling the otherwise invisible fact of sexual preference. There is a

---

5. Wertham, p. 188.

6. Wertham, p. 190.

7. **Noel Coward** (1899–1973)   British playwright, actor, and composer known for witty, sophisticated comedies.—EDS.

8. See, for example, the newspaper stories on "how to spot" homosexuals printed in Britain in the fifties and sixties, and discussed in Jeffrey Weeks, *Coming Out: Homosexual Politics in Britain* (London: Quartet, 1979).

difference, though, between sporting the secret symbols of a subculture if you form part of that subculture and the elephantine spot-the-homo routine that Wertham performs.

Bat-fans have always responded angrily to Wertham's accusation. One calls it "one of the most incredible charges . . . unfounded rumours . . . sly sneers"[9] and the general response has been to reassert the masculinity of the two heroes, mixed with a little indignation: "If they had been actual men they could have won a libel suit."[10] This seems to me not only to miss the point, but also to *reinforce* Wertham's homophobia —it is only possible to win a libel suit over an "accusation" of homosexuality in a culture where homosexuality is deemed categorically inferior to heterosexuality.

Thus the rush to "protect" Batman and Robin from Wertham is simply the other side to the coin of his bigotry. It may reject Wertham, cast him in the role of dirty-minded old man, but its view of homosexuality is identical. Mark Cotta Vaz thus describes the imputed homosexual relationship as "licentious" while claiming that in fact Bruce Wayne "regularly squired the most beautiful women in Gotham city and presumably had a healthy sex life."[11] Licentious versus healthy—Dr. Wertham himself could not have bettered this homophobic opposition.

Despite the passions aroused on both sides (or rather the two facets of the same side), there is something comic at the heart of this dispute. It is, simply, that Bruce and Dick are *not* real people but fictional constructions, and hence to squabble over their "real" sex life is to take things a little too far. What is at stake here is the question of reading, of what readers do with the raw material that they are given. Readers are at liberty to construct whatever fantasy lives they like with the characters of the fiction they read (within the limits of generic and narrative credibility, that is). This returns us to the unfortunate patients of Dr. Wertham:

> One young homosexual during psychotherapy brought us a copy of *Detective* comic, with a Batman story. He pointed out a picture of "The Home of Bruce and Dick," a house beautifully landscaped, warmly lighted and showing the devoted pair side by side, looking out a picture window. When he was eight this boy had realized from fantasies about comic book pictures that he was aroused by men. At the age of ten or eleven, "I found my liking, my sexual desires, in comic books. I think I put myself in the position of Robin. I did want to have relations with Batman . . . I remember the first time I came across the page mentioning the "secret batcave." The thought of Batman and Robin

9. Phrases taken from Chapters 5 and 6 of Mark Cotta Vaz, *Tales of the Dark Knight: Batman's First Fifty Years* (London: Futura, 1989).

10. Les Daniels, *Comix: A History of Comic Books in America* (New York: Bonanza Books, 1971), p. 87.

11. Cotta Vaz, pp. 47 and 53.

living together and possibly having sex relations came to my
mind . . ."[12]

Wertham quotes this to shock us, to impel us to tear the pages of *Detective*
away before little Tommy grows up and moves to Greenwich Village,
but reading it as a gay man today I find it rather moving and also highly
recognizable.

What this anonymous gay man did was to practice that form of
bricolage[13] which Richard Dyer has identified as a characteristic reading
strategy of gay audiences.[14] Denied even the remotest possibility of
supportive images of homosexuality within the dominant heterosexual
culture, gay people have had to fashion what we could out of the
imageries of dominance, to snatch illicit meanings from the fabric of
normality, to undertake a corrupt decoding for the purposes of satisfying
marginalized desires.[15] This may not be as necessary as it once was, given
the greater visibility of gay representations, but it is still an important
practice. Wertham's patient evokes in me an admiration, that in a period
of American history even more homophobic than most, there he was,
raiding the citadels of masculinity, weaving fantasies of oppositional desire. What effect the dread Wertham had on him is hard to predict, but
I profoundly hope that he wasn't "cured."

It wasn't only Batman who was subjected to Dr. Doom's bizarre
ideas about human sexuality. Hence:

> The homosexual connotation of the Wonder Woman type of story is
> psychologically unmistakable. . . . For boys, Wonder Woman is a
> frightening image. For girls she is a morbid ideal. Where Batman is
> anti-feminine, the attractive Wonder Woman and her counterparts are
> definitely anti-masculine. Wonder Woman has her own female follow-
> ing . . . Her followers are the "Holiday girls," i.e. the holiday girls,
> the gay party girls, the gay girls.[16]

Just how much elision can be covered with one "i.e."? Wertham's
view of homosexuality is not, at least, inconsistent. Strong, admirable
women will turn little girls into dykes—such a heroine can only be seen
as a morbid ideal."

---

12. Wertham, p. 192.

13. bricolage   A new object created by reassembling bits and pieces of other
objects; here, gay-identified readings produced from classic texts.—EDS.

14. Richard Dyer, ed., *Gays and Film,* 2nd Edition (New York: Zoetrope, 1984),
p. 1.

15. See Richard Dyer, "Judy Garland and Gay Men," in Dyer, *Heavenly Bodies*
(London: BFI, 1987) and Claire Whitaker, "Hollywood Transformed: Interviews with
Lesbian Viewers," in Peter Steven, ed., *Jump Cut: Hollywood, Politics and Counter-Cinema*
(Toronto: Between the Lines, 1985).

16. Wertham, pp. 192–3.

Crazed as Wertham's ideas were, their effectiveness is not in doubt. The mid-fifties saw a moral panic about the assumed dangers of comic books. In the United States companies were driven out of business, careers wrecked, and the Comics Code introduced. This had distinct shades of the Hays Code[17] that had been brought in to clamp down on Hollywood in the 1930s, and under its jurisdiction comics opted for the bland, the safe, and the reactionary. In Britain there was government legislation to prohibit the importing of American comics, as the comics panic slotted neatly into a whole series of anxieties about the effects on British youth of American popular culture.[18]

And in all of this, what happened to Batman? He turned into Fred   20
MacMurray from *My Three Sons*. He lost any remaining edge of the shadowy vigilante of his earliest years, and became an upholder of the most stifling small-town American values. Batwoman and Batgirl appeared (June Allyson and Bat-Gidget) to take away any lingering doubts about the Dynamic Duo's sex lives. A 1963 story called "The Great Clayface-Joker Feud" has some especially choice examples of the new, squeaky-clean sexuality of the assembled Bats.

Batgirl says to Robin, "I can hardly wait to get into my Batgirl costume again! Won't it be terrific if we could go on a crime case together like the last time? (sigh)." Robin replies, "It sure would, Betty (sigh)." The elder Bats look on approvingly. Batgirl is Batwoman's niece—to make her a daughter would have implied that Batwoman had had (gulp) sexual intercourse, and that would never do. This is the era of Troy Donohue and Pat Boone,[19] and Batman as ever serves as a cultural thermometer, taking the temperature of the times.

The Clayface/Joker business is wrapped up (the villains of this period are wacky conjurors, nothing more, with no menace or violence about them) and the episode concludes with another tableau of terrifying heterosexual contentment. "Oh Robin," simpers Batgirl, "I'm afraid you'll just have to hold me! I'm still so shaky after fighting Clayface . . . and you're so strong!" Robin: "Gosh Batgirl, it was swell of you to calm me down when I was worried about Batman tackling Clayface alone." (One feels a distinct Wertham influence here: If Robin shows concern about Batman, wheel on a supportive female, the very opposite of a "morbid ideal," to minister in a suitably self-effacing way.) Batwoman here seizes her chance and tackles Batman: "You look worried about Clayface, Batman . . . so why don't you follow Robin's example and let me soothe you?" Batman can only reply "Gulp."

---

17. **Hays Code**   The 1930 Motion Picture Production Code, which described in detail what was morally acceptable in films.—Eds.

18. See Barker.

19. **Troy Donohue and Pat Boone**   Clean-cut, all-American-boy stars from the 1950s and 1960s.—Eds.

Gulp indeed. While it's easy simply to laugh at strips like these, knowing as we do the way in which such straight-faced material would be mercilessly shredded by the sixties' TV series, they do reveal the retreat into coziness forced on comics by the Wertham onslaught and its repercussions. There no doubt were still subversive readers of *Batman*, erasing Batgirl on her every preposterous appearance and reworking the Duo's capers to leave some room for homoerotic speculation, but such a reading would have had to work so much harder than before. The *Batman* of this era was such a closed text, so immune to polysemic interpretation, that its interest today is only as a symptom—or, more productively, as camp. "The Great Clayface-Joker Feud" may have been published in 1963, but in every other respect it is a fifties' text. If the 1960s began for the world in general with the Beatles, the 1960s for Batman began with the TV series in 1966. If the Caped Crusader had been all but Werthamed out of existence, he was about to be camped back into life.

The Camped Crusader and the Boys Wondered

Trying to define "camp" is like attempting to sit in the corner of a circular room. It can't be done, which only adds to the quixotic appeal of the attempt. Try these:

To be camp is to present oneself as being committed to the marginal with a commitment greater than the marginal merits.[20]

Camp sees everything in quotation marks. It's not a lamp but a "lamp"; not a woman but a "woman". . . . It is the farthest extension, in sensibility, of the metaphor of life as theatre.[21]

Camp is . . . a way of poking fun at the whole cosmology of restrictive sex roles and sexual identifications which our society uses to oppress its women and repress its men.[22]

Camp was and is a way for gay men to re-imagine the world around them . . . by exaggerating, stylizing and remaking what is usually thought to be average or normal.[23]

Camp was a prison for an illegal minority; now it is a holiday for consenting adults.[24]

---

20. Mark Booth, *Camp* (London: Quartet, 1983), p. 18.
21. Sontag, p. 109.
22. Jack Babuscio, "Camp and the Gay Sensibility," in Dyer, ed., *Gays and Film*, p. 46.
23. Michael Bronski, *Culture Clash: The Making of Gay Sensibility* (Boston: South End Press), p. 42.
24. Philip Core, *Camp: The Lie that Tells the Truth* (London: Plexus), p. 7.

All true, in their way, but all inadequate. The problem with camp   25
is that it is primarily an experiential rather than an analytical discourse.
Camp is a set of attitudes, a gallery of snapshots, an inventory of postures,
a modus vivendi, a shop-full of frocks, an arch of eyebrows, a great big
pink butterfly that just won't be pinned down. Camp is primarily an
adjective, occasionally a verb, but never anything as prosaic, as earth-
bound, as a noun.

Yet if I propose to use this adjective as a way of describing one or
more of the guises of Batman, I need to arrive at some sort of working
definition. So, for the purposes of this analysis, I intend the term "camp"
to refer to a playful, knowing, self-reflexive theatricality. *Batman,* the
sixties' TV series, was nothing if not knowing. It employed the codes of
camp in an unusually public and heavily signalled way. This makes it
different from those people or texts who are taken up by camp audiences
without ever consciously putting camp into practice. The difference may
be very briefly spelled out by reference to Hollywood films. If *Mildred
Pierce*[25] and *The Letter*[26] were taken up *as* camp, teased by primarily gay
male audiences into yielding meaning not intended by their makers, then
Whatever Happened to Baby Jane?[27] is a piece of self-conscious camp,
capitalizing on certain attitudinal and stylistic tendencies known to exist
in audiences. *Baby Jane* is also, significantly, a 1960s' film, and the 1960s
were the decade in which camp swished out of the ghetto and up into
the scarcely prepared mainstream.

A number of key events and texts reinforced this. Susan Sontag
wrote her *Notes on Camp,* which remains the starting point for researchers
even now. Pop Art[28] was in vogue (and in *Vogue*) and whatever the more
elevated claims of Lichtenstein,[29] Warhol,[30] and the rest, their artworks
were on one level a new inflection of camp. The growing intellectual
respectability of pop music displayed very clearly that the old barriers
that once rigidly separated high and low culture were no longer in force.
The James Bond films, and even more so their successors like *Modesty*

25. ***Mildred Pierce*** 1945 murder mystery film that traces the fortunes of a homemaker who breaks with her husband.—EDS.

26. ***The Letter*** 1940 murder movie whose ending was changed to satisfy moral
standards of the time.—EDS.

27. ***Whatever Happened to Baby Jane?*** Macabre 1962 film about an ex–child
movie star living in an old Hollywood mansion.—EDS.

28. **Pop Art** Art movement, begun in the 1950s, that borrowed images and
symbols from popular culture, particularly from commercial products and mass media,
as a critique of traditional fine art.—EDS.

29. **Lichtenstein** Roy Lichtenstein (1923–   ), American artist at the center of
the Pop Art movement, best known for melodramatic comic-book scenes.—EDS.

30. **Warhol** Andy Warhol (1930?–87), pioneering Pop artist known for reproducing stereotyped images of famous people, such as Marilyn Monroe, and of commercial
products, such as Campbell's Soup cans.—EDS.

Blaise, popularized a dry, self-mocking wit that makes up one part of the multifaceted diamond of camp. And on television there were *The Avengers, The Man from UNCLE, Thunderbirds,* and *Batman.*

To quote the inevitable Sontag, "The whole point of Camp is to dethrone the serious. . . . More precisely, Camp involves a new, more complex relation to 'the serious.' One can be serious about the frivolous, frivolous about the serious."[31]

The problem with Batman in those terms is that there was never anything truly serious to begin with (unless one swallows that whole portentous Dark Knight charade, more of which in the next section). Batman in its comic book form had, unwittingly, always been camp— it was serious (the tone, the moral homilies) about the frivolous (a man in a stupid suit). He was camp in the way that classic Hollywood was camp, but what the sixties' TV series and film did was to overlay this "innocent" camp with a thick layer of ironic distance, the self-mockery version of camp. And given the long associations of camp with the homosexual male subculture, Batman was a particular gift on the grounds of his relationship with Robin. As George Melly put it, "The real Batman series were beautiful because of their unselfconscious absurdity. The remakes, too, at first worked on a double level. Over the absorbed children's heads we winked and nudged, but in the end what were we laughing at? The fact they didn't know that Batman had it off with Robin."[32]

It was as if Wertham's fears were being vindicated at last, but his 1950s' bigot's anguish had been supplanted by a self-consciously hip 1960s' playfulness. What adult audiences laughed at in the sixties' *Batman* was a camped-up version of the fifties they had just left behind.

Batman's lessons in good citizenship ("We'd like to feel that our efforts may help every youngster to grow up into an honest, useful citizen"[33]) were another part of the character ripe for ridiculing deconstruction—"Let's go, Robin, we've set another youth on the road to a brighter tomorrow" (the episode "It's How You Play the Game"). Everything the Adam West Batman said was a parody of seriousness, and how could it be otherwise? How could anyone take genuinely seriously the words of a man dressed like that?

The Batman/Robin relationship is never referred to directly; more fun can be had by presenting it "straight," in other words, screamingly camp. Wertham's reading of the Dubious Duo had been so extensively aired as to pass into the general consciousness (in George Kelly's words,

30

---

31. Sontag, p. 116.
32. George Melly, *Revolt Into Style: The Pop Arts in the 50s and 60s* (Oxford: Oxford University Press, 1989 [first published 1970]), p. 193.
33. "The Batman Says," *Batman* #3 (1940), quoted in Cotta Vaz, p. 15.

"We all knew Robin and Batman were pouves"[34]), it was part of the fabric of *Batman,* and the makers of the TV series proceeded accordingly.

Consider the Duo's encounter with Marsha, Queen of Diamonds. The threat she embodies is nothing less than heterosexuality itself, the deadliest threat to the domestic bliss of the Bat-couple. She is even about to marry Batman before Albert intervenes to save the day. He and Batman flee the church, but have to do so in the already decorated Batmobile, festooned with wedding paraphernalia including a large "Just Married" sign. "We'll have to drive it as it is," says Batman, while somewhere in the audience a Dr. Wertham takes feverish notes. Robin, Commissioner Gordon, and Chief O'Hara have all been drugged with Marsha's "Cupid Dart," but it is of course the Boy Wonder who Batman saves first. The dart, he tells Robin, "contains some secret ingredient by which your sense and your will were affected," and it isn't hard to read that ingredient as heterosexual desire, since its result, seen in the previous episode, was to turn Robin into Marsha's slobbering slave.

We can tell with relief now, though, as Robin is "back in fighting form" (with impeccable timing, Batman clasps Robin's shoulder on the word "fighting"). Marsha has one last attempt to destroy the duo, but naturally she fails. The female temptress, the seductress, the enchantress must be vanquished. None of this is in the least subtle (Marsha's cat, for example, is called Circe) but this type of mass-market camp can't afford the luxury of subtlety. The threat of heterosexuality is similarly mobilized in the 1966 feature film, where it is Bruce Wayne's infatuation with Kitka (Catwoman in disguise) that causes all manner of problems.

A more interesting employment of camp comes in the episodes where the Duo battle the Black Widow, played by Tallulah Bankhead. The major camp coup here, of course, is the casting. Bankhead was one of the supreme icons of camp, one of its goddesses, "Too intelligent not to be self-conscious, too ambitious to bother about her self-consciousness, too insecure ever to be content, but too arrogant ever to admit insecurity, Tallulah personified camp."[35]

A heady claim, but perhaps justified, because the Black Widow episodes are, against stiff competition, the campiest slices of *Batman* of them all. The stories about Bankhead are legendary—the time when on finding no toilet paper in her cubicle she slipped a ten dollar bill under the partition and asked the woman next door for two fives, or her whispered remark to a priest conducting a particularly elaborate service and swinging a censor of smoking incense, "Darling, I love the drag, but your purse is on fire"—and casting her in *Batman* was the final demonstration of the series' commitment to camp.

---

34. Melly, p. 192.
35. Core, p. 25.

The plot is unremarkable, the usual Bat-shenanigans; the pleasure lies in the detail. Details like the elderly Bankhead crammed into her Super-Villainess costume, or like the way in which (through a plot detail I won't go into) she impersonates Robin, so we see Burt Ward miming to Bankhead's voice, giving the unforgettable image of Robin flirting with burly traffic cops. Best of all, and Bankhead isn't even in this scene but the thrill of having her involved clearly spurred the writer to new heights of camp, Batman has to sing a song to break free of the Black Widow's spell. Does he choose to sing "God Bless America"? Nothing so rugged. He clutches a flower to his Bat chest and sings Gilbert and Sullivan's "I'm Just a Little Buttercup." It is this single image, more than any other, that prevents me from taking the post–Adam West Dark Knight at all seriously.

The fundamental camp trick which the series pulls is to make the comics speak. What was acceptable on the page, in speech balloons, stands revealed as ridiculous once given audible voice. The famous visualized sound effects (URKKK! KA-SPLOOSH!) that are for many the fondest memory of the series work along similar lines. Camp often makes its point by transposing the codes of one cultural form into the inappropriate codes of another. It thrives on mischievous incongruity.

The incongruities, the absurdities, the sheer ludicrousness of Batman were brought out so well by the sixties' version that for some audience there will never be another credible approach. I have to include myself here. I've recently read widely in postsixties Bat-lore, and I can appreciate what the writers and artists are trying to do, but my Batman will always be Adam West. It's impossible to be somber or pompous about Batman because if you try the ghost of West will come Bat-climbing into your mind, fortune cookie wisdom on his lips and keen young Dick by his side. It's significant, I think, that the letters I received from the editors of this book began "Dear Bat-Contributor."[36] Writers preparing chapters about James Joyce or Ingmar Bergman do not, I suspect, receive analogous greetings. To deny the large camp component of Batman is to blind oneself to one of the richest parts of his history.

Is There Bat-Life After Bat-Camp?

The international success of the Adam West incarnation left Batman high and dry. The camping around had been fun while it lasted, but it hadn't lasted very long. Most camp humor has a relatively short life span, 40

---

36. This essay originally appeared in an anthology, *The Many Lives of the Batman: Critical Approaches to a Superhero and His Media.*—EDS.

new targets are always needed, and the camp aspect of Batman had been squeezed dry. The mass public had moved on to other heroes, other genres, other acres of merchandising, but there was still a hard Bat-core of fans to satisfy. Where could the Bat go next? Clearly there was no possibility of returning to the caped Eisenhower, the benevolent patriarch of the 1950s. That option had been well and truly closed down by the TV show. Batman needed to be given his dignity back, and this entailed a return to his roots.

This, in any case, is the official version. For the unreconstructed devotee of the Batman (that is, people who insist on giving him the definite article before the name), the West years had been hell—a tricksy travesty, an effeminizing of the cowled avenger. There's a scene in *Midnight Cowboy* where Dustin Hoffman tells Jon Voight that the only audience liable to be receptive to his cowboy clothes are gay men looking for rough trade. Voight is appalled—"You mean to tell me John Wayne was a fag?" (quoted, roughly, from memory). This outrage, this horror at shattered illusions, comes close to encapsulating the loathing and dread the campy Batman has received from the old guard of Gotham City and the younger born-again Bat-fans.

So what has happened since the 1960s has been the painstaking reheterosexualization of Batman. I apologize for coining such a clumsy word, but no other quite gets the sense that I mean. This strategy has worked, too, for large audiences, reaching its peak with the 1989 film. To watch this and then come home to see a video of the 1966 movie is to grasp how complete the transformation has been. What I want to do in this section is to trace some of the crucial moments in that change, written from the standpoint of someone still unashamedly committed to Bat-camp.

If one wants to take Batman as a Real Man, the biggest stumbling block has always been Robin. There have been disingenuous claims that "Batman and Robin had a blood-brother closeness. Theirs was a spiritual intimacy forged from the stress of countless battles fought side by side"[37] (one can imagine what Tallulah Bankhead might say to *that*), but we know otherwise. The Wertham lobby and the acolytes of camp alike have ensured that any Batman/Robin relationship is guaranteed to bring on the sniggers. Besides which, in the late 1960s, Robin was getting to be a big boy, too big for any shreds of credibility to attach themselves to all that father-son smokescreen. So in 1969 Dick Grayson was packed off to college and the Bat was solitary once more.

This was a shrewd move. It's impossible to conceive of the recent, obsessive, sturm-und-drang Batman with a chirpy little Robin getting

---

37. Cotta Vaz, p. 53.

in the way.[38] A text of the disturbing power of *The Killing Joke*[39] could not have functioned with Robin to rupture the grim dualism of its Batman/Joker struggle. There was, however, a post–Dick Robin, but he was killed off by fans in that infamous telephone poll.[40]

It's intriguing to speculate how much latent (or blatant) homophobia lay behind that vote. Did the fans decide to kill off Jason Todd so as to redeem Batman for unproblematic heterosexuality? Impossible to say. There are other factors to take into account, such as Jason's apparent failure to live up to the expectations of what a Robin should be like. The sequence of issues in which Jason/Robin died, *A Death in the Family,* is worth looking at in some detail, however, in order to see whether the camp connotations of Bruce and Dick had been fully purged.

The depressing answer is that they had. This is very much the Batman of the 1980s, his endless feud with the Joker this time uneasily stretched over a framework involving the Middle East and Ethiopia. Little to be camp about there, though the presence of the Joker guarantees a quota of sick jokes. The sickest of all is the introduction of the Ayatollah Khomeini, a real and important political figure, into this fantasy world of THUNK! and THER-ACKK! and grown men dressed as bats. (As someone who lived in the part of England from which Reagan's planes took off on their murderous mission to bomb Libya, I fail to see the humor in this cartoon version of American foreign policy: It's too near the real thing.)

Jason dies at the Joker's hands because he becomes involved in a search for his own origins, a clear parallel to Batman's endless returns to *his* Oedipal scenario. Families, in the Bat-mythology, are dark and troubled things, one more reason why the introduction of the fifties versions of Batwoman and Batgirl seemed so inappropriate. This applies only to real, biological families, though; the true familial bond is between Batman and Robin, hence the title of these issues. Whether one chooses to read Robin as Batman's ward (official version), son (approved fantasy), or lover (forbidden fantasy), the sense of loss at his death is bound to be devastating. Batman finds Robin's body and, in the time-honored tradition of Hollywood cinema, is at least able to give him a loving em-

38. A female Robin is introduced in the *Dark Knight Returns* series, which, while raising interesting questions about the sexuality of Batman, which I don't here have the space to address, seems significant in that the Dark Knight cannot run the risk of reader speculation that a traditionally male Robin might provoke.

39. **The Killing Joke** Graphic novel by Alan Moore, Brian Bolland and John Higgins (New York: DC Comics 1988).—EDS.

40. **telephone poll** In a 1988 issue of the *Batman* comic, a "post-Dick Robin," Jason Todd, was badly injured in an explosion, and readers were allowed to phone the publisher to vote on whether he should be allowed to survive.—EDS.

brace. Good guys hug their dead buddies, only queers smooch when still alive.

If the word "camp" is applied at all to the eighties' Batman, it is a label for the Joker. This sly displacement is the cleverest method yet devised of preserving Bat-heterosexuality. The play that the texts regularly make with the concept of Batman and the Joker as mirror images now takes a new twist. The Joker is Batman's "bad twin," and part of that badness is, increasingly, an implied homosexuality. This is certainly present in the 1989 film, a generally glum and portentous affair except for Jack Nicholson's Joker, a characterization enacted with venomous camp. The only moment when this dour film comes to life is when the Joker and his gang raid the Art Gallery, spraying the paintings and generally camping up a storm.

The film strives and strains to make us forget the Adam West Batman, to the point of giving us Vicki Vale as Bruce Wayne's lover, and certainly Michael Keaton's existential agonizing (variations on the theme of why-did-I-have-to-be-a-Bat) is a world away from West's gleeful subversion of truth, justice and the American Way. This is the same species of Batman celebrated by Frank Miller: "If your only memory of Batman is that of Adam West and Burt Ward exchanging camped-out quips while clobbering slumming guest-stars Vincent Price and Cesar Romero, I hope this book will come as a surprise. . . . For me, Batman was never funny. . . ."[41]

The most recent linkage of the Joker with homosexuality comes in *Arkham Asylum,* the darkest image of the Bat-world yet. Here the Joker has become a parody of a screaming queen, calling Batman "honey pie," given to exclamations like "oooh!" (one of the oldest homophobic clichés in the book) and pinching Batman's behind with the advice, "Loosen up, tight ass." He also, having no doubt read his Wertham, follows the pinching by asking, "What's the matter? Have I touched a nerve? How is the Boy Wonder? Started shaving yet?" The Bat-response is unequivocal: "Take your filthy hands off me . . . Filthy degenerate!"

Arkham Asylum is a highly complex reworking of certain key aspects of the mythology, of which the sexual tension between Batman and the Joker is only one small part. Nonetheless the Joker's question "Have I touched a nerve?" seems a crucial one, as revealed by the homophobic ferocity of Batman's reply. After all, the dominant cultural construction of gay men at the end of the 1980s is as plague carriers, and the word "degenerate" is not far removed from some of the labels affixed to us in the age of AIDS.

41. Frank Miller, "Introduction," *Batman: Year One* (London: Titan, 1988).

Batman: Is He or Isn't He?

The one constant factor through all of the transformations of Batman has been the devotion of his admirers. They will defend him against what they see as negative interpretations, and they carry around in their heads a kind of essence of batness, a Bat-Platonic Ideal of how Batman should really be. The Titan Books reissue of key comics from the 1970s each carry a preface by a noted fan, and most of them contain claims such as "This, I feel, is Batman as he was meant to be."[42]

Where a negative construction is specifically targeted, no prizes for guessing which one it is: "you . . . are probably also fond of the TV show he appeared in. But then maybe you prefer Elvis Presley's Vegas years or the later Jerry Lewis movies over their early stuff . . . for me, the definitive Batman was then and always will be the one portrayed in these pages."[43]

The sixties' TV show remains anathema to the serious Bat-fan precisely because it heaps ridicule on the very notion of a serious Batman. *Batman* the series revealed the man in the cape as a pompous fool, an embodiment of superseded ethics, and a closet queen. As Marsha, Queen of Diamonds, put it, "Oh Batman, darling, you're so divinely square." Perhaps the enormous success of the 1989 film will help to advance the cause of the rival Bat-archetype, the grim, vengeful Dark Knight whose heterosexuality is rarely called into question (his humorlessness, fondness for violence, and obsessive monomania seem to me exemplary qualities for a heterosexual man). The answer, surely, is that they needn't be mutually exclusive.

If I might be permitted a rather camp comparison, each generation has its definitive Hamlet, so why not the same for Batman? I'm prepared to admit the validity, for some people, of the swooping eighties' vigilante, so why are they so concerned to trash my sixties' camped crusader? Why do they insist so vehemently that Adam West was a faggy aberration, a blot on the otherwise impeccably butch Bat-landscape? What *are* they trying to hide?

If I had a suspicious frame of mind, I might think that they were protesting too much, that maybe Dr. Wertham was on to something when he targeted these narratives as incitements to homosexual fantasy. And if I want Batman to be gay, then, for me, he is. After all, outside of the minds of his writers and readers, he doesn't really exist.

42. Kim Newman, "Introduction," *Batman: The Demon Awakes* (London: Titan, 1989).

43. Jonathan Ross, "Introduction," to *Batman: Vow from the Grave* (London: Titan, 1989).

Reading the Text

1. Summarize the objections Fredric Wertham makes to Batman in *Seduction of the Innocent*.
2. In a paragraph, write your own explanation of what Medhurst means by "camp."
3. What evidence does Medhurst supply to demonstrate that Batman is a gay character?
4. Explain what Medhurst means by his closing comment: "And if I want Batman to be gay, then, for me, he is. After all, outside of the minds of his writers and readers, he doesn't really exist."

Reading the Signs

1. Do you agree with Medhurst's argument that the Batman and Robin duo were really a covert homosexual couple? Write an essay arguing for or challenging his position, being sure to study his evidence closely. You may want to visit your campus's media library to see if they have file tapes of old *Batman* shows, or read contemporary reviews of *Batman,* to gather evidence for your own essay.
2. Compare Medhurst's analysis of Batman to Tania Modleski's analysis of *Dead Poets Society* (p. 278). In what ways is the homoeroticism in *Batman* and *Dead Poets Society* either suppressed or revealed? How are any differences in the treatment of homoeroticism signs of attitude changes toward homosexuality between the 1960s and late 1980s?
3. Check your college library for a copy of Fredric Wertham's *Seduction of the Innocent*. Then write your own critique of Wertham's attack on Batman.
4. Buy a few copies of the current *Batman* comic book, and write an essay in which you explain Batman's current sexual orientation.
5. Visit your college library and obtain a copy of Susan Sontag's "Notes on Camp" (included in Sontag's collections *Against Interpretation* and *The Susan Sontag Reader)*. How would Sontag interpret the character of Batman?
6. Drawing upon Medhurst's essay and Richard Herrell's "The Symbolic Strategies of Chicago's Gay and Lesbian Pride Day Parade" (p. 643), write an essay in which you explore the relationship between camp and gay sensibility.

GEORGE H. LEWIS

From Common Dullness to Fleeting Wonder:
The Manipulation of Cultural Meaning in the
Teenage Mutant Ninja Turtles Saga

||||||||||||||||||||||||||||||||||||||||||||||||

The Turtles have come a long way since their inception in 1983 in a
black-and-white underground comic book. Today, in a particularly strik-
ing instance of the commodifying power of a consumer society, they have
become an industry unto themselves, spawning movies, TV shows, cer-
eals, clothing fashions, and toys, toys, and more toys. In this study of
the Teenage Mutant Ninja Turtles saga, George H. Lewis (b. 1943)
sets their story in the context of the classical American "monomyth," in
which a solitary hero (or in this case, band of heroes) emerges from
obscurity to rescue society from evil forces, and, having restored peace and
harmony, rides off into the sunset—or splashes back down into the
sewer. Thus, the Turtles join American heroes like Natty Bumppo, the
Lone Ranger, and even Batman in their archetypal struggle against
wickedness. Lewis, a professor in the Department of Sociology and
Anthropology at the University of the Pacific, writes on many areas of
popular culture, including music, shopping malls, food, and media.

Heroes must act their ages.
         – MARSHALL FISHWICK: *The Hero American Style* (1969)

Cowabunga! Let's rock, dudes!
         – RAPHAEL: *Teenage Mutant Ninja Turtle Adventures* (1988)

Of all the kid heroes of the past few years, the most popular by far are the Teenage Mutant Ninja Turtles, who have by now, in addition to starring in two on-going and different sets of comic book adventures, also been featured in two motion pictures (with a third film on the way), a Saturday morning television cartoon show, a rock concert tour (with accompanying cassette and CD), and mall openings and fast-food outlet appearances too numerous to mention. In 1990, in addition to the popularity of Ninja Turtle cereal, bubble bath, TV dinners, trading cards, fruit juices, and T-shirts, Ninja Turtle toys outsold all others, both across the year and for the hyped-up Christmas season. For young America, it is clear, the Ninjas are where it's at in the early 1990s.

These unlikely heroes made their debut in 1983 in a black-and-white comic book drawn by Kevin Eastman and Peter Laird. Laird, trying to eke out a living with free-lance illustrating, had been introduced to Eastman, an amateur cartoonist working as a short-order cook, by the editor of a local comic magazine (Simpson 1990:59). The two formed

Mirage Studios in Dover, New Hampshire, where, as Laird tells it, the turtles were born:

> At that time, Mirage Studios was just us, sitting around in our living room, watching TV and drawing. One night, in a particularly silly mood, Kevin doodled up a pencil drawing of a turtle wearing a mask, with nunchakus strapped to its forearms . . . the goofiness continued, with Kevin penciling a drawing of four turtles, each with a different martial arts–type weapon. (Laird 1988)

Eastman, deciding "a name for these critters was in order," dubbed them Ninja Turtles. Laird, drawing on two of the most popular themes in comic books of the time, tacked "Teenage Mutant" onto the name. Thus, in an evening of lightheaded, absurdist fun, the mythic turtles sprang to life.

The American Monomyth and the Turtles Tale

Although many adults view the Turtles as just the latest moneymaking fad foisted off on their kids by the culture industry, and are seriously concerned with them only in the context of the amount of ultraviolence they feel is a part of their appeal, the fact is these "Heroes on a Half Shell," as their best-selling theme song labels them, are more closely connected to traditional heroic themes in American culture than most might imagine.

Robert Jewett and John Shelton Lawrence, in *The American Monomyth* (1977), document a mythic form that can be traced through American popular culture from Cooper's Leatherstocking tales through the creation of such classic heroes as John Wayne and Disney's Davy Crockett—and on, even to the 1980s cinematic reincarnations of Superman and Batman.

The form and structure of this myth is derived from what Joseph Campbell, in his *The Hero with a Thousand Faces* (1949), called the classical monomyth. This plot of heroic action has been modified, as Jewett and Lawrence point out, in the American version, in which our heroes—reenacting the old rites of separation, initiation, and return to community—venture forth from what Fishwick calls "the world of common dullness to the region of fleeting wonder" (1972:4). In the myth, a community in a relatively harmonious paradise is threatened by evil. Normal institutions fail to contend with this threat. A selfless superhero emerges, usually reluctantly, to attempt to eradicate this evil, many times moved to action by the threat of danger to a young, "innocent" woman. The superhero's first attempt may well be met with failure, as he has some flaw that the evil force knows of and exploits. Moving out of the community, the superhero connects with natural and supernatural forces which allow him to correct the flaw (or override it).

(This movement *out* of the community may or may not show up in the American version of the myth, although it is almost inevitable in its classical form.)

Thus aided by fate, the superhero returns. His decisive victory restores the community to its paradisal condition. The superhero then recedes into obscurity—or rides off into the sunset! Although, as Cawelti has noted (1976), the American pop culture hero has, in the last 15 years, become more a violent avenger than a restorer of justice, his traditional function in the myth is one of restoring harmony to the community. The Lone Ranger exposed the evil banker who had been cheating the homesteaders. Gary Cooper faced down four gunslingers at high noon on the streets of Hadleyville. Batman (in his earlier comic book version) rid the streets of Gotham City of the Joker and the Penguin.

This restorative function of the hero, as acted out in traditional American popular culture, is quite evident in the adventures of the Teenage Mutant Ninja Turtles. Although there is a good deal of physical violence involved in these tales, it is most all of a hand-to-hand-combat variety. Unlike GI Joe or the Masters of the Universe, the Turtles are not violent avengers who use explosive technology and the weapons of overkill to blow away the bad guys. Instead, they may even beat the bad guys with no use of violence whatsoever. In one Saturday morning cartoon episode, for example, the Turtles confront some punks who have robbed an apartment, scaring them away without ever throwing a punch. As Michelangelo exclaims, "You see, there are ways of settling disputes without violence."

The major focus, in the Turtle tales, is on the social meaning of individual action and the reestablishment of order to their world. This comes through strongly in the story line of their feature film which, in turn, was adapted from the original comic book saga of Laird and Eastman.

A crime wave is plaguing New York City and the police are ineffective—largely because they do not take seriously the idea that this amount of crime could be caused by young boys, coordinated and running in gangs. The only one who is bringing heat on the establishment is a young female newscaster—April O'Neil—who publicizes both the crime wave and the ineffectiveness of city hall and the police on her nightly newscasts.

The four turtles, who would be content to hang out in their pad deep in New York City's sewer system eating pizza and watching TV, are drawn into action when they happen to see April being attacked in a dark alley by a youth gang. They drive off the attackers and retreat into the sewers unseen, cracking jokes as they go. ("We were awesome! Yeah! Bossa Nova! Uhh . . . Chevy Nova? Hahaha. . . .")

However, one of the turtles (Raphael) loses his weapon—a Japanese sai—in the battle. April scoops it into her purse, thus giving Raphael an excuse to look for her, in hopes of recovering it. This sets up a confrontation in a deserted subway station between April and members of the evil Foot Clan—soldiers of the master villain The Shredder—who is behind the crime wave and wants to put April off the air. Raphael breaks up the attack and carries April, like a miniature King Kong carrying Faye Wray, down through the subway tunnel to the sewers and the Ninja Turtles' pad, which they share with their Zen master, a giant rat named Master Splinter.

In the course of swift-moving later events, Master Splinter is abducted by The Shredder and his Foot Soldiers and the Turtles' pad is trashed. Splinter is taken to The Shredder's hideout and chained to the wall. Meanwhile, the highly emotional Raphael has a clash with another of the Turtles (Leonardo) and storms out of April O'Neil's apartment alone. He is attacked by the Foot Clan, beaten badly, and thrown through the skylight of April's apartment, where the other three Turtles are hanging out. The building burns. And April and the Turtles escape in April's battered Volkswagen van.

They retreat to the country, and the abandoned farmhouse of April's deceased father. There, in this quiet, rural environment, they rest, perfecting their various skills while Raphael recovers from his beating.

Leonardo, the intellectual and spiritual Turtle, makes a "mind contact" with Splinter, and calls together the Turtles, who have been grieving for their Master and wallowing in self-doubt and guilt for having allowed him to be captured. The four of them sit around a campfire in the woods and together call up the image of Splinter, who tells them: "You have learned the greatest truth of the Ninja—that ultimate mastery comes not of the body, but of the mind. Together, there is nothing your four minds cannot accomplish. Help each other, draw upon one another, and always remember the true force that bonds you, the same as that which brought me here tonight. I love you all, my sons. . . ."

United in love, the Turtles embrace while tears slip down their green cheeks. Then, with their newly gained knowledge and power, they journey back to the city to rescue Splinter and confront and conquer The Shredder and his dread Foot Clan. Having rid the city of its crime problem, they return exultantly to their hideout in the sewer to watch April O'Neil on TV, crack jokes among themselves, and eat mondo amounts of pizza.

Folk Tales, Popular Culture, and Myth: Variations on a Theme

Recalling the traditional American monomyth, as sketched out previously, it is clear that the plot of the Ninja Turtle film (which, in turn, is derived from the original comic book series), follows the monomyth in an uncannily close manner. The Turtles would rather eat pizza than fight. They are drawn into the conflict by reacting to danger aimed at a young woman. Raphael's hot temper is the flaw that defeats them on their first attempt against The Shredder. Removing themselves from the community, they connect with nature in the rural American countryside, correcting the flaw and gaining spiritual insight. Armed with this new knowledge about themselves, and united in mind and spirit, they return to the city, rescue Splinter, destroy the evil, and vanish—into the sewers instead of the sunset (but one is allowed *some* variation on the theme!).

Another variation, this time an important one, is the abduction and rescue of Master Splinter instead of the innocent young woman, who is the one captured, if anyone is, in the traditional myth. In the 1990s, by contrast, the young liberated female moves to the side of the Turtles as an heroic partner (after her initial distress gets them into the fray in the first place), and the abducted figure (who in the myth represents innocence, purity, and love) becomes the father figure. But what a shift in father figures! Master Splinter is raising his "sons" alone, teaching them the skills and moral codes necessary to conduct their lives. He detests violence and admonishes Raphael about his temper and anger. ("I have tried to channel your anger, Raphael, but more remains. Anger clouds the mind. Turned inward, it is an unconquerable enemy . . .")

Splinter is wise and teaches that harmony, cooperation, and love are the ultimate weapons. In a word, he is a socioemotional leader—closer to the traditional, nurturing role model of the mom (combined with the wise elder—a rare figure in our popular culture) than he is to the macho role model of the male that characters such as G.I. Joe represent.

One has to look to the evil and merciless Shredder to find a violent [20] and dark macho authority figure with his domineering and unnatural passion for power, wealth, and revenge (Warner 1990, 127). It is no accident that The Shredder, in his earlier more human incarnation in Japan, was Oroku Saki, a jealous student of Yoshi Hamato, the Master of the Ninja clan (who was Master Splinter in *his* previous incarnation). In their earlier conflict, Oroku Saki defeated Yoshi Hamato in a bitter fight for power and the love of a beautiful woman, Tang Shen—a classic acting out of the Oedipus myth. Now the two, as Master Splinter and The Shredder (note the similarity in literal meaning of their names), are good and evil, the light and the dark, the classic duality in which the existence of each makes sense only in relation to the other.

The Splinter/Shredder character is not the only composite character in the Ninja myth. As Master Splinter teaches, the four Turtles are, symbolically, four facets of a complete and fully realized super individual. Raphael is known for his hot temper and emotionality. With Leonardo, who is strongly intellectual, they represent the classic conflict between emotion and intellect that echoes through the mythic tales of our culture.

The other two turtles represent success in social and technological skills respectively. Michelangelo is the cool party/surfer dude—the one who knows how to handle himself in any situation. Donatello is a master of mechanical things. He is the one who invents (and keeps running) the Turtles' various technological contraptions—from their mobile automatic pizza throwing weapon to the Turtles' airship. Donatello also understands computers and the complexities of the electronic world of microchips, video, and passage into other dimensions.

The colors of their headbands and belts reflects their major orientation. Raphael's is a hot red in color, while Michelangelo, who also deals in warmer emotional matters, is orange. The intellectual Leonardo has cool, blue attire—while Donatello, the mechanical one, is a mixture of cool blue and red—a royal shade of purple.

Taken together, like many superhero teams, the four Ninja Turtles are far greater than the sum of their parts. This uniquely American wrinkle on the superhero, the smoothly functioning team, is reflective of our faith in bureaucratic models—like a football team or a military unit, we win when our plugged-in specialist selves each play their part. And yet, even here, the Turtles seem to be subverting the form—it is, really, their comraderie, their sense of small-group community, which is of more importance than their specialized skills, or their ability to smoothly mesh them together. Turtles, like the young adolescents who idolize them, have a need for "ganging," and the security that such group behavior provides.

Ninja Bricolage: The Raiding of American Pop Culture

In addition to reinventing the traditional American monomyth, the   25
Ninja Turtles have been cultural raiders—gleefully pulling bits and pieces of American pop culture out of context and reassembling it for their own purposes. Cultural references from comics, video, cartoons, and film are cleverly woven into the fabric of their mythic world in, to use Umberto Eco's phrase, a playful type of semiotic guerilla warfare (Eco 1973:100). For example, "cowabunga" comes from the Howdy Doody Show,[1] where it was used by Chief Thunderthud, the Indian founder of Doodyville. "Dude," of course, is 1990s hip kid street-speak which— although ultimately derived from the Western "dude" of "dude ranch" connotation—was first used in this way by inner-city minority youth. Employed by Chicanos in East Los Angeles, the term signified a cool, together person. From the youth of these inner-city ghettos, the term spread, in California, to the white suburbs, becoming part of "surfer-speak," and then a stable part of the hip teen vocabulary of the 1980s—

---

1. ***Howdy Doody Show*** Television's first popular children's show, first broadcast 1947–1950, featuring a puppet.—EDS.

along with terms such as "rad" and "mondo," both of which show up regularly in Turtle talk (Lewis 1991).

The location of the Turtles in the New York sewer system also ties in, thematically, with our folk and popular culture. For many years there has been an "urban legend" circulating around the country concerning giant alligators in the New York City sewer system (Brunvand 1981:90–98). They got there, so the legend goes, because they were bought as pets when they were very tiny and flushed down toilets in the city by moms and dads when they began to get too big, or when the child had lost interest in them. This urban legend was used as the basis of the campy 1970s film *Alligator!* (which also satirized the successful *Jaws*—a large, water-based creature fighting back against the human race). Here, the Turtles are the good guys, in a clever inversion, but they grow from small pets that (in this case, by accident) have been dropped into the sewer system.

Other folk and pop cultural references in the Turtle myth include villains that parallel those found in various 1950s and 1960s films, from *The Fly* to *Texas Chainsaw Massacre*. Superman has appeared (as an overweight, petulant lout) in the comic book version, as have several characters from the Black Lagoon. Even The Shredder has a decidedly Darth Vader look to him, especially in the movie version of the tale.

The whole idea of mutant turtles (created by their exposure to a radioactive green slime in the sewers) recalls the dozen of movies of the 1950s with the theme of giant, radioactively mutated animals roaming the earth. A youth-oriented film of the early 1980s, *The Toxic Avenger,* spoofed this whole theme, while merging it with the concept of the superhero, as does the Turtle myth.

The transformation of the Turtles from lovable, slow, cuddly creatures into lean mean fighting machines reflects a tradition of transformation in our superheros. The Lone Ranger was transformed from a regular peace official by the vengeful energy he gained when his comrades were slaughtered around him in an ambush. Clark Kent, a mild-mannered reporter, looks for phone booths and becomes Superman. Billy Batson transforms himself into Captain Marvel by uttering the word "Shazam." Batman, Spiderman, Wonder Woman—all are ordinary, rather ineffectual humans who can transform themselves into powerful superheroes—an idea most appealing to young children and adolescents, who are still in the process of developing a self-identity, and who many times feel powerless, ineffectual, and frustrated in the adult world that surrounds them.

This concept of transformation (Englehardt 1986:91) has reached its 30 zenith in kid culture with the Japanese-originated "transformer" toys, comics, and cartoons, in which shape-shifts are made from machine to robot/humanoid and back again. These powerful figures probably can be traced back to the popularity of *The Bionic Man* on American TV, and to the line of toys he inspired. From there, one can move forward to Robo-Cop and The Transformers. And in the Ninja Turtles, The Shredder ("transformed" from a martial arts expert) looks surprisingly like one of these Japanese transformer toys himself.

The Turtles also directly reference the 1980s craze for things oriental in our popular culture, from Kung Fu films with Bruce Lee and the Karate Kid, to the latest samurai epic (whether it be *Shogun* or the newest Kurosawa film), to the fascination with oriental philosophies and the "mysterious wisdom" of the East that Master Splinter so playfully embodies. Those who have criticized the Turtles (especially the film version) as racist and anti-Japanese are perhaps missing the point. Although it is true that Japan-bashing has become increasingly popular in America, and the bad guys in the film all hail from Japan and are depicted as devious, violent, and deadly, one must remember that Master Splinter is also from Japan. And so is the philosophy he imparts to the Turtles, who use it (and Japanese forms of the martial arts) to defeat the bad guys in the end.

Critics such as these also miss the point that a large amount of what goes on in Turtle culture is satire and spoof. When April O'Neil, about to be attacked by the Foot Clan in the subway, cracks "What . . . Am I behind on my Sony payments again?" we have a joke that has more to do with American consumer habits than it does any type of racism. These sorts of cultural references are meant to be funny—it is no accident that the four turtles are named after the cultural paragons of the Western adult world's "holy" renaissance, and by a mutant rat, at that! (Splinter got the names from an art book he found discarded in the sewer—a further comment on current American cultural priorities and values.) This type of satire—the mocking of icons of adult culture (Fiske 1989), or the bricolagic[2] rearranging of them to create bizarre, "absurd" messages (Clark 1990)—is often seen in the cultural material of adolescents and preadolescents, from *Mad* magazine through the Teenage Mutant Ninja Turtles in both their original, teen-oriented comic book version and in the cartoon and video versions designed for the younger audience.

Inversions: Questioning the Values of Adult Culture

A related aspect of playing with the symbols of culture is that of inversions. Not only are objects rearranged, as in bricolage, the standard cultural meanings associated with these objects are inverted. This cultural phenomenon, seen in areas as seemingly unrelated as punk styles (Hebdige 1979), carnivals (Bakhtin 1968), and professional wrestling (Fiske

---

2. **bricolagic**   Characteristic of bricolage, objects constructed from bits and pieces of other objects.—EDS.

1987:243–255), is common in the culture of the culturally powerless—like American adolescents. It is also very much evident in the saga of the Ninja Turtles.

Not only are turtles unlikely heroes, they come from a class of objects—reptiles—that are almost universally used in American culture, cartoon or otherwise, to signify villains. Although snakes are the heaviest signifiers (perhaps because of the Judeo-Christian equation of the snake as the devil in the Garden of Eden), other reptiles, such as lizards, alligators, and crocodiles are commonly cast as villains in cartoon stories. With the Turtles, this point of inversion is underscored by having their wise and kind mentor, Master Splinter, exist in the form of a rat—another of the common symbols of viciousness and evil in our culture, as seen in texts ranging from James Cagney's famous "you dirty rat" to the fright film *Willard* and the works of Stephen King.

Sewers, where the Ninja Turtles live and where they were magically transformed into their heroic forms, are also signifiers of dirt, dark, and death in our culture. Heroes are to come from humble beginnings, it is true. But they live in clean, well-lighted places, not in the dark tunnels of our refuse, sluggishly festering deep beneath our urban feet.

A third cultural inversion is that of mutation itself. Warner has pointed out that mutants almost always appear as villains in cartoons (1990:123), and also in our culture at large. As Stephen King remarks in *Danse Macabre,* there is an equation in our culture of mutant and monster. He refers to John Wyndham's novel, *Rebirth,* in which the protagonist of the novel has plaques hung in his home reading, "Keep True the Stock of the Lord," "Blessed is the Norm," and "Watch Thou for the Mutant" (King 1981:201). Mutations always challenge the status quo and, because of this, are grand symbols for cultural inversion. The Ninjas—and Master Splinter—are mutants (as admittedly are two minor villains, Rock Steady and Be Bop). In contrast to the master villain Shredder, who is a natural, highly physically endowed human being, the heroes of this saga are mutant, sewer-living reptiles.

Although there are many other minor cultural inversions in the stories, two more are worthy of note. One is the treatment of April, the Turtles' female sidekick. As previously mentioned, the monomyth would dictate that the young woman in the story be virtuous, weak, and in need of saving. In the Ninja Turtle story, April is young and in a glamorous profession—television newscasting. Although she does need rescuing in the story, she proves herself to be both physically and emotionally strong—and bright. Without her help, the Turtles could not defeat the Shredder and his Foot Clan Soldiers. As a strong, positive female role model, April flies in the face of a good deal of traditional American popular culture. Although she is not the only "liberated" female figure in contemporary American cartoons—there is Miss Bianca in *The Res-*

cuers, for example—she is probably the most fully realized, and her portrayal in the çomic book series is extremely sensitive and enlightened.

Finally, there is the character of Casey Jones, the teenage crime fighter who aids the Turtles most significantly in their rural isolation—where they prepare for their final battle with the Shredder. Jones acts as a sort of "big brother" figure for the Turtles—helping Donatello, for example, repair an old truck at the farm. While they work, the two engage in typical teen/male name calling, back and forth: "Barfaroni." "Camel Breath." "Duck Fart." "Gack Face." "OK. Now, turn it (the engine) over."

Jones, also used to some extent as a romantic foil for April in the film, is an alienated urban teen who has, independently of the Turtles, become fed up with the violence of "his" city. Acting alone (with no family, parents, or friends), Jones is battling the urban punks of the city when he is first encountered by the Turtles.

Clearly, Casey Jones fits into the American monomyth well—a   40 teenage hero, fighting for what he believes in the corrupted urban landscape of adults. And his name is, of course, significant in this respect. Casey Jones has been an American hero from his runaway-train folk ballad days to his appearance in a hit counterculture song by the Grateful Dead in the early 1970s.

But now we have the delightful inversion. Casey Jones wears a hockey goalie's mask, to disguise himself. Not only are masks, when they cover the whole face (not just the eyes), an accepted feature of villains, *this* mask is an especially potent symbol. It is the mask that Jason,[3] the demented teen killer, wears in his long string of gory slasher films. So here we have a teen, disguised as one the adult and older teen culture knows as deeply evil being—in this inversion—perhaps an even *better* fit to the traditional American mythic hero than are the Turtles themselves.

The Character of Evil

One cannot conclude a discussion of the Ninja Turtles saga without some further attention being paid the villains of the stories. The Shredder, as the primary source of evil, is a dark, domineering character with an insatiable thirst for power and the ultimate destruction of Master Splinter and the Ninja Turtles. As such, he typifies on the surface the sort of villain most usually found in cartoon stories. As Warner has pointed out, deviant character in cartoon villains is visually reified. Villains consistently

---

3. **Jason** The villain in the *Friday the 13th* films.—EDS.

have their moral status linked to their appearance, "their face and bodies express their basic characters . . ."; this "suggests to viewers that deviance originates genetically, not socially. . . ." Villains are "bad seeds . . . they lie, cheat, steal, and covet; they abuse their associates, behave selfishly, act mercilessly" (1990:119–120). Evil, in a word, is biological or psychological, not social, in origin. Blocked opportunity structures in a society, or outrage at a societally accepted set of values or social conditions that is perceived to be wrong, for example, have nothing to do with transgressions against society in cartoon land. Evil is evil. Standards are universal. Just as in the American monomyth—and in the minds of many middle Americans.

The Shredder fits this notion of evil perfectly. A Darth Vader type, he is encased in heavy body armor with razor-sharp spikes bristling from his shoulders and his wrists. He wears a heavy metal helmet which also wraps around his face, revealing only his eyes, which glow with menace (a common feature of cartoon villains). His black cloak, which he sweeps around himself for dramatic effect, suggests Vader from *Star Wars,* as does the amplified breathing that overlays his speaking voice in the feature film. As with many cartoon master villains, the Shredder is athletic and physically powerful, with a stress on his male secondary sexual characteristics. And yet, in the Ninja saga, the ultimate nature of good and evil is questioned, by making the Shredder the ying to Master Splinter's yang. There can be no ultimate evil without ultimate good, the Ninja epic seems to be saying—the two are inextricably intertwined—a bit more complex depiction of evil than is traditionally found in cartoon stories (Warner 1990).

The Shredder's closest associates, whom he abuses constantly, are the mutants Rock Steady and Be Bop, a wart hog and a rhino that he—the Shredder—mutated into dull-witted, mesomorphic punk rockers, complete with purple spike hair and bondage chains. These bumbling characters, like most secondary villains, lend a comedic element to evil—the Shredder's dark plans are constantly being scrambled by this bumbling twosome. Still, as laughable as they are, Be Bop and Rock Steady are both stupid *and* dangerous—a combination that is common in our mythic conception of "bad" guys as flawed and inferior, and thus, naturally destined for ultimate defeat by the moral forces of right. In reality, these moral forces of right, in the 1970s in Great Britain and America, created a moral panic concerning teen punk rockers—who, as Hebdige (1979) and others have described—were labeled by the media (and ultimately by the public) as deviant, deranged, and laughable—even as they were pronounced morally dangerous. That this establishment attitude shows up in the Ninja story is interesting. Ultimately, in this cartoon saga, the punk "threat" is seen to be of little real significance. Anyone (meaning adults) who, in real life, feels threatened by punk rockers and their styles is really missing the point, the Ninjas seem to be saying.

The other major villain in the Turtle saga is Krang, the alien from   45
"Dimension X." Krang, a quivering pink brain with octopus-like tentacles, has dreams of invading Earth with his soldiers, and is constantly
in conflict with the Shredder as to who of the two will be the more
dominant. Krang has sharp, fanglike teeth (a sure mark of a villain) and
is clearly a spoof on the adult American culture's distrust of intellectuality.
In middle-American culture, "brains" are suspect. Existing in some dimension other than our own, they are to be distrusted when they are
evilly clever, like Krang, and ridiculed as not understanding the "real
world" when they take exception to (or ignore) self-evident middle-
American cultural truths. Krang takes this position one step further along
in spoof, as he manufactures a huge, Frankenstein-like hulking body in
which to move himself around when he visits Earth. Krang sits in the
stomach cavity of the body, and manipulates it with his tentacles—
equating the self-serving greed of the stomach with his type of insatiable
intellect, while at the same time drawing on a whole host of pop cultural
images of alien-controlled monsters. The spoofed message is clear—if
you allow it, these "alien" intellects can—and will—bend you to their
will, and you will be no better than the walking corpses of George
Romero's brilliantly satiric *Living Dead* films, which Krang's image
evokes.

But the Ninja epic does not stop here, with respect to villains. To
keep the plots moving in the steadily lengthening list of comic books
and TV cartoon shows, there is Rat-Man (a Schwarzenegger type whose
name is a clever reference to Bat Man); Don Turtellini (Godfather and
the Mafia); Baxter Stockman (the mad scientist/fly combination, drawn
from the 1950s classic film *The Fly*); Leatherhead (an oblique reference
to the baddie in *Texas Chainsaw Massacre*); the Triceratons (human/
dinosaur creatures); and even the Teenage Mutant Punk Frogs, to name
but a few of the secondary villains who have appeared in these adventures. These villains, drawn cleverly from American pop culture myths,
are another way in which the Ninja Turtle epic playfully comments back
upon our commonly held concepts of good and evil, even as it presents
these concepts to a new generation.

Conclusion

In sum, the Teenage Mutant Ninja Turtle saga is one in which the
traditional American monomyth is resurrected, then cleverly played with
in its contemporary American pop cultural context. As John Clarke has
pointed out:

> Together, object and meaning constitute a sign, and, within any
> one culture, such signs are assembled, repeatedly, into characteristic
> forms of discourse. However, when the bricoleur re-locates the sig-

nificant object in a different position within that discourse, using the same overall repertoire of signs, or when that object is placed within a different total ensemble, a new discourse is constituted, a different message conveyed. (Clarke 1976:197)

For adolescents and young Americans, this is the appeal of the Ninja Turtles—heroes on a half shell indeed—who spoofingly turn adult popular culture upside down, even as they use its elements to create new messages for their own young audience.

WORKS CITED

Bakhtin, Michael. *Rabelais and His World*. Cambridge, Mass.: MIT Press, 1968.

Brunvand, Jan Harold. *The Vanishing Hitchhiker*. New York: Norton, 1981.

Campbell, Joseph. *The Hero with a Thousand Faces*. New York: Meridian Books, 1949.

Cawelti, John. *Adventure, Mystery and Romans*. Chicago: Univ. of Chicago Press, 1976.

Clarke, John. "Pessimism Versus Populism: The Problematic Aspects of Popular Culture," in Richard Butsch (ed.). *For Fun and Profit*. Philadelphia: Temple Univ. Press: 28–46, 1990.

Clarke, John. "Style" in Stuart Hall, et al. (eds.). *Resistance Through Rituals*. London: Hutchinson: 180–198, 1976.

Eco, Umberto. "Social Life as a Sign System," in David Robey (ed.). *Structuralism*. London: Cape, 1973.

Englehardt, Tom. "The Shortcake Strategy," in Todd Gitlin (ed.). *Watching Television*. New York: Pantheon: 68–110, 1986.

Fishwick, Marshall. *The Hero American Style*. New York: David McKay, 1969.

Fishwick, Marshall, Ray Browne and Michael Marsden. *Heroes of Popular Culture*. Bowling Green, OH: Popular Press, 1972.

Fiske, John. *Television Culture*. London: Methuen, 1987.

Fiske, John. *Understanding Popular Culture*. Boston: Unwin Hyman, 1989.

Hebdige, Dick. *Subculture: The Meaning of Style*. London: Methuen, 1979.

Jewett, Robert and John Shelton Lawrence. *The American Monomyth*. New York: Anchor, 1977.

King, Stephen. *Danse Macabre*. New York: Everest House, 1981.

Laird, Peter. *Teenage Mutant Ninja Turtles Adventures*. Haydenville, Mass.: Mirage Studios, 1988.

Lewis, George H. "From GI Joe to the Ninja Turtles," *World & I*, 1991.

Simpson, Janice. "Lean, Green, On the Screen," *Time*, April: 59, 1990.

Warner, Priscilla Kiehnle. "Fantastic Outsiders: Villains and Deviants in Animated Cartoons," in Clinton Sanders (ed.). *Marginal Conventions: Popular Culture, Mass Media and Social Change*. Bowling Green, OH: Popular Press: 117–130, 1990.

Reading the Text

1. Trace the history of the Teenage Mutant Ninja Turtles, as outlined by Lewis.
2. How, according to Lewis, do the Turtles function as heroes?
3. How are the Turtles amalgams of American pop culture?

4. What does Lewis mean by saying that the Turtles "invert" traditional cultural values?

Reading the Signs

1. Read or review Gary Engle's "What Makes Superman So Darned American?" (p. 309). In class, form two teams, and debate whether the Turtles would qualify as true "American heroes," in Engle's terms.
2. Watch a current episode of *Teenage Mutant Ninja Turtles* on television, and write a semiotic analysis of it.
3. Lewis claims that April O'Neil is a "strong, positive female role model." Argue for or against his claim, basing your argument on your viewing of at least one episode of the show. To guide your analysis, you may want to consult Emily Prager's "Our Barbies, Ourselves" (p. 353) and Susan Faludi's "Teen Angels and Tart-Tongued Witches" (p. 219) for other discussions of the images of women in popular culture.
4. Study the Turtles in light of Linda Seger's ("Creating the Myth," p. 250) analysis of popular heroic stereotypes. How would Seger analyze the Turtles' heroic status?
5. Peter Rainer ("Antihero Worship," p. 318), Gary Engle ("What Makes Superman So Darned American?," p. 309), and George Lewis all describe popular culture characters who function as heroes. Read or review all three essays, and write an essay in which you explore what the word "hero" means to Americans in the late twentieth century.

EMILY PRAGER

Our Barbies, Ourselves

—————————————————————————

||||||||||||||||||||||||||||||||||||||||||||||||||||||||||||||

Little girls throughout America should know that Barbie is not drawn to scale. In this tongue-in-cheek essay on the role Barbie has played in her life, Emily Prager (b. 1952) reveals the damaging effect of a doll that establishes such an impossible standard of physical perfection for little girls—and for little boys who grow up expecting their girlfriends to look like Barbie. When not contemplating what Barbie has done to her, Emily Prager is an essayist and fiction writer who has published for The National Lampoon, The Village Voice, *and* Penthouse, *among other magazines. Her books include a work of historical fiction for children,* World War II Resistance Stories; *a book of humor,* The Official I Hate Videogames Handbook; *and works of fiction such as* Eve's Tattoo *(1991) and* Clea and Zeus Divorce *(1987).*

I read an astounding obituary in the *New York Times* not too long ago. It concerned the death of one Jack Ryan. A former husband of Zsa Zsa Gabor, it said, Mr. Ryan had been an inventor and designer during his lifetime. A man of eclectic creativity, he designed Sparrow and Hawk missiles when he worked for the Raytheon Company, and, the notice said, when he consulted for Mattel he designed Barbie.

If Barbie was designed by a man, suddenly a lot of things made sense to me, things I'd wondered about for years. I used to look at Barbie and wonder, What's wrong with this picture? What kind of woman designed this doll? Let's be honest: Barbie looks like someone who got her start at the Playboy Mansion. She could be a regular guest on *The Howard Stern Show*. It is a fact of Barbie's design that her breasts are so out of proportion to the rest of her body that if she were a human woman, she'd fall flat on her face.

If it's true that a woman didn't design Barbie, you don't know how much saner that makes me feel. Of course, that doesn't ameliorate the damage. There are millions of women who are subliminally sure that a thirty-nine-inch bust and a twenty-three-inch waist are the epitome of lovability. Could this account for the popularity of breast implant surgery?

I don't mean to step on anyone's toes here. I loved my Barbie. Secretly, I still believe that neon pink and turquoise blue are the only colors in which to decorate a duplex condo. And like many others of my generation, I've never married, simply because I cannot find a man who looks as good in clam diggers as Ken.

The question that comes to mind is, of course, Did Mr. Ryan design   5
Barbie as a weapon? Because it *is* odd that Barbie appeared about the same time in my consciousness as the feminist movement—a time when women sought equality and small breasts were king. Or is Barbie the dream date of weapons designers? Or perhaps it's simpler than that: Perhaps Barbie is Zsa Zsa if she were eleven inches tall. No matter what, my discovery of Jack Ryan confirms what I have always felt: There is something indescribably masculine about Barbie—dare I say it, phallic. For all her giant breasts and high-heeled feet, she lacks a certain softness. If you asked a little girl what kind of doll she wanted for Christmas, I just don't think she'd reply, "Please, Santa, I want a hard-body."

On the other hand, you could say that Barbie, in feminist terms, is definitely her own person. With her condos and fashion plazas and pools and beauty salons, she is definitely a liberated woman, a gal on the move. And she has always been sexual, even totemic. Before Barbie, American dolls were flat-footed and breastless, and ineffably dignified. They were created in the image of little girls or babies. Madame Alexander was the queen of doll makers in the fifties, and her dollies looked like Elizabeth Taylor in *National Velvet*. They represented the kind of girls who looked perfect in jodhpurs, whose hair was never out of place, who grew up to be Jackie Kennedy—before she married Onassis. Her dolls' boyfriends were figments of the imagination, figments with large portfolios and three-piece suits and presidential aspirations, figments who could keep dolly in the style to which little girls of the fifties were programmed to become accustomed, a style that spasm-ed with the sixties and the appearance of Barbie. And perhaps what accounts for Barbie's vast popularity is that she was also a sixties woman: into free love and fun colors, anticlass, and possessed of real, molded boyfriend, Ken, with whom she could chant a mantra.

But there were problems with Ken. I always felt weird about him. He had no genitals, and, even at age ten, I found that ominous. I mean, here was Barbie with these humongous breasts, and that was OK with the toy company. And then, there was Ken with that truncated, unidentifiable lump at his groin. I sensed injustice at work. Why, I wondered, was Barbie designed with such obvious sexual equipment and Ken not? Why was his treated as if it were more mysterious than hers? Did the fact that it was treated as such indicate that somehow his equipment, his essential maleness, was considered more powerful than hers, more worthy of the dignity of concealment? And if the issue in the mind of the toy company was obscenity and its possible damage to children, I still object. How do they think I felt, knowing that no matter how many water beds they slept in, or hot tubs they romped in, or swimming pools they lounged by under the stars, Barbie and Ken could never make love? No matter how much sexuality Barbie possessed, she would never turn Ken on. He would be forever withholding, forever detached. There was a loneliness about Barbie's situation that was always disturbing. And twenty-five years later, movies and videos are still filled with topless women and covered men. As if we're all trapped in Barbie's world and can never escape.

God, it certainly has cheered me up to think that Barbie was designed by Jack Ryan. . . .

Reading the Text

1. Why does Prager say "a lot of things made sense" to her after she learned Barbie was designed by a man?
2. What is Prager's attitude toward Ken?
3. How do Madame Alexander dolls differ from Barbies?

Reading the Signs

1. Bring a toy to class and, in same-sex groups, discuss its semiotic significance; you may want to focus particularly on how the toys may be intended for

one gender or another. Then have each group select one toy and present your interpretation of it to the whole class. What gender-related patterns do you find in the presentations?

2. Think of a toy you played with as a child, and write a semiotic interpretation of it, using Prager's essay as a model. Be sure to consider differences between your childhood response to the toy and your current response.

3. Did you have a Barbie doll when you were a child? If so, write a journal entry in which you explore what the doll meant to you when you were young and how Prager's essay has caused you to rethink your attitudes.

4. Consider how Jack Ryan, the creator of Barbie, would defend his design. Write a letter, as if you were Ryan, addressed to Prager in which you justify Barbie's appearance and refute Prager's analysis.

5. Barbie can be seen as embodying not only America's traditional gender roles but also its consumerist ethos. Visit a toy store to learn what "accessories" one can buy for Barbie, and then write an essay in which you explore the extent to which she illustrates the "hunger for more" described by Laurence Shames (see "The More Factor," p. 25).

WANDA COLEMAN
Say It Ain't Cool, Joe

||||||||||||||||||||||||||||||||||||||||||||||||||||||

In 1988, R.J.R. Nabisco revived the old figure of Joe Camel and turned him into a too-cool-to-be-true cartoon smoothie designed to pitch Camels to a preteen market. The Camel people deny that Joe Camel is aimed at children, of course, but when this debonair dromedary has a higher recognition value among American children than Cheerios or Kelloggs, one has to wonder. Even Antonia Novello, U.S. Surgeon General in 1992, wondered enough to wage an unsuccessful attempt to abolish Joe Camel ads from the nation's billboards, bus stops, and magazines. Wanda Coleman (b. 1946) joins the attacks on Joe Camel, but with a difference: She offers the perspective of an African-American woman concerned with Joe's impact on children in our inner cities. Coleman, author of Mad Dog Black Lady *(1979), is an Emmy Award–winning television writer and poet who lives and performs in Los Angeles.*

Boy, oh boy, there's Joe, sportin' those Polaroid peepers, looking rakishly Mediterranean with hot babes and hotter cars. His hair looks like Moammar Kadafi's. The tuxedoed dome-nose has all the sleek arrogance of a shah exiled to Malibu.

I like Joe Camel. And I don't smoke. Not out of the closet anyway.
And Camels? Never. But . . .

In Afro-American street parlance, Joe the Camel is a player. Life is
a game and he's winning it. He runs in the fast lane. And he's about as
gangsterish as it comes. The cat—er, dromedary—is too cool Old
School. (Consult your Digital Underground[1] on TNT Recordings.)

If I didn't know better, I'd say Joe was patterned after one of my
father's old cronies. Doc was the original "crip," meaning physically
challenged. But that didn't stop any action. He hustled his way around
South-Central with one crutch on his best days, a wheelchair on his
worst. According to his own legend, he had lost one leg in World War II,
but rumor was that he'd sacrificed the gam in some unsavory back-alley
adventure.

In spite of his cop-and-blow existence, Doc always sported highly   5
polished wingtip kicks, though one shoe was always curiously devoid of
mass. As Mama would say, he was "sharp as a tack." And generous. One
of his philanthropic pleasures was formal-dress tea parties, where he gave
us munchkins a crash course on etiquette, Perle Mesta–style. He paid
polite attention to me and charmed my little socks off—the adult who
takes a child seriously is always an attraction.

Doc smoked. He carried the first gold cigarette case I ever saw. It
was impressive to watch him slip it from the pocket of his pin-striped
vest. Thing about Doc was that, no matter how vulnerable he might've
been, he was not to be pitied or messed with. A gat[2] was concealed in
the creases of his threads.

And therein lies the appeal of Joe Camel as a clever selling gizmo
and tobacco kingpin's dream.

Underneath Joe's Cheshire cat–smug macho is a deeper message.
Joe's not just another lung-collapse peddler. He's a self-respect maven.
In rural bottoms and urban ghettos nationwide, rife with runaways and
bored, unemployed youth, there's a serious shortage of self-esteem. Like
Doc or Joe, you can fire up a coffin nail for instant attitude, the easiest
way to strike a pose.

Face it. Joe Camel has life-style appeal. He's rich and he's infamous.
And he runs with the pack. There's Joe the suave, white-on-white
betuxed academic. If you ain't got it, you can fake his "smooth philosophy" by lighting up. Or you can rack 'em up for Pool Shark Joe cuz
he's about to run the table.

In his stingy fedora, Hard Pack Joe and his Wide cousins have all   10
the Hollywood charisma of William Bendix breathing down Robert
Mitchum's neck in *The Big Steal* or Brando in *The Godfather*.

---

1. **Digital Underground** A rap group.—EDS.
2. **gat** A gun.—EDS.

Beachcomber Joe has done his share of Venice Beach schmoozing, no doubt sipping Long Island iced tea on the volleyball court. Calypso Joe opens the doors of Club Camel on some tiny Caribbean isle where the cane grows tall and the money laundering is easy.

Joe's crimey, Eddie Camel, was a bead-wearing, apple-capped, paintbrush-totin', long-haired flower child in the sixties. But today he's a loose-lipped, slack-collared, tam-topped, neo-bebop jazz drummer. Bustah (note the idiomatic black spelling) Camel undergoes a similar transformation, and only his electric guitar remains the same.

I can't resist poking fun at ol' Joe. But underneath the fun, the birth of his cool is linked to the birth of survival strategies that have allowed the black male to withstand the relentlessness of racism. It is the cool personified by Malcolm X, Miles Davis, Willie Brown, and Ice Cube. To be cool is to be laid-back black.

But Joe Camel is offensive. Not only because cigarettes can be addictive and debilitating but because, at root, old Joe's shtick is plain-and-simple racist. He's a composite of little-understood cultural traits designed to sucker in youngsters, especially black children. And that ain't cool.

You dig?   15

Reading the Text

1. How, according to Coleman, is the character Joe Camel used to sell cigarettes?
2. What parallels does Coleman see between Joe Camel and "Doc"?
3. Why does Coleman believe Joe Camel is "racist"?

Reading the Signs

1. In class, form teams and debate whether the Joe Camel campaign should be banned on the grounds that it inappropriately uses an attractive cartoon character to peddle a dangerous product to children. In researching your arguments, consult the issue of the *Journal of the American Medical Association* devoted entirely to tobacco use (vol. 266, no. 22, December 11, 1991) and the First Amendment controversies discussed in Chapter Six of this text.
2. Read or review Richard Majors's "Cool Pose: The Proud Signature of Black Survival" (p. 471), and using his essay as your critical framework, refute or defend Coleman's claim that Joe Camel is essentially a black character who makes a special appeal to African-American children.
3. Discuss in class the tone that Coleman adopts. Why does she use a nonacademic, "homegirl" style in her essay?
4. Using Coleman's selection as a model, write an essay in which you explore the appeal of the Marlboro Man. Be sure to note the differences in the audiences to which the two characters appeal.

5. Compare Joe Camel with other cartoon characters that target children (you might read or review Andy Medhurst's "Batman, Deviance, and Camp," p. 323, and George Lewis's "From Common Dullness to Fleeting Wonder," p. 340). Write an essay in which you explore how cool or camp characters especially appeal to children.
6. Interview younger siblings or other children you know, and ask them about their familiarity with Joe Camel. Then write an essay defending, refuting, or modifying Coleman's argument.

McCREA ADAMS

Advertising Characters: The Pantheon of Consumerism

<hr>

||||||||||||||||||||||||||||||||||||||||||||||||||||||||||||||||

From the Quaker Oats Quaker and Betty Crocker to Joe Isuzu and Spuds MacKenzie, American advertisers have been inventing "person-alities" to pitch the product since the nineteenth century. In this semiotic survey of America's advertising characters, McCrea Adams (b. 1952) traces the mythological descent of such figures and their eventual en-shrinement at the heart of commercial culture. But not all such characters are invented; genuine social heroes may be enlisted as well. The result? A teacher may show her class a picture of George Washington and hear her students identify him as "someone who sold stuff on TV"—or maybe just Joe Camel in a wig. McCrea Adams, who wrote this essay as a UCLA student, has published articles on poetry and popular music history. A book and film reviewer for the Dow Jones and Prodigy on-line computer systems, Adams currently is a project editor at Salem Press and, on the side, a rock-and-roll keyboardist.

Advertising characters, those people or animals that symbolize various products, have been with us for a long time. The Quaker Oat Quaker appeared in 1877; Psyche, the White Rock Soda girl, debuted in 1894. The twentieth century was only four years old when the Campbell's Soup Kids arrived. Betty Crocker was born, full-grown, in the mid-1930s.[1] Back in Psyche's youth, when neither advertising nor psychology were huge fields of their own, these characters were created by people trying to sell their own products. Usually someone at the manufacturing company would dream up what seemed to be an appropriate identifying symbol for their product. No one is sure, for example,

<hr>

1. "Cherubic But Not as Chubby," *Time,* Apr. 4, 1983, p. 60.

exactly how the chick that symbolizes Bon Ami cleanser began, but apparently a company founder, in the nineteenth century, started wrapping soap bars in paper with a little chick design on it; the enigmatic "hasn't scratched yet" slogan was not added until later.[2]

Advertising characters and symbols can be seen as part of a continuum of fictions and fantasies given life by the restless, fertile human imagination. Further back than recorded history, mythical or religious beings were created and attributed with fantastic exploits and superhuman powers. Oral traditions passed down descriptions and tales of these "characters" before writing on papyrus was invented, let alone radio and television. The gods of ancient Egypt, the Greek gods on Mount Olympus, the Norse gods, and the pantheon of Nigeria's Yoruba people all are extensions of these prehistoric traditions. The gods and superheroes of Finnish mythology present an interesting similarity to modern advertising characters in that beings from ancient times and those of a much more recent era coexist in the same cycles of stories. Ad characters, too, inhabit a syncretic world in which Moe (Three Stooges) Howard stands beside Albert Einstein and where Leonardo da Vinci fumbles ineffectually in a modern, high-tech office. The ancient Romans adapted the Greek gods to their own culture, just as modern advertising adapts characters from the past, both real and mythical. And the birth of an advertising "being" can seem as mysterious and lost in antiquity as that of any mythical creature. Clarence Birdseye, for example, was a real frozen-food pioneer (born December 9, 1886), but he has been in the character pantheon so long that he now seems fictitious.

The Yoruba pantheon includes a character called Eshu who frequently appears in mythology: the "trickster," that supernatural being dedicated to confusing things, to befuddling and bedeviling us poor mortals. The relationship of the trickster to advertising is too obvious to require much discussion, but suffice it to say that without illusion, trickery, and magical transformations, the power of our advertising gods would be lessened considerably. We even have a double-trickster: Joe Isuzu, the lying car salesman for Isuzu, lets us laugh at the advertising "trick" even as he sells us cars. The Yoruba pantheon also includes a god of iron, Ogun, who has evolved into the god of war and transportation; nowadays he is the god who protects a city dweller's Mercedes. As our ad characters are, Ogun is a powerful "transformer"—and, like them, he is both transformer and transformed, since he himself has changed through time.[3]

Unlike religions, which seek to make sense of the cosmos and create a way to deal with mortality, folk tales and their heroes evolved largely

---

2. *Nation's Business,* March, 1981, pp. 70–71.

3. Dr. Donald Cosentino provided information on the Yoruba in UCLA lectures in 1987.

as a source of entertainment. They also, however, often typify a culture's valued qualities, such as strength or mental agility. They represent the oral tradition in a secular context with fables of giants (such as Jack's nemesis atop the beanstalk), mythical animals, heroes such as Paul Bunyan, and tales of witches and fairies. Now, in the world of television, we have the Jolly Green Giant and the Keebler elves, ably personifying the apparently valued ability to invent new frozen foods and cookies. Television, in effect, has provided us with an artificial, electronic oral tradition, entering our minds through visual and audio stimuli.

Ellen Weis is the director of San Francisco's Museum of Modern   5
Mythology, which has a collection of over three thousand artifacts, including an eight-foot plastic Jolly Green Giant and a motorized Buster Brown display from 1915. "Every society has mythology," Weis says. "In some societies it's religion. Our religion is consumerism."[4] She points out that some mythical beings were half man, half god, and that advertising characters are half man, half product. Both are "given enormous credence in their society. Just look at Cap'n Crunch." When she says that one "can really learn a lot from an original drawing of Elsie the Cow," many things come to mind—fertility, the milk of human kindness, the relationship between humans and nature, and perhaps even the fact that Hindus hold the cow to be sacred.

Psychologist Carol Moog, who does "psychological semiotics" for advertising agencies, similarly has explored the meaning of Lever Brothers' Snuggle fabric-softener teddy bear: "The bear is an ancient symbol of aggression, but when you create a teddy bear, you provide a softer, nurturant side." This combination is the "perfect image for a fabric softener that tames the rough texture of clothing," according to Moog.[5] She advised Lever Brothers to keep Snuggle genderless and avoid mixing Snuggle with live humans in ads. "To keep the magic, it has to be just Snuggle and the viewer communicating. The teddy bear acts as a bridge between the consumer's rational and more instinctual, emotional side." Notice the supernatural overtones and the intimation of a sort of prayer. Another media observer, perhaps only half-jokingly, went so far as to call Snuggle "the anti-Christ."[6] Ellen Weis again: "These images get into our subconscious and stay with us for life. It's very important to be aware of how powerful they are." Not everyone agrees with these sorts of evaluations; as George Lois, chairman of Lois Pitts Gershon Pon, puts it, "These psychologists tend to be overly intellectual and a little tutti-frutti."

4. Carrie Dolan, "Why is Capt. Crunch a Little Like Zeus?" *Wall Street Journal,* Feb. 1, 1988, pp. 1, 20.

5. Ronald Alsop, "Agencies Scrutinize Their Ads for Psychological Symbolism," *Wall Street Journal,* June 11, 1987, p. 27.

6. Christina Bauman, personal communication.

An early phase of advertising in the United States that might be termed "protoadvertising" evolved during the nineteenth century. Prime examples include the "Wild West" show and the hundreds of tonics and elixirs identified with a "doctor" who had supposedly created them to cure whatever ailed one. Here again are links with myth and power. In the first case, the reality of "the West" blurs into a re-creation of it, with some of the real characters (Wild Bill Hickok, Buffalo Bill Cody) themselves—now trickster figures—helping to smudge the lines between reality and legend, person and performer. In the second, a fabricated character ("Dr. Whoever") is presented as the inventor of a patent medicine.

As the twentieth century progressed, radio and then television became filled with advertisements, and newspapers and magazines continued to bombard us with them; the streets filled with billboards, and the sky with skywriting and banners. Something had changed. There were too many gods in the pantheon and too many doctors selling us tonic. As advertising became a billion-dollar industry and television entered nearly every American home, the messages of advertising and the various characters and symbols used to convey those messages multiplied almost beyond comprehension. Life in the information society is now cluttered with sensory input of all kinds, and advertising is the most unrelenting demander of our attention. Rhetoric has been dubbed "the art of saying nothing finely," but the rhetoric of advertising is the art of saying nothing incessantly. We try our best to screen it out, turn it off, scoff at it, curse at it, laugh at it. But it is pervasive, and its characters—real, unreal, alive, animated—invade our consciousness, invited or not.

Because of this invasion, the lines between reality and fiction no longer seem very clear. Actors sell products as themselves, as anonymous pitchmen, or as created characters, and what's the difference? They are all transformed into tricksters before the camera. ("I'm an actor," John Carradine once intoned in a bank commercial, "but I'm not acting now.") Politicians in turn sell themselves as products—packaged, prepared characters. How much difference is there really between the two Ronalds, McDonald and Reagan? Quite possibly the viewer, or reader, or consumer no longer notices or cares what is real and what is not. Television, in particular, streams on endlessly, real and unreal side by side in a funny and terrible jumble of images and sounds, all trivialized by the constant yammering of commercials.

Deities in the Pantheon

The pantheon of advertising characters contains far more beings than we can recall at one time. Some have been short-lived, others have lasted for ninety years or more. Juan Valdez grows our coffee and Mrs. Olsen   10 brews it, although Joe DiMaggio and Mr. Coffee have given her some competition. Madge tells us how to have younger-looking hands; Mr. Clean and the Brawny man help us mop the floor. The lonely Maytag repairman waits for a phone call. Mr. Goodwrench fixes the car, Mrs. Paul makes fish sticks, Aunt Jemima serves pancakes, and Joe Isuzu lies.

Some distinctions can be drawn among the various types of advertising characters and spokespeople, provided we bear in mind that such classifications are not as clear and clean as they might at first appear. One basic distinction is between representations of real people and depictions of created characters. Within the "real" category are celebrities as themselves, corporate spokespersons as themselves, and "person-in-the-street" testimonials. Within the "created" realm are actors strongly identified with particular characters (e.g., Charmin's Mr. Whipple); actors representing a character with no unique actor identification (the Marlboro Man, for example); and actors as unnamed people shown doing things in commercials—primarily various versions of having fun. There are also cartoon characters, both still and animated (a classic is Speedy Alka-Seltzer).

Characters frequently transcend the boundaries between categories, however. Mr. Whipple is played by a live actor but has also been turned into a drawing used on packaging; conversely, symbols spawn actors to portray them. The haziest division perhaps is between created characters and "real" celebrities. The fictional Rosie of Rosie's Diner, for example, appears in an ad with Rosey Grier, making jokes about what a good name Rosie is and teaching him that Bounty really is the "quicker-picker-upper."

Cartoon characters, as well as live characters, can be either created specifically for a product or appropriated from elsewhere. Cap'n Crunch was created by Jay Ward's animation studio specifically for the cereal itself (as was Tony the Tiger, by a different studio, for Sugar Frosted Flakes). Hanna-Barbera's Flintstones, on the other hand, have been taken from their "real" world of Bedrock and used as pitchmen for at least two wildly divergent products. The first, strange as it may seem today, was Winston cigarettes, back when Winston cosponsored the original TV show in the sixties; another, more recently, has been their namesake, Flintstones vitamins. Charles M. Schulz's Peanuts gang has sold all kinds of things, including insurance for Metropolitan Life. Even the voice behind so many cartoons, Mel Blanc, has done one of those American Express "unrecognized celebrities" ads.

Some agencies created a sympathetic, "real" character for an actor to portray, while others take a more exaggerated approach. The "Sparkletts man" is a prime example of the former. Warm, friendly, handsome, competent, he happily drove his green Sparkletts truck around under sunny California skies while reciting happy, humorous rhymes about himself "and Sparkletts water makin' friends." Mr. Whipple aptly embodies the second (although he certainly has plenty of company). Played by ex-vaudevillian Dick Wilson, he first appeared in October, 1964, uttering "the whine heard round the world: 'Please don't squeeze the Charmin.'"[7] Wilson helped make Charmin the best-selling toilet paper in the United States; he now earns a handy six-figure income for about sixteen days of filming a year. Interestingly, both these actors received so much exposure from their commercials that they soon became celebrities in their own right. Again, they are not alone; Mrs. Olsen, the Bartles and James characters, and more recently Joe Isuzu can be counted among their ranks.

Actor Jim Varney plays a character named Ernest P. Worrell, created   15 by Nashville agency Carden & Cherry, who sticks his head in the window while saying "Hey, Vern!" Varney's Ernest is supposed to represent someone in everyone's neighborhood—"the guy who drives you crazy yet cracks you up as he's doing it."[8] Well, maybe; at any rate, the Vern/ Ernest commercials are used to sell a variety of products in over a hundred local markets. And in one of those odd quirks of show business, Ernest P. Worrell somehow became the lead character in a feature film, *Ernest Saves Christmas.* (The best analogue that comes to mind is the recent feature starring Cassandra Peterson's Elvira character. As a camp horror-movie host, Elvira is about as close to being a commercial character as one can get without actually being one.)

Nobody's Perfect: Troubles on Olympus

The power attributed to advertising spokespersons—be they real or invented—is manifest in the problems they can create. The Federal Trade Commission announced in 1978 that it would begin putting pressure on stars involved in ads that make verifiably false claims. Pat Boone agreed to stop promoting an ineffective acne cream; former astronaut Gordon Cooper stopped advertising an automobile gas valve. In 1985, former football star Johnny Unitas was sued by two investors in a Florida financial services firm for misrepresenting a product he endorsed in a radio ad. The suit argued, their attorney said, that "a celebrity has some obligation to . . . make sure he is not being used in a scheme of fraud." Some entertainment agents and lawyers now require indemnification clauses holding the advertisers responsible for any fines levied against their clients.[9]

---

7. "Mr. Whipple, Dick Wilson, Wraps 20th Year," *People,* Nov. 12, 1984, p. 151.
8. Rudy Maxa and Bina Kiyonaga, "Hey, Vern," *People,* Dec. 2, 1985, p. 121.
9. "A Celebrity Malpractice?" *Newsweek,* Dec. 23, 1985, p. 66.

Other problems occur as well. Bill Cosby, for example, has sold so many different products that some say it is hard to identify him with any one campaign. His "overexposure" was blamed by one expert for the failure of E. F. Hutton's 1986 campaign featuring Cosby. Distinguished actor John Houseman, very effective when promoting financial house Smith Barney, was a flop at selling Big Macs. "I can't imagine John Houseman ever having been in a McDonald's," noted adman Jay Chiat.[10]

The J. Walter Thompson agency failed to sell Burger King's burgers with its huge ($40 million) campaign built around a search for the mysterious (fictional) "Herb," who had never eaten a Whopper. The public was completely uninterested. Thompson president Steve Bowen reflected that Herb never should have been revealed as a nerd, as he finally was. "Herb should have been Robert Redford," he claimed. "In reality, everything in life is aspirational, even fast food."[11] Note that Herb and Redford are viewed (albeit whimsically) as inhabitants of the same reality. Since we only "know" Redford from his fictional roles, there are many permutations of the Robert Redford persona. Similarly, Bill Cosby has been a comedian, a spy, a teacher (Chet Kincaid), and a doctor with a lawyer wife (Cliff Huxtable). And he has sold for Jell-O, Coke, Ford, Texas Instruments, and E. F. Hutton. Cosby and Redford are both changelings—and tricksters of the highest order.

Another sort of problem befell Ivory Soap executives, who were horrified when the media discovered that the woman whose portrait graced their boxes of "99 44/100 % pure" detergent was Marilyn Chambers, an adult film star. This was overexposure of quite a different sort than Cosby's. In this case, the advertising character—the fiction—snagged on an unacceptable reality. The performers in pornographic movies, after all, really do perform explicit sexual acts, and this is *too* real for the world of selling. Ironically, advertising, which thrives on the sexual tease, must evade the actuality of intercourse. Ads give glimpses, magic shiny moments. Look but don't touch, they say; look and go buy. They attempt to create the urge, but place their products as the necessary middle step to obtaining satisfaction.

While human spokespersons are the most problematic for advertisers, nothing is exempt from controversy. Even man's best friend can end up in hot water. Anheuser-Busch's Spuds MacKenzie made a big splash when he arrived, a forty-seven-pound English bull terrier who sometimes appeared with "a trio of spandexed honeys" called the Spudettes.[12] Spuds's message, according to Budweiser manager Joe Corcoran, is that

20

10. Christy Marshall, "It Seemed Like a Good Idea at the Time," *Forbes,* Dec. 28, 1987, p. 98.

11. Ibid.

12. Bernice Kanner, "Top Dog: Spudsmania," *New York,* Sept. 28, 1987, pp. 20–23.

"you can be a hip, happy trendsetter like Spuds." No information was revealed about the "real" Spuds—advertisers insisted they wanted to preserve the mystique—although Spuds himself did hit the talk-show circuit. Toward the end of 1987 Spuds got some bad press, not because of complaints about the degrading ads with dancing bimbos, but for reportedly being a female posing as a male. Then, as if such deceptions were not bad enough, she or he soon stood accused of being a pit bull.

A more serious concern is whether Spuds may be a corrupting influence on young people. The Spuds campaign, centering as it does on a household pet (and being aimed at the lowest common denominator), may well appeal to children way below the drinking age. Federal authorities refused to act on complaints about the matter. Ohio's liquor commission, however, has long had a regulation prohibiting the use of Santa Claus in ads that "might entice children to drink," and in December of 1987, it was considering whether to ban Budweiser Christmas promos and packaging that pictured Spuds MacKenzie dressed up as Santa.[13] A surprising number of mythological overtones, it must be noted, appear in these anecdotes about Spuds MacKenzie. Spuds is a Dionysian figure and, as an animal surrounded by women, is certainly a relative of the satyr. His sexual ambiguity is reminiscent of Tiresius and Hermaphroditus. He also has folkloric ties with Saint Nicholas/Santa Claus and, in adults' fears that children will be enticed to follow him, with the Pied Piper of Hamlin.

The Pantheon from Hell

Although there are intriguing similarities between advertising characters and beings from folklore, mythology, and religion, the ways in which they differ are crucial. Religion and folklore come from the human capacity, even compulsion, to imagine the unseen. Humans want to understand things—and if we can't, we at least want to come up with a plausible and entertaining story. We create art; we have a language that can depict a past behind the moment, a future before it. That is what makes humans human; that is what we are. The supernatural is born of a sense of mystery and wonder. The characters of advertising, on the other hand, are created not to help understand the universe but to move the merchandise. In a sense, they even help to hide the truth by concealing the workings of the capitalist universe. They are self-consciously created by committees who have probed the mysteries by doing market research and studying the psychology of the consumer. Advertising characters muddle the past and diminish the future into a time when new

---

13. "Spuds, You Dog," *Newsweek,* Dec. 14, 1987, p. 68.

consumption will occur. They represent the loss of mystery, and its replacement by an empty mechanistic cycle of watching and buying.

Mark Crispin Miller points out that television and its advertising have become so self-referential, and often so slyly self-mocking, that the viewer no longer has a standard by which to judge them:

> As advertising has become more self-referential, it has also become harder to distinguish from the various other features of our media culture. . . . TV is suffused with the enlightened irony of the common man, the "little guy," or—to use a less dated epithet—the smart shopper. . . . Whatever was a source of pleasure in the past is now derided by and for the knowing, whether it's . . . the silent movies derisively excerpted in the ads for Hershey or Toshiba, or the cowboy pictures lampooned by Philip Morris . . . or the Mona Lisa as ridiculed to sell Peter Pan peanut butter.[14]

Miller calls this ongoing derision "compulsive trashing." It permeates advertising, and the use of historical figures as advertising characters is one of the ways it manifests itself. Benjamin Franklin and Thomas Jefferson have represented banks, and George Washington and Abraham Lincoln have been used in innumerable pitches—especially in the month of February. Ralph Nader complained in an open letter to President Reagan that while it isn't illegal, "using revered leaders from our nation's past as salespeople or hawkers [is] in the realm of sleaziness."[15] Nader wrote that a teacher reported holding up a picture of Washington and having a child identify him as someone who sold stuff on TV. Historical figures are often used in gag ads, making the "trashing" overt. Historical entertainment figures are also used and abused. Laurel and Hardy look-alikes, for example, have sold windshield wipers. And in a very strange case, IBM's agency built a successful campaign around an imitator of Charlie Chaplin's Tramp character. Remember that in the most famous scene in Chaplin's film *Modern Times,* the Tramp was whirled wildly about by the huge gears and belts of a gigantic industrial machine. There is a terrible irony in the perverting of the pathetic, loner Tramp figure into a character selling computers for IBM, a gigantic, impersonal "machine" of the postindustrial age.

The Tramp campaign and all "historical" campaigns smudge the line 25 between the real and the fictitious. In a very real way, the question eventually becomes "What is reality?" Television programming and advertisements present a stream of images in which fiction and nonfiction are nearly indistinguishable; news, entertainment, and advertising all look

14. Mark Crispin Miller, "Deride and Conquer," in *Watching Television,* Todd Gitlin, ed. (New York: Pantheon Books, 1986). The excerpts are scattered throughout Miller's essay, which begins on p. 183.

15. "Would Honest Abe Lie to You?" *Consumer Reports,* Sept. 1985, p. 567.

more and more alike. The Tramp was a fiction, created by Chaplin; he was then recreated by an actor imitating Chaplin as the Tramp. The crucial distinction is that Chaplin's Tramp was art, whereas IBM's Tramp is pure commerce. The danger is that we may be presented with so much slick, dazzling commerce that we no longer care about the art or the history. Consumer entertainment is, after all, very convenient. The George Washington pitching products on TV is in some ways more real than the other—this one can be seen "in the flesh," before our very eyes. This unreal television world has at least partially displaced the other. A consumer survey taken in early 1985 showed that 93 percent of the people polled remembered who Mr. Clean was, although he hadn't been on the air for years, but only 56 percent knew who George Bush was.[16]

The artificial pantheon of advertising beings represents not a link with our history and culture but a break from any meaningful sense of who we are. Advertising presents a self-perpetuating cycle of clichés based only on older clichés. A comedian once complained about the ad campaign for Country Time lemon drink that boasted it "tastes just like good old-fashioned lemonade." He said, Hey, wait a minute, folks; lemonade isn't something from our past, some long-forgotten secret. Anyone can make it, any time; you only need lemons, water, and sugar. But the culture of consumerism would prefer that we forget that.

The lying Joe Isuzu character represents something even darker. He embodies a disillusionment, a sense that there are no ethics left in our society. Indeed, we have heard so much news about illegality and deception in Washington and on Wall Street that the cliché of the sleazy car salesman seems a fitting symbol for a large corporation. Trickster Joe Isuzu lies and—since the audience is in on the joke—tells us to laugh it off. Isuzu lies to sell cars, politicians lie to get elected, and we've all been lied to so much that we find it hard to believe anything. The creators of the pantheon of consumerism must go to ever greater lengths to capture our attention and remind us that advertising characters, the gods of commerce, are our heroes and protectors. Kurt Vonnegut once remarked that when he tried to think about what American culture was, all that came to mind were television commercials. With every passing year, that observation seems more valid.

Reading the Text

1. According to Adams, why is the use of characters an especially effective strategy for selling products?

---

16. Mark N. Vamos, "New Life for Madison Avenue's Old-time Stars," *Business Week,* Apr. 1, 1985, p. 94.

2. What differences are there in the impact of fictional and real advertising characters?
3. What problems may arise when using characters as an advertising strategy?

Reading the Signs

1. In class, brainstorm on the blackboard as many advertising characters as you can, drawing both from Adams's essay and your own experience. With your class, categorize the characters, perhaps according to Adams's fictional and real groups, or according to gender, ethnicity, or profession. Then discuss the significance of your categories. How do the different groups appeal to consumers to buy their products? What do they reveal about American values?

2. Explore in a journal entry the appeal of Joe Camel, keeping in mind both Adams's essay and Wanda Coleman's "Say It Ain't Cool, Joe" (p. 356).

3. Select one of the products from the "Portfolio of Ads" (pp. 156–165), and sketch a new character that could serve as an advertising representative of that product. Then write an essay in which you explain how your character would act as a sign. How would it sell the product? What values would it project?

4. Adams quotes Ellen Weis of San Francisco's Museum of Modern Mythology as saying "Every society has mythology. In some societies, it's religion. Our religion is consumerism." Write an essay defending or refuting Weis's claim. To support your position, you can draw upon your own behavior as a consumer and your observations of others; you may also want to read or review Laurence Shames's "The More Factor" (p. 25).

5. In recent years, athletic shoe companies have transformed real athletes into characters to sell their products (for instance, Nike's Bo Jackson "just do it" campaign). Analyze the appeal of one such campaign, basing your analysis on specific examples of ads (you might watch some sports shows on television for broadcast ads, or study an issue of *Sports Illustrated* for print ads).

GERARD JONES, RON RANDALL, AND RANDY ELLIOTT

Doomed by Deconstructo

||||||||||||||||||||||||||||||||||||||||||||||||||||||||||||||

*Since the 1960s, a philosophical movement known as "deconstruction"
has caused professors of everything from English literature to legal theory
to question the fundamental principles and presuppositions of their disciplines. Deconstruction takes as one of its most important premises the
semiotic conviction that language is a reflection of cultural codes, not a
signifier of truth or reality. Thus, this movement can be seen as undermining the truth claims of every science and intellectual system, for if
our knowledge is relative to the linguistic system in which it is constructed,
how can we know anything that is outside the system?*

*In this fanciful excerpt from a DC Comics series starring the heroes
of the Justice League Europe, cartoonists Gerard Jones, Ron Randall,
and Randy Elliott illustrate what it would be like if a deconstructive
critic got loose in the world of superheroes. This excerpt shows the
introduction of Deconstructo—and the Justice League's response to him.
Alas, even the citadel of semiotics might come crashing down!*

Reading the Signs

1. How does Deconstructo illustrate the description of deconstruction given
   in the headnote? Note particularly the target of his attacks, and his aphor-
   isms (e.g., "There is no meaning").
2. Discuss in class your interpretation of the appearance of Deconstructo.
   What is the significance of his clothing and hair style? How, in short, are
   we expected to "read" him by his appearance? How does he compare with
   the Justice League characters? You might consult Elizabeth Wilson's "Oppositional Dress" (p. 45).
3. In what way could this comic be considered "postmodern" (see the introduction to Chapter Four, p. 233)? Be sure to take into account the appearance of Batman in the section reprinted here.
4. What sort of hero would Robert Ray ("The Thematic Paradigm," p. 241)
   call Deconstructo? Write an essay in which you explore Deconstructo's
   status as a hero.
5. Visit a comic book store and buy one of the new, socially conscious comics,
   such as *Brotherman,* a comic book for African-Americans. Write a semiotic
   analysis of it, describing how it uses the comic genre to reach new audiences
   with new messages.

PART TWO

ISSUES

6.   SPEAK NO EVIL: THE POLITICS OF FREE SPEECH

7.   A GATHERING OF TRIBES: MULTICULTURAL SEMIOTICS

8.   STREET SIGNS: GANG CULTURE IN THE U.S.A.

9.   YOU'VE COME A LONG WAY, MAYBE: GENDER CODES IN
     AMERICAN CULTURE

10. JOURNALS OF THE PLAGUE YEARS: THE SOCIAL
     MYTHOLOGY OF AIDS

The Parental Advisory Label is a registered certification mark of the Recording Industry of America.

CHAPTER SIX

SPEAK NO EVIL

The Politics of Free Speech

Imagine that you're in an editing group reading a classmate's essay and you find something in the writing that you find personally offensive. What would you do? Ask the author to change it (after all, you *are* an editor giving your advice)? What if the author gets defensive and refuses to change the offending passage on the grounds of his or her First Amendment rights to free speech? How would you feel then? And how would you feel about the First Amendment?

Free speech: Who, in principle, could be against it? And yet who, in practice, hasn't run into *something* that has made you want to draw the line *somewhere?* At this very moment you may have such an issue raging on your own campus. Maybe it's a fraternity songbook, or a visit by a speaker from the Nation of Islam. Has your campus struggled with a "hate speech" code? Which side are you on? How would you defend your position?

The essays in this chapter show you what a range of writers say about freedom of expression, but the fact is, there's no easy answer. No sensitive person could be in *favor* of hate speech, but many enlightened people are equally concerned with what might happen once our constitutionally guaranteed rights to freedom of speech are tampered with, in even the slightest way. The result is a kind of deadlock that leaves room for a semiotic analysis of the framework behind each position but not for a simple answer as to which side is right.

From a semiotic perspective, the battle over the First Amendment cuts to the heart of the nature of political culture. The issues are basic. Who gets to speak, the semiotician asks, and who gets to decide who speaks? What is protected speech, and where do we draw the line? Or do we draw the line? Defenders of the First Amendment tend to take a very broad position on the matter, insisting that no lines at all be drawn between permitted and unpermitted expression. Virtually anything beyond shouting "Fire!" in a crowded theater or uttering explicitly threatening "fighting words" is protected speech, from this point of view. Thus, when the American Nazis were forbidden by a municipal ordinance from marching in full Nazi regalia through a neighborhood populated by Holocaust survivors in Skokie, Illinois, in the 1970s, they were represented in their court challenge by the American Civil Liberties Union. Though the organization knew that it would lose many of its supporters, the ACLU chose to stand upon a strict interpretation of the First Amendment's words: "Congress shall make no law respecting an establishment of religion, or prohibiting the free exercise thereof; or abridging the freedom of speech, or of the press; or the right of the people peaceably to assemble, and to petition the Government for a redress of grievances." In effect, the ACLU took the position that the text of the First Amendment is clear and unambiguous and so not open to adjustment to suit special conditions.

Well, what do *you* think? If a Nazi group wanted to organize a parade through your neighborhood, would you side with the ACLU, or would you argue that surely the line has to be drawn somewhere? What if the group wanted to parade past an elementary school? A synagogue?

If you're not so sure that the First Amendment should protect everything, you're not alone. Though believers in free speech, some feminist critics, for example, have decried the misogynistic lyrics of many rap and heavy metal songs, arguing that if a choice must be made between the safety of women and the sanctity of free expression, safety should come first. Similarly, students and faculty who grew up laughing along with George Carlin's classic comic routine on the seven words you can't use on radio or television have drawn up lists of their own of "fighting words" that should be deleted from university campuses.

Meanwhile the political right, the traditional force for censorship in America, has advocated restricting a wide range of art, from Robert Mapplethorpe exhibits to Ice-T's lyrics. The National Endowment for the Arts's sponsorship of works that offend the taste of conservative legislators and their constituents has resulted in unprecedented restrictions upon which works may be funded by NEA grants. Funded artists have even been required to sign a kind of decency oath by which they pledge not to offend religious or sexual sensibilities. Such restrictions actually represent a compromise, for the original goal of some legislators, such as Senator Jesse Helms, was to eliminate the NEA altogether.

For its part, the Supreme Court, though currently conservative, has taken a rather broad stance on the First Amendment, upholding the freedom to burn both the American flag and Ku Klux Klan–style crosses. A recent legal decision absolving the heavy metal band Judas Priest from responsibility for the suicidal behavior of two of its fans has signalled yet another instance of judicial unwillingness to restrict free speech. But the courts *are* getting uneasy. Rap music is touching a nerve.

Rap and Race

For at the same time that the courts were exonerating white metallists, the distributors of 2 Live Crew's "As Nasty as They Wanna Be" album were being prosecuted with some initial success. Eventually, the prosecutions failed on appeal due to the court system's history of protecting speech that is found to be merely offensive. But speech that is threatening is another matter. The courts have held since 1942 that "fighting words"—speech that may incite someone to violence—are not protected under the terms of the First Amendment. Such a legal precedent may eventually lead to restrictions on lyrics like the ones found in Ice-T's 1992 rap "Cop Killer," which includes the lines "I'm 'bout to bust some shots off/I'm 'bout to dust some cops off." Though Ice-T claims that his rap is simply an artist's dramatic interpretation of the sort of thing a gangster might say, he eventually asked his distributor, Time Warner, to pull the number from future cuts of his album rather than face the potential legal and commercial consequences of a growing national uproar against him. In the end, Time Warner simply cut Ice-T loose.

You probably can recall the whole flap. What did you think at the time? Did you feel that something of your own culture, your own music, was under attack? Or did you sympathize with the position of police officers who felt that songs like "Cop Killer" endangered their lives? What did your friends think? Would you feel comfortable discussing the issue in class, or would you fear that the whole matter is too sensitive?

Likely as not, any discussion of rap lyrics you might have with your friends would eventually end up in a discussion of race as well. For as *Newsweek* recognized in a June 29, 1992, cover story, "Rap and Race," the ruckus over rap is a projection, in code, of a deeper division in American society. You may see rap as youth music, but in many quarters it is seen as race music. Indeed, *Newsweek* quoted someone in the country music industry who attributed the soaring popularity of country music singers like Garth Brooks to a white backlash against rap. Think of your own high school experience: Were the kids who went for rap the same as those who were heavy metal fans? How does race affect society's response to the two kinds of music? Does it influence the current

Discussing the Signs of Free Speech

List on the blackboard all the possible names for the different ethnic groups represented in your class, being sure not to censor yourselves. Then discuss the significance of these names. Which would you not use under any circumstance? Which might you use, and when? Which would you use only at home or with members of the same ethnicity? Would you use any only with members of different ethnicities?

popularity of grunge music, the Seattle sound? Then consider: Have heavy metal or grunge lyrics met with the same opposition as raps?

Policing Language

Whether spoken, written, or rapped, language, in short, is rarely politically innocent. "Sticks and stones may break your bones, but names will really hurt you" is the political reality of the sign. Should you doubt the power of "mere" signs and symbols, consider that some twenty years after the fact, Los Angeles Dodger fans still recall (or are not allowed to forget by the Dodger management) how Rick Monday once rescued an American flag in the Dodger outfield seconds before it could be torched by a group of demonstrators before a game in the early seventies. By 1988, in the wake of the Supreme Court decision that ruled that flag burning was protected by the First Amendment, legislators on both sides of the aisle called for a constitutional amendment just to protect the flag.

Words, of course, also count as politically charged signs. Consider the statement you make every time you identify yourself as, say, an African-American, rather than a "black" or "Negro," or as a "Latina" rather than an "Hispanic." What are you saying to the world when you use these words? How do they empower you? Can you tell your classmates, especially if they aren't from your own racial group, why you want them to use the name for you that you yourself use? How do you feel if they refuse?

For the semiotician, the restrictions placed upon speech provide a particularly striking field for analysis. A semiotic analysis, for example, can begin with the dos and don'ts of speech and expression, probing what a culture permits and prohibits to determine the cultural forces and mythologies behind its speech codes. This is as true in America as anywhere else, for while we like to tell ourselves that we are free to say whatever we want, a moment's reflection shows that this is not true. Think of all the things you can't say in public. What are the sources of those taboos? Do you tailor your speech to your company? How, and why?

Such questions can help you see how the politics of discourse, of the means by which accepted and prohibited speech are determined, is a central feature of your daily life. Our students have described arguments in class over whether to use the word "murder" or "assassination" when referring to the death of Martin Luther King, Jr., for example. Have you ever gotten into an argument over what to call the civil disturbances in Los Angeles in the spring of 1992? Was it "unrest" or an "uprising," a "riot" or a "rebellion"? Can you decode someone's political position on the basis of the words they use? Think of some examples from your own experience. Do you spell the word "women" with a "y"—as in "womyn"—and if so, why? Do you say "people of color" rather than "minorities" or "nonwhites"? Again, if so, why?

PC or Not PC

Your choice of language, of course, is often shaped by the habits and preferences of the groups with which you study, work, and live. Indeed, the force of such social pressure has been granted its own label by its detractors: "political correctness." At one time or another, you have probably felt the pressure to be "politically correct" in one discussion or another. Especially prevalent on college campuses, the PC controversy tends to appear when students and faculty feel that they are implicitly or explicitly expected to adopt certain political positions. You can probably think of a number of examples without any difficulty. The question for semiotic inquiry is not whether you should adopt such positions or whether it is right or wrong that a given political tone should prevail on your college campus. Rather, the semiotic question is: What precisely is the significance of the PC debate? What does it mean?

Consider what is at stake in any PC controversy, whether it involves banning fraternity songbook lyrics, the adoption of a "friendly speech" code, or the more generalized feeling that you are not welcome to espouse some political positions on campus. First, you need to look at the larger cultural system in which such phenomena function. Take the most recent election in your state. What political positions were the candidates pressured to adopt or reject? What were they expected to say about crime, for example, or gay rights? If you think they were free to say whatever they believed about such issues, consider how President Bill Clinton, who had stuck his neck out in 1993 on the controversy over gays in the military, found himself unable to be in Washington on the day of the gay and lesbian march that spring. What forces, do you think, made it appear to the president that the "politically correct" thing to do would be to accept an invitation to speak in Boston that day?

|||||||||||||||||||||||||||||||||||||||||||||||||||||||||||||||||||||||||||||||||||||||||||||||||||||||||||||||||||||||||||

Exploring the Signs of Free Speech

Have you ever had an experience in which you've wanted to "silence"
another person or group? In your journal, explore your response to
this experience. What motivated you to want to restrict the speech of
others? Did you act upon your desires, and if so, did you meet with
resistance? Would you feel the same way today?

But of course, when people shape their language and politics to suit
their perception of public opinion in the nonacademic world, this is not
called PC behavior. From a semiotic perspective, however, it is no
different from what goes on on a college campus; it just tends to run in
the opposite political direction. This is not the way it is described, of
course. Rather, politicians are urged to stick to the "mainstream" of
public opinion, but "mainstream" is just another code word for a certain
political dominance. Who, after all, gets to decide just what the "mainstream" is?

The semiotic lesson, in short, is that both on the campus and in the
larger political arena, the name of the game is "power." Those who are
in a position to dominate in a political controversy don't tend to acknowledge this, however, putting the problem instead in terms of right
and wrong (as in "I'm right and you're wrong"). But once again, who
gets to decide questions of right and wrong? When everyone has an
opinion, where can we turn for absolute assurance?

The Politics of Interpretation

If you long for a place to stand where "truth" and not power will
be your guide in making political decisions, consider the politics of
constitutional interpretation. In America, the U.S. Constitution is supposed to be the document that can point us objectively to the "truth."
But look at what happens every time a key provision of the Constitution
comes up for review. Partisans from all over the political map weigh in
to explain why their reading of the text is the correct one, and the case
moves from court to court, only stopping at the Supreme Court. That
doesn't mean that Supreme Court justices have a magic key to decode
the language of the Constitution, however: They just get the last word.
Indeed, the reason we have a Supreme Court is to ensure that the
potentially endless round of legal interpretation ends *somewhere*. That's
why so much political maneuvering occurs every time a Supreme Court
nomination is made.

Of course, the political nature of judicial interpretation is usually masked by accusations of "playing politics" directed by each side against the other in a constitutional controversy or high court nomination, but the fact is that interpretation, especially constitutional interpretation, is always a matter of playing politics. Most of us like to think that we have the key to the truth, but when we unlock the doors to our opinions we find interpretations, contingencies, not fixed truths.

To acknowledge the political nature of interpretation, even the interpretation of such fundamental texts as the First Amendment, doesn't mean giving up your opinions: It only means bringing to light the full force of your beliefs and those of others. The readings in this chapter may present issues on which you hold strong opinions, but look not only at the content of the issues but at the language in which they are expressed. Pay close attention to the power relations that are at play: Whose interests are at stake in the debate? How does a given position privilege those who hold it? Seeing that your opinions represent your interests doesn't have to invalidate them; it may make you fight for them all the more.

The Readings

This chapter begins addressing free speech issues by looking close to home, at how the issue has affected college campuses. First Nat Hentoff surveys various campus speech code controversies—especially at Stanford University—and finds both a threat to fundamental free speech rights and an implicit double standard whereby some groups may be maligned but not others. Thomas Grey, a Stanford law professor, provides a counterargument in the next selection; he both proposes a framework for a friendly speech code at Stanford and supplies a legal justification for his proposals. Cornel West's "Diverse New World" presents a case for opening up the literary canon at a time of profound ethnic change in America—a position that Todd Gitlin partly endorses in his historical description of the multiculturalist movement and partly criticizes in his warning against making cultural difference a tribalistic absolute. Richard Goldstein follows with an analysis of the basic dilemma that the battle for the First Amendment presents to many progressive thinkers who believe, on the one hand, in the importance of free speech, and on the other, in the need to protect historically vulnerable groups from oppression. Reflecting a similar ambivalence, Barbara Ehrenreich at once decries the "cheap" rebelliousness of raps such as Ice-T's "Cop Killer" and finds in the rapper's easy posturing a reason not to boycott his words. In a coauthored opinion piece, Elaine Lafferty and Tammy Bruce are less sure, pointing out that if cops are going to get upset by "cop-killing" raps, then it's time for mainstream America to hear the misogynistic lyrics that rappers and metallists have been intoning for years. James Crawford's overview of the "English Only" movement profiles the nativist backlash against non-English-speaking immigrants while calling for a multilingual policy that will help unite Americans rather than divide them on linguistic lines. Finally, Gloria Anzaldúa's "How to Tame a Wild Tongue" provides a linguistic and political analysis of Chicano/Chicana speech, showing how important language is to one's sense of personal identity and what differences exist within what appears to be a single linguistic community.

NAT HENTOFF

"Speech Codes" on the Campus and Problems of Free Speech

If you've ever found yourself hesitating to speak up in class for fear that your words might be attacked for being "politically incorrect," then Nat Hentoff's scathing indictment of the "friendly speech" movement now sweeping through American universities may strike a chord. Especially outraged by the speech-limiting proposals at Stanford University, Hentoff (b. 1925) argues that the effect of such codes is to silence not conservative students whose campus newspapers gleefully mock PC discourse, but liberal students who feel intimidated by their more radical classmates and professors. Hentoff also argues that a double standard is at work in the "friendly speech" movement, whereby speech against "unprotected" groups and unpopular opinions may be tolerated and even encouraged. For many years the dean of culture critics at the Village Voice, *Nat Hentoff is also a columnist for the* Washington Post *and a staff writer at* The New Yorker. *In a long career of writing about civil rights and social issues, Hentoff has written numerous books on jazz, politics, education, and free speech.*

During three years of reporting on anti–free-speech tendencies in higher education, I've been at more than twenty colleges and universities—from Washington and Lee and Columbia to Mesa State in Colorado and Stanford.

On this voyage of initially reverse expectations—with liberals fiercely advocating censorship of "offensive" speech and conservatives merrily taking the moral high ground as champions of free expression —the most dismaying moment of revelation took place at Stanford.

In the course of a two-year debate on whether Stanford, like many other universities, should have a speech code punishing language that might wound minorities, women, and gays, a letter appeared in the *Stanford Daily.* Signed by the African-American Law Students Association, the Asian-American Law Students Association, and the Jewish Law Students Association, the letter called for a harsh code. It reflected the letter and the spirit of an earlier declaration by Canetta Ivy, a black leader of student government at Stanford during the period of the grand debate. "We don't put as many restrictions on freedom of speech," she said, "as we should."

Reading the letter by this rare ecumenical body of law students (so pressing was the situation that even Jews were allowed in), I thought of twenty, thirty years from now. From so bright a cadre of graduates, from so prestigious a law school would come some of the law professors, civic leaders, college presidents, and even maybe a Supreme Court justice of the future. And many of them would have learned—like so many other university students in the land—that censorship is okay provided your motives are okay.

The debate at Stanford ended when the president, Donald Kennedy,   5 following the prevailing winds, surrendered his previous position that once you start telling people what they can't say, you will end up telling them what they can't think. Stanford now has a speech code.

This is not to say that these gags on speech—every one of them so overboard and vague that a student can violate a code without knowing he or she has done so—are invariably imposed by student demand. At most colleges, it is the administration that sets up the code. Because there have been racist or sexist or homophobic taunts, anonymous notes or graffiti, the administration feels it must *do something.* The cheapest, quickest way to demonstrate that it cares is to appear to suppress racist, sexist, homophobic speech.

Usually, the leading opposition among the faculty consists of conservatives—when there is opposition. An exception at Stanford was law professor Gerald Gunther, arguably the nation's leading authority on constitutional law. But Gunther did not have much support among other faculty members, conservative or liberal.

At the University of Buffalo Law School, which has a code restricting speech, I could find just one faculty member who was against it. A liberal, he spoke only on condition that I not use his name. He did not want to be categorized as a racist.

On another campus, a political science professor for whom I had great respect after meeting and talking with him years ago, has been silent—students told me—on what Justice William Brennan once called "the pall of orthodoxy" that has fallen on his campus.

When I talked to him, the professor said, "It doesn't happen in my   10 class. There's no 'politically correct' orthodoxy here. It may happen in other places at this university, but I don't know about that." He said no more.

One of the myths about the rise of PC (politically correct) is that, coming from the left, it is primarily intimidating conservatives on campus. Quite the contrary. At almost every college I've been, conservative students have their own newspaper, usually quite lively and fired by a muckraking glee at exposing "politically correct" follies on campus.

By and large, those most intimidated—not so much by the speech codes themselves but by the Madame Defarge–like spirit behind them —are liberal students and those who can be called politically moderate.

I've talked to many of them, and they no longer get involved in class discussions where their views would go against the grain of PC righteousness. Many, for instance, have questions about certain kinds of affirmative action. They are not partisans of Jesse Helms or David Duke, but they wonder whether progeny of middle-class black families should get scholarship preference. Others have a question about abortion. Most are not prolife, but they believe that fathers should have a say in whether the fetus should be sent off into eternity.

Jeff Shesol, a recent graduate of Brown and now a Rhodes scholar at Oxford, became nationally known while at Brown because of his comic strip, "Thatch," which, not too kindly, parodied PC students. At a forum on free speech at Brown before he left, Shesol said he wished he could tell the new students at Brown to have no fear of speaking freely. But he couldn't tell them that, he said, advising the new students to stay clear of talking critically about affirmative action or abortion, among other things, in public.

At that forum, Shesol told me, he said that those members of the 15 left who regard dissent from their views as racist and sexist should realize that they are discrediting their goals. "They're honorable goals," said Shesol, "and I agree with them. I'm against racism and sexism. But these people's tactics are obscuring the goals. And they've resulted in Brown no longer being an open-minded place." There were hisses from the audience.

Students at New York University Law School have also told me that they censor themselves in class. The kind of chilling atmosphere they describe was exemplified last year as a case assigned for a moot court competition became subject to denunciation when a sizable number of law students said it was too "offensive" and would hurt the feelings of gay and lesbian students. The case concerned a divorced father's attempt to gain custody of his children on the grounds that their mother had become a lesbian. It was against PC to represent the father.

Although some of the faculty responded by insisting that you learn to be a lawyer by dealing with all kinds of cases, including those you personally find offensive, other faculty members supported the rebellious students, praising them for their sensitivity. There was little public opposition from the other students to the attempt to suppress the case. A leading dissenter was a member of the conservative Federalist Society.

What is PC to white students is not necessarily PC to black students. Most of the latter did not get involved in the N.Y.U. protest, but throughout the country many black students do support speech codes. A vigorous exception was a black Harvard law school student during a debate on whether the law school should start punishing speech. A white student got up and said that the codes are necessary because without them, black students would be driven away from colleges and thereby deprived of the equal opportunity to get an education.

A black student rose and said that the white student had a hell of a nerve to assume that he—in the face of racist speech—would pack up his books and go home. He's been familiar with that kind of speech all his life, and he had never felt the need to run away from it. He'd handled it before and he could again.

The black student then looked at his white colleague and said that   20
it was condescending to say that blacks have to be "protected" from racist speech. "It is more racist and insulting," he emphasized, "to say that to me than to call me a nigger."

But that would appear to be a minority view among black students. Most are convinced they do need to be protected from wounding language. On the other hand, a good many black student organizations on campus do not feel that Jews have to be protected from wounding language.

Though it's not much written about in reports of the language wars on campuses, there is a strong strain of anti-Semitism among some—not all, by any means—black students. They invite such speakers as Louis Farrakhan, the former Stokely Carmichael (now Kwame Touré), and such lesser but still burning bushes as Steve Cokely, the Chicago commentator who has declared that Jewish doctors inject the AIDS virus into black babies. That distinguished leader was invited to speak at the University of Michigan.

The black student organization at Columbia University brought to the campus Dr. Khallid Abdul Muhammad. He began his address by saying: "My leader, my teacher, my guide is the honorable Louis Farrakhan. I thought that should be said at Columbia Jewniversity."

Many Jewish students have not censored themselves in reacting to this form of political correctness among some blacks. A Columbia student, Rachel Stoll, wrote a letter to the *Columbia Spectator:* "I have an idea. As a white Jewish American, I'll just stand in the middle of a circle comprising . . . Khallid Abdul Muhammad and assorted members of the Black Students Organization and let them all hurl large stones at me. From recent events and statements made on this campus, I gather this will be a good cheap method of making these people feel good."

At UCLA, a black student magazine printed an article indicating   25
there is considerable truth to the *Protocols of the Elders of Zion.*[1] For months, the black faculty, when asked their reactions, preferred not to comment. One of them did say that the black students already considered the black faculty to be insufficiently militant, and the professors didn't want to make the gap any wider. Like white liberal faculty members on other campuses, they want to be liked—or at least not too disliked.

---

1. ***Protocols of the Elders of Zion*** Documents forged by anti-Semites and introduced in the late nineteenth century as "proof" of an international Jewish conspiracy. —EDS.

Along with quiet white liberal faculty members, most black professors have not opposed the speech codes. But unlike the white liberals, many honestly do believe that minority students have to be insulated from barbed language. They do not believe—as I have found out in a number of conversations—that an essential part of an education is to learn to demystify language, to strip it of its ability to demonize and stigmatize you. They do not believe that the way to deal with bigoted language is to answer it with more and better language of your own. This seems very elementary to me, but not to the defenders, black and white, of the speech codes.

Consider University of California president David Gardner. He has imposed a speech code on all the campuses in his university system. Students are to be punished—and this is characteristic of the other codes around the country—if they use "fighting words"—derogatory references to "race, sex, sexual orientation, or disability."

The term "fighting words" comes from a 1942 Supreme Court decision, *Chaplinsky* v. *New Hampshire,* which ruled that "fighting words" are not protected by the First Amendment. That decision, however, has been in disuse at the high court for many years. But it is thriving on college campuses.

In the California code, a word becomes "fighting" if it is directly addressed to "any ordinary person" (presumably, extraordinary people are above all this). These are the kinds of words that are "inherently likely to provoke a violent reaction, *whether or not they actually do.*" (Emphasis added.)

Moreover, he or she who fires a fighting word at any ordinary person   30
can be reprimanded or dismissed from the university because the perpetrator should "reasonably know" that what he or she has said will interfere with the "victim's ability to pursue effectively his or her education or otherwise participate fully in university programs and activities."

Asked Gary Murikami, chairman of the Gay and Lesbian Association at the University of California, Berkeley: "What does it mean?"

Among those—faculty, law professors, college administrators—who insist such codes are essential to the university's purpose of making *all* students feel at home and thereby able to concentrate on their work, there has been a celebratory resort to the Fourteenth Amendment.

That amendment guarantees "equal protection of the laws" to all, and that means to all students on campus. Accordingly, when the First Amendment rights of those engaging in offensive speech clash with the equality rights of their targets under the Fourteenth Amendment, the First Amendment must give way.

This is the thesis, by the way, of John Powell, legal director of the American Civil Liberties Union, even though that organization has now formally opposed all college speech codes—after a considerable civil war among and within its affiliates.

The battle of the amendments continues, and when harsher codes   35
are called for at some campuses, you can expect the Fourteenth
Amendment—which was not intended to censor *speech*—will rise again.

A precedent has been set at, of all places, colleges and universities,
that the principle of free speech is merely situational. As college administrators change, so will the extent of free speech on campus. And invariably, permissible speech will become more and more narrowly defined. Once speech can be limited in such subjective ways, more and
more expression will be included in what is forbidden.

One of the exceedingly few college presidents who speaks out on
the consequences of the anti–free-speech movement is Yale University's
Benno Schmidt:

> Freedom of thought must be Yale's central commitment. It is not
> easy to embrace. It is, indeed, the effort of a lifetime. . . . Much
> expression that is free may deserve our contempt. We may well be
> moved to exercise our own freedom to counter it or to ignore it. But
> universities cannot censor or suppress speech, no matter how obnox-
> ious in content, without violating their justification for existence. . . .
>
> On some other campuses in this country, values of civility and
> community have been offered by some as paramount values of the
> university, even to the extent of superseding freedom of expression.
>
> Such a view is wrong in principle and, if extended, is disastrous
> to freedom of thought. . . . The chilling effects on speech of the
> vagueness and open-ended nature of many universities' prohibitions
> . . . are compounded by the fact that these codes are typically enforced
> by faculty and students who commonly assert that vague notions of
> community are more important to the academy than freedom of
> thought and expression. . . .
>
> This is a flabby and uncertain time for freedom in the United
> States.

On the Public Broadcasting System in June, I was part of a Fred
Friendly panel at Stanford University in a debate on speech codes versus
freedom of expression. The three black panelists strongly supported the
codes. So did the one Asian-American on the panel. But then so did
Stanford law professor, Thomas Grey, who wrote the Stanford code, and
Stanford president Donald Kennedy, who first opposed and then embraced the code. We have a new ecumenicism of those who would
control speech for the greater good. It is hardly a new idea, but the mix
of advocates is rather new.

But there are other voices. In the national board debate at the ACLU
on college speech codes, the first speaker—and I think she had a lot to
do with making the final vote against codes unanimous—was Gwen
Thomas.

A black community college administrator from Colorado, she is a   40
fiercely persistent exposer of racial discrimination.

She started by saying, "I have always felt as a minority person that we have to protect the rights of all because if we infringe on the rights of any persons, we'll be next."

"As for providing a nonintimidating educational environment, our young people have to learn to grow up on college campuses. We have to teach them how to deal with adversarial situations. They have to learn how to survive offensive speech they find wounding and hurtful."

Gwen Thomas is an educator—an endangered species in higher education.

Reading the Text

1. Why does Hentoff claim that liberal and moderate students are the ones most likely to be intimidated by speech codes?
2. In your own words, describe Hentoff's attitude toward "political correctness."
3. How do blacks and Jews tend to view speech codes differently, according to Hentoff?
4. Why does Hentoff say black community college administrator Gwen Thomas "is an educator—an endangered species in higher education"?

Reading the Signs

1. In your journal, explore the impact of political correctness on your own behavior as a student. Have you ever felt uncomfortable expressing your opinions in class, especially on controversial topics? If so, what led to your discomfort? Do you think a campus speech code would have helped? If you have never felt silenced in class, why do you think that's the case?
2. Does your college campus have its own speech code? If so, obtain the text of the code and write an essay in which you explain whether you believe it would, in Hentoff's words, make "all students feel at home and thereby able to concentrate on their work." If not, do you believe your campus should institute one? To develop your argument, you might interview students of different ethnicities to determine their opinions; you might also consult Thomas Grey, "Responding to Abusive Speech on Campus: A Model Statute" (p. 392) and Richard Goldstein, "Hate Speech, Free Speech, and the Unspoken" (p. 411).
3. As Hentoff explains, many believe campus speech codes are necessary to "insulate" minority students from offensive language. Write an essay in which you argue whether white students, too, deserve such protections. As you write your essay, imagine specific scenarios in which students, both white and nonwhite, might be the target of "fighting words," and then examine whether they equally need "insulation."
4. Has there been an incident on your campus that involves offensive speech or "fighting words"? If so, divide the class into two teams, and debate

whether the presence of speech codes would have relieved or exacerbated the controversy.

5. Write an imaginary letter to Stanford student Canetta Ivy in which you support, refute, or modify her assertion that "We don't put as many restrictions on freedom of speech as we should."

THOMAS C. GREY

Responding to Abusive Speech on Campus: A Model Statute

|||||||||||||||||||||||||||||||||||||||||||||||||

Successful legal challenges to the "friendly speech" codes adopted by such schools as the University of Wisconsin have caused the proponents of these codes to write them with an eye to future litigation. In this selection, Thomas Grey (b. 1941) lays out the plan for Stanford's speech code that has drawn so much attention from free speech defenders and opponents of PC discourse. Remarking that private universities are not bound by the First Amendment, Grey tries to construct a code that will honor free speech rights while protecting students from racial and sexual verbal harassment. Thomas Grey, who received his law degree from Yale University, is the Nelson Bowman Sweitzer and Marie B. Sweitzer Professor of Law at Stanford University. In addition to many legal articles, Grey is the author of The Wallace Stevens Case: Law and the Practice of Poetry *(1991) and editor of* The Legal Enforcement of Morality *(1983).*

In recent years, Stanford, like many other American universities, has witnessed a number of incidents in which students have abused their colleagues with racist and homophobic speech. Authorities have had to decide what, if any, forms of abusive speech should be held to violate the university's student code of conduct. There has been much debate on campus about how to balance competing values of nondiscrimination and decency on the one hand and free expression on the other.

The campus disciplinary system is governed by an Honor Code, which covers offenses against academic integrity, and a Fundamental Standard, which requires students to show "such respect for the rights of others as is expected of good citizens." Over the years, this latter provision has been enforced mainly against physical assaults and property offenses committed on campus. In matters implicating freedom of expression, Stanford, though a private university not bound by the First

Amendment, has nonetheless committed itself in recent years to complying with federal constitutional free speech doctrine.

As a teacher at Stanford Law School who has served on the campus judicial council, I have proposed the following provision for adoption by the university's legislative body. The proposal attempts to mesh a concept drawn from antidiscrimination policy—the idea that maintaining a hostile environment may constitute invidious discrimination—with one of the recognized, though controversial, exceptions to the First Amendment's ban on content-based restriction of free expression—the so-called "fighting words" doctrine.[1]

I believe that racist, homophobic, and other types of abusive speech are serious problems. I also think that some of the efforts to deal with these problems threaten to stifle salutary debate on issues involving race, sexual preference, and other concerns. Here I have tried to define for prohibition a limited form of expression that is discriminatory, assaultive, and plays no essential part in the exposition of ideas. I offer it for discussion and for whatever practical help it may provide to others who are trying to deal with verbal abuse on American campuses.

Free Expression and Discriminatory Harassment

1. Stanford is committed to the principles of free inquiry and free   5
expression. Students have the right to hold and vigorously defend and
promote their opinions, thus entering them into the life of the university,
there to flourish or wither according to their merits. Respect for this
right requires that students tolerate even expression of opinions which
they find abhorrent. Intimidation of students by other students in their

---

1. Editorial note [from *Reconstruction*]: Below Professor Grey describes "fighting words" as "words, pictures or other symbols that, by virtue of their form are commonly understood to convey direct and visceral hatred or contempt for human beings on the basis of their sex, race, color, handicap, religion, sexual orientation, or national and ethnic origin." The term became part of federal constitutional law in 1942 when the Supreme Court upheld the conviction of a person prosecuted for having called a police officer "a God damned racketeer" and "fascist." According to the Court

> There are certain well-defined and narrowly limited classes of speech, the prevention and punishment of which have never been thought to raise any Constitutional problem. These include the lewd and obscene, the profane, the libelous, and the insulting or "fighting" words—those which by their very utterance inflict injury or tend to incite an immediate breach of the peace. It has been well observed that such utterances are no essential part of any exposition of ideas, and are of such slight social value as a step to truth that any benefit that may be derived from them is clearly outweighed by the social interest in order and morality.

Chaplinsky v. *New Hampshire,* 315 U.S. 568, 571–72 (1942).

exercise of this right, by violence or threat of violence, is therefore considered to be a violation of the Fundamental Standard.

2. Stanford is also committed to principles of equal opportunity and nondiscrimination. Each student has the right of equal access to a Stanford education, without discrimination on the basis of sex, race, color, handicap, religion, sexual orientation, or national and ethnic origin. Harassment of students on the basis of any of these characteristics contributes to a hostile environment that makes access to education for those subjected to it less than equal. Such discriminatory harassment is therefore considered to be a violation of the Fundamental Standard.

3. This interpretation of the Fundamental Standard is intended to clarify the point at which protected free expression ends and prohibited discriminatory harassment begins. Prohibited harassment includes discriminatory intimidation by threats of violence, and also includes personal vilification of students on the basis of their sex, race, color, handicap, religion, sexual orientation, or national and ethnic origin.

4. Speech or other expression constitutes harassment by personal vilification if it:

> a. is intended to insult or stigmatize an individual or a small number of individuals on the basis of their sex, race, color, handicap, religion, sexual orientation, or national and ethnic origin; and
>
> b. is addressed directly to the individual or individuals whom it insults or stigmatizes; and
>
> c. makes use of "fighting" words or nonverbal symbols.

In the context of discriminatory harassment, "fighting" words or nonverbal symbols are words, pictures, or other symbols that, by virtue of their form, are commonly understood to convey direct and visceral hatred or contempt for human beings on the basis of their sex, race, color, handicap, religion, sexual orientation, or national and ethnic origin.

Comments

The Fundamental Standard requires that students act with "such respect for . . . the rights of others as is demanded of good citizens." Some incidents in recent years on campus have revealed doubt and disagreement about what this requirement means for students in the sensitive area where the right of free expression can conflict with the right to be free of invidious discrimination. This interpretation is offered for enactment by the Student Conduct Legislative Council to provide students and administrators with some guidance in this area.

The interpretation first restates, in Sections 1 and 2, existing university policy on free expression and equal opportunity respectively. 10

Stanford has affirmed the principle of free expression in its Policy on Campus Disruption, committing itself to support "the rights of all members of the university community to express their views or to protest against actions and opinions with which they disagree." The university has likewise affirmed the principle of nondiscrimination, pledging itself in the Statement of Nondiscriminatory Policy not to "discriminate against students on the basis of sex, race, color, handicap, religion, sexual orientation, or national and ethnic origin in the administration of its education policies." In Section 3, the interpretation recognizes that the free expression and equal opportunity principles conflict in the area of discriminatory harassment, and draws the line for disciplinary purposes at "personal vilification" that discriminates on one of the bases prohibited by the university's nondiscrimination policy.

1. *Why prohibit "discriminatory harassment," rather than just plain harassment?* Some harassing conduct would no doubt violate the Fundamental Standard whether or not it was based on one of the recognized categories of invidious discrimination—for example, if a student, motivated by jealousy or personal dislike, harassed another with repeated middle-of-the-night phone calls. Personal vilification that is not discriminatory might in some circumstances fit within the same category. The question has thus been raised why we should then define *discriminatory* harassment as a separate violation of the Fundamental Standard.

The answer is suggested by reflection on the reason why the particular kinds of discrimination mentioned in the university's Statement on Nondiscriminatory Policy are singled out for special prohibition. Obviously it is university policy not to discriminate against *any* student in the administration of its educational policies on any arbitrary or unjust basis. Why then enumerate "sex, race, color, handicap, religion, sexual orientation, and national and ethnic origin" as specially prohibited bases for discrimination? The reason is that, in this society at this time, these characteristics are the target of socially pervasive invidious discrimination. Persons with these characteristics tend to suffer the special injury of *cumulative* discrimination: They are subjected to repetitive stigma, insult, and indignity on the basis of a fundamental personal trait. In addition, for members of certain vulnerable groups, a long history closely associates verbal abuse with intimidation by physical violence, so that vilification is experienced as assaultive in the strict sense. It is the cumulative and socially pervasive discrimination, often linked to violence, that distinguishes the intolerable injury of wounded identity caused by discriminatory harassment from the tolerable, and relatively randomly distributed, hurt of bruised feelings that results from single incidents of ordinary personally motivated name-calling, a form of hurt that we do not believe the Fundamental Standard protects against.

2. *Does not "harassment" by definition require repeated acts by the individual charges?* No. Just as a single sexually coercive proposal can constitute prohibited sexual harassment, so can a single instance of vilification constitute prohibited discriminatory harassment. The reason for this is, again, the socially pervasive character of the prohibited forms of discrimination.

3. *Why is intent to insult or stigmatize required?* Student members of groups subject to pervasive discrimination may be injured by unintended insulting or stigmatizing remarks as well as by those made with the requisite intent. In addition, the intent requirement makes enforcement of the prohibition of discriminatory harassment more difficult, particularly since proof beyond a reasonable doubt is required to establish charges of Fundamental Standard violations.

Nevertheless, I believe that the disciplinary process should only be invoked against intentionally insulting or stigmatizing utterances. The kind of expression defined in Section 4(c) does not in my view reach the level of "fighting words" unless used with intent to insult. For example, a student who heard members of minority groups using the standard insulting terms for their own group in a joking way among themselves might—trying to be funny—insensitively use those terms in the same way. Such a person should be told that this is not funny, but should not be subject to disciplinary proceedings.   15

The threat of prosecution for possibly thoughtless or insensitive misuses of the kind of terminology or symbolism defined in Section 4(c) also creates the danger of chilling campus discussion of race, gender, and other sensitive issues, in which these terms and symbols will naturally be mentioned, and where some may naturally mistake quotation or mention for deliberately insulting use. Confining the disciplinary offense of harassment to intended direct insults or fighting words, backed by the requirement of proof beyond a reasonable doubt, should prevent any serious chilling effect of this kind, thus preserving the necessary breathing space for vigorous and free debate on these topics.

4. *Why is only vilification of "a small number of individuals" prohibited and how many are too many?* The principle of free expression creates a strong presumption against prohibition of speech based upon its content. Narrow exceptions to this presumption are traditionally recognized, among other categories, for speech that is defamatory or assaultive, and (a closely related category) for speech that constitutes "fighting words." The interpretation adopts the concept of "personal vilification" to help spell out what constitutes the prohibited use of fighting words in the discrimination context. Personal vilification is a narrow category of intentionally insulting or stigmatizing statements *about* individuals (4a), directed *to* those individuals (4b), and expressed in viscerally offensive form (4c).

This excludes "group defamation"—insulting statements concerning social groups directed to the campus or the public at large. The purpose of this limitation is to give extra breathing space for vigorous public debate on campus, protecting even extreme and offensive utterance in the public context against the potentially chilling effect of the threat of disciplinary proceedings.

The expression "small number" of individuals in 4(a) (rather than "group" or "determinate group") is meant to make clear that prohibited personal vilification does not include "group defamation" as that term has been understood in constitutional law and in campus debate. The clearest case for application of the prohibition of personal vilification is the face-to-face insult of one individual by another. Of course more than one person can be insulted face to face, and vilification by telephone is not essentially different from vilification that is literally face to face.

For reasons such as these, the exact contours of the concept of insult to "a small number of individuals" cannot be defined with mechanical precision. One limiting restriction is that the requirements of 4(a) and 4(b) go together, so that a "small number" of persons must be no more than can be and are "addressed directly" by the person conveying the vilifying message.

For example, I believe that a poster placed in the common area of a student residence might be found to constitute personal vilification of all the students living in that residence who possess the characteristic subject to attack. Any such finding would depend, however, upon an individualized determination of the knowledge and intent of the person or persons placing the poster.

5. *What do "fighting words" have to do with fighting?* The term "fighting words" means words (or other forms of expression) so intolerable in our society that they are likely in normal circumstances to provoke violent response. The expression has become a term of art in connection with free speech issues. The term does not imply that violence is considered an acceptable or appropriate response, even to discriminatory vilification; disciplinary proceedings are meant to substitute for, not supplement, violent response. The term also does not mean that a threat or prediction of violent response can by itself turn protected speech into unprotected "fighting words"; any such principle would establish a veto over free expression on the part of anyone willing to threaten violence. Nor, for similar reasons, should the term be read to imply that an actual threat or likelihood of violent response is a necessary element for application of the "fighting words" concept; statements that in themselves constitute "fighting words" do not become protected speech simply because their immediate victims are, for example, such disciplined practitioners of nonviolence, or so physically helpless, or so cowed and demoralized, that they do not, in context, pose a realistic physical threat. In my view,

"fighting words" should be considered essentially equivalent to words that would justify imposition of tort liability for intentional infliction of emotional distress.

6. *What is the point of the terms "by virtue of their form" and "commonly understood" in the definition of "fighting words"?* These terms in Section 4(c) are meant to limit vilification to expression using epithets or pictorial representations that are, as a matter of general social consensus, recognized as gut-level insults to those with the characteristic in question. The restrictive term "by virtue of their form" is meant to exclude charges of harassment being brought on the basis that certain social and political views are in and of themselves, simply by virtue of their *content,* offensive and insulting to members of groups that they concern. Thus under this interpretation, the expression of racist, sexist, homophobic, or blasphemous views as such, even with the intent to insult, and personally directed to those known to be vulnerable to that kind of insult, does not by itself violate the Fundamental Standard.

What is required in addition is that the *form* of expression used must include the standard abusive epithets or their equivalents—for example, terms such as "nigger," "kike," "faggot," or the use of KKK symbols directed at African-American students or Nazi symbols directed at Jewish students. The expression "commonly understood" is added to *narrow* the discretion of enforcement authorities; it is meant to ensure that forms of expression thought to be insulting or offensive by a social group or certain members of a group do not qualify as vilification unless those forms of expression are generally so understood across society as a whole. For example, the Confederate flag, though experienced by many African Americans as a racist endorsement of slavery and segregation, is still widely enough accepted as an appropriate symbol of regional identity and pride that it would not, in my view, fall within the "commonly understood" restriction.

7. *Does not the narrow definition of vilification imply approval of all "pro-   25 tected expression" that falls outside the definition?* Not every form of speech or conduct that is "protected" in the sense of being immune from disciplinary sanction is thereby approved or endorsed by the Stanford community. For example, while interference with free expression by violence or threat of violence violates the Fundamental Standard, less overt forms of silencing of diverse expression, such as too-hasty charges of racism, sexism, and the like, generally do not. Yet the latter form of silencing is hurtful to individuals and bad for education; as such, it is to be discouraged, though by means other than the disciplinary process.

Similarly, while personal vilification violates the Fundamental Standard, even extreme expression of racial hatred and contempt does not, as long as it is not addressed to individuals. Yet the latter form of speech causes real harm and it can and, in my opinion, should be sharply denounced throughout the university community. Less extreme expressions of bigotry (including off-hand remarks that embody harmful stereotypes) are also hurtful to individuals and bad for education. They too should be discouraged, though again by means other than the disciplinary process.

In general, the disciplinary requirements that form the content of the Fundamental Standard are not meant to be a comprehensive account of good citizenship within the Stanford community. They are meant only to set a floor of minimum requirements of respect for the rights of others, requirements that can be reasonably and fairly enforced through a disciplinary process. The Stanford community should expect much more of itself by way of tolerance, diversity, free inquiry, and the pursuit of equal educational opportunity than can possibly be guaranteed by any set of disciplinary rules.

8. *Is the proposal consistent with the First Amendment?* Though Stanford as a private university is not bound by the First Amendment as such, it has for some years taken the position that, as a matter of policy, it would treat itself as so bound. I agree with the policy, and I believe that this proposal is consistent with First Amendment principles as the courts have developed them. However no court has ruled on the constitutionality of a harassment restriction based on the "fighting words" concept, and no one can guarantee that this approach will prove acceptable. What in my view is virtually certain is that any broader approach, for example one that proceeds on the basis of a theory of group defamation, or (like the University of Michigan regulation recently struck down by a federal court) on the basis of the tendency of speech to create a hostile environment, without restriction to "fighting words" (or some equivalent such as "intentional infliction of serious emotional distress"), will be found by courts applying current case law to be invalid.

Reading the Text

1. How does Grey's code attempt to enact Stanford's "Fundamental Standard"?
2. What distinction does Grey make between "discriminatory" and "plain" harassment?
3. Why does Grey believe that his code does not violate First Amendment rights?
4. Why is "group defamation" excluded from the code?

Reading the Signs

1. Writing as if you were Nat Hentoff ("'Speech Codes' on the Campus and Problems of Free Speech," p. 385), compose a letter to Grey in which you

try to persuade him that speech codes are not only unnecessary but potentially dangerous.

2. In his code, Grey excludes some "hurtful" forms of expression, such as
   hasty charges of racism and casual expressions of bigotry, from disciplinary
   sanctions. In class, divide into two teams, and debate whether such expressions ought to be included in speech codes.

3. Grey's code implicitly singles out hate speech against historically victimized
   groups as needing university control; abusive speech against historically
   dominant groups (such as Caucasians, Christians, heterosexuals) does not
   appear to be a violation of the code. Do you believe that framing the code
   according to the target of hate speech is appropriate? Write an essay in
   which you explore this issue, basing your argument on real or hypothetical
   cases of hate speech on your campus.

4. Read or review Peter Lyman's "The Fraternal Bond as a Joking Relationship" (p. 611), and write an essay in which you apply Grey's code to the
   fraternity stunts that Lyman describes. Would the fraternity's actions count
   as "discriminatory harassment," according to the code? Does it violate the
   "Fundamental Standard" that the code is intended to uphold?

5. If your campus has a speech code, compare it with the code that Grey
   wrote for Stanford. What similarities and differences do you see? Depending
   on your perspective, which do you find a more effective way of protecting
   students or, conversely, the greater infringement on freedom of speech?

CORNEL WEST
Diverse New World

|||||||||||||||||||||||||||||||||||||||||||||||

*While critics of multicultural education such as the late Allan Bloom
rail against what they see as the trashing of Western civilization in the
current restructuring of the literary canon, proponents point out that the
Eurocentric point of view simply leaves out too much of cultural history.
In this argument for a multicultural canon, Cornel West (b. 1953)
argues not for the dismantling of the Western tradition but for its
enrichment through the inclusion of the many non-European voices that
have contributed to world culture. In an America that is increasingly
multicultural and multiracial in its own demographic makeup, it only
makes sense to take advantage of diversity, West argues, rather than
resist it. Cornel West is a professor of religion at Princeton University,
where he directs the Afro-American Studies Program. His publications
include* The American Evasion of Philosophy: A Genealogy
of Pragmatism *(1989),* The Ethical Dimensions of Marxist

Thought *(1991)*, Race Matters *(1993)*, *and* Keeping Faith: Philosophy and Race in America *(1993)*.

We are grappling with the repercussions and implications of what it means to live now forty-six years after the end of the age of Europe. This age began in 1492, with the encounter between Europeans and those who were in the New World, with the massive expulsion of Jews in Spain, and with the publication of the first Indo-European grammar books in 1492. It continued through World War II, the concentration camps, and the shaking of the then-fragile European maritime empires. Forty-six years later is not a long time for that kind of fundamental glacier shift in civilizations that once dominated the world.

Analyzing multiculturalism from a contemporary philosophical perspective, and looking at its roots especially among the professional managerial strata, in museums, in galleries, in universities and so forth, is an attempt to come to terms with how we think of universality when it has been used as a smokescreen for a particular group. How do we preserve notions of universality given the fact that various other particularities—traditions, heritages, communities, voices, and what have you—are moving closer to the center of the historical stage, pushing off those few voices which had served as the centering voices between 1492 and 1945?

The United States has become the land of hybridity, heterogeneity, and ambiguity. It lacks the ability to generate national identity and has an inferiority complex vis-à-vis Europe, and the United States must deal with indigenous people's culture, including the scars and the dead bodies left from its history. Expansion across the American continent trampled the culture and heritages of degraded, hated, haunted, despised African peoples, whose backs would constitute one fundamental pillar for the building of the United States and for the larger industrializing processes in Europe.

Within the multiculturalist debate, leading Afrocentric and Africanist thinkers Leonard Jeffries and Molefi Asante articulate a critical perspective that says they are tired of the degradation of things African. On this particular point, they're absolutely right. However, they don't have a subtle enough sense of history, so they can't recognize ambiguous legacies of traditions and civilizations. They refuse to recognize the thoroughly hybrid culture of almost every culture we have ever discovered. In the case of Jeffries, this lack of subtlety slides down an ugly xenophobic slope—a mirror image of the Eurocentric racism he condemns.

We need to see history as in part the cross-fertilization of a variety of different cultures, usually under conditions of hierarchy. That's thoroughly so for the United States. For example, jazz is the great symbol of American culture, but there's no jazz without European instruments or

African polyrhythms. To talk about hybrid culture means you give up all quest for pure traditions and pristine heritages.

Yes, black folk must come up with means of affirming black humanity. Don't just read Voltaire's great essays on the light of reason—read the "Peoples of America," in which he compares indigenous peoples and Africans to dogs and cattle. Don't read just Kant's *Critique of Pure Reason,* read the moments in *The Observations of the Sublime,* in which he refers to Negroes as inherently stupid. It's not a trashing of Kant. It's a situating of Kant within eighteenth-century Germany, at a time of rampant xenophobia, along with tremendous breakthroughs in other spheres. An effective multicultural critique recognizes both the crimes against humanity and the contributions to humanity from the particular cultures in Europe.

We have to demystify this notion of Europe and Eurocentrism. Europe has always been multicultural. Shakespeare borrowed from Italian narratives and pre-European narratives. When we think of multiculturalism, we're so deeply shaped by the American discourse of positively valued whiteness and negatively valued blackness, that somehow it's only when black and white folk interact that real multiculturalism's going on. The gradation of hybridity and heterogeneity is not the same between the Italians and the British, and the West Africans and the British. But "Europe" is an ideological construct. It doesn't exist other than in the minds of elites who tried to constitute a homogeneous tradition that could bring together heterogeneous populations—that's all it is.

In looking at history with a subtle historical sense, I also have in mind the fundamental question: What do we have in common? By history, I mean the human responses to a variety of different processes over time and space—various social structures that all human beings must respond to. In responding to these circumstances, the problem has been that most of us function by a kind of self-referential altruism, in which we're altruistic to those nearest to us, and those more distant, we tend to view as pictures rather than human beings. Yet, as historical beings, as fallen and fallible historical beings, we do have a common humanity. We must not forget our long historical backdrop. The present is history—that continues to inform and shape and mold our perceptions and orientations.

On the political level, multiculturalism has much to do with our present-day racial polarization—which is in many ways gender polarization, especially given the vicious violence against women, and sexual-orientation polarization with increased attacks on gays and lesbians. These conflicts, mediated or not mediated, reverberate within bureaucratic structures, and within the larger society.

Certain varieties of multiculturalism do have a politics. Afrocentrism 10 is an academic instance of a longer black nationalist tradition, and it does have a politics and a history. Black nationalism is not monolithic—there's a variety of different versions of black nationalism. In so many slices of the black community, with the escalation of the discourse of whiteness and blackness, racism escalates, both in terms of the life of the mind as well as in practices. We're getting a mentality of closing of ranks. This has happened many, many times in the black community; and it takes a nationalist form in terms of its politics. Black nationalism politics is something that has to be called for what it is, understood symptomatically, and criticized openly. It's a question of, if you're really interested in black freedom, I am too—will your black nationalist view in education, will your black nationalist view in politics deliver the black freedom that you and I are interested in? You're upset with racism in Western scholarship. I am too, and some white folk are too.

As democratic socialists, we have to look at society in a way that cuts across race, gender, region, and nation. For most people in the world, their backs are against the wall. When your back is against the wall, you're looking for weaponry: intellectual and existential weaponry to sustain yourself and your self-confidence and your self-affirmation in conditions that seemingly undermine your sense of possibility; political weaponry to organize, mobilize, to bring your power to bear on the status quo.

If you're Afro-American and you're a victim of the rule of capital, and a European Jewish figure who was born in the Catholic Rhineland and grew up as a Lutheran, by the name of Karl Marx, provides certain analytical tools, then you go there. You can't find too many insightful formulations in Marx about what it is to be black; you don't go to Marx for that. You go to Marx to keep track of the rule of capital, interlocking elites, political, banking, financial, that's one crucial source of your weaponry. You don't care where you get it from, you just want to get people off of your back.

If you want to know what it means to be black, to be African in Western civilization and to deal with issues of identity, with bombardment of degrading images, you go to the blues, you go to literature, you go to Du Bois's[1] analysis of race, you go to Anna Julia Cooper's[2] analysis of race. For what it means to be politically marginalized, you go to a particular tradition that deals with that.

To gain a universal perspective, the left must have a moral focus on suffering. Once you lose that focus, then you're presupposing a certain level of luxury that is all too common among the professional managerial strata in their debates. Their debates begin to focus on who's going to get what slice of what bureaucratic turf for their bid for the mainstream, for middle-class status. Now, that for me is one slice of the struggle, but

---

1. **W.E.B. Du Bois** (1868–1963)   Historian who studied the lives of blacks in America and leading opponent of racial discrimination.—EDS.
2. **Anna Julia Cooper** (1858–1964)   Educator and civil rights leader who researched slavery.—EDS.

it's just a slice. The center of the struggle is a deeper intellectual and political set of issues: understanding the larger historical scope, the post-European age, the struggles of Third World persons as they attempt to deal with their identity, their sense of economic and political victimization. We need to not only understand but also to assist people trying to forge some kinds of more democratic regimes, which is so thoroughly difficult.

Let's not package the debate in static categories that predetermine the conclusion that reinforces polarization—that's the worst thing that could happen. Polarization paralyzes all of us—and we go on our middle-class ways, and the folk we're concerned about continue to go down the drain.

The political challenge is to articulate universality in a way that is not a mere smokescreen for someone else's particularity. We must preserve the possibility of universal connection. That's the fundamental challenge. Let's dig deep enough within our heritage to make that connection to others.

We're not naive, we know that argument and critical exchange are not the major means by which social change takes place in the world. But we recognize it has to have a role, has to have a function. Therefore, we will trash older notions of objectivity, and not act as if one group or community or one nation has a god's-eye view of the world. Instead we will utilize forms of intersubjectivity that facilitate critical exchange even as we recognize that none of us are free of presuppositions and prejudgments. We will put our arguments on the table and allow them to be interrogated and contested. The quest for knowledge without presuppositions, the quest for certainty, the quest for dogmatism and orthodoxy and ridigity is over.

Reading the Text

1. Why does West see the period betwen 1492 and 1945 as significant?
2. What does West mean by saying that "'Europe' is an ideological construct"?
3. What sort of curriculum does West recommend for African-American students? For students of other races?

Reading the Signs

1. Do you agree with West's charge that the United States has an "inferiority complex vis-à-vis Europe"? Discuss in class what West means by this statement and whether you share his position.
2. West only implicitly outlines his vision of an ideal multicultural curriculum. Write an essay in which you explain what you think his curriculum would be like. What sort of authors and historical figures would be studied? Would

anything in the "traditional" curriculum be deleted? Share your essay with your classmates.

3. Examine the curriculum of the courses you are taking this quarter or semester. To what extent do they reflect West's "diverse new world"? If they don't resemble West's vision of the ideal education, what changes would you suggest?

4. West expresses some reservations about the views of black nationalists such as Leonard Jeffries and Molefi Asante. Visit your college library, and research one such thinker. Then write an essay in which you compare and contrast the black nationalist's views with West's perspective.

5. West identifies himself as a socialist scholar. What response might a middle-class African-American, such as Sam Fulwood III ("The Rage of the Black Middle Class," p. 462), have to his positions? Writing as if you were Fulwood, compose a letter to West responding to his vision of a "diverse new world."

TODD GITLIN
On the Virtues of a Loose Canon

‖‖

"Let's face it," Todd Gitlin (b. 1943) bluntly says in this analysis of the PC controversy, "Some of the controversy over the canon and the new multiculturalism has to do with the fact that the complexion of the United States—on campuses and in the country as a whole—is getting darker." Locating the issue in an historical context, Gitlin takes on both sides of the debate. He scolds the political right for exaggerating the goals of the multiculturalists and for ignoring that the literary canon has always been in motion. At the same time, Gitlin warns that if cultural difference is celebrated for its own sake to the exclusion of the commonalities all Americans can share, the result can be a divisive tribalism that a truly inclusive multicultural education should avoid. One of the founders of the 1960s radical group Students for a Democratic Society and a prolific writer on American popular and political culture, Todd Gitlin is a professor of sociology and director of the mass communications program at the University of California, Berkeley. His publications include The Whole World Is Watching *(1980),* Inside Prime Time *(1985), and* The Sixties: Years of Hope, Days of Rage *(1987).*

I understand the "political correctness" controversy as the surface of a deeper fault line—a trauma in American cultural identity.

America's current identity crisis was precipitated by several events. First, the collapse of the Cold War denied the United States an opponent in the tug-of-war between capitalism and communism. When the enemy let go of the rope, the American "team"—constituted to hold the line against tyranny—was dropped on its collective ass. We are now on the prowl for a new enemy, something or someone to mobilize against: Noriega, drugs, Satan, Saddam Hussein, or the newest bogey: "political correctness"—a breed of left-wing academic intolerance and exclusion that ends up shackling not only free speech but free-flowing intellectual inquiry—a perversion of a sensible multicultural program of tolerance and inclusion.

Though political correctness is rightly condemned for its flights of excess, opponents often fail to separate multiculturalism from the PC version of tribalism. Indeed, some of the right's intolerance is aimed not at the message but at the messengers: immigrants of color—mostly Asian and Hispanic—whose numbers have greatly increased on campuses since the sixties. These groups, along with African-Americans and women, now want access—not just to the corridors of the academy but to its curriculum.

Let's face it: Some of the controversy over the canon and the new multiculturalism has to do with the fact that the complexion of the United States—on its campuses and in the country as a whole—is getting darker. In 1960, 94 percent of college students were white. Today almost 20 percent are nonwhite or Hispanic and about 55 percent are women.

It is the confluence of these events—the end of the Cold War and the transformation of the "typical American"—that appears to have stirred up a particularly vocal reaction at this time to the multicultural movement within the academy. Just note the degree of alarm, the alacrity with which the media have jumped on this issue. *Newsweek,* the *Atlantic Monthly,* the *New Republic,* and *New York* jumped up with cover stories on race, multiculturalism, and the politically correct movement on college campuses. The *New York Times* has given extensive coverage to the PC trend. And George Bush, knowing a no-risk issue when he sees it, recently gave the commencement address to the University of Michigan at Ann Arbor on "the new intolerance" of political correctness sweeping college campuses, what he called "the boring politics of division and derision"—an ironic comment coming from the man who elevated race baiting, through his Willie Horton commercials, to an art form. 5

In important ways, hysteria rules the response to multiculturalism. Academic conservatives who defend a canon, tight or loose, sometimes sound as if American universities were fully and finally canonized until the barbarians showed up to smash up the pantheon and install Alice Walker and Toni Morrison in place of the old white men. These conservatives act as if we were floating along in an unadulterated canon until sixties radicals came along and muddied the waters. Moreover, the hysterics give the misleading impression that Plato and St. Augustine have been banned.

The tight canonists don't take account, either, of the fact that the canon has always been in flux, constantly shifting under our feet. Literary historian Leo Marx made the point recently that when he was in school it was a fight to get good, gay Walt Whitman into the canon, and to get John Greenleaf Whittier, Henry Wadsworth Longfellow and James Russell Lowell out.

Still, without doubt there *has* been a dilution of essential modes of critical reasoning, the capacity to write, and a general knowledge of the contours of world history and thought. And this is to be deplored and resisted.

Indeed, there is a side of the academic conservatives argument I agree with. There are a shocking number of students not only in run-of-the-mill segments of higher education but in elite institutions who are amazingly uneducated in history, literature, and the fundamentals of logic, who don't know the difference between an argument and an assertion. There *is* a know-nothing mood in some quarters which refuses to understand that the ideas and practices of many a dead white male have been decisive in Western—and therefore world—history.

But the stupidification of our students cannot be blamed simply on 10 shifts in the canon. Cultural illiteracy has crept into our educational process for a variety of reasons. In fact, America's higher illiteracy—to call it by a name Thorstein Veblen might have appreciated—is largely a function of the so-far irresistible force of popular culture as the shaper of popular discourse. By popular discourse, I mean not only the way we speak on the street but the way we speak as presidents and presidential candidates. This is a culture in which "read my lips" or "make my day" constitutes powerful and persuasive speech.

We live in a sound-bite culture, one that has taken antielitism as its sacred principle. In the United States, to master a vocabulary that is superior to the mediocre is to be guilty of disdain, of scorning democracy. Though conservatives will not be happy to hear about it, this leveling principle has the full force of market capitalism working for it, a force that insists the only standard of value is consumer sovereignty—what people will buy. Since what people will buy are slogans and feel-good pronouncements, it is not surprising that schools and universities have degraded themselves in a frantic pursuit of the lowest common denominator.

The Perils of PC

This said, we must also condemn the bitter intolerance emanating from much of the academic left—steadily more bitter with each passing Republican year as students who feel politically helpless go looking for targets of convenience. The right exaggerates the academic left's power to enforce its prejudices, but is rightly appalled by a widespread self-righteous illiberalism. Academic freedom—the irreducible prerequisite of a democratic society—goes by the board when students at Berkeley and Michigan disrupt classes (whether of a prejudiced anthropologist or a liberal sociologist, respectively). With the long-overdue withering away of Marxism, the academic left has degenerated into a loose aggregation of margins—often cannibalistic, romancing the varieties of otherness, speaking in tongues.

In this new interest-group pluralism, the shopping center of identity politics makes a fetish of the virtues of the minority, which, in the end, is not only intellectually stultifying but also politically suicidal. It creates a kind of parochialism in which one is justified in having every interest in difference and no interest in commonality. One's identification with an interest group comes to be the first and final word that opens and terminates one's intellectual curiosity. As soon as I declare I am a Jew, a black, a Hispanic, a woman, a gay, I have no more need to define my point of view.

It is curious and somewhat disturbing that this has become a position on the left since, as Isaiah Berlin has eloquently pointed out in his essays on nationalism, adherents of these views walk head-on into the traditional nationalist trap—a trap that led participants of the German Sturm und Drang movement[1] against French cultural imperialism, in the end, to Fascism, brutal irrationalism, and the oppression of minorities.

But there is an interesting difference between the German Sturm   15
und Drang and our own "Storm and Stress" reaction to monochromatic presentations of history and literature. The Romantics of that period were opposing a French-imposed imperialism. What imperialism is being imposed in the United States? Is it the hegemony of Enlightenment ideals of reason and equality, the values of universalism?

If America's multiculturalism means respect for actual difference, we should uphold and encourage this reality against the white-bread, golden-arch version of Disneyland America.

On the other hand, if multiculturalism means there is nothing but difference, then we must do everything we can to disavow it. We cannot condone the creation by the left of separate cultural reservations on which to frolic. There *are* unities—to recognize, to appreciate, deplore, or whatever, but at least to acknowledge. There is America's strange admixture of individualism and conformity. There is the fact of American military, political, cultural, and—still—economic power on a world scale. There are shared myths that cut across tribal lines. We may deplore the ways in which America recognizes itself. Indeed, the Persian Gulf

---

1. **Sturm und Drang movement**   German for "storm and stress," an eighteenth-century literary movement that exalted nature, emotion, and human individualism.—EDS.

War, the Academy Awards, or the Super Bowl are not high notes in the symphony of civilization, though that is when our culture seems to collectively acknowledge itself. Nonetheless, the United States is also a history, an organization of power and an overarching culture. The world is interdependent and America is not simply a sum of marginalities.

Authentic liberals have good reason to worry that the elevation of "difference" to a first principle is undermining everyone's capacity to see, or change, the world as a whole. And those who believe that the idea of the left is an idea of universal interdependence and solidarity— of liberty, equality, fraternity-and-sorority—have reason to mourn the sectarian parochialism of the academic left. To mourn and to organize, so that the right does not, by default, monopolize the legacy of the Enlightenment.

From Particularism to Pluralism

We badly need a careful accounting of the intellectual, social, and cultural nature and roots of the new illiteracies and conformities—as well as the academy's high-level efforts to integrate hitherto submerged materials and populations.

It is not a contradiction to say that America has a real culture and   20
also say that this culture is conflicted, fragile, constantly in need of shoring up. The apparent contradiction is only its complexity. In fact, the identity we promote by way of giving lip service to certain ideals about life, liberty and the pursuit of happiness is riddled with contradiction, or at least with tension. Ours is not a relaxed or natural ideology, nor was the French Revolution's program of liberty, equality, fraternity. The point is that we can't maximize all values simultaneously.

That is why part of the multicultural program is very important. What is required in a general multicultural program, which is *not* a program for group narcissism, is an understanding of one's own vantage point but also the vantage point of others. If we don't infuse multiculturalism with a respect for the other, all we have is American-style tribalism—a perfect recipe for a home-grown Yugoslavia.[2]

Reading the Text

1. What does Gitlin mean by the "trauma of American cultural identity"?
2. Gitlin agrees with some liberal and some conservative arguments in the multicultural debate. In what ways does Gitlin align himself with both sides of the controversy?

---

2. **Yugoslavia** An allusion to the deep divisions and conflicts among the different ethnicities that composed the former Yugoslavia.—EDS.

3. What does Gitlin consider the "perils of PC"?
4. Summarize in your own words Gitlin's attitudes toward a multicultural curriculum.

Reading the Signs

1. Compare and contrast Gitlin's attitudes toward political correctness with Nat Hentoff's ("'Speech Codes' on the Campus and Problems of Free Speech," p. 385). What difference does it make that Gitlin is a college professor teaching at a multicultural campus while Hentoff is a journalist?
2. Interview two faculty members at your campus, one known for "liberal" views, the other for "conservative." Ask them about their views on political correctness and multiculturalism and how their own scholarship has or has not been affected by these issues. Use the results of your interviews to formulate an argument about the impact of the PC and multicultural controversies on teaching and scholarship.
3. Gitlin notes that the political correctness debate has been featured in the popular media, including magazines such as *Newsweek* and the *Atlantic Monthly*. Visit your college library, and research the treatment of this issue in three or four magazines (check the *Reader's Guide to Periodical Literature* for the magazines Gitlin mentions and for others). Do the articles you've found demonstrate the "degree of alarm" that Gitlin sees in popular media? What attitude toward colleges and universities do you find in the magazines? Does the image of college life and learning communicated in the magazines correspond to your own observations and experiences as a college student? Use your research to formulate an essay about the media's depiction of university life and controversies.
4. Gitlin blames popular culture for the "stupidification of our students." Write an essay in which you support, challenge, or modify his claim. What attitudes are implicit in his term "stupidification"? Do you think *Signs of Life in the U.S.A.*, which focuses on popular culture, contributes to "stupidification"?
5. Explore how ethnic studies are taught on your college campus. You might start by studying your school catalogue, and then visit ethnic studies departments and programs and interview staff, students, and faculty. Use your research to formulate an essay in which you argue whether your school's ethnic studies group teaches what Gitlin calls "group narcissism," or conversely, "a general multicultural program."

RICHARD   GOLDSTEIN

Hate Speech, Free Speech, and the Unspoken

‖‖‖

The battle for the First Amendment is particularly troubling for liberal thinkers who endorse not only freedom of speech but also the right to be free from verbal and symbolic abuse. In this broad review of the legal and moral issues at stake in the free speech controversy, Richard Goldstein (b. 1944) exemplifies the conflicting impulses of a progressive writer. "To ban hate speech from public discourse would indeed be unconscionable and dangerous," he writes, adding, "to restrict it in private or coercive situations is a matter of common decency and political urgency." At a time when skinhead racism, the Nazis, and the Ku Klux Klan are all on the rise, Goldstein's conviction that we have to draw the line somewhere is especially poignant and challenging: for where are we to draw it? The executive editor of the Village Voice, *Richard Goldstein writes on mass culture and sexual politics and is the author of, among other books,* Reporting the Counterculture *(1989).*

Edward J. Cleary, a Minneapolis attorney and civil libertarian, had never argued a case before the Supreme Court. Now, he rose before the justices intoning, "This is the hour of danger for the First Amendment." He was not referring to the high court's decision allowing the government to curb speech by doctors who counsel patients on abortion in federally funded clinics. He was not referring to the Court's recent rulings that permit the owners of factories and malls to ban leafletting, soliciting, and union organizing—even in the parking lot. He was not referring to the congressional ban on funding for offensive art. It might be argued that any or all of these represent a stark retreat from the imperatives of the First Amendment. But for Edward J. Cleary the greatest danger to free expression comes from an attempt to punish hate speech.

Cleary was arguing against a St. Paul ordinance that defines as disorderly conduct the placing of "a symbol, object, appellation, characterization, or graffiti [that] arouses anger, alarm, or resentment in others on the basis of race, color, creed, religion, or gender." The St. Paul ordinance makes it a misdemeanor to display a burning cross or a swastika. And so, when a pack of skinheads who had been drinking together burned a cross on a black family's lawn, they were charged with fourth-degree assault and an additional bias-related misdemeanor. One of the young defendants has challenged that statute, which Cleary calls "so broad it opens the door to eviscerating the whole First Amendment."

The Minnesota Supreme Court agreed—up to a point. It ruled that, although the St. Paul ordinance is too broad, localities could prohibit "conduct that is not protected by the First Amendment." Relying on a fifty-year-old precedent in which the U.S. Supreme Court allowed states to regulate what is called "fighting words," the Minnesota justices upheld St. Paul's right to outlaw epithets that incite immediate violence. The original fighting words, ironically, had nothing to do with race. In 1942, a Mr. Chaplinsky had been convicted for calling a New Hampshire marshal "a damned fascist" and "a God-damned racketeer." Fifty years later, these insults would barely bring a blush to the cheeks of a talk-show guest, and to many civil libertarians, the shifting impact of offensive language illustrates the inherently discriminatory nature of this concept. But supporters of the St. Paul ordinance concur with the 1942 ruling that there are words "which by their very utterance inflict injury." In the intervening years, however, the Supreme Court has never upheld a conviction for "fighting words." This is the murky legal landscape the justices are now revisiting.

The Court will rule on the St. Paul statute at a time of heightened awareness about acts of bias, when many states have enacted ordinances that increase the penalties for hate crimes, allowing the assailant's use of epithets to be introduced as evidence of intent. And many campuses have adopted codes of conduct that curb expression deemed offensive to racial, ethnic, or sexual minorities, as well as women. Civil libertarians are taking aim at these codes and laws, hoping the Supreme Court will rescind the concept of fighting words on which they are founded. Most readers of this magazine [*Tikkun*] would probably agree with Nadine Strossen of the American Civil Liberties Union (ACLU) that "once the government is allowed to punish any speech based upon its content, free expression exists only for those with power." But most of us would also agree that hate speech bears a tangible relationship to violent behavior —we hear Hitler's anti-Semitic rantings and we think Holocaust. We also know that the current explosion of hate speech in America is not an isolated phenomenon. There has been a demonstrable rise in bias-related incidents, including anti-Semitic and antigay violence: More than twice the number of bias crimes occurred in New York City during the first three months of 1992 than in the same period of the previous year and anti-Semitic incidents, according to the Anti-Defamation League, are at a fourteen-year high; and federal statistics show that gay bashing, too, is on the rise. Even allowing for more vigilant reporting of such incidents life is clearly more dangerous for whole groups of Americans —people of color, Jews, women, and gays.

This perception of crisis is why hate speech has become a divisive 5
issue among progressives. The distressing force of the current backlash against hard-won minority rights creates a fundamental conflict between our commitment to free expression and our desire to protect and preserve the victims of abuse. The result is an aching uncertainty about where to draw the line. Though we might be loath to see the state curb the

political process or intervene in cultural production, few of us would put a pack of white kids hurling epithets at a black woman on a dark street in the same category. Yet most of us are aware that suppressing speech often rebounds against the victim in unforeseen ways. For example, campus codes banning speech that offends people on the basis of their race can be and have been used to prevent black activists from insulting whites. And epithets can be ambiguous in their intent: By appropriating terms of insult, Queer Nation, a radical gay cadre, and Niggers With Attitude, a militant rap group, transform them into expressions of solidarity. How can the law possibly regulate something as fundamentally subjective as symbolic expression? And yet, given the power of symbols to incite fear and loathing, not to mention violence, how can it not?

The most compelling case for regulating hate speech is when it targets an individual and occurs in a setting where violence is a real possibility. Most civil libertarians would agree that the perpetrators ought to be punished regardless of whether their threat is limited to speech. The ACLU's *Policy Statement on Free Speech and Bias on College Campuses* affirms that codes "aimed at restricting acts of harassment, intimidation, and invasion of privacy are consistent with the ACLU's reading of the First Amendment." The difficulty begins when words or other forms of symbolic expression are banned without regard to their context. Civil libertarians assert that the best way to insure the safety of individuals while preserving freedom of speech is to ban acts of "terrorism" without regard to their content. Such "content-neutral" statutes would not punish racist, sexist, or homophobic speech; rather, they would deal with the context in which such statements occur. But is there no difference between being called "brown-eyed" and "nigger" in a dark alley? Is the content of expression never terroristic? What about statements that carry such a legacy of violence that they can only be interpreted as a threat?

The burning cross has a tangible meaning, grounded in its historical connection with lynching—as the skinheads who snuck into Russ Jones's yard well knew. "I don't see the free speech problem here," Jones told one journalist, "because burning a cross on someone's lawn is a direct threat, and how can a threat of violence be protected?" The perpetrators could be punished under local statutes that define such trespasses on private property as a form of assault. What Jones is looking for is a redress directly related to the meaning and context of the skinheads' act. The anonymous nature of this cross burning, and the fact that it singled Jones out, make the incident different in impact and intent from a cross burning at a public event. A similar distinction can be made between statements in a classroom that are deemed anti-Semitic and a swastika scrawled on a Jewish student's dormitory door.

The St. Paul statute makes no mention at all of context; it could be read as banning the display of offensive symbols at a performance or a political rally. On the other hand, the ACLU's guidelines make no exception for the tangible impact of epithets. Strossen argues that "the intentional infliction of emotional distress" should never be a criterion for curbing speech. The fact that such distress is inflicted solely on the basis of someone's gender or membership in a minority group makes no difference: The ACLU falls back on its traditional counsel that bad speech should be answered by "more speech." But most victims of hate speech would argue that there is no effective way to answer an epithet short of violence or flight.

To understand why, consider the etymology of these words and their relationship to the body. Epithets work precisely because they target the aspect of identity that is the greatest source of vulnerability—usually an aspect of the body as well. Racial epithets focus on the ineffaceable fact of skin color; anti-Semitic epithets suggest that, even when no such identifiable mark exists, a Jew can be singled out from others—as if this affiliation were so consuming that it renders someone physically distinct. A similar dynamic underlies antigay slurs: One is identified as "queer," as if sexual practice were the sum total of one's being. (Even the word "faggot," connoting sexual servitude, becomes a summation of identity.) Then there are the epithets of gender, so many of which relate to female genitalia. Here, as in racial epithets, something physically innate becomes the source of abuse. And that certain something is precisely what renders one vulnerable to specific forms of violence: rape, lynching, genocide, gay bashing. Epithets are part of a system of dominance and control: They are threats that have a history of being carried out.

This history of categorization and oppression through the body   10
makes it all but impossible to respond to an epithet in an effective manner. If a woman who had been called a "cunt" were to reply with the anatomical equivalent—"prick"—the impact would not be the same, since men are rarely punished because they have penises. By the same token, epithets that refer to white people are rarely effective, because they do not connote a history of oppression based on skin color. Jewish epithets for Christians—"goy," "shiksa"—are bandied about in mixed company because they do not place the recipient in any sense of danger; and a gay epithet for heterosexuals, like the word "breeder," may cause offense but it hardly conjures up images of violence or even subservience. Indeed, fecundity, masculinity, Christianity, and a white skin are all marks of superior status in American society. So what is the speech that can answer an epithet? A "robust response," to use the ACLU's language, might be to call the perpetrator a bigot, but that designation—unlike skin color or gender—can be denied. For the victim of hate speech, there are usually only two alternatives: Ignore it or prepare to fight.

The case now before the Supreme Court is a right-winger's dream, since it pits the ACLU against the NAACP, the ADL, and People for the American Way. This is certainly not the first time these groups have been on different sides of an issue, but defending the right of Nazis to march in Skokie is an enterprise with limited consequences. The scope of this case is far broader, as is the effect it could have on antibias codes and statutes across the country. If the Court undermines most of these ordinances, it could open a major rift between civil-rights activists and civil libertarians, two progressive constituencies that have long shared a common agenda. This conflict would have much in common with the battles over crime and punishment that drove a wedge through the Left in the seventies. Then, as now, progressives found it impossible to reconcile safety and civil liberties to the satisfaction of the victimized; then, as now, racial resentment lay just below the surface of the debate. What makes the collision over hate speech so distressing, from a progressive perspective, is that it has brought civil libertarians into an alliance with social conservatives, while minority activists who stood with the ACLU are now on the other side.

To many civil libertarians, that is just the point. The ACLU is not an organization of the Left or the Right, they argue, but a nonpartisan coalition to defend the Bill of Rights. Over the past twenty-five years, however, the ACLU's commitment has gone well beyond these parameters to embrace civil rights, gay rights, and reproductive rights. A generation of activists in all these areas has grown up with the ACLU on its side. But not all civil libertarians still honor that bond. It has become apparent in recent years that the conscience of a civil libertarian can coexist with socially conservative views on abortion, homosexuality, and civil rights.

To examine these contradictions is to realize that this conflict stems from powerfully different perspectives. Those who would curb hate speech are, for the most part, of a different class and caste than those who would allow it in the name of freedom. But these distinctions pale before the psychic conflict between those who feel endangered by epithets and those who do not. To the former, civil libertarians can seem insensitive; to the latter, activists can seem censorious.

Furthermore, both sides in this debate can argue from equally bitter experience, either that curbing hate speech opens the door to regulation of ideas by shifts in the political world, or that permitting hate speech empowers bigots and compounds the helplessness of minorities. Victims of hate speech, be they black, Jewish, female, or gay, can easily see betrayal in the principled defense of hate speech, just as civil libertarians can feel a special rage when the beneficiaries of their lifelong struggle turn on the very ideas that made these movements possible. These currents swirl beneath the surface of debates on hate speech, as both sides ask the unspoken question, Which side are you on?

That question has been vastly complicated by the recent addition of 15 gender as a category of oppression, at a time when some feminists equate pornography with hate speech and demand that it be similarly repressed.

No wonder there are two Nadine Strossens. One writes a persuasively argued monograph in the *Duke Law Journal,* assuring minority activists that the ACLU's position is not absolute and urging them to come together with civil libertarians to find ways to stop harassment that are consistent with the First Amendment. Strossen's conciliatory tone was aimed at a black professor who had written a monograph in the same issue questioning the ACLU's stance. She is nowhere near as kind to feminists who demand legal redress for sexual insults. Appearing on a PBS panel discussion of hate speech, Strossen snaps at a woman who wants curbs on catcalling by men, "I have no problem with being told I'm good-looking." This exchange suggests that the anxieties ignited by this debate go well beyond the immediate issue. "Now we have minorities and feminists and the left allied with fundamentalists, . . ." Strossen recently told the *New York Times.* "To them group rights are more important than individual rights." To which a victim of hate speech might reply: "Why is my security less important to you than my oppressor's rights?"

Stripped of this mutual sense of betrayal, the hate speech impasse is not impossible to resolve. The ACLU supports sexual harassment statutes barring words directed at individuals that undermine their ability to function as students or employees. Campus codes that protect minorities against abuse in their homes or dormitory rooms are also acceptable, as is the regulation of speech that is "an essential element of violent or unlawful activity." In her piece for the *Duke Law Journal* Strossen writes that racially harassing speech "should be neither absolutely protected nor absolutely prohibited," a position many activists share. And yet the case currently before the Supreme Court has taken on the tone of recent crusades against "political correctness," complete with the specter of an America ruled by minority and feminist thought police. Edward Cleary's brief against the St. Paul ordinance envisions legislatures courting political support by endlessly "enlarging the list of protected groups while precluding unpopular minority expressions." The result would be a nightmare of truly Orwellian proportions, as public (and even private) discourse becomes subject to a politically charged process of review.

Granted that this is a possibility, and that no one would really be safe from racism or sexism if it came to pass. But the domination of America by censorious minorities is far less likely to occur than its obverse: the resurgence of right-wing authoritarianism and its traditional system of repressing minorities, assertive women, and homosexuals. Recent rulings by the Supreme Court suggest that the current majority—fashioned over twelve years of conservative government—is hastening to restore that system. Consider what is likely to happen if the Court forcefully overturns the "fighting words" precedent: The ripple effects will make prosecutors (and officials at state universities) reluctant to punish acts of racial and sexual harassment; cross burnings and the brandishings of swastikas will proliferate, along with sexist and homophobic taunting; the anxiety of minorities will be heightened, and with it, their rage. Of course, the free exchange of hatred could also generate an upsurge of activism. But the same Supreme Court that unleashes hate speech could very well hamper the right of its victims to organize. Consider the implications of permitting federal funders to regulate the speech of doctors in abortion clinics; that same Court could easily permit employers to fire workers who reveal their homosexuality, on the grounds that sodomy is still a criminal act in many states. The same Court that recently allowed the owners of businesses to curb the speech of labor organizers could easily rule that Congress may regulate the content of federally funded art—including its politics.

We are entering an era of conservative judicial activism unknown in this nation since the days of Jim Crow. The values we learned to apply vigorously, confident that they would produce a better deal for the downtrodden, the deviant, and the dissenting, are now being used for very different purposes. This is the political environment in which Edward Cleary rose to argue his case. He is right to argue that the First Amendment is our best defense against authoritarianism, but it is also true that nothing about freedom of expression is absolute; each generation sets its own standard—that, too, is part of the constitutional process. And the strategy of today's majority may well be to free up hate speech while suppressing expressions of dissent. Many legal scholars think the Supreme Court will dismantle the concept of "fighting words." If that occurs, it will be incumbent on civil libertarians to find another way to deal with social reality. For there is nothing intangible about epithets, and their newfound respectability is the sign of an authoritarian time. To ban hate speech from public discourse would indeed be unconscionable and dangerous; to restrict it in private or coercive situations is a matter of common decency and political urgency. And to ignore the context of speech entirely is to discard the time-honored advice that the unintended consequences of any social policy are always more important than the intended ones.

Reading the Text

1. How does Goldstein account for the recent rise in hate speech in America?
2. In your own words, summarize what Goldstein sees as the most compelling reason for considering regulations on hate speech.
3. How does Goldstein explain the difference between hate speech that targets historically oppressed groups and that which targets historically dominant groups?

4. What is Goldstein's attitude toward the St. Paul, Minnesota, ordinance restricting hate speech?

Reading the Signs

1. Research one of the nonacademic cases that Goldstein mentions (such as the Bush administration's "gag order" prohibiting doctors from counseling patients on abortion in federally funded clinics), and write a well-documented essay in which you argue for or against the institution of speech restrictions in this case.
2. One of the problems with the hate speech controversy, Goldstein argues, is the "aching uncertainty about where to draw the line." In class, discuss what sorts of hate speech, if any, you would argue for restricting in some way. Be sure to consider different targets of hate speech—such as ethnic minorities, Jews, women, gays—and the different effects the speech might have on their targets.
3. Do you agree that there's a difference between "statements made in a classroom that are deemed anti-Semitic and a swastika scrawled on a Jewish student's dormitory door"? In your journal, explore what your response to these two incidents would be if you were a college administrator in charge of student conduct. Then share your response with your class.
4. Do you agree with some feminists that pornography should be equated with hate speech? Write an essay in which you support, refute, or complicate this position, being sure to base your argument on the legal principles that Goldstein mentions.
5. Goldstein assumes that the hate speech issue will be decided by a largely conservative Supreme Court. To what extent is this assumption still valid? Research the ways in which the Court's profile has changed since Goldstein published his article in 1992, focusing on the attitudes toward First Amendment rights held by the justices.

BARBARA EHRENREICH
Ice-T: Is the Issue Creative Freedom?

||||||||||||||||||||||||||||||||||||||||||||||||||||||||||

In the early 1990s, rap triggered a round of calls for boycotts and censorship, though the word was seldom used by those opposing this music. First, 2 Live Crew made headlines when its best-selling album "As Nasty As They Wanna Be" caused the prosecution of some of the record store owners who sold it. In 1992, Ice-T's song "Cop Killer" inspired furious debate between those horrified by the song's threats of violence against police and those arguing that freedom of speech is more important than freedom from offense. In the following selection, Barbara Ehrenreich examines the "Cop Killer" controversy, finding that the song's shallow posturing makes it hard to take its threats very seriously. A free-lance writer and lecturer, Ehrenreich (b. 1941) is co-chairperson of Democratic Socialists of America. Her recent books include Fear of Falling: The Inner Life of the Middle Class *(1989),* The Worst Years of Our Lives: Irreverent Notes from a Decade of Greed *(1990), and a novel,* Kipper's Game *(1993).*

Ice-T's song "Cop Killer" is as bad as they come. This is black anger—raw, rude, and cruel—and one reason the song's so shocking is that in postliberal America, black anger is virtually taboo. You won't find it on TV, not on the *McLaughlin Group* or *Crossfire,* and certainly not in the placid features of Arsenio Hall or Bernard Shaw. It's been beaten back into the outlaw subcultures of rap and rock, where, precisely because it is taboo, it sells. And the nastier it is, the faster it moves off the shelves. As Ice-T asks in another song on the same album, "Goddamn what a brotha gotta do / To get a message through / To the red, white, and blue?"

But there's a gross overreaction going on, building to a veritable paroxysm of white denial. A national boycott has been called, not just of the song or Ice-T, but of all Time Warner products. The president himself has denounced Time Warner as "wrong" and Ice-T as "sick." Ollie North's Freedom Alliance has started a petition drive aimed at bringing Time Warner executives to trial for "sedition and anarchy."

Much of this is posturing and requires no more courage than it takes to stand up in a VFW hall and condemn communism or crack. Yes, "Cop Killer" is irresponsible and vile. But Ice-T is as right about some things as he is righteous about the rest. And ultimately, he's not even dangerous—least of all to the white power structure his songs condemn.

The "danger" implicit in all the uproar is of empty-headed, suggestible black kids, crouching by their boom boxes, waiting for the word. But what Ice-T's fans know and his detractors obviously don't is that "Cop Killer" is just one more entry in pop music's long history of macho hyperbole and violent boast. Flip to the classic-rock station, and you might catch the Rolling Stones announcing "the time is right for violent revoloo-shun!" from their 1968 hit "Street Fighting Man." And where were the defenders of our law-enforcement officers when a white British group, the Clash, taunted its fans with the lyrics: "When they kick open your front door / How you gonna come / With your hands on your head / Or on the trigger of your gun?"

"Die, Die, Die Pig" is strong speech, but the Constitution protects strong speech, and it's doing so this year more aggressively than ever. The Supreme Court has just downgraded cross burnings to the level of bonfires and ruled that it's no crime to throw around verbal grenades like "nigger" and "kike." Where are the defenders of decorum and social stability when prime-time demagogues like Howard Stern deride African-Americans as "spear chuckers"?

More to the point, young African-Americans are not so naive and suggestible that they have to depend on a compact disc for their sociology lessons. To paraphrase another song from another era, you don't need a rap song to tell which way the wind is blowing. Black youths know that the police are likely to see them through a filter of stereotypes as miscreants and potential "cop killers." They are aware that a black youth is seven times as likely to be charged with a felony as a white youth who has committed the same offense, and is much more likely to be imprisoned.

They know, too, that in a shameful number of cases, it is the police themselves who indulge in "anarchy" and violence. The U.S. Justice Department has received 47,000 complaints of police brutality in the past six years, and Amnesty International has just issued a report on police brutality in Los Angeles, documenting forty cases of "torture or cruel, inhuman, or degrading treatment."

Menacing as it sounds, the fantasy in "Cop Killer" is the fantasy of the powerless and beaten down—the black man who's been hassled once too often ("A pig stopped me for nothin'!"), spread-eagled against a police car, pushed around. It's not a "responsible" fantasy (fantasies seldom are). It's not even a very creative one. In fact, the sad thing about "Cop Killer" is that it falls for the cheapest, most conventional image of rebellion that our culture offers: the lone gunman spraying fire from his AK-47. This is not "sedition"; it's the familiar, all-American, Hollywood-style pornography of violence.

Which is why Ice-T is right to say he's no more dangerous than George Bush's pal Arnold Schwarzenegger, who wasted an army of cops in *Terminator 2*. Images of extraordinary cruelty and violence are marketed every day, many of far less artistic merit than "Cop Killer." This is our free market of ideas and images, and it shouldn't be any less free for a black man than for other purveyors of "irresponsible" sentiments, from David Duke to Andrew Dice Clay.

Just, please, don't dignify Ice-T's contribution with the word *sedition*.   10
The past masters of sedition—men like George Washington, Toussaint-Louverture, Fidel Castro, or Mao Zedong, all of whom led and won armed insurrections—would be unimpressed by "Cop Killer" and probably saddened. They would shake their heads and mutter words like "infantile" and "adventurism." They might point out that the cops are hardly a noble target, being, for the most part, honest working stiffs who've got stuck with the job of patrolling ghettos ravaged by economic decline and official neglect.

There is a difference, the true seditionist would argue, between a revolution and a gesture of macho defiance. Gestures are cheap. They feel good, they blow off some rage. But revolutions, violent or otherwise, are made by people who have learned how to count very slowly to 10.

Reading the Text

1. Why does Ehrenreich feel that the protests over "Cop Killer" are an "overreaction"?
2. What evidence does Ehrenreich present to show that songs such as "Cop Killer" are not really dangerous?
3. What parallels does Ehrenreich see between "Cop Killer" and other music and films?

Reading the Signs

1. Do you agree with Ehrenreich's claim that opponents of "Cop Killer" are overreacting? Write an essay in which you support, refute, or modify her position, being sure to cite specific lyrics as part of your argument. As you develop your essay, you may want to consult Elaine Lafferty and Tammy Bruce's "Suddenly, They Hear the Words" (p. 422) for an alternative perspective and Richard Goldstein's "Hate Speech, Free Speech, and the Unspoken" (p. 411) for a discussion of First Amendment issues.
2. Ehrenreich states that "'Cop Killer' is the fantasy of the powerless and beaten down." In class, discuss what response bell hooks (p. 190) would have to this statement and to Ehrenreich's assessment of the controversy over the song.
3. When it comes to "offensive" art, distinctions are often made between adults and children as the audience for such art. In class, debate whether such distinctions should be made, and if so, how. Be sure to consider specific cases of "offensive" art, such as controversial rap lyrics or pornography. Do adults have a responsibility to protect children from certain kinds of art? Whose rights should take precedence: the rights of children or the rights of artists?
4. Popular music has often raised controversy and prompted attempts to "control" controversial content. Research in your college library controversial artists from other decades (such as Elvis Presley in the 1950s and the Beatles in the 1960s), and discover what attempts were made to "sanitize" them. Then write an essay in which you explore the efficacy of attempts to control popular artists.
5. What is your opinion of the PMRC warning label on controversial albums? To develop your essay, interview students from a variety of ethnicities and political persuasions. Do consumers pay attention to the label? Do parents use it to control their children's music-listening habits? Are there any instances in which you think it is legitimate for parents to prohibit their children from listening to certain artists?

ELAINE LAFFERTY AND TAMMY BRUCE

Suddenly, They Hear the Words

‖‖‖

In the aftermath of the 1992 L.A. riots, a rapper named Ice-T found himself at the center of a national controversy over rap lyrics with his song "Cop Killer." As Elaine Lafferty and Tammy Bruce note in this opinion piece for the Los Angeles Times, *conservative men didn't object when rap and heavy metal lyrics seemed to encourage violence against women, but they really got their dander up when the music came down against the police. "Now you know how it feels," Lafferty and Bruce tell those who said nothing when women were the targets of pop music but who eagerly organized a national crusade when the cops came under attack. Elaine Lafferty is a Los Angeles–based writer, and Tammy Bruce is the president of the Los Angeles chapter of the National Organization for Women.*

It has long been profitable in pop music to wax rhapsodic about torturing, raping, and killing women. When a few souls complained about a Motley Crüe tune about a man in a padded cell thinking of his late girlfriend: "Laid out cold / now we're both alone / But killing you helped me keep you home," one newsweekly wondered how anyone could not recognize the lyric as a "joke."

Yes, there have been voices raised against the growing violence against women in movies, books, and lyrics, but there have been more voices dismissing the complainers as humorless prigs, censoring crusaders or, worse, just unhip. "It's just a book, or a movie or a song, it doesn't mean anything" is the response. Or: "Sure it's yucky, but there's no connection between this stuff and violence in society."

Now police are the target, in a song by Ice-T, and suddenly a broad consensus develops. In a flash of perspicacity, community leaders recognize that this music just may encourage real people to commit real acts of violence, so the condemnation cavalry rushes in, from the Los Angeles City Council to Ollie North to George Bush, who calls the song "sick" and its distribution "wrong."

The point here is not to discuss the merits of the song "Cop Killer" or the wisdom of a boycott of Time Warner. The issue is why a critical consensus emerges when the targets of violence are police. In fact, the song preceding "Cop Killer" on Ice-T's record talks of immolating a woman, beating her with a Louisville Slugger, and finishing the task with a "handy carving knife." Where is the moral outrage from our elected officials and community leaders?

When lyrics describe women being raped and dismembered, the imagery is breezily defended as some kind of mythic/gothic theme. When the group N.W.A. raps about tying a woman to a bed, raping her, and then killing her with a .44 magnum in their song "One Less Bitch," some people decry the language but defend the music as representative of the rage of the streets.

Fine. But it is no mistake that among the acknowledgements on Ice-T's album cover are nods to their white misogynistic predecessors Metallica, Megadeth, and Guns n' Roses, all heavy-metal groups whose lyrics degrade women.

If you want to criticize Ice-T for "Cop Killer," fine. But understand that women have been the targets of this kind of lyrical assault for years. Welcome to the club, guys.

Reading the Text

1. Why do Lafferty and Bruce conclude by saying "Welcome to the club, guys"?
2. What is Lafferty and Bruce's attitude toward violence against police in popular songs?
3. Why do Lafferty and Bruce call Metallica, Megadeth, and Guns n' Roses the "white misogynistic predecessors" of Ice-T?

Reading the Signs

1. What is your opinion of the misogynistic lyrics that Lafferty and Bruce describe? Write a journal entry in which you describe your response to lyrics that describe rape and torture of women. Then share your entry with same-sex groups in class.
2. Research the controversy over Ice-T's song "Cop Killer," and write an essay in which you argue whether Lafferty and Bruce's argument is valid. Were the song's critics more upset by the *target* of the song's violence than by the violence itself?
3. Have a class member bring a controversial rap album to class and play a few songs. Then debate the significance of the songs that you've listened to. Are they signs of "the rage of the street," as Lafferty and Bruce put it? Or are they, in Barbara Ehrenreich's words (p. 418), just "posturing"?
4. Lafferty and Bruce note that many white heavy metal bands sing lyrics just as misogynistic as some rap lyrics, then ask "Where is the moral outrage from our elected officials and community leaders?" Write an essay in which you answer their question, exploring why white bands have not been

equally condemned for their offensive lyrics. To develop your essay, you might consult Lisa A. Lewis, "Male-Address Video" (p. 182).

JAMES CRAWFORD

Hold Your Tongue: The Question of Linguistic Self-Determination

|||||||||||||||||||||||||||||||||||||||||||||||||

Like the end of the nineteenth century, the last quarter of the twentieth century has been a period of massive immigration to America. But while the immigrants of a century ago were mostly of European origin, today's immigrants come mainly from Asian and Central American nations. In this analysis of the movement, spawned by a nativistic backlash, that attempted to establish English as America's official tongue, James Craw-ford (b. 1949) warns against the possible consequences of restrictions on the languages Americans may use. "Tyrannies of the majority are ultimately self-defeating," he warns, "national unity cannot be coerced." Raising free speech issues that encompass the language in which we speak rather than the content, Crawford suggests that the future harmony of an ethnically diverse America depends upon today's linguistic freedom. James Crawford is a free-lance writer who focuses on language and education issues. In addition to Hold Your Tongue: Bilingualism and the Politics of "English Only" *(1992), from which this selection is taken, he is the author of* Bilingual Education *(1989) and the editor of* Language Loyalties: A Source Book on the Official English Controversy *(1992).*

"English is under attack," warns a new movement of civic activists. Two decades ago this idea would have struck most Americans as bizarre: the histrionics of literati, or perhaps a Dadaist[1] charade. But in the uneasy eighties it attracted mass support. "Defend our common language!" became the rallying cry. No one had to ask, "From whom?"

Immigration to the United States has increased noticeably in recent years and, more important, its source countries have changed. In 1965, Congress abolished the national-origins quota system, a racially restrictive policy that long favored northwestern Europeans and virtually excluded

---

1. **Dadaist** Member of an experimental art movement, begun 1916, that rebelled against traditional artistic styles.—EDS.

Asians. As late as the 1950s Europe was still supplying more than half of all immigrants to the United States. By the 1980s the Third World was providing 85 percent of them, not counting the undocumented.[2] These newcomers were far less familiar, racially and culturally, and so was their speech. After half a century of decline, minority tongues were suddenly more audible and, to many Americans, more dissonant as well.

In 1981, for the first time, Congress entertained a proposal to designate English as the official language of the United States. The sponsor was Senator S. I. Hayakawa of California, a Canadian immigrant of Japanese ancestry who believed that concessions to linguistic minorities had gone too far. "English has long been the main unifying force of the American people," he asserted. "But now prolonged bilingual education in public schools and multilingual ballots threaten to divide us along language lines." A semanticist by profession, Hayakawa was best known for his college text, *Language in Thought and Action,* which explores a wide range of obstacles to effective communication. Oddly, the book never mentions bilingualism, a problem that seems to have escaped the author's notice until he entered politics.

On retiring from the Senate, in 1983 Hayakawa helped to found U.S. English, a Washington lobby to promote his constitutional English Language Amendment and similar measures at the state level. He served as the group's "honorary chairman" until his death in 1992. Started on a shoestring, U.S. English claimed 400,000 dues-paying members by decade's end. Over that time it raised and spent approximately $28 million on campaigns to "preserve the status" of English—or, more precisely, to limit public uses of other languages. Whether such restrictions are intended to encompass all or selected government programs, schools, broadcast media, workplaces, business advertising, and other domains have remained matters of dispute. Proponents have issued contradictory statements. Some have pressed merely to give English legal recognition, while others have sought to outlaw all public services in other tongues, up to and including emergency 911 operators,[3] and to crack down on private sector bilingualism as well.

------

2. In the 1950s the top five countries of origin were Germany, Canada, Mexico, the United Kingdom, and Italy; in the 1980s they were Mexico, the Philippines, Vietnam, Korea, and China (including Taiwan). Asian immigration increased from 6 percent of the total in the 1950s to 43 percent in 1986.

3. Incredible as this may seem, Dr. Robert Melby, chairman of the Florida English campaign, called for the abolition of bilingual 911 assistance during a public debate in Miami, as reported by United Press International (*Diario Las Américas,* March 22, 1985). A year later he reiterated the same argument during an interview: "Everybody calling the emergency line should have to learn enough English so they can say 'fire' or 'emergency' and give the address. I would [learn that much Spanish] if I was living in Mexico." Asked whether his proposal might not lead to needless tragedies, the Tampa optometrist responded that "loss of life" had already occurred in cases where bilingual operators were

The new guardians of English achieved few tangible changes in   5
language policy during the 1980s. They did succeed, however, in placing
a polarizing issue on the national agenda, a debate—conducted almost
entirely in English—that produced misunderstanding and mistrust on all
sides. Throughout the country language differences became a lightning
rod for ethnic tensions:

> In Elizabeth, New Jersey, a city whose residents are 30 percent
> Hispanic, the mayor instituted a "Speak-English-Only" rule for
> city workers while performing their duties, except when other
> languages were needed to communicate with members of the
> public. He insisted it was "discourteous for City employees to
> converse in other than English in front of other City employees."

> A San Diego grand jury denounced schooling in languages other
> than English as "un-American." It asserted that "bilingual edu-
> cation promotes a type of cultural apartheid in that it encourages
> a dual society."

> Koreans in Philadelphia secured the city's permission to purchase
> and erect street signs in their native language. Posted in a racially
> mixed neighborhood, the signs soon became targets for vandal-
> ism and angry protests and had to be removed. Local German
> Americans, betraying an ignorance of their own history, ob-
> jected that their ancestors had never enjoyed such advantages.

> A cooperative apartment building in Broward County, Florida,
> voted to restrict residency to persons able to speak and read the
> English language. "We screen everyone for the protection of
> our tenants," explained the co-op's president. "We don't want
> undesirables living here. And if we can't communicate with
> people, it creates a real burden."

> At a concert near Boston, when Linda Ronstadt and a mariachi
> band performed music from her recent album, *Canciones de mi
> Padre,* some members of the audience began to chant: "Sing in
> English." As Ronstadt continued to sing in Spanish, two hundred
> fans walked out.

> Responding to complaints from African-American constituents
> about Korean, Arab, and Hispanic merchants, an alderman in
> Chicago proposed that anyone seeking a retail grocer's license
> should have to pass an English-proficiency test. "If you don't
> know English, you can't understand the laws," he said. "You
> have to know more than Mexican."

---

unavailable. It was "an unrealistic dream," Melby added, for non-English speakers to
expect emergency services in numerous languages; see James Crawford, "Conservative
Groups Take Aim at Bilingual-Education Programs," *Education Week,* March 19, 1986,
pp. 1, 14.

What is at issue for policymakers is how to address the practical reality of bilingualism within a framework of democratic principles. While this is partly a matter of managing resources—balancing costs and benefits—it is primarily one of defining rights. By nature the process will be political; that is, it will involve conflicting interests and symbols. Yet, to be productive, it must dispense with global analogies and focus on tangible problems.

For individuals there are two kinds of rights that must be clarified: freedom from discrimination on the basis of language and affirmative steps to overcome language barriers. The first category would seem rather straightforward and noncontroversial. As we have seen, the Supreme Court has increasingly treated language discrimination as a surrogate for national-origin discrimination, which is prohibited both by statute and by the U.S. Constitution. It should be a simple matter to codify these precedents in federal law so that they are widely understood. Who would oppose this basic principle of fairness? Senator Richard Shelby, for one. At the behest of U.S. English, the Alabama Democrat has proposed legislation that would, among other things, amend the Civil Rights Act of 1964 to include an explicit ban on language-based discrimination, *but for English speakers only*. How courts would interpret this implied departure from equal protection is uncertain. Some might now question the Equal Employment Opportunity Commission's fair-practice guidelines for linguistic minorities; even the *Lau v. Nichols* precedent on special help for LEP students could be subject to challenge. Private-sector employers could be vulnerable to lawsuits if they hired or promoted workers for their bilingual skills. Shelby's so-called Language of Government Act would also prohibit any "official act"[4] by federal

---

4. As in Arizona's Proposition 106, much unclarity surrounds this term. Shelby's bill, S. 434, and a similar measure sponsored by Representative Bill Emerson, H. R. 123, include the following definition:

(2) The term 'official' means governmental actions, documents, or policies that are enforceable with the full weight and authority of the Government, but does not include—

   (A) actions, documents, or policies that are purely informational or educational;
   (B) actions, documents, or policies that are not enforceable in the United States;
   (C) actions that protect the public health or safety;
   (D) actions that protect the rights of victims of crimes or criminal defendants; and
   (E) documents that utilize terms of art or phrases from languages other than English.

This wording raises more questions than it answers. As "enforceable actions" would federal civil and administrative proceedings—e.g., immigration hearings—be included in the ban? As "informational documents," would bilingual voter aids be exempted? What about contracts, treaties, and trade negotiations with foreign governments—would

agencies or employees "that requires the use of a language other than English"—in effect, requiring the government itself to discriminate. At minimum, Americans should reject such mean-spirited restrictions.

A more difficult, though no less urgent, task is to formulate an affirmative policy for bilingual public services that is both equitable and realistic. There is no question of accommodating 160 languages at once, as some obstructionists have suggested, or of creating an entitlement to language assistance for any non-English speaker at any time. A sound policy must reflect both numbers and need. Naturally these will vary, depending on the languages spoken in a given community and the government services at issue. Take a hypothetical American city, recently transformed by newcomers whose English is limited, and assume that 20 percent of local residents are native speakers of Spanish, 5 percent speak Vietnamese, and another 5 percent speak either Cantonese, Tagalog, Gujarati, Armenian, or Polish. Should the city ensure that court interpreters and 911 operators are available in all these languages? Definitely. In which tongues besides English should it provide brochures on low-income energy assistance? Probably in Spanish and Vietnamese and in the others if practical, since non-English speakers are among those likely to need help. Should it translate property tax bills into every language? Probably not, considering the expense and the alternatives for providing assistance, although printing them in Spanish might prove cost-effective.

It would be best to leave such decisions to local or state governments, which are already responding to these needs (if somewhat haphazardly). No doubt many jurisdictions would welcome guidance on what kinds of accommodations are reasonable. Yet in areas where minorities remain powerless to secure help through normal political channels, federal mandates may be necessary, especially where due process or public safety is involved. Neither cost nor administrative convenience can excuse policies that result in the denial of fundamental rights or essential services. Less vital needs may be balanced against practical exigencies. Demographic formulas could be devised, as under the Voting Rights Act, to trigger a jurisdiction's obligation to provide certain kinds of help, say, bilingual drivers' tests, and special oversight could be authorized in localities with a documented history of discrimination. The operative principle, which should be applied wherever possible, is one of simple equality under the law. Rights that individuals would otherwise enjoy, including free access to government, must not be limited on account of language ability.

More complex questions of democracy arise regarding minorities   10 whose native tongues have been excluded or repressed or both, yet

---

the U.S. government have to act in English only? Once again the philosophy seems to be: Let the courts sort it out.

survive as valued means of self-expression. Does justice demand that such communities be granted extraordinary rights—beyond equality as individuals and freedom of communication in private contexts? Should they be offered, in effect, an exemption from "the primacy of English," with guarantees of native-language services and assistance in undoing the damage wrought by forced "Americanization"? On the other hand, can we extend these special rights without fostering resentment and divisiveness, not only between Anglos and non-Anglos, but among linguistic minorities who are treated differently? Can we create legal privileges on the basis of ethnicity without encouraging tribalism?

In jurisdictions where a single minority language has been historically dominant and continues to be so, these questions are easily settled. Residents of Puerto Rico—whether they choose statehood or not—should have every right to preserve their Spanish heritage and to resist further attempts to anglicize the island. Or they should be able to move toward bilingualism, appeasing a growing stratum of Puerto Ricans that favors greater use of English. But whatever the outcome, it should be a decision by Puerto Ricans, not by outsiders.

This same principle should apply on the Navajo, Tohono O'odham, and other reservations where Indian tongues remain viable. In addition, as past targets of cultural genocide, indigenous Americans should have a special claim on subsidies to maintain or revive their languages and teach them to their young. The Hawaiian language, reduced to fewer than two thousand native speakers, is now beginning to make a comeback, thanks to private efforts like the Pûnana Leo ("Language Nest") immersion program for preschoolers. But preventing the extinction of indigenous tongues must be understood as preserving cultural treasures that belong, in a sense, to all Americans—a public responsibility. Besides expanding educational assistance, the federal government should finance tribally controlled projects in language revival.

The question of linguistic self-determination is a much closer one for Spanish speakers in the Southwest, now reduced to minority status in all but a few locales. A substantial percentage of these Hispanics are recent immigrants, and in any case, they are rapidly becoming anglicized. Nevertheless, Spanish remains a significant, if not a dominant, tongue in many parts of the region, where it antedates English by nearly three centuries. Surveys have repeatedly shown that Mexican-Americans (like most other linguistic minorities) want their children to learn English, but not to lose their native tongue in the process. For this sizable group of U.S. citizens, it would seem hard to justify a restriction of language choice—to insist that maintaining Spanish should be a private matter, not a public right—purely on the basis of "majority rule" by relative newcomers to their homeland. To do so would be equivalent to justifying an Official Spanish policy for Dade County, or an Official Chinese policy for Monterey Park, should local voters decide to enact them.

Such acts of retribution against English speakers seem unlikely. Yet tomorrow's balkanization thrives on today's denial of minority rights. This remains the essential folly of English Only, whether it affects immigrants or indigenous Americans, groups or individuals, people with historic claims or newcomers seeking a modicum of fairness. Tyrannies of the majority are ultimately self-defeating. At a juncture in our national experience when ideals of community seem elusive and fellow countrymen seem fractionated into selfish clans, it is worth remembering, to paraphrase the Supreme Court in *Meyer* v. *Nebraska,* that—however advantageous the goal may appear—national unity cannot be coerced. "American" identity cannot be propagated, nor ethnic harmony assured, by means that contradict our founding principles.

Reading the Text

1. What are the goals of the English-only movement?
2. How have recent changes in the ethnic makeup of America led to the popularity of English-only initiatives, according to Crawford?
3. What, for Crawford, are the free speech issues involved in the debate over language restrictions?
4. What is Crawford's attitude toward bilingualism?

Reading the Signs

1. In class, discuss the examples of attempts to restrict language difference that Crawford mentions early in his essay. Do you consider these attempts to designate English as the preferred language appropriate? Why or why not? Are some cases clearer than others? Why or why not?
2. Visit your college library and research U.S. English's attempt to add an English Language Amendment to the Constitution in the 1980s. Then write an argumentative essay in which you explain why you support or oppose U.S. English's goals.
3. Interview at least four students whose families have immigrated to the United States, and ask them about their use of language. When did they learn English, and what languages do they and their relatives use? Do they feel comfortable using their family's language around native Americans? Have they ever been required to use English? Use the results of your interviews to formulate an essay in which you explore the importance of language as a means of self-expression.
4. Do you agree with Crawford's proposals about which bilingual services should be provided to residents of his hypothetical city (see p. 428)? Write an essay in which you support, refute, or modify his proposals.
5. To what extent is the American identity dependent on the exclusive use of the English language? In class, explore this question by first brainstorming on the blackboard qualities you believe are part of being "American." Then

examine your brainstormed list: To what extent is communicating in English essential? Use your results to discuss the merits or problems of the English-only movement.

GLORIA ANZALDÚA

How to Tame a Wild Tongue

IIIIIIIIIIIIIIIIIIIIIIIIIIIIIIIIIIIIIIIIIIIIIIIIIIIIIIII

How would you feel if your teacher scolded you when you tried to tell her how to pronounce your name? That is the opening anecdote in Gloria Anzaldúa's linguistic analysis of Mexican-American speech. Showing that the language of Chicanos and Chicanas differs not only from the speech of Anglos but from the speech of other Hispanic groups, Anzaldúa provides a detailed description of the history and significance of her mother tongue. Language is not simply an instrument for communication, she suggests, it is a sign of identity. "So if you really want to hurt me," Anzaldúa concludes, "talk badly about my language." A lecturer at the University of California, Santa Cruz, Gloria Anzaldúa is a writer and editor whose books include This Bridge Called My Back: Writings by Radical Women of Color *(1983),* Haciendo Caras: Making Face/Making Soul *(1990) and* Borderlands/La Frontera: The New Mestiza *(1987), from which this selection is taken.*

"We're going to have to control your tongue," the dentist says, pulling out all the metal from my mouth. Silver bits plop and tinkle into the basin. My mouth is a mother lode.

The dentist is cleaning out my roots. I get a whiff of the stench when I gasp. "I can't cap that tooth yet, you're still draining," he says.

"We're going to have to do something about your tongue," I hear the anger rising in his voice. My tongue keeps pushing out the wads of cotton, pushing back the drills, the long thin needles. "I've never seen anything as strong or as stubborn," he says. And I think, how do your tame a wild tongue, train it to be quiet, how do you bridle and saddle it? How do you make it lie down?

Who is to say that robbing a people of its language is less violent than war?
— RAY GWYN SMITH[1]

---

1. Ray Gwyn Smith, *Moorland Is Cold Country*, unpublished book.

I remember being caught speaking Spanish at recess—that was good for three licks on the knuckles with a sharp ruler. I remember being sent to the corner of the classroom for "talking back" to the Anglo teacher when all I was trying to do was tell her how to pronounce my name. "If you want to be American, speak 'American.' If you don't like it, go back to Mexico where you belong."

"I want you to speak English. *Pa' hallar buen trabajo tienes que saber hablar el inglés bien. Qué vale toda tu educación si todavía hablas inglés con un* 'accent,'"[2] my mother would say, mortified that I spoke English like a Mexican. At Pan American University, I, and all Chicano students were required to take two speech classes. Their purpose: to get rid of our accents.

Attacks on one's form of expression with the intent to censor are a violation of the First Amendment. *El Anglo con cara de inocente nos arrancó la lengua.*[3] Wild tongues can't be tamed, they can only be cut out.

Overcoming the Tradition of Silence

Ahogadas, escupimos el oscuro.
Peleando con nuestra propia sombra
el silencio nos sepulta.[4]

En boca cerrada no entran moscas. "Flies don't enter a closed mouth" is a saying I kept hearing when I was child. *Ser habladora* was to be a gossip and a liar, to talk too much. *Muchachitas bien criadas,* well-bred girls don't answer back. *Es una falta de respeto*[5] to talk back to one's mother or father. I remember one of the sins I'd recite to the priest in the confession box the few times I went to confession: talking back to my mother, *hablar pa' 'tras, repelar. Hocicona, repelona, chismosa,* having a big mouth, questioning, carrying tales are all signs of being *mal criada.*[6] In my culture they are all words that are derogatory if applied to women—I've never heard them applied to men.

---

2. *Pa' hallar buen trabajo tienes que saber hablar el inglés bien. Qué vale toda tu educación si todavía hablas inglés con un* 'accent.'   To find a good job you have to know how to speak English well. What good is all your education if you still speak English with an accent?—EDS.

3. *El Anglo con cara de inocente nos arrancó la lengua.*   The Anglo with an innocent-looking face made us shut up. Translated literally: "pulled our tongues out."—EDS.

4. *Ahogadas, escupimos el oscuro. / Peleando con nuestra propia sombra / el silencio nos sepulta.*   Drowned, we spit in the dark. / Fighting with our own shadow / the silence buries us.—EDS.

5. *Es una falta de respeto*   It's a lack of respect.—EDS.

6. *mal criada*   Ill-bred.—EDS.

The first time I heard two women, a Puerto Rican and a Cuban,   5
say the word "*nosotras,*"[7] I was shocked. I had not known the word
existed. Chicanas use *nosotros*[8] whether we're male or female. We are
robbed of our female being by the masculine plural. Language is a male
discourse.

> *And our tongues have become*
> *dry   the wilderness has*
> *dried out our tongues   and*
> *we have forgotten speech.*
> — IRENA KLEPFISZ[9]

Even our own people, other Spanish speakers *nos quieren poner candados en la boca.*[10] They would hold us back with their bag of *reglas de
academia.*[11]

Oyé como ladra: el lenguaje de la frontera[12]

Quien tiene boca se equivoca.[13]
— MEXICAN SAYING

"*Pocho,* cultural traitor, you're speaking the oppressor's language by
speaking English, you're ruining the Spanish language," I have been
accused by various Latinos and Latinas. Chicano Spanish is considered
by the purist and by most Latinos deficient, a mutilation of Spanish.

But Chicano Spanish is a border tongue which developed naturally.
Change, *evolución, enriquecimiento de palabras nuevas por invención o
adopción*[14] have created variants of Chicano Spanish, *un nuevo lenguaje.
Un lenguaje que corresponde a un modo de vivir.*[15] Chicano Spanish is not
incorrect, it is a living language.

---

7. **nosotras** We, female form.—EDS.

8. **nosotros** We, male form.—EDS.

9. Irena Klepfisz, "*Di rayze aheym* / The Journey Home," in *The Tribe of Dina: A
Jewish Women's Anthology,* Melanie Kaye/Kantrowitz and Irena Klepfisz, eds. (Montpelier,
VT: Sinister Wisdom Books, 1986), 49.

10. **nos quieren poner candados en la boca.**   They want us to put padlocks on our
mouths.—EDS.

11. **reglas de academia** Academic rules.—EDS.

12. **Oyé como ladra: el lenguaje de la frontera**   Listen how it barks: the language
of the borderlands.—EDS.

13. **Quien tiene boca se equivoca.**   Whoever has a mouth makes mistakes.—EDS.

14. **evolución, enriquecimiento de palabras nuevas por invención o adopción**   Evolution, enrichment of new words by invention or adoption.—EDS.

15. **un nuevo lenguaje. Un lenguaje que corresponde a un modo de vivir.**   A new
language. A language that matches a way of living.—EDS.

For a people who are neither Spanish nor live in a country in which Spanish is the first language; for a people who live in a country in which English is the reigning tongue but who are not Anglo; for a people who cannot entirely identify with either standard (formal, Castillian) Spanish or standard English, what recourse is left to them but to create their own language? A language which they can connect their identity to, one capable of communicating the realities and values true to themselves— a language with terms that are neither *español ni inglés*,[16] but both. We speak a patois, a forked tongue, a variation of two languages.

Chicano Spanish sprang out of the Chicanos' need to identify our-   10
selves as a distinct people. We needed a language with which we could communicate with ourselves, a secret language. For some of us, language is a homeland closer than the Southwest—for many Chicanos today live in the Midwest and the East. And because we are a complex, hetero- geneous people, we speak many languages. Some of the languages we speak are:

1. Standard English
2. Working class and slang English
3. Standard Spanish
4. Standard Mexican Spanish
5. North Mexican Spanish dialect
6. Chicano Spanish (Texas, New Mexico, Arizona, and California have regional variations)
7. Tex-Mex
8. *Pachuco* (called *caló*)

My "home" tongues are the languages I speak with my sister and brothers, with my friends. They are the last five listed, with 6 and 7 being closest to my heart. From school, the media and job situations, I've picked up standard and working-class English. From Mamagrande Locha and from reading Spanish and Mexican literature, I've picked up Standard Spanish and Standard Mexican Spanish. From *los recién llegados*,[17] Mexican immigrants, and *braceros*,[18] I learned the North Mexican dialect. With Mexicans I'll try to speak either Standard Mexican Spanish or the North Mexican dialect. From my parents and Chicanos living in the Valley, I picked up Chicano Texas Spanish, and I speak it with my mom, younger brother (who married a Mexican and who rarely mixes Spanish with English), aunts, and older relatives.

With Chicanas from *Nuevo México* or *Arizona* I will speak Chicano Spanish a little, but often they don't understand what I'm saying. With

---

16. *español ni inglés* Spanish nor English.—EDS.
17. *los recién llegados* The recently arrived.—EDS.
18. *braceros* Laborers.—EDS.

most California Chicanas I speak entirely in English (unless I forget). When I first moved to San Francisco, I'd rattle off something in Spanish, unintentionally embarrassing them. Often it is only with another Chicana *tejana*[19] that I can talk freely.

Words distorted by English are known as anglicisms or *pochismos.* The *pocho* is an anglicized Mexican or American of Mexican origin who speaks Spanish with an accent characteristic of North Americans and who distorts and reconstructs the language according to the influence of English.[20] Tex-Mex, or Spanglish, comes most naturally to me. I may switch back and forth from English to Spanish in the same sentence or in the same word. With my sister and my brother Nune and with Chicano *tejano* contemporaries I speak in Tex-Mex.

From kids and people my own age I picked up *Pachuco. Pachuco* (the language of the zoot suiters) is a language of rebellion, both against Standard Spanish and Standard English. It is a secret language. Adults of the culture and outsiders cannot understand it. It is made up of slang words from both English and Spanish. *Ruca* means girl or woman, *vato* means guy or dude, *chale* means no, *simón* means yes, *churro* is sure, talk is *periquiar, pigionear* means petting, *que gacho* means how nerdy, *ponte águila* means watch out, death is called *la pelona.* Through lack of practice and not having others who can speak it, I've lost most of the *Pachuco* tongue.

Chicano Spanish

Chicanos, after 250 years of Spanish/Anglo colonization, have de-   15
veloped significant differences in the Spanish we speak. We collapse two adjacent vowels into a single syllable and sometimes shift the stress in certain words such as *maíz / maiz, cohete / cuete.* We leave out certain consonants when they appear between vowels: *lado / lao, mojado / mojao.* Chicanos from South Texas pronounce *f* as *j* as in *jue (fue).* Chicanos use "archaisms," words that are no longer in the Spanish language, words that have been evolved out. We say *semos, truje, haiga, ansina,* and *naiden.* We retain the "archaic" *j,* as in *jalar,* that derives from an earlier *h* (the French *halar* or the Germanic *halon* which was lost to standard Spanish in the sixteenth century), but which is still found in several regional dialects such as the one spoken in South Texas. (Due to geography, Chicanos from the Valley of South Texas were cut off linguistically from

---

19. *tejana* Female Texan.—EDS.
20. R. C. Ortega, *Dialectología Del Barrio,* trans. Hortencia S. Alwan (Los Angeles, CA: R. C. Ortega Publisher & Bookseller, 1977), 132.

other Spanish speakers. We tend to use words that the Spaniards brought over from Medieval Spain. The majority of the Spanish colonizers in Mexico and the Southwest came from Extremadura—Hernán Cortés was one of them—and Andalucía. Andalucians pronounce *ll* like a *y*, and their *d*'s tend to be absorbed by adjacent vowels: *tirado* becomes *tirao*. They brought *el lenguaje popular, dialectos y regionalismos.*[21])

Chicanos and other Spanish speakers also shift *ll* to *y* and *z* to *s.*[22] We leave out initial syllables, saying *tar* for *estar*, *toy* for *estoy*, *hora* for *ahora* (*cubanos* and *puertorriqueños* also leave out initial letters of some words). We also leave out the final syllable such as *pa* for *para*. The intervocalic *y*, the *ll* as in *tortilla, ella, botella*, gets replaced by *tortia* or *tortiya, ea, botea*. We add an additional syllable at the beginning of certain words: *atocar* for *tocar*, *agastar* for *gastar*. Sometimes we'll say *lavaste las vacijas*, other times *lavates* (substituting the *ates* verb endings for the *aste*).

We use anglicisms, words borrowed from English: *bola* from ball, *carpeta* from carpet, *máchina de lavar* (instead of *lavadora*) from washing machine. Tex-Mex argot, created by adding a Spanish sound at the beginning or end of an English word such as *cookiar* for cook, *watchar* for watch, *parkiar* for park, and *rapiar* for rape, is the result of the pressures on Spanish speakers to adapt to English.

We don't use the word *vosotros / as* or its accompanying verb form. We don't say *claro* (to mean yes), *imagínate*, or *me emociona*, unless we picked up Spanish from Latinas, out of a book, or in a classroom. Other Spanish-speaking groups are going through the same, or similar, development in their Spanish.

Linguistic Terrorism

Deslenguadas. Somos los del español deficiente.[23] *We are your linguistic nightmare, your linguistic aberration, your linguistic* mestisaje,[24] *the subject of your* burla.[25] *Because we speak with tongues of fire we are culturally crucified. Racially, culturally, and linguistically* somos huérfanos[26] *—we speak an orphan tongue.*

---

21. Eduardo Hernandéz-Chávez, Andrew D. Cohen, and Anthony F. Beltramo, *El Lenguaje de los Chicanos: Regional and Social Characteristics of Language Used by Mexican Americans* (Arlington, VA: Center for Applied Linguistics, 1975), 39.

22. Hernandéz-Chávez, xvii.

23. **Deslenguadas. Somos los del español deficiente.** Foul-mouthed. We are the ones with deficient Spanish.—EDS.

24. **mestisaje** Mongrels.—EDS.

25. **burla** Ridicule.—EDS.

26. **somos huérfanos** We are orphans.—EDS.

Chicanas who grew up speaking Chicano Spanish have internalized the belief that we speak poor Spanish. It is illegitimate, a bastard language. And because we internalize how our language has been used against us by the dominant culture, we use our language differences against each other.

Chicana feminists often skirt around each other with suspicion and   20 hesitation. For the longest time I couldn't figure it out. Then it dawned on me. To be close to another Chicana is like looking into the mirror. We are afraid of what we'll see there. *Pena.* Shame. Low estimation of self. In childhood we are told that our language is wrong. Repeated attacks on our native tongue diminish our sense of self. The attacks continue throughout our lives.

Chicanas feel uncomfortable talking in Spanish to Latinas, afraid of their censure. Their language was not outlawed in their countries. They had a whole lifetime of being immersed in their native tongue; generations, centuries in which Spanish was a first language, taught in school, heard on radio and TV, and read in the newspaper.

If a person, Chicana or Latina, has a low estimation of my native tongue, she also has a low estimation of me. Often with *mexicanas y latinas* we'll speak English as a neutral language. Even among Chicanas we tend to speak English at parties or conferences. Yet, at the same time, we're afraid the other will think we're *agringadas* because we don't speak Chicano Spanish. We oppress each other trying to out–Chicano each other, vying to be the "real" Chicanas, to speak like Chicanos. There is no one Chicano language just as there is no one Chicano experience. A monolingual Chicana whose first language is English or Spanish is just as much a Chicana as one who speaks several variants of Spanish. A Chicana from Michigan or Chicago or Detroit is just as much a Chicana as one from the Southwest. Chicano Spanish is as diverse linguistically as it is regionally.

By the end of this century, Spanish speakers will comprise the biggest minority group in the United States, a country where students in high schools and colleges are encouraged to take French classes because French is considered more "cultured." But for a language to remain alive it must be used.[27] By the end of this century English, and not Spanish, will be the mother tongue of most Chicanos and Latinos.

So, if you want to really hurt me, talk badly about my language. Ethnic identity is twin skin to linguistic identity—I am my language. Until I can take pride in my language, I cannot take pride in myself. Until I can accept as legitimate Chicano Texas Spanish, Tex-Mex, and

---

27. Irena Klepfisz, "Secular Jewish Identity: Yidishkayt in America," in *The Tribe of Dina,* Kaye/Kantrowitz and Klepfisz, eds., 43.

all the other languages I speak, I cannot accept the legitimacy of myself.
Until I am free to write bilingually and to switch codes without having
always to translate, while I still have to speak English or Spanish when I
would rather speak Spanglish, and as long as I have to accommodate the
English speakers rather than having them accommodate me, my tongue
will be illegitimate.

I will no longer be made to feel ashamed of existing. I will have my   25
voice: Indian, Spanish, white. I will have my serpent's tongue—my
woman's voice, my sexual voice, my poet's voice. I will overcome the
tradition of silence.

> *My fingers*
> *move sly against your palm*
> *Like women everywhere, we speak in code. . . .*
> — MELANIE KAYE/KANTROWITZ[28]

Reading the Text

1. Why does Anzaldúa blend Spanish and English in her selection?
2. How does Anzaldúa's language contribute to her sense of identity, in her
   view?
3. What are the essential features of Chicano Spanish, according to Anzaldúa?
4. What does Anzaldúa mean by "linguistic terrorism"?

Reading the Signs

1. Anzaldúa sees her language in political terms. Write a personal essay in
   which you explore the significance of your native language to you. If, like
   Anzaldúa, you too see your language politically, describe an incident that
   motivated you to feel this way. If you don't view language as she does,
   consider why your experiences have led you to an alternative view of
   language.
2. Writing as if you were Gloria Anzaldúa, compose a hypothetical letter to
   the U.S. English organization, arguing for your right to speak in your native
   tongue. Consult James Crawford, "Hold Your Tongue: The Question of
   Linguistic Self-Determination" (p. 424) and Ada María Isasi-Diaz, "Hispanic in America: Starting Points" (p. 503) to develop your letter.
3. In class, discuss the effect of Anzaldúa's blending of English and Spanish
   and imagistic and analytic language. How does such blending contribute

---

28. Melanie Kaye/Kantrowitz, "Sign," in *We Speak in Code: Poems and Other Writ-*
ings (Pittsburgh, PA: Motheroot Publications, Inc., 1980), 85.

to the points she is making? What different impact would the essay have if it were written all in English?

4. How might Anzaldúa respond to the cross-cultural struggles that Dorinne K. Kondo ("On Being a Conceptual Anomaly," p. 477) experiences? Writing as if you were Anzaldúa, compose a letter to Kondo in which you help Kondo come to terms with her struggles.

5. How do you think Ron Maydon (interview, p. 515) might respond to Anzaldúa's selection? Write a dialogue between Maydon and Anzaldúa, being sure to consider issues of gender as well as ethnicity. Share your dialogue with your class.

"I think there's a pretty simple reason Jackie and I are so comfortable with each other. We see the world as more than just black and white."

©1992 The Cherokee Group

CHAPTER SEVEN

A GATHERING OF
TRIBES

Multicultural Semiotics

Who are you? A simple question. Ask it of a classmate, of yourself. "Who are you?" What's the answer? Did your classmate give her name? Did you? Or did each of you answer differently? Did you say "I am an American"? Or did you say "I am an African-American," or an "Asian-American," or a "Latino," or a "Native American"? Would you answer "I am a European-American" or a "Jewish-American"? However you answered the question, can you say why you answered as you did?

To ask how you identify yourself and why you do so as you do is to begin to probe the semiotics of race and culture in America's multicultural society. You may have strong feelings on the matter, some of you believing that it is essential that all Americans think of themselves as *Americans,* others thinking just as strongly that your racial and cultural identity comes first. In either case, your beliefs reflect a world view, or cultural mythology, that guides you in your most fundamental thoughts about your identity. Let's look at those myths for a moment.

Say you feel that all American citizens should view themselves simply as Americans, without all the hyphens. If so, your feelings reflect a basic cultural mythology best known as the myth of the American "melting pot." This is the belief that America offers all of its citizens the opportunity to blend together into one harmonious whole that will erase the many differences among us on behalf of a new, distinctly American, identity. This belief has led many immigrants to seek to assimilate into what they perceive as the dominant American culture, shedding the specific cultural characteristics that may distinguish them from what they see as the American norm. And it is a belief that stands behind some of the most generous impulses in our culture—at least ideally.

But what if you don't buy this belief? What if, as far as you are concerned, you're proud to belong to a different community, one that differs from the basically Anglo-Saxon culture that has become the dominant, and normative, culture for assimilation? Or what if you and your people have found that you were never really allowed to blend in anyway, that in spite of the promise, the melting pot was never meant for you? If so, how does the myth of the melting pot look to you? Does it look the same as it would to someone who never had any trouble assimilating, or never needed to, because he or she already belonged to the dominant culture?

To see that the myth of the melting pot looks different depending upon who is looking at it is to see why it is so precious to some Americans and so irrelevant to others. It is to realize again the fundamental semiotic precept that our social values are culturally determined rather than inscribed in the marble of absolute truth. This may be difficult to accept, especially if you and your classmates all come from the same culture and hence all hold the same values. But if you know people who are different, you might want to ask them how the myth of the melting pot looks from their perspective. Does it look like an ideal for our nation to strive to achieve? Or does it look like an invitation to cultural submission? It all depends upon who's looking.

We Are the People

All cultures have their own traditional ways of identifying themselves, and most begin by assuming that their culture is normative. It's not just Anglo-Saxon America, in other words, that presumes its centrality in the order of things. We can see how groups of people implicitly believe in their privileged place in the world by looking at the names with which they identify themselves. Take the members of the largest Native-American tribe in the United States. To the rest of the world, they are known as the "Navajos." This is not the name the "Navajos" use among themselves, however, for the word "Navajo" does not come from their language. In all likelihood, the name was given to them by neighboring Pueblo Indians, for whom the term "Navahu" means "large area of cultivated lands." But in the language of the Navajo, which is quite different from that of the Pueblo Indians, they are not the people of the tilled fields. They are, quite simply, "The People," the most common English translation of the word "diné," the name by which the Navajo know themselves.

||||||||||||||||||||||||||||||||||||||||||||||||||||||||||||||||||||||||||||||||||||||||||||||||||||||||||||||||||||||||||||||||||||||||||||||||||||

Exploring the Signs of Race

In your journal, reflect on the question, "Who are you?" How does your ethnicity contribute to your sense of self? Are there other factors that contribute to your identity? If so, what are they and how do they relate to your ethnicity? If you don't perceive yourself in ethnic terms, why do you think that's the case?

||||||||||||||||||||||||||||||||||||||||||||||||||||||||||||||||||||||||||||||||||||||||||||||||||||||||||||||||||||||||||||||||||||||||||||||||||||

Or take the Hmong tribe of Southeast Asia. "Hmong" simply means "person," so to say "I am a Hmong" implicitly states "I am a person." While it is not the case that when a Navajo says "I am diné," or a Hmong says "I am Hmong," they mean "I am a human being and the rest of you aren't," we still find inscribed within the unconscious history of these ancient tribal names the trace of a belief found within many a tribal name: the sense that one's own tribe comes first in the order of things. Thus in the film *Little Big Man* (1970), the Cheyenne Indians who adopt Jack Crabb refer to themselves simply as "the human beings," while hidden in the ancient roots of the modern word "Aryan" (a word that is reflected in the national names of Iran and Ireland) is a sense of nation or peoplehood: "Aryan" once simply meant "the people."

Things are not really so different in America, even though our name for ourselves is derived from the name of a fifteenth-century navigator, Amerigo Vespucci. For in essence, we have tried to make America itself a tribe, and we too conceive of ourselves as a specially favored people. Indeed, our Pledge of Allegiance includes the phrase "one nation, under God," as if America alone enjoyed such a privilege. Just think how often America has tried to define itself as the richest, most powerful, most blessed nation on earth, the center to which all other peoples are to be compared.

But when we try to identify what, precisely, the American tribe is, we run into trouble. With so many races and cultures living together in this land, it is difficult to say which should have the privilege of becoming the standard by which the others are identified—or if there even should be a standard. The "melting pot" metaphor, after all, presumes that American assimilation means assimilating to the culture of a particular tribe of white, Anglo-Saxon protestantism.

And so, as we enter a multicultural era, it seems best to take the semiotic approach, to regard America as a tissue of mythologies, and to see ourselves as *peoples* rather than the People. The first step, then, is to recognize that cultural "absolutes" really reflect cultural mythologies, and in this way we may level the playing field as we investigate a multicultural society, asking, "Who are *we*?"

Culture or Race?

As you consider the cultural bases for your own sense of personal identity, you may object that race stands outside the cultural realm and within the natural realm of biology. But even biological issues are subject to cultural interpretation. In 1970, for example, the state of Louisiana passed a law (since repealed) that identified anyone as "black" whose veins flowed with at least a one-thirty-second share of "Negro blood." A woman with a similar share in her blood sued the state in 1982 to have her racial classification changed from "black" to "white," and lost. So, what *is* she? What she believes herself to be, or what the state defines her to be? Either way, her racial identity becomes more a matter of cultural and political determination than a natural fact.

Similarly, the great majority of those who identify themselves as "Indians" or "Native Americans" have considerable amounts of non-Indian blood in their veins. At present, anyone who can demonstrate a twenty-five percent share of Native American blood will be legally identified as such, but there is political pressure among Native-American groups themselves to broaden the blood requirements to increase the number of legally identifiable "Indians." Conversely, among Jews, or-thodoxy requires that to be identified as a Jew one's mother must be Jewish, and there is resistance to any tampering with this ancient rab-binical definition, even though many individuals with Jewish fathers and non-Jewish mothers consider themselves Jewish.

And so culture, the promptings of ideology rather than biology, makes its voice heard in what may appear to be the most natural of human identifications. But in current racial discourse, culture impinges in quite another way as well. You can see this at work in the very word "multiculturalism." If taken literally, a call for multicultural education could simply mean a call to introduce more Scandinavian, or French, or Greek, or Irish culture into a school curriculum. After all, these groups represent a broad range of cultures whose differences may be far more pronounced than the cultural differences between middle-class American families of African, Latin American, or European ancestry. But the word is not intended to be taken literally, of course. In practice, "multicultural" means "multiracial," and while this codification may strike some as a form of political euphemism, there are some sound reasons, in the con-text of American history, for so linking culture and race.

For unlike the relatively homogeneous nations of Europe, where social divisions have been inscribed largely along class lines, America has been obsessed with racial difference almost from the beginning. Though class divisions are important in America, it is race that defines our sense of social identity. This obsession with racial difference has had its own cultural effects, such that it makes perfect sense to speak, for instance, of African-Americans as a culture as well as a race. It makes sense because a history of slavery and racial oppression molded a New World culture that can be quite different from the Old World cultures of Africa. The American experience of the descendants of the African people who were dragged in chains to these shores, in other words, has produced a new culture (not without its own local distinctions) that is indeed African-*American,* but whose outward signs begin with the color of one's skin.

Culture Matters

With the recent arrival of a new wave of immigrants to American shores—a wave whose potential for effecting widespread cultural change rivals that of the great influx of eastern and southern Europeans at the turn of the century—the confluence of race and culture in American society has produced a new set of social challenges and conflicts. A nation that endured a devastating civil war over the issue of human slavery has traditionally perceived racial conflict in black-and-white terms, but the equations of cultural difference are no longer so neatly balanced. There are too many other races and cultures to take into account.

Where the rest of the country, for example, viewed the civil disturbances in Los Angeles in the spring of 1992 as a classic expression of black rage against white oppression, those living in L.A. knew that it wasn't this simple. Despite the media's almost exclusive focus on these two groups (*U.S. News & World Report*'s cover read, for instance, "Black vs. White: The New Fears"), a good half of those involved came from the city's largely Central American barrios. And herein lies another distinction. A census form will employ the same term for people of either Mexican or Central American origin—"Hispanic" or "Latino"—but to use this term in the context of the civil unrest is imprecise, for L.A.'s more-established Chicano population largely stayed out of the action during the days of rage.

More importantly, the focus on black-white conflict in L.A. obscured a different sort of conflict. The nation's newspapers and TV screens focused on the Rodney King beating, but how many people outside of L.A. were aware of the Latasha Harlins case? This case, which involved the shooting death of an African-American girl by a Korean-American shopkeeper, was just as important as the King beating in L.A.'s black community. The King case was the last straw, but the Harlins case, which resulted in the shopkeeper's being sentenced to five years' probation for the killing, really touched a nerve only a few months before the uprising, so much so that Korean-American shops were specially targeted for destruction during the unrest.

The simmering conflict between African-Americans and Korean-Americans is well known to anyone living in New York or Los Angeles, and it provides a particularly good example of what the semiotics of

||||||||||||||||||||||||||||||||||||||||||||||||||||||||||||||||||||||||||||||||||||||||||||||||||||||||||||||||||||||

Discussing the Signs of Race

In class, discuss which of several metaphors—melting pot, salad bowl, and layer cake are among the most common—you think best describes the racial composition of America. If you don't think any of the familiar metaphors capture America's racial makeup, then invent your own.

cultural difference is all about. For the racial differences between these groups go hand in hand with cultural differences that are equally potent sources of conflict. The Korean cultural code, for example, holds that it is impolite to make direct eye contact with other people, a practice that many African-American customers of Korean-American shops have interpreted as a gesture of racial disdain. Similarly, Korean women traditionally are taught to avoid direct physical contact with men and so may drop a man's change on a store counter rather than hand it to him directly. For an African-American customer, this may seem like another act of disrespect. To complicate the cultural confusion further, black immigrants from the West Indies are used to bargaining for the things they buy, particularly for produce. Thus, it may be perfectly natural for such a person to haggle over the price of an apple in a Korean-owned grocery. To the owner, however, this looks like the next thing to shoplifting (indeed, Latasha Harlins was shot during an argument that ensued when she offered to pay less for a pint of orange juice than was marked on the bottle).

Of course, larger socioeconomic issues are at work here as well—recent immigrants and long-time black citizens alike are tossed into the same underclass and forced to struggle among themselves for political and economic power—but the cultural issues cannot be dismissed. Sometimes it's the small things that count most (like how one perceives the price of a bottle of orange juice), and a semiotic sensitivity to such differences can head off the larger explosions.

The Multicultural Debate

Exploring the outline of a cultural mythology is not the same as attacking it, though it may seem to be under attack if it is *your* culture under investigation. This is perfectly natural, for not only our values but, as we have seen, our very sense of identity comes to us through our cultures. Thus, it can come as a shock to be told that one's cultural world view is just that: one world view among many. And when a traditionally dominant culture is challenged by other groups intent upon winning a share of cultural and political power for themselves, bewilderment can turn into backlash.

Try to think of an instance where your cultural values clashed with someone else's. Can you see why the other person may have felt threatened by your difference of opinion? Do you wish that that other person could just, for once, see things from your point of view? Would it be good to come to some sort of agreement about the matter, or would you prefer to have your own views triumph? If you'd like to find a way to agreement, how would you go about it?

As you consider the particular cultural differences that really matter to you, you may well find yourself up against the problem of cultural relativism. Relativism is the view that all values are relative to their social contexts and that there is no single standard by which to judge them. Indeed, opponents of multicultural education often point to the specter of relativism as a point in their favor. "How," they ask, "can we have a civil society if we can't agree on one set of values?" The monocultural position is, in effect, that America has successfully molded the many peoples and cultures in this land together into one harmonious nation (or at least is on its way to such a union) and is now being split apart by the trend toward multiculturalism. But what are the cultural assumptions behind this belief? What sort of culture do the opponents of multicultural education take for granted?

It's not that the opponents of multicultural education necessarily oppose the existence of other cultures in America. Usually, they hold the traditional American value of tolerance for difference even as they argue for a monocultural sense of nationhood. But "tolerance" itself looks tricky when we come to analyze it in cultural terms. It has rarely occurred to the dominant culture in America that people don't want to be "tolerated," that tolerance assumes a position of social and moral superiority from which one magnanimously chooses to allow other people to exist. From a semiotic perspective, tolerance is absurd in its traditional expression. It is the freedom to found your own country club because you have been blackballed from all the existing ones.

And that is one reason why multiculturalism is so threatening to those who oppose it. It doesn't call for more tolerance; it doesn't even call for acceptance (acceptance, too, implies a social superior who is in the position of accepting). Rather, multiculturalism calls for something closer to negotiation, a round-table dialogue presuming the participation of cultural equals who have come together to work out a complex restructuring of society. This negotiation can't take place, however, if everyone at the table presumes that their culture is the one true perspective. The United States has never had to negotiate like this before, so there is nothing ready made to put on the table for discussion. The first step is simply for everyone to get a chance to tell their story. That is what a multicultural education is about. The next, more challenging step, is to come up with a new story in which everyone can feel included.

The Readings

This chapter focuses on the ways that race and culture provide a sense of identity for Americans, beginning with Michael Omi's survey of how race works as a sign in popular American culture. Sam Fulwood III's personal testimony in "The Rage of the Black Middle Class" shows the conflict that the American Dream presents to African-Americans who have attempted to assimilate into a white, middle-class world. Richard Majors interprets the poses and signaling systems used for survival by African-American males. Dorinne K. Kondo reflects on her own sense of ethnic identity, offering insights into the contrasting cultural inheritances of Japanese-Americans, while Fan Shen provides a personal analysis of the role his Chinese heritage played in his experience as a student of freshman composition. From a Native-American perspective, Leslie Marmon Silko relates storytelling traditions to the sense of self and personal identity that prevails in her Pueblo culture. Then Ada María Isasi-Diaz describes the way Hispanics define themselves and how their definitions differ from the one-size-fits-all definitions of a census form. Finally, Studs Terkel's interviews of a Caucasian schoolteacher, a Mexican-American businessman, and a white woman who is struggling economically display the personal testimonies of three Americans in a complex, and changing, multiracial America.

MICHAEL OMI

In Living Color: Race and American Culture

Though many like to think that racism in America is a thing of the past, Michael Omi argues that racism is a pervasive feature in our lives, one that is both overt and inferential. Using race as a sign by which we judge a person's character, inferential racism invokes deep-rooted stereotypes, and as Omi shows in his survey of American film, television, and music, our popular culture is hardly immune from such stereotyping. Indeed, when ostensibly "progressive" programs like Saturday Night Live *can win the National Ethnic Coalition of Organizations' "Platinum Pit Award" for racist stereotyping in television, and comedians like Andrew Dice Clay command big audiences and salaries, one can see popular culture has a way to go before it becomes colorblind. The author of* Racial Formation in the United States: From the 1960s to the 1980s *(with Howard Winant, 1986), Michael Omi is a sociologist who teaches in the Asian-American/Ethnic Studies program at the University of California, Berkeley.*

In February 1987, Assistant Attorney General William Bradford Reynolds, the nation's chief civil rights enforcer, declared that the recent death of a black man in Howard Beach, New York and the Ku Klux Klan attack on civil rights marchers in Forsyth County, Georgia were "isolated" racial incidences. He emphasized that the places where racial conflict could potentially flare up were "far fewer now than ever before in our history," and concluded that such a diminishment of racism stood as "a powerful testament to how far we have come in the civil rights struggle."[1]

Events in the months following his remarks raise the question as to whether we have come quite so far. They suggest that dramatic instances of racial tension and violence merely constitute the surface manifestations of a deeper racial organization of American society—a system of inequality which has shaped, and in turn been shaped by, our popular culture.

In March, the NAACP released a report on blacks in the record industry entitled "The Discordant Sound of Music." It found that despite the revenues generated by black performers, blacks remain "grossly underrepresented" in the business, marketing and A & R (Artists and Repertoire) departments of major record labels. In addition, few blacks

---

1. Reynold's remarks were made at a conference on equal opportunity held by the bar association in Orlando, Florida. *The San Francisco Chronicle* (7 February 1987).

are employed as managers, agents, concert promoters, distributors, and retailers. The report concluded that:

> The record industry is overwhelmingly segregated and discrimination is rampant. No other industry in America so openly classifies its operations on a racial basis. At every level of the industry, beginning with the separation of black artists into a special category, barriers exist that severely limit opportunities for blacks.[2]

Decades after the passage of civil rights legislation and the affirmation of the principle of "equal opportunity," patterns of racial segregation and exclusion, it seems, continue to characterize the production of popular music.

The enduring logic of Jim Crow is also present in professional sports. In April, Al Campanis, vice president of player personnel for the Los Angeles Dodgers, explained to Ted Koppel on ABC's *Nightline* about the paucity of blacks in baseball front offices and as managers. "I truly believe," Campanis said, "that [blacks] may not have some of the necessities to be, let's say, a field manager or perhaps a general manager." When pressed for a reason, Campanis offered an explanation which had little to do with the structure of opportunity of institutional discrimination within professional sports:

> [W]hy are black men or black people not good swimmers? Because they don't have the buoyancy. . . . They are gifted with great musculature and various other things. They're fleet of foot. And this is why there are a lot of black major league ballplayers. Now as far as having the background to become club presidents, or presidents of a bank, I don't know.[3]

Black exclusion from the front office, therefore, was justified on the basis of biological "difference."

The issue of race, of course, is not confined to the institutional arrangements of popular culture production. Since popular culture deals with the symbolic realm of social life, the images which it creates, represents, and disseminates contribute to the overall racial climate. They become the subject of analysis and political scrutiny. In August, the National Ethnic Coalition of Organizations bestowed the "Golden Pit Awards" on television programs, commercials, and movies that were deemed offensive to racial and ethnic groups. *Saturday Night Live,* regarded by many media critics as a politically "progressive" show, was singled out for the "Platinum Pit Award" for its comedy skit "Ching

5

---

2. Economic Development Department of the NAACP, "The Discordant Sound of Music (A Report on the Record Industry)," (Baltimore, Maryland: The NAACP, 1987), pp. 16–17.

3. Campanis's remarks on *Nightline* were reprinted in *The San Francisco Chronicle* (April 9, 1987).

Chang" which depicted a Chinese storeowner and his family in a derogatory manner.[4]

These examples highlight the *overt* manifestations of racism in popular culture—institutional forms of discrimination which keep racial minorities out of the production and organization of popular culture, and the crude racial caricatures by which these groups are portrayed. Yet racism in popular culture is often conveyed in a variety of implicit, and at times invisible, ways. Political theorist Stuart Hall makes an important distinction between *overt* racism, the elaboration of an explicitly racist argument, policy, or view, and *inferential* racism which refers to "those apparently naturalized representations of events and situations relating to race, whether 'factual' or 'fictional,' which have racist premises and propositions inscribed in them as a set of *unquestioned assumptions.*" He argues that inferential racism is more widespread, common, and indeed insidious since "it is largely *invisible* even to those who formulate the world in its terms."[5]

Race itself is a slippery social concept which is paradoxically both "obvious" and "invisible." In our society, one of the first things we notice about people when we encounter them (along with their sex/ gender) is their *race*. We utilize race to provide clues about *who* a person is and *how* we should relate to her/him. Our perception of race determines our "presentation of *self,*" distinctions in status, and appropriate modes of conduct in daily and institutional life. This process is often unconscious; we tend to operate off of an unexamined set of *racial beliefs.*

Racial beliefs account for and explain variations in "human nature." Differences in skin color and other obvious physical characteristics supposedly provide visible clues to more substantive differences lurking underneath. Among other qualities, temperament, sexuality, intelligence, and artistic and athletic ability are presumed to be fixed and discernible from the palpable mark of race. Such diverse questions as our confidence and trust in others (as salespeople, neighbors, media figures); our sexual preferences and romantic images; our tastes in music, film, dance, or sports; indeed our very ways of walking and talking are ineluctably shaped by notions of race.

Ideas about race, therefore, have become "common sense"—a way of comprehending, explaining, and acting in the world. This is made painfully obvious when someone disrupts our common sense understandings. An encounter with someone who is, for example, racially

---

4. Ellen Wulfhorst, "TV Stereotyping: It's the 'Pits'," *The San Francisco Chronicle* (August 24, 1987).

5. Stuart Hall, "The Whites of Their Eyes: Racist Ideologies and the Media," in George Bridges and Rosalind Brunt, eds. *Silver Linings* (London: Lawrence and Wishart, 1981), pp. 36–37.

"mixed" or of a racial/ethnic group we are unfamiliar with becomes a source of discomfort for us, and momentarily creates a crisis of racial meaning. We also become disoriented when people do not act "black," "Latino," or indeed "white." The content of such stereotypes reveals a series of unsubstantiated beliefs about who these groups are, what they are like, and how they behave.

The existence of such racial consciousness should hardly be surpris- 10 ing. Even prior to the inception of the republic, the United States was a society shaped by racial conflict. The establishment of the Southern plantation economy, Western expansion, and the emergence of the labor movement, among other significant historical developments, have all involved conflicts over the definition and nature of the *color line*. The historical results have been distinct and different groups have encoun- tered unique forms of racial oppression—Native Americans faced gen- ocide, blacks were subjected to slavery, Mexicans were invaded and colonized, and Asians faced exclusion. What is common to the experi- ences of these groups is that their particular "fate" was linked to histor- ically specific ideas about the significance and meaning of race.[6] Whites defined them as separate "species," ones inferior to Northern European cultural stocks, and thereby rationalized the conditions of their subor- dination in the economy, in political life, and in the realm of culture.

A crucial dimension of racial oppression in the United States is the elaboration of an ideology of difference or "otherness." This involves defining "us" (i.e., white Americans) in opposition to "them," an im- portant task when distinct racial groups are first encountered, or in historically specific periods where preexisting racial boundaries are threatened or crumbling.

Political struggles over the very definition of who an "American" is illustrates this process. The Naturalization Law of 1790 declared that only free *white* immigrants could qualify, reflecting the initial desire among Congress to create and maintain a racially homogeneous society. The extension of eligibility to all racial groups has been a long and protracted process. Japanese, for example, were finally eligible to become naturalized citizens after the passage of the Walter-McCarran Act of 1952. The ideological residue of these restrictions in naturalization and citizenship laws is the equation within popular parlance of the term "American" with "white," while other "Americans" are described as black, Mexican, "Oriental," etc.

Popular culture has been an important realm within which racial ideologies have been created, reproduced, and sustained. Such ideologies

---

6. For an excellent survey of racial beliefs see Thomas F. Gossett, *Race: The History of an Idea in America* (New York: Shocken Books, 1965).

provide a framework of symbols, concepts, and images through which we understand, interpret, and represent aspects of our "racial" existence.

Race has often formed the central themes of American popular culture. Historian W. L. Rose notes that it is "curious coincidence" that four of the "most popular reading-viewing events in all American history" have in some manner dealt with race, specifically black/white relations in the south.[7] Harriet Beecher Stowe's *Uncle Tom's Cabin,* Thomas Ryan Dixon's *The Clansman* (the inspiration for D. W. Griffith's *The Birth of a Nation*), Margaret Mitchell's *Gone with the Wind* (as a book and film), and Alex Haley's *Roots* (as a book and television miniseries), each appeared at a critical juncture in American race relations and helped to shape new understandings of race.

Emerging social definitions of race and the "real American" were   15
reflected in American popular culture of the nineteenth century. Racial and ethnic stereotypes were shaped and reinforced in the newspapers, magazines, and pulp fiction of the period. But the evolution and ever-increasing sophistication of visual mass communications throughout the twentieth century provided, and continues to provide, the most dramatic means by which racial images are generated and reproduced.

Film and television have been notorious in disseminating images of racial minorities which establish for audiences what these groups look like, how they behave, and, in essence, "who they are." The power of the media lies not only in their ability to reflect the dominant racial ideology, but in their capacity to shape that ideology in the first place. D. W. Griffith's forementioned epic *Birth of a Nation,* a sympathetic treatment of the rise of the Ku Klux Klan during Reconstruction, helped to generate, consolidate, and "nationalize" images of blacks which had been more disparate (more regionally specific, for example) prior to the film's appearance.[8]

In television and film, the necessity to define characters in the briefest and most condensed manner has led to the perpetuation of racial caricatures, as racial stereotypes serve as shorthand for scriptwriters, directors, and actors. Television's tendency to address the "lowest common denominator" in order to render programs "familiar" to an enormous and diverse audience leads it regularly to assign and reassign racial characteristics to particular groups, both minority and majority.

Many of the earliest American films deal with racial and ethnic "difference." The large influx of "new immigrants" at the turn of the

---

7. W. L. Rose, *Race and Region in American Historical Fiction: Four Episodes in Popular Culture* (Oxford: Clarendon Press, 1979).

8. Melanie Martindale-Sikes, "Nationalizing 'Nigger' Imagery Through *Birth of a Nation,*" paper prepared for the 73rd Annual Meeting of the American Sociological Association (September 4–8, 1978) in San Francisco.

century led to a proliferation of negative images of Jews, Italians, and Irish which were assimilated and adapted by such films as Thomas Edison's *Cohen's Advertising Scheme* (1904). Based on an old vaudeville routine, the film featured a scheming Jewish merchant, aggressively hawking his wares. Though stereotypes of these groups persist to this day,[9] by the 1940s many of the earlier ethnic stereotypes had disappeared from Hollywood. But, as historian Michael Winston observes, the "outsiders" of the 1890s remained: "the ever-popular Indian of the Westerns; the inscrutable or sinister Oriental; the sly, but colorful Mexican; and the clowning or submissive Negro."[10]

In many respects the "Western" as a genre has been paradigmatic in establishing images of racial minorities in film and television. The classic scenario involves the encircled wagon train or surrounded fort from which whites bravely fight off fierce bands of Native American Indians. The point of reference and viewer identification lies with those huddled within the circle—the representatives of "civilization" who valiantly attempt to ward off the forces of barbarism. In the classic Western, as writer Tom Engelhardt observes, "the viewer is forced behind the barrel of a repeating rifle and it is from that position, through its gun sights, that he receives a picture history of Western colonialism and imperialism."[11]

Westerns have indeed become the prototype for European and   20
American excursions throughout the Third World. The cast of characters may change, but the story remains the same. The "humanity" of whites is contrasted with the brutality and treachery of nonwhites; brave (i.e., white) souls are pitted against the merciless hordes in conflicts ranging from Indians against the British Lancers to Zulus against the Boers. What Stuart Hall refers to as the imperializing "white eye" provides the framework for these films, lurking outside the frame and yet seeing and positioning everything within, it is "the unmarked position from which . . . 'observations' are made and from which, alone, they make sense."[12]

Our "common sense" assumptions about race and racial minorities in the United States are both generated and reflected in the stereotypes presented by the visual media. In the crudest sense, it could be said that

---

9. For a discussion of Italian, Irish, Jewish, Slavic, and German stereotypes in film, see Randall M. Miller, ed., *The Kaleidoscopic Lens: How Hollywood Views Ethnic Groups* (Englewood, N.J.: Jerome S. Ozer, 1980).

10. Michael R. Winston, "Racial Consciousness and the Evolution of Mass Communications in the United States," *Daedalus*, vol. III, No. 4 (Fall 1982).

11. Tom Engelhardt, "Ambush at Kamikaze Pass," in Emma Gee, ed., *Counterpoint: Perspectives on Asian America* (Los Angeles: Asian American Studies Center, UCLA, 1976), p. 270.

12. Hall, "Whites of Their Eyes," p. 38.

such stereotypes underscore white "superiority" by reinforcing the traits, habits, and predispositions of nonwhites which demonstrate their "inferiority." Yet a more careful assessment of racial stereotypes reveals intriguing trends and seemingly contradictory themes.

While all racial minorities have been portrayed as "less than human," there are significant differences in the images of different groups. Specific racial minority groups, in spite of their often interchangeable presence in films steeped in the "Western" paradigm, have distinct and often unique qualities assigned to them. Latinos are portrayed as being prone toward violent outbursts of anger; blacks as physically strong, but dim-witted; while Asians are seen as sneaky and cunningly evil. Such differences are crucial to observe and analyze. Race in the United States is not reducible to black/white relations. These differences are significant for a broader understanding of the patterns of race in America, and the unique experience of specific racial minority groups.

It is somewhat ironic that *real* differences which exist within a racially defined minority group are minimized, distorted, or obliterated by the media. "All Asians look alike," the saying goes, and indeed there has been little or no attention given to the vast differences which exist between, say, the Chinese and Japanese with respect to food, dress, language, and culture. This blurring within popular culture has given us supposedly Chinese characters who wear kimonos; it is also the reason why the fast-food restaurant McDonald's can offer "Shanghai McNuggets" with teriyaki sauce. Other groups suffer a similar fate. Professor Gretchen Bataille and Charles Silet find the cinematic Native American of the Northeast wearing the clothing of the Plains Indians, while living in the dwellings of Southwestern tribes:

> The movie men did what thousands of years of social evolution could not do, even what the threat of the encroaching white man could not do; Hollywood produced the homogenized Native American, devoid of tribal characteristics or regional differences.[13]

The need to paint in broad racial strokes has thus rendered "internal" differences invisible. This has been exacerbated by the tendency for screenwriters to "invent" mythical Asian, Latin American, and African countries. Ostensibly done to avoid offending particular nations and peoples, such a subterfuge reinforces the notion that all the countries and cultures of a specific region are the same. European countries retain their distinctiveness, while the Third World is presented as one homogeneous mass riddled with poverty and governed by ruthless and corrupt regimes.

---

13. Gretchen Bataille and Charles Silet, "The Entertaining Anachronism: Indians in American Film," in Randall M. Miller, ed., *Kaleidoscopic Lens,* p. 40.

While rendering specific groups in a monolithic fashion, the popular cultural imagination simultaneously reveals a compelling need to distinguish and articulate "bad" and "good" variants of particular racial groups and individuals. Thus each stereotypic image is filled with contradictions: The bloodthirsty Indian is tempered with the image of the noble savage; the *bandido* exists along with the loyal sidekick; and Fu Manchu is offset by Charlie Chan. The existence of such contradictions, however, does not negate the one-dimensionality of these images, nor does it challenge the explicit subservient role of racial minorities. Even the "good" person of color usually exists as a foil in novels and films to underscore the intelligence, courage, and virility of the white male hero.

Another important, perhaps central, dimension of racial minority [25] stereotypes is sex/gender differentiation. The connection between race and sex has traditionally been an explosive and controversial one. For most of American history, sexual and marital relations between whites and nonwhites were forbidden by social custom and by legal restrictions. It was not until 1967, for example, that the U.S. Supreme Court ruled that antimiscegenation laws were unconstitutional. Beginning in the 1920s, the notorious Hays Office, Hollywood's attempt at self-censorship, prohibited scenes and subjects which dealt with miscegenation. The prohibition, however, was not evenly applied in practice. White men could seduce racial minority women, but white women were not to be romantically or sexually linked to racial minority men.

Women of color were sometimes treated as exotic sex objects. The sultry Latin temptress—such as Dolores Del Rio and Lupe Velez— invariably had boyfriends who were white North Americans; their Latino suitors were portrayed as being unable to keep up with the Anglo-American competition. From Mary Pickford as Cho-Cho San in *Madame Butterfly* (1915) to Nancy Kwan in *The World of Suzie Wong* (1961), Asian women have often been seen as the gracious "geisha girl" or the prostitute with a "heart of gold," willing to do anything to please her man.

By contrast, Asian men, whether cast in the role of villain, servant, sidekick, or kung fu master, are seen as asexual or, at least, romantically undesirable. As Asian American studies professor Elaine Kim notes, even a hero such as Bruce Lee played characters whose "single-minded focus on perfecting his fighting skills precludes all other interests, including an interest in women, friendship, or a social life."[14]

The shifting trajectory of black images over time reveals an interesting dynamic with respect to sex and gender. The black male characters in *The Birth of a Nation* were clearly presented as sexual threats to "white

---

14. Elaine Kim, "Asian Americans and American Popular Culture" in Hyung-Chan Kim, ed., *Dictionary of Asian American History* (New York: Greenwood Press, 1986), p. 107.

womanhood." For decades afterwards, however, Hollywood consciously avoided portraying black men as assertive or sexually aggressive in order to minimize controversy. Black men were instead cast as comic, harmless, and nonthreatening figures exemplified by such stars as Bill "Bojangles" Robinson, Stepin Fetchit, and Eddie "Rochester" Anderson. Black women, by contrast, were divided into two broad character types based on color categories. Dark black women such as Hattie McDaniel and Louise Beavers were cast as "dowdy, frumpy, dumpy, overweight mammy figures": while those "close to the white ideal," such as Lena Horne and Dorothy Dandridge, became "Hollywood's treasured mulattoes" in roles emphasizing the tragedy of being of mixed blood.[15]

It was not until the early 1970s that tough, aggressive, sexually assertive black characters, both male and female, appeared. The "blaxploitation" films of the period provided new heroes (e.g., *Shaft, Superfly, Coffy,* and *Cleopatra Jones*) in sharp contrast to the submissive and subservient images of the past. Unfortunately, most of these films were shoddy productions which did little to create more enduring "positive" images of blacks, either male or female.

In contemporary television and film, there is a tendency to present and equate racial minority groups and individuals with specific social problems. Blacks are associated with drugs and urban crime, Latinos with "illegal" immigration, while Native Americans cope with alcoholism and tribal conflicts. Rarely do we see racial minorities "out of character," in situations removed from the stereotypic arenas which scriptwriters have traditionally embedded them in. Nearly the only time we see young Asians and Latinos of either sex, for example, is when they are members of youth gangs, as *Boulevard Nights* (1979), *Year of the Dragon* (1985), and countless TV cop shows can attest to.

Racial minority actors have continually bemoaned the fact that the roles assigned them on stage and screen are often one-dimensional and imbued with stereotypic assumptions. In theater, the movement towards "blind casting" (i.e., casting actors for roles without regard to race) is a progressive step, but it remains to be seen whether large numbers of audiences can suspend their "beliefs" and deal with a Latino King Lear or an Asian Stanley Kowalski. By contrast, white actors are allowed to play anybody. Though the use of white actors to play blacks in "black face" is clearly unacceptable in the contemporary period, white actors continue to portray Asian, Latino, and Native American characters on stage and screen.

Scores of Charlie Chan films, for example, have been made with white leads (the last one was the 1981 *Charlie Chan and the Curse of the*

30

---

15. Donald Bogle, "A Familiar Plot (A Look at the History of Blacks in American Movies)," *The Crisis,* Vol. 90, No. 1 (January 1983), p. 15.

Dragon Queen). Roland Winters, who played Chan in six features, was once asked to explain the logic of casting a white man in the role of Charlie Chan: "The only thing I can think of is, if you want to cast a homosexual in a show, and you get a homosexual, it'll be awful. It won't be funny . . . and maybe there's something there."[16]

Such a comment reveals an interesting aspect about myth and reality in popular culture. Michael Winston argues that stereotypic images in the visual media were not originally conceived as representations of reality, nor were they initially understood to be "real" by audiences. They were, he suggests, ways of "coding and rationalizing" the racial hierarchy and interracial behavior. Over time, however, "a complex interactive relationship between myth and reality developed, so that images originally understood to be unreal, through constant repetition began to *seem* real."[17]

Such a process consolidated, among other things, our "common sense" understandings of what we think various groups should look like. Such presumptions have led to tragicomical results. Latinos auditioning for a role in a television soap opera, for example, did not fit the Hollywood image of "real Mexicans" and had their faces bronzed with powder before filming because they looked too white. Model Aurora Garza said, "I'm a real Mexican and very dark anyway. I'm even darker right now because I have a tan. But they kept wanting to make my face darker and darker."[18]

Historically in Hollywood, the fact of having "dark skin" made an   35
actor or actress potentially adaptable for numerous "racial" roles. Actress Lupe Velez once commented that she had portrayed "Chinese, Eskimos, Japs, squaws, Hindus, Swedes, Malays, and Japanese."[19] Dorothy Dandridge, who was the first black woman teamed romantically with white actors, presented a quandary for studio executives who weren't sure what race and nationality to make her. They debated whether she should be a "foreigner," an island girl, or a West Indian.[20] Ironically, what they refused to entertain as a possibility was to present her as what she really was, a black American woman.

The importance of race in popular culture is not restricted to the visual media. In popular music, race and race consciousness has defined, and continues to define, formats, musical communities, and tastes. In the

---

16. Frank Chin, "Confessions of the Chinatown Cowboy," *Bulletin of Concerned Asian Scholars,* Vol. 4, No. 3 (Fall 1972).

17. Winston, "Racial Consciousness," p. 176.

18. *The San Francisco Chronicle,* September 21, 1984.

19. Quoted in Allen L. Woll, "Bandits and Lovers: Hispanic Images in American Film," in Miller, ed., *Kaleidoscopic Lens,* p. 60.

20. Bogle, "Familiar Plot," p. 17.

mid-1950s, the secretary of the North Alabama White Citizens Council declared that "Rock and roll is a means of pulling the white man down to the level of the Negro."[21] While rock may no longer be popularly regarded as a racially subversive musical form, the very genres of contemporary popular music remain, in essence, thinly veiled racial categories. "R & B" (Rhythm and Blues) and "soul" music are clearly references to *black* music, while Country & Western or heavy metal music are viewed, in the popular imagination, as *white* music. Black performers who want to break out of this artistic ghettoization must "cross over," a contemporary form of "passing" in which their music is seen as acceptable to white audiences.

The airwaves themselves are segregated. The designation "urban contemporary" is merely radio lingo for a "black" musical format. Such categorization affects playlists, advertising accounts, and shares of the listening market. On cable television, black music videos rarely receive airplay on MTV, but are confined instead to the more marginal BET (Black Entertainment Television) network.

In spite of such segregation, many performing artists have been able to garner a racially diverse group of fans. And yet, racially integrated concert audiences are extremely rare. Curiously, this "perverse phenomenon" of racially homogeneous crowds takes place despite the color of the performer. Lionel Richie's concert audiences, for example, are virtually all-white, while Teena Marie's are all-black.[22]

Racial symbols and images are omnipresent in popular culture. Commonplace household objects such as cookie jars, salt and pepper shakers, and ashtrays have frequently been designed and fashioned in the form of racial caricatures. Sociologist Steve Dublin in an analysis of these objects found that former tasks of domestic service were symbolically transferred onto these commodities.[23] An Aunt Jemima-type character, for example, is used to hold a roll of paper towels, her outstretched hands supporting the item to be dispensed. "Sprinkle Plenty," a sprinkle bottle in the shape of an Asian man, was used to wet clothes in preparation for ironing. Simple commodities, the household implements which help us perform everyday tasks, may reveal, therefore, a deep structure of racial meaning.

A crucial dimension for discerning the meaning of particular stereo-   40
types and images is the *situation context* for the creation and consumption of popular culture. For example, the setting in which "racist" jokes are

21. Dave Marsh and Kevin Stein, *The Book of Rock Lists* (New York: Dell Publishing Co., 1981), p. 8.

22. *Rock & Roll Confidential,* No. 44 (February 1987), p. 2.

23. Steven C. Dublin, "Symbolic Slavery: Black Representations in Popular Culture," *Social Problems,* Vol. 34, No. 2 (April 1987).

told determines the function of humor. Jokes about blacks where the teller and audience are black constitute a form of self-awareness; they allow blacks to cope and "take the edge off" of oppressive aspects of the social order which they commonly confront. The meaning of these same jokes, however, is dramatically transformed when told across the "color line." If a white, or even black, person tells these jokes to a white audience, it will, despite its "purely" humorous intent, serve to reinforce stereotypes and rationalize the existing relations of racial inequality.

Concepts of race and racial images are both overt and implicit within popular culture—the organization of cultural production, the products themselves, and the manner in which they are consumed are deeply structured by race. Particular racial meanings, stereotypes, and myths can change, but the presence of a *system* of racial meanings and stereotypes, of racial ideology, seems to be an enduring aspect of American popular culture.

The era of Reaganism and the overall rightward drift of American politics and culture has added a new twist to the question of racial images and meanings. Increasingly, the problem for racial minorities is not that of misportrayal, but of "invisibility." Instead of celebrating racial and cultural diversity, we are witnessing an attempt by the right to define, once again, who the "real" American is, and what "correct" American values, mores, and political beliefs are. In such a context, racial minorities are no longer the focus of sustained media attention; when they do appear, they are cast as colored versions of essentially "white" characters.

The possibilities for change—for transforming racial stereotypes and challenging institutional inequities—nonetheless exist. Historically, strategies have involved the mobilization of political pressure against an offending institution(s). In the late 1950s, for instance, "Nigger Hair" tobacco changed its name to "Bigger Hare" due to concerted NAACP pressure on the manufacturer. In the early 1970s, Asian-American community groups successfully fought NBC's attempt to resurrect Charlie Chan as a television series with white actor Ross Martin. Amidst the furor generated by Al Campanis's remarks cited at the beginning of this essay, Jesse Jackson suggested that a boycott of major league games be initiated in order to push for a restructuring of hiring and promotion practices.

Partially in response to such action, Baseball Commissioner Peter Ueberroth announced plans in June 1987 to help put more racial minorities in management roles. "The challenge we have," Ueberroth said, "is to manage change without losing tradition."[24] The problem with respect to the issue of race and popular culture, however, is that the *tradition* itself may need to be thoroughly examined, its "common sense"

---

24. *The San Francisco Chronicle* (June 13, 1987).

assumptions unearthed and challenged, and its racial images contested and transformed.

Reading the Text

1. Describe in your own words the difference between overt and inferential racism.
2. Why, according to Omi, is popular culture so powerful in shaping America's attitudes toward race?
3. What relationship does Omi see between gender and racial stereotypes?
4. How have racial relations changed in America during the 1980s, in Omi's view?

Reading the Signs

1. In class, brainstorm on the blackboard stereotypes, both "good" and "bad," attributed to specific racial groups. Then discuss the possible sources of these stereotypes. In what ways have they been perpetuated in popular culture, including movies, television, advertising, music, and consumer products? What does your discussion reveal about popular culture's influence on our most basic ways of seeing the world?
2. Omi explains that the "situation context" can determine the impact of racially charged comments and images. Apply his concept of "situation context" to the experiences of the African-Americans described in Sam Fulwood III's "The Rage of the Black Middle Class" (p. 462). Why are some of the experiences painful reminders of living in a racist society, while others have a therapeutic effect?
3. Rent a videotape of *Gone with the Wind* and view the film. Write a semiotic essay in which you analyze how race operates as a sign in this movie. How, to use Omi's terms, does the film create, reproduce, and sustain racial ideologies in America? What does its racial ideology reveal about its status as a "classic" American film?
4. Rent a videotape of *Malcolm X* and view the film. Then, using Omi's essay as your critical framework, write an essay in which you explore how this film may reflect or redefine American attitudes toward racial identity and race relations. To develop your essay, you may want to consult Shelby Steele's "Malcolm X" (p. 287), Peter Rainer's "Antihero Worship" (p. 318), or Valerie Boyd's *Atlanta Journal and Constitution* interviews (p. 296).
5. Buy an issue of a magazine targeted to a specific ethnic readership, such as *Hispanic, Ebony,* or *Transpacific,* and study both its advertising and its articles. Then write an essay in which you explore the extent to which the magazine accurately reflects that ethnicity or, in Omi's words, appeals to readers as "colored versions of essentially 'white' characters."

SAM   FULWOOD   III

The Rage of the Black Middle Class

||||||||||||||||||||||||||||||||||||||||||||||||||||

> *Though a period of violence and upheaval, the sixties were also a time*
> *of hope, especially for the American civil rights movement. A new*
> *American Dream appeared, one that promised a colorblind society where*
> *all Americans could live together as one and racial differences would no*
> *longer matter. Writing a quarter-century after the assassination of Martin*
> *Luther King, Jr., Sam Fulwood III (b. 1956) surveys the legacy of the*
> *civil rights movement and finds it wanting. In America, the color of your*
> *skin still matters, even for African-Americans who have moved into the*
> *suburban middle class. Torn between his desire to maintain a comfortable*
> *middle-class existence and his rage at still feeling alien in a largely white*
> *world, Fulwood shares his disappointment and his sense of betrayal in*
> *this essay, originally written for the* Los Angeles Times Magazine.
> *Can African-Americans join the middle class and still retain their sense*
> *of ethnic identity? Fulwood, a correspondent for the* Los Angeles
> Times's *Washington bureau, isn't so sure. He is currently at work on*
> *a book based on this essay, to be published by New American Library.*

Race awareness displaced my blissful childhood in 1969.

I was then in the sixth grade at Oaklawn Elementary, a three-year-old school built on the edge of my neighborhood in Charlotte, N.C. Everybody knew that one day little white boys and girls would attend classes there, but at the time, the sparkling new rooms contained only black students and teachers.

Some gossips believed that the school was built less to accommodate the affluent black families in the poorly served northwest neighborhood than to anticipate the demands of white parents who never would have allowed their precious little ones to sit in our old ramshackle schoolhouse.

None of this mattered to me. I was simply proud of the school and confident that nothing would detour my short walk to and from its library and lunchroom, my two favorite places in the building. My contentment was coldly jolted on one beautiful spring day, when Principal Gwen Cunningham's voice crackled over the intercom, summoning me to her office for a chat about my future.

Mrs. Cunningham, a proper and proud black woman, knew that   5
my father was a Presbyterian minister and my mother was an elementary school teacher, the perfect pair of parents for unchallenged credentials into black society's elite. She was convinced, on the advice of my teach-

ers, that I should be among the first students from her elementary school to attend the nearest white junior high school the following year. This was an honor, she declared. Mrs. Cunningham countered any arguments I attempted about staying at the neighborhood school. As if I needed additional persuading, she stated: "I am absolutely certain that you can hold your own with the best [white students] at Ranson Junior High."

Suddenly, I was different from my friends and classmates, slightly better prepared to "hold my own." Moreover, it was my duty to my race to blaze a path for other blacks to follow. Mrs. Cunningham didn't know it, but she had set my life on a new course. I had been tapped, in the words of Yale law professor Stephen L. Carter, into the fraternity of "best blacks," an unofficial grouping of people selected to lead the way toward improved racial understanding and uplift.

I evolved that day into a race-child, one who believed that he would illuminate the magnificent social changes wrought by racial progress. Overt racial barriers were falling, and I, among the favored in Charlotte's black middle class, thought my future would be free of racism, free of oppression. I believed I was standing on the portico of the Promised Land.

Now, as the twentieth century seeps away, I am waking from my blind belief in the American Dream. I feel betrayed and isolated. I am angrier than I've ever been.

Lest anyone misunderstand, this is a new and troubling sensation. I was born to cheerfully embrace integration of the races, not to sulk back into a segregated world in despair. I was among that virgin group of black men and women for whom legal segregation was less a cruel reality and more historical (some say forgotten) fact. Nobody ever called me a nigger.

But now, for the first time, I am no longer running away from the   10
questions that I've spent a lifetime denying would ever be posed: Is American society the race-blind haven that black people of my parents' generation had hoped it would be for their children? If not, what alternative do we have? I have no answers.

Although racial tensions continue to escalate, few blacks or whites seem willing to spend the resources—both fiscal and human—to ease the strain of living separate lives. Rather, a form of Balkanization is occurring, with race and class separating us. My generation—called the "new black middle class" by one sociologist—is so disillusioned by the persistent racism that continues to define and limit us that we are abandoning efforts to assimilate into the mainstream of society. I see no end to this trend.

In 1967, as the civil rights movement gathered steam, about 266,000 black American households earned an inflation-adjusted $50,000 or more, the government definition of affluence. In 1989, the number of such households had grown to more than one million. Prosperity for middle-class blacks soared so fast and so high during the past three decades that some of us no longer remember the way things used to be.

My parents used to bristle with anger whenever I teased them about being "richer" than other black families we knew. Their displeasure stemmed from a closer identification with poor black people than with neighbors and friends who in their nicer houses and fancier cars appeared "too big for their britches." In my parents' generation, poverty and black were synonymous. When my father and now-deceased mother were married in the early 1950s, about 55% of black Americans were living below the official poverty line. Although my father knows that only a third of the nation's blacks remain poor—with less than 10% confined to an "underclass" of persistent poor—he still associates himself with the underdog.

That attitude was evident during the recent Clarence Thomas Supreme Court confirmation battle. Much of Thomas' support among blacks stems from his up-by-the-bootstraps background. In contrast, Oklahoma law professor Anita Hill's polished demeanor was perceived by many working-class blacks as elitist, something they couldn't identify with.

But those views seem to be fading relics of the civil rights generation. 15 Younger, wealthier, better-educated black Americans associate less—and, therefore, identify less—with their poor cousins. We zoom past crack houses in bright, shiny cars with our windows and doors locked tight. We live in the suburbs and send our children to private academies. The world of a black middle-class achiever is a self-protective cocoon, separate from poor blacks and all whites.

I don't know what to tell my four-year-old daughter, Amanda, who is developing an awareness of her own racial and class identity, when difficult questions arise about her place in society. Recently she shocked her mother and me by declaring that when she grows up, she intends to "be white" like one of her classmates.

For the moment, the issue is dormant because simple answers will satisfy her. Clearly, the time is coming when I will need a better answer. And, I am sure, I will *not* repeat the blind beliefs of my youth. I don't want my daughter to be a second-generation "best black," her childhood twisted by the mistaken belief that race will one day be unimportant in her life.

My parents, born in rural North Carolina in the first quarter of this century, never questioned the inequities of the segregated South, but they demanded that life for my brother and me would be different. By an act of Protestant willpower, they sheltered us from the lingering traces of Jim Crow and imbued in us a belief that the evils of the outside world—I never heard the word *racism* in our household—could be made to disappear. If I worked hard, nothing was impossible.

A telling incident occurred in the early sixties—I don't really remember it, but the family has recalled the tale so often that it has become part of our history—when my younger brother, George, and I were turned away from a donkey ride outside Clarks' department store.

George noticed the bright red, blue, and green neon lights in the   20
store's parking lot. That's where the donkeys, tethered to a pole in the asphalt, slowly paced in a hay-filled circle. Other kids were riding the animals; we begged our parents to let us ride, too.

Exactly what was said by the teenage white attendant, my parents never repeated. The upshot was clear, however: He wasn't going to let us ride. As decent and law-abiding Negroes, my parents accepted the snub without argument or question. As the four of us walked back to our car with George and me in full-throated retreat, my parents' embarrassment remained veiled—until George (I am sure it was George) asked my father why they wouldn't let us ride.

"The people who own the animals don't want colored people riding them," he said in a statement-of-fact voice. "Only whites."

"Well, we can come back tomorrow," George demanded in the imperious voice that only a child can summon. "We can wear false faces. Maybe then they'll let us ride."

As the family version of this story goes, Momma lost it right then at the mere thought of her little ones hiding behind plastic masks for a ride on a funky donkey. The sight of her tears reignited our crying and provoked Daddy into a rare flash of anger. "You're not wearing any false faces, and you're not riding the damn donkeys," he said. "So forget it. This never happened."

Were it not for the dramatic social changes that transpired during   25
my childhood, I doubt that, decades later, my family would have been able to joke about the episode. I carried their laughter over the retelling of that story into adulthood as a lesson in the inevitability of the changes occurring around me. I was certain that by the time I turned thirty-five, no one would care what color I was. All that mattered would be whether I carried a green, gold, or platinum American Express card.

I was born in 1956 and came of age as the Great Society of the late 1960s closed. Author and scholar David Bradley defined that period as the "Years of the Black" in a seminal essay in the May, 1982, issue of *Esquire*. Bradley called it a "fascinating epoch" during which benevolent, wealthy and white liberals, driven by the guilt of their forefathers' sins and the rantings of Afro'd, heat-packing, shades-wearing militants, persuaded politicians and activists to swallow an expensive set of social programs meant "to conceal evidence of a scandalous past or present."

I have kept a clipping of Bradley's autobiographical essay—titled "Black and American, 1982" and subtitled "There are no good times to be black in America, but some times are worse than others"—since it was published. At that time, I was embarking on my career as a reporter at my hometown newspaper with the naive notion that my ambition and ability would carry me to unlimited vistas. I was convinced that someday I would respond to Bradley, challenging his pessimism and extolling my triumph. I would declare that the Rev. Martin Luther King, Jr.'s, Great Black American Dream had been fulfilled in my generation. Mine would be the first in this nation's history to be judged "by the content of their character, not the color of their skin."

Sadly, almost a decade later, I must admit that Bradley, a professor of English at Temple University, was right to say that it is impossible "to give a socially meaningful description of who I am and what I've done without using the word black." This is painful, because it means I must accept his corollary: "Nothing I shall ever accomplish or discover or earn or inherit or buy or sell or give away—nothing I can ever do—will outweigh the fact of my race in determining my destiny."

As a child of the post–civil rights black bourgeoisie, I was a primary beneficiary of the protest generation and, therefore, among its most hopeful supporters. Today, we sons and daughters of those who faced the dogs, water hoses, and brutal cops are turning away from our parents' great expectations of an integrated America. Many middle-class black executives are moving out of their corporate roles to create fulfilling jobs that serve black customers. Black colleges are experiencing a renaissance. Black organizations—churches, fraternities, sororities, and professional groups—are attracting legions of new members. And, most surprising to me, upscale blacks are moving to neighborhoods that insulate them from the slings and arrows of the larger society.

Two years ago, I lived in the conspicuously affluent, middle-class 30 black suburban neighborhood of BrookGlen, about 15 miles from downtown Atlanta. My neighbors were proud of their large homes and loved to entertain. One warm, summer evening, a backyard gathering fell suddenly silent as a car, marked with a local realtor's logo and containing a white couple, cruised slowly through the subdivision. Finally, one of my neighbors spoke up. "What are they looking for?" he asked bitterly. "I hope they don't find anything they like. Otherwise, there goes the neighborhood." The message was clear: Even affluent whites would ruin the sanctuary of our community.

Many of the black men and women who have come to accept this reality appear to fit neatly within the system among their white peers. They own the symbols of success. But deep inside, they are unhappy, knowing they are not accepted as equals by their white colleagues or acquaintances.

"This will be an ethnic party," says my friend Marian Holmes, inviting me to a dinner at her home in one of the few predominantly white neighborhoods in Washington. "It will be just us, no white people."

Holmes is no racist. Quite the contrary, she worries that her world is not black enough. Nearly all of her colleagues at the *Smithsonian* magazine, where she works as an editor, are white. She is comfortable with them, frequently entertaining coworkers at her home and being entertained in theirs. Even so, she seemed perplexed by her urge to host a dinner party of only black guests. It was something she couldn't remember ever having done, and now it seemed imperative. For the first time in her forty-two years, Holmes was taking stock of the fact that being black was an inescapable fact of her life.

Perhaps, like me, it hit her when Jennifer, her five-year-old daughter, began asking the tough questions: "Mommy, why aren't there more black people in the world?"

"That's an odd question for a black child living in Washington to   35
ask," Holmes says. "But then, you know, it made sense that she would ask me something like that. There aren't very many black people in her world, which includes home, neighborhood, and school."

Pam Harris, a forty-one-year-old accountant with an Atlanta real estate management firm and one of my Atlanta neighbors, says the folks who live in her BrookGlen subdivision are proud that their community is composed of black doctors, attorneys, executives, and college professors.

"All of us have been made to feel that we have to be validated by whites to be good people and good at what we do," Harris says. "But we don't want to be validated. By living in an all-black, middle-class community, it lets us know that we're good, and there are not any of them around staring us in the face to prove it so.

"So much goes on at the job that [black professionals] have to endure, the slights and negative comments and feelings that we're unwanted," she continues. "When we have to work around them all day, by the time I come home I don't want to have to deal with white people any more."

It's a form of self-segregation, a defense against the pain of being rejected or misunderstood. One friend has coined the term "white folks overload" to explain the fits of frustration that she says black people experience from prolonged exposure to white people. With that in mind, she and her husband consciously sought out a predominantly black neighborhood in Los Angeles—View Park—as a place to begin a family. "I can't see [whites] everyday," she explained. "It's not that I dislike them or anything, but there's a membrane of coping that you have to wear to be around them."

I know what she means. Whites rarely seem at ease in my company, 40
unless they are in control of the environment. By outnumbering and
outmanning me at virtually every turn, they compel me to adapt my
view of the world, even my own sense of self, to their majoritarian
biases. Trying to explain my life to white people, who just don't care to
understand, is taxing and, ultimately, not worth the trouble. Sort of like
singing "Swing Low, Sweet Chariot" *en francais*. Why bother? Once
translated, it's just not the same song.

After cultivating an image, a personality, and a set of career trophies
that I assumed would be eagerly embraced by the larger society, I am
maddened to learn that the color black is the foremost thing that whites
see in me. I am reminded of the words of the black sergeant in Charles
Fuller's *A Soldier's Play:* "You got to be like them! And I was! I was—
but the rules are fixed. . . . It doesn't make any difference. They still
hate you!"

This revelation first appeared to me while on assignment in the dusty
South African township of Duduza, about 30 miles west of Johannesburg.
My guide, Alexander Monteodi, pointed out that every fifth house or
so on one street had been torched, apparently by black activists opposed
to the apartheid government. Monteodi, who was the founder of the
Duduza Civic Association, a community self-improvement group, explained that the charred remains "were the houses of the briefcase toters,"
those middle-class blacks set up by authorities to serve as examples for
disgruntled blacks to emulate.

"The government wants to create a black middle class for us to look
up to," Monteodi said. "Here in all this despair, they believe that those
misguided blacks working for them in those city offices will serve as role
models for the rest of us stuck here. It's crazy. All of us can't be middle
class."

This pinprick of a comment burst my balloon. I am black and middle
class in America. Have I been set up, framed like a pretty picture of
upward mobility for other blacks—in America, across the globe—to
replicate? Monteodi shrugged. "You live there, I don't," he said softly.

I wanted to scream. In South Africa, I first challenged the status quo 45
of my soul. I no longer wanted to play the game. Being "middle class"
suddenly was an epithet, another way of saying I wanted to be white, a
rejection of being black and American.

More than a generation ago, a black sociologist named E. Franklin
Frazier ignited a blaze of angst that still burns within black America by
publishing *The Black Bourgeoisie*, a scathing denunciation of black American pseudoaristocracy. The 1955 book touched raw nerves among old-
line, fair-skinned black families who affected the manners, dress, and
behavior of whites. These blacks, Frazier contended, lived "largely in a
world of make-believe; the masks which they wear to play their sorry

roles conceal the feelings of inferiority and of insecurity and the frustrations that haunt their inner lives."

After two world wars and the migration of large numbers of blacks
from the rural South to the industrial centers in northern cities, the
complexion of the black middle class grew darker as "pure Negroes"
displaced the mulatto elites, Frazier explained. In fact, skin pigmentation
declined as the mark of rank among middle-class blacks, giving way to
white collars and salaried jobs as the assumed price of acceptance among
whites. Frazier observed that black professionals—"doctors, dentists and
lawyers, and even teachers"—set the standards for what it takes "to
achieve status and recognition in American society."

But Thomas L. Johnson, a thirty-four-year-old urologist in Los
Angeles, told me that advanced education and professional achievement
provide no vaccination against an outbreak of racist behavior from
whites. "All through high school, college and medical school, I was
around liberal [white students]," he said one evening at his home. "As I
spent more time around them and we all got older, I really discovered
they were pseudo-liberals from the sixties, who would hang around
black people, smoke dope with some of us, maybe even date black
women. But when it's time to settle down and raise their families, they
revert to their roots of racism."

An example: "I was playing in a team tennis tournament here in Los
Angeles last year at a white country club," he says. "My team is all black,
and the team we were playing was all white, and we were winning when
one of the white guys became frustrated. The scene deteriorated as he
lost more and more points and started an argument with a black guy on
my team.

"As they argued over a point, the white guy shouted: 'Well, what   50
if I call you a nigger?'" Johnson says, rolling his eyes in disgust at the
memory. "I didn't expect that kind of behavior from these so-called
'upper-class' whites. But what shocked me even more was that other
whites heard him use the 'N word,' and their attitude was like 'That's
no big deal, let's play some tennis.' They didn't seem the least bit shocked
and failed to react. White people refuse to understand how much that
hurt and how insulted we were by the racist remark and their acceptance
of it.

"On one level, I guess I always thought this would happen," he says.
"But I'm taken aback now that I'm experiencing it firsthand. I know
racism exists, but I never expected it to happen to me."

In his 1988 book, *The New Black Middle Class,* Bart Landry argues
that a "chance simultaneous occurrence" of civil rights activism and
national prosperity between 1960 and 1970 generated "the most radical
changes in black social structure" in the nation's history.

Moreover, Landry, a sociologist at the University of Maryland, suggests that the civil rights movement was "at first a movement with

middle-class goals—desegregation of public accommodations." This shouldn't come as a surprise because the sit-ins and nonviolent protests that swept through the South and, later, the nation, were led by middle-class blacks, who wanted to move closer to a white standard of living. Many were college students who expected one day to earn big salaries working in large, white-owned corporations and to spend their new-found wealth on the luxuries traditionally reserved for white people.

As they assimilated, black folks lost their soul and rhythm, their willingness to laugh out loud in public, even their outrage at oppression—both real and imagined. Recently, for example, a luncheon companion scolded me for ordering fried chicken. "I can't believe you did that," she said, sputtering with embarrassment and contempt. "That's the sort of thing I would expect an ignorant person who's never been in a restaurant before to do. How would you feel if your [white] co-workers saw you getting all greasy eating that?" This black woman, who owns both undergraduate and law-school degrees, has become so well-educated that she now knows better than to appear ignorant before white people by eating chicken in public.

So what does all this mean?   55

I am reluctant to predict the future. Despite what my heart wants to believe, I can't escape thinking that white America, which stopped short of embracing middle-class blacks at the moment we most wanted inclusion, may have already lost its opportunity. The refusal of the larger society to embrace us, combined with our unwillingness to return to the ghetto, is likely to result in even more isolation, frustration, and desperation. And, worst of all, more anger. As one who once wanted to live and work and play snuggled within the American Dream, I am putting a fresh coat of pain on my cocoon.

There, in the safety of that betwixt-and-between state, I stand wobbly, unaccepted by whites who do not regard me as their equal and hovering aloof from poorer blacks, separated from them by a flimsy wrapper of social status. I straddle two worlds and consider neither home.

Reading the Text

1. What were Fulwood's boyhood expectations of adult life?
2. Why do Fulwood's black middle-class friends engage in "self-segregation"?
3. What evidence does Fulwood present to show covert racism on the part of middle-class white people?
4. Why does Fulwood say "I straddle two worlds and consider neither home"?

Reading the Signs

1. In a journal entry, explore your own responses to Fulwood's essay. If you are a person of color, have you shared some of the frustrations and anger

that Fulwood expresses? How have your experiences been similar or different? If you are Caucasian, how do you respond to the "white folks overload" and the voluntary segregation described by Fulwood's friends? How might such segregation compare with the historical segregation imposed upon blacks?

2. Research the extent to which the alienation from mainstream society that Fulwood describes is prevalent among blacks on your campus. Interview at least five African-Americans (they can be students, staff, or faculty), and ask them about their experiences and aspirations. Then write an essay in which you compare your findings with the experiences Fulwood describes.

3. To what extent do the African-Americans described by Fulwood illustrate the theory of identity evolution postulated by William E. Cross, Jr. (see Minabere Ibelema, "Identity Crisis: The African Connection in African American Sitcom Characters," p. 198)? Write an essay in which you apply Cross's theory to Fulwood's friends, being sure to discuss why the theory either does or does not explain their experiences.

4. Compare Fulwood's friends with the middle-class African-Americans quoted by Valerie Boyd (see "The Word on *Malcolm X*," p. 296). In what ways are their concerns about ethnicity and racial injustice similar? What differences do you find in their comments?

5. Fulwood says he is angry because the color black is, for white people, the primary sign of his identity. In class, brainstorm on the board ways in which "whiteness" can function as a sign in American society. Then discuss your results. What patterns emerge in your list? In what ways does the significance of "whiteness" depend on the ethnicity of the interpreter?

RICHARD   MAJORS

Cool Pose: The Proud Signature of Black Survival

One of the signs you read in everyday life is the body language of the people you meet. But often we can misread this language, especially when we do not know the cultural context in which it is "spoken." In this descriptive analysis of African-American body language, Richard Majors explains the postures adopted by men whose physical and psychic survival may depend on the face they present to the world. Reading the signs of "cool pose," Majors argues, can be essential to racial understanding. Richard Majors is associate professor of psychology at the University of Wisconsin, Eau Claire, and is the cofounder of the National Council of African American Men, as well as the Journal of African American Males. *He is coauthor, with Janet Mancini Billson, of* Cool Pose *(1992).*

Just when it seemed that we black males were beginning to recover from past injustices inflicted by the dominant white society, we find once again that we are being revisited in a similar vein. President Reagan's deemphasis of civil rights, affirmative action legislation, and social services programs; the rise of black neoconservatives and certain black feminist groups; harshly critical media events on television (e.g., the CBS documentary "The Vanishing Family—Crisis in Black America") and in films (e.g., *The Color Purple*); and the omnipresent problems of unemployment and inadequate health care, housing, and education—all have helped to shape a negative political and social climate toward black men. For many black men this period represents a new black nadir, or lowest point, and time of deepest depression.

Black people in general, and the black man in particular, look out on a world that does not positively reflect their image. Black men learned long ago that the classic American virtues of thrift, perseverance, and hard work would not give us the tangible rewards that accrue to most members of the dominant society. We learned early that we would not be Captains of Industry or builders of engineering wonders. Instead, we channeled our creative energies into construction of a symbolic universe. Therefore we adopted unique poses and postures to offset the externally imposed "zero" image. Because black men were denied access to the dominant culture's acceptable avenues of expression, we created a form of self-expression—the "Cool Pose."[1–3]

Cool Pose is a term that represents a variety of attitudes and actions that serve the black man as mechanisms for survival, defense, and social competence. These attitudes and actions are performed using characterizations and roles as facades and shields.

Cool Culture

Historically, coolness was central to the culture of many ancient African civilizations. The Yorubas of Western Nigeria (900 B.C. to 200 A.D.) are cited as an example of an African civilization where cool was integrated into the social fabric of the community.[4] Uses of cool ranged from the way a young man carried himself before his peers to

---

1. Majors, R. G. & Nikelly, A. G., "Serving the Black Minority: A New Direction in Psychotherapy," *J. for Non-white Concerns,* 11:142–151 (1983).

2. Majors, R. G., "The Effects of 'Cool Pose': What Being Cool Means," *Griot,* pp. 4–5 (Spring, 1985).

3. Nikelly, A. G. & Majors, R. G. "Techniques for Counseling Black Students," *Techniques: J. Remedial Educ. & Counseling,* 2:48–54 (1986).

4. Bascom, W., *The Yoruba of Southwestern Nigeria* (New York: Holt, Rinehart & Winston, 1969).

the way he impressed his elders during the initiation ritual. Coolness helped to build character and pride for individuals in such groups and is regarded as a precolonial cultural adaptation. With the advent of the modern African slave trade, cool became detached from its indigenous cultural setting and emerged equally as a survival mechanism.

Where the European saw America as the promised land, the African saw it as the land of oppression. Today, reminders of black America's oppressive past continue in the form of chronic underemployment, inadequate housing, inferior schools, and poor health care. Because of these conditions many black men have become frustrated, angry, confused, and impatient.

To help ease the pain associated with these conditions, black men have taken to alcoholism, drug abuse, homicide, and suicide. In learning to mistrust the words and actions of dominant white people, black males have learned to make great use of "poses" and "postures" which connote control, toughness, and detachment. All these forms arise from the mistrust that the black males feel toward the dominant society.

For these black males, particular poses and postures show the white man that "although you may have tried to hurt me time and time again, I can take it (and if I am hurting or weak, I'll never let you know). They are saying loud and clear to the white establishment, "I am strong, full of pride, and a survivor." Accordingly, any failures in the real world become the black man's secret.

The Expressive Life-style

On the other hand, those poses and postures that have an expressive quality or nature have become known in the literature as the "expressive life-style."[5] The expressive life-style is a way in which the black male can act cool by actively displaying particular performances that emphasize creative expression. Thus, while black people historically have been forced into conciliatory and often demeaning positions in American culture, there is nothing conciliatory about the expressive life-style.

This dynamic vitality will not be denied even in limited stereotypical roles—as demonstrated by Hattie McDaniel, the maid in *Gone with the Wind,* or Bill "Bojangles" Robinson as the affable servant in the Shirley Temple movies. This abiding need for creative self-expression knows no bounds and asserts itself whether on the basketball court or in dancing. We can see it in black athletes—with their stylish dunking of the basketball, their spontaneous dancing in the end zone, and their different styles of handshakes (e.g., "high fives")—and in black entertainers with

---

5. Rainwater, L., *Behind Ghetto Walls* (Chicago: Aldine, 1970).

their various choreographed "cool" dance steps. These are just a few examples of black individuals in their professions who epitomize this creative expression. The expressive life-style is a dynamic—not a static —art form, and new aesthetic forms are always evolving (e.g., "rap-talking" and breakdancing). The expressive life-style, then, is the passion that invigorates the demeaning life of blacks in White America. It is a dynamic vitality that transforms the mundane into the sublime and makes the routine spectacular.

A Cultural Signature

Cool Pose, manifested by the expressive life-style, is also an aggres-   10
sive assertion of masculinity. It emphatically says "White man, this is my turf. You can't match me here." Though he may be impotent in the political and corporate world, the black man demonstrates his potency in athletic competition, entertainment, and the pulpit with a verve that borders on the spectacular. Through the virtuosity of a performance, he tips the socially imbalanced scales in his favor. "See me, touch me, hear me, but, white man, you can't copy me." This is the subliminal message which black males signify in their oftentimes flamboyant performance. Cool Pose, then, becomes the cultural signature for such black males.

Being cool is a unique response to adverse social, political, and economic conditions. Cool provides control, inner strength, stability, and confidence. Being cool, illustrated in its various poses and postures, becomes a very powerful and necessary tool in the black man's constant fight for his soul. The poses and postures of cool guard, preserve, and protect his pride, dignity, and respect to such an extent that the black male is willing to risk a great deal for it. One black man said it well: "The white man may control everything about me—that is, except my pride and dignity. That he can't have. That is mine and mine alone."

The Cost

Cool Pose, however, is not without its price. Many black males fail to discriminate the appropriate uses of Cool Pose and act cool much of the time, without regard to time or space.[6] Needless to say, this can cause severe problems. In many situations a black man won't allow himself to express or show any form of weakness or fear or other feelings and emotions. He assumes a facade of strength, held at all costs, rather

---

6. Majors, R. G., "Cool Pose: A New Hypothesis in Understanding Anti-Social Behavior in Lower SES Black Males," unpublished manuscript.

than "blow his front," and thus his cool. Perhaps black men have become so conditioned to keeping up their guard against oppression from the dominant white society that this particular attitude and behavior represent for them their best safeguard against further mental or physical abuse. However, this same behavior makes it very difficult for these males to let their guard down and show affection, even for people that they actually care about or for people that may really care about them (e.g., girlfriends, wives, mothers, fathers, "good" friends, etc.).

When the art of being cool is used to put cool behaviors ahead of emotions or needs, the result of such repression of feelings can be frustration. Such frustrations sometimes cause aggression which often is taken out on those individuals closest to such men—other black people. It is sadly ironic, then, that the same elements of cool that allow for survival in the larger society may hurt black people by contributing to one of the more complex problems facing black people today—black-on-black crime.

Further, while Cool Pose enables black males to maintain stability in the face of white power, it may through inappropriate use render many of them unable to move with the mainstream or evolve in healthy ways. When misused, cool can suppress the motivation to learn, accept or become exposed to stimuli, cultural norms, aesthetics, mannerisms, values, etiquette, information, or networks that could help them overcome problems caused by white racism. Finally, in a society which has as its credo, "A man's home is his castle," it is ironic that the masses of black men have no castle to protect. Their minds have become their psychological castle, defended by impenetrable cool. Thus, Cool Pose is the bittersweet symbol of a socially disesteemed group that shouts, "We are" in the face of a hostile and indifferent world that everywhere screams, "You ain't."

Cool and the Black Psyche

To be fully grasped, Cool Pose must be recognized as having gained ideological consensus in the black community. It is not only a quantitatively measured "social reality" but a series of equally "real" rituals of socialization. It is a comprehensive, officially endorsed cultural myth that became entrenched in the black psyche with the beginning of the slave experience. This phenomenon has cut across all socioeconomic groups in the black community, as black men fight to preserve their dignity, pride, respect, and masculinity with the attitudes and behaviors of Cool Pose. Cool Pose represents a fundamental structuring of the psyche of the black male and is manifested in some way or another in the daily activities and recreational habits of most black males. There are few other social or psychological constructs that have shaped, directed, or con-

15

trolled the black male to the extent that the various forms of coolness have. It is surprising, then, that for a concept that has the potential to explain problems in black male and black female relationships, black-on-black crime, and black-on-black pregnancies, there is such limited research on this subject.

In the final analysis, Cool Pose may represent the most important yet least researched area with the potential to enhance our understanding and study of black behavior today.

Reading the Text

1. Summarize in your own words the "cool pose" and the "expressive life-style" adopted by black men.
2. Why, according to Majors, has it been necessary for black men to channel their "creative energies into construction of a symbolic universe"?
3. What are the benefits and problems associated with the cool pose, as Majors sees them?

Reading the Signs

1. Use Majors's argument about the cool pose to extend or modify Wanda Coleman's explanation in "Say It Ain't Cool, Joe" (p. 356) for why the Joe Camel character is so attractive to inner-city youth.
2. Majors acknowledges that one aspect of cool pose, the expressive life-style, may also be part of black racial stereotypes. To what extent could Majors be accused of stereotyping black men himself by attributing to them the expressive life-style? To support your argument, you might examine particular examples of the groups Majors mentions (black athletes or entertainers) and read or review Michael Omi's "In Living Color: Race and American Culture" (p. 449) for his comments on racial stereotyping.
3. Analyze the body language and expressive style of males who belong to another American ethnic group. How do they compare with the style of black males as described by Majors? How might you account for any similarities or differences?
4. In what ways do the African-Americans discussed in Sam Fulwood III's "The Rage of the Black Middle Class" (p. 462) adopt a cool pose or a "zero image"? In what circumstances do they adopt either personal style? Use your answers to these questions to formulate an essay in which you explain how personal style can be a survival mechanism.
5. How do the survival and expressive strategies of black males compare with those of another traditionally oppressed group, homosexuals? Read or review Richard K. Herrell's "The Symbolic Strategies of Chicago's Gay and Lesbian Pride Day Parade" (p. 643), and compare the expressive strategies described there with Major's notion of cool pose. What similarities and

differences do you find? As you write, remember that the parade is a ritual event, not everyday life.

D O R I N N E   K.   K O N D O

On Being a Conceptual Anomaly

IIIIIIIIIIIIIIIIIIIIIIIIIIIIIIIIIIIIIIIIIIIIIIIIIIIIIIIIIIII

Imagine going back to your ancestral homeland and finding yourself being judged for your inability to fit in perfectly with people of your ancestry. That's what happened to Dorinne Kondo, a Japanese American anthropology professor who went back to Japan to live and study and found herself being criticized for her American accent when speaking Japanese. Noting how, for the Japanese, "race, language, and culture are intertwined," Kondo tells how she was "a living oxymoron" to her Japanese hosts, who were astonished by this visitor who looked Japanese but who lacked Japanese "cultural competence." At the same time, as an American woman, Kondo found herself astonished by the gender roles of Japanese society whereby "men—even the sweetest, nicest ones —ask for a second helping of rice merely by holding out their rice bowls to the woman nearest the rice cooker." Dorinne Kondo holds the MacArthur Associate Professorship of Women's Studies in the Anthropology Department at Pomona College. She is the author of Crafting Selves: Power, Gender, and Discourses of Identity in a Japanese Workplace *(1990), from which this selection is excerpted.*

As a Japanese American,[1] I created a conceptual dilemma for the Japanese I encountered. For them, I was a living oxymoron, someone

---

1. Said, Edward. *Orientalism*. New York: Pantheon. 1978. The issue of what to call ourselves is an issue of considerable import to various ethnic and racial groups in the United States, as the recent emphasis on the term "African American" shows. For Asian Americans, the term "Oriental" was called into question in the sixties, for the reasons Said enumerates: the association of the term with stereotypes such as Oriental despotism, inscrutability, splendor, exoticism, mystery, and so on. It also defines "the East" in terms of "the West," in a relationship of unequal power—how rarely one hears of "the Occident," for example. Asian Americans, Japanese Americans included, sometimes hyphenate the term, but some of us would argue that leaving out the hyphen makes the term "Asian" or "Japanese" an adjective, rather than implying a half-and-half status: i.e., that one's loyalties/identities might be half Japanese and half American. Rather, in the terms "Asian American" and "Japanese American," the accent is on the "American," an important political claim in light of the mainstream tendency to see Asian Americans as somehow more foreign than other kinds of Americans.

who was both Japanese and not Japanese. Their puzzlement was all the greater since most Japanese people I knew seemed to adhere to an eminently biological definition of Japaneseness. Race, language, and culture are intertwined, so much so that any challenge to this firmly entrenched conceptual schema—a white person who speaks flawlessly idiomatic and unaccented Japanese, or a person of Japanese ancestry who cannot—meets with what generously could be described as unpleasant reactions. White people are treated as repulsive and unnatural—*hen na gaijin,* strange foreigners—the better their Japanese becomes, while Japanese Americans and others of Japanese ancestry born overseas are faced with exasperation and disbelief. How can someone who is racially Japanese lack "cultural competence"?[2] During my first few months in Tokyo, many tried to resolve this paradox by asking which of my parents was "really" American.

Indeed, it is a minor miracle that those first months did not lead to an acute case of agoraphobia, for I knew that once I set foot outside the door, someone somewhere (a taxi driver? a salesperson? a bank clerk?) would greet one of my linguistic mistakes with an astonished "Eh?" I became all too familiar with the series of expressions that would flicker over those faces: bewilderment, incredulity, embarrassment, even anger, at having to deal with this odd person who looked Japanese and therefore human, but who must be retarded, deranged, or—equally undesirable in Japanese eyes—Chinese or Korean. Defensively, I would mull over the mistake of the day. I mean, how was I to know that in order to "fillet a fish" you had to cut it "in three pieces"? Or that opening a bank account required so much specialized terminology? Courses in literary Japanese at Harvard hadn't done much to prepare me for the realities of everyday life in Tokyo. Gritting my teeth in determination as I groaned inwardly, I would force myself out of the house each morning.

For me, and apparently for the people around me, this was a stressful time, when expectations were flouted, when we had to strain to make sense of one another. There seemed to be few advantages in my retaining an American persona, for the distress caused by these reactions was difficult to bear. In the face of dissonance and distress, I found that the desire for comprehensible order in the form of "fitting in," even if it meant suppression of and violence against a self I had known in another context, was preferable to meaninglessness. Anthropological imperatives to immerse oneself in another culture intensified this desire, so that acquiring the accoutrements of Japanese selfhood meant simultaneously constructing a more thoroughly professional anthropological persona.

---

2. White, Merry. *The Japanese Overseas: Can They Go Home Again?* New York: Free Press, 1988. Offers an account of the families of Japanese corporate executives who are transferred abroad and who often suffer painful difficulties upon reentering Japan.

This required language learning in the broadest sense, mastery of culturally appropriate modes of moving, acting, and speaking. For my informants, it was clear that coping with this anomalous creature was difficult, for here was someone who looked like a real human being, but who simply failed to perform according to expectation. They, too, had every reason to make me over in their image, to guide me, gently but insistently, into properly Japanese behavior, so that the discrepancy between my appearance and my cultural competence would not be so painfully evident. I posed a challenge to their senses of identity. How could someone who *looked* Japanese not *be* Japanese? In my cultural ineptitude, I represented for the people who met me the chaos of meaninglessness. Their response in the face of this dissonance was to *make* me as Japanese as possible. Thus, my first nine months of fieldwork were characterized by an attempt to reduce the distance between expectation and inadequate reality, as my informants and I conspired to rewrite my identity as Japanese.

My guarantor, an older woman who, among her many activities, was a teacher of flower arranging, introduced me to many families who owned businesses in the ward of Tokyo where I had chosen to do my research. One of her former students and fellow flower-arranging teachers, Mrs. Sakamoto, agreed to take me in as a guest over the summer, since the apartment where I was scheduled to move—owned by one of my classmates in tea ceremony—was still under construction. My proclivities for "acting Japanese" were by this time firmly established. During my stay with the Sakamotos, I did my best to conform to what I thought their expectations of a guest / daughter might be. This in turn seemed to please them and reinforced my tendency to behave in terms of what I perceived to be my Japanese persona.

My initial encounter with the head of the household epitomizes this   5 mirroring and reinforcement of behavior. Mr. Sakamoto had been on a business trip on the day I moved in, and he returned the following evening, just as his wife, daughter, and I sat down to the evening meal. As soon as he stepped in the door, I immediately switched from an informal posture, seated on the *zabuton* (seat cushion) to a formal greeting posture, *seiza*-style (kneeling on the floor) and bowed low, hands on the floor. Mr. Sakamoto responded in kind (being older, male, and head of the household, he did not have to bow as deeply as I did), and we exchanged the requisite polite formulae, I requesting his benevolence, and he welcoming me to their family. Later, he told me how happy and impressed he had been with this act of proper etiquette on my part. "Today's young people in Japan," he said, "no longer show such respect. Your grandfather must have been a fine man to raise such a fine granddaughter." Of course, his statements can hardly be accepted at face value. They may well indicate his relief that I seemed to know something of proper Japanese behavior, and hence would not be a complete nuisance to them; it was also his way of making me feel at home. What is important to note is the way this statement was used to elicit proper Japanese behavior in future encounters. And his strategy worked. I was left with a warm, positive feeling toward the Sakamoto family, armed with an incentive to behave in a Japanese way, for clearly these were the expectations and the desires of the people who had taken me in and who were so generously sharing their lives with me.

Other members of the household voiced similar sentiments. Takemisan, the Sakamotos' married daughter who lived in a distant prefecture, had been visiting her parents when I first moved in. A few minutes after our initial encounter, she observed, "You seem like a typical Japanese woman" (*Nihon no josei, to iu kanji*). Later in the summer, Mrs. Sakamoto confided to me that she could never allow a "pure American" (*junsui na Amerikajin*) to live with them, for only someone of Japanese descent was genetically capable of adjusting to life on *tatami* mats, using unsewered toilets, sleeping on the floor—in short, of living Japanese style. Again, the message was unambiguous: My "family" could feel comfortable with me insofar as I was—and acted—Japanese.

At first, then, as a Japanese American I made sense to those around me as a none-too-felicitous combination of racial categories. As fieldwork progressed, however, and my linguistic and cultural skills improved, my informants seemed best able to understand me by placing me in meaningful cultural roles: daughter, guest, young woman, student, prodigal Japanese who had finally seen the light and come home. Most people preferred to treat me as a Japanese—sometimes an incomplete or unconventional Japanese, but a Japanese nonetheless. Indeed, even when I tried to represent myself as an American, others did not always take heed. For instance, on my first day on the job at the confectionery factory, Mr. Satō introduced me to the division chief as an "American student," here to learn about the business and about the "real situation" (*jittai*) of workers in small enterprise. Soon it became clear that the chief remembered "student," but not "American." A week or so later, we gathered for one of our noon meetings to read from a pamphlet published by an ethics school. The owner came, and he commented on the theme of the day, *ketsui* (determination). At one point during his speech, he singled me out, praising my resolve. "If Kondō-san had been an ordinary young woman, she might never have known Japan." I stared at my shoes, my cheeks flaming. When the exercise finished, I hurried back to my work station. Akiyama-san, the division head, approached me with a puzzled expression on his face. *"Doko desu ka?"* he asked. (Where is it? —in other words, where are you from?) And after my reply, he announced loudly to all: "She says it's America!"

My physical characteristics led my friends and coworkers to emphasize my identity as Japanese, sometimes even against my own intentions and desires. Over time, my increasingly "Japanese" behavior served temporarily to resolve their crises of meaning and to confirm their assumptions about their own identities. That I, too, came to participate enthusiastically in this recasting of the self is a testimonial to their success in acting upon me.

Conflict and Fragmentation of Self

Using these ready-made molds may have reduced the dissonance in my informants' minds, but it served only to increase the dissonance in my own. What occurred in the field was a kind of fragmenting of identity into what I then labeled Japanese and American pieces, so that the different elements, instead of fitting together to form at least the illusion of a seamless and coherent whole—it is the contention of this book that selves which are coherent, seamless, bounded, and whole are indeed illusions—strained against one another. The war was not really—or only—between Japanese and American elements, however. Perhaps it had even more to do with the position of researcher versus one of daughter and guest. In one position, my goal had to be the pursuit of knowledge, where decisive action, independence, and mastery were held in high esteem. In another, independence and mastery of one's own fate were out of the question; rather, being a daughter meant duties, responsibilities, and *inter*dependence.

The more I adjusted to my Japanese daughter's role, the keener the   10
conflicts became. Most of those conflicts had to do with expectations surrounding gender, and, more specifically, my position as a young woman. Certainly, in exchange for the care the Sakamotos showed me, I was happy to help out in whatever way I could. I tried to do some housecleaning and laundry, and I took over the shopping and cooking for Mr. Sakamoto when Mrs. Sakamoto was at one of the children's association meetings, her flower-arranging classes, or meetings of ward committees on juvenile delinquency. The cooking did not offend me in and of itself; in fact, I was glad for the opportunity to learn how to make simple Japanese cuisine, and Mr. Sakamoto put up with my sometimes appalling culinary mistakes and limited menus with great aplomb. I remember one particularly awful night when I couldn't find the makings for soup broth, and Mr. Sakamoto was fed "*miso* soup" that was little more than *miso* dissolved in hot water. He managed to down the tasteless broth with good grace—and the trace of a smile on his lips. (Of course, it is also true that although he was himself capable of simple cooking, he would not set foot in the kitchen if there were a woman in the house.) Months after I moved out, whenever he saw me he would say with a sparkle in his eye and a hint of nostalgic wistfulness in his voice, "I miss Dōrin-san's salad and sautéed beef," one of the "Western" menus I used

to serve up with numbing regularity. No, the cooking was not the problem.

The problem was, in fact, the etiquette surrounding the serving of food that produced the most profound conflicts for me as an American woman. The head of the household is usually served first and receives the finest delicacies; men—even the sweetest, nicest ones—ask for a second helping of rice by merely holding out their rice bowls to the woman nearest the rice cooker, and maybe, just maybe, uttering a grunt of thanks in return for her pains. I could never get used to this practice, try as I might. Still, I tried to carry out my duties uncomplainingly, in what I hope was reasonably good humor. But I was none too happy about these things "inside." Other restrictions began to chafe, especially restrictions on my movement. I had to be in at a certain hour, despite my "adult" age. Yet I understood the family's responsibility for me as their guest and quasi-daughter, so I tried to abide by their regulations, hiding my irritation as best I could.

This fundamental ambivalence was heightened by isolation and dependency. Though my status was in some respects high in an education-conscious Japan, I was still young, female, and a student. I was in a socially recognized relationship of dependency vis-à-vis the people I knew. I was not to be feared and obeyed, but protected and helped. In terms of my research, this was an extremely advantageous position to be in, for people did not feel the need to reflect my views back to me, as they might with a more powerful person. I did not try to define situations; rather, I could allow other people to define those situations in their culturally appropriate ways, remaining open to their concerns and their ways of acting in the world. But, in another sense, this dependency and isolation increased my susceptibility to identifying with my Japanese role. By this time I saw little of American friends in Tokyo, for it was difficult to be with people who had so little inkling of how ordinary Japanese people lived. My informants and I consequently had every reason to conspire to recreate my identity as Japanese. Precisely because of my dependency and my made-to-order role, I was allowed—or rather, *forced*—to abandon the position of observer. Errors, linguistic or cultural, were dealt with impatiently or with a startled look that seemed to say, "Oh yes, you are American after all." On the other hand, appropriately Japanese behaviors were rewarded with warm, positive reactions or with comments such as "You're more Japanese than the Japanese." Even more frequently, correct behavior was simply accepted as a matter of course. *Naturally* I would understand, *naturally* I would behave correctly, for they presumed me to be, *au fond*, Japanese.

Identity can imply unity or fusion, but for me what occurred was a fragmentation of the self. This fragmentation was encouraged by my own participation in Japanese life and by the actions of my friends and acquaintances. At its most extreme point, I became "the Other" in my own mind, where the identity I had known in another context simply collapsed. The success of our conspiracy to recreate me as Japanese reached its climax one August afternoon.

It was typical summer weather for Tokyo, "like a steam bath" as the saying goes, so hot the leaves were drooping limply from the trees surrounding the Sakamotos' house. Mrs. Sakamoto and her married daughter, Takemi, were at the doctor's with Takemi's son, so Mr. Sakamoto and I were busy tending young Kaori-chan, Takemi-san's young daughter. Mr. Sakamoto quickly tired of his grandfatherly role, leaving me to entertain Kaori-chan. Promptly at four P.M., the hour when most Japanese housewives do their shopping for the evening meal, I lifted the baby into her stroller and pushed her along ahead of me as I inspected the fish, selected the freshest-looking vegetables, and mentally planned the meal for the evening. As I glanced into the shiny metal surface of the butcher's display case, I noticed someone who looked terribly familiar: a typical young housewife, clad in slip-on sandals and the loose, cotton shift called "home wear" (*hōmu wea*), a woman walking with a characteristically Japanese bend to the knees and a sliding of the feet. Suddenly I clutched the handle of the stroller to steady myself as a wave of dizziness washed over me, for I realized I had caught a glimpse of nothing less than my own reflection. Fear that perhaps I would never emerge from this world into which I was immersed, inserted itself into my mind and stubbornly refused to leave, until I resolved to move into a new apartment, to distance myself from my Japanese home and my Japanese existence.

For ultimately, this collapse of identity was a distancing moment. It led me to emphasize the *differences* between cultures and among various aspects of identity: researcher, student, daughter, wife, Japanese, American, Japanese American. In order to reconstitute myself as an American researcher, I felt I had to extricate myself from the conspiracy to rewrite my identity as Japanese. Accordingly, despite the Sakamotos' invitations to stay with them for the coming year, I politely stated my intentions to fulfill the original terms of the agreement: to stay just until construction on my new apartment was complete. In order to resist the Sakamotos' attempts to recreate me as Japanese, I removed myself physically from their exclusively Japanese environment.

Thus, both the fragmentation of self and the collapse of identity were results of a complex collaboration between ethnographer and informants. It should be evident that at this particular point, my informants were hardly inert objects available for the free play of the ethnographer's desire. They themselves were, in the act of being, actively interpreting and trying to make meaning of the ethnographer. In so doing, the people I knew asserted their power to act upon the anthropologist. This was their means for preserving their own identities. Understanding, in this context, is multiple, open-ended, positioned—although that positioning can shift dramatically, as I have argued—and pervaded by relations of power. These power-imbued attempts to capture, recast, and rewrite each other were for us productive of understandings and were, existentially, alternately wrenching and fulfilling.

Reading the Text

1. Why do the native Japanese find Kondo to be a "conceptual anomaly"?
2. Why did Kondo feel increasing inner conflict as her Japanese hosts grew increasingly comfortable with her "Japanese" identity?
3. What unfamiliar gender roles did Kondo face in Japan, and how did she respond to them?
4. Why does Kondo say her Japanese hosts engaged in a "conspiracy" to rewrite her identity as Japanese?

Reading the Signs

1. If you have ever experienced a cultural identity crisis similar to that described by Kondo, discuss it in your journal. What factors precipitated this crisis? Explore your own responses and those of people around you.
2. Writing as if you were Kondo, compose a letter to Fan Shen (see "The Classroom and the Wider Culture: Identity as a Key to Learning English Composition," p. 485) in which you explain Shen's problems in his composition class. What advice might Kondo give Shen for coping with the alternative cultural norms he is facing in the classroom?
3. In class, freewrite for fifteen minutes on what you believe are the most important components of your identity. Then, in small groups (racially mixed if possible), discuss your results. How much of your identity is determined by ethnic origin? What other cultural factors have influenced your self-image? How does your freewriting compare with that of others in your group, and how can you account for both similarities and differences?
4. Kondo describes the importance of food rituals as signs of cultural identity and bonding. Write an essay in which you discuss the particular eating rituals of your ethnic group, being sure to discuss not simply their personal significance to you but also their significance to the group.
5. Kondo describes the "fragmentation of self" she experienced when she adopted "ready-made molds," or cultural norms, to conform to her hosts' expectations. Use her notion of "fragmentation of self" to explain the anguish felt by the African-Americans in Sam Fulwood III's "The Rage of the Black Middle Class" (p. 462). How are Fulwood's interviewees suffering a similar identity crisis? How does an important difference—the fact that his interviewees are Americans living in America—affect their attitudes?

FAN SHEN

The Classroom and the Wider Culture: Identity as a Key to Learning English Composition

||||||||||||||||||||||||||||||||||||||||||||||||||||||||||||

Writing conventions involve more cultural presuppositions and mythologies than we ordinarily recognize. Take the current practice of using the first-person singular pronoun "I" when writing an essay. Such a convention presumes an individualistic world view, which can appear very strange to someone coming from a communal culture, as Fan Shen relates in this analysis of the relation between culture and composition. Hailing from the People's Republic of China, where the group comes before the individual in social consciousness, Shen describes what it was like to move to the United States and have to learn a whole new world view to master the writing conventions that he himself now teaches as an assistant professor at Rockland Community College. A translator as well as a writer and teacher, Fan Shen has translated three books from English to Chinese and has written numerous articles for Chinese publications.

One day in June 1975, when I walked into the aircraft factory where I was working as an electrician, I saw many large-letter posters on the walls and many people parading around the workshops shouting slogans like "Down with the word 'I'!" and "Trust in masses and the Party!" I then remembered that a new political campaign called "Against Individualism" was scheduled to begin that day. Ten years later, I got back my first English composition paper at the University of Nebraska–Lincoln. The professor's first comments were: "Why did you always use 'we' instead of 'I'?" and "Your paper would be stronger if you eliminated some sentences in the passive voice." The clashes between my Chinese background and the requirements of English composition had begun. At the center of this mental struggle, which has lasted several years and is still not completely over, is the prolonged, uphill battle to recapture "myself."

In this paper I will try to describe and explore this experience of reconciling my Chinese identity with an English identity dictated by the rules of English composition. I want to show how my cultural background shaped—and shapes—my approaches to my writing in English and how writing in English redefined—and redefines—my *ideological* and *logical* identities. By "ideological identity" I mean the system of values that I acquired (consciously and unconsciously) from my social and cultural background. And by "logical identity" I mean the natural (or Oriental) way I organize and express my thoughts in writing. Both had to be modified or redefined in learning English composition. Becoming aware of the process of redefinition of these different identities is a mode of learning that has helped me in my efforts to write in English, and, I hope, will be of help to teachers of English composition in this country. In presenting my case for this view, I will use examples from both my composition courses and literature courses, for I believe that writing papers for both kinds of courses contributed to the development of my "English identity." Although what I will describe is based on personal experience, many Chinese students whom I talked to said that they had had the same or similar experiences in their initial stages of learning to write in English.

Identity of the Self: Ideological and Cultural

Starting with the first English paper I wrote, I found that learning to compose in English is not an isolated classroom activity, but a social and cultural experience. The rules of English composition encapsulate values that are absent in, or sometimes contradictory to, the values of other societies (in my case, China). Therefore, learning the rules of English composition is, to a certain extent, learning the values of Anglo-American society. In writing classes in the United States I found that I had to reprogram my mind, to redefine some of the basic concepts and values that I had about myself, about society, and about the universe, values that had been imprinted and reinforced in my mind by my cultural background, and that had been part of me all my life.

Rule number one in English composition is: Be yourself. (More than one composition instructor has told me, "Just write what *you* think.") The values behind this rule, it seems to me, are based on the principle of protecting and promoting individuality (and private property) in this country. The instruction was probably crystal clear to students raised on these values, but, as a guideline of composition, it was not very clear or useful to me when I first heard it. First of all, the image or meaning that I attached to the word "I" or "myself" was, as I found out, different from that of my English teacher. In China, "I" is always subordinated to "We"—be it the working class, the Party, the country, or some other collective body. Both political pressure and literary tradition require that "I" be somewhat hidden or buried in writings and speeches; presenting the "self" too obviously would give people the impression of being disrespectful of the Communist Party in political writings and boastful in scholarly writings. The word "I" has often been identified with another "bad" word, "individualism," which has become a synonym for selfishness in China. For a long time the words "self" and "individualism" have had negative connotations in my mind, and the negative force of the words naturally extended to the field of literary studies. As a result, even if I had brilliant ideas, the "I" in my papers always had to show some modesty by not competing with or trying to stand above the names of ancient and modern authoritative figures. Appealing to Mao or other Marxist authorities became the required way (as well as the most "forceful" or "persuasive" way) to prove one's point in written discourse. I remember that in China I had even committed what I can call "reversed plagiarism"—here, I suppose it would be called "forgery"—when I was in middle school: willfully attributing some of my thoughts to "experts" when I needed some arguments but could not find a suitable quotation from a literary or political "giant."

Now, in America, I had to learn to accept the words "I" and "self" as something glorious (as Whitman did), or at least something not to be ashamed of or embarrassed about. It was the first and probably biggest step I took into English composition and critical writing. Acting upon my professor's suggestion, I intentionally tried to show my "individuality" and to "glorify" "I" in my papers by using as many "I's" as possible—"I think," "I believe," "I see"—and deliberately cut out quotations from authorities. It was rather painful to hand in such "pompous" (I mean immodest) papers to my instructors. But to an extent it worked. After a while I became more comfortable with only "the shadow of myself." I felt more at ease to put down *my* thoughts without looking over my shoulder to worry about the attitudes of my teachers or the reactions of the Party secretaries, and to speak out as "bluntly" and "immodestly" as my American instructors demanded.

But writing many "I's" was only the beginning of the process of redefining myself. Speaking of redefining myself is, in an important sense, speaking of redefining the word "I." By such a redefinition I mean not only the change in how I envisioned myself, but also the change in how *I* perceived the world. The old "I" used to embody only one set of values, but now it had to embody multiple sets of values. To be truly "myself," which I knew was a key to my success in learning English composition, meant *not to be my Chinese self* at all. That is to say, when I write in English I have to wrestle with and abandon (at least temporarily) the whole system of ideology which previously defined me in myself. I had to forget Marxist doctrines (even though I do not see myself as a Marxist by choice) and the Party lines imprinted in my mind and familiarize myself with a system of capitalist/bourgeois values. I had to put aside an ideology of collectivism and adopt the values of individualism. In composition as well as in literature classes, I had to make a fundamental adjustment: If I used to examine society and literary materials through the microscopes of Marxist dialectical materialism and historical materialism, I now had to learn to look through the micro-

5

scopes the other way around, i.e., to learn to look at and understand the world from the point of view of "idealism." (I must add here that there are American professors who use a Marxist approach in their teaching.)

The word "idealism," which affects my view of both myself and the universe, is loaded with social connotations, and can serve as a good example of how redefining a key word can be a pivotal part of redefining my ideological identity as a whole.

To me, idealism is the philosophical foundation of the dictum of English composition: "Be yourself." In order to write good English, I knew that I had to be myself, which actually meant not to be my Chinese self. It meant that I had to create an English self and be *that* self. And to be that English self, I felt, I had to understand and accept idealism the way a Westerner does. That is to say, I had to accept the way a Westerner sees himself in relation to the universe and society. On the one hand, I knew a lot about idealism. But on the other hand, I knew nothing about it. I mean I knew a lot about idealism through the propaganda and objections of its opponent, Marxism, but I knew little about it from its own point of view. When I thought of the word "materialism"—which is a major part of Marxism and in China has repeatedly been "shown" to be the absolute truth—there were always positive connotations, and words like "right," "true," etc., flashed in my mind. On the other hand, the word "idealism" always came to me with the dark connotations that surround words like "absurd," "illogical," "wrong," etc. In China "idealism" is depicted as a ferocious and ridiculous enemy of Marxist philosophy. Idealism, as the simplified definition imprinted in my mind had it, is the view that the material world does not exist; that all that exists is the mind and its ideas. It is just the opposite of Marxist dialectical materialism which sees the mind as a product of the material world. It is not too difficult to see that idealism, with its idea that mind is of primary importance, provides a philosophical foundation for the Western emphasis on the value of individual human minds, and hence individual human beings. Therefore, my final acceptance of myself as of primary importance—an importance that overshadowed that of authority figures in English composition—was, I decided, dependent on an acceptance of idealism.

My struggle with idealism came mainly from my efforts to understand and to write about works such as Coleridge's *Biographia Literaria* and Emerson's "Over-Soul." For a long time I was frustrated and puzzled by the idealism expressed by Coleridge and Emerson—given their ideas, such as "I think, therefore I am" (Coleridge obviously borrowed from Descartes) and "the transparent eyeball" (Emerson's view of himself)— because in my mind, drenched as it was in dialectical materialism, there was always a little voice whispering in my ear "You are, therefore you think." I could not see how human consciousness, which is not material, could create apples and trees. My intellectual conscience refused to let me believe that the human mind is the primary world and the material world secondary. Finally, I had to imagine that I was looking at a world with my head upside down. When I imagined that I was in a new body (born with the head upside down) it was easier to forget biases imprinted in my subconsciousness about idealism, the mind, and my former self. Starting from scratch, the new inverted self—which I called my "English Self" and into which I have transformed myself—could understand and *accept,* with ease, idealism as "the truth" and "himself" (i.e., my English Self) as the "creator" of the world.

Here is how I created my new "English Self." I played a "game" similar to ones played by mental therapists. First I made a list of (simplified) features about writing associated with my old identity (the Chinese Self), both ideological and logical, and then beside the first list I added a column of features about writing associated with my new identity (the English Self). After that I pictured myself getting out of my old identity, the timid, humble, modest Chinese "I," and creeping into my new identity (often in the form of a new skin or a mask), the confident, assertive, and aggressive English "I." The new "Self" helped me to remember and accept the different rules of Chinese and English composition and the values that underpin these rules. In a sense, creating an English Self is a way of reconciling my old cultural values with the new values required by English writing, without losing the former.

An interesting structural but not material parallel to my experiences in this regard has been well described by Min-zhan Lu in her important article, "From Silence to Words: Writing as Struggle" (*College English* 49 [April 1987]: 437–48). Min-zhan Lu talks about struggles between two selves, an open self and a secret self, and between two discourses, a mainstream Marxist discourse and a bourgeois discourse her parents wanted her to learn. But her struggle was different from mine. Her Chinese self was severely constrained and suppressed by mainstream cultural discourse, but never interfused with it. Her experiences, then, were not representative of those of the majority of the younger generation who, like me, were brought up on only one discourse. I came to English composition as a Chinese person, in the fullest sense of the term, with a Chinese identity already fully formed.

Identity of the Mind: Illogical and Alogical

In learning to write in English, besides wrestling with a different ideological system, I found that I had to wrestle with a logical system very different from the blueprint of logic at the back of my mind. By "logical system" I mean two things: the Chinese way of thinking I used to approach my theme or topic in written discourse, and the Chinese critical/logical way to develop a theme or topic. By English rules, the first is illogical, for it is the opposite of the English way of approaching a topic; the second is alogical (nonlogical), for it mainly uses mental pictures instead of words as a critical vehicle.

THE ILLOGICAL PATTERN

In English composition, an essential rule for the logical organization of a piece of writing is the use of a "topic sentence." In Chinese composition, "from surface to core" is an essential rule, a rule which means that one ought to reach a topic gradually and "systematically" instead of "abruptly."

The concept of a topic sentence, it seems to me, is symbolic of the values of a busy people in an industrialized society, rushing to get things done, hoping to attract and satisfy the busy reader very quickly. Thinking back, I realized that I did not fully understand the virtue of the concept until my life began to rush at the speed of everyone else's in this country. Chinese composition, on the other hand, seems to embody the values of a leisurely paced rural society whose inhabitants have the time to chew and taste a topic slowly. In Chinese composition, an introduction explaining how and why one chooses this topic is not only acceptable, but often regarded as necessary. It arouses the reader's interest in the topic little by little (and this is seen as a virtue of composition) and gives him/her a sense of refinement. The famous Robert B. Kaplan "noodles" contrasting a spiral Oriental thought process with a straight-line Western approach ("Cultural Thought Patterns in Inter-Cultural Education," *Readings on English as a Second Language,* Ed. Kenneth Croft, 2nd ed., Winthrop, 1980, 403–10) may be too simplistic to capture the preferred pattern of writing in English, but I think they still express some truth about Oriental writing. A Chinese writer often clears the surrounding bushes before attacking the real target. This bush-clearing pattern in Chinese writing goes back two thousand years to Kong Fuzi (Confucius). Before doing anything, Kong says in his *Luen Yu (Analects),* one first needs to call things by their proper names (expressed by his phrase "Zheng Ming" 正名). In other words, before touching one's main thesis, one should first state the "conditions" of composition: how, why, and when the piece is being composed. All of this will serve as a proper foundation on which to build the "house" of the piece. In the two thousand years after Kong, this principle of composition was gradually formalized (especially through the formal essays required by imperial examinations) and became known as "Ba Gu," or the eight-legged essay. The logic of Chinese composition, exemplified by the eight-legged essay, is like the peeling of an onion: Layer after layer is removed until the reader finally arrives at the central point, the core.

Ba Gu still influences modern Chinese writing. Carolyn Matalene   15
has an excellent discussion of this logical (or illogical) structure and its
influence on her Chinese students' efforts to write in English ("Con-
trastive Rhetoric: An American Writing Teacher in China," *College English* 47 [November 1985]: 789–808). A recent Chinese textbook for
composition lists six essential steps (factors) for writing a narrative essay,
steps to be taken in this order: time, place, character, event, cause, and
consequence (*Yuwen Jichu Zhishi Liushi Jiang* [*Sixty Lessons on the Basics
of the Chinese Language*], Ed. Beijing Research Institute of Education,
Beijing Publishing House, 1981, 525–609). Most Chinese students (including me) are taught to follow this sequence in composition.

The straightforward approach to composition in English seemed to
me, at first, illogical. One could not jump to the topic. One had to walk
step by step to reach the topic. In several of my early papers I found that
the Chinese approach—the bush-clearing approach—persisted, and I
had considerable difficulty writing (and in fact understanding) topic sentences. In what I deemed to be topic sentences, I grudgingly gave out
themes. Today, those papers look to me like Chinese papers with forced
or false English openings. For example, in a narrative paper on a trip to
New York, I wrote the forced/false topic sentence, "A trip to New
York in winter is boring." In the next few paragraphs, I talked about the
weather, the people who went with me, and so on, before I talked about
what I learned from the trip. My real thesis was that one could always
learn something even on a boring trip.

THE ALOGICAL PATTERN

In learning English composition, I found that there was yet another
cultural blueprint affecting my logical thinking. I found from my early
papers that very often I was unconsciously under the influence of a
Chinese critical approach called the creation of "yijing," which is totally
non-Western. The direct translation of the word "yijing" is: yi, "mind
or consciousness," and jing, "environment." An ancient approach which
has existed in China for many centuries and is still the subject of much
discussion, yijing is a complicated concept that defies a universal definition. But most critics in China nowadays seem to agree on one point,
that yijing is the critical approach that separates Chinese literature and
criticism from Western literature and criticism. Roughly speaking, yijing
is the process of creating a pictorial environment while reading a piece
of literature. Many critics in China believe that yijing is a creative process
of inducing oneself, while reading a piece of literature or looking at a
piece of art, to create mental pictures, in order to reach a unity of nature,
the author, and the reader. Therefore, it is by its very nature both creative
and critical. According to the theory, this nonverbal, pictorial process

leads directly to a higher ground of beauty and morality. Almost all critics in China agree that yijing is not a process of logical thinking—it is not a process of moving from the premises of an argument to its conclusion, which is the foundation of Western criticism. According to yijing, the process of criticizing a piece of art or literary work has to involve the process of creation on the reader's part. In yijing, verbal thoughts and pictorial thoughts are one. Thinking is conducted largely in pictures and then "transcribed" into words. (Ezra Pound once tried to capture the creative aspect of yijing in poems such as "In a Station of the Metro." He also tried to capture the critical aspect of it in his theory of imagism and vorticism, even though he did not know the term "yijing.") One characteristic of the yijing approach to criticism, therefore, is that it often includes a description of the created mental pictures on the part of the reader/critic and his/her mental attempt to bridge (unite) the literary work, the pictures, with ultimate beauty and peace.

In looking back at my critical papers for various classes, I discovered that I unconsciously used the approach of yijing, especially in some of my earlier papers when I seemed not yet to have been in the grip of Western logical critical approaches. I wrote, for instance, an essay entitled "Wordsworth's Sound and Imagination: The Snowdon Episode." In the major part of the essay I described the pictures that flashed in my mind while I was reading passages in Wordsworth's long poem, *The Prelude*.

> I saw three climbers (myself among them) winding up the mountain in silence "at the dead of night," absorbed in their "private thoughts." The sky was full of blocks of clouds of different colors, freely changing their shapes, like oily pigments disturbed in a bucket of water. All of a sudden, the moonlight broke the darkness "like a flash," lighting up the mountain tops. Under the "naked moon," the band saw a vast sea of mist and vapor, a silent ocean. Then the silence was abruptly broken, and we heard the "roaring of waters, torrents, streams/Innumerable, roaring with one voice" from a "blue chasm," a fracture in the vapor of the sea. It was a joyful revelation of divine truth to the human mind: the bright, "naked" moon sheds the light of "higher reasons" and "spiritual love" upon us; the vast ocean of mist looked like a thin curtain through which we vaguely saw the infinity of nature beyond; and the sounds of roaring waters coming out of the chasm of vapor cast us into the boundless spring of imagination from the depth of the human heart. Evoked by the divine light from above, the human spring of imagination is joined by the natural spring and becomes a sustaining source of energy, feeding "upon infinity" while transcending infinity at the same time. . . .

Here I was describing my own experience more than Wordsworth's. The picture described by the poet is taken over and developed by the reader. The imagination of the author and the imagination of the reader are thus joined together. There was no "because" or "therefore" in the paper. There was little *logic*. And I thought it was (and it is) criticism. This seems to me a typical (but simplified) example of the yijing approach. (Incidentally, the instructor, a kind professor, found the paper interesting, though a bit "strange.")

I am not saying that such a pattern of "alogical" thinking is wrong —in fact some English instructors find it interesting and acceptable— but it is very non-Western. Since I was in this country to learn the English language and English literature, I had to abandon Chinese "pictorial logic," and to learn Western "verbal logic."

If I Had to Start Again

The change is profound: Through my understanding of new meanings of words like "individualism," "idealism," and "I," I began to accept the underlying concepts and values of American writing, and by learning to use "topic sentences" I began to accept a new logic. Thus, when I write papers in English, I am able to obey all the general rules of English composition. In doing this I feel that I am writing through, with, and because of a new identity. I welcome the change, for it has added a new dimension to me and to my view of the world. I am not saying that I have entirely lost my Chinese identity. In fact I feel that I will never lose it. Any time I write in Chinese, I resume my old identity, and obey the rules of Chinese composition such as "Make the 'I' modest," and "Beat around the bush before attacking the central topic." It is necessary for me to have such a Chinese identity in order to write authentic Chinese. (I have seen people who, after learning to write in English, use English logic and sentence patterning to write Chinese. They produce very awkward Chinese texts.) But when I write in English, I imagine myself slipping into a new "skin," and I let the "I" behave much more aggressively and knock the topic right on the head. Being conscious of these different identities has helped me to reconcile different systems of values and logic, and has played a pivotal role in my learning to compose in English.

Looking back, I realize that the process of learning to write in English is in fact a process of creating and defining a new identity and balancing it with the old identity. The process of learning English composition would have been easier if I had realized this earlier and consciously sought to compare the two different identities required by the two writing systems from two different cultures. It is fine and perhaps even necessary for American composition teachers to teach about topic sentences, paragraphs, the use of punctuation, documentation, and so on, but can anyone design exercises sensitive to the ideological and logical differences that students like me experience—and design them so they can be introduced at an early stage of an English composition class? As

I pointed out earlier, the traditional advice "Just be yourself" is not clear and helpful to students from Korea, China, Vietnam, or India. From "Be yourself" we are likely to hear either "Forget your cultural habit of writing" or "Write as you would write in your own language." But neither of the two is what the instructor meant or what we want to do. It would be helpful if he or she pointed out the different cultural/ideological connotations of the word "I," the connotations that exist in a group-centered culture and an individual-centered culture. To sharpen the contrast, it might be useful to design papers on topics like "The Individual vs. The Group: China vs. America" or "Different 'I's' in Different Cultures."

Carolyn Matalene mentioned in her article (789) an incident concerning American businessmen who presented their Chinese hosts with gifts of cheddar cheese, not knowing that the Chinese generally do not like cheese. Liking cheddar cheese may not be essential to writing English prose, but being truly accustomed to the social norms that stand behind ideas such as the English "I" and the logical pattern of English composition—call it "compositional cheddar cheese"—is essential to writing in English. Matalene does not provide an "elixir" to help her Chinese students like English "compositional cheese," but rather recommends, as do I, that composition teachers not be afraid to give foreign students English "cheese," but to make sure to hand it out slowly, sympathetically, and fully realizing that it tastes very peculiar in the mouths of those used to a very different cuisine.

Reading the Text

1. Why does Fan Shen say English composition is a cultural and social activity?
2. What are the differences between Western and Chinese views of the self, according to Shen?
3. What does Shen mean by the "yijing" approach to writing?
4. In a paragraph, summarize the process by which Fan Shen learned to write English composition essays.

Reading the Signs

1. In your journal, brainstorm ways in which you were brought up to either assert your individuality or subordinate yourself to group interests (you might consider involvement in sports or school activities). Then stand back and consider your brainstormed list. To what extent were you raised with a "Western" concept of self? How do your ethnic background and gender affect your sense of self-identity?
2. Compare and contrast Fan Shen's experience in his composition class with

that of Anna (see Elizabeth Chiseri-Strater, "Anna," p. 635). How do ethnicity and gender shape each writer's experiences?

3. In class, discuss the extent to which your classes, including your writing class, assume Western styles of learning and discourse. Then write an essay discussing the results of your discussion, using the "yijing" approach that Fan Shen describes. Read your essay aloud in class.

4. Using Fan Shen's notions of Western and non-Western styles of self, categorize the cool pose style described by Richard Majors ("Cool Pose: The Proud Signature of Black Survival," p. 471). How is the self conceived of in the cool pose? How might that conception of self operate as a survival strategy for blacks in American culture?

5. Has anything you have learned in your writing class felt "foreign" to you? Write a list, as Fan Shen did, in which you name features about writing that come "naturally" to you and then list those that seem "unnatural." Then study your lists. Which features seem culturally determined and which seem linked to your own personality and way of thinking? Can you make such a distinction? How can these lists help you as a writer?

L E S L I E   M A R M O N   S I L K O
Language and Literature from a Pueblo Indian Perspective

||||||||||||||||||||||||||||||||||||||||||||||||||||||||||||

One of America's best-known Native-American writers, Leslie Marmon Silko (b. 1948) gained national attention in 1977 with the publication of her novel Ceremony, *where she blends the conventions of the European novel with Laguna mythic traditions to tell the story of a mixed-blood Laguna veteran home from Vietnam. In this essay, Silko describes the mythologies of the Pueblo Indians, retelling the Pueblo creation story and explaining the essential place of storytelling and of the land in which the stories are told, in maintaining tribal cohesion and identity. The recipient of a MacArthur Foundation grant, Silko lives and writes in Arizona, near the Laguna homeland from which she derives her literary power and inspiration. She has also published a collection of poems,* Laguna Woman *(1974), and a collection of short stories,* Storyteller *(1981). Her most recent work is a novel,* Almanac of the Dead *(1992).*

This "essay" is an edited transcript of an oral presentation. The "author" deliberately did not read from a prepared paper so that the audience could experience firsthand one dimension of the oral tradition—non-linear structure. Her remarks were intended to be heard, not read.

Where I come from, the words that are most highly valued are those which are spoken from the heart, unpremeditated and unrehearsed. Among the Pueblo people, a written speech or statement is highly suspect because the true feelings of the speaker remain hidden as he reads words that are detached from the occasion and the audience. I have intentionally not written a formal paper to read to this session because of this and because I want you to hear and to experience English in a nontraditional structure, a structure that follows patterns from the oral tradition. For those of you accustomed to a structure that moves from point A to point B to point C, this presentation may be somewhat difficult to follow because the structure of Pueblo expression resembles something like a spider's web—with many little threads radiating from a center, crisscrossing each other. As with the web, the structure will emerge as it is made and you must simply listen and trust, as the Pueblo people do, that meaning will be made.

I suppose the task that I have today is a formidable one because basically I come here to ask you, at least for a while, to set aside a number of basic approaches that you have been using and probably will continue to use in approaching the study of English or the study of language; first of all, I come to ask you to see language from the Pueblo perspective, which is a perspective that is very much concerned with including the whole of creation and the whole of history and time. And so we very seldom talk about breaking language down into words. As I will continue to relate to you, even the use of a specific language is less important than the one thing—which is the "telling," or the storytelling. And so, as Simon Ortiz has written, if you approach a Pueblo person and want to talk words or, worse than that, to break down an individual word into its components, ofttimes you will just get a blank stare, because we don't think of words as being isolated from the speaker, which, of course, is one element of the oral tradition. Moreover, we don't think of words as being alone: Words are always with other words, and the other words are almost always in a story of some sort.

Today I have brought a number of examples of stories in English because I would like to get around to the question that has been raised, or the topic that has come along here, which is what changes we Pueblo writers might make with English as a language for literature. But at the same time I would like to explain the importance of storytelling and how it relates to a Pueblo theory of language.

So first I would like to go back to the Pueblo Creation story. The reason I go back to that story is because it is an all-inclusive story of creation and how life began. Tséitsínako, Thought Woman, by thinking of her sisters, and together with her sisters, thought of everything which is, and this world was created. And the belief was that everything in this world was a part of the original creation, and that the people at home realized that far away there were others—other human beings. There is even a section of the story which is a prophesy—which describes the origin of the European race, the African, and also remembers the Asian origins.

Starting out with this story, with this attitude which includes all things, I would like to point out that the reason the people are more concerned with story and communication and less with a particular language is in part an outgrowth of the area [pointing to a map] where we find ourselves. Among the twenty Pueblos there are at least six distinct languages, and possibly seven. Some of the linguists argue—and I don't set myself up to be a linguist at all—about the number of distinct languages. But certainly Zuni is all alone, and Hopi is all alone, and from mesa to mesa there are subtle differences in language—very great differences. I think that this might be the reason that what particular language was being used wasn't as important as what a speaker was trying to say. And this, I think, is reflected and stems or grows out of a particular view of the story—that is, that language *is* story. At Laguna many words have stories which make them. So when one is telling a story, and one is using words to tell the story, each word that one is speaking has a story of its own too. Often the speakers or tellers go into the stories of the words they are using to tell one story so that you get stories within stories, so to speak. This structure becomes very apparent in the storytelling, and what I would like to show you later on by reading some pieces that I brought is that this structure also informs the writing and the stories which are currently coming from Pueblo people. I think what is essential is this sense of story, and story within story, and the idea that one story is only the beginning of many stories, and the sense that stories never truly end. I would like to propose that these views of structure and the dynamics of storytelling are some of the contributions which Native American cultures bring to the English language or at least to literature in the English language.

First of all, a lot of people think of storytelling as something that is done at bedtime—that it is something that is done for small children. When I use the term "storytelling," I include a far wider range of telling activity. I also do not limit storytelling to simply old stories, but to again go back to the original view of creation, which sees that it is all part of a whole; we do not differentiate or fragment stories and experiences. In the beginning, Tséitsínako, Thought Woman, thought of all these things, and all of these things are held together as one holds many things together in a single thought.

So in the telling (and today you will hear a few of the dimensions of this telling) first of all, as was pointed out earlier, the storytelling always includes the audience and the listeners, and, in fact, a great deal of the story is believed to be inside the listener, and the storyteller's role

5

is to draw the story out of the listeners. This kind of shared experience grows out of a strong community base. The storytelling goes on and continues from generation to generation.

The Origin story functions basically as a maker of our identity— with the story we know who we are. We are the Lagunas. This is where we came from. We came this way. We came by this place. And so from the time you are very young, you hear these stories, so that when you go out into the wider world, when one asks who you are, or where are you from, you immediately know: We are the people who came down from the north. We are the people of these stories. It continues down into clans so that you are not just talking about Laguna Pueblo people, you are talking about your own clan. Within the clans there are stories which identify the clan.

In the Creation story, Antelope says that he will help knock a hole in the earth so that the people can come up, out into the next world. Antelope tries and tries, and he uses his hooves and is unable to break through; and it is then that Badger says, "Let me help you." And Badger very patiently uses his claws and digs a way through, bringing the people into the world. When the Badger clan people think of themselves, or when the Antelope people think of themselves, it is as people who are of *this* story, and this is *our* place, and we fit into the very beginning when the people first came, before we began our journey south.

So you can move, then, from the idea of one's identity as a tribal person into clan identity. Then we begin to get to the extended family, and this is where we begin to get a kind of story coming into play which some people might see as a different kind of story, though Pueblo people do not. Anthropologists and ethnologists have, for a long time, differentiated the types of oral language they find in the Pueblos. They tended to rule out all but the old and sacred and traditional stories and were not interested in family stories and the family's account of itself. But these family stories are just as important as the other stories—the older stories. These family stories are given equal recognition. There is no definite, pre-set pattern for the way one will hear the stories of one's own family, but it is a very critical part of one's childhood, and it continues on throughout one's life. You will hear stories of importance to the family —sometimes wonderful stories—stories about the time a maternal uncle got the biggest deer that was ever seen and brought back from the mountains. And so one's sense of who the family is, and who you are, will then extend from that—"I am from the family of my uncle who brought in this wonderful deer, and it was a wonderful hunt"—so you have this sort of building or sense of identity.

There are also other stories, stories about the time when another uncle, perhaps, did something that wasn't really acceptable. In other words, this process of keeping track, of telling, is an all-inclusive process

10

which begins to create a total picture. So it is very important that you know all of the stories—both positive and not so positive—about one's own family. The reason that it is very important to keep track of all the stories in one's own family is because you are liable to hear a story from somebody else who is perhaps an enemy of the family, and you are liable to hear a version which has been changed, a version which makes your family sound disreputable—something that will taint the honor of the family. But if you have already heard the story, you know your family's version of what *really* happened that night, so when somebody else is mentioning it, you will have a version of the story to counterbalance it. Even when there is no way around it—old Uncle Pete did a terrible thing—by knowing the stories that come out of other families, by keeping very close watch, listening constantly to learn the stories about other families, one is in a sense able to deal with terrible sorts of things that might happen within one's own family. When a member of one's own family does something that cannot be excused, one always knows stories about similar things which happened in other families. And it is not done maliciously. I think it is very important to realize this. Keeping track of all the stories within the community gives a certain distance, a useful perspective which brings incidents down to a level we can deal with. If others have done it before, it cannot be so terrible. If others have endured, so can we.

The stories are always bringing us together, keeping this whole together, keeping this family together, keeping this clan together. "Don't go away, don't isolate yourself, but come here, because we have all had these kinds of experiences"—this is what the people are saying to you when they tell you these other stories. And so there is this constant pulling together to resist what seems to me to be a basic part of human nature: When some violent emotional experience takes place, people get the urge to run off and hide or separate themselves from others. And of course, if we do that, we are not only talking about endangering the group, we are also talking about the individual or the individual family never being able to recover or to survive. Inherent in this belief is the feeling that one does not recover or get well by one's self, but it is together that we look after each other and take care of each other.

In the storytelling, then, we see this process of bringing people together, and it works not only on the family level, but also on the level of the individual. Of course, the whole Pueblo concept of the individual is a little bit different from the usual Western concept of the individual. But one of the beauties of the storytelling is that when something happens to an individual, many people will come to you and take you aside, or maybe a couple of people will come and talk to you. These are occasions of storytelling. These occasions of storytelling are continuous; they are a way of life.

Storytelling lies at the heart of the Pueblo people, and so when someone comes in and says, "When did they tell the stories, or what time of day does the storytelling take place?" that is a ridiculous question. The storytelling goes on constantly—as some old grandmother puts on the shoes of a little child and tells the child the story of a little girl who didn't wear her shoes. At the same time somebody comes into the house for coffee to talk with an adolescent boy who has just been into a lot of trouble, to reassure him that *he* got into that kind of trouble, or somebody else's son got into that kind of trouble too. You have this constant ongoing process, working on many different levels.

One of the stories I like to bring up about helping the individual in   15 crisis is a recent story, and I want to remind you that we make no distinctions between the stories—whether they are history, whether they are fact, whether they are gossip—these distinctions are not useful when we are talking about this particular experience with language. Anyway, there was a young man who, when he came back from the war in Vietnam, had saved up his Army pay and bought a beautiful red Volkswagen Beetle. He was very proud of it, and one night drove up to a place right across the reservation line. It is a very notorious place for many reasons, but one of the more notorious things about the place is a deep arroyo behind the place. This is the King's Bar. So he ran in to pick up a cold six-pack to take home, but he didn't put on his emergency brake. And his little red Volkswagen rolled back into the arroyo and was all smashed up. He felt very bad about it, but within a few days everybody had come to him and told him stories about other people who had lost cars to that arroyo. And probably the story that made him feel the best was about the time that George Day's station wagon, with his mother-in-law and kids in the back, rolled into that arroyo. So everybody was saying, "Well, at least your mother-in-law and kids weren't in the car when it rolled in," and you can't argue with that kind of story. He felt better then because he wasn't alone anymore. He and his smashed-up Volkswagen were now joined with all the other stories of cars that fell into that arroyo.

There are a great many parallels between Pueblo experiences and the remarks that have been made about South Africa and the Caribbean countries—similarities in experiences so far as language is concerned. More specifically, with the experience of English being imposed upon the people. The Pueblo people, of course, have seen intruders come and intruders go. The first they watched come were the Spaniards; while the Spaniards were there, things had to be conducted in Spanish. But as the old stories say, if you wait long enough, they'll go. And sure enough, they went. Then another bunch came in. And old stories say, well, if you wait around long enough, not so much that they'll go, but at least their ways will go. One wonders now, when you see what's happening to technocratic-industrial culture, now that we've used up most of the sources of energy, you think perhaps the old people are right.

But anyhow, our experience with English has been different because the Bureau of Indian Affairs schools were so terrible that we never heard of Shakespeare. There was Dick and Jane, and I can remember reading that the robins were heading south for winter, but I knew that all winter the robins were around Laguna. It took me a long time to figure out what was going on. I worried for quite a while about the robins because they didn't leave in the winter, not realizing that the textbooks were written in Boston. The big textbook companies are up here in Boston and *their* robins do go south in the winter. But this freed us and encouraged us to stay with our narratives. Whatever literature we received at school (which was damn little), at home the storytelling, the special regard for telling and bringing together through the telling, was going on constantly. It has continued, and so we have a great body of classical oral literature, both in the narratives and in the chants and songs.

As the old people say, "If you can remember the stories, you will be all right. Just remember the stories." And, of course, usually when they say that to you, when you are young, you wonder what in the world they mean. But when I returned—I had been away from Laguna Pueblo for a couple of years, well more than a couple of years after college and so forth—I returned to Laguna and I went to Laguna-Acoma high school to visit an English class, and I was wondering how the telling was continuing, because Laguna Pueblo, as the anthropologists have said, is one of the more acculturated pueblos. So I walked into this high school English class and there they were sitting, these very beautiful Laguna and Acoma kids. But I knew that out in their lockers they had cassette tape recorders, and I knew that at home they had stereos, and they were listening to Kiss and Led Zeppelin and all those other things. I was almost afraid, but I had to ask—I had with me a book of short fiction (it's called *The Man to Send Rain Clouds* [New York: Viking Press, 1974]), and among the stories of other Native American writers, it has stories that I have written and Simon Ortiz has written. And there is one particular story in the book about the killing of a state policeman in New Mexico by three Acoma Pueblo men. It was an act that was committed in the early fifties. I was afraid to ask, but I had to. I looked at the class and I said, "How many of you heard this story before you read it in the book?" And I was prepared to hear this crushing truth that indeed the anthropologists were right about the old traditions dying out. But it was amazing, you know, almost all but one or two students raised their hands. They had heard that story, just as Simon and I had heard it, when we were young. That was my first indication that storytelling continues on. About half of them had heard it in English, about half of them had heard it in Laguna. I think again, getting back to one of the original statements, that if you begin to look at the core of the importance of the language and how it fits in with the culture, it is the *story* and the feeling of the story which matters more than what language it's told in.

Reading the Text

1. Why do the Pueblo people mistrust written language, according to Silko?
2. What does Silko mean by saying that "the storyteller's role is to draw the story out of the listeners"?
3. How, according to Silko, do stories create a "clan identity"?

Reading the Signs

1. Silko comments on the importance of family stories to Pueblo social life. Divide the class into small groups, and have each group member narrate a story from his or her family. Then, in your groups, discuss the family stories and your response to them. How do the stories become a "shared experience," in Silko's terms?
2. Write an essay in which you reflect on the importance of storytelling in your own family. Which stories have become family traditions? Can you speculate about why? How do the stories shape your "sense of who the family is, and who you are"?
3. Compare and contrast the Pueblo creation story with the Judeo-Christian creation story in the Bible. What different world views are implied in each story? Are there any similarities?
4. Silko's essay is an edited transcript of an oral presentation. Read all or part of her selection aloud in class, and discuss what differences the oral recitation makes. As a listener, do you focus on different aspects of the selection? To what extent is your understanding of her ideas modified?
5. Compare the Pueblo mode of storytelling with the *yijing* approach described by Fan Shen ("The Classroom and the Wider Culture: Identity as a Key to Learning English Composition," p. 485). How do both differ from the Western logical patterns? How do they reflect their culture's world views?
6. Compare the role of storytelling in Pueblo culture with the role of language in Chicano culture as described by Gloria Anzaldúa ("How to Tame a Wild Tongue," p. 431). What role does each play in forming personal and cultural identity? How does each compare with traditionally Western attitudes toward language? What are the consequences of imposing on each culture different modes of communication?

A D A   M A R Í A   I S A S I - D I A Z

Hispanic in America: Starting Points

||||||||||||||||||||||||||||||||||||||||||||||||||||||||||

"Hispanic," "Latino," "Latina," "Chicano," "Chicana"—all these words are used to name the fastest-growing ethnic group in America. But what it means to be Hispanic in America, and what all the names mean, is not well understood by those outside the Spanish-speaking community, argues Ada María Isasi-Diaz (b. 1943) in this "working paper" designed to improve cultural understanding. From their language to their religion to their communal mythos, Hispanics are different from the rest of America, Isasi-Diaz asserts, and that difference "is not seen as an enrichment but as a threat." To defuse the situation, mainstream America must be taught more about their Spanish-speaking neighbors, a task that Isasi-Diaz begins in this essay. The author of Hispanic Women: Prophetic Voice in the Church *(with Yolanda Tarango, 1988), and the 1982 recipient of the Chicago Catholic Women's Woman of the Year award, Isasi-Diaz lives and writes in New York.*

The twenty-first century is rapidly approaching and with it comes a definitive increase in the Hispanic population of the United States. We will soon be the most numerous ethnic "minority"—a minority that seems greatly problematic because a significant number of us, some of us would say the majority, behave differently from other immigrant groups in the United States.

Our unwillingness to jump into the melting pot; our insistence on maintaining our own language; our ongoing links with our countries of origin—due mostly to their geographic proximity and to the continuous flow of more Hispanics into the United States; and the fact that the largest groups of Hispanics, Mexican Americans and Puerto Ricans, are geographically and politically an integral part of this country: These factors, among others, make us different. And the acceptance of that difference, which does not make us better or worse than other groups but simply different, has to be the starting point for understanding us. What follows is a kind of working paper, a guide toward reaching that starting point.

A preliminary note about terminology. What to call ourselves is an issue hotly debated in some segments of our communities. I use the term "Hispanic" because the majority of the communities I deal with include themselves in that term, though each and every one of us refers to ourselves according to our country of origin: Cubans, Puerto Ricans,

Mexican Americans, etc. What I do wish to emphasize is that *"Latina/o"* does *not* have a more politicized or radical connotation than "Hispanic" among the majority of our communities. In my experience it is most often those outside our communities who insist on giving *Latina/o* such a connotation. The contrary, however, is true of the appellation, *"Chicana/o,"* which does indicate a certain consciousness and political stance different from but not necessarily contrary to the one of those who call themselves Mexican Americans.

The way Hispanics participate in this society has to do not only with us, but also with U.S. history, economics, politics, and society. Hispanics are in this country to begin with mostly because of U.S. policies and interests. Great numbers of Mexican Americans never moved to the United States. Instead, the border crossed *them* in 1846 when Mexico had to give up today's Southwest in the Treaty of Guadalupe-Hidalgo. The spoils of the Spanish American War at the end of the nineteenth century included Puerto Rico, where the United States had both military and economic interests. Without having any say, that nation was annexed by the United States.

Cuba suffered a somewhat similar fate. The United States sent troops   5
to Cuba in the midst of its War of Independence against Spain. When Spain surrendered, the United States occupied Cuba as a military protectorate. And though Cuba became a free republic in 1902, the United States continued to maintain economic control and repeatedly intervened in Cuba's political affairs. It was, therefore, only reasonable that when Cubans had to leave their country, they felt they could and should find refuge here. The United States government accepted the Cuban refugees of the Castro regime, giving them economic aid and passing a special law making it easy for them to become residents and citizens.

As for more recent Hispanic immigrants, what can be said in a few lines about the constant manipulation by the United States of the economies and political processes of the different countries of Central America? The United States, therefore, has the moral responsibility to accept Salvadorans, Guatemalans, Hondurans, and other Central Americans who have to leave their countries because of political persecution or hunger. In short, the reasons Hispanics are in the United States are different from those of the earlier European immigrants, and the responsibility the United States has for our being here is vastly greater.

In spite of this difference, many people believe we Hispanics could have become as successful as the European immigrants. So why haven't we? For one thing, by the time Hispanics grew in numbers in the United States, the economy was no longer labor-intensive. Hispanics have lacked not "a strong back and a willingness to work," but the opportunity to capitalize on them. Then, unlike the European immigrants who went west and were able to buy land, Hispanics arrived here after homestead-ing had passed. But a more fundamental reason exists: racism. Hispanics are considered a nonwhite race, regardless of the fact that many of us are of the white race. Our ethnic difference has been officially construed as a racial difference: In government, businesses, and school forms "His-panic" is one of the choices under the category *race*.

No possibility exists of understanding Hispanics and being in dia-logue with us unless the short exposition just presented is studied and analyzed. The starting point for all dialogue is a profound respect for the other, and respect cannot flourish if the other is not known. A commit-ment to study the history of Hispanics in the United States—from the perspective of Hispanics and not only from the perspective presented in the standard textbooks of American history—must be the starting point in any attempt to understand Hispanics.

A second obstacle to dialogue is the prevalent insistence in this country that one American Way of Life exists, and it is the best way of life for everybody in the world. The melting pot concept has provided a framework in which assimilation is a must, and plurality of cultures an impossibility. Hispanic culture is not seen as an enrichment but as a threat. Few understand that Hispanic culture provides for us, as other cultures do for other peoples, guidelines for conduct and relationships, a system of values, and institutions and power structures that allow us to function at our best. Our culture has been formed and will continue to be shaped by the historical happenings and the constant actions of our communities—communities in the United States that are influenced by what happens here as well as in our countries of origin.

It is only within our own culture that Hispanics can acquire a sense   10 of belonging, of security, of dignity, and of participation. The ongoing attempts to minimize or to make our culture disappear will only create problems for the United States. They engender a low sense of identity that can lead us to nonhealthy extremes in our search for some self-esteem. For us, language is the main means of identification here in the United States. To speak Spanish, in public as well as in private, is a political act, a means of asserting who we are, an important way of struggling against assimilation. The different state laws that forbid speak-ing Spanish in official situations, or militate against bilingual education, function as an oppressive internal colonialism that ends up hurting U.S. society.

The majority of Hispanics are U.S. citizens who have lived here all of our lives. To engage with us, Americans belonging to the dominant group, as well as to different marginalized racial and ethnic groups, must be open to new possibilities, to new elements becoming part of the American Way. Above all, they must reach beyond the liberal insistence on individualism, now bordering on recalcitrant self-centeredness. This is all the more urgent given the importance of community and family in Hispanic culture. Community for us is so central that we understand personhood as necessarily including relationship with some form of community. Family has to do not only with those to whom we are immediately related or related only by blood; it is a multilayered structure constituted by all those who care, all those to whom we feel close, who share our interests, commitments, understandings, and to whom we will always remain faithful. This sense of family is closer to the model that is becoming prevalent in the United States instead of the now almost mythical nuclear family. Indeed, Hispanics have much to contribute to the changing concept of family in this society.

The importance of community also finds expression in the way we relate to others at our work places. Our business contacts and dealings have at their center personal relationships much more than institutionalized procedures and structures. It is often better to know someone, even someone who knows someone, than to present the best plan, have the highest bid, or be the first one there. And the very prosperous Hispanic businesses that do exist here, though limited in number when one considers that more than 18 million Hispanics live in this country, clearly show that the way we do business can also be successful.

Hispanics know that we wear our emotions pinned on our sleeves, that we express what we believe and feel quite readily. Not to feel deeply seems to us to diminish our sense of humanity. We do not find it valuable to hide our subjectivity behind a so-called objectivity and uniform ways of dealing with everyone. We proudly and quickly express our opinions. For us time is to be used to further and enjoy our sense of community. It is more important to wait for everyone to be present than to start a meeting exactly on time. It is more important to listen to everybody and to take time to dwell on the personal than to end a meeting on time.

And those who want to deal with Hispanics need to know that conscience plays a very prominent role in our lives because we live life intensely. We do not take anything lightly, whether it is play, work, love, or, unfortunately, hate. We often think in ethical terms even in inconsequential matters. This intensity and insistence in giving serious consideration to almost all aspects of life are a constitutive element of our high sense of honor, our way of talking about our standard of morality and personhood, which we are willing to defend no matter the cost.

Finally, those who wish to understand Hispanics need to know that   15
our religious practices—what is often referred to as *religiosidad popular*—express our close relationship with the divine. A personal relationship with God and the living-out of that relationship in day-to-day life is

much more important to us than establishing and maintaining relationships with church structures and going to church on Sundays. Christianity, and specifically Roman Catholicism, are an intrinsic part of Hispanic culture—something not always understood and taken into consideration in this secular culture. Many of the cultural traditions and customs still prevalent today in Hispanic communities are closely entwined with religious rituals. Processions, lighting candles, relating to the saints, arguing and bartering with God through *promesas*—all of these are not only a matter of religion but a matter of culture.

The dominant groups in U.S. society must acknowledge that Hispanics have much to contribute to the United States and that in order to do so we must be allowed to be who we are. Meanwhile, the dominant groups in society, especially, need to be open to cultural, religious, social, and even organizational pluralism. The nations that have failed and disappeared from the map of our world are not those that have been open to change but rather those that insist on rigidity, uniformity, and believing they are better than others. That is what should be adamantly opposed in the United States—not a multiplicity of language, cultures, and customs.

Reading the Text

1. Why, according to Isasi-Diaz, are Hispanics "different" from other immigrant groups in the United States?
2. What are the problems with the melting-pot concept for Hispanics?
3. What are the characteristics of Hispanic culture that Isasi-Diaz says mainstream American society must better understand?

Reading the Signs

1. Isasi-Diaz claims that the Hispanic immigrant experience is different from that of European immigrants because of racism. Visit your college library and research the immigrant experience of Southern and Eastern Europeans in the early part of the twentieth century (if you wish, you may also interview some such immigrants or their relatives). Use your research to formulate a well-documented essay that supports, modifies, or refutes her claim.
2. Interview at least five people of Hispanic background and ask them how they prefer to label their ethnicity (e.g., Chicano, Latino, and so forth) and why. How does the label work as a sign of their cultural identity? How do your interviewees feel about other labels? Use the results of your interviews to formulate an essay about the importance of terminology in creating cultural identity. To develop your essay, you may want to consult Gloria Anzaldúa's "How to Tame a Wild Tongue" (see p. 431).

3. Isasi-Diaz lists obstacles to understanding Hispanic culture that are prevalent in American society. Select an ethnic group other than Hispanics, and write your own list of obstacles to understanding that culture. What are the essential values and world views of that group? Share your list with your class.

4. Isasi-Diaz laments that many Americans seem to blame Hispanics for not being as successful as other immigrant groups. Read or review Michael Omi's "In Living Color: Race and American Culture" (p. 449), and write an essay in which you explore how popular culture may have contributed to this attitude toward Hispanics. As you develop your essay, try to generate your own examples from popular culture, in addition to drawing upon Omi's.

5. Isasi-Diaz says that the history of Hispanics needs to be studied "from the perspectives of Hispanics and not only from the perspective presented in the standard textbooks of American history." Find some of these "standard textbooks" in your college library, and examine them for their view of Hispanics and their contributions to American society. Then write an essay in which you critique their treatment of Hispanic culture, being sure to discuss both what's included and what's omitted from the textbooks.

STUDS TERKEL

Speaking About Race

|||||||||||||||||||||||||||||||||||||||||||||||||||||||

Studs Terkel (b. 1912) has been letting Americans tell their own stories for a quarter century as America's most prominent oral historian. A Pulitzer Prize winner in nonfiction for "The Good War": An Oral History of World War II (1985), Terkel's interviews with ordinary Americans give us a glimpse into their thoughts and lives, and let us hear their voices, with all the pain and humor, anger and pride preserved. In Race: How Blacks and Whites Think and Feel About the American Obsession *(1992), from which these interviews are excerpted, Terkel tackles what is perhaps America's most intractable social dilemma. Here Terkel lets the people speak for themselves, from a white high school teacher to a Mexican-American businessman to a white welfare recipient, each one telling the story of his or her own experience with race in America. A broadcaster at WFMT radio in Chicago as well as a prolific author and interviewer, Terkel also holds a law degree from the University of Chicago.*

Peter Soderstrom

He is a high school teacher in a suburb bordering a large Midwestern city. It had been, for decades, an all-white, predominantly WASP, middle-class enclave. Since World War II, it has undergone gradual, though considerable, changes. Today, it has an extensive black community, working-class as well as middle-class. It is fairly well integrated.

I'm a teacher, trying to do the right thing. It's becoming more and more difficult.

I was a student here in the late sixties. I even eat lunch with some of my former teachers. It's interesting to see the same place and walk the same halls, and see it in a wholly different way.

My dad was very active in civil rights, and I remember marching with him through the streets of this town for an open-housing ordinance. We carried signs, and people were throwing little round cherry bombs at us.

One of the reasons I liked working at this school rather than at an all-white suburb was the mix of races. I wanted that for my own children, too. As I look back over these five years, I think I came in with a very idealistic idea.

As a beginning teacher, I was given low-level classes. Kids that need   5 remedial help. They were predominantly black. As I gained years there, I started getting honors classes. They were overwhelmingly white. Right now I have one black child in my honors class, out of twenty-seven.

This was startling to me. I realized these honors classes get a lot of attention because these are things the school can boast about. It took me a while to catch on: Why, as a beginning teacher, did I get remedial classes? It was a stunning realization. It's like giving doctors the emergency room to train on. Here's where it really requires the specialist, the veteran. With the years, you work your way out of these remedial classes. You gain the clout to say no.

I found that unfair to the kids and unfair to me as a teacher. There isn't a focused curriculum for these kids. The problem's so perplexing that nobody really knows where to go with it. These kids need a person who knows what he's doing. I work with remedial kids now by choice, but I still don't know quite how to do it.

My honors classes are easy. You come up with one question and they fly with it. You don't have problems with writing and reading skills.

The school is very responsive to the community. Parents who can and do make a big fuss get things to happen. These kids in the low-level classes don't have a voice; their parents don't make their voices heard. When I have a parents'-conference night, almost every honors parent will show up. All you have to do is say, "Fred's doing great. He's a splendid student." The low-level kids, I get one or two parents. Those are the ones you really need to talk to.

As the son of a father who took lots of heat for his stand on civil rights, I am now being considered a racist. This word is coming at me now, and it's very startling. I've been fairly active in the halls. If a kid's in the wrong place at the wrong time, I'll go up and talk to him. Frequently I'm hit with a confrontation. The kid will just yell at me, degrade me; or it's just a complete dismissal: "You have no right asking me this stuff."

When the bell rings, you're supposed to be in your class. That has become quite lax. There are kids coming in from other schools, and we don't know which are ours and which are outside students. We have problems with graffiti, with drug stuff, with weapons brought in.

I just had a bad one. I wrote a kid up, a behavioral referral: This kid was doing this, such-and-such. It calls for disciplinary action. I heard this loud yelling and a running halt outside my door. I came out. "Where are you supposed to be? Do you have a pass?" They didn't. So I wrote it up, which is my job.

Two nights ago, while I was at home, I got a call about six o'clock. It was this boy's father. He said, "I want to know the details, I want to straighten this out. I just got this in the mail, a Saturday detention." The kid's supposed to come to school on Saturday and serve some time. He was furious with me. I said another teacher was there who saw it. He said, "What's that teacher's name? I'll find him."

At ten that night, he calls me at home again. "I just talked to that teacher and he doesn't know a damn thing about it. Whatever is happening at that school is bullshit." Finally, after going round and round, I said, "I'm a professional and I'll be happy to deal with you during those professional hours." He said, "I understand now. I'm the lowly black man and you are the professional and I have to come up to your professional level. Is that all the help I'm going to get from you?" And I said, "For tonight." He hung up.

The next morning, I walked into the office and the phone was ringing. The dean was on the phone. This boy's mother is furious and his father was on his way. The first thing he said to me when he got there was, "I don't like your attitude, I don't like anything about you. I like shit more than I like your attitude." That's how the conversation started.

He was concerned that I had said it was a man who witnessed it and it turned out to be a woman. He said, "Tell me, do you know the difference between a man and a woman?" It was crazy. At the end of the conversation, we found that the boy had lied. He sort of came down, but said, "I want you to know there are lots of kids who think you're a racist." Then he stood up and shook my hand. By way of apology, he said, "I hope you understand, one, I thought my son was telling the truth, and, two, everybody thinks you're a racist."

An administrator called me in. She's had reports from teachers as well as other kids that I'm confrontational and go after black kids more than white kids. I had to do a lot of soul-searching. You get called racist over and over again, you start thinking, "Am I looking for black kids? When I see a black kid coming, what am I thinking? Is it different than if I see a little girl with blond hair coming toward me?" I don't know, I don't know. It's hard to say I'm not a racist, and to prove it I have to say that most of the problems are black.

There's this idea that I don't stop white kids. Not true. But— [*Pause.*]—I just thought of something. The white kids and I banter, not a confrontation. I'm more like their parent figure. I just realized that I approach white kids in a way similar to black teachers approaching black kids. I think we exude signals we may not have control over.

As I picture myself going up to a black kid, I just wonder if it's a readying. Getting ready for something.

For a battle?   20

Whatever it is I'm preparing for. I've worked hard to approach them, maybe stick my hands in my pockets to appear more casual. It doesn't work.

Putting your hands in your pockets. Do you think they might fear you have a weapon?

Wait a minute! [*Pause.*] Even though that's so outside the realm of possibilities for me, even have a pocket knife in my pocket—what does it mean in that kid's world? To me, hands in your pocket is my dad jingling his change. A very warm sound to me. What does it mean in that kid's world, so different from mine?

I just remembered something. One of my students was expelled; he had a gun. A couple of kids got into an argument. One kid ran home, got his father's gun, and brought it to school. Another kid took the gun away from him and he handed it to my student, who didn't know what to do with it. He passed it on to an older kid, who took the first kid aside, calmed him down, gave him back the gun, which he took back home.

The school expelled everybody involved—my student, who held it   25 for one second, the older boy who calmed things down, everybody. The authorities felt the gun should have been given to the administrators or the correct personnel. A parent stood up at a board meeting, someone not involved, and said, "How unfeeling of you. Shame on you, not to understand that in his world, if he had turned that gun in to the authorities, the other kid, excited, would have done him in. You're imposing your world on this kid. Don't you understand?"

I have friends among the black teachers. Some of them are as concerned about the kids as I am. They say we're not going to get anywhere unless we make the difficult truth known and admit it. Other teachers move in a pocket and say: What's the problem? You'll find they are teaching the honors classes. They walk through the hall and don't try to stop trouble when they see it. You can choose not to see anything; it's easy.

The problem is not really in the classroom, where the kids know you and you know them. It's when they become anonymous in the halls. A lot of people are pushing for ID badges. I think it would be really good. To identify the kid who belongs in the school, you cut down on his anonymity.

We're doing *Raisin in the Sun* in all three levels of my classes. Reading the text. The remedial kids are thrilled by the fact that I'm doing the same book with them as with the honors and the two-levels. "Are we caught up with them?" "Are we ahead of them?" We're talking about racism and experiences with it. I was surprised at some of the things they told me openly. One girl said, "We know you. You're not a racist." When I'm accused, I say, "Come talk to my kids. The ninety kids who would bear the brunt if I were a racist."

When I sat in the same room with that angry father, we really saw each other and he came to know I was not really a threat. I looked in the mirror before I came there. I was real nervous about this meeting. It was just to be he and I and the dean, who was black. I looked so white, so middle-class white in the mirror. I was dressed casually, but it bothered me that I looked so white. [*Laughs.*] I don't know what I mean by that.

I walked in and there he is, wearing a kind of working vest and a 30 flannel shirt and boots caked with clay. A construction worker. I saw this disparity between us and it bothered me. I saw him only once since then, although he lives only two blocks from me. I saw him standing on his stoop. I don't think we're on great terms. I still think he hates my attitude.

The dean backs me very much. The school's been embroiled in a lot of trouble recently and he's been pushing for change. He really feels the problem is largely black and the black community needs to deal with it. He took me aside and said, "You know in your heart you're not a racist. You just have to let it go." It's an easy accusation to make and extremely difficult to disprove.

I'm glad to see the year end, and I feel I'm really going to do some soul-searching on this. What am I doing when I walk up to these kids that incites them so much? I have been told I set these kids off. There's something.

If there are kids yelling to each other across the hall and disturbing my class, I'm going to say something. I'll just say, "Keep it down." Immediately they'll say, "What the fuck's bothering you? I know all about you, I've heard about you." It's immediate, real quick.

Another teacher, a gentle, gracious person, told me that whenever the kids get mad at her they call her a racist. Whenever they feel good about her, they say, "We know you're not a racist, we were just kidding." Then all of a sudden they'll get mad at her again and call her a racist. It's almost a game.

Do black teachers come out and discipline the kids? 35

Yeah, but they have a whole other way, makes us all envious. It's a different vernacular. I've seen black teachers walk up to some kid who's being feisty and angry, put his arm around him, and say, "Come on, what is all this?" The kid just changes, is transformed. Suddenly he's a kid. I couldn't possibly. I'd look like an idiot!

It's not the arm so much as the way they can banter. Words, phrases that have nothing to do with my experience. The idiom and a rhythm. I can't touch, I can't get near it. A whole different style. We're all products of the way we were brought up. What does an adult do when a kid says, "Fuck off"? I don't have anything to fall back on. I don't know what to do next, I'm frustrated. Many of them in their experience don't have a treatment of respect, a sense of what authority is. So there the two of us are: I not knowing what to say next, he not knowing what to say next. It gets all bungled up.

I have a black friend at school. She's a secretary in the office. She came up to me on several occasions and said, "You just have to learn to talk to black kids, and I'm going to teach you." There's never been a time when we can get together. I think it would be really interesting.

I get mad, but the Swede in me tries to control it and lets me know it's not constructive. Yet we end up yelling at each other. I'm an adult, I'm a teacher: "You can't talk to me that way." It's funny as I say it, because I've said it so many times. I just feel so appalled. And humiliated, too. Really humiliated. I need to deal with that in myself. I've been told to back off because I'm going to have trouble. I know some kids have threatened me. I know I've caused trouble because I'm being confrontational. My last period of the day is free, so I leave before three though I'm supposed to stay till four. I leave because I know I'm not going to deal well with it. A friend said, "It's like watching somebody burn out."

We have a whole new type of kid. There are those who say, "You 40 should have been here in the sixties." In the sixties, there was a cause, there was a feeling of hope. Now there's no cause. There's just incredible meanness. I'm not talking about just black kids. I'm talking about an egocentric society, from the top down. They say every new generation has conflict with the older generation. But there's something very different here.

This year has really made me look at myself and see what is going on. What word am I looking for? To reevaluate. Am I becoming a racist? Of my new batch of kids, two-thirds will be black. I know exactly what I'm going to get. Am I prejudging? Prejudiced? What's happening to me?

The school's always saying call the parents, call the parents. You call, the line is dead, it's been disconnected, they've never heard of the person. I realize at this moment, that kid probably just has no family life. And I don't even bother to try and search it out. To me, that's prejudicial. Why am I becoming that? This survival thing. You're dealing with so many kids, trying to get through so much.

We've had several board meetings that have been absolutely packed. Usually nobody comes, but when we talk about discipline, everybody shows up. There are black parents who say, "We have to stop turning to the school and should start cleaning up our own homes here." There are other parents who say, "You have teachers who look at black kids in a different way and have different expectations."

I'll be teaching two remedial classes this summer. I have one girl who's in desperate need of special education. In the community there's a stigma attached to it. Her parent is refusing to have her tested, necessary to get in. The girl can barely put a sentence together, can barely comprehend what we're doing. Yet she stays in my classroom, which is not doing her or anybody any good. Things move so slowly that there she stays.

Odd thing, though, with this girl. We did *Romeo and Juliet*. We'd 45 listen to a recording, chunks at a time. She was the first that would go up and be able to interpret what she had just heard. She just had this innate way. I can't understand it.

I'd keep trying to get them to keep their eyes on the book because I think it would be good for them. They do so little reading. They'd not look at the book, but they'd *hear* everything. And they understood it.

Yet, there's a bravado about doing poorly. I used to put on the board grades of people who did well on a test. They'd get so much heat and ribbing from the other kids, I stopped doing it. It's almost as damaging as putting up poor grades. The bright kids are called nerds. Mostly they say, "You're acting white."

One kid had typed his paper. It was a harsh essay, thoughtful. I held it up for everybody to see that he typed it. They all thought he was a jackass for going to all that trouble. He never did it again.

I feel like a white missionary down in an area where I don't belong. I'm saying here's my religion, education. It worked great for me, it's going to work great for you, too. They don't buy it. That's what you believe in. You're one of the ministers of it. But these kids do have to find a way to live in a world where they're going to have bosses, authority figures all over the place.

Do I ever compliment the slower kids? Constantly. It's something   50
they're extremely responsive to. At first I had to force myself to do so. It sounded phony. I'd say, "That's not quite right, but it's a good thought." But now I say, "You've done a good job," and it doesn't sound phony at all.

Ron Maydon

"I'm a forty-two-year-old Mexican-American, born and raised on the South-east side of Chicago. I have worked since I was sixteen. I lied about my age, so I could make some money. While going to college, I worked summers in the steel mill, side by side with my late father."

His father's flight from Mexico, across the border, is a walking, hitchhiking saga; town to town; odd jobs picking cotton in Texas, peeling potatoes at the Rice Hotel; gandy-dancing for the railroads; water boy in a Chicago steel mill.

"We are a God-fearing, religious family. Every Sunday we're in church, my mother, my sister and me. 'You take a few knocks coming up,' my mother used to say. 'That's why God gave you more padding in the butt, so it could be spanked.' She and my father both worked hard."

He is fair-complexioned and could easily pass for an Anglo, if he wished. He does not. "Throughout my life, I've been a proud nationalistic Mexican-American."

Hispanics are used as a buffer, and also a wedge, between white and black communities. Show me a white community and a black community and I'll show you an adjoining community between both. We're kind of a geographic Ping-Pong ball. Whites may let us move into their neighborhood because they've got a choice. "We'll take the lesser of the two evils," they say. They make it seem like they're doing us a big favor.

I call him a dumb Hispanic, the one who moves into a white community and is not even greeted as a neighbor. He thinks it's a miracle from God that he was let in. Or he did it on his own. "Oh wonderful! I've been accepted." He thinks he's moved up the ladder socially. I tell him, "Look, dummy, the only reason you're here is because right behind you are the blacks about to move in. They'll use you to hold off the blacks, and when they move, you'll stay here as the buffer." They're under the illusion that they're accepted. Of course they're not.

Because I could pass for Anglo, I got a bird's-eye view, an inside view of a racist country. I kind of snuck behind enemy lines. A kamikaze. When I was playing football in high school, they thought I was Italian or Greek. I got to hear comments about Mexicans. I'd immediately stand up, and the next thing I'm in a fistfight. "Oh, Ron, I'm sorry, I didn't mean you." "Who the fuck did you mean?" I've heard it all and it has gotten me angry and inspired and determined to keep fighting. I know how they really feel.

When my name confused the other kids, they'd ask me what I was. I said, "I'm an American." Today I'd say, "I'm an American of Mexican descent."

I don't like the word "Hispanic." It sounds nice and says nothing.   5
Which Hispanic? Mexican? Cuban? Puerto Rican? Every ten years, the United States government census gives us a new label. Spanish-Americans. Latinos. Chicanos. It's a lot like black labels.

Economically, the Puerto Rican is the lowest-income, least educated of the Hispanic community. They are our blacks. We look on the Mexican-Americans as the Polacks, the Polish-Americans. Family-oriented, hardworking, Catholic. The white Cubans are our Jews: the professionals, pharmacists, doctors, lawyers. Know why? After Batista lost, Castro sent them here. They were the elite, the landlords, the robber barons, the well-to-do. They were the ones with the money. They didn't like to identify with the Indians or the racially mixed Cubans. They came here with skills, education, and money they had socked away. They took over Florida. They're successful up and down the coast. They don't like black Cubans. There's racism in the Spanish community as anywhere else.

I would get into some arguments with dark-complected Latinos. They'd make racist remarks about blacks: "Niggers are getting everything." I'd say, "Look, you so-and-so, black as you are, you got a lot of nerve talking about blacks. You've been a victim of discrimination as much as blacks. You're the new niggers, you dummies."

I guess you'd call me a community activist, working for a black-Latino coalition. Our own people were calling us nigger-lovers. We had to let them know the police were beating the shit out of us, too. We organized the first Mexican-American march on police brutality in 1971.

I'm a strong believer in minority coalitions. Whatever gains the Hispanic community has made, we have piggy-backed on the black movement. I say every time the blacks make political, economic, and social gains, hooray for them, because we get some of the fallout. They sneeze, we catch cold. They make inroads, we get hired. There are also problems in the black-Hispanic coalition. It's really a mixed bag.

The black community says they haven't made any progress. But the   10
Hispanic sees the blacks as moving up and taking over. It's piggy-move-

up. We're on the bottom of the totem pole. We're the busboys, the new
ditchdiggers, the new laborers. We see Hispanics on the assembly line
with a black supervisor, a black boss.

Historically, it's always been so. The Irish dumped on the Italians.
The last one in gets the shit. So we're the latest. The Asians are behind
us, but they're intellectually making the greatest gains. The Japanese may
be getting lazy and the Koreans, the Jews of the Asian community, are
working hard round the clock.

There are two kinds of Hispanics: the ethnic and the racial. The first
identify with the whites and act, think, and try to be like them. But
there are those who say: "We don't have a low self-esteem. We know
where we stand. We know we're not black or white. We're in the middle
and not trying to be either."

The Hispanics who believe they are white often try interracial marriages. Personally, I'm against that. When I get married, it will be to a
Mexican woman. My kids will be one-hundred-percent Mexican. I'll
be frank with you, I don't want to see halfbreeds. It's a personal preference. When I wake up Sunday morning, I want *menudo* or *carnitas* or
chorizo and eggs. I don't want to have to go through a historical explanation to my Anglo wife of what I want. We're going to dance to the
same tune. I'm not nationalistic to the point of being blind to the cultures
of others. But what I want you to know we're definitely Mexican-
American and proud.

This is not a melting pot. It's more of a layered cake. I believe we're
a pluralistic society. This city is divided by viaducts, railroad crossings,
thoroughfares. We say: This is Polish, this is Italian, this is Jewish, this is
a Mexican community. Live and let live, but we must maintain our
identity.

Once you lose your identity, your whole psyche is twisted. You're   15
at the whim of anything that occurs in a society. I don't want to be a
Mexican Fritz Mondale, who wanted to be everything to everybody
and wound up being nothin' to no one.

In our country at this time, there is latent and blatant racism. You
meet these closet racists who are condescending and patronizing, but
deep inside they don't really want us.

This is part of the racism between Hispanics and blacks. I know
some nationalistic black activists. I understand where they're coming
from. I have no problems with them. I ask myself, Are blacks capable of
racism? Of course. Are Hispanics capable of racism? Of course. I think
these two extremes are going to have some kind of come-together. There
has to be some serious coalition-building if we're going to live side by
side.

We'll have to work on the Hispanic Uncle Toms, who do everything
they can to ingratiate themselves, to please their white racist neighbors.
Tio Tacos we call them. A Tio Taco is worse than an Uncle Tom.

You don't find many Hispanics living in black areas, period. If they do, they're residual, the last ones left. I know this city like the back of my hand. I was a paramedic for three years and a building inspector for three.

We have Hispanic huppies, urban professionals. The huppies, the   20
buppies, and the yuppies are living alongside one another on the lake-front. Junior execs. It's a real paradox they find themselves in, the His-panics and the blacks. On the one hand, we say: Get an education, get that degree, make a better life. But when they leave the old neighbor-hood, they're sell-outs. Uncle Toms, Tio Tacos. The rest of the people say, "You're too good, you don't come around anymore. You've made it now and you can't talk to us."

This is the crisis of the black and Hispanic professional. They're in two worlds. Some talk of depression and suicide. Should we say: "Don't make any progress and stay put?"

As for role models, we have very few. Up until recently, we haven't had a Martin Luther King or a Harold Washington. We don't have people breaking the ice. We have a few unrecognized, unsung heroes anonymously chipping away. Mostly in the neighborhoods.

The only time you see Hispanics on TV, it's a street gang, an im-migration raid, a drug bust. If I landed here from Mars and turned on the TV, I'd say, "All these people named Sánchez, Gómez, Rodríguez and García are troublemakers. You better get them out of this country. Every time I turn around, they're taking away a job and they're illegal."

On the lowest rung of the Mexican society is the illegal. He, she cannot surface. He had come here to earn a living, to send money back home to mom. They're terrified of exposure. They will go to the su-permercado to buy their Mexican food products. They will listen to Mexican radio and watch Mexican TV and stay in hiding.

To Hispanics, the word "minorities" is a code word for blacks. I   25
fault both communities. The blacks were too exclusive and didn't try to recruit us, get us involved. The Hispanics were not aggressive enough, didn't say, "Cut us in or cut it out." I blame the Church for our fault. It's always been, "Whatever your plight is, accept it. God will take care of you later." Look at its history in Mexico.

The Mexican loves the authoritarian personality. He loves to be told what to do. The strong church, the strong father figure. But there's a contradiction here, too. It's still the mother who holds the family to-gether. The father gives the appearance: "I wear the pants. I'm the *chingón,* the bad so-and-so." His perception is that he must be assertive. Yet the little Anglo supervisor calls him every dirty name in the book: wetback, illegal, spic, greaser. He chews him out. And he meekly says, "Yes, sir, no, sir, I'm sorry." He comes home and asserts himself as the main man.

His kids and wife are thinking, 'You could have beat the shit out of
the little Anglo, but you didn't say nothin'. You come home and take it
out on us." That's what's happening right now in Hispanic families. But
the father is just finding out you can't talk tough at night and be a sissy
during the day. If you're going to be a man, be a man twenty-four hours
a day, not part-time. Now the mother and kids are saying: To hell with
the damn job. Your self-respect is worth more than that four-dollar-an-
hour job. You should have grabbed him and kicked the shit out of him.

It's a new sign. It's one of the first indications that we're going to
make serious attempts to break down the barriers of racism. We're seeing
this at college and high-school levels.

But we're also seeing Hispanic street gangs fight black street gangs.
This may go on for years. The guy will say, "I fought with this black
kid twenty years ago. He came into our neighborhood. I just don't like
niggers now." He'll remember, "It was a black kid shot at me." The
black kid will remember, "It was a Mexican cracked me over the head.
I just don't like grease balls."

The fights are over drugs and turf and money and gang signs. We're   30
having trouble in four high schools right now. That is what's happening
in this country now. We're turning on each other. Whites will blame
the blacks. Blacks will blame the Hispanics and vice-versa. Hispanics will
say of affirmative action, "They hired seventeen blacks and one Hispanic." They're using us against them.

In the sixties, everyone was more aware. We always lived next door
and worked with blacks. We were car-pooling because we didn't have
any money. We shared lunches together. We went to school together.
We worked in the stockyards together. We worked in the steel mills
together. We worked in the fields together, migrant workers, side by
side. We were in the same boat and it was sinking.

Now because of racial consciousness, groups are trying to assert their
identity and get their share of the American pie. The economic pie is
not big enough for anybody, not the way it's divided. Now we're competitors. We're not allies, we're adversaries. We're on a collision course.

I don't know if many Hispanics view affirmative action as a program
to benefit them. They don't really identify with it. Many Hispanics
believe affirmative action is a black program. We don't aggressively apply,
seek out. I've heard that from every college recruiter: "Send me Hispanics." How many get their degree and do something about it? Few. I
see signs of change. The kids are becoming more aggressive and are not
going to take the bullshit their mom and dad did.

Our women have never been recognized. Mexican-American
women have never received their just due. They've held our family
together, period. Our women have taken the abuse, kept their mouths
shut: "Don't tell anybody." Dad comes home drunk. He's a real man

now. The boss has told him off and he's taking it out on his wife. We have a saying: "When Anglos drink, they drink to forget. When Mexicans drink, they drink to remember."

I see a duality in the Mexican community. The wedding, the Christ- 35
mas ceremony, the stores, the music, the food, the art, the culture. We must never lose our identity. But I also want assimilation. We can't carry it off alone, separately.

We're at a crucial period in black-Hispanic relations. Do we want to be identified with whites or blacks? I think we're schizophrenic now. We really don't have a sense of where we fit. We're the buffer.

Margaret Welch

Everyone thinks that if you try hard enough, you can make it in America. I thought so too, but when I found myself a widow at age thirty-three, with two children to support, and forced to go on public aid, I discovered how the welfare system works.

I have tried hard to make a better life for myself and my girls. I have studied hard to get an A average after being out of school for sixteen years, and it hurts to have to give up my dream, but the system won't let me out of the 'welfare class.' There are a great many of us who want out of the welfare class, but the system won't let us out.

— *Margaret Welch, Letters to the Editor,*
CHICAGO TRIBUNE, *March 26, 1987*

She had come to Chicago five years ago from Tennessee. Her second husband "walked out," leaving her with two girls, nine and five.

The image people have of public aid is black women with a lot of kids. Before I went on public aid, I had that impression: The more babies you have, the more money you get. I realized that you get three dollars a day if you have another baby. That's not going to raise a kid. I thought they were freeloaders, who like to live off other people. But when I was forced on public aid, my opinion changed. I was on an even keel with them. We all sat there in the office and waited five or six hours at a time. They weren't getting special treatment. They were having hard times, too.

What gets me is this:

I'm on public aid. I'm trying to stay in school and apply for all these scholarships. Blacks and Hispanics have hollered so much, they've got these scholarships. Even single white men can get scholarships if they have kids. But it's hard for a single white woman to get a scholarship, because you're not a minority.

If you're a woman, you're supposed to take care of your kids if you're left alone with them. If men are left with kids, it's "Oh, that poor guy." All the women in the neighborhood are cooking and bringing him food and finding hand-me-down clothes for the kids and babysit for free, so he's not stuck at home. Everybody's helping him. But if you're a white woman and your husband has walked out leaving her with kids—forget it.

I've just registered for my last year in nursing school. I won't be able   5
to go back because the scholarship I got last year was just denied me. They said it was a Hispanic scholarship and enough Hispanics applied, so I lost out. It just hit me. This week. I can't afford the tuition, so I don't know if I'm ever going back.

At this school, they have the American Indian club that gives scholarships. Even a Thai club. Of course there are black scholarships. But none for the single white woman. My dad was half-Cherokee. Maybe I can qualify as a half-Cherokee. [*Laughs.*]

I went on public aid when my job at the hot-dog stand ended and my house burned down. I lost everything. On public aid, they gave me $711. That was supposed to get me an apartment, replace all my furniture and all the kids' clothes. The cheapest apartment called for a $600 deposit. It doesn't leave anything.

I noticed a poster on the wall: Public aid helps returning to school. I had a GED. I took the test and placed into the highest class. They were telling me about the scholarships and said I was a cinch. I got one last year and carried straight A's. But I found out last week I'm not a minority and out.

There goes my 86 average and my dream of becoming a registered nurse. It's something I've always wanted and never thought possible. I got so close. "I'm sorry, but this time we have enough Hispanics."

This is the first time in my life I'm really mad this way. It's a new   10
feeling for me, and I don't know how to deal with it. My boyfriend is Mexican and my best girlfriend is Puerto Rican and very black. I've never been prejudiced, but why the hell are you doing this to me? I've been through enough. I was widowed at seventeen and married again and my husband took off, leaving me with two kids. Just because I'm white, I don't get something?

Always on TV, whenever you hear blacks making speeches, it's "White people won't let us do this or that; we're put down." All of a sudden, they're giving me the short end.

Who is "they"?

The minorities. No, I don't mean that. I'm not saying they're doing bad. They band together and speak out when they're hurt and get something done. Right now, I'm just upset. I'm mad at people in general. Women in my position are being denied something because of the racial issue. It's crazy.

I *never, never* had any racist feelings. In that small country town, I never distinguished between people because of color. There's black people living in my building. We get along great. I've never looked at myself as better than they are. But with this scholarship thing, I *deserved* it. Just because their skin's darker than mine, why should they get it and I don't? It's the first time I've had feelings like this and it makes me very uncomfortable. All this happened last week and it's hard to deal with. I'm really torn apart. Last week, I was on the point of saying, "To hell with it. I'm going back to Tennessee with my girls to raise corn and beans."

I feel like I've been robbed of a chance to finish school. I had it   15 counted down. I already had a job promised me in a hospital. I would be making $15 an hour for the first time in my life. I could feed my kids without begging, borrowing, or stealing. Selling food stamps is considered stealing. I get $308 a month to live on. My rent's $250. So that leaves me $58. You can't pay lights and gas and everything else. So you end up selling a few food stamps to buy laundry detergent.

For food, you buy a lot of rice and flour, make tortillas. That's all your kids have. They're the ones who are punished, whether you're white, black, or anything else. I was so sure that in a year, I'd have a job where I could feed my kids without feeling the way I do. I wouldn't have them laughed at in school because they get free meals. They wouldn't have to suffer that any more. Now . . .

My Puerto Rican black friend and I always applied for the same scholarships. We were always among the top in grades. She was straight A's all the way. We were promised jobs at the same hospital. We were in school together since the first day. This year, she got the scholarship, I didn't. She came to the house and said, "Don't be mad at me." I'm not. She's still my best friend. It's just—*why?*

We were sitting in my truck. I told her I got my letter. She ran out, checked her mail, and she's gotten hers. We didn't open them until we were together. She could tell by the look on my face. "What's the matter?" "I didn't get it. Did you?" She mumbled, "Yeah," and wouldn't let me see her letter. For a minute I was so mad at her. "I just want to kill you." [*Laughs.*] We're still great friends. I'm glad she's making it, she deserves it.

I think blacks are going ahead. They speak out, they fight for their rights, and they're getting them. We're almost afraid of them and let them push us back.

If you see one black guy walking by, it's okay. But if you see three   20 or four standing on a corner, you cross to the other side of the street. I was mugged about two years ago by a couple of Hispanic guys. Now if I see several Hispanics standing together, I cross the street.

Suppose there were three or four tough-looking white guys?

I'd just walk through them. I'm a tough ol' hillbilly girl. I worked in taverns as soon as I got old enough. I wore my jeans and cowboy boots and I'd jump in the middle of the barroom with any of them, grab my pool stick. I've never been scared of a fight. I'm a big woman. I can handle myself.

Not far from my house is a motorcycle gang, Hell's Henchmen. They have their Harley-Davidsons, tattoos, and beards. When I was tending bar, I'd walk past them at two, three in the morning by myself and not think anything of it. But there's no way I'd walk by a black club.

I myself really don't feel hostility, but I feel that a lot of whites are becoming more and more afraid of blacks. It's like "We're letting them learn to read and write and they're taking over." I don't feel that. My Mexican boyfriend says the neighborhood is running down. He gets mad because the blacks band together and push you around. I argue with him, we disagree. So we don't talk much about it.

Somehow, people have to talk about this. You shouldn't feel "I'm   25 too dumb to get up and say something"; talk in your words, say whatever. If enough people talk, good ideas may come out of it. Nobody wants to give up whatever power they got. To me, that's the whole thing, power.

You see the old slave-day movies. They were scared of their masters, their owners. They did what they were told. It seems like they've almost turned the tables. It's like we're scared to stand up against them now.

In the small town where I was from, we had our part and there was nigger town. They stayed there and never came out. They'd just come in, get groceries, and leave. They just didn't mix. They didn't bother anybody and we didn't bother them. When I moved to the city, everybody was together all of a sudden.

Would you prefer it the old way?

No-o-o-o! When I went to City-Wide College, my supervisor was a black lady. She just knew when there was something wrong. I'd sit at my desk half-crying. I'd gotten my second five-day notice that month to move out of my apartment. One of my classmates told her. When I came back from my break, there was a check on my desk to cover my rent. I tried to pay her back, but she said, "No, that's my gift to you." I would never have dreamed there was a black person like that when I was in Tennessee.

I don't believe black people should be pushed back. But I don't feel   30 because I'm white, I should be either. It goes both ways. I don't think the gap is that big on a street level, not in my neighborhood. But when you get into the bureaucracy, business, and school, it's those big people making the noise.

I myself am not intimidated. I would never have written that letter to the *Tribune*. I wouldn't have made it through three years of college. I got married when I was sixteen and dropped out of high school. I never dreamed I'd go to college. Here I am two semesters away from my graduation. It looks like I'm stopped for a while, but you can't sit back and never open your mouth.

Reading the Text

1. Why has Peter Soderstrom been accused of being a racist?
2. What different styles of communication are used by white and black teachers in Soderstrom's school?
3. Why does Soderstrom himself wonder, "Am I prejudging? Prejudiced? What's happening to me?"
4. What is Ron Maydon's attitude toward other ethnic groups?
5. What, for Maydon, constitutes Hispanic identity?
6. Explain in your own words why Maydon sees Hispanics as a "buffer" between blacks and whites in America.
7. Why does Margaret Welch say she "*never, never* had any racist feelings"?
8. How have Welch's experiences shaped her attitudes toward other ethnicities?

Reading the Signs

1. What advice would Richard Majors ("Cool Pose: The Proud Signature of Black Survival," p. 471) give Peter Soderstrom in dealing with African-American students? Writing as if you were Majors, compose a letter to Soderstrom, explaining how he might respond to black students and read the signs of their body language more accurately.
2. Both Peter Soderstrom and Sam Fulwood III ("The Rage of the Black Middle Class," p. 462) begin their selections by recalling the promise of the 1960s civil rights movement in their youth. Compare and contrast their responses to the subsequent history of race relations in America, and their own personal attitudes toward race. How might you account for any differences in their attitudes?
3. Compare Ron Maydon's view of Hispanic culture with that of Ada María Isasi-Diaz ("Hispanic in America: Starting Points," p. 503). What are their views of assimilation? How do they each view other ethnic groups and the various groups that constitute Hispanic culture?
4. Ron Maydon ranks various ethnic groups, including the different nationalities that form Hispanic culture. Write an essay in which you explain your response to this ranking. What do you think is Maydon's motivation? What is the significance of his comparisons among groups (e.g., "the white

Cubans are our Jews")? As you formulate your response, you might consult Dorinne K. Kondo's "On Being a Conceptual Anomaly" (p. 477) for her comments on the power of "ready-made molds" to shape racial and cultural expectations.

5. Working in small groups, role-play a conversation on interracial relations between Margaret Welch, Sam Fulwood III ("The Rage of the Black Middle Class"), Peter Soderstrom, and Ron Maydon. Then report the tenor of the conversation to the rest of the class. How do the whole class's conversations compare?

6. Margaret Welch observes that she is denied scholarship help because of her ethnicity. Research your school's policy on race-based financial awards, and write an essay in which you support, challenge, or change that policy. To develop your essay, you might interview students from a number of different ethnicities.

7. Both Margaret Welch and Peter Soderstrom reflect on whether they themselves are racist. Compare their responses to this issue. How do their reflections relate to their external actions and public behavior? How might their thoughts be shaped by their life experiences? Which, if either, do you find a more sympathetic character, and why?

8. How does race operate as a sign in the lives of Margaret Welch and Ron Maydon? How do you account for any differences in their attitudes toward race?

Photograph copyright © 1993 by Robert Daniel Ullman / Design Conceptions.

STREET SIGNS

Gang Culture in the U.S.A.

In the last chapter we asked a simple enough question: "Who are you?" In this chapter, we begin with an apparently simpler one: "Where are you from?" Have you ever been asked this? Probably often. Have you ever been asked it by a group of guys standing on a street corner, in a tone not of inquiry but of challenge? If you have, or if you might in the future, you'd better know exactly what the question really means. And how to answer it.

Because in the code language of a typical American street gang, "Where are you from?" isn't really a question. It's more an assertion, a statement. If you know the code, you know what that statement is. It means, "This is our turf and we don't recognize you." It means, "We think you belong on a different turf, a different street." It means, "As far as we're concerned, you're from another gang, and unless you can show us otherwise, you're in real trouble." And so the answer often given by teens in America's inner cities is, "I'm not from anywhere," which means, "I don't belong to a gang." And sometimes this is enough to prevent a fight. Sometimes it's not.

For those of you who have never been exposed to the codes of street gang culture, this might all sound peculiar. But for those of you who have lived in neighborhoods where every street, apartment building, wall, and lamppost has been claimed by one gang or another, this simple question, "Where are you from?" and the knowledge of how properly to answer it, might be an essential part of your survival equip-

527

ment. Indeed, it is hard to think of any semiotic system of such particular importance to American youth as the codes of gang culture, for even if you do not belong to a gang, your knowledge of gang signaling systems can be important street knowledge, whether you live in the city or a suburb, for the American street gang is no longer a phenomenon exclusive to the inner city.

Think for a moment of the signs and signals of the gang code that you do know. What forms of dress, or posture, or hand signaling, or speech are you aware of? How much can you decode? Have you ever used such signs? How? And for what purpose?

The Semiotics of the Street

The explosive growth of street gangs in America has effectively taken what was once a hidden, marginalized social phenomenon and put it on the center stage of American culture, especially youth culture. To be sure, street gangs are hardly new to American society, the first appearing among nineteenth-century Irish immigrants in lower Manhattan. But in the 1990s, gangs have transcended their traditional boundaries of slum, ghetto, and barrio to become one of America's most prominent, if troubling, subcultures, a subculture whose elaborate linguistic, clothing, and behavioral codes are not only known but admired and emulated by teens around the country, regardless of their race, class, or geographical region. Courted by fashion designers, Hollywood producers, record labels, talk-show hosts, and even civic leaders (in the aftermath of the L.A. riots of 1992, captains of the Bloods and the Crips were treated, some commentators complained, like ambassadors of independent nations), gangsters, homeboys, cholos, gangstas, what-have-you, aren't just thugs anymore. They have become a major component of American popular and commercial culture, offering to the semiotician at least three major avenues of analytic approach.

First, you can analyze the elaborate codes and rituals of the gangs themselves, the signaling systems by which gangs communicate to each other and to the world outside who they are and, sometimes, what they mean to do. Second, the commodification of the gang subculture can be interpreted as part of a larger economic culture in which apparently anything can be transformed into a product for commercial exploitation. And third, you may look at the powerful attraction that ethnic urban gangs—especially black gangs—have held for suburban white teens, whose fascination with the visible imagery of gangsterism has made its commercial exploitation possible. We'll look briefly at these three approaches here, leaving you to extend and develop the interpretations to follow.

‖‖‖

Discussing the Signs of Gangs

In class, discuss the reasons you think many middle-class youths have been attracted to the signs of gang culture, ranging from clothing styles and music to tagging and graffiti. Do these different signs mean the same thing to middle-class gangs as they do to inner-city gangs? Try to formulate your own explanation of this phenomenon.

The Writing on the Wall

We'll start with the signaling systems of the gangs themselves, for surely the semiotics of the street starts with the street, where, scrawled upon walls, streetlights, billboards, traffic signs, sidewalks, overpasses, trees . . . in short, anything that doesn't move (check that; Dumpsters, panel vans, buses, and, of course, subway cars move) may be found the intricate graffiti of the modern gang. Gang graffiti was apparently invented by Latino gangs in L.A. about seventy years ago, but it has proliferated with the invention of spray paint. Though outsiders complain that they can't for the life of them figure out what all those squiggles and sharp angles mean, they are, in effect, part of an elaborate code whose conventions are highly standardized. Have you ever noticed just how similar in appearance gang graffiti is, from the round-letter script of a quick spray job or Magic Marker run, to the several-foot-high printed letters that rise upon a wall in massive jagged blocks to shout out a gang's initials? This standardization is no accident: Within a gang, older homeboys teach younger initiates the techniques of the graffiti guerrilla, while suburban wannabes may carefully practice their own technique by copying what they see in graffiti-scarred neighborhoods. In this way, a standard repertoire of styles is passed from generation to generation and from social class to social class. Replicating a gang's signature, in effect, is a sign of membership and group identity.

What is more, the codes of gang graffiti can be racially distinguishable as well. At least in Los Angeles, Latino gang graffiti tends to be written in block letters, while black gangs go for the scrawled, squiggly script. There is even a racial difference in gang nicknaming. Latino gang monikers chosen by a gangster's homeboys tend to distinguish his most striking characteristics—"Shorty" is a common gang tag in Los Angeles— while black gangsters may name themselves with more intimidating labels like "Bullet."

The names of the gangs themselves seem to differ both racially and regionally. The first Irish gangs in New York sported names like the

Shirt Tails, the Plug Uglies, and the Roach Guards, and New York gang labels still sound like the names of rock groups and social clubs (e.g., the Sandmen, the Sex Boys, and the Montauk Chestbreakers). On the other hand, Chicago gangs, whose memberships may number in the thousands, often sound like the vast institutions that, in essence, they are, boasting names like the Blackstone Rangers and the Black Disciples. While in L.A. the Bloods and the Crips (and their many subcohorts, which sport names like the "Eight Trey Crips") are the best-known gang names, Latino gangs, which are numerically superior, tend to choose gang handles that identify their 'hood and that can be abbreviated in three-letter tags (BVN for Barrio Van Nuys and VST for Valerio Street were particularly common tags in the authors' former neighborhood), a practice emulated by the rap group N.W.A.

Gang names are tagged for territorial purposes. Generally, they mark the boundaries of a gang's turf and proliferate at the margins of a territory or where turf lines are in dispute. Of course, gang labels may be sprayed deliberately within the turf of another gang as a challenge. And then again, they may be scrawled in places—like freeway overpasses—that no gang could claim as a territory but that will be seen by other gangs —and everyone else—as a sign of the gang's ubiquity and daring (how do they get up on those freeway signs anyway?).

There is a code for crossing out gang tags as well. Gangsters don't paint *out* an offending tag (unless they've been caught by the police and are made to pay antigraffiti penance), they paint *over* it. An "X" spray-painted over another gang tag (or "placa," as Latino gangs call them) is a sign of disrespect, a "dis" mark. A lot of taunting is going on out there, as one may see several tags superimposed over each other in a messy blot that looks like the sort of thing that happens when a computer printer jams. Gangs also line out another gang's graffiti, but notice the color of the line. A black line might just be a "dis" mark, but a red line (at least in L.A.) means that a drive-by against the offending gang is being planned. A spray-painted number "187" is another such sign: It refers to the California state penal code number for homicide. Finally, as the spread of crack cocaine (and the resulting arms race) among gangs has dramatically raised the level of violence in the gang subculture, a code for the dead has been devised. Now walls serve not only as turf markers and tag opportunities but as environmental obituaries as well, with the names of the slain sentimentally inscribed alongside pledges for revenge or simply covered with spray-painted "clouds" of glory.

Such are some of the conclusions drawn by adult interpreters of gang graffiti. But perhaps they are missing the point. As the private language of what is, in essence, a youth culture, gang graffiti may well have meanings that have eluded professional interpretation. Here your own experience may offer you insights that are invisible to others. Are the interpretations gathered here correct? What does graffiti mean to you and your friends? What, in short, have we left out?

The difficulty of nailing down the meaning of graffiti is increased by the proliferation of "taggers," who more often than not don't belong to formal gangs but work alone or in "crews" or "posses." Here the possibilities for interpretation become almost unlimited, because every tagger may be the author of a new private code whose meaning may be apparent only to himself or herself and a few friends. Interpreting such codes may require that you ask questions that adults often cannot ask or will certainly not receive answers to if they do ask.

The Signs of Gang Identity

Nevertheless, we may say that, in general, gang symbolism exists for purposes of identification: personal, communal, and territorial. Gang colors, tags, nicknames, hand signals, slogans, dress, and even posture precisely identify the gang member, who frequently feels no other sense of identity in an environment of deteriorating neighborhoods and hopeless poverty. In many cases, the gang takes the place of the family that has collapsed and provides protection as well as community.

Identifying yourself within the code of gang semiotics can be a tricky matter, however. On the one hand, the ability to let a potential enemy know right away that you belong to a gang of fellow homeys who will avenge you if anyone decides to mess with you can be a source of protection on dangerous streets. On the other hand, that very identity can provoke an attack, especially if you stray into another gang's territory. Indeed, gang members may feel that a reputation for being tough— enhanced by the right uniform and the right posture of menacing cool —will protect them.

But as with swaggering gunfighters of the Old West, sending the signal of toughness often invites countertoughness. This can prove particularly disastrous for the legions of teens, from barrio, ghetto, and suburb, who do not belong to gangs but dress as if they do. Again and again after a drive-by shooting, police records report that the victims, shot while hanging out on a street corner or lawn, did not belong to a gang. And yet, kids still yank their Raiders cap on backward, pull on a blue scarf, and take a walk in a red-scarf neighborhood. The situation has become so dangerous that suburban as well as urban schools around the country are devising dress codes to forbid the wearing of gang fashions on campus, while schools in Los Angeles have banned red or blue clothing, due to their adoption by the myriad factions of Bloods and Crips as gang colors. Here too students often have a different take on the matter than do adults. What is your response to antigang dress codes? Do they work? Would you have felt more comfortable in high school with such codes in place, or not? Do you feel that such codes violate your First Amendment rights to freedom of expression?

Gangsta Chic

The fact that the dangers inherent in gang attire haven't reduced its allure, that schools have tried to force students not to dress in certain ways, is itself significant, showing how the codes of gang culture have been adopted by the middle classes. Gang fashion (hip-hop), gang music (rap), and gang violence (exploited in movie after movie, from *Colors* to *Boyz in the Hood*) are, quite simply, big business in a marketplace that extends far beyond the ghettos and barrios where the codes of gang culture originate. Sales of baggy, oversized pants, overalls (worn un-strapped or single-strapped), baseball caps, team sweats and jackets, and Nike basketball shoes (worn unlaced one year, laced the next) have bounded beyond the gangs who first favored them to adolescents who line up to adopt the gangsta look. Just think of Luke Perry on *Beverly Hills, 90210,* whose multimillionaire character sports the latest in overall chic, while even Michael Jackson, the crossover star who opposed gang violence in "Beat It," got into the act, donning black leather and chains to out-gangsta the gangstas in "Bad."

Still, corporate America can miss the point. A few years ago, L.A. Gear gambled that a Michael Jackson–designed sneaker might really do well among teen consumers. The shoe flopped. If you recall the shoe— a black leather hightop festooned with silver chains and buckles—per-haps you could explain just what went wrong.

You might also be able to explain why graffiti, which most adults regard as a form of vandalism, is viewed both as a mode of artistic expression and as a model for fashion design among its fans. Why are "graffiti"-styled sports glasses and bicycle frames popular? Why do high-fashion models appear in front of graffiti-spattered walls in teen-wear displays? Only the consumers of such fashions can really answer these questions.

You Say You Want a Revolution

But something more exists behind the cultural significance of gang culture than fashion alone. Have you ever felt that the defiance of the gangs provides an outlet for your own feelings of rebelliousness or dis-content? Are you making a social statement by aligning yourself with gang signals? Do the raps of Ice-T, Ice Cube, N.W.A., Public Enemy, and 2 Live Crew express your rage?

Exploring the Signs of Gangs

Imagine that a younger brother or sister confided in you that he or she is planning to join a gang, whether urban or suburban. In your journal, reflect on what your response would be, perhaps by writing a dialogue with your sibling. Would you try to stop gang involvement, and what reasons would you give? Would you encourage or ignore it? What advice would you give your sibling?

Or is it all just fashion? Misspelling words (especially using the letter "z" instead of "s" for a plural, as in "Boyz"), wearing baseball caps backward and shoelaces untied, and spouting violent raps were gestures originally intended at once to disturb and distinguish, to identify the urban gangster while outraging mainstream white America. But as has been so often the case in American racial politics, what was once condemned in the dominated class soon came to be consumed by the dominators. Just as bop and the blues, once marginalized as "Negro music" and kept off mainstream radio, metamorphosed into white-dominated rock-and-roll, so too have the emblems of gang culture—especially those of black gangs—been co-opted by white America. The symbols of disaffection become fashion symbols. Images of social despair return as dollar signs in a commercial cornucopia.

It is thus significant that it is the black gang that has supplied most of the imagery of commercial gangsterism. Though Hispanic gangs make up more than half of L.A.'s street gangs, for example, the cholo style sets fewer trends. Suburban gangsta wannabes (even the word "gangsta" originates in the ghetto) emulate not the prison-inspired styles of Latino East L.A. (for instance, below-the-knee cutoffs and close-cropped hair) but rather the professional sports–inspired styles of the black gangs, designs that send them running to the Raiders and Reebok and Nike. Though there are Latino rappers, the sound that can claim that it's "straight outa Compton"—one of the last predominantly black communities in a city where Latinos are the majority population—gets all the attention. When Edward James Olmos made a film about Latino gangs in L.A., *American Me,* the movie received local press attention but nothing like the national media stakeouts that occur every time a new film about black gangs appears.

Thus, one of the enduring ironies of American race relations makes its way into the semiotics of the street. Though young African-American males may be the most socially oppressed demographic group in America, B-boys are also the trendsetters for white youth. From generation to generation, black America has provided young white America with metaphors of oppression, with symbols and analogies to use in their own struggles. You might want to begin your thinking about gang culture with this phenomenon. Do you believe that it is valid for white middle-class youths to adopt the symbols of the underclass to express themselves? Does it in any way trivialize the social conditions behind the growth of gangs to turn street gangs into fashion plates? Or does the crossing over of gang culture into middle-class culture exert a unifying force among the young that can be used to solve social problems that have been historically ignored? Such questions only you can answer, for you are part of the code in a way that your teachers and parents are not.

The Readings

Carl Rogers's "Children in Gangs" inaugurates our readings in this chapter by providing a broad overview of youth gangs in America. Our next selection takes you to Los Angeles—a city that has been called the gang capital of the United States—where Léon Bing's interview with a gangster named "Faro" provides a raw insight into the world of the Bloods and Crips, America's most famous gangs. Anne Campbell then takes us to New York, where she studies members of "girl gangs" and analyzes their relationship to male gangsters, showing how the women, rather than representing female independence and power in the gangster world, are often little more than satellites of their male cohorts. Our next reading, "Signs of the Street: A Conversation," presents an interview conducted by the authors of this book with a group of current and former gang members now attending classes at the West Valley Occupational Center in Los Angeles. Here, the students speak of the styles and signaling systems now current among L.A.'s gangs, describe what gang membership means to them, and offer their opinions of the suburban wannabes who copy them. Next, James Diego Vigil's description of the clothing, speech patterns, and personal styles of cholo gangs illustrates the complex signaling systems used by youth gangs, while Seth Mydans's report on the growth of white gangs charts the expansion of the gang phenomenon out of the inner city and into the suburbs, where middle-class wannabes play out the life-styles of urban gangsters in a 1990s version of rebels without a cause. Finally, we include an illustration from *Teen Angels* Magazine, a home-grown publication put together by gang members to communicate with each other and to express their sense of their world.

CARL ROGERS

Children in Gangs

||||||||||||||||||||||||||||||||||||||||||||||||||||||||||

Street gangs are nothing new to American life, having originated among Irish immigrants in the early nineteenth century. But never before have there been so many gangs in America, nor have the ages of their members been so young. In this journalistic overview of gangs in America, written for a European audience, Carl Rogers shows how today's street gangs differ from the romanticized image popularized by the musical West Side Story. *In particular, the advent of crack cocaine has helped "to transform gangs into drug trafficking criminal organizations"—and may have changed forever the lives of inner-city youth. Rogers is the vice-president of the American National Council on Child Abuse and Family Violence located in Washington, D.C., and is in charge of public policy for the organization.*

The 1980s witnessed the explosive resurgence of an historic American urban social problem: children and youth in gangs. From New York to Los Angeles, from Chicago to Miami, over forty-five American cities have an identified youth gang problem.

The number of youth gangs in the United States is on the rise and their involvement in the drug trade is resulting in dramatic increases in gang-related violence—including homicide—and arrests for criminal activities in almost every American city. The scope and the nature of the problem vary widely from city to city, but it has been estimated that over 50,000 children and youths are gang members in the city of Los Angeles and that there are over 600 youth gangs in California alone.

Popularized in the 1950s musical *West Side Story,* youth gangs have been a recurring social problem in U.S. cities at least since the second half of the nineteenth century. Their emergence and growth, primarily in poor, urban neighborhoods, were frequently fueled by successive waves of immigrants arriving in the United States, and were symptomatic of the problems these groups encountered in trying to adapt to a new and at times radically different culture. Today many youth gangs continue to reflect the difficulties of assimilation of immigrant populations.

Youth gangs are usually defined as groups of young people who frequently engage in illegal activity on a group basis. They are usually territorial in nature, identifying with a particular neighborhood and protecting their "turf" from encroachment by other gangs. Better organized gangs often control economically motivated crime such as burglary, extortion, or drug trafficking at the neighborhood level. They may also sell "protection" from criminal activity to legitimate merchants. Youth gangs usually identify themselves by a name ("Crips" and "Bloods" are the names of two Los Angeles–based gangs), and may further distinguish themselves by a particular style or color of clothing, by use of symbols, or by wearing certain kinds of jewelry.

A Million Dollars a Week from Crack

The recent dynamic growth of youth gangs and related violence is   5
directly attributed by most sources to the increased sale of cocaine, particularly in the form known as "rock" or "crack." This lucrative illegal activity is helping to transform gangs into drug trafficking criminal organizations. In 1988 Los Angeles police officials acknowledged that they were aware of at least four gangs in their city grossing over one million dollars per week through the sale of cocaine. A recent article in *Time* ironically noted that the crack cocaine trade may be one of the biggest job programs for inner-city youth in the United States.

One reason why children become involved in drug trafficking is that the laws governing juvenile crime are more lenient than those governing adult crime. Ironically, as the U.S. "war on drugs" has intensified, with both increasing arrests for drug trafficking and more severe penalties for adults convicted of drug-related crime, the value of youth gang members has increased. While an adult convicted of selling drugs in most states is subject to a mandatory prison sentence of anywhere from two years to life imprisonment, a young person under the age of eighteen will seldom be committed to a correctional facility for a first offense, and even if committed is not subject to mandatory sentence lengths. It has become both increasingly profitable and safer for adult criminals to enroll children and youths in the drug-trafficking business.

Peewees and Wannabees

The average age of youth gang members continues to decline. Most experts place the figure at around thirteen to fifteen years of age, while law enforcement officials in Los Angeles, Chicago, and other cities note that children as young as nine or ten years are frequently found in today's gangs. These young recruits, often called "peewees" (slang for little members) or "wannabees" (slang for "want to be" gang members), become casually involved with older gang members who live in their neighborhood, attend their school, or are members of their own families. Initially, younger children may be asked to perform "favors" for older gang members—to watch for police in the neighborhood, or to deliver packages which may contain drugs, money, or weapons. In exchange, the children often receive expensive gifts or money.

As they demonstrate their trustworthiness and reliability, these children assume more difficult and more dangerous roles. Children as young as ten or eleven years of age are frequently involved in gang-related drug trafficking. Younger children are routinely employed as "spotters" watching and reporting on police activity in their neighborhood to other gang members, as "weapons carriers" for older gang members, or in other roles, and earn anywhere from two hundred dollars per week to one hundred dollars per day. "Runners," usually slightly older children, may earn up to three hundred dollars per day keeping street-corner dealers supplied with drugs from a hidden cache. Enterprising youths as young as fifteen or sixteen may advance to the level of street-corner dealers, routinely earning between four hundred dollars and one thousand dollars per day. In a particularly good market such as New York City, authorities indicate that dealers can make up to three thousand dollars per day.

Few dealers, however, work full time, and two different studies in Washington, D.C., would suggest that a street-corner dealer's average earnings are more likely to be in the range of four thousand dollars to seven thousand dollars per month. In contrast, most states in the United States set a minimum employment age of sixteen years, and most legal entry-level jobs available to young people pay less than forty dollars per day, or approximately eight hundred dollars per month.

Once a child is involved with a gang, it may be virtually impossible   10
for him to quit. Gang membership usually leads to truancy and ultimately dropping out of school, closing off escape from a criminal life-style through education. The gang member also finds it difficult to give up a more lucrative life-style in exchange for unemployment or employment at minimum wage.

The gang member who attempts to quit is also subject to social pressures to continue his or her involvement. At best, attempting to leave the gang may lead to social ostracism; at worst it may lead to direct intimidation.

Impoverished Inner-city Neighborhoods

To truly understand the youth gang problem it is important to understand the social context within which the gangs emerge. First, they are almost universally a product of impoverished urban neighborhoods, where unemployment routinely exceeds 20 percent of the work force and in some cases exceeds 50 percent. Families consist overwhelmingly of single mothers with children and often rely primarily on public assistance for their livelihood. Nationally, 20 percent of all children in the United States live in families at or below the established federal poverty level. In many inner-city neighborhoods this figure approaches 100 percent. These communities are characterized by generally high crime rates, limited legitimate business activity or employment opportunities, and poorly functioning public education systems.

In contrast to the phenomenon of street children in many Third World countries, or to the problem of runaway or "throw-away" children (children, usually teenagers, expelled from their homes by their parents), most youth gang members live at home with their families. Some parents actively support their child's gang involvement or are totally indifferent, but most parents do care. Even the best-intentioned parent, however, can find it difficult, if not impossible, to keep his or her child from becoming involved with a local gang. Every neighborhood has its history of gang revenge against individual children or their families for resisting the gang. The combined factors of intimidation on the one hand and some financial support on the other eventually result in tacit collusion on the part of these parents. An uneasy truce develops where the parent, while not condoning or supporting the child's gang involvement, nonetheless does little to try to stop this involvement and welcomes the child's periodic financial contributions to the family budget.

So far, the overall public policy approach to this social problem has focused on three broad strategies: suppression of drug use and drug trafficking; suppression of youth gangs; and prevention of youth involvement in gangs. To date, while national statistics suggest an overall decline in the use of illegal drugs, this decline appears to have had little effect on the growth of the gangs or on the frequency of gang-related violence. Similarly, attempts at direct suppression of the gangs through law enforcement activities appear to have had limited effects, despite the mobilization of extensive resources. It is argued by many, however, that these efforts have slowed the growth and spread of gangs. Alternatively, some have suggested that efforts at gang suppression through arrest and detention of gang members actually lead to increased levels of gang-related violence as other gangs compete for control of territories once controlled by the suppressed gang.

Most experts agree that the only viable long-term solution to the 15 problem is to prevent children and youths from getting involved in gangs in the first place. Most current programs seek to provide support for high-risk children and their families. They focus on children between the ages of six and fourteen, since it appears to be generally agreed that prevention efforts must begin before young people develop well-established patterns of delinquent behavior or become seriously involved with gangs. Key elements in many of these programs include the provision of social and recreational activities, and educational assistance, as well as efforts to prevent the children from dropping out of school and to enhance their self-confidence and self-esteem. The success of prevention efforts ultimately depends on whether these children and young people have a sense of hope in their own future and a belief that through their own efforts they can lead useful, productive lives.

Reading the Text

1. Why, according to Rogers, have gangs made a resurgence in the last few years?
2. What link does Rogers see between youth gangs and the drug trade?
3. Why is the age of gang members continuing to decline?
4. Why do law enforcement attempts to control gangs so often fail, in Rogers's view?

Reading the Signs

1. Rogers points out that youth gangs in the 1950s were popularized in *West Side Story*. Rent a videotape of this film, and then compare the image of gangs it presents with a more recent gang-oriented film, such as *Angel Town*. In what ways do the images of gangs differ in the two films? Is one film more "realistic" than the other, or do they represent gang life equally well? As you develop your essay, you might consult any of the other selections in this chapter.
2. Rogers wrote this selection for a European audience. What image of America does he communicate to his European readers? What assumptions does he make about gangs and, particularly, inner-city neighborhoods? Use your responses to these questions to formulate a critique of Rogers's essay.
3. Rogers claims that gangs are usually "territorial in nature, identifying with a particular neighborhood and protecting their 'turf' from encroachment by other gangs." To what extent do Faro (see Léon Bing, "Faro," p. 540) and Connie (see Anne Campbell, "The Praised and the Damned," p. 544) demonstrate this characteristic?
4. At the close of his essay, Rogers describes some proposed solutions to the gang "problem." In class, discuss whether these solutions are likely to be effective. What other solutions might you suggest? Are there aspects of gang involvement that the experts have neglected to consider?
5. Rogers assumes that gang involvement is motivated primarily by negative social factors. Do you feel his assumption is valid, or are there other factors that might motivate one to join a gang? Read or review "Faro" by Léon Bing (p. 540), "The Praised and the Damned" by Anne Campbell (p. 544), and "Signs of the Street: A Conversation" (p. 560), and write an essay in which you support, refute, or modify Rogers's assumption.

LÉON BING
Faro

‖‖‖‖‖‖‖‖‖‖‖‖‖‖‖‖‖‖‖‖‖‖‖‖‖‖‖‖‖‖‖‖‖‖‖‖

For many teens today, something about gangsterism, even the violence, is glamorous. But as Léon Bing (b. 1950) reveals in this portrait of Faro—a homeless, half-starving gang member from South Central L.A.—there is nothing glamorous about it at all. Armed and dangerous, Faro has only to "look crazy" at someone, and be looked at crazy in return, to justify a casual homicide. The simple act of showing up on the wrong turf can mean death in an undeclared war zone where, to survive, you have to know how to hold your face and what neighborhoods to avoid. Sometimes the signs are no more visible than a street sign, and you can never know when death, blazing away with an AK-47, may wheel up in a battered sedan. Léon Bing is a former fashion model turned journalist whose work has appeared in Rolling Stone, L.A. Weekly, *and* Harper's. *She is the author of the best-selling book* Do or Die *(1991), from which this selection is taken.*

He is seventeen years old, and he is homeless. I met him through one of his homeboys on whose couch he has been sleeping for the past week. This is how he lives, from couch to couch, or in a sleeping bag, or in the back seat of a parked car. A couple of days in one place, maybe two weeks in another. He does not remember the last time he went to school, and he does not know how to read or write. He is as close to invisibility as it is possible to be.

The reason he's talking is because his friend has vouched for me. We are in my car because I have to run some errands, and I want to save time, so I have decided to take this kid—Faro—along. He sits next to me, looking out the window. His mouth is slightly open, and I can see that his teeth are small and straight. The tip of his tongue is almost, but not quite, the exact shade of raspberry sherbet. His hair has been sectioned into a myriad of tiny braids, each with a blue rubber band at the tip. He is wearing shabby sweats and busted-down Nike hightops. He is very thin; the bones of his wrists stick knobbily out of the elastic cuffs of his hooded jacket, which is at least two sizes too small for him.

We ride in silence for a while, and then I ask him about his family. It takes him a long time to answer, and when he does, his voice is soft, controlled.

"My mother, she died from a drug overdose. I got a grandmother, but she gonna go the same way—she just wanderin' the streets day and night, lookin' for handouts so she can fix herself a pipe. My brother got killed in a holdup three years ago."

I ask which end of the gun his brother was at, and Faro looks at me   5
in surprise. It is the first time we have made any kind of eye contact.
He has sixty-year-old eyes set down in that seventeen-year-old face.
Graveyard eyes.

"Most people think he was holdin' the gun." He almost smiles; it is
a pained expression. "He wasn't but eight years old. He was lookin' at
comic books in a 7-Eleven and some dude come in to rob the place."
He turns away to look out the window. "The homies give him a nice
funeral. I used to have a picture of him, laid out, in my scrapbook. It
got lost."

He continues to look out the window. We are moving through an
intersection where the streets are torn and gaping with road work. A
pneumatic drill is blasting, and Faro winces a little at the sound. As we
come to a stoplight a Mustang convertible pulls up on Faro's side of the
car. The driver and the guy in the passenger seat are both young, both
black. Their haircuts, called "fades," are highly styled, carefully constructed flattops with geometric designs etched into the closely shaven
sides.

"See them two dudes?" Faro's voice, unaccountably, has dropped to
a whisper. I nod my head.

"I'm gonna look crazy at 'em. You watch what they do." He turns
away from me, and I lean forward over the wheel so that I can watch
the faces on the two guys. The driver, sensing that someone is looking
at him, glances over at my car. His eyes connect with Faro's, widen for
an instant. Then he breaks the contact, looks down, looks away. And
there is no mistaking what I saw there in his eyes: It was fear. Whatever
he saw in Faro's face, he wasn't about to mess with it.

Faro giggles and turns back toward me. He looks the same as he did   10
before to me: a skinny, slightly goofy-looking kid. The light changes
and the Mustang speeds away, turning right at the next corner. I ask
Faro to "look crazy" for me. He simply narrows his eyes. That's all. He
narrows his eyes, and he looks straight at me and everything about his
face shifts and changes, as if by some trick of time-lapse photography. It
becomes a nightmare face, and it is a scary thing to see. It tells you that
if you return his stare, if you challenge this kid, you'd better be ready to
stand your ground. His look tells you that he doesn't care about anything,
not your life and not his.

I ask Faro what would have happened if the guy had looked crazy
back.

"Then we woulda got into it."

"With me sitting here next to you? Are you kidding?" I can hear
an edge of shrillness in my voice.

He laughs softly. "Never woulda happened. That was just some
damn preppy out on his lunch hour."

But if he *had* returned the challenge. What then?   15

"Then I woulda killed him."

My eyes slide over his skinny silhouette. No way can he be hiding a weapon under that sweatsuit. He smiles slyly and pats the top of his right shoe. I peer down and there, unbelievably, is the glint of metal. I look up at Faro's face, and without knowing why, I'm shocked. I feel as if he has betrayed me, and it makes me angry.

"What you expect? This ain't no game." He is disgusted.

"You played a game with that guy, though, didn't you? That whole thing was a game."

"And what kinda game *you* playin', lady? You come on down here,   20
and you ask a whole lotta questions, and then when it get too real fo' you, you start in hollerin' like somebody dis'ed you." Cold, icy anger in his voice. His eyes are narrowed again; this time it's for real. I want to meet the challenge, I want to defend myself, but what he's saying is true. I got mad when it got too real.

"You're right, you know."

"Ye-eeeeh."

"I get scared. And then I guess I get mad."

"Be like that with me sometime, too." We are both beginning to relax again.

"So I can ask questions again."   25

"Ye-eeeeh."

We pass a group of little kids, five- and six-year-olds, walking in line behind their teacher. As they get to the corner, the teacher raises both arms in readiness to cross the street, signaling for the children to do the same. All of them lift their arms high over their heads, like holdup victims, following the teacher to the other side.

"I watch out for the little kids in my neighborhood. So gangs who we don't get along with"—he names several sets, both Bloods and Crips—"don't come in and shoot 'em up. All them I just named, they come in and shoot us up, then we catch one of 'em slippin'[1] and it's all over for them."

He is looking at the children as he talks. His voice is soft, but somehow it is not calm.

"Like there was this fool, this enemy nigger from our worst enemy   30
set, and he was with his wife and his baby. They was walkin' down there near Vermont, where he had no business bein'. He was slippin' bad and we caught him. We was in a car, all homies, and I was like, 'Let's pop this dumb nigger, let's empty the whole clip in him.'" Faro turns to look at me, as if he wants to make sure I understand what he is saying. "We had an AK—two-barrel banana clips, two sides—and I just . . ." He hesitates only for an instant. "I just wanted to make him pay."

---

1. being careless; not watching your back.—BING'S NOTE.

Careful to keep my voice as soft as his, I ask him what it was he wanted the guy to pay for.

"For all our dead homeboys. For bein' our enemy. For slippin' so bad." He is warming to his subject, his voice is coming alive now. "You gotta understand—enemy got to pay just for bein' alive." He is quiet for a moment, then he gives a little hitch of his shoulders, like a prizefighter, and he goes on. He is animated now, reliving the event for me. "I was like 'fuck it, Cuz—I'm gonna strap this shit to the seat and I'm just gonna *work* it.'" He twists around to face the passenger door and mimes the action of holding and aiming an AK-47 rifle. "So I strapped it to the seat, like this, and we circled around and pulled up on this nigger from two blocks away, crept up on him slow like, and I just gave it to him." Faro begins to jerk and buck there in his seat as the imaginary weapon in his hands fires automatically. "*Pah-pah-pah-pah-pah-pah-pah!* You know, just let him have it. Just emptied the whole . . ." He is wholly caught up in his recollection, inflamed with it, drunk with it. "I lit his ass *up!* I killed him—shot his baby in the leg—crippled his wife!" He is facing me again, his eyes fixed on some point just to the left of mine. "She in a wheelchair now, I heard, wearin' a voicebox, 'cause one of the bullets caught her in the throat." Then, in afterthought, "The baby okay."

We are silent for a moment; when Faro speaks again his voice is a fusion of bad feelings: despair, remorse, a deep, biting resentment. "I just lit his whole family up and . . ." He sucks in air, holds it a couple of seconds, puffs it out. "It was like, damn, Cuz—I killed him, that was my mission, but still—his whole family." He shakes his head several times, as if he cannot will himself to believe his own story. Then he places the tip of one index finger on the glass next to him and taps it in a nervous, rhythmic beat. "That's a crazy world out there, and we livin' in it."

"Dying in it, too."

The finger stops tapping.   35

"If you die, you die. Most gangbangers don't have nothin' to live for no more, anyway. That why some of 'em be gangbangin'."

He seems to sense what it is that I'm thinking.

"I ain't just talkin' 'bout myself, either. I'm talkin' for a lotta gangbangers. They mothers smokin' dope. Or somebody shot somebody else's mother, and that person figure if they gangbang they got a chance to get 'em back." He is silent again for a beat or two. Then, "People don't have nothin' to live for if they mother dead, they brother dead, they sister dead. What else they got to live for? If people in yo' family is just dyin', if the person you love the most, the person who love *you* the most be dead, then what else *do* you got to live for?"

"Yourself."

It's as if I hadn't spoken; he doesn't even hear me.   40

"I tell you this—you see enough dyin', then you be ready to die yourself, just so you don't have to see no more of death."

Reading the Text

1. Why does Bing say that Faro is "as close to invisibility as it is possible to be"?
2. What sort of sign is "looking crazy"?
3. Why does Faro feel he and his friends were duty-bound to kill the rival gang member and wound his family?

Reading the Signs

1. In your journal, explore your response to Faro's story. Do you feel sympathy or hostility toward him? What does gang involvement mean to him? Does Faro's story change your attitudes toward gangs in any way?
2. Read or review Seth Mydans's "Not Just the Inner City: Well-to-Do Join Gangs" (p. 587). What value might Faro's story hold for the suburban gang wannabes whom Mydans describes?
3. How might Richard Majors ("Cool Pose: The Proud Signature of Black Survival," p. 471) explain Faro's body language and even actions? Write an essay in which you apply Majors's analysis of African-American stylistic choices to Faro, being sure to discuss ways Faro does and does not illustrate Majors's argument.
4. In class, discuss how adequately Carl Rogers's "Children in Gangs" (p. 535) explains Faro's actions and gang involvement.

ANNE CAMPBELL

The Praised and the Damned

||||||||||||||||||||||||||||||||||||||||||||||||||||||||

The popular image of the gang subculture is overwhelmingly masculine, but a large—and growing—number of female gangsters have evolved their own codes and styles. But, as Anne Campbell shows in this anthropological case study excerpted from The Girls in the Gang *(1991), girl gangs tend to exist in a symbiotic—and subordinate— relationship to all-male cohorts. Far from representing a feminist version of street gang culture, female gangs seem locked in a prefeminist era in which women are perceived as the sexual and criminal servants of the men with whom they associate. Anne Campbell teaches at the School*

of Criminal Justice, Rutgers University, and is also the author of Girl
Delinquents *(1981) and (with John J. Gibbs)* Violent Transactions
(1986).

Cops bust up gang rumble on IND tracks
by Philip Messing

> *A bloody subway rumble involving three notorious Manhattan youth
> gangs—armed with a sawed-off rifle, baseball bats, metal-studded bracelets,
> and chains—was narrowly averted last night on the tracks of a Manhattan
> train station.*
>
> *Ten well-armed members of the Renegades and the Chosen Ones
> jumped over turnstiles at the IND's 168th St. downtown subway station to
> chase three members of The Sandmen [sic], a rival gang, police said.*
>
> *"If they had been caught, they would have definitely been hurt badly,"
> said plainclothes Transit Officer Noel Negron.*
>
> *Negron and his partner, Officer Lenko Kaica, who were standing on the
> platform, joined in the chase, which continued in the southbound subway
> tunnel and ended in a nearby park.*
>
> *Police searched the area and found a sawed-off rifle, leather bracelet with
> metal studs, leather belts, a baseball bat, and a bandolier with several empty
> bullet casings.*
>
> *Four youths—including Samuel (Sinbad) Gonzalez, president of the
> Chosen Ones—were arrested and charged with illegal weapons possession,
> defacing a firearm, criminal trespass and theft of services.*
>
> *The rest of the gang members escaped.*
>
> *Police said the Renegades and Chosen Ones had joined forces after the
> Sandmen beat up a member of the Chosen Ones and looted an apartment of
> the rival gang's president.*
>
> *— New York Post,* THURSDAY, OCTOBER 9, 1980

Connie is the leader of the Sandman Ladies, a female affiliate of the
Sandman based in Manhattan's Upper West Side. On October 9, 1980,
we were sitting together outside the city-owned apartment block in
which she lived. Concrete benches and tables had thoughtfully been
provided for the leisure hours of the residents, which, given the unemployment rate of the occupants, tended to be many. The seats had been
taken over that day by the gang members, who shifted uneasily between
surveying Broadway and Amsterdam avenues and returning to smoke,
drink, and talk at our table. Between Connie and I lay a brown paper
bag, which might have been taken for a beer can hidden from the police.
Gino, the leader of the Sandman, was at a downtown gang community
center, attempting to straighten things out between the Chosen Ones,
the Renegades, and his own gang. In his absence, Connie was in charge.
Conversation was stilted and tense, and Connie interrupted anyone who

spoke too long or too much, dispatching them to the corner to look out. At 3:30 Connie announced she had to go pick up her kid from school. The guys were told to keep watch. She pushed the bag toward me, telling me to use it if I needed it. It contained a .32-caliber gun. With that, Connie put on her sunglasses and left to collect her two-year-old daughter from the nursery.

In New York City there may be as many as four hundred gangs with a total membership between 8,000 and 40,000. Ten percent of those members are female, ranging in age from fourteen to thirty. Some are married and many have children. They are blamed as the inciters of gang feuds; they are described as "passive, property and promiscuous." They are accused of being more vicious than any male; they are praised for being among the few with enough power to curb male gang crime. For some they represent the coming of age of urban women's liberation, for others the denial of the best qualities of womanhood. The contradictions of their position have provoked speculation among the police, the media, and the public about their reasons for joining, their roles and way of life. Despite the volumes written on male gang members, however, little is actually known about the girls, the standard reason being that girls constitute such a small proportion of gang members and are responsible for an even smaller number of gang crimes. Writers have also found male gangs, apart from their criminological interest, to be revealing in far wider sociological and psychological ways.[1] Gangs have been discussed in terms of societal structure, class relations, rites of passage in adolescence, group cohesion, ecological pressures, learning mechanisms, even linguistic usage. Yet in most of these accounts too, girls are invisible or appear as a footnote, an enigma, an oddity.

Little enough is known in terms of hard numbers on the size of the gang problem generally, let alone on girls' involvement. In the sixties,

---

1. On societal structure see A. K. Cohen, *Delinquent Boys: The Culture of the Gang* (Glencoe, Ill.: Free Press, 1955); R. K. Merton, *Social Theory and Social Structure* (Glencoe, Ill.: Free Press, 1957); R. A. Cloward and L. E. Ohlin, *Delinquency and Opportunity* (Glencoe, Ill.: Free Press, 1960). On class relations see W. B. Miller, "Lower Class Culture as a Generating Milieu of Gang Delinquency," *Journal of Social Issues, 14* (1958): 5–19; E. Stark, "Gangs and Progress: The Contribution of Delinquency to Progressive Reform," in D. F. Greenberg (ed.), *Crime and Capitalism* (Palo Alto, Calif.: Mayfield, 1981). On rites of passage see H. Block and A. Niederhoffer, *The Gang: A Study of Adolescent Behavior* (New York: Philosophical Library, 1958). On group cohesion see M. Klein and L. Crawford, "Groups, Gangs and Cohesiveness," in J. F. Short (ed.), *Gang Delinquency and Delinquent Subcultures* (New York: Harper & Row, 1968). On ecological pressures see F. M. Thrasher, *The Gang* (Chicago: University of Chicago Press, 1927); C. Shaw, *Delinquency Areas* (Chicago: University of Chicago Press, 1929). On learning mechanisms see E. Sutherland and D. Cressey, *Criminology,* 10th ed. (New York: Lippincott, 1978). On linguistic usage see W. Labov, *Language in the Inner City* (Philadelphia: University of Pennsylvania Press, 1970).

for example, it was widely believed that gangs had finally disappeared. Absorbed into youth politics, some argued. Fighting in Vietnam, said others, or turned into self-destructive junkies. It seems likely that their disappearance was a media sleight of hand.[2] New York stopped reporting gang stories and the rest of the country followed suit. Gangs die out and are reincarnated regularly by the media whenever news is slow. As a phenomenon they have never been fully put to rest. When a crime involving a few teenagers from a poor area makes news, gangs "reappear" in New York City. When gangs return, they are not reinvented. Though they may be inactive for a few months or a few years, they are quietly living in the tradition and culture that has sustained them for over a hundred years in the United States.

Statistics on gang membership have only been available since the 1970s when police departments in major cities became sufficiently concerned about the problem to set up Gang Intelligence Units. In 1975, sociologist Walter Miller attempted to document the size of the gang problem in a government report.[3] He was criticized not only by academics but by members of the very police departments he interviewed for relying on gross estimates which in many cases were contaminated by changes in recording methods and poor record keeping. Often they were no more than informed guesses to unanswerable questions.

A more approachable question is the extent to which the roles girls   5 play in the gang have changed over time, but even this is not without difficulties. In reviewing a hundred years of writing on female gang involvement, it is difficult to separate the true nature of girls' involvement from the particular interpretive stance of the writer (usually male), whose moral or political view most probably reflects the prevailing community standards. These must have affected the girls too and the nature of their involvement in the gang. Nevertheless, certain themes appear consistently throughout the writing and reveal important factors in the girls' participation, as constants and as historical changes in their roles.

---

2. Estimating the size of gang membership generally has been a problem. Few cities keep statistics on gang membership and those that do use different definitions of gang, gang membership, and gang crime. These matters and the role of the New York City media are discussed in W. B. Miller, *Violence by Youth Gangs and Youth Groups as a Crime Problem in Major American Cities* (Washington, D.C.: U.S. Government Printing Office, 1975), and in W. B. Miller, "Gangs, Groups and Serious Youth Crime," in D. Schichor and D. Kelly (eds.), *Critical Issues in Juvenile Delinquency* (Lexington: Lexington Books, 1980). A more recent estimate of New York gang membership suggests that numbers have declined to 4,300 members in 86 gangs. This decline was contemporaneous with the dismantling of the Police Gang Intelligence Units in Brooklyn and the Bronx and so may represent a less sensitive estimate. See J. A. Needle and W. V. Stapleton, *Police Handling of Youth Gangs* (Washington, D.C.: U.S. Department of Justice, 1983).

3. Miller, *Violence by Youth Gangs and Youth Groups.*

Two factors can help in interpreting the roles of the girls. The first is the girls' class value orientation—their desire and ability to be upwardly mobile in terms of their life-style. Gang girls are almost unanimously working- or lower-class from the point of view of their parents' income and educational and employment status, but class value orientation is distinct from the reality of social class itself. Some of the girls described, while working-class, show a distinct desire to climb the social ladder. They value middle-class concerns such as the deferment of immediate gratification, long-term planning, and the desirability of self-improvement, and they also are able to deal effectively with middle-class institutions such as school and work. In the literature they are held up as "good girls." "Good girls" are feminine girls. It has been traditional to equate femininity with middle-class attributes (being well-groomed, charming, polite, passive, and modest), while masculinity is associated with working-class stereotypes (being direct, confrontational, nonverbal, physical).

Among the "good girls," some want to assume traditional complementary roles toward males. They look forward to a future as Good Wives, dependent financially and emotionally upon a man, living in a clean, decent apartment (perhaps not quite in the area of town to which they aspire) with children who are well dressed and who will grow up to better themselves in a respectable job as clerks or carpenters. Although this girl associates with a boy from the neighborhood gang, her aim is to save him from his rowdy friends who are clearly a bad element, bringing out the worst in him.

Some "good girls" assume relations with men that are not complementary but similar. These are the Independent Women. Ideally, they hope to go to college and become self-supporting with a decent job, as nurses, secretaries, or bank clerks. They may want children but do not want the financial dependence associated with total reliance on a man's income. If worse comes to worst, they will obtain welfare child allowance and raise the kids alone or with the help of their mother. They associate with the gang but only as an adolescent phase. They may go a little crazy as teenagers, but they are not lowlifes or bums. Nor do they plan to spend their lives in a grubby apartment, taking the children upstate on a bus every weekend to visit their father in prison.

The majority of gang girls, however, have a static class value orientation. They are not tortured by dreams of upward mobility and have a realistic view of their chances of success in society. They have not done well in school, and when they have money, they spend it (often when they don't have it as well). They watch television specials about the rich and famous but understand that, short of a win on the numbers, those life-styles are extravagant dreams. They certainly are not interested in the intermediate status of a lower-middle-class suburban life-style. Like the boys in the neighborhood, they enjoy excitement and trouble, which break the monotony of a life in which little attention is given to the future. They like sharp clothes, loud music, alcohol, and soft drugs. They admire toughness and verbal "smarts." They may not be going anywhere, but they make the most of where they are. Authority, in the shape of school, parents, and police, is the enemy but a welcome one since it generates confrontations and livens things up. Because these girls accept a lower-class value system, they are represented in the literature as "bad girls." Men may find dignity by being straightforward, unpretentious, and working class, but women do not.

Among the "bad girls," as within the "good girls," some take the   10 traditional complementary role toward their men. Boyfriends take precedence over same-sex friendships, and boys are the ones who really matter. Because of this, these girls see other girls as possible rivals and are constantly on their guard. The major focus of their quest for excitement lies in romances with the boys in which they assume a passive role. This passivity can make them the victims of unscrupulous males who may lead them into prostitution or drug addiction. Even if such a dramatic fate is avoided, their undisguised interest in sexual relationships has led them to be branded as Sex Objects by many writers (in spite of the fact that boys who show a similar interest in sex avoid this kind of labeling). The only time this type of girl escapes her passivity is when she provokes fights within and between male gang members by her promiscuous sexual behavior and her treacherous revelation of one boy's secrets to another. But even in this, her behavior has a traditional female quality: scheming, divisive, and nonconfrontational.

Some "bad girls" choose to compete with males on their own terms and are therefore considered in the literature as Tomboys. They insist on accompanying their men to gang rumbles and on joining in. They pride themselves on being tough and take particular pride in fighting and beating male gang members. To prove their toughness, they emulate typically male crimes such as robbery, burglary, and auto theft, and some achieve the distinction of being arrested and, more rarely and therefore more prestigiously, of being sent to jail. Like the males, they have strong same-sex friendships within the gang and pride themselves on their solidarity.

However, Sex Objects and Tomboys have much in common. Both have romantic and sexual relationships with the boys in the gang, but Tomboys give equal attention to their female friends. Both will engage in fights with female rivals for their man, but Tomboys fight for other reasons as well, whereas Sex Objects feel that fighting is usually a man's job. Both will use their femininity in the service of the gang by acting as spies with other nearby gangs, by luring unsuspecting male victims into situations where they are robbed or assaulted by the boys, and by carrying concealed weapons for the boys since as females they cannot be searched on the street by male officers.[4]

These types of roles tend to suggest a no-win situation for gang girls. As Sex Objects, they are cheap women rejected by other girls, parents, social workers, and ironically, often by the boys themselves. As Tomboys, they are resented by boys and ridiculed by family and friends who wait patiently for them to "grow out of it." Among lower-class women, the Independent Woman, as often as not, raises her children in an all-female household. In so doing, she becomes the target of government, academic, and media concern by those who accuse her of rearing a new cycle of delinquents or, if she works, of ousting the male from the labor force by taking low wages. Among the black population especially, as feminist writer Michele Wallace suggests, a covert war between the sexes may exist because of the male's perception of the Independent Woman as "castrating."[5] Clearly the most socially acceptable role is that of Good Wife. Yet even here the Woman is often characterized as the fun-spoiling petty bourgeoise who takes the high-spirited male away from his gang friends to a future of shopping expeditions and diaper changing. Perhaps this is an overdrawn picture, yet in a classic account of male gang life by William Whyte one can almost hear a groan from the author as two members of the Norton Street Gang fall in love with socially aspiring girls and leave their old street friends behind.[6]

A Day with Connie

Connie lives in the Upper West Side of Manhattan on the thirteenth floor of a project apartment building. You can spot her windows easily from the ground. A Puerto Rican flag hangs from one and heads bob in and out of the other to check what's happening on the street. Inside, the lobby is painted a pale lavatorial green and echoes with the laughter and shrieks of children in the nursery on the ground floor. It smells of a musty scent that covers the odor of chemical used to control cockroaches.

---

4. This discussion of class value orientation draws upon the work of Cohen, *Delinquent Boys,* especially his discussion of "college boys" and "corner boys," and of Miller, "Lower Class Culture as a Generating Milieu of Gang Delinquency." The views of these theorists on the value systems of gang members have been considered incompatible. The literature on female gang membership suggests that girls from the same class background differ in their adherence to middle- versus lower-class values or focal concerns.

5. M. Wallace, *Black Macho and the Myth of Superwoman* (New York: The Dial Press, 1978).

6. W. F. Whyte, *Street Corner Society: The Social Structure of an Italian Slum* (Chicago: University of Chicago Press, 1943).

The two elevators operate spasmodically. A ten-minute wait is not unusual.

No one answers Connie's door at first because the knocking is   15
drowned out by the thundering bass of the rap disco blasting out of radio
speakers. The door's spyhole cover opens, swings shut, and OK is standing there. He waves me through, smiling with exaggerated politeness.
In the corner of the living room, the color television is on with the
sound turned down, and quiz-show hosts grin and chatter idiotically. JR
is stretched out luxuriously on the sofa beneath a giant Sandman insignia
depicting a hooded face on an iron cross, which hangs on the wall. He
wears a yellow T-shirt that proudly states "I love Brooklyn," in graffiti
writing and a leather vest. A bottle of Colt 45 beer rests on the floor
next to him. Mico is in the kitchen, helping Connie bag up marijuana
for the day.

Connie, perched on a stool, looks up and smiles. She wears no
makeup and her hair, scrupulously clean, falls around her face. She is
small—five feet two—but the tall stool gives her a certain stature. Up
high by the window, she can see down onto the street. She is wearing
a check blouse, jeans, and two belts, one with a demonic goat's head
and the other apparently a chain from a BSA motorcycle. At the side of
one belt is a small leather case that holds a knife. Connie always carries
a flick knife and always in a visible place—as long as it is not a switchblade
(which shoots the blade forward from the handle) and it is not concealed,
the police will leave her alone. I pull up a chair and the three of us talk
over the blare of the radio, yelling to make ourselves heard or leaning
together conspiratorially to catch some complicated story.

In the mornings, Connie and Suzie, her daughter, get up early at
7:30. Suzie is fourteen, taller than her mother, and very capable. The
girlfriend of Connie's six-year-old son Raps comes by to pick him up
and often she dresses and feeds him as well. He is out of the house by
8:30. JJ, Connie's youngest son, has to be dressed and given breakfast
along with baby Dahlia. She and Suzie take him to school, put Dahlia
in the nursery downstairs, and sometimes manage to eat breakfast together in a donut shop. By 9:30 the kids are usually dispatched for the
day.

This particular Friday, Suzie has stayed home to help out and hang
around. Gino, Connie's husband and leader of the Sandman, is not going
to work today and is sleeping through the early morning hubbub. Connie
is happy to have all her family around her. As we talk, she bags up with
a dexterity she has developed over years—snipping up the grass and
packing it into tiny yellow envelopes. She seals each with Scotch tape
and then, with a small piece of cardboard, scrapes another bagful from
the white plastic bowl. We talk about jealousy. Connie leans over and
pulls a notebook out of the kitchen drawer. Each page has neat paragraph

entries, the visible results of years of sitting, thinking, bagging, and talking. She writes down each new insight about life and relationships.

This morning she announces that she has to get on with her "automated routines," so she gets up, washes the dishes, puts a pile of dirty T-shirts into the washing machine, and lights a cigarette. OK is now listening to the radio through headphones, but the volume is so loud that we can all hear it. JR has turned up the television and sits absorbed by a soap opera. Connie runs out of cigarettes and OK is sent to the store to buy a pack of Kools. Connie tells me about when she had Suzie at fifteen. After her fourth child at twenty-eight, Connie "closed down the factory." "I felt like a damn incubator. There has got to be some balance in life, but who should decide who's to live and who's to die?" she ponders as she slaps Scotch tape onto the tiny bags.

At one o'clock, Wolfy from the Satan's Wheels in the South Bronx arrives. He has a black handkerchief around his head, held in place by a piece of string, and wears a T-shirt and a cutoff denim jacket without gang insignia or "patches." Patches seen on the subway cause trouble. The guys get up to greet him as he comes into their clubhouse. They exchange news from different clubs, and Connie and I sit by, half-listening from the kitchen. From the bedroom comes a warm roar and Gino appears with arms outstretched to Wolfy. "Hey, hey, what's up?" They embrace and Gino's presence as leader is felt.   20

Connie divides the plastic bags and hands them to some of the guys who pull on their leather jackets and denim patches with SANDMAN MC NYC on the back and go out for the day to the street. Gino, wearing a black leather biker's cap with his leather jacket, jeans, and motorcycle boots, comes over and kisses Connie. Then he leaves to go down with the guys.

At 1:30, Shorty arrives. She is small and curly-haired, perhaps only nineteen. She is gang member Sinbad's girlfriend and wears her denim jacket over a blue sweatshirt. To be Sinbad's girlfriend is not a direct entry into the Sandman Ladies, however. She must prove her capability, just like anyone else who wants to join, and she has not yet earned her patches. Connie will decide when she deserves the title Sandman Lady. Connie says that she doesn't care about a girl's fighting history; what she looks for in a possible member are brains. Shorty is still learning. Later, when she answers the door and leaves it ajar as she tells Connie who it is, Connie tells her never, never to leave the door open. How does she know that someone they don't want to see isn't out there about to walk right in? Shorty nods. She sits in the living room quietly watching and listening to everything.

Connie's favorite song plays on the radio. She jumps up and whistles for Suzie to come in from the bedroom. Together they take over the living room floor, doing the hustle. Suzie acts the male's part perfectly, with minimum body movement and an expression of total boredom. At the end of the song, Suzie walks back to the bedroom and Connie, out of breath, laughs to herself. At 1:45, Connie's mother phones from Queens. Connie talks with her mother frequently on the phone but does not see her often. Her mother disapproves of the club, and Connie feels caught between duty and love.

Everything is quiet now. Family members have gone their ways for the day, and only Shorty sits quietly in the next room, clutching a hankie. Connie tells me more of her life story. When she was nineteen—eleven years ago—her father died. She shows me one of the letters he wrote to her while he was in the hospital for drug treatment. The handwriting is scrupulously neat. He complains that the doctors think he is crazy and tells Connie that if anything should happen to him, she should investigate it. He writes with great pride about Connie's new career in nursing and about his beautiful granddaughter (Suzie). Among his letters, Connie finds some official papers. One is a charge sheet from the police or a court, signed by a doctor, testifying that her father was found unfit to plead because of "imbecility." The other is a telegram from the hospital telling her that he is dead and asking her to make funeral arrangements. Connie never saw the death certificate and never knew what her father died from. Now she remembers his injunction and feels guilty. She never did check the circumstances of his death. She looks at the clock; it's time to go pick up the kids.

Halfway to the elevator Connie runs back to the apartment to get her sunglasses. Last week she got beaten up. Her nose was broken, she had stitches, and both her eyes puffed out. The swelling has gone down, but two plum-colored circles remain around her eyes. Until they go, the sunglasses are compulsory public wear. She has also changed into a pair of dark red boots—lovingly cared for with daily doses of cold cream—that are pulled over her jeans. Over her blouse, she wears a fur-lined leather jacket, a couple of sizes too big, and on top of that her patches. Sewn on the denim jacket are the full colors of the club: SAND-MAN NYC LADIES. With Shorty, we go into the weak afternoon sunshine. 25

Outside on a bench, Gino is recounting to the gang how the police beat him up when he had tuberculosis: "They beat the TB right out of me!" Sitting on the stone bench and the wall are seven club members all with their colors on. Wolfy and Lalla, a girl of twenty who deals around the area, are there too. Lalla wears a baseball cap back to front and a red jacket. She looks young and jumpy in comparison to Connie, severe and feminine, who sits on the stone chess table listening quietly while her husband speaks. Gino's story gets increasingly boisterous, and there is much laughter as they slap one another's hands in appreciation of the tale. The group appears insulated and self-contained. Their uniform jacket patches and their red bandannas divide them from the rest of the world. Nevertheless, neighbors, janitors, social workers, mothers of children who share Dahlia's nursery greet them as they pass, and Gino and the group wave back or shout "Hi. What's up?"

Dahlia stumbles out of the front lobby, watched by her teacher. She heads straight for Connie who picks her up, kisses her, and switches her shoes, which Dahlia has put on the wrong feet. Gino kisses Dahlia hello, and he and Connie decide who will go to pick up JJ from school. Gino goes, since he is usually at work these days and misses the daily ritual.

Every so often, someone approaches one of the group—the guy who is "holding" that day. The drug deal is transacted quietly. The girls sit separately. We talk about the neighborhood, about fights, about men. Now and again one of the guys asks for a cigarette or tells Connie something in Spanish connected with today's business. At the end of the day, all the money goes to Connie, who does the bookkeeping. Connie gives Suzie a couple of dollars from the roll of bills in her pocket to take Dahlia to the store to buy some candy. Today Dahlia gets some marsh-mallows, but Connie doesn't generally approve. She doesn't want her to get a taste for too much sugar.

Gino returns, and now the whole family is together. Raps, six years old, tells about a fight he had at school: "Yeah, I really dogged him. I fucked up his shit." Gino teases him about his ten-year-old girlfriend, offering some fatherly advice: "You tell that bitch that she can't carry your gaddam books to school no more." Everyone laughs except Raps, who looks down, embarrassed. He likes the attention but doesn't really know what is so funny. The teenage girls from the project are coming home from junior high school. As they pass, they greet Connie with a kiss, exchange a few words, kiss her cheek again, and go inside. They all know her and Suzie. Members of the club who have been at work or school arrive one at a time until there are fifteen of us. We each throw in a couple of dollars, and JC goes off to the liquor store. He returns with small plastic cups, a bottle of Coke, and some Bacardi rum. The girls' drinks are poured into the cups and are very strong. Sinbad notices me sipping at mine and instructs me to "Drink like a *woman*." The guys pass the liquor bottle around, drinking theirs neat. Before each one drinks, he pours a little of the rum on the ground in memory of those who are dead or in jail. The bottle ends up on the stone chess table in front of the girls, and the guys gravitate toward it. Gino and Wolfy speak half to each other and half to the kids who climb on and off the benches, threatening to upset the liquor. Raps drops his lollipop on the ground, and Gino picks it up, wipes it off, and pours Bacardi over it to sterilize it. Raps puts it back in his mouth and grimaces.

The conversation turns to Gino's time in Vietnam, where, he tells   30
us, he was a combat photographer. He tells how many of the injuries he saw were perpetrated by the Americans on themselves when incendiary bombs were dropped short of target or when machines backfired. He

was injured in the leg, but when the U.S. Army withdrew, his medical papers were lost. Now he has no way to prove that he is entitled to veteran's compensation, unless he were to take his case to court and that would cost him thousands. "If I had that kind of money, I wouldn't need their damn compensation, right?" Gino interrupts the story to wave and yell at a guy across the street who is something of a local celebrity because he had a role in *The Wiz*. Gino also sees two guys in surplus army jackets crossing the street—plainclothes cops. Gino watches as they enter a flower shop, which is a local drug-dealing center. Later, a local guy comes over to tell Gino that he followed them but they split up and went different ways.

It's 4:50 and it's getting colder. Gino announces we are going to a party tonight at the house of the president of Satan's Wheels in the Bronx. Upon hearing of the party, Connie, who has been standing back with Shorty, occasionally chatting to her, decides it is a good time to give Shorty her first patches. They disappear upstairs to sew them on her jacket and to check that Suzie can baby-sit. As we sit drinking, the daylight fades quickly. People coming home from work pass the apartment building in a steady stream. Some stare curiously at the group. Others, more familiar, simply hurry past. The light in the lobby spills out onto the concrete in front and the yellow streetlights come on.

Connie and Shorty return. Shorty spins around triumphantly to show off her new patches: LADY NYC. Later she will earn her final patch: SANDMAN. The guys yell and whistle and, led by Gino, pour bottles of beer over her head in traditional gang congratulations. She squeals. It's very cold by now and her hair is soaking wet, but she smiles and flicks back her curls with the back of her hand. Sinbad hugs her proudly.

Connie disappears and returns with a sandwich wrapped in silver foil from a local Spanish store. We pass it around and share it with the kids who have come downstairs. By now there are about twenty of us. From time to time, one of the guys comes over and looks through my notebook, curious to see what I have written down today. They borrow my pen to make illustrations, additions, or subtractions. Connie and I stand together. She points out females who pass by, some friends and some potential enemies. I am shivering from the cold, but Connie teases me that my knees are knocking at the thought of going to the South Bronx. There is talk that the Satan's Wheels will send a van to pick up everyone. That would be better than going by subway. On the subway, twenty people dressed in gang colors attract attention, which often leads to problems with the police. But the Sandman must wear their colors as a sign of pride in their club if they are going to another club's turf. Maybe they'll carry them over their arms on the train and put them on when they get out. Some of the guys who have come from work look tired. Gino tells them to watch out for being burned. If they fall asleep at the party he will set fire to their pants, a disciplinary custom that reminds members always to be on their guard when they are away from their own area.

Gino announces that we will go by subway but no one is to wear colors on the train. Five of us take the kids and their various toys and carts up to the apartment. Suzie has two girlfriends over for the evening and is playing disco music. Connie leaves a small bag of grass for them. Suzie tries for a pint of Bacardi too, but Connie refuses. Dahlia cries for her mother but quiets down when Suzie picks her up. We go downstairs after I have been given a plain denim jacket so I won't look completely out of place.

OK and Shorty carry down motorcycle helmets, which they offer to Gino. Gino asks what the hell they are for. OK protests that Gino told him to bring them. Gino says he didn't. OK mumbles some curse and turns away. Gino loses his temper and begins yelling at him. Everyone freezes and watches to see what will happen. OK does not say a word. Gino berates him for not listening, for not following orders, for being insolent. Wolfy, even though it is not his gang, joins in: "He's your leader. You'd better damn well respect him." OK, head down, walks away. Gino does not let up: "And don't you be sulking like that neither." OK seems to look happier afterward. Gino's threat to leave him chained to the iron fence at the edge of the project buildings is forgotten.

We walk in twos and threes to the subway station five or six blocks away. Gino stops to urinate behind a wall. I walk on with the Hulk, talking about his future, his school, his clothes. Connie calls out, "Hey, where's Annie?" She is looking out for me all the time. At the subway, Wolfy and I walk down the steps while the rest of the group gathers at the entrance. I put my token in the stile, but Wolfy walks through the swing doors without paying. The subway clerk calls him back, but he walks on. When Gino and the others appear, the clerk has already picked up the phone to call the transit police. Gino intervenes and pays everyone's fare, including Wolfy's. On the platform, he bawls Wolfy out, telling him it's crazy to get the cops down for the measly fare. Gino shows a roll of money in his pocket to reinforce the point. This is, after all, their turf. They have to use the subway all the time, so why make trouble? Wolfy is a guest and, as such, he should respect their turf.

Gino tells us to split up because we look too conspicuous in a group. Connie, Shorty, and I walk down the platform. Near us two black girls are casually rolling a joint. Connie watches them—there is something about their manner that she doesn't like. When we get on the train, one of them leans on the center post of the car, ignoring the available seats. Connie walks over and leans on the opposite post four feet away, staring at her through her dark glasses. They stare each other down, but the other girl breaks first. She looks away, then at her feet, then gets off the train. We change trains at 182nd Street. A train pulls in, but it's not the one we want to take. Inside a car, a man in his thirties, dressed in a suit, smiles at us. It isn't clear to me whether he is leering or laughing at us. As the train pulls away, Shorty smashes her fist at the window where his face is. He jumps back and the train disappears. Shorty clutches her hand. In a few minutes, it begins to swell and turn red, but she does not mention it.

We board our train. Two Puerto Rican girls are standing by the door, whispering and laughing. Connie watches them, wondering whether to "bug them out." She approaches them, but I cannot hear what is said. One girl reaches into her bag and pulls out some gum, offering Connie a stick. She takes one and offers it to me. I decline. Connie pops it in her mouth and leans over to kiss the girl on the cheek. Connie is smiling. The girls look pleased, embarrassed, and confused. The guys walk up and down the train in ones and twos, checking that everybody is on and knows where to get off. Although they are carrying their colors over their arms, they look conspicuous in their chains, boots, and bandannas. Some have sheath knives in their waistbands. Passengers watch their comings and goings uneasily.

We get off the train and climb the unlit stairs to the street. The guys take the girls' arms to guide us up. Several young girls are standing by the subway entrance. They seem excited at our arrival and particularly interested in Connie and Shorty with their patches. As we cross the street, Sinbad authoritatively holds up his hand to halt the oncoming traffic. We straggle along a side street, and Gino peers down an alleyway to a handball court where some kids are playing by floodlight. The game breaks up, and after a few seconds one of them appears in patches: FLAMES NYC. It is Felix, a friend of Gino. He greets all of us and cordially offers a small plastic cup of vodka and grapefruit juice, which we pass around. He has recently redesigned his club patches—from a swastika into a more complex design with a skull set in red and orange flames—and turns around so we can admire them. I reach out to touch them, wondering how he got such a complicated design so professionally done. Connie pulls my hand back and tells me that it is forbidden to touch someone's patches. And there are rituals surrounding them: They can never be taken off carelessly, but must be folded and laid down safely, they must always be worn with boots, never with sneakers.

Felix decides to escort us through his turf to the party, which is 40 several blocks away. He is on good terms with Satan's Wheels. We walk on down dark streets with huge empty tenements on either side. Doorways are covered heavily with graffiti and smell of urine. Connie, Shorty, and I walk at the rear, and Sinbad turns every few yards to make sure we are keeping up. Connie advises me to sit quietly at the party and be careful that nothing I do be misunderstood. I am white and, as such, am considered to be available property. Don't say too much and stick close to her, Connie says. We gaze around at the buildings. We are both completely out of our territory, although Connie points a few blocks

downtown to where she lived briefly years ago. She tells me this isn't a
real nice area. Broken bottles crunch under our feet. Finally we halt
outside a grocery store, waiting while Gino and Felix finish their discussion.

We walk into an old tenement building. The huge hallway is painted
crimson and lit by long fluorescent tubes. Initials and names are embla-
zoned on the walls. We walk up one flight of stairs and ring a doorbell.
After a few minutes, we are let in and walk down a hallway. Three or
four girls are sitting in a bedroom through some French doors. Gino
greets the guys in the club who are in the kitchen drinking, and Connie
goes into the bedroom. In perfect Spanish and very politely she introduces herself as head of the Sandman Ladies and thanks the girls for their
hospitality. They are much younger than she is and struggle to summon
an equally dignified reply. They are dressed casually, but when they
reappear several minutes later, they have put on sweatshirts that say
PROPERTY OF SATAN'S WHEELS NYC, with the name of their particular man underneath. Connie tells me that *her* girls don't belong to any
man.

We all assemble in the living room. Connie points out that the room
is "typically Spanish"—velour-patterned sofa and many mementos on
the tables and shelves; dolls, candles, crucifixes. The Satan's Wheels move
the sound system into the room. Bottles of beer and Bacardi are passed
around, interspersed with joints. When the music comes on, it is heavy
rock—Stones, Led Zeppelin, Pink Floyd—and is deafening. Conversation is possible only by leaning right up against the other person's ear.
The main lights go out, and the room is lit only by three ultraviolet
lights, which illuminate eyes, teeth, and the white in jacket patches. One
by one people begin to dance. Connie sits next to me on the sofa with
her back straight.

It is the Hulk's sixteenth birthday. Suddenly the lights are switched
on and he is drenched by several bottles of beer. He waves his arms,
apparently enjoying the experience. The floor is awash with liquid, but
one of the Satan's Wheels later mops up. Everyone is also scrupulously
careful to flick their cigarette ashes into ashtrays, rather than on the floor.
Amid the apparent chaos, there is a definite order. The Hulk moves
around the room, embracing every member of the club, and by the end,
we are all nearly as wet as he is. Gino spends most of the evening in the
kitchen, discussing club business with the Flames and Satan's Wheels.
Connie and I sit together drinking. Everybody is loosening up. Chino
gets his beard set alight as a reminder that he is getting a little too loose.
He climbs onto the fire escape and peers down, announcing that he is
contemplating suicide. Then he laughs.

Connie and I, as we drink more, consider the implications of everything in the world being a product of our imagination. If we wished it
all away now, only *we* would remain, suspended sixty feet in the air,

discussing this very thought. A guy next to me searches vainly for some matches. I hand him some and Connie warns me about body contact. If you touch someone accidentally, they may take it the wrong way. I move away from him, suddenly aware that I have been half-leaning on him. Connie motions me to lean forward and tells me that if we keep talking together, maybe the guys will assume that I'm with her. That way, I'll be safe. Gino returns to sit by us. He and some other guys are throwing a bottle back and forth with eyes closed, a kind of test of everybody's reaction speed. I notice Connie's hands loose in her lap but ready in case it is thrown her way. The music changes to disco—a whole album side of it—and Connie gets up to dance alone.

It is after midnight and I decide to leave. Connie forces twenty   45
dollars into my hand for a cab. Gino assigns two guys to walk me to the taxi office. Everybody yells goodnight, and I make my way back home.

Reading the Text

1. Why, according to Campbell, has so little been written about female gang members?
2. What are the various roles that female gang members are seen as playing?
3. Why has Connie achieved the status of leader of the Sandman Ladies?
4. How must Campbell, as a nongang white woman, adjust her verbal and body language when she is with the gang members?

Reading the Signs

1. In class, write on the board the various roles that female gang members assume ("Sex Objects," "Tomboys," and so forth). Discuss the extent to which these roles are available for "mainstream" women not involved with gangs. What do these roles say about the power of gender roles in both mainstream cultures and countercultures?
2. Compare the male and female gang members whom Campbell describes. What does gang involvement seem to mean to each gender? What different roles do males and females play in the gang? Use your observations to formulate an argument about gender roles in Connie's gang; you may want to consult Holly Devor's "Gender Role Behaviors and Attitudes" (p. 603) as you write your essay.
3. Write an essay in which you explore the nature of the relationship among the gang members described in this selection. In what ways does Connie's gang operate as a "family"? And to what extent does her gang redefine traditional notions of what an American family is like?
4. How do symbols and rituals work to define Connie's gang as a group? Write a semiotic reading of the signs that the Sandman Ladies use to communicate gang affiliation, both to outsiders and to each other.

5. To what extent do the gang members described by Campbell share the "hunger for more" that Laurence Shames discusses (p. 25)? How do you account for your conclusions?

SONIA MAASIK
AND JACK SOLOMON

Signs of the Street: A Conversation

||||||||||||||||||||||||||||||||||||||||||||||||||||

Too often, gangs are interpreted by adults—especially white middle-class professionals—who have no personal experience of gang life, nor any direct knowledge of the social conditions in which youth gangs flourish. One of the best ways to learn about gangs, however, is to speak with those who are associated with them. To see what the kids themselves had to say, the authors of this book visited a Los Angeles high school that offers former gang members an opportunity to complete their secondary school education. The following conversation reveals what a group of some twenty-five students at the West Valley Occupational Center school think about such issues as gang fashion, suburban wannabes, and the value that gang membership holds for those who belong to them. All names of students have been changed to protect their identity.

Can you describe for us what sorts of clothing you see on the streets these days?

JORGE: Baggy pants, skate clothes, stuff like that. Look around, and everybody wears baggy pants.

Do you know when people started wearing baggy pants? About?

JORGE: Well, early you know, like maybe in the forties or back in the thirties.

LUIS: It came out with the zoot suits.   5

OSCAR: Well, gang members had to like the same thing, you know. Gangsters still stay the same.

JORGE: Designers are wearing baggy pants, just like gangs. Recently, everybody's started wearing them within probably the past what? Maybe year, two, three years.

MIKE: It started getting really crazy around two years ago.

JORGE: You know about sagging? Where they used to sag a long time ago?

LUIS: Oh, that started about, like, forty years ago. I think sagging came   10
out with the black people first. It started with the brothers.

HANK: It was rappers that came first. Remember that song about saggin'
pants? It was Ice-T.

RUDY: And colors. You know, a guy may wear like red, mustard colors.
And other guys wear dark colors. Everyone belongs in a group, and
you can tell him by the way he dresses.

*How are Nikes these days? A few years ago Nikes were just the shoe. What's
going on now?*

HANK: They're gangbanger shoes.

OSCAR: A lot of crooks wore 'em. And the Bloods would wear the all-   15
red ones with a little red stripe, but now they're trying to get
conservative and they wear black and then have just a little red
somewhere. They like dressing down, but they'll let you know
where they're from.

Any sneakers that you just wouldn't be seen dead in?

TONY: Crow Wings! They're just cheap, you know, you can get 'em at
Penney's for like 10 bucks.

RUDY: Reeboks are cool. Everybody wears Reeboks.

OSCAR: Converse. Converse, man. Converse.

HANK: Converse are gangbanger shoes.   20

LATISHA: Some taggers like the versatile Converse. They have lowtops,
hightops, different colors, suede, you know, like that.

*Is there anything that you wouldn't wear at school, but would wear at home or
in your neighborhood?*

OSCAR: Pajamas!

LUIS: You wouldn't wear clothes with your gang on it. You can't wear
that in school 'cuz you get in trouble. Or clothes in remembrance
of a friend that died.

BRIAN: You can't even wear a hat to school, 'cuz they think it's gang-   25
related.

*Two guys here are wearing shorts: one pair are blue denim cutoffs and the other
are plaid cutoffs. Do you read those two guys differently?*

JORGE: Geeks, geeks! That's a skater.

And the plaid is what?

GARY: Surfer.
TERESA: And gangsters wear cutoff Dickies.   30

What do cutoffs say to guys on the street?

JORGE: You're a gang member. And they have to be Dickies. The make
 is important. The brand style.
TERESA: And they're ironed. All the gang members iron. They can't be
 all wrinkled. They want to show their respect, that they care for
 themselves.
LUIS: Gangsters are the ones that crease it, even their boxer shorts, man!
 It's the respect they have when they go on the street. They want
 people to see that they try to look good for other people.
TERESA: Well, you're not going to see a gang member going in the   35
 street with wrinkled clothes, you know? They just don't look right.

Is there anything else that they do to show respect?

ALICIA: Short haircuts. It's got to be clean cut. It shows they respect
 themselves and they want respect for their gang.
OSCAR: And bald people. Bald means that they're gangbangers.

Bald is a code word. Do you really mean shaven head?

MIKE: Well, it means two different things. One's a gangbanger. But my   40
 head's shaved all the way around, all the way under and I have hair
 on top. When I shaved my head, I shaved it clean. Because I'm not
 Hispanic or I'm not black, I immediately looked skinhead. So it has
 something to do with the color you are. I have a goatee and a full
 shaved head. I was fully labeled a skinhead, right off.

*I don't think there are any skinheads in the room now. That way nobody needs
to feel defensive. What about the skinheads? What do you think about them?*

TONY: They're mostly all white power.
MIKE: That's bull, dude. They're not.
BRIAN: You're so wrong, dude. You guys have such a misconception
 of the skinheads. There are so many skinhead groups that are totally
 against racism and stuff like that. Like shark skinheads.

MIKE: There's a lot of groups like that, you know there's groups like   45
Ghost Town Skinheads and there're Nazi skinheads and stuff like that.

BRIAN: But there's Peace Punk, stuff like that. And they won't wear
leather and stuff like that or do things like killing animals or hurting
the environment. And people just have misconceptions and think
that if you're white and got a shaved head, you're like a Nazi, you're
a skinhead and you're a racist toward everyone. But that's not the
way it is.

LATISHA: Don't you think that that's the image they project to us? And
that image is what most of the skinheads are about?

BRIAN: That's what you see, that's what you see on the media. That's
what you see on TV.

LATISHA: Okay, so what makes the difference if I see a white guy
walking down the street and he just baldheaded? I have never met
one skinhead who ain't racist toward a black person.

MIKE: I think everyone pretty much has a little bit of racism in them.   50
Everybody's against every race.

BRIAN: But there's a lot of different groups, I'm telling you. See, the
media makes it seem like skinheads are, you know, the epitome of
racist people. The majority of skinheads are probably racist, but a
lot of them are not. People give skinheads bad names and that's not
cool.

Is it useful to you to be able to figure people out by the way they dress?

TONY: On the street, yeah. If you're walking by yourself, and you see
a bunch of people, you just don't want to get involved.

MIKE: You know that people mess with each other out on the streets.
Me and him, we were just skating at a parking lot and a car full of
guys drives up and they scream out some names. They scream out
these nicknames, and if we start talking back, then that's how things
happen, you know. Just by their appearance you can see stuff coming. Their cars even tell you.

JORGE: Yeah, Impalas and Regals, '65 Impalas.   55

You can read a car real quick?

MANY: Yeah.

What are the cars?

HANK: Cadillacs, Regals, Impalas, older cars.

LUIS: In the olden days, they used to drive old cars. Now they're trying   60 to keep the tradition of those old cars. All you see today is pure *raza*,[1] just driving old cars so they look good.

How do you and your friends in your neighborhoods feel when you see in movies or on television or on the streets obviously rich, generally white kids trying to dress up like gangsters? What do you think when you see that?

TERESA: Stupid!

JORGE: We laugh at them. We laugh.

OSCAR: They try to dress like us, they're trying to make a statement, like they are like we are. But if somebody approach 'em or something, they'd be the first one to back down and run away or something like that. And that ain't cool.

TERESA: They're trying to be like everybody else, trying to fit in.   65

TONY: They're just wannabes.

When I ask you where you're from, what does that question really mean?

JORGE: What gang we're from, what neighborhood.

LUIS: You know what? They can dress like gangs, but they have to show it. They have to prove themselves.

So it's something more than just the clothing?   70

LUIS: You gotta have heart for it.

JORGE: A lot of people that dress up like that, they're starting in rich, rich areas, they're starting to like get their own little gangs and they're starting to tag up the walls there, and they're starting to do the same stuff that's going on out here.

RUDY: They imitate everybody else, they try to dress the same way.

So if it's your own style, it's cool, but, if you try to take somebody else's style that you haven't earned, that's kind of dumb?

TERESA: There's a lot of people, just to fit in they'll dress like gangsters,   75
but they ain't about shit. They're punks. It's true, man. Say, my brother or my cousin sees someone dressed like a gangster and they ask, "Where were you from?" He says, "I'm not from nowhere, I just like the way I dress." He straight out says it. He acts like he's from somewhere, but he's just scared to say he's afraid, but that's stupid. Why you gonna dress like that if you're not gonna be down for your group?

---

1. **raza**   Refers to *la raza,* the race or Hispanic people.—EDS.

I've heard that some guys like to wear tattoos and those tattoos mean something. Why do people tattoo?

OSCAR: Most Chicanos, they like getting tattoos, like naked girls, Aztec warriors. It has to do with *la raza,* to do with their race. See, other guys, other races, they can get other kinds of tattoos, like cats, like lions.
BRIAN: That's like a totally different thing.

I notice the letters. Why'd you pick those letters (points to Gothic lettering on one student's tattoo)?

LUIS: Because that's like gang letters. It's the old style.   80
LATISHA: I think the Hispanics started it, but black people like it too, you know.

What about the three dots on the hand? Is that where they go?

ALICIA: Um, like about right here *(points),* between my thumb and my first finger. You can put them anywhere else too. You could put 'em on the elbow or the wrist.

What if you saw somebody from the suburbs with three dots that obviously weren't really tatoos, but just kind of a wash-off tattoo, with three dots on their wrist, what would you think?

JORGE: I'd ask 'em why it's there and what kind of life do you have?   85
TERESA: A fake tattoo! Like, what are they trying to prove? To make it look hard?
BRIAN: If you can't take the ink, don't draw on yourself. If you're not down to getting drawn on, then, you know, don't start playing with pens drawing things.
TERESA: I know, but what are they trying to prove? If they get one, then get a real one.
OSCAR: One thing I want to point out, see, it doesn't really matter the way you dress.
LUIS: Yeah. Because you can dress the dorkiest-assed person on the   90
planet, but you could be still a gang member, and if you're that gang member and dress so dorky you could have a lot of heart for that gang that you're from. It doesn't really matter how you dress. You could dress like some different type of style, but still you have heart for that neighborhood that you got jumped in to. It doesn't matter the way you dress. It doesn't.
OSCAR: It's how people perceive you, how people look at you. All that matters is what you have inside your heart.

MIKE: It's what society puts on teens. It's the way society says, "This is how these people dress, this is how these people dress, this is how these people dress." No questions. And it's fucked up. It sucks.

TERESA: But you know what? The media puts everything so wrong when they talk about kids, but it's not the story.

Can you think of something that's really dead wrong that the media does?

LUIS: Oh, yeah. Like in the news or in radio, when they talk about   95
gangs, like Hispanic gangs. They make us look bad. They always talk about the things we do bad, like, "Oh, another drive-by," but they never talk about when one of us Hispanics graduates or does something good, become a doctor or something like that. They only talk about the bad about us and that's one thing I don't really understand. Why do they have to talk about things that are bad about us? I think there's good stuff and there's bad stuff here. Like us, you know, everybody in this class, we're *raza,* they're black, they're white, but we go to this school, we can learn and try to make something of our lives.

JORGE: Man, I'm a gang member, but I don't go up against society. I'm gonna be up there on top of everybody else, we can do it too, you know. It don't matter the way that you dress. I could be gang member, but hey, I'm smart too. I could do the same thing other people could do.

LUIS: Yeah, I could go to college.

OSCAR: Last night, I was listening to the radio and they were talkin' about gangs, and I didn't like it, 'cuz they were talkin' about just the bad part: We kill people and we shank.

JORGE: Well, you don't?

OSCAR: No . . . all gang members don't. Most gang members get into   100
a gang because they're scared of other people, you know. They need somebody to be around, they need a base, like a family, 'cuz see, most gang members don't have love at home so they join the neighborhood. They want the love your family can't give you.

LUIS: It's like, say your mom and your dad are ignoring you or something, you go to your neighborhood, and they pay attention to you, you know, they cheer you up. They're there for you, they give you love.

OSCAR: Let's say if I got kicked outta my house, I could go with my homeboy right here, I could go to his house and kick back as long as I want. You know, they'd take care of me.

LUIS: We're always there for each other. No matter what. Thick and thin. We're family.

OSCAR: I'm gonna show you guys. You guys want to hear a rap about love?

TONY: All right! Listen, listen.

105

OSCAR: All right, here we go . . . (*rapping*) This is a story about a young kid, about his life and things he did. Young kid, he wants to join a gang. He wanta live his life in the fast lane. Hold out with the troubles in the neighborhood, doing little things that he never should. Robbing, stealing, beating up *gente*,[2] rocking around saying things like these. Dressed down, khakis and a white T-shirt standing proud and tall. *Todos vatos, todos vatos*[3] they jump me in. I want to gangbang with you, my friends, and todos step to the *calle*,[4] rock it down to L.A. from the *valle*.[5] It was accomplished, you did what I said, when he made the promise. He promised himself one day he'll be a man. I don't think they truly understand. He gonna grow like one day working, now he's watching his back in order to live, so he tries the gang. For the very first time, first time in his life that he got high. He dropped out of school at the age of twelve. People said he messed up, he said, "Oh, well." He doesn't care about anything, 'cuz now he steps on up to cocaine. He could care less about the things he lost, because this is the story about a rebel without a cause.

(*Applause.*) *What do you guys think when you hear that? Where did rap come from?*

HANK: It's just like nursery rhymes. A nursery rhyme is a rap. All you gotta do is speed it up or slow it down.

LATISHA: Yeah, it's like poetry. Before it was just instinct, it just happened. But now they really rappin' mean stuff.

TERESA: They rap to make a record, but now they're rappin' to mean something. Messages are being sent by rap.

110

We're interested in what you understand when you see graffiti on the wall, how you can know who did it and what it means. There're all sorts of differences, aren't there?

HANK: First of all, you know who it is 'cuz they write their name on the wall. Then you'll basically know what gang they are. Anywhere you go, you can tell if it's a tagger writing or if it's gang writing.

---

2. *gente*   People.—EDS.
3. *todos vatos*   All these guys.—EDS.
4. *calle*   Street.—EDS.
5. *valle*   Valley.—EDS.

How?

JORGE: By the way they write. Most taggers kinda handwrite, mostly handwriting with a big, big spray can. You know, gangbangers they do block letters, little blocklike letters. They use different kinds of letters, different styles.

LATISHA: There's another thing with taggers. When I used to tag—I 115
don't do it anymore—but when I used to hang with a tagger crew, when we wrote, we used different kinds of ink, like scribe and streaks. Being original, you can cut half of one and cut half of the other and put it in one pen and make it double like it's rainbow color.

What's a scribe?

LATISHA: Scribe is when you carve it on a window. You can carve your name on it.

TERESA: It looks like crayon chalk. You can carve wood and you can carve it in a bus window.

What do you think when you see people in the suburbs becoming taggers?

JORGE: They're trying to prove a point. 120
OSCAR: They're trying to get their space. That's what everybody wants in this whole world, you know, to gain your respect. And writing on the wall is doing it or the way you dress is doing it. There's all kinds of ways of gaining respect. That's what everybody wants. No matter what race you're from, you know, black, white, Hispanic. The point is, everybody just wants respect, okay? Sometimes being in the gangs gets you that respect or being a tagger gets you that respect from other taggers. You know, it depends where you're coming from.

LATISHA: That's true, because when I was in junior high I used to gangbang with a Mexican gang, me and another black girl. I tried to go with them because I used to get picked on by a lot of girls, because I came from a small town, I used to be like a school girl. Everybody used to pick on me and then I was talking with one of my friends and she was in the gang and she was like, "Well, you can come kick it with us." But after a while, kicking it became more. I started dressing like them and doing my hair like them, everything. And I just changed completely. Then I got picked on again for acting like a Mexican girl wannabe. But when I walked with them and we all walked around that junior high, we all had respect and they all looked at me like, you know, "I ain't gonna mess with her." But then, after that, I went to taggers because I found out that the Mexicans didn't really want to hang with me. The taggers I went to were an all–black gang in L.A., and then I had respect with them too.

LUIS: You see, in the old days, the way we, *la raza,* used to get respect was by throwing one on one. Fighting. But now, no one don't throw no blows at each other, they just pull out a gun and bam, right there. One minute just takes your life away.

ALICIA: Another thing about the imitation is that I know a lot of gangsters think taggers try to imitate them by carrying a gun or something.

TERESA: Actually there's a lot of real gangsters, who are older, like in 125 their twenties and stuff, they always say that the taggers are trying to copy them. When they see them, they chase them out of their 'hood.

Any other stories you want to tell?

TONY: Sometimes you're going down the street, and you see a gang member by the way he's dressed. But sometimes he's not even a gang member, you know, his clothes don't necessarily mean he's in a gang. He wears it for his race. They just want to get their own respect by themselves.

OSCAR: Many people think that, when gang members go to a white party, everybody treats 'em different. Just like about two weeks ago, I went to some white party and I asked for something to drink, and people just gave it to me and they wanted to open it up for me. They gave me respect. I swear to God, man, he opened it for me and he said, "Here you go, would you like anything else?"

TONY: That's what they do in the stores, they try to just hurry up and give you what you want before you get mad and you tear up something.

HANK: I know if I get mad I'm gonna tear up something and then leave. 130 Somebody say I can't have something and I ask politely and they look at you like you got shit on your face. And you be ready to swing on somebody, real quick. And that's what they trying not to have. They don't want to get in a fight with you 'cuz they know you kick ass.

OSCAR: Yeah, when you go to the store, the first thing they say is, "Do you need something?"

HANK: I get sweat all the time. Every time I walk through a store, I get sweat, I get followed, I get asked questions. Every time.

Reading the Text

1. How is clothing used as a signaling system on the street?
2. What is the value of gang membership, according to the students?

3. What attitudes do the students have toward suburban gang wannabes?
4. How do the students feel about skinheads?

Reading the Signs

1. Gang culture is often depicted in the media as a counterculture. Basing your discussion on the students' comments, write an essay in which you explore the extent to which this depiction is valid. Why do you think, for instance, that Luis so frequently refers to tradition and *la raza*?
2. In class, have one student sing Oscar's rap, and discuss your responses to it.
3. What role does gang membership have in forming a teen's identity, especially a teen living in the inner city? Write an essay in which you formulate your own argument. In addition to "Signs of the Street: A Conversation," you might consult Léon Bing's "Faro" (p. 540) and Anne Campbell's "The Praised and the Damned" (p. 544).
4. What response do you think the students would have to Carl Rogers's "Children in Gangs" (p. 535)? In class, role-play a conversation between Rogers and some or all of the students, being sure to articulate issues on which they might agree as well as disagree.
5. "Respect" frequently surfaces as an issue in the students' conversation. In your journal, compare what respect means to the students with what it means to you. Do you define respect in similar ways, and if so, how? If not, how do you define it? What might you say to the students about their notions of respect?

JAMES   DIEGO   VIGIL

Gang Styles: Cholo Dress and Body Adornment, Speech, Demeanor, Partying, and Car Culture

||||||||||||||||||||||||||||||||||||||||||||||||||

Thanks to Hollywood, the dress codes of L.A.'s most notorious street gangs, the Bloods and the Crips, are well known throughout the country. Less well known is the fact that most street gangs in Los Angeles are Hispanic, and that the "cholo"—or Hispanic—subculture has its own dress codes and signaling systems that have nothing to do with red and blue bandannas. In this study of the semiotics of the cholo style, James Diego Vigil (b. 1938) describes the clothes, cars, body language, and life-style of L.A.'s Hispanic street gangs as they appeared in the 1980s. Things have changed some since Vigil's study, however. Khakis and plaids have been replaced by baggy black Dickies chinos and white T-shirts, and the "bald," or shaven-headed, look is in. But no matter what look prevails at any given time, Vigil's study shows how gang styles are signaling systems used both to bond the gang together and to warn outsiders at a glance with whom they are dealing. James Diego Vigil is a professor of anthropology at the University of Southern California and is the author of Barrio Gangs: Street Life and Identity in Southern California *(1988), from which this selection is excerpted, in addition to* From Indians to Chicanos: A Sociocultural History *(1980) and* Cultura Chicana *(with Steve Arvizu and Sam Rios, 1985).*

Group affiliation often entails embracing the external signs that characterize the group. Gangs, like many youth groups, are notorious for encouraging their members to dress, talk, and act in a certain way to show that they belong and identify with peers. Such behavior serves a number of purposes. Aside from the obvious show of group conformity, gang members also have practical reasons for adopting this image. Clothing is usually the first signal that novitiates send out to advertise their new social and personal identity.

George Barker (1950, 1972) has long reminded us that the cultural and linguistic differences among Mexican Americans stemmed in large measure from the effects of Anglo-American culture contact. Particularly noteworthy was the tendency among the American-born youth to establish their own group cultural style (at first known as *pachuco*) and to "correspondingly reject the conventional social standards of the Anglo and Mexican communities" (p. 46).

Cholo Dress

It is fairly certain that the cholo subcultural experiences helped produce the clothing styles. As with other low-income people who try to stretch their dollars, the cholos have sought to find dependable, comfortable, durable, and reasonably priced clothing; even the expensive shirts and shoes are recognized as long-wearing and lasting. Cost considerations have also influenced the cholos to limit the wardrobe to simple and interchangeable items. One good shirt and several T-shirts and pants of the same make and color are usually almost all that are needed for a wardrobe. Borrowing and exchanging clothes among friends, especially of shirts that have a different plaid design and color, is a way to expand one's wardrobe and is a fairly common intragroup habit.

The cholo style began about the same time that the group was recognized as an urban problem source. The perpetuation of the style stems in part from present youngsters' desiring to maintain the traditions of the past; in fact, the recent hit play (1978) and movie (1981) *Zoot Suit* and popular barrio-oriented magazines like *Low Rider* and *Q.V.* have generated renewed interest in these styles, with some shops, like El Pachuco in Fullerton, specializing in such wear. Thus, along with the functionality of the clothing style, barrio tradition plays a significant role. It is a way to identify with the past, one's roots so to speak, by dressing like someone from the past.

Although the style has undergone slight variations and additions, it nevertheless has remained relatively unchanged through the decades. Khaki pants, for example, became fashionable after World War II and the Korean War. It was the youngsters' way to identify with older brothers and relatives who had been in the armed services, especially those serving in such elite bodies as the paratroopers and marines. Although other pant styles (e.g., "counties" or "Frisco" bluejeans, a carry-over from county detention facilities) have also been used, it is the khakis that have persisted. Today, the pants are "stylish" if they are large and baggy (some even call them "baggies"), heavily starched with a crease that wearers try not to bend, and worn with a long and unrolled hem hiding the heels of the shoes. Ironically, and perhaps predictably, the pants style stemmed from public sources—military and penal; there is even a cutoff, below-the-knees jeans style and, lately, other multicolored styles that have been introduced by youth just out of a penal institution.

Shirt and shoe styles have remained remarkably stable over time. Creatively combining two types of shirts from the 1940–1950 period (e.g., long sleeve nonvariated gabardine and short-sleeved plaid "Sir Guys"), the present-day cholo relies on the long-sleeved plain shirt, known generically as "pendletons." Worn with all buttons fastened, shirt tails outside, often in an oversized fit, the pendletons usually are darker hued and complement the lighter tan khakis. If the weather is warm, a person might methodically drape the shirt over a forearm and instead sport a bright white crew-neck T-shirt or tank top undershirt. Shoes are usually of two kinds: the long, tapered-toe Imperials, similar to the Florsheim french-toes of earlier decades (but less expensive), and either Hush Puppies or deck shoes, known as "winos." Imperials are kept highly polished, and with the starched khakis and clean T-shirt or pendleton, a cholo shows a great deal of pride in dress appearance. Trench coats are not as common as before, but one still observes cholos who wear them.

Hair styles and head adornments have also contributed to the distinctiveness of the cholo. Similar to other prison-life influences, the current hair style is shortly cropped, about one-half to an inch of hair, combed straight back, and neatly trimmed around the ears and neck to affect a rather conservative appearance reflective of youth camp and prison requirements; sometimes a hair net is worn to train unruly hair to stay down. Earlier styles were longer, especially during the pachuco "greasy-kid-stuff" era and to a lesser degree the 1960s "hippie" period. Head adornments, beginning with broad-brimmed fedoras of the 1940s, have always been a major feature of dress. While some individuals might occasionally sport such hats, the present custom is to wear a stingy-brim version or a watchcap beanie and baseball cap, depending on personal resources and tastes. Since the 1960s Chicano movement emphasized indigenous customs, it has become fashionable to wear bandanas around the head, much like a "Barrio Warrior" (Frias 1982); lately, earrings also have become commonplace.

Young females in every barrio have also taken up this style and with slight variations have fashioned a chola appearance, especially for those who identify with the gang. Obviously, some dress items differ; blouses and female T-shirts and polo shirts replaced the male types, and cords and regular jeans joined the "baggies" and khaki pants wear. The manner of arranging the hair has remained rather traditional, in that Mexican women appear, beginning in the 1940s at least, to prefer long, natural hair. Cholas favor this natural look, as their tresses flow in long strands down their back and the sides of their head. Facial makeup, especially around the eyes, is quite a different story, as a lot of mascara and white shadow base paint are the custom. Long, fake eyelashes and overly plucked eyebrows with new thin eyebrows drawn in higher on the forehead stand out in the white eye-shadow background that covers all of the area around the eyes—from the bottom of the eyes to the eyebrows, and from the corner of each eye to the temple region. This "peacock-hued eye shadow beneath thin, high eyebrows," as one observer said (Morrison 1983), is an integral part of the chola front. Dark, heavily applied lipstick complements the eye makeup.

The style has become pervasive throughout Southern California, for it is the easiest cholo facet to adopt. Without thinking, talking, feeling, or acting, one can just dress up and appear to be a cholo in the eyes of observers. Some adopt the style because it is both fashionable and adaptive. In effect, it conjures up the image of a group behind you, even if you are not what you represent. There is a certain amount of security created in that pause when an observer has to think about your social ties. It often works as a deterrent. However, it can also operate as a challenge, especially to a rival barrio observer.

Adoption of the dress style marks one's closer associations to the   10
barrio gang. Of the over one-half of the youngsters who spoke of the style, most mentioned it as a source of group affiliation. Joining the gang often meant dressing like the others. There is even a change in behavior when the dress style is adopted, like when someone dons a uniform or fancy clothes, as I observed on numerous occasions with Want-to-Be's (someone who desires to be like a cholo and so dresses and acts the part). Descriptions of group thinking, behavior, and events are often punctuated by mentioning how they were dressed. A twenty-year-old female from East Los Angeles said during an interview: "When we wanted revenge [for a gang retaliation] we would go to their part of town in our Levi's and khakis really creased and a boyfriend's pendleton. We

thought we were fancy. But nobody could whip our ass." For most, then, dress style aids group identification. However, some individuals were very flexible about shifting to other dress styles when a new image was required. This was a way of managing their social front when they had another purpose in mind. An El Hoyo sixteen-year-old male made this point quite clear in an interview, even though he was a regular gang member: "But this girlfriend I have isn't a chola. When I go over to my girlfriend's house, I dress regular, with slacks and a dress shirt, and walk regular, without trying to be a *chingón*."

Wizard, a regular gang member (whose life history case was noted earlier), exhibited the same flexibility: "I used to wear football jerseys and things like that to look not like a cholo, but to look more respectable. . . ."

Having undergone the choloization process early in life, there was no question that these males were recognized and accepted as cholos. Changing their dress, for them, meant changing social roles, especially to confuse observers. Changing dress styles can also be understood as a matter of survival: One can remain incognito when visiting a girlfriend or committing a crime or, as in the cases of Latinos and some Chicanos on the periphery of cholo life, avoid trouble by giving the appearance that one is "trouble." One eighteen-year-old male from Ontario, however, describes how an otherwise normal youth social activity can be tainted by appearance: "Dressing like a bad *vato* doesn't pay off because to every party and dance you go it seems that someone always has to hit you up. . . . they treat you like you are from a different world."

Clothes help create this different world. However, other gestural and demeanor patterns also reflect the cholo style. Though cholo attire is important and comprises a large proportion of the total social image, it must be examined in the context of other image characteristics.

Nicknames, Tattoos, and *Placas*

Body adornments in the form of tattoos are a worldwide practice and in recent decades have become a common-enough occurrence for street youth in American cities. Explanations for this phenomenon are varied—adolescent body concerns, peer conformity, and hidden sadomasochistic desires—but in the Chicano case it appears to largely revolve around personal and social issues. The personal nickname and barrio name that make up the tattoo reflect this reality. Nicknames are created and assigned by fellow gang members to signify acceptance, and a person who places a tattoo on his or her body (nickname and barrio) confirms the alliance. Often there are public "tattoos" in the form of *placas* (literally, plaques, but used to indicate graffiti) on walls and fences to publicize a person's affiliation and commitment (Poirier 1982). The use of tattoos and placas to demonstrate personal identity in the gang is, thus, a gesture of multiple origins.

Nicknames, or stylized regular names, are often the centerpiece of   15 personal tattoos and public graffiti, a habit often associated with gangs (Bloch and Niederhoffer 1958:99). In part, it is the adolescent's way to capture and caricature peer quirks and by the naming make them accepted and normal; it's as if poking fun publicly works to destigmatize a funny or odd personal quality. Although a nickname may be acquired earlier, it usually comes in junior high when gang affiliations materialize. While it affirms group membership, it also grants personal anonymity. According to some gang researchers, self-image problems are at the root: ". . . influences convey to the adolescent that he is a person of very little worth. It is hardly surprising that he then seeks a more favorable definition of himself" (Cartwright et al. 1975:66). In some ways, a nickname allows a person to lay aside a fragmented ego and take on an ego created in the barrio.

As in other barrios, members in one early klika of an East Los Angeles gang also used and are referred to by their regular names; some have a diminutive form, like Juanito and Tu-Tu. The sources of nicknames can be separated into two basic categories: personal appearances and quirks.

> Personal appearance nicknames (with explanations) include:
>   Chaparro (Shorty)
>   Trokitas (Truck, shaped like one)
>   Freddie Narizón (Freddie Big Nose)
>   Gorilla (pronounced the Spanish way)
>   Huero (light or white skin, spelled the cholo way)
>   Midnite (either because of dark skin, or stays up late)
>   Chuco (dresses and acts cool, like a *pachuco*)
>   Orejón (big ears, or eavesdropper)
>   Tony Fatbox (fat and boxlike body)
>   Fish (face resembles fish)
>   Bobby Gordo (Bobby Fatso)
>
> Some with an ethnic twist:
>   Philip Flip (Filipino)
>   Black Phillip
>   Chilino (Chilean)
>
> Personal quirk nicknames include:
>   Rudy Bubble Gum
>   Lefty
>   Chesshound (likes to play chess)
>   Tony Spring (good at getting bail, springing guys)
>   Deep Purple (likes song of the same name, also dark skin)

Some nicknames have multiple meanings, such as Hando (from cholo word *jando,* meaning "money," but also someone who always has funds); Sapito (from Sapo, "lucky" or "chance," or Frog, but also diminutive, meaning "little one"); Ruco ("old man," but also "wise counselor"); and Black Bart (bearded, but also good robber like historical character). Youths aspiring to the esteem of former renowned gang members may adopt that individual's nickname, prefixing it with "Li'l" (i.e., Little), as in Li'l Crow or Li'l Wino.

Nicknaming provides avenues for proving commitment and unwavering group loyalty. An indelible imprint, like a tattoo, is like a barrio imprimateur, locking a person in for what the group seemingly considers life. Members wear their tattoos with pride and gain a certain amount of status and adulation from barrio onlookers, especially siblings and younger individuals who look up to them. Often one's level of gang identity can be gauged by the amount and type of tattoo. Some might only place a small dot (●) or cross (†) on their hand, between the thumb and forefinger, while others, especially the committed *veteranos,* might cover large parts of the body with a very elaborate art form. (Many of the latter have a practical reason for this, as tattoos help hide injection "marks" when they are "using.")

The symbolism of the tattoo is also expressed in the graffiti on public walls and buildings, that is, the *placaso* (graffiti) is a nickname, barrio, and *klika* signature. Usually stylized, the tattoos vary from professional to homemade. Similarly, the quality of graffiti differs as to number of items, size, degree of artistic ingenuity, and type of painting/drawing material used. Although the public views graffiti as an example of antisocial, delinquent defacement of public and private property, the activity is perceived somewhat differently by gang members themselves. Sometimes romantic liaisons still appear (Freddie *y* Stella) and recently sociopolitical slogans and causes were common, but most graffiti is gang-related.

At one level, it is a way to declare territorial dominance. Gang members proudly put their placas in their barrio, in areas that are being contested with neighboring rival barrios, or in the enemy barrio itself, as a form of boasting much like Plains Indians' "counting coup." At another level, as many interviewed members have verified and I have confirmed in cruising with them, the *placas* are a way to gain attention and recognition from the general public—"I always wonder what people think of when they ride by and see the name 'Puppet' there. Do they think of me?" And there are the barrio youth interested in personal matters—"I know the guys from that barrio know who I am. They've seen my *placas* in their neighborhood." For all these reasons, *placas* are usually quite accessible to the public view as the writers place them near major roads and street frontage structures. (This fact contrasts with Robert George Reisner's [1968] explanation in his book *Graffiti,* where he maintains that writers put messages in undetected places that only reach a limited number of viewers.) The prideful boasting of the placas also accounts for the frequency with which rival gang members cover them over or, more frequently, append written insults to them.

The placas vary in stylistic devices (especially over time) and are encoded in current barrio idioms. In general, however, the message in the graffiti is direct and pointed toward other gang members, who will be well acquainted with the conventions employed. The following personal example is one type of message, with the definition added for clarification:

EL
= The (*El* is masculine, *La* is feminine; in cholo speech, the article is often used with first names, as it is with personal titles.)

PEGLEG
= PEGLEG (nickname)

DE
= From

32nd
= Gang name (32nd Street)

-R-
= We're the best (*rifamos*)

C/S
= Jointly means: There is nothing you can do about it; don't touch; or anything you do to this, twice to you (*con safos*).

One other barrio example would be:

Los NEiGBoRHOOD = Gang (*los neighborhood*)

To-TAL = United (*total*)

CoNTROZZA = Controls (*controlla*)

Such messages, obviously, constitute an extension of face-to-face challenges and often serve to aggravate tensions among rival gangs.

Although much of the gang graffiti is crudely put together (especially insults written over the original claims), not infrequently the *placas* display linguistic invention and aesthetic creativity. They are likely to be found on shop and business walls, fences, bridges, apartment houses, and private garages. Although sacred objects are generally considered unmarkable, the prohibition is not fully honored, as is clear from the placas covering many local churches in Los Angeles. Generally, barrio and nonbarrio residents frown on the graffiti. Some barrios have had programs to eliminate or curb the proliferation of "eyesores." One way was to paint historical or cultural murals, popular since the 1960s Chicano movement (Zucker 1978), on surfaces the gang members would then refrain from *plaqueando.* Many of these murals, however, have by now been altered substantially by graffiti.

Cholo Kinesics

As Haviland (1980:102) has noted, "kinesics is a system of postures, facial expressions, and bodily notions which convey messages." Like other subcultures, the cholo subculture has a distinctive body language. The messages that are conveyed are direct and simple and usually emanate from the facial and bodily demeanor of the individual; the eyes, mouth, and hands are particularly demonstrative. The sometimes stoic, even sullen, cholo kinesics usually portray a posture of being in control of the situation. Such an attitude probably evolved to assuage and manage the traumatic and stressful life experiences, especially the endemic fears engendered by street pressures. This attempt to gain a sense of personal efficacy becomes a particularly important task during the adolescent's age/sex role clarification phase.

Movement is generally methodical, deliberate, and smooth, whether walking out of the front door, pulling a pack of cigarettes out of a front shirt pocket and getting the cigarette out to meet the match, passing out beer to comrades, or sizing up a new group of people with a steady gaze. A walk to the corner, for example, especially when one is alone, will typically be at a leisurely gait, with stiffly postured shoulders and head leaning very slightly back, and eyes fixed forward. 25

Proxemic behavior is also stylized. Interpersonal encounters are typically characterized by participants stopping short of arm's length from each other and staring directly toward one another, to signify readiness to meet a potential challenge. Shortly, one participant will speak or simply step away calmly, with a last sideward glance to indicate disinterest but continued readiness. Stepping directly toward the other, however, is to issue the awaited challenge.

Gesturing is also common. Head movements often serve to punctuate other facial expressions: the mouth's corners downturned and the head slightly jerked back to indicate, "What's going on?"; the eyes motioning in the direction of a person or object and the head nodding in the same direction to show concern or interest, like "Who or what is that?"; or the hands with the index finger and thumb, like a gun, pointed and directed to a person or object that is negatively sanctioned or has a *leva* (social avoidance) thrown on it, with the head held down, eyes avoiding object, to complement the message.

Sometimes a hand, eye, or mouth movement, or a combination thereof, is the sole gesture, but more generally verbal messages accompany it. As an illustration, a gesture relaying one's fearlessness or fearfulness can be conducted with one hand and fingers that approximate human physiology. For indicating courage, the hand and fingers are cupped as if holding a heavy ball and sagged slightly downward, accompanied by the phrase "¡*Tiene huevos!*" (He has balls). For showing anxiety or apprehension, the hand and fingers, with the thumb meeting the fingers, are formed as a cone with the fingers and thumb simulating a moving body aperture (a twitching rectum) and the phrase uttered is, "¡*Está escamado!*" (He's afraid).

Much of the cholo physical presence revolves around managing inner psychic tension. Although early childhood was a tearful, painful experience for many, it must be forgotten and replaced by a more forebearing adolescent and young adult demeanor. The stoic attitude is especially useful in assuaging feelings of fear. Regular gang members, as creators and carriers of the subculture, are much more proficient at this, with peripheral and other fringe members following in that order. The projection of this image is sometimes undertaken with the expectation of an audience, as if in guarded preparation for any mistakes that would indicate a weak link to observers. For many peripheral members, as noted, it is a way of disguising personal apprehension and trepidation by taking on group-sanctioned mannerisms.

Cholo Speech

Among the most remarkable aspects of the cholo subculture is the development of its unique forms of speech. This linguistic phenomenon is widely characterized as a result of strains and stresses in the acculturation process: "Pidgins arise as makeshift adaptations, reduced in structure and use, no one's first language; creoles are pidgins become primary languages. Both are marginal, in the circumstances of their origin, and in the attitudes towards them on the part of those who speak one of the languages from which they derive" (Hymes 1971:3). Carey McWilliams (1968) noted the southwestern United States cultural milieu in which this creativity blossomed: "It is in the speech of the city gangs, 'the *pachuco* patois,' that the attempt to fuse the two languages is most clearly apparent. . . . Anglicizing Spanish and Hispanicizing English as it suits their purpose and often coining an expression of their own."

Contemporary cholos reflect somewhat similar historical conditions and experiences, which create this type of language style (R. Sánchez 1983). In large part, this speech style is merely a carryover from the early *pachuco* days when the words were first concocted. In fact, much of the word tradition has been lost through the generations, for it was much richer and varied in its earlier form, much as the *pachuco* life-style has also changed. Language usage back then was much more bilingual (or trilingual, if one includes the patois) (Griffith 1948), thus creating a more productive cultural crucible for word invention. Today barrio gang talk is mostly English, and the degree of Spanish and cholo terms that are spoken is dependent on the tradition and generational history of the barrio; in a fashion, it is one way to show loyalty and allegiance to remnants of Mexican culture or, more basically, "us" against "them."

The association between talking like a cholo and group identity and membership is clear. Many individuals indicated in interviews that they actually shifted their speech pattern to conform to group expectations when the situation warranted; and I observed this phenomenon on several occasions. Especially noteworthy is how communication in this manner occurred when outsiders—for example, various law enforcement and criminal justice authorities—were around, much as if the group required a secret code to shield its members from the intrusions of untrustworthy strangers. Many words, of course, refer to group-related features. In addition to the constant use of exclamatory phrases like ¡Órale! (Hey! Hello!), ese or esa (say, you, he, or she), and vato or vata (guy or chick), there was regular mention of barrio (their neighborhood) networks or allegiances. Friends and associates are called by their first name or nickname, but the use of other socially bonding utterances, like camarada, carnal, vato, or homeboy, is also quite common. An age cohort in the gang is designated a klika, as noted. Both major ethnic groups from whom the cholo style derived are now considered outsiders and are given racial epithets rather than ethnic names: Anglos are called gabachos (with sometimes a long emphasis on the middle syllable of the word for special opprobrium), while Mexican nationals are referred to as chúntaros or "chunts." This attitude toward Anglos and Mexicans tends to confirm their own in-group solidarity as cholos. Other terms often allude to group activities, such as getting locote (being drunk, high, and crazy or acting that way), becoming trucha (alert), throwing chingazos (fighting, throwing blows), showing cora (heart, compassion), and declaring rifamos (we rule). Much of the usage of phrases like vato loco (crazy dude) and placaso (graffiti writing of ego and barrio name on buildings and walls) also is group centered. Other words for objects, such as lisa (shirt), vaisa (hands), calcos (shoes), pisto (liquor), cantón (house), and so on, are regularly used, but the words that hint at group associations and the strengthening of social ties provide particular insight to the functions of cholo speech.

Dictionaries of barrio (Fuentes and López 1974) and pachuco (Serrano 1979) words have been compiled, so there is no need to elaborate here on the working, contemporary terminologies in usage. The words and their usage stemmed from the choloization process initially and in subsequent decades have become another facet of the cholo "image." For individuals and barrios that are presently still in the midst of choloization, such as Tercera Flats (Third Street Flats) in East Los Angeles, the image is shaped by living conditions. But adoption of cholo talk, similar to adopting the dress style, is also a general requisite for group membership,

espccially aiding the identity-conscious fringe gang members. The use
of the patois helps reify gang solidarity, even if only a few choice words
are known.

Cholo "Partying"

"Partying," to a cholo, means a number of things—although its
varied meanings almost always imply that, first, homies (homeboys from
the barrio) are involved and that, second, some form of intoxicants are
available. The number of participants (ranging from two or three to
dozens) and the types of inebriants (from beer and/or wine to hard
drugs) may vary, but the essence of partying remains the same. The
context of partying can be very casual—a few guys sitting around,
talking, and getting high—or more formally structured. The more common casual variety may involve gatherings on a front porch or lawn, in
a car (moving or parked), at a local hangout, or at a park. The outdoor
casual gatherings often include one or more individuals playing a *lira*
(guitar) and the others joining in singing old Mexican *canciones* (rancheras,
boleros, corridos, and other rural, folksy tunes).

While these casual get-togethers sometimes include females, they   35
are more often all male. (Gang girls similarly gather with one another,
although substance use tends to be slightly less intense, musical instruments are rare, and the songs they sing are more apt to be "oldies-but-
goodies," that is, music derived from the black "rhythm and blues"
tradition and Chicano creations based on it.) Partying between the sexes
usually involves slightly more structured settings, such as house parties
or neighborhood dances. Neighborhood baptisms, birthdays, weddings,
and anniversaries also occasion parties to celebrate the events, and gang
members often mix with neighbors and relatives from the barrio at these
events. At the predominantly cholo house parties and dances, dancing is
typically a slow, rhythmic rocking from side to side by couples closely
embraced; music with a quicker tempo generally thins out the dancers
on the floor. In some of the more isolated and Mexican-oriented barrios,
canciones, rather than "oldies-but-goodies," will be played; both types of
music evoke sentimental moods and romantic ideas. At the more generalized family-and-friends gatherings in which cholos mix, elders'
choice of music is apt to prevail—"Tex-Mex" or swing music is commonly heard.

Parties—in part because of the heavy drug and alcohol consumption—often are marred by fights. Since gang members often carry
knives or even handguns to such events—especially outside their own
barrio—the violence can frequently occasion serious injury or even
death. This is especially the case when members of different barrio gangs

are invited to the same celebrations or when gang members "crash" an affair to which they were not invited.

Car Culture: The Cholo Style

The automobile is a focal concern of youth culture. Chicano "low-riding" evolved in the context of American adaptation to youth patterns (Trillen and Koren 1978; West 1976). The cholo image of a controlled, calm, and cool demeanor has affected this style, and I particularly enjoyed excursions on the streets observing it. The car style is distinctive, too, with lowered rear ends (or all around), either permanent or temporary (with hydraulic lifts of the type that raise or lower truck tailgates). This lowered vehicle can be an older 1940s or more recent 1970s model (usually a General Motors vehicle, especially a Chevrolet); it may be regular in appearance or highly decorated (multicolored paint jobs, sparkling wheels, rich leather or velvet upholstery, and so on). The image of the driver is a slumped-back low silhouette and the drive is smooth and slow. There is both form and function to low-riding, for it is a look and an operation. It has been suggested that Chicanos fashioned this style to demonstrate their difference from Anglos and "Anglicized" ways (West 1976:76). Although unintentional, there are ethnic contrasts, even though in recent years Anglos have borrowed from the Chicano variant. Most of the cholos interviewed and observed for this study considered low-riding in a positive light, as a way to socialize and court, usually when "high"; but there is also an occasional chase scene or confrontation stemming from the activity.

The first generations to participate in this car pattern were *pachucos,* although it was then referred to as cruising. Community and social workers attempted to redirect street youth by establishing car/social clubs in the 1950s, a practice still common in some gang worker programs (Sample 1984). These programs provided alternatives, and, with some inroads, these car/social clubs helped guide the *pachuco* tradition and formulate highly elaborate low-riding style. Great amounts of time and money are today expended on cars by such groups and a quintessentially institutionalized pattern has resulted. *Low-rider* magazine was very popular in the 1970s and 1980s. To complement (or generate) such media hype, car shows and the weekend car cruising in different barrios (most clearly East Los Angeles's Whittier Boulevard, the "granddaddy" of them all, where sheriffs now block the route) add to the tradition.

Street youth find it difficult to join such costly and organized activities, even though some crossover cholos can mix with the car/social club types. Cholo low-riding, in fact, is different from the flashy "clubber" style. Cholos have a taste for a more or less informal, casual run of stock cars, due to limited resources. To them, to customize a car means renovating an older 1940–1950s model. Of course, this is in line with their penchant for tradition, such as in language and dress.

Youth car cultural patterns often entail matters of masculinity and maturation. Bloch and Niederhoffer (1958:131) have suggested the idea of the car as a *churinga,* an object or place in which an Australian aborigine's soul resides: ". . . can it be denied that the youthful owner of an automobile does not likewise put his 'heart and soul' into his car? He adjusts it, tunes it, cleans it, polishes it, communes with it, cherishes it." Cholos have infused their cars with their style, if not their hearts; and the nicknames for cars reflect this casual habit—"Earth Angel," "96 Tears," and so on.

The car has become a social instrument to aid the youths' sexual and maturity goals. Social encounters and interactions are generated in a new cultural way. The smooth, methodical walk that carries the cholo forward is repeated in the car movement. Slumping back, peering over the steering wheel and sill are all ways of turning an attitude into a practice. The vehicle's sounds must also measure up. An almost inaudible slow-moving engine is sometimes "revved up" to release a lowered-tone rumble from the dual exhaust system. The driver's cool image is thus complemented by cool sounds. With this look and sound, the car is easily managed. Street and male considerations have shaped this style. Slow driving helps human eye contact and creates opportunities for favorable responses from onlookers (eye movements, smiles, words, gestures). Social interaction becomes the raison d'être for driving, and why move quickly when it is social contacts one desires? Use of the car in this fashion increases territorial coverage and thus opportunities to meet more people, particularly members of the opposite sex. (However, regular peer interactions of both sexes are also common.) The low silhouette contributes to the male image of being deliberate in talk and gestures. Such posturing requires time, which cruising allows, and it produces expediencies for males and females to court each other.

Social interaction cruising is clearly the most important use of the car among cholos. It is also used as a private sanctuary when it is parked. Like so many other hangouts, someone's car is a regular meeting spot to talk, get high, drink, and just conduct normal social intercourse; sometimes it's stationed in the same spot almost every day.

There is a great amount of pride in owning a cruiser car. A seventeen-year-old male from San Gabriel, in an interview, said that his "'62 Chevy was something I was proud of. But I needed money one time and I had to sell it for $200.00. The one thing I was proud of." Putting a great amount of time and energy into cars is also a way of demonstrating pride. Several individuals whom I have observed boasted about working on engines. One twenty-year-old male from Chino gave this answer to a query on why Chevrolets were so common among Chicanos: ". . . they know the engine well. Your father had a Chevy and showed you how to change the oil and how to switch engines . . . Yeah, to have a good time the guys would have a couple of beers and a whole bunch would get under the engine. They don't even have to say the make of the car, you know it's a Chevy when someone says, 'Hey, I just bought a '56 with skirts.'"

Although cruising and social interaction in one's barrio are appreciated, it is much more exciting to cruise another barrio. Doing so generates opportunities for liaisons, specifically meeting members of the opposite sex. Many a courting relationship has been initiated in this way, some even ending up as permanent dating arrangements. There are pitfalls to this courting method, however, for barrio youth groups are often extremely hostile toward any outsiders who appear to be "messing around" with one of their own (often a relative). As an example of such attitudes, a young girl, sixteen, from Cucamonga explained in an interview how she and her friends react to intruders: ". . . three carloads of girls from Ontario were here and gunning their motors at some of the guys at the corner. When they got to where we were at, we started stoning them 'cause they were yelling Ontario *rifamos* [we-from-Ontario-rule], so we started calling them *putas* and Ontario *putos.* Then this guy went by and we stopped him [car] and asked him to take us and chase those girls out, so we chased them out." A male, twenty-five, from the same barrio, said: "We would go to Upland or Ontario and pick up girls and bring them to Cuca to cruise. The guys from there would chase us out, throwing bottles and rocks. But we used to do the same thing to them when they used to come to Cuca."

Interestingly, although many illegal chases, bumping incidents, and   45
fights spin off from cruising forays, only a few of our informants reported incidents that involved other criminal activity. In one interview, a male, nineteen, from Chino gave this account of cruising and dealing: "We were cruising one night in my Monte Carlo looking for people to buy dope. It was a slow night, so my friend dropped me off at my girlfriend's. I let him drive the car. About a half an hour later the police pulled him over. They searched the car and found the drugs [reds and cocaine]." Generally, such stories are rare and occur more often with barrio members who have become crime-oriented. Cruising, as we have seen, is definitely a social affair, even though some individuals instigate and create other goals.

Conclusion

This admixture in the car culture of stylistic elements, social activities, and, less frequent but more widely noticed, violence and criminal actions holds true in general for the subculture of the gang. Through the decades the gang subculture has established itself as an alternative coping strategy with socialization and enculturation processes of its own. Only a small percentage of the barrio youth population is attracted to it, and of that number an even smaller portion become thoroughly immersed in it, usually members of the underclass or the most marginal ones. The external reasons for the variance in involvement and participation are multiple—type and degree of family stress, amount of street socialization, peer and model influences, barrio traditions and sense of territoriality, and so on. However, there are also reasons intrinsic to the gang subculture. The fact that the gang mixes functional (i.e., *palomilla*) and problematic (i.e., street survival) activities informs us about the personal choices that operate in gang life. Some youngsters can largely ignore or avoid those customs that are detrimental or damaging yet still be considered (by themselves and others) a part of the gang, "someone from the barrio." Most members of a gang know, understand, and accept the personal differences within the group and thus maintain various expectations for each individual.

Usually it is outsiders, including especially law enforcement and the media, who tend to lump all members together regardless of their personal degree of gang involvement and commitment. In large part, these observers have based their assessment on the visual characteristics of the gang, particularly the dress, demeanor, and other easily practiced signs. As we have seen, there are other social and cultural dynamics that need to be considered in understanding the gang subculture. What needs to be clarified is the distinction between the cholo experience, for example, the transitional phase of being in the middle of two cultural traditions, and the varied group customs and habits that arise as a result of that experience. As noted, some patterns are quite normal and functional while others are definitely problematic, and both are found in the gang.

References

Barker, G. C.
  1950   *Pachuco, an American-Spanish Argot and Its Social Function in Tucson, Arizona.* Tucson: University of Arizona Press.
  1972   *Social Functions of Language in a Mexican-American Community.* Tucson: University of Arizona Press.
Bloch, H. A., and A. Niederhoffer
  1958   *The Gang: A Study in Adolescent Behavior.* New York: Philosophical Library.
Cartwright, Desmond S., B. Tomson, and H. Schwartz
  1975   *Gang Delinquency.* Monterey, Calif.: Brooks/Cole.
Fuentes, Dagoberto, and José A. López
  1974   *Barrio Language Dictionary.* La Puente, Calif.: Sunburst Enterprises.
Griffith, Beatrice
  1948   *American Me.* Boston: Houghton Mifflin Co.
Haviland, William A.
  1980   *Cultural Anthropology.* New York: Holt, Rinehart, and Winston.

Hymes, Dell, ed.
   1971   *Pidginization and Creolization of Languages.* London: Cambridge University Press.
McWilliams, C.
   1968   *North from Mexico—the Spanish-Speaking People of the United States.* New York: Greenwood Press.
Morrison, Patt
   1983   "Gang Girls Get a Hint at What They Could Be." *Los Angeles Times,* March 29.
Poirier, Mike
   1982   *Street Gangs of Los Angeles County.* Los Angeles: Self-Published. P.O. Box 60481, Los Angeles, CA 90060.
Reisner, Robert G.
   1968   *Graffiti.* New York: Canyon Books.
Sample, Herbert A.
   1984   "Youth Gangs Take a Shine to Custom Cars." *Los Angeles Times,* February 5.
Sánchez, Rosaura
   1983   *Chicano Discourse: Socio-historic Perspectives.* Rowley, Mass.: Newbury House Publishers.
Serrano, Rudolfo A.
   1979   *Dictionary of Pachuco Terms.* Bakersfield: California State University, Bakersfield.
Trillen, Calvin, and Edward Koren
   1978   "Our Far-Flung Correspondents: Low and Slow, Mean and Clean." *The New Yorker,* July 10.
West, Ted
   1976   "Scenes from a 'Revolution: Low and Slow.'" *Car and Driver,* August.
Zucker, Martin
   1978   "Walls of Barrio Are Brought to Life by Street Gang Art." *Smithsonian,* October.

Reading the Text

1. What are the characteristics of cholo fashion, as described by Vigil?
2. Of what value are nicknames and *placas* to gang identity?
3. According to Vigil, what is the distinctive body language of cholo culture?
4. Why are cars significant to young cholos, and in what ways?

Reading the Signs

1. Vigil describes the external signs that indicate group affiliation among gangs. In your journal, consider a group to which you belong (a group you belonged to in high school would also work). How does the group use signs to communicate group identity? Consider clothing, language, nicknames, and forms of behavior. How do you signal insider status to outsiders? What happens if outsiders "borrow" your group's signs?
2. Would you describe cholo style as being primarily "oppositional" in Elizabeth Wilson's terms (see "Oppositional Dress," p. 45), or "traditional," or a combination of the two? Write an essay in which you argue for your

position, being sure to support your argument with specific examples of
cholo style.

3. How would Vigil explain the fashion preferences of the students speaking
   in "Signs of the Street: A Conversation" (p. 560)?

4. Compare and contrast cholo body language with that of African-American
   males as described in Richard Majors's "Cool Pose: The Proud Signature
   of Black Survival" (p. 471). How do you account for any similarities—and
   differences—you might find?

5. Why might group identity be so important to young gang members? Is its
   significance different than it is for "mainstream" groups? To develop your
   own argument, consult, in addition to Vigil, Anne Campbell's "The Praised
   and the Damned" (p. 544), Léon Bing's "Faro" (p. 540), and Carl Rogers's
   "Children in Gangs" (p. 535).

S E T H   M Y D A N S

Not Just the Inner City: Well-to-Do Join Gangs

*Though originally a subculture born of poverty and racial oppression,
youth gangs are becoming increasingly attractive to white suburban "wannabes" for whom gang membership constitutes a particularly effective
way of rebelling against their parents. While, as Seth Mydans (b. 1946)
points out in this* New York Times *article, the "copycat" or "yuppie"
gangs have not yet demonstrated widespread involvement in "serious"
criminal activity, they have shown a penchant for graffiti vandalism and
weapons carrying. But playing gangster can get dangerous. Dabbling
with gangs may appear to some middle-class wannabes as a sign of
solidarity with a racial underclass, but with drive-by shootings now
involving anyone caught in the wrong place at the wrong time, the
romantic allure of gangsterism is becoming less attractive. A national
correspondent for the* New York Times *based in Los Angeles, Seth
Mydans is a career journalist who has served as a foreign correspondent
stationed in the former Soviet Union, England, the Philippines, and
Thailand. He currently focuses on race, immigration, and urban problems.*

In suburban Hawthorne, social workers tell of the police officers
who responded to a report of gang violence, only to let the instigators
drive away in expensive cars, thinking they were a group of teenagers
on their way to the beach.

In Tucson, Ariz., a white middle-class teenager wearing gang colors died, a victim of a drive-by shooting, as he stood with black and Hispanic members of the Bloods gang.

At Antelope Valley High School in Lancaster, Calif., about 50 miles north of Los Angeles, 200 students threw stones at a policeman who had been called to help enforce a ban on the gang outfits that have become a fad on some campuses.

Around the country, a growing number of well-to-do youths have begun flirting with gangs in a dalliance that can be as innocent as a fashion statement or as deadly as hard-core drug dealing and violence.

The phenomenon is emerging in a variety of forms. Some affluent   5 white youths are joining established black or Hispanic gangs like the Crips and Bloods; others are forming what are sometimes called "copy-cat" or "mutant" or "yuppie" gangs.

The development seems to defy the usual socioeconomic explanations for the growth of gangs in inner cities, and it appears to have caught parents, teachers, and law-enforcement officers off guard.

Police experts and social workers offer an array of reasons: a mis-guided sense of the romance of gangs; pursuit of the easy money of drugs; self-defense against the spread of established hard-core gangs. And they note that well-to-do families in the suburbs can be as empty and loveless as poor families in the inner city, leaving young people searching for a sense of group identity.

Furthermore, "kids have always tried to shock their parents," said Marianne Diaz-Parton, a social worker who works with young gang members in the Los Angeles suburb of Lawndale, "and these days be-coming a gang member is one way to do it."

A member of the South Bay Family gang in Hermosa Beach, a twenty-one-year-old surfer called Road Dog who said his family owned a chain of pharmacies, put it this way: "This is the nineties, man. We're the type of people who don't take no for an answer. If your mom says no to a kid in the nineties, the kid's just going to laugh." He and his friends shouted in appreciation as another gang member lifted his long hair to reveal a tattoo on a bare shoulder: "Mama tried."

Separating their gang identities from their home lives, the South Bay   10 Family members give themselves nicknames that they carry in elaborate tattoos around the backs of their necks. They consented to interviews on the condition that only these gang names be used.

The gang's leader, who said he was the son of a bank vice president, flexed a bicep so the tattooed figure of a nearly naked woman moved suggestively. Voicing his own version of the basic street philosophy of gang solidarity, the leader, who is called Thumper, said, "If you want to be able to walk the mall, you have to know you've got your boys behind you."

From Cool to Dead

For young people who have not been hardened by the inner city, an attitude like this, if taken into the streets, can be dangerous, said Sgt. Wes McBride of the Los Angeles Sheriff's Department, who has gathered reports on the phenomenon from around the country.

"They start out thinking it's real cool to be a gang member," he said. "They are 'wannabes' with nothing happening around them to show them it's real dangerous, until they run afoul of real gang members, and then they end up dead."

In California's palm-fringed San Fernando Valley, said Manuel Velasquez, a social worker with Community Youth Gang Services, a private agency, "there are a lot of kids who have no business being in gangs who all of a sudden are going around acting like gang members."

"They play the part," he went on. "They vandalize. They do graffiti. 15 They do all kinds of stuff. But when it comes down to the big stuff, it's: 'Wait a minute. That's enough for me. I want to change the rules.' And then they realize it's a little bit too late."

There are few statistics on middle-class involvement in gangs, and officials are reluctant to generalize about its extent or the form it is taking. But reports of middle-class gang activity come from places as disparate as Denver, Seattle, Tucson, Portland, Dallas, Phoenix, Chicago, Minneapolis, Omaha, and Honolulu.

Sgt. John Galea, until recently the head of the youth gang intelligence unit of the New York City Police Department, said that although there was no lack of youth violence in the city, organized street gangs as such were not a serious problem.

The South Bay Family, in Hermosa Beach, has evolved over the past five years from a group of bouncers for a rock band to a full-fledged streetwise, well-armed gang. But for the most part, white gangs, or white members of minority gangs, have just begun to be noticed in the past few months.

"Parents Are Totally Unaware"

"I think it's a new trend just since the latter part of 1989, and it's really interesting how it's getting out to suburban areas," said Dorothy Elmore, a gang intelligence officer for the Portland Police Bureau in Oregon. "We've got teachers calling up and saying: 'We've got some Bloods and Crips here. What's going on?'

"It's definitely coming from two-parent families, working class to 20 middle class to upper middle class, predominantly white," she went on.

"The parents are totally unaware of the kind of activity these kids are doing."

In Tucson, Sgt. Ron Zimmerling, who heads the Police Department's gang unit, said that "Kids from even our country-club areas were suddenly joining gangs."

After the drive-by shooting last summer in which a white teenager was killed, he said, he asked a black gang member about another white youth who had attached himself to the gang. "I don't know," the black member replied. "He just likes to hang out."

The phenomenon is better established but still relatively new in the Los Angeles area, the nation's gang capital.

"We have covered parties where I'm totally shocked at the mixture of people who are there," said Mrs. Diaz-Parton, of Community Youth Gang Services in Lawndale. "Your traditional Hispanic gang member is next to this disco-looking person who is next to a preppie guy who looks like he's getting straight A's on his way to college."

Bandannas and Baseball Caps

Irving G. Spergel, a sociology professor at the University of Chicago   25
who studies gangs, emphasized that the phenomenon accounts for a very small part of the nation's gang problem, which is centered in inner cities. He said the four thousand to five thousand neo-Nazi skinhead groups around the country, which have their own style and ideology, were a separate and worrisome problem.

More trivial, but still troubling to school officials, is a trend toward gang fashions in some high schools and junior high schools. In Los Angeles, Phoenix, Tucson, and several California suburbs, students have staged demonstrations to protest bans on wearing certain colors, bandannas, jewelry, or baseball caps that can be a mark of gang membership.

Bare chests, tattoos, Budweiser beer, and a televised hockey game seemed to be the fashion one recent Saturday evening at an extremely noisy gathering of members of the South Bay Family in a small house in a middle-class neighborhood near the Pacific Coast Highway in Hermosa Beach. There were knives and a deer rifle in evidence, and some said they had pistols.

Asked about the gang's philosophy, Bam Bam, the son of a professor at the University of Southern California, shouted, "Right or wrong, your bros are your bros!"

"Another thing that goes good here is peace," said Road Dog loudly.

"Peace by force, man," shouted Porgy, who said his father was vice   30
president of a plastics company.

"No drug dealing!" shouted Tomcat, the son of a stockbroker.

"Quit lying to him, man," said Little Smith. "There's drugs everywhere."

On a more reflective note, away from the crowd in a small back room, Porgy said: "There is no justification. We do what we do because we want to. I don't blame my mother. She did the best she could."

Reading the Text

1. Why do some teenagers become gang "wannabes," according to Mydans?
2. Which signs of gang involvement are typically adopted by suburban gang members?
3. How can suburban kids' "dallying" with gangs be seen as a "fashion statement"?

Reading the Signs

1. Write a dialogue between the students interviewed in "Signs of the Street: A Conversation" (p. 560), and the suburban gang wannabes described in Mydans's essay. Share your dialogue with your classmates.
2. Compare the suburban gang involvement with that of inner-city gang members. What differences—and similarities—do you see in motivation and external signs of gang affiliation? To develop your argument, consult "Signs of the Street: A Conversation" (p. 560), Anne Campbell, "The Praised and the Damned" (p. 544), and Léon Bing, "Faro" (p. 540).
3. How might Scott Poulson-Bryant ("B-Boys," p. 56) explain the phenomenon of gang wannabes?
4. Compare the nicknames and symbols of group affiliation that the suburban gang member adopts with those adopted by cholo gangsters (see James Diego Vigil, "Gang Styles: Cholo Dress and Body Adornment, Speech, Demeanor, Partying, and Car Culture," p. 570). What differences, if any, do you find in frame of cultural reference and ideology?
5. In class, discuss your responses to the son of the bank vice president who claims, "If you want to be able to walk the mall, you have to know you've got your boys behind you"? Have you ever known anyone like that? Why do you think he makes such a claim?

TEEN ANGELS *MAGAZINE*

Summertime

||||||||||||||||||||||||||||||||||||||||||||||||

The public image of the American street gang has been carefully constructed by Hollywood and the record industry. In this illustration from Teen Angels *Magazine, a self-described "'Gang' Rights Activist News Agency" associated with the American Civil Liberties Union, you can see how L.A.'s Hispanic gang members view themselves. Composed mostly of letters, photos, and illustrations submitted by its readers,* Teen Angels *serves as a forum for gangsters to let each other know who they are and what they're thinking.*

Reading the Signs

1. Read or review James Diego Vigil's "Gang Styles: Cholo Dress and Body Adornment, Speech, Demeanor, Partying, and Car Culture" (p. 570). Using Vigil's essay as your critical framework, analyze the image of gang members depicted in "Summer Time."
2. In class, discuss the gender roles depicted in "Summer Time." You might consult Holly Devor, "Gender Role Behaviors and Attitudes," p. 603.
3. To what extent do Faro (Léon Bing, "Faro," p. 540) and the students speaking in "Signs of the Street: A Conversation" (p. 560) express attitudes and world views similar to those depicted in "Summer Time"? Use your observations to write an essay in which you argue whether "Summer Time" presents an idealized or realistic vision of gang life.
4. What response might Connie (Anne Campbell, "The Praised and the Damned," p. 544) have to "Summer Time"? In class, role-play a conversation between Connie and the artist who drew this illustration, being sure to articulate the reasons for Connie's response.
5. Sketch your own vision of a group to which you belong. Present it to you class, and give a semiotic reading of it.

CHAPTER NINE

YOU'VE COME
A LONG WAY,
MAYBE

Gender Codes in American Culture

Stand by for a moment, men, this question's for the women in the class. Now, have you ever found yourself fantasizing about taking to the road with a woman friend, free to go wherever you want and to do whatever you please, including fighting back against the goons who might harass you on your way? In your fantasy, do you see yourself as willing to go out in a blaze of glory, like Butch Cassidy and the Sundance Kid, rather than give in and return home, defeated and domesticated? Maybe this fantasy sounds a bit extreme, but in 1992 a cinema fantasy very much like it became one of the surprise hits of the season, demonstrating just how powerful a fantasy it was for thousands of American women. Do you remember the movie it appeared in?

You probably do. The film, of course, was *Thelma and Louise,* and we begin with it because it is an exceptionally accurate sign of the state of gender consciousness in America in the early nineties. *Thelma and Louise* is one of those movies that instantly transcends the earthly realm of the box office to soar into the stratosphere of myth. Its mythic potency is quite simple. Playing upon the archetypal figure of the male warrior bond—a heroic archetype that extends from the Old Testament's David and Jonathan to Hollywood's Mel Gibson and Danny Glover—*Thelma and Louise* offers American women a new twist on the old story. For *this* time the hard-living, tough-talking, and straight-shooting warrior duo is female, and as a result their violent ride to glory became an immediate cultural icon.

Why? Because *Thelma and Louise* breaks the rules. Shucking off the age-old gender norm that tells women to compete with each other *for* men rather than bond together in defense *against* them, the movie emerges as a sign of a resurgent feminism in the American nineties, an indicator (along with *Fried Green Tomatoes,* another of that season's surprisingly successful films featuring two women who bond together in friendship) that women are not content with the "new traditionalism" so enthusiastically promoted throughout the eighties by such movies as *Fatal Attraction*. Instead, one could hear women exclaiming to each other in the wake of such gender conflicts as the Anita Hill–Clarence Thomas face-off in the Supreme Court confirmation hearings, "I wish that Thelma and Louise were here."

All right, guys, now it's your turn. Did you see *Thelma and Louise?* Did you go by yourself? With a girlfriend? With some other guys? How did the movie make you feel? Did you have the sense that somehow the rules were being changed?

Discovering the Myths of Gender

If you felt uneasy about *Thelma and Louise,* you aren't alone. For in its reversal of traditional gender roles, its dramatization of two women appropriating the parts of glamorous male outlaws, *Thelma and Louise* demonstrates that the codes governing male and female behavior in America are reversible. For some men, this represents a threat to traditional male authority, while for some women, Thelma and Louise's violent behavior is no improvement on the behavior of men. In either case, the film has caused viewers of both sexes to examine their own gender assumptions, to see just how many assumptions they have.

In semiotic terms, *Thelma and Louise* suggests that our beliefs about the appropriate social roles for men and women are as much a product of the dominant gender *myths* of our culture as of actual biological differences. Think of some such myths. Traditionally, for example, the myths that govern courtship in America have held that it is "natural" for a man to pay the expenses on a date and even to be responsible for all the logistics, including providing transportation and a destination. But there is no natural or biological reason for this to be so. It's just a cultural expectation, one that now is changing. Ask yourself: Who pays when you date? Who drives? Who chooses where to go? If your answer is not always "the guy," then you yourself are part of a cultural shift, a readjusting of a gender myth.

Still, the myths die hard. In 1993, two women were disqualified in their bids to become the first female attorney general when it was discovered that they had hired illegal immigrants as nannies for their children. The issue had never come up when only men were nominated for

‖‖

Exploring the Signs of Gender

In your journal, explore the expectations about gender roles that you grew up with. What gender norms were taught by your family, either overtly or implicitly? Have you ever had any conflicts with your parents over "natural" gender roles? If so, how did you resolve them? Do you think your gender-related expectations today are the same you had when you were a child?

government posts; according to the gender mythology of America, men aren't responsible for arranging for child care. But when a woman was nominated, child care arrangements suddenly mattered. All the fuss that ensued provided a prime example of the power of the gender myths of our society.

It is one of the major tasks of cultural semiotics to expose the outlines of such gender myths to show how deeply they influence our lives. In conducting your own examination of the gender myths that influence your life, you should recognize the difference between the biological category of *sex* and the cultural category of *gender*. Your sex is determined by your chromosomes, but your gender goes beyond your sex into the roles that society has determined are appropriate for you. Your sex, in other words, is your birthright, but the roles you play in society are largely determined by your culture. In everyday life, however, this distinction between the natural category of sex and the cultural category of gender is blurred because socially determined gender roles are regarded as naturally defined sexual necessities. Western culture traditionally has assumed, for instance, that women naturally are the attractive sex, designed to be looked at, while men are natural voyeurs, made to do the looking. This myth is related to the belief that the male sex drive is far more active than the female's. Both myths are represented in a tradition of European art, which is filled with female nudes, but hardly any male ones. Just consider how *Playboy* and *Penthouse* enjoy subscriptions in the millions, while *Playgirl* struggles along in the shadows.

If you think this is obviously the way of nature, consider ancient Greek art, which, from its introduction of the *kouros* (a sculpted figure of a nude male) into art more than two thousand years ago, was at least as interested in the male form as the female. The example of the Greeks tells us that there is nothing in nature to dictate whose body, male or female, will be considered more attractive. At the same time, the Greeks can show us just how much we presume that the roles our gender myths define for us will be heterosexually oriented. For as ancient Greece reminds us, cultures may be homoerotic as well.

Even the standards of beauty that men as well as women are held to are culturally determined. The ideal medieval woman, for example, was short, slender, high-waisted, small-breasted, and boasted a high, domed forehead whose effect she enhanced by shaving her hairline. By the Renaissance, she had filled out considerably, and in the paintings of Peter Paul Rubens could appear positively pudgy by today's standards (we even have an adjective, "Rubenesque," for well-padded feminine beauty). In more recent times, we have seen a shift from the hourglass figures of the fifties to the aerobically muscled hard bodies of the eighties and early nineties. You may assume that this is it, the last stop, the one truly beautiful body, but stick around. Wait to see what's hot in bodies in the years to come.

Men, too, have seen their bodily ideals change over time. The ideal man of the eighteenth century, for example, was a rather heavyset fellow, rounded in appearance, and with a hint of a double chin, while today's ideal (especially in the corporate world) has square-hewn features and a jutting jaw (cleft if possible: Just look at some ads for business-oriented services to see what today's businessman wants to look like). Now think for a moment: What would you look like if you had the choice? Would you look like the ideal man of the 1950s or 1960s? Would you be long and lean, or well-sculpted courtesy of Nautilus?

Take another gender myth that our culture holds as a wholly natural reflection of the difference between the sexes. Women, the myth declares, are naturally intuitive and emotional (recall the Nike campaign featuring "emotional" sportswomen), while men are held to be rational and controlled. Or again: Men are naturally aggressive, while women are passive. Note the pattern: Male and female traits are lined up in neat sets of opposites that are justified through an appeal to nature. But nature isn't bound by categories. After all, have you ever seen a female bear defending her young?

Backlash

Because of the political stakes involved, the semiotic unmasking of gender myths has not gone unchallenged in America. For once a myth has been identified, it can be questioned or altered. Thus, in the wake of the feminist revival of the seventies, the eighties saw something of a backlash. It became culturally fashionable to embrace a "new traditionalism" that really meant going back to the old mythology that had been questioned the decade before. Indeed, only five years before the appearance of *Thelma and Louise, Time* had declared that feminism was dead, that Wonder Woman and the ERA were henceforth to be regarded as things of the past, as obsolete as Nehru jackets and Earth shoes.

The media exulted. More and more women, the media exclaimed, were becoming worried about their "biological clocks" and whether their careers were adequate compensation for the traditional roles they supposedly left behind in the seventies. Thanks to an article by Felice Schwartz in the *Harvard Business Review,* a new myth emerged about businesswomen who were now willing to settle for a kind of second-class corporate citizenship (christened the "mommy track") rather than miss out on the joys of motherhood. The postfeminist era, the media declared, had arrived.

According to Susan Faludi's study of the phenomenon, *Backlash,* such declarations were simply part of a nationwide assault upon the women's movement, an invention of "trends" that had little basis in reality but whose effect was to create some of the very anxieties that were eagerly predicted. To convince American women to return home and have children (as all women should do, according to the traditional mythology), the media showered us with unsubstantiated stories of yuppie infertility, angst, and fears of spinsterhood. Meanwhile, parenting became one of the top pop cultural activities of the decade. Returning to "traditional values"—which in the code of the eighties meant returning to the docile gender roles imposed on women in the fifties and sixties—became the media's new theme. Suddenly everyone wanted to get into the baby game. Can you think of some movies or TV shows from the last few years that exemplify this trend? How have children become our newest media stars?

At the same time, the very word "feminism" itself was demonized. Women around the country, from the college campus to the kitchen, insisted to interviewers that "yes of course they were for women's rights, but they were not feminists." Have you ever found yourself making the same declaration? Why? What images come to mind when you think of the word "feminist"? Are those images realistic, or are they, too, myths? And whether you are male or female, what reactions do you get when you do declare that you are a feminist?

Perhaps because of the controversy, the image of feminism in America today is a potent one. Just consider what happened to Hillary Rodham Clinton during the presidential campaign of 1992. An outspoken feminist with a successful corporate career of her own, she had gone on record declaring that she was not the type to stay at home and bake cookies. Quite a ruckus ensued, much of which was generated by women who denounced her supposed arrogance and defended their own choice to accept the traditional woman's role as homemaker. The image of the typical feminist, for such women, was that of a privileged, college-educated white woman who sneered at women who weren't as successful as she, and while this image, like so many images, was mostly myth, Bill Clinton deemed it safest to remove his wife from the campaign spotlight until the election was safely won.

Discussing the Signs of Gender

In small same-sex groups, brainstorm your ideas of what makes the other gender physically attractive, then list your brainstormed ideas on the blackboard. Discuss the lists as a whole class. What patterns do you see in the lists created by females and males? How do you respond to the other gender's lists?

At the same time, America's consumer culture was finding its own way of shaping the image of a feminist. In campaigns like Virginia Slims's long-running pitch for cigarettes, women have been invited to imagine themselves as liberated consumers, free at last to smoke when and where they please. The "new woman" who appears in so many ads today is someone who will go out and buy her own Honda without male supervision or will choose a new hair color "just for herself." She will purchase Esprit fashions because she is politically aware, or Nike sportswear because she believes in herself. But what is really happening? Why would advertisers adopt a "feminist" stance to sell their products? How are they appealing to their market?

The Revenge of the Gorgon

America's consumer culture is perfectly comfortable with the image of the feminist as an avid, if independent, shopper (look at the heroine of the cartoon strip "Cathy"), but things get dicey when women assert themselves in other ways, especially sexually. Our culture is quite happy with a woman who is sexually *available,* but not when she is a sexual *aggressor.* And when she is both aggressive and bisexual, then America really gets uncomfortable. The horrific nature of the Sharon Stone character in the film *Basic Instinct* is a potent sign of just how America views the image of the sexually predatory, bisexual woman. She becomes, in short, a monster.

Women with their own ideas about sexuality have been considered this way for a long time. Consider the ancient Greek legend of Perseus and Medusa. Medusa is the name of a monster with the body of a woman, a head curling with writhing snakes, and a stare that reduces men to stone. By cutting off Medusa's head, Perseus became one of the heroes of Greek mythology. But that's only when the tale is read from a traditional perspective. From a feminist perspective, it looks quite different.

For the writhing snakes on Medusa's head suggest other snakes, the two snakes held in the grasp of figurines unearthed in the ruins of the ancient Minoan culture of Crete. Perhaps you've seen her: the image of a goddesslike woman holding two snakes in her hands, standing imperiously in a bare-breasted pose. There is a possibility that the ancient Minoans worshipped her in what may have been a matriarchal, or women-centered, culture. But that culture was eventually overrun by the patriarchal Greeks and the beautiful Minoan snake goddess vanished. Medusa, as read in a feminist key, is the goddess's patriarchal replacement: a warning to powerful women. For a modern parallel, consider how a woman with "big hair" (say, a snaky perm) is viewed in the male-dominated corporate world. Isn't she, too, shorn of her locks by a male-defined dress code and forced to appear less sexy in the workplace and, hence, less threatening?

For feminist semioticians, such myths as Medusa's reflect a continuous history of male control, and what men have attempted especially to control is female sexuality. Consider how our culture still encourages young men to "sow their wild oats" but raises its collective eyebrows at the sexually active woman. Indeed, in the traditional sexual mythology, women are offered only three roles: the part of the virginal bride (soon to be a socially approved mother), of the whore, and of the castrating witch (these last two roles may be mixed, as in the figure of Delilah, who is both whore and castrator in the biblical story of Samson's fall). Now, recall *Basic Instinct*. How is the Sharon Stone character like Delilah? Which role does the Michael Douglas character want Stone to play? Is there a "witch" figure in the cast too? How, in short, is *Basic Instinct* a veritable display case of America's traditional sexual mythology?

Iron John

Men, too, may find themselves bound in by mythic images. Men are supposed to be warriors (he who flinches is a "coward") and studs (have you ever said "What a stud!" to mean "What a great guy"?). Just think of the typical Big Man on Campus. Is he not likely to be an athlete (the warrior role on a school campus) and a sexual star? What do you think of the guy who avoids athletics and doesn't "score"? How popular is he, and with whom?

The men's movement in America, currently led by such writers as Robert Bly, has arisen alongside the women's movement to challenge the traditional masculine gender roles that require men to be aggressive, competitive, and unemotional. In his bestseller *Iron John,* Bly calls for an exploration of both the masculine and the feminine side of male being. Thus, Bly's drum-beating warrior has a sensitive side, which distinguishes him from the sort of Conan the Barbarian hero that America's popular culture continues to go for. How else could we explain the rise of Arnold Schwarzenegger to the top of the Hollywood heap?

Indeed, the images that are shaping your own sense of gender identity are playing now at a theater near you. Start there, or with TV or MTV. What are you being told about your sexual identity? What stars are you supposed to emulate? What images do you try to avoid? What does a "real man" look like on screen? How about a "real woman"? Do you ever wish that they would just "get real"?

The Readings

Our chapter begins with Holly Devor's analysis of gender roles and how men and women manipulate the signs by which we traditionally communicate our gender identity. Peter Lyman's study of the codes that govern college fraternity behavior provides an insight into the male bonding rituals that are still enshrined within the Greek system. Next, blending archetypal cultural analysis with a bit of Zen Buddhism, Robert Bly compares the four-stage male initiation rituals of preindustrial cultures to the disrupted initiation patterns of modern men. Robin Tolmach Lakoff follows by looking at language as a gendered sign, showing how the form as well as the content of our speech reflects gender coding and relations of power. Next Deborah Tannen looks at the way women are always "marked" in our society: No detail of a woman's appearance, from her hair to her shoes to her very name, fails to send a gender-coded message about her. Elizabeth Chiseri-Strater provides a case study of the difference between women and men as speakers, writers, and readers in a representative composition class, where women see learning as a cooperative "conversation," while male students tend to see it as a competitive debate. Finally, Richard K. Herrell provides a semiotic analysis of the messages sent by the Chicago Gay and Lesbian Pride Day Parade, tracing the changes in the parade to changes in the gay community since the Stonewall riot of 1969.

Gender Role Behaviors and Attitudes

IIIIIIIIIIIIIIIIIIIIIIIIIIIIIIIIIIIIIIIIIIIIIIIIIIIIIIIIII

*"Boys will be boys, and girls will be girls": Few of our cultural my-
thologies seem as natural as this one. But in this exploration of the
gender signals that traditionally tell what a "boy" or "girl" is supposed
to look and act like, Holly Devor (b. 1951) shows how these signals
are not "natural" at all but instead are cultural constructs. While the
classic cues of masculinity—aggressive posture, self-confidence, a tough
appearance—and the traditional signs of femininity—gentleness, passivity, strong nurturing instincts—are often considered "normal," Devor
explains that they are by no means biological or psychological necessities.
Indeed, she suggests, they can be richly mixed and varied, or to paraphrase the old Kinks song, "Lola," "Boys can be girls and girls can be
boys." Holly Devor teaches in the Women's Studies Program at Simon
Fraser University and is the author of* Gender Blending: Confronting the Limits of Duality *(1989), from which this selection is excerpted.*

Gender Role Behaviors and Attitudes

The clusters of social definitions used to identify persons by gender
are collectively known as "femininity" and "masculinity." Masculine
characteristics are used to identify persons as males, while feminine ones
are used as signifiers for femaleness. People use femininity or masculinity
to claim and communicate their membership in their assigned, or chosen,
sex or gender. Others recognize our sex or gender more on the basis of
these characteristics than on the basis of sex characteristics, which are
usually largely covered by clothing in daily life.

These two clusters of attributes are most commonly seen as mirror
images of one another with masculinity usually characterized by dominance and aggression, and femininity by passivity and submission. A
more evenhanded description of the social qualities subsumed by femininity and masculinity might be to label masculinity as generally concerned with egoistic dominance and femininity as striving for cooperation or communion.[1] Characterizing femininity and masculinity in such

---

1. Maccoby, Eleanor. *Social Development: Psychological Growth and the Parent-Child
Relationship* (New York: Harcourt, Brace, Jovanovich, 1980), p. 217. Egoistic dominance
is a striving for superior rewards for oneself or a competitive striving to reduce the
rewards for one's competitors even if such action will not increase one's own rewards.
Persons who are motivated by desires for egoistic dominance not only wish the best for

a way does not portray the two clusters of characteristics as being in a hierarchical relationship to one another but rather as being two different approaches to the same question, that question being centrally concerned with the goals, means, and use of power. Such an alternative conception of gender roles captures the hierarchical and competitive masculine thirst for power, which can, but need not, lead to aggression, and the feminine quest for harmony and communal well-being, which can, but need not, result in passivity and dependence.

Many activities and modes of expression are recognized by most members of society as feminine. Any of these can be, and often are, displayed by persons of either gender. In some cases, cross-gender behaviors are ignored by observers, and therefore do not compromise the integrity of a person's gender display. In other cases, they are labeled as inappropriate gender role behaviors. Although these behaviors are closely linked to sexual status in the minds and experiences of most people, research shows that dominant persons of either gender tend to use influence tactics and verbal styles usually associated with men and masculinity, while subordinate persons, of either gender, tend to use those considered to be the province of women.[2] Thus it seems likely that many aspects of masculinity and femininity are the result, rather than the cause, of status inequalities.

Popular conceptions of femininity and masculinity instead revolve around hierarchical appraisals of the "natural" roles of males and females. Members of both genders are believed to share many of the same human characteristics, although in different relative proportions; both males and females are popularly thought to be able to do many of the same things, but most activities are divided into suitable and unsuitable categories for each gender class. Persons who perform the activities considered appropriate for another gender will be expected to perform them poorly; if they succeed adequately, or even well, at their endeavors, they may be rewarded with ridicule or scorn for blurring the gender dividing line.

The patriarchal gender schema currently in use in mainstream North American society reserves highly valued attributes for males and actively supports the high evaluation of any characteristics which might inadvertently become associated with maleness. The ideology underlying the schema postulates that the cultural superiority of males is a natural outgrowth of the innate predisposition of males toward aggression and

5

---

themselves but also wish to diminish the advantages of others whom they may perceive as competing with them.

2. Judith Howard, Philip Blumstein, and Pepper Schwartz, "Sex, Power, and Influence Tactics in Intimate Relationships," *Journal of Personality and Social Psychology* 51 (1986), pp.102–109; Peter Kollock, Philip Blumstein, and Pepper Schwartz, "Sex and Power in Interaction: Conversational Privileges and Duties," *American Sociological Review* 50 (1985), pp. 34–46.

dominance, which is assumed to flow inevitably from evolutionary and biological sources. Female attributes are likewise postulated to find their source in innate predispositions acquired in the evolution of the species. Feminine characteristics are thought to be intrinsic to the female facility for childbirth and breastfeeding. Hence, it is popularly believed that the social position of females is biologically mandated to be intertwined with the care of children and a "natural" dependency on men for the maintenance of mother-child units. Thus the goals of femininity and, by implication, of all biological females are presumed to revolve around heterosexuality and maternity.[3]

Femininity, according to this traditional formulation, "would result in warm and continued relationships with men, a sense of maternity, interest in caring for children, and the capacity to work productively and continuously in female occupations.[4] This recipe translates into a vast number of proscriptions and prescriptions. Warm and continued relations with men and an interest in maternity require that females be heterosexually oriented. A heterosexual orientation requires women to dress, move, speak, and act in ways that men will find attractive. As patriarchy has reserved active expressions of power as a masculine attribute, femininity must be expressed through modes of dress, movement, speech, and action which communicate weakness, dependency, ineffectualness, availability for sexual or emotional service, and sensitivity to the needs of others.

Some, but not all, of these modes of interrelation also serve the demands of maternity and many female job ghettos. In many cases, though, femininity is not particularly useful in maternity or employment. Both mothers and workers often need to be strong, independent, and effectual in order to do their jobs well. Thus femininity, as a role, is best suited to satisfying a masculine vision of heterosexual attractiveness.

Body postures and demeanors which communicate subordinate status and vulnerability to trespass through a message of "no threat" make people appear to be feminine. They demonstrate subordination through a minimizing of spatial use: People appear feminine when they keep their arms closer to their bodies, their legs closer together, and their torsos and heads less vertical than do masculine-looking individuals. People also look feminine when they point their toes inward and use their hands in small or childlike gestures. Other people also tend to stand closer to people they see as feminine, often invading their personal space, while people who make frequent appeasement gestures, such as smiling,

---

3. Chodorow, Nancy. *The Reproduction of Mothering: Psychoanalysis and the Reproduction of Mothering* (Berkeley: University of California Press, 1978), p. 134.

4. Jon K. Meyer and John E. Hoopes, "The Gender Dysphoria Syndromes: A Position Statement on So-Called 'Transsexualism,'" *Plastic and Reconstructive Surgery* 54 (Oct. 1974), pp. 444–51.

also give the appearance of femininity. Perhaps as an outgrowth of a subordinate status and the need to avoid conflict with more socially powerful people, women tend to excel over men at the ability to correctly interpret, and effectively display, nonverbal communication cues.[5]

Speech characterized by inflections, intonations, and phrases that convey nonaggression and subordinate status also make a speaker appear more feminine. Subordinate speakers who use more polite expressions and ask more questions in conversation seem more feminine. Speech characterized by sounds of higher frequencies are often interpreted by listeners as feminine, childlike, and ineffectual.[6] Feminine styles of dress likewise display subordinate status through greater restriction of the free movement of the body, greater exposure of the bare skin, and an emphasis on sexual characteristics. The more gender distinct the dress, the more this is the case.

Masculinity, like femininity, can be demonstrated through a wide variety of cues. Pleck has argued that it is commonly expressed in North American society through the attainment of some level of proficiency at some, or all, of the following four main attitudes of masculinity. Persons who display success and high status in their social group, who exhibit "a manly air of toughness, confidence, and self-reliance" and "the aura of aggression, violence, and daring," and who conscientiously avoid anything associated with femininity are seen as exuding masculinity.[7] These requirements reflect the patriarchal ideology that masculinity results from an excess of testosterone, the assumption being that androgens supply a natural impetus toward aggression, which in turn impels males toward achievement and success. This vision of masculinity also reflects the ideological stance that ideal maleness (masculinity) must remain untainted by female (feminine) pollutants.

Masculinity, then, requires of its actors that they organize themselves and their society in a hierarchical manner so as to be able to explicitly quantify the achievement of success. The achievement of high status in one's social group requires competitive and aggressive behavior from those who wish to obtain it. Competition which is motivated by a goal of individual achievement, or egoistic dominance, also requires of its

10

---

5. Erving Goffman, *Gender Advertisements* (New York: Harper Colophon Books, 1976); Judith A. Hall, *Non-Verbal Sex Differences: Communication Accuracy and Expressive Style* (Baltimore: Johns Hopkins University Press, 1984); Nancy M. Henley, *Body Politics: Power, Sex and Non-Verbal Communication* (Englewood Cliffs, New Jersey: Prentice Hall, 1979); Marianne Wex, *"Let's Take Back Our Space": "Female" and "Male" Body Language as a Result of Patriarchal Structures* (Berlin: Frauenliteraturverlag Hermine Fees, 1979).

6. Karen L. Adams, "Sexism and the English Language: The Linguistic Implications of Being a Woman," in *Women: A Feminist Perspective,* 3rd edition, ed. Jo Freeman (Palo Alto, Calif.: Mayfield, 1984), pp. 478–91; Hall, pp. 37, 130–37.

7. Pleck, Joseph H. *The Myth of Masculinity* (Cambridge, Mass.: M.I.T. Press, 1981), p. 139.

participants a degree of emotional insensitivity to feelings of hurt and loss in defeated others, and a measure of emotional insularity to protect oneself from becoming vulnerable to manipulation by others. Such values lead those who subscribe to them to view feminine persons as "born losers" and to strive to eliminate any similarities to feminine people from their own personalities. In patriarchally organized societies, masculine values become the ideological structure of the society as a whole. Masculinity thus becomes "innately" valuable and femininity serves a contrapuntal function to delineate and magnify the hierarchical dominance of masculinity.

Body postures, speech patterns, and styles of dress which demonstrate and support the assumption of dominance and authority convey an impression of masculinity. Typical masculine body postures tend to be expansive and aggressive. People who hold their arms and hands in positions away from their bodies, and who stand, sit, or lie with their legs apart—thus maximizing the amount of space that they physically occupy—appear most physically masculine. Persons who communicate an air of authority or a readiness for aggression by standing erect and moving forcefully also tend to appear more masculine. Movements that are abrupt and stiff, communicating force and threat rather than flexibility and cooperation, make an actor look masculine. Masculinity can also be conveyed by stern or serious facial expressions that suggest minimal receptivity to the influence of others, a characteristic which is an important element in the attainment and maintenance of egoistic dominance.[8]

Speech and dress which likewise demonstrate or claim superior status are also seen as characteristically masculine behavior patterns. Masculine speech patterns display a tendency toward expansiveness similar to that found in masculine body postures. People who attempt to control the direction of conversations seem more masculine. Those who tend to speak more loudly, use less polite and more assertive forms, and tend to interrupt the conversations of others more often also communicate masculinity to others. Styles of dress which emphasize the size of upper body musculature, allow freedom of movement, and encourage an illusion of physical power and a look of easy physicality all suggest masculinity. Such appearances of strength and readiness to action serve to create or enhance an aura of aggressiveness and intimidation central to an appearance of masculinity. Expansive postures and gestures combine with these qualities to insinuate that a position of secure dominance is a masculine one.

Gender role characteristics reflect the ideological contentions underlying the dominant gender schema in North American society. That

---

8. Goffman, *Gender Advertisements;* Hall; Henley; Wex.

schema leads us to believe that female and male behaviors are the result of socially directed hormonal instructions which specify that females will want to have children and will therefore find themselves relatively helpless and dependent on males for support and protection. The schema claims that males are innately aggressive and competitive and therefore will dominate over females. The social hegemony of this ideology ensures that we are all raised to practice gender roles which will confirm this vision of the nature of the sexes. Fortunately, our training to gender roles is neither complete nor uniform. As a result, it is possible to point to multitudinous exceptions to, and variations on, these themes. Biological evidence is equivocal about the source of gender roles, psychological androgyny is a widely accepted concept. It seems most likely that gender roles are the result of systematic power imbalances based on gender discrimination.[9]

Reading the Text

1. List the characteristics that Devor describes as being traditionally "masculine" and "feminine."
2. What relationship does Devor see between characteristics considered masculine and feminine?
3. How does Devor explain the cultural belief in the "superiority" of males?
4. How, according to Devor, do speech and dress communicate gender roles?

Reading the Signs

1. In small same-sex groups, brainstorm lists of traits that you consider "masculine" and "feminine," then have each group write their lists on the board. Compare the lists produced by male and female groups. What patterns of differences or similarities do you see? To what extent do the traits presume a heterosexual orientation? How do you account for your results?
2. Study the speech patterns, styles of dress, and other nonverbal cues communicated by your friends during a social occasion, such as a party, trying not to reveal that you are observing them for an assignment. Then write an essay in which you analyze these cues used by your friends. To what extent do your friends enact the traditional gender roles Devor describes?
3. Look through a popular magazine, such as *Vogue, Rolling Stone,* or *Gentlemen's Quarterly,* for advertisements that depict men and women interacting with each other. Then write an essay in which you interpret the body postures of the models, using Devor's selection as your framework for analysis. How do males and females typically stand? To what extent do the

---

9. Howard, Blumstein, and Schwartz; Kollock, Blumstein, and Schwartz.

models enact stereotypically masculine or feminine stances? To develop
your essay, consult Diane Barthel, "A Gentleman and a Consumer," p. 128.
4. Devor argues that female fashion traditionally has restricted body movement
while male styles of dress have commonly allowed freedom of movement.
In class, discuss whether this gender division is still true today, being sure
to consider a range of clothing types (e.g., athletic wear, corporate dress,
party fashion, and so forth).
5. Compare the gender norms of Japanese society as described by Dorinne K.
Kondo (see "On Being a Conceptual Anomaly," p. 477) to the norms of
North American society that Devor outlines in her selection. Use the details
of your comparison to formulate an overall argument about the roles of
each gender in the two cultures.

PETER LYMAN
The Fraternal Bond as a Joking Relationship

*Let's face it: College fraternities aren't Boy Scout troops. With the
reported incidence of fraternity-based date rapes on the rise and controversies about songbooks with racially and sexually offensive lyrics raging
at universities from coast to coast, the Greeks are looking increasingly
out of step with contemporary standards of behavior. But as Peter Lyman
(b. 1940) shows in this anthropological study of the fraternal world
view, the aggressiveness, the stunts, the ribald drinking songs are all part
of a bonding ritual by which the boys group together in defense against
what they see as threats from the worlds of work and of women. Being
cool, and being tough, mean being in control for young men who feel
the world slipping out of their grasp. Peter Lyman is university librarian
and dean of libraries at the University of Southern California, where
his research interests include the sociology of emotions and the sociology
of information.*

One evening during dinner, forty-five fraternity men suddenly broke
into the dining room of a nearby campus sorority, surrounded the thirty
women residents, and forced them to watch while one pledge gave a
speech on Freud's theory of penis envy as another demonstrated various
techniques of masturbation with a rubber penis. The women sat silently
staring downward at their plates listening for about ten minutes, until a
woman law student who was the graduate resident in charge of the house
walked in, surveyed the scene, and demanded, "Please leave immedi-

ately!" As she later described that moment, "There was a mocking roar from the men, 'It's tradition.' I said, 'That's no reason to do something like this, please leave!' And they left. I was surprised. Then the women in the house started to get angry. And the guy who made the penis envy speech came back and said to us, 'That was funny to me. If that's not funny to you I don't know what kind of sense of humor you have, but I'm sorry.'"

That night the women sat around the stairwell of their house discussing the event, some angry and others simply wanting to forget the whole thing. They finally decided to ask the university to require that the men return to discuss the event. When university officials threatened to take action, the men agreed to the meeting. I was asked by both the men and the women involved to attend the discussion as a facilitator, and was given permission to write about the event as long as I concealed their identities.

In the women's view, the joke had not failed because of its subject; they considered sexual jokes to be a normal part of the erotic joking relationship between men and women. They criticized its emotional structure, the mixture of sexuality with aggression and the atmosphere of physical intimidation in the room. Although many of the men individually regretted the damage to their relationship with women friends in the group, they argued that the special group solidarity created by the initiation was a unique form of masculine friendship that justified the inconvenience caused the women.

Fraternal group bonding in everyday life frequently takes the form of *joking relationships,* in which men relate to each other by exchanging insults and jokes in order to create a feeling of solidarity that negotiates the latent tension and aggression they feel toward each other (Radcliffe-Brown, 1959). The humor of joking relationships is generally sexual and aggressive, and frequently consists of sexist or racist jokes. As Freud (1960:99) observed, the jokes men direct *toward* women are generally sexual, tend to be clever (like double entendres), and have a seductive purpose; but the jokes that men tell *about* women in the presence of other men tend to be sexist rather than intimate or erotic, and use hostile and aggressive rather than clever verbal forms. In this case study, joking relationships will be analyzed to uncover the emotional dynamics of fraternal groups and the impact of fraternal bonding upon relationships between men and women.

The Girls' Story

The women had frequently been the target of fraternity initiation 5 rites in the past, and generally enjoyed this joking relationship with the men, if with a certain ambivalence. "There was the naked Christmas

Carol event, they were singing 'We wish you a Merry Christmas,' and 'Bring on the hasty pudding' was the big line they liked to yell out. And they had five or six pledges who had to strip in front of the house and do naked jumping jacks on the lawn, after all the women in the house were lined up on the steps to watch." The women did not think these events were hostile because they had been invited to watch, and the men stood with them watching, suggesting that the pledges, not the women, were the targets of the joke. This defined the joke as sexual, not sexist, and part of the normal erotic joking relation between "guys and girls." Still, these jokes were ritual events, not real social relationships. One woman said, "We were just supposed to watch, and the guys were watching us watch. The men set up the stage and the women are brought along to observe. They were the controlling force, then they jump into the car and take off."

At the meeting with the men, two of the women spoke for the group while eleven others sat silently in the center, surrounded by about thirty men. The first woman began, "Your humor was pretty funny as long as it was sexual, but when it went beyond sexual to sexist, then it became painful. You were saying 'I'm better than you.' When you started using sex as a way of proving your superiority, it hurt me and made me angry."

The second woman said that the fraternity's raid had the tone of a rape. "I admit we knew you were coming over, and we were whispering about it. But it went too far, and I felt afraid to say anything. Why do men always think about women in terms of violating them, in sexual imagery? You have to understand that the combination of a sexual topic with the physical threat of all of you standing around terrified me. I couldn't move. You have to realize that when men combine sexuality and force, it's terrifying to women."

Many of the women began by saying, "I'm not a feminist, but. . . ," to reassure the men that although they felt angry, they hoped to reestablish the many individual friendships that had existed between men and women in the two groups. In part the issue was resolved when the women accepted the men's construction of the event as a joke, although a failed joke, transforming a discussion about sexuality and force into a debate about good and bad jokes.

For an aggressive joke to be funny, and most jokes contain some hostility, the joke teller must send the audience a cue that says "this is meant as a joke." If accepted, the cue invokes special social rules that "frame" the hostile words that are typical of jokes, ensuring they will not be taken seriously. The men had implicitly sent such a cue when they stood *next* to the women during the naked jumping jacks. Verbal aggression mediated by the joke form will generally be without later consequences in the everyday world, and will be judged in terms of the formal intention of jokes, shared play and laughter.

In accepting the construction of the event as "just a joke" the women   10
absolved the men of responsibility for their actions by calling them "little
boys." One woman said, "It's not wrong, they're just boys playing a
prank. They're little boys, they don't know what they're doing. It was
unpleasant, but we shouldn't make a big deal out of it." In appealing to
the rules of the joke form (as in saying "That was funny to me, I don't
know what kind a sense of humor you have"), the men sacrificed their
personal friendships with the women in order to protect the feelings of
fraternal solidarity it produced. In calling the men "little boys" the
women were bending the rules of friendship, trying to preserve their
relationships to the guys by playing a patient and nurturing role.

The Guys' Story

Aside from occasional roars of laughter, the men interrupted the
women only once. When a woman began to say that the men had
obviously intended to intimidate them, the men loudly protested that
the women couldn't possibly judge their intentions, that they intended
the whole event only as a joke, and the intention of a joke is, by
definition, just fun.

At this point the two black men in the fraternity intervened to
explain the rules of male joking relationships to the women. In a sense,
they said, they agreed with the women, being the object of hostile jokes
is painful. As they described it, the collective talk of the fraternity at
meals and group events was entirely hostile joking, including many racist
jokes. One said, "I've had to listen to things in the house that I'd have
hit someone for saying if I've heard them outside." The guys roared with
laughter, for the fraternal joking relation consisted almost entirely of
aggressive words that were barely contained by the convention that joke
tellers are not responsible for what they say.

One woman responded, "Maybe people should be hit for saying
those things, maybe that's the right thing to do." But the black speaker
was trying to explain the rules of male joke culture to the women, "If
you'd just ignored us, it wouldn't have been any fun." To ignore a joke,
even though it makes you feel hurt or angry, is to be cool, one of the
primary masculine ideals of the group.

Another man tried to explain the failure of the joke in terms of the
difference between the degree of "crudeness" appropriate "between
guys" and between "guys and girls." He said, "As I was listening to the
speech I was both embarrassed and amused. I was standing at the edge
of the room, near the door, and when I looked at the guys I was laughing
but when I looked at the girls I was embarrassed. I could see both sides
at the same time. It was too crude for your sense of propriety. We have

a sense of crudeness you don't have. That's a cultural aspect of the difference between girls and guys."

The other men laughed as he mentioned "how crude we are at the house," and one of the black men added, "You wouldn't believe how crude it gets." Many of the men later said that although they individually found the jokes about women vulgar, the jokes were justified because they were necessary for the formation of the fraternal bond. These men thought that the mistake had been to reveal their crudeness to the women; this was "in bad taste."

In part the crudeness was a kind of "signifying" or "dozens," a ritual exchange of intimate insults that creates group solidarity. "If there's one theme that goes on it's the emphasis on being able to take a lot of ridicule, of shit, and not getting upset about it. Most of the interaction we have is verbally abusing each other, making disgusting references to your mother's sexuality, or the women you were seen with, or your sex organ, the size of your sex organ. And you aren't cool unless you can take it without trying to get back." Being cool is an important male value in other settings as well, like sports or work; the joking relationship is a kind of training that, in one guy's words, "teaches you how to keep in control of your emotions."

But the guys themselves would not have described their group as a joking relationship or fraternal bond, they called it friendship. One man said that he had found perhaps a dozen guys in the house who were special friends, "guys I could cry in front of." Another said, "I think the guys are very close, they would do nearly anything for each other, drive each other places, give each other money. I think when they have problems about school, their car, or something like that, they can talk to each other. I'm not sure they can talk to each other about problems with women though." Although the image of crying in front of the other guys was often mentioned as an example of the intimacy of the fraternal bond, no one could actually recall anyone in the group ever crying. In fact crying would be an admission of vulnerability which would violate the ideals of "strength" and "being cool."

The women interpreted the sexist jokes as a sign of vulnerability. "The thing that struck me the most about our meeting together," one said, "was when the men said they were afraid of trusting women, afraid of being seen as jerks." One of the guys added, "I think down deep all the guys would love to have satisfying relationships with women. I think they're scared of failing, of having to break away from the group they've become comfortable with. I think being in a fraternity, having close friendships with men is a replacement for having close relationships with women. It'd be painful for them because they'd probably fail." These men preferred to relate to women as a group at fraternity parties, where they could take women back to their rooms for quick sex without commitments.

Sexist jokes also had a social function, policing the boundaries of the group, making sure that guys didn't form serious relationships with girls and leave the fraternity (cf. Slater, 1963). "One of the guys just acquired a girlfriend a few weeks ago. He's someone I don't think has had a woman to be friends with, maybe ever, at least in a long time. Everybody has been ribbing him intensely the last few weeks. It's good natured in tone. Sitting at dinner they've invented a little song they sing to him. People yell questions about his girlfriend, the size of her vagina, does she have big breasts." Thus, in dealing with women, the group separated intimacy from sex, defining the male bond as intimate but not sexual (homosocial), and relationships with women as sexual but not intimate (heterosexual).

The Fraternal Bond in Men's Life Cycle

Men often speak of friendship as a group relationship, not a dyadic 20 one, and men's friendships often grow from the experience of shared activities or risk, rather than from self-disclosing talk (cf. Rubin, 1983:130). J. Glenn Gray (1959:89–90) distinguishes the intimate form of friendship from the comradeship that develops from the shared experience of suffering and danger of men at war. In comradeship, he argues, the individual's sense of self is subordinated to a group identity, whereas friendship is based upon a specific feeling for another that heightens a sense of individuality.

In this case, the guys used joking relationships to suspend the ordinary rules and responsibilities of everyday life, placing the intimacy of the fraternal group in competition with heterosexual friendships. One of the men had been inexpressive as he listened to the discussion, but spoke about the fraternity in a voice filled with emotion, "The penis envy speech was a hilarious idea, great college fun. That's what I joined the fraternity for, a good time. College is a stage in my life to do crazy and humorous things. In ten years when I'm in the business world I won't be able to carry on like this [loud laughter from the men]. The initiation was intended to be humorous. We didn't think through how sensitive you women were going to be."

This speech gives the fraternal bond a specific place in the life cycle. The joking relationship is a ritual bond that creates a male group bond in the transition between boyhood and manhood: after the separation from the family where the authority of mothers limits fun, but before becoming subject to the authority of work. One man later commented on the transitional nature of the fraternal bond, "I think a lot of us are really scared of losing total control over our own lives. Having to sacrifice our individuality. I think we're scared of work in the same way we're scared of women." The jokes expressed hostility toward women because an intimate friendship with a woman was associated with "loss of control," namely the risk of responsibility for work and family.

Most, but not all, of the guys in the fraternity were divided between their group identity and a sense of personal identity that was expressed in private friendships with women. Some of the guys, like the one who could "see both sides" as he stood on the edge of the group during the initiation, had reached a point of leaving the fraternity because they couldn't reconcile the tension between his group identity and the sense of self that he felt in his friendships with women.

Ultimately the guys justified the penis envy joke because it created a special kind of male intimacy. But although the fraternal group was able to appropriate the guys' needs for intimacy and commitment it is not clear that it was able to satisfy those needs, because it defined strength as shared risk taking rather than a quality of individual character or personality. In Gray's terms, the guys were constructing comradeship through an erotic of shared activities with an element of risk, shared danger, or rule breaking such as sports, paramilitary games, wild parties, and hostile jokes. In these contexts, strength implied the substitution of a group identity for a personal code that might extend to commitment and care for others (cf. Bly 1982).

In the guys' world, aggression was identified with strength, and defined as loss of control only if it was angry. The fraternal bond was built upon an emotional balance between aggression and anger, for life of the group centered upon the mobilization of aggressive energies in rule-governed activities, especially sports and games. In each arena aggression was defined as strength (toughness) only when it was rule-governed (cool). Getting angry was called "losing control," and the guys thought they were most likely to lose control when they experienced themselves as personally dependent, that is, in relationships with women and at work. The sense of order within fraternal groups is based upon the belief that all members are equally dependent upon the rules, and that no *personal* dependence is created within the group. This is not true of the family or of relations with women, both of which are intimate, and, from the guys' point of view, are "out of control" because they are governed by emotional commitments.

The guys recognized the relationship between their male bond and the work world by claiming that "high officials of the University know about the way we act, and they understand what we are doing." Although this might be taken as evidence that the guys were internalizing their fathers' norms and thus inheriting the rights of patriarchy, the guys described their fathers as slaves to work and women, not as patriarchs. It is striking that the guys would not accept the notion that men have more power than women; to them it is not men who rule, but work and women that govern men.

References

Bly, Robert. (1982) "What men really want: An interview with Keith Thompson." *New Age* 30–37, 50–51.

Freud, Sigmund. (1960) *Jokes and Their Relation to the Unconscious.* New York: W. W. Norton.

Gray, Glenn J. (1959) *The Warriors: Reflections on Men in Battle.* New York: Harper.

Radcliffe-Brown, Alfred. (1959) *Structure and Function in Primitive Society.* Glencoe: The Free Press.

Rubin, Lillian. (1983) *Intimate Strangers.* New York: Harper & Row.

Slater, Phillip. 1963) "On Social Regression." *The American Sociological Review* 28: 339–364.

Reading the Text

1. Summarize in your own words the differences between male joke culture and female joke culture.
2. How, according to Lyman, did the black fraternity members play a different role than the whites in the meeting with the female students?
3. Why did the women interpret the fraternity stunt as a "sign of vulnerability"?
4. What is the difference between intimacy and comradeship, in Lyman's terms?

Reading the Signs

1. In small same-sex groups, brainstorm ways in which both the men and women could have more effectively signaled their intentions and responses to the fraternity stunt incident. How, in other words, might you alter the situation so that all parties involved would have considered the joke a joke? Then share your group's suggestions with the whole class. Do you see any patterns in the suggestions provided by male and female groups?
2. Using Holly Devor's "Gender Role Behaviors and Attitudes" (p. 603) as your critical framework, write an essay explaining the extent to which the fraternity members were enacting traditionally masculine roles and the sorority women were enacting traditionally feminine roles.
3. Interview members of fraternities and sororities on campus to learn if pranks similar to the one Lyman describes occur. If so, ask both males and females about the motivation behind the pranks and their responses to them. Then write an essay in which you explore the pranks' significance to the men and women who participate in them. Do you find gender differences among your interviewees? Do all parties find such pranks equally funny? Is the source of the humor the same for both groups?
4. Compare the value of being cool for the fraternity men with the "cool pose" adopted by African-American males (see Richard Majors, "Cool Pose: The Proud Signature of Black Survival," p. 471). How can each be

seen as a mechanism for surviving in the world? How do class and ethnicity affect the meaning of being cool for each group?

5. Think of a group with which you have close relations (it could be a fraternity or sorority; a club; a political, sports, or religious group; or simply a group of friends). In your journal, reflect on the ways you've bonded with others in the group. What signs do you send to each other—and to outsiders—to indicate your solidarity? What difference does it make that your group is same-sex or mixed? Is your relationship with group members, in Lyman's terms, more intimate or more comradely?

6. One of the current controversies on campuses across the nation involves fraternity pranks and songbooks, which often include racially charged and sexually violent lyrics. Do you think there should be restrictions on such pranks or songbooks, as have been instituted on many college campuses? In class, form two teams and debate this issue, focusing on a controversy at your own campus or elsewhere (research this issue by first checking the *Readers' Guide to Periodical Literature* in your library). To develop your arguments, you might consult Nat Hentoff, "'Speech Codes' on the Campus and Problems of Free Speech," p. 385, and Thomas C. Grey, "Responding to Abusive Speech on Campus: A Model Statute," p. 392.

ROBERT BLY

Men's Initiation Rites

||||||||||||||||||||||||||||||||||||||||||||||||||||||||||||

Though less influential and less politically active than the women's movement, the men's movement in America has also contributed to a readjustment of the way we perceive gender. Just as feminism has caused women to explore their relationships to their mothers and grandmothers, so has the men's movement prompted men to rediscover their fathers. But as Robert Bly (b. 1926), one of the high priests of the men's movement, suggests in this analysis of male initiation rites, modern industrial culture makes it very difficult for men to bond with their fathers and, hence, to separate from them in a psychically healthy way. Through an exploration of the archetypal stages of male initiation that can be exemplified in ancient and preindustrial cultures, Bly traces the path that modern men are missing in their "messy" progress toward manhood. The author of Iron John: A Book About Men *(1990), one of the bibles of the men's movement, Robert Bly is one of America's best-known poets and translators, who began to explore the father-son relationship in his poems long before the men's movement came onto the scene.*

The ancient rites of male initiation were complicated and subtle experiences which could be imagined better as a continual spiral than as a walk down a road. The spiral could be described as a year which repeats itself in seasons. The four seasons of male development amount to four stages, four steps, and four events, though we all know that seasons run into each other, and repeat.

The four seasons, or stages, I'll discuss here are bonding with and separation from the mother; bonding with and separation from the father; finding of the male mother; and the interior marriage or marriage with the Hidden Woman.

Bonding with and Separation from Mother

The first event is bonding with the mother and separation from the mother. Bonding of the son with the mother usually goes quite well in this country, though we could distinguish between instantaneous birth-bonding and a later, slower emotional bonding. The medical profession has adopted birth practices involving harsh lights, steel tables, painful medicines, and, most harmful of all, the infant's isolation for long periods, all of which damage the birth bond. Joseph Chilton Pearce has written of that movingly in *The Magical Child* (Dell). Mothers can sometimes repair that bonding later by careful attention to their sons' needs, by praise, carrying, talking, protecting, comforting—and many mothers do exactly that. Most American men achieve a successful bonding with the mother. It is the *separation* from the mother that doesn't go well.

When the world of men is submerged in the world of technology and business, it seems to the boy that cool excitement lies there, and warm excitement with the mother; money with the father, food with the mother; anxiety with the father, assurance with the mother; conditional love with the father, and unconditional love with the mother. All over the United States we meet women whose thirty-five-year-old sons are still living at home. One such woman told me that her divorce brought her freedom from the possessiveness of her husband, who wanted her home every night, etc. But she had noticed last week that her son said, "Why are you going out so much in the evenings?" In recent years the percentage of adult sons still living at home has increased; and we can see much other evidence of the difficulty the male feels in breaking with the mother: the guilt often felt toward the mother; the constant attempt, usually unconscious, to be a nice boy; lack of male friends; absorption in boyish flirtation with women; attempts to carry women's pain, and be their comforters; efforts to change a wife into a mother; abandonment of discipline for "softness and gentleness"; a general confusion about maleness. These qualities are all simple human characteristics, and yet when they, or a number of them, appear together, they point toward a failure in the very first stage of initiation. Ancient initiation practices, still going on in many parts of the world, solve this problem decisively through active intervention by the older males. Typically, when three or four boys in a tribe get to be eight to twelve years old, a group of older men simply appears at the houses one night, and takes them from their mothers, with whom the boys never live again. They may return, but often with faces covered with ash, to indicate that they are now "dead" to their mothers, who in their part return this play by crying out in mourning when they see their sons again, and acting out rituals otherwise done for the dead.

Bonding with and Separation from Father

The second season of initiation is bonding with the father and sep-   5
aration from the father. Before the Industrial Revolution this event took place with most sons. But this bonding requires many hours in which the bodies of the father and son sit, stand, or work close to each other, within a foot or two. The average father in the United States talks to his son less than ten minutes a day. And that talk may be talk from a distance, such as "Is your room cleaned up?" or "Are you on drugs?" As we know, the psyche of the child interprets the death of a parent personally; that is, the psyche regards it as a failure on the child's part: "If I had been worthy, my parent would not have died." So the psyche of the small son interprets without question the father's absence from the house for hours and hours each day as evidence of the same unworthiness. The German psychiatrist Alexander Mitscherlich in his book *Society Without the Father* (Tavistock Publications) gives an image still more startling. He declares that when a son does not witness his father at work through the day and through the year, a hole develops in the son's psyche, and that hole fills with demons. Dustin Hoffman played such a son in *Marathon Man:* The son does not bond with the father then, but on the contrary a magnetic repulsion takes place, for by secret processes the father becomes associated in the son's mind with demonic energy, cold evil, Nazis, concentration camp guards, evil capitalists, agents of the CIA, powers of world conspiracy. Some of the fear felt in the sixties by young leftist men ("Never trust anyone over thirty") came from that well of demons.

The severance that the Norwegian immigrant male, for example, experienced when he lost his old language in which feelings naturally expressed themselves—and the Polish immigrant, and the German immigrant—affected the ability of these men to talk to their sons, and their sons to their sons. We might add to that the frontier mentality, whose pressure of weather, new land, building, plowing, etc. left almost all feeling activities—music appreciation, novel reading, poetry recital —to women. This request to women that they carry on "feeling" activities obviously deepened the crisis, because the boy then learns cultural feeling, verbal feeling, discrimination of feeling almost entirely from his mother. Bonding requires physical closeness, a sense of protection, approval of one's very being, conversation in which feelings and longings can step out, and some attention which the young male can feel as *care for the soul*. The boy in the United States receives almost all of these qualities, if he receives them at all, from the mother, and so his bonding takes place with her, not with the father. If bonding with the father does not take place, how can separation from the father take place? There are many exceptions to this generalization, of course, but most of the exceptions I met were in men who worked in some physical way with their fathers, as carpenters, woodcutters, musicians, farmers, etc.

American men in general cannot achieve separation from the father because they have not achieved bonding with the father; or more exactly, our bonding with the father goes on slowly, bit by bit, often beginning again, after the remoteness of adolescence, at the age of thirty-five or so; and of course this gradual bonding over many years slows up the separation as well, so that the American man is often forty or forty-five before the first two events of initiation have taken place completely enough to be felt as events. The constant attempt by young males working in popular music to play a music their fathers never played or heard suggests an inability to bond with their fathers. The fathers in their turn feel puzzled, rejected, inadequate, and defeated. So many American fathers if they answer the phone when a son or daughter calls will usually say after a moment: "Here is your mother."

Male Mother

A third event in the ancient male initiation was the appearance of the male mother, and we'll call that the essential event. John Layard, who gained much of his knowledge of male initiation from his years with the Stone-Age tribes of Malekula, declares in his study called *The Celtic Quest* (Spring Publications) that Arthur was a male mother. "Arthur" may have been the name traditionally given to such an initiator centuries before he became King Arthur. In the ancient Mabinogion[1] story "Culhwch and Olwen," Arthur is the keeper of a castle to which the young male initiate gains entry. Though male, Arthur's kingdom, Layard says, "has to be 'entered' as though it were a woman." Layard continues: "This entry into the male world which is a 'second mother' is what all initiation rites are concerned with." When Arthur has accepted the invader, he details the things he will not give to the young man,

---

1. **Mabinogion**   Welsh prose epic.—EDS.

which are ship, cloak, sword, shield, dagger, and Guinevere, his wife. He then asks the boy, "What do you want?" Culhwch says, "I want my hair trimmed." Then "Arthur took a golden comb and shears with loops of silver, and combed his head." The younger male places his head, or his consciousness, into the hands of an older man he trusts, and by that act he is symbolically freed from his bonds both to his mother and to his father.

Our culture lacks the institution of the male mother: The memory of it seems to have dropped into forgetfulness. We receive only one birth, from the mother, even though Jesus insisted on the importance of a second birth. We lose the meaning of his metaphor by interpreting it as a conversion experience. It was a new birth from the male, and it is possible that Jesus himself provided this second birth to young men. The Australian aborigines to this day arrange an experience of male birth that the sons do not forget: They construct a sort of tunnel of sticks and brush twenty to thirty feet long, and at the proper moment put the boys in at one end, and receive them, surrounded by the tremendous male noise of the bullroarers, at the other end, and immediately declare them to be born out of the male body for once and for all—a new boy, a new body, a new spirit, a man at last.

This experience, of course, implies the willingness of the older males to become male mothers, and so exhibit the protectiveness, self-sacrificing generosity and soul-caring that the female mother traditionally shows. In Africa, males of the Kikuyu tribe take boys who are hungry and terrified, after a day's fasting, and sit them down among adult males around a fire late at night. Each adult male then cuts his arm with a knife and lets his blood flow into a gourd which is passed on to the young boys to drink, so that they can see and taste the depth of the older males' love for them. By this single ceremony, the boy is asked to shift from female milk to male blood.

It is Arthur's kindness, savvy, spiritual energy, his store of psychic knowledge, his willingness to lead, guide, and welcome the young male which we lack in American ritual, when, for example, the initiating power is held by sergeants, priests, or corporate executives. The qualities I've mentioned above cannot appear together, or only rarely, in those three roles because we have forgotten the male mother role. We need to rethink the purpose of a male mother and how he achieves that purpose. The old apprentice system in crafts and arts through the Middle Ages and Renaissance accomplished initiation for some young men, but the mass university lectures of today cannot provide it—nor can workshop classes of twenty. Pablo Casals was a male mother to some young men; William Carlos Williams to others, and there are always a few marvelous teachers or woodsmen here and there who understand the concept and embody it. By and large, however, one would say that if the American male does achieve the first two events—bonding with and separation from the mother, bonding with and separation from the father—he will come up short on this third step. A man needs to look decisively for a male mother, but he cannot look if the culture has not even retained the concept in its storehouse of possibilities. The men around Arthur were healthy because he nourished them, and they expected it.

The Invisible Czarina

We notice that the male mother, or primary initiator, is not one's personal father; so by this third step, the male passes beyond the realm of his personal mother and father. He also expands his conception of women beyond the roles of wife, girlfriend, mistress, chick, movie actress, model. The predominant figure in the fourth stage is the Invisible Czarina, or Elena the Wise, as some Russian fairy tales call her, and in the fourth season it is the man's task to marry her. Edward Schieffel, in *Rituals of Manhood,* writing about contemporary male rituals in New Guinea, reports that in the Kaluli tribe the young boys sometimes find in the pool below a waterfall during ceremonies a "stone bride," which they can identify because it moves on its own. We see here again a connection being made with a secret, powerful, and usually helpful woman who is not a living woman. The fourth step does not aim then at a hardening or intensification of maleness, but rather at a deepening of feeling toward the religious life. We can immediately see the connection with the worship of the woman in Arthurian legend, the image of Mona Lisa in Italy, "Diotima" in Socrates' Greece, and lunar substance that contributes to the creation of "gold" that is the aim of alchemy. The "woman by the well" preserves in many European fairy tales and in the New Testament the memory of the Hidden Woman. In Celtic initiation, Arthur guides the young male toward the marriage with her; she is in fact the Olwen ("white trace" or "track of the moon") mentioned in the title of the Celtic story, "Culhwch and Olwen."

The fourth season therefore represents an astonishing leap into the other world and a love for a radiance of the yin. Initiation results in less dependence on living women or "strong" women, less fear of the feminine and creation of the more balanced older man that Zen and Tibetan traditions, to name only these two, aim at. Western culture has retained a dim memory of this fourth stage; and when most men today imagine initiation, a fourth stage like this is probably not a part of their imaginative scenario, even though the Wild Man story or "Iron Hans" ends like so many Grimm Brothers tales, in a marriage. The twentieth-century Spanish poet Antonio Machado retained a very lively memory of Elena or the Hidden Woman, about whom he wrote a number of poems. This poem he wrote around 1900:

Close to the road we sit down one day,
our whole life now amounts to time, and our sole concern
the attitudes of despair that we adopt
while we wait. But She will not fail to arrive.

I want to emphasize that the ancient view of male development implies a spiral movement rather than a linear passage through clearly defined stages, with a given stage finished once and for all. As men, we go through all stages in a shallow way, then go back, live in several stages at once, go through them all with slightly less shallowness, return again to our parents, bond and separate once more, find a new male mother, and so on and so on. The old initiation systems having been destroyed, and their initiators gone, no step is ever done cleanly, just as we don't achieve at twelve a clean break with our mothers. So a quality of male initiation as we live it in the culture is a continual returning. Gradually and messily over many years a man achieves this complicated or subtle experience; it is very slow.

Reading the Text

1. Summarize in your own words the four stages of male development that Bly describes.
2. What is the difference between a male mother and a female mother, according to Bly?
3. Why does Bly emphasize that he considers male development to be a "spiral" movement?
4. How does modern society differ from ancient societies, in Bly's view?

Reading the Signs

1. Write a journal entry in which you explore your response to Bly's essay. If you are male, do you recognize the patterns he claims characterize the experiences of boys growing up today, such as distant fathers? If you are female, how do you respond to Bly's ignoring of the experiences of girls growing up?
2. How might Bly interpret the fraternity pranks described in Peter Lyman's "The Fraternal Bond as a Joking Relationship" (p. 609)? To what extent do you think the rituals Lyman describes are part of the "four seasons" of male development that Bly discusses? Is the bonding that occurs among the fraternity members similar to the sort of bonding that Bly finds critical to male development?
3. Bly has been a leading force in the emergence of the men's movement, which parallels the women's movement in many ways. In class, discuss whether you think there is a need for a men's movement.
4. Bly would argue for a redefinition of gender roles in our society. In small

groups, discuss what redefined gender roles might mean. What different roles for men and women, heterosexuals and homosexuals, would you suggest? Read or review Holly Devor's "Gender Role Behaviors and Attitudes" (p. 603) before you begin your discussion.

5. Read Bly's *Iron John,* his fullest exploration of the need for a men's movement, and write a critique of it. How persuaded are you that men need the sort of psychic renewal that Bly imagines?

ROBIN TOLMACH LAKOFF
Women's Language

||||||||||||||||||||||||||||||||||||||||||||||||||

Do the men in your class tend to dominate during class discussion? Do the women tend to contribute by asking questions? According to Robin Tolmach Lakoff's (b. 1942) linguistic analysis of women's speech patterns, such tendencies may be expected in an environment where the prevailing gender codes compel men to be aggressive and women to be conciliatory. In all cultures, Tolmach argues, women's speech patterns reflect the gender codes of their society, and that wherever one looks, women's speech is defined as "illogical" in comparison with the "logical" norms of male speech. The very form of our speech is political, Lakoff argues in this excerpt from Talking Power: The Politics of Language in Our Lives *(1990), reflecting the politics of gender in society. Robin Tolmach Lakoff is professor of linguistics at the University of California, Berkeley. Her books include* Language and Woman's Place *(1975),* Face Value: The Politics of Beauty *(with Raquel Scherr, 1984), and* Father Knows Best: The Use and Abuse of Power in Freud's Case of Dora *(1993).*

The characteristic ways of communication that have been identified as typical of women range in English over the whole of the linguistic repertoire, from sounds to word choice to syntactic features to pragmatic and conversational options, with the preponderance in the latter categories. In this, gender-related diversity differs from regional and social dialects, whose most noticeable and numerous variations from the standard cluster in the phonology and the lexicon. This difference makes sense because dialects develop in isolation from one another as a result of the instability of linguistic forms and influence from other languages. But gender-related differences have a strong psychological component: They are intimately related to the judgments of members of a culture about how to be and think like a good man or woman. So the characteristic forms cluster at the end of the linguistic spectrum most related to psychological expression. Also anomalous, if we were disposed to consider women's linguistic patterns as one sort of social dialect, is the fact that they persist despite intense and constant fraternization with speakers of the standard; most dialects tend to erode if speakers are constantly exposed to the standard language. Gender differences in language arise not because male and female speakers are isolated from each other, but precisely because they live in close contiguity, which constantly causes comparisons and reinforces the need for polarization—linguistic and otherwise. As is true of many types of dialects and special linguistic forms, some speakers of women's language, but few speakers of the standard (male language), are able to *code-switch*, that is, use the nonstandard form in some contexts, the standard in others. Women in business or professional settings often sound indistinguishable from their male counterparts. Speakers of nondominant forms must be bilingual in this way, at least passively, to survive; speakers of the dominant form need not be. (So women don't generally complain that men's communication is impossible to understand, but the battle cry "What do women want?" has echoed in one form or another down the centuries.)

Also striking is that some form of women's language exists in every culture that has been investigated with these questions in mind. The same forms are found in language after language. These special forms may differ from one language to another, but most functional characteristics of women's language are widespread, an unremarkable fact since the language represents behavior supposedly typical of women across the majority of cultures: alleged illogic, submissiveness, sexual utility to men, secondary status.

Reality and Interpretation

As an example of how one form may represent different functions in different cultures, consider . . . the Malagasy special use of conversational logic.[1] Because information in that culture is more precious than it is for us, the prudent speaker hoards any that he acquires, to the point of speaking in a way we would consider deliberately misleading, in violation of the rules of conversational logic; although to our eyes, neither a breach of politeness nor self-protection is involved. But this strategy is typical only of male Malagasy speakers. Women do just the

---

1. Keenan, E. O. 1976. "The Universality of Conversational Postulates." *Language in Society* 5:67–80.

reverse: speak directly and to the point (unless there are obvious reasons to do otherwise). As a result, women are considered poor communicators: They just don't know how to behave in a conversation, don't know how to transmit information properly, and are therefore illogical.

In other words, the Malagasy stereotype of women is identical to ours: Women don't handle the flow of information properly. But the explicit behavior that gives rise to the stereotype is diametrically opposite in the two cultures. So it cannot be that the basis of the stereotype is a universal Aristotelian logical principle. No one decides what communication is intrinsically "logical," then notices that women don't do it, and therefore rationally determines that women are illogical. It's rather the reverse. The dominant group first notices the ways in which the nondominant differ from themselves. They do not think to attribute such differences to external necessity imposed by themselves, or to differences in cultural expectations. Instead, they assume the difference must be due to some deep intrinsic physical and/or psychological distinction that irrevocably divides the sexes: The need for polarization is very strong. Then they decide that there must be some principled difference between men and women to explain the discrepancy. Women are the other; the other is the worse. (That is already given knowledge.) So there is something about women's minds or bodies that makes them be, think, and speak worse than men. Then what men (ideally) do is called "logical." Therefore women's ideal style is "illogical." Whatever is characteristic of the male in a culture will be defined and identified within that culture as "right" or "logical" behavior. Since women are the other, anything they do that is different will be assigned to the opposite pole. Changing their style will not help. If they change it so as to be the same as that of men, they will be seen not as logical beings in their own newfound right, but as men *manqué* or uppity persons striving for privileges they don't deserve. Anything else they do will be seen as illogical, regardless of its form.

Characteristics of Women's Language

Numerous traits have been said to characterize women's forms of speech in this culture. Not all women use them, and probably no one uses them all the time. (They are, for instance, more likely to show up in informal social circumstances than in business settings.) Men sometimes use them, either with different meanings or for individual special reasons. (Gay men imitate some of them.)[2]

---

2. Jespersen, O. 1921. "The Woman," in *Language: Its Nature, Development, and Origin,* chapter 13. New York: W. W. Norton.

1. Women often seem to hit phonetic points less precisely than men: lisped *s*'s, obscured vowels.
2. Women's intonational contours display more variety than men's.[3]
3. Women use diminutives and euphemisms more than men ("You nickname God's creatures," says Hamlet to Ophelia).
4. Women make more use of expressive forms (adjectives not nouns or verbs and, in that category, those expressing emotional rather than intellectual evaluation) more than men: *lovely, divine.*
5. Women use forms that convey impreciseness: *so, such.*
6. Women use hedges of all kinds more than men.
7. Women use intonation patterns that resemble questions, indicating uncertainty or need for approval.
8. Women's voices are breathier than men's.
9. Women are more indirect and polite than men.
10. Women won't commit themselves to an opinion.
11. In conversation, women are more likely to be interrupted, less likely to introduce successful topics.[4]
12. Women's communicative style tends to be collaborative rather than competitive.
13. More of women's communication is expressed nonverbally (by gesture and intonation) than men's.
14. Women are more careful to be "correct" when they speak, using better grammar and fewer colloquialisms than men.

All of these characteristics can be seen as instantiating one or more of the roles women are supposed to play in this culture. Also notable is the fact that, as suggested by several items on this list, women have communicatively more options than men, more channels legitimately open to them. (That should be seen as a plus, but nonverbal signals are often stigmatized as distracting, and variety in intonation as hysterical.) At the same time, what they may express, and to whom, is more severely limited. This ambivalence is not unique to language: In many ways, it can be said that women are more constrained in their behavior than men (professionally, sexually); yet less in others (dress, home-versus-career options).

Other generalizations: Womanly communicative behavior is imprecise and indirect (both characteristic of female deference politeness, actually or symbolically leaving interpretation up to the hearer); nonpow-

----

3. Lakoff, R. 1975. *Language and Woman's Place.* New York: Harper & Row. This claim is discussed, for instance, along with numbers 3 through 7.

4. Zimmerman, D.; and West, C. 1975. "Sex Roles, Interruptions and Silences in Conversations." In B. Thorne and N. Henley, eds., *Language and Sex: Difference and Dominance.* Rowley, Mass.: Newbury House.

erful or nonseeking of power; and more capable of expressing emotions (a trait scorned by the "logical").

The superficial forms themselves may change slightly over time. The way "ideal" women spoke in the 1930s movies (think of Katharine Hepburn or Jean Harlow) is not that of 1950s (Doris Day or Marilyn Monroe), or 1970s (Jane Fonda or Jill Clayburgh) movie heroines. Specific traits shift, but all involve some of the preceding assumptions, for our assessment of their femininity and therefore desirability (and hence ultimately movie bankability) is dependent on stereotypes embedded in the culture.

Reading the Text

1. How, according to Lakoff, can women be considered "bilingual"?
2. What are the most striking differences between male and female linguistic patterns, as Lakoff sees them?
3. Why does Lakoff include the example from the Malagasy culture in her essay?

Reading the Signs

1. Study the speech patterns of a woman friend as she speaks both to other women and to men. Then write an essay in which you analyze your friend's linguistic behavior, applying Lakoff's list of traits characterizing women's speech,
2. In small same-sex groups, discuss which of Lakoff's characteristics of women's language (if any) you think are accurate, thinking of your own speech patterns and those of friends. Then share the small-group results with the whole class. Do any gender-related patterns emerge?
3. What would a list of men's speech characteristics look like? Don't just reverse Lakoff's list, but create your own by observing men speaking in both formal and informal circumstances. After you've created your list, write an essay in which you explore the significance of gender differences in speech patterns.
4. To what extent can Lakoff's theory about the gender differences in speech patterns explain the misunderstandings between males and females described in Peter Lyman's "The Fraternal Bond as a Joking Relationship" (p. 609)?
5. Do you agree with Lakoff that gay men imitate some of women's forms of speech? Write an essay illustrating, refuting, or elaborating on this claim, basing your argument in part on interviews with gay men that you conduct. Ask them about their own opinions about their speech patterns and observe those patterns for yourself.
6. At the close of her essay, Lakoff points to movies as showing that, despite superficial changes in women's speech, the traits she describes tend to

remain constant in our culture. Test Lakoff's assertion by watching a sampling of movies from three different decades (either rent videotapes or watch them at your school's media library). As you watch the movies, study the speech patterns of the female characters, particularly the leads, looking for the female traits Lakoff lists. Then use the results of your analysis to support, challenge, or modify Lakoff's argument.

DEBORAH TANNEN
Wears Jump Suit. Sensible Shoes. Uses Husband's Last Name.

||||||||||||||||||||||||||||||||||||||||||||||||||||||||||||||||

If you use the pronoun "s/he" when writing, or write "women and men" rather than "men and women," you are not just writing words: You are making a statement that may "mark" you as being a "feminist." In this analysis of the way everything a woman does marks her in some way or other—from writing and speaking to the way she dresses and styles her hair—Deborah Tannen (b. 1945) reveals the asymmetrical nature of gender semiotics in our culture. Wearing makeup or not wearing makeup sends a signal about a woman, whereas a man without makeup sends no signal at all. Tannen's analysis shows how what men do is implicitly considered the norm in society, and so is relatively neutral, while women's difference inevitably marks them, "because there is no unmarked woman." University Professor in Linguistics at Georgetown University, Deborah Tannen is the author of the best-selling book You Just Don't Understand: Women and Men in Conversation *(1986), as well as ten other books.*

Some years ago I was at a small working conference of four women and eight men. Instead of concentrating on the discussion I found myself looking at the three other women at the table, thinking how each had a different style and how each style was coherent.

One woman had dark brown hair in a classic style, a cross between Cleopatra and Plain Jane. The severity of her straight hair was softened by wavy bangs and ends that turned under. Because she was beautiful, the effect was more Cleopatra than plain.

The second woman was older, full of dignity and composure. Her hair was cut in a fashionable style that left her with only one eye, thanks to a side part that let a curtain of hair fall across half her face. As she looked down to read her prepared paper, the hair robbed her of bifocal vision and created a barrier between her and the listeners.

The third woman's hair was wild, a frosted blond avalanche falling over and beyond her shoulders. When she spoke she frequently tossed her head, calling attention to her hair and away from her lecture.

Then there was makeup. The first woman wore facial cover that made her skin smooth and pale, a black line under each eye and mascara that darkened already dark lashes. The second wore only a light gloss on her lips and a hint of shadow on her eyes. The third had blue bands under her eyes, dark blue shadow, mascara, bright red lipstick and rouge; her fingernails flashed red.

I considered the clothes each woman had worn during the three days of the conference: In the first case, man-tailored suits in primary colors with solid-color blouses. In the second, casual but stylish black T-shirts, a floppy collarless jacket and baggy slacks or a skirt in neutral colors. The third wore a sexy jump suit; tight sleeveless jersey and tight yellow slacks; a dress with gaping armholes and an indulged tendency to fall off one shoulder.

Shoes? No. 1 wore string sandals with medium heels; No. 2, sensible, comfortable walking shoes; No. 3, pumps with spike heels. You can fill in the jewelry, scarves, shawls, sweaters—or lack of them.

As I amused myself finding coherence in these styles, I suddenly wondered why I was scrutinizing only the women. I scanned the eight men at the table. And then I knew why I wasn't studying them. The men's styles were unmarked.

The term "marked" is a staple of linguistic theory. It refers to the way language alters the base meaning of a word by adding a linguistic particle that has no meaning on its own. The unmarked form of a word carries the meaning that goes without saying—what you think of when you're not thinking anything special.

The unmarked tense of verbs in English is the present—for example, *visit*. To indicate past, you mark the verb by adding *ed* to yield *visited*. For future, you add a word: *will visit*. Nouns are presumed to be singular until marked for plural, typically by adding *s* or *es*, so *visit* becomes *visits* and *dish* becomes *dishes*.

The unmarked forms of most English words also convey "male." Being male is the unmarked case. Endings like *ess* and *ette* mark words as "female." Unfortunately, they also tend to mark them for frivolousness. Would you feel safe entrusting your life to a doctorette? Alfre Woodard, who was an Oscar nominee for best supporting actress, says she identifies herself as an actor because "actresses worry about eyelashes and cellulite, and women who are actors worry about the characters we are playing." Gender markers pick up extra meanings that reflect common associations with the female gender: not quite serious, often sexual.

Each of the women at the conference had to make decisions about hair, clothing, makeup and accessories, and each decision carried meaning. Every style available to us was marked. The men in our group had made decisions, too, but the range from which they chose was incomparably narrower. Men can choose styles that are marked, but they don't have to, and in this group none did. Unlike the women, they had the option of being unmarked.

Take the men's hair styles. There was no marine crew cut or oily longish hair falling into eyes, no asymmetrical, two-tiered construction to swirl over a bald top. One man was unabashedly bald; the others had hair of standard length, parted on one side, in natural shades of brown or gray or graying. Their hair obstructed no views, left little to toss or push back or run fingers through and, consequently, needed and attracted no attention. A few men had beards. In a business setting, beards might be marked. In this academic gathering, they weren't.

There could have been a cowboy shirt with string tie or a three-piece suit or a necklaced hippie in jeans. But there wasn't. All eight men wore brown or blue slacks and nondescript shirts of light colors. No man wore sandals or boots; their shoes were dark, closed, comfortable, and flat. In short, unmarked.

Although no man wore makeup, you couldn't say the men didn't   15
wear makeup in the sense that you could say a woman didn't wear makeup. For men, no makeup is unmarked.

I asked myself what style we women could have adopted that would have been unmarked, like the men's. The answer was none. There is no unmarked woman.

There is no woman's hair style that can be called standard, that says nothing about her. The range of women's hair styles is staggering, but a woman whose hair has no particular style is perceived as not caring about how she looks, which can disqualify her from many positions, and will subtly diminish her as a person in the eyes of some.

Women must choose between attractive shoes and comfortable shoes. When our group made an unexpected trek, the woman who wore flat, laced shoes arrived first. Last to arrive was the woman in spike heels, shoes in hand and a handful of men around her.

If a woman's clothing is tight or revealing (in other words, sexy), it sends a message—an intended one of wanting to be attractive, but also a possibly unintended one of availability. If her clothes are not sexy, that too sends a message, lent meaning by the knowledge that they could have been. There are thousands of cosmetic products from which women can choose and myriad ways of applying them. Yet no makeup at all is anything but unmarked. Some men see it as a hostile refusal to please them.

Women can't even fill out a form without telling stories about   20
themselves. Most forms give four titles to choose from. "Mr." carries no

meaning other than that the respondent is male. But a woman who checks "Mrs." or "Miss" communicates not only whether she has been married but also whether she has conservative tastes in forms of address —and probably other conservative values as well. Checking "Ms." declines to let on about marriage (checking "Mr." declines nothing since nothing was asked), but it also marks her as either liberated or rebellious, depending on the observer's attitudes and assumptions.

I sometimes try to duck these variously marked choices by giving my title as "Dr."—and in so doing risk marking myself as either uppity (hence sarcastic responses like "Excuse *me!*") or an overachiever (hence reactions of congratulatory surprise like "Good for you!").

All married women's surnames are marked. If a woman takes her husband's name, she announces to the world that she is married and has traditional values. To some it will indicate that she is less herself, more identified by her husband's identity. If she does not take her husband's name, this too is marked, seen as worthy of comment: She has *done* something; she has "kept her own name." A man is never said to have "kept his own name" because it never occurs to anyone that he might have given it up. For him using his own name is unmarked.

A married woman who wants to have her cake and eat it too may use her surname plus his, with or without a hyphen. But this too announces her marital status and often results in a tongue-tying string. In a list (Harvey O'Donovan, Jonathan Feldman, Stephanie Woodbury McGillicutty), the woman's multiple name stands out. It is marked.

I have never been inclined toward biological explanations of gender differences in language, but I was intrigued to see Ralph Fasold bring biological phenomena to bear on the question of linguistic marking in his book *The Sociolinguistics of Language.* Fasold stresses that language and culture are particularly unfair in treating women as the marked case because biologically it is the male that is marked. While two X chromosomes make a female, two Y chromosomes make nothing. Like the linguistic markers *s, es,* or *ess,* the Y chromosome doesn't "mean" anything unless it is attached to a root form—an X chromosome.

Developing this idea elsewhere Fasold points out that girls are born   25
with fully female bodies, while boys are born with modified female bodies. He invites men who doubt this to lift up their shirts and contemplate why they have nipples.

In his book, Fasold notes "a wide range of facts which demonstrates that female is the unmarked sex." For example, he observes that there are a few species that produce only females, like the whiptail lizard. Thanks to parthenogenesis, they have no trouble having as many daughters as they like. There are no species, however, that produce only males. This is no surprise, since any such species would become extinct in its first generation.

Fasold is also intrigued by species that produce individuals not involved in reproduction, like honeybees and leaf-cutter ants. Reproduction is handled by the queen and a relatively few males; the workers are sterile females. "Since they do not reproduce," Fasold said, "there is no reason for them to be one sex or the other, so they default, so to speak, to female."

Fasold ends his discussion of these matters by pointing out that if language reflected biology, grammar books would direct us to use "she" to include males and females and "he" only for specifically male referents. But they don't. They tell us that "he" means "he or she," and that "she" is used only if the referent is specifically female. This use of "he" as the sex-indefinite pronoun is an innovation introduced into English by grammarians in the eighteenth and nineteenth centuries, according to Peter Mühlhäusler and Rom Harré in *Pronouns and People*. From at least about 1500, the correct sex-indefinite pronoun was "they," as it still is in casual spoken English. In other words, the female was declared by grammarians to be the marked case.

Writing this article may mark me not as a writer, not as a linguist, not as an analyst of human behavior, but as a feminist—which will have positive or negative, but in any case powerful, connotations for readers. Yet I doubt that anyone reading Ralph Fasold's book would put that label on him.

I discovered the markedness inherent in the very topic of gender   30 after writing a book on differences in conversational style based on geographical region, ethnicity, class, age, and gender. When I was interviewed, the vast majority of journalists wanted to talk about the differences between women and men. While I thought I was simply describing what I observed—something I had learned to do as a researcher—merely mentioning women and men marked me as a feminist for some.

When I wrote a book devoted to gender differences in ways of speaking, I sent the manuscript to five male colleagues, asking them to alert me to any interpretation, phrasing, or wording that might seem unfairly negative toward men. Even so, when the book came out, I encountered responses like that of the television talk show host who, after interviewing me, turned to the audience and asked if they thought I was male-bashing.

Leaping upon a poor fellow who affably nodded in agreement, she made him stand and asked, "Did what she said accurately describe you?" "Oh, yes," he answered. "That's me exactly." "And what she said about women—does that sound like your wife?" "Oh yes," he responded. "That's her exactly." "Then why do you think she's male-bashing?" He answered, with disarming honesty, "Because she's a woman and she's saying things about men."

To say anything about women and men without marking oneself as either feminist or anti-feminist, male-basher or apologist for men seems as impossible for a woman as trying to get dressed in the morning without inviting interpretations of her character.

Sitting at the conference table musing on these matters, I felt sad to think that we women didn't have the freedom to be unmarked that the men sitting next to us had. Some days you just want to get dressed and go about your business. But if you're a woman, you can't, because there is no unmarked woman.

Reading the Text

1. Explain in your own words what Tannen means by "marked."
2. Why does Tannen say that men have the option of being "unmarked"?
3. What significance does Tannen see in Ralph Fasold's biological explanations of linguistic gender difference?

Reading the Signs

1. Do you agree with Tannen's assumption that men have the luxury of remaining "unmarked" in our society? Do you think it's possible to be purely "unmarked"? To develop your essay, you might interview some men, particularly those who elect to have an unconventional appearance, and read Elizabeth Wilson's "Oppositional Dress" (p. 45).
2. In class, survey the extent to which the males and females in your class are "marked" or "unmarked," in Tannen's terms, studying such signs as clothing and hair style. Do the males tend to have "unmarked" styles, while the women tend to send a message by their choices? Discuss the results of your survey, and reflect on the validity of Tannen's claims.
3. Interview at least five women who are married, and ask them about their choice of names: Did they keep their "own" name, adopt their husband's, or opt for a hyphenated version? What signals do they want to send about their identity through their names? Use the results of your interviews to write a reflective essay on how our names function as signs, particularly as gender-related signs.
4. Apply Tannen's concept of being "marked" to Sam Fulwood III's "The Rage of the Black Middle Class" (p. 462). To what extent might Fulwood say that being black in American society is to be ethnically "marked"?
5. What would an unmarked appearance for women be like? Write a speculative essay in which you imagine the features of an unmarked female appearance. Share your essay with your class.

ELIZABETH CHISERI-STRATER
Anna

Traditionally, academic study has valued intellectual objectivity and emotional detachment. Learning is viewed as a kind of contest, a debate in which the side with the most data wins. Feminist scholars believe that this reflects a male intellectual paradigm that may not be appropriate for female learners. In this case study of a female college student named Anna, Elizabeth Chiseri-Strater (b. 1943) traces the writing and learning process of a woman for whom education is most effective when it is personal and experiential rather than objective and cognitive. An ethnographer who specializes in literacy and composition, Elizabeth Chiseri-Strater is an assistant professor at the University of North Carolina, Greensboro. She has published Academic Literacies *(1990), from which this selection was taken, and articles on journal writing and collaborative learning.*

Anna confided in me that she felt Prose Writing should be a year-long course: "I wish this class were continuing into next semester because I think there's a lot in this class in terms of people. . . . I put so much into it. And I've been doing a lot of meaningful writing and now I'm going to have to stop." Her reason for favoring this class over others was that "it's so personal." Personalized knowledge is valued by Anna, who contrasts prose writing with other coursework in which she's made to look at explicit knowledge rather than rely on what Polyani has identified as tacit knowing. Tacit knowing, Polyani suggests, is more fundamental than explicit knowing: "We know more than we can tell; we can tell nothing without relying on our awareness of things we may not be able to tell" (Emig 1977, 151).

In Prose Writing class, Anna is an active participant in what educators from Dewey through Rosenblatt have described as transactional learning. For Anna, this participation does not come without some effort on her part. One of my field notes refers to the tension that precedes Anna's talk in the whole-group discussions: "She always seems nervous before she talks: I can sense when she has something to say just by watching her body, particularly her hands." When she speaks, she does so quickly. Later, Anna comments on her muted speech style as she contrasts it with Carlos's: "Carlos I just wanted to hit! Because he talks so slowly, I think. Not that there's anything wrong with talking slowly. I speak so fast." Anna's evaluative response is typical: questioning—why Carlos's talk bothers her; nonjudgmental—nothing wrong with it; and somewhat self-effacing—I speak too fast.

Anna's participation in her writing class was like her membership in a dance troupe: She was prompt and prepared, she participated regularly, and she practiced on her own. She was a part of this community in the way her dance company formed a tightly knit group. Along with others in Prose Writing, Anna engaged in the many conversations that took place there. Had I never followed her into another setting, I would not have understood that for her to be an active speaker was unusual, that her usual role was silence.

The authors of *Women's Ways of Knowing* (Belenky et al. 1986) have identified the beginning stage of some women's thinking as "silence"— a description that reflects the important metaphor of "voice" in understanding women's growth as thinkers.[1] Anna explains that she found it easier to speak up in her composition course because "I could back up what I said. It all came from inside of my head." Composition courses rub against the model of the student as blank text, as unfilled bottle, by *valuing* the experiences and feelings students develop from inside of them to speak out, to read and write from the "inside out" (Atwell 1985). In a course like Donna's, students are invited to play what Peter Elbow has called "the believing game," which makes composition studies so different from other academic communities where the "doubting game" stands as the dominant epistemology (Elbow 1973).

Anna also values listening. She describes three of her female professors, including Donna, as "really knowing how to listen." Anna describes her dance teacher, in particular, as "a really *caring* person." Nel Noddings suggests that caring involves receptivity and engrossment rather than projection and analysis (1984, 30). Such empathy with others comes through listening, which for many women is a positive stance as well as an active and demanding process (Belenky et al. 1986, 37). When I suggested to Anna that she didn't talk as much as Nick and Carlos in her reading group she said, "I felt I talked a lot," and then reflected, "Maybe I just thought a lot."

Vygotsky has stressed the importance of outer speech or dialogue in the development of inner thought and cognitive growth (Vygotsky 1978). Yet listening, without the support of talk, can eliminate women from full participation in the academic conversation, affording them the spectator and outsider role, as members of the audience rather than members of the troupe.

---

1. Voice has become an important term for describing women in the work of different feminist thinkers. Writers Adrienne Rich (*On Lies, Secrets, and Silence*, 1979) and Tillie Olsen (*Silences*, 1978) employ the metaphors of voice and silence extensively. Developmental psychologist Carol Gilligan works with the concept of voice in her book (*In a Different Voice*, 1982) on women's moral development to show how women's growth contrasts with that of men. And Nadya Aisenberg and Mona Harrington in their recent study (*Women of Academe: Outsiders in the Sacred Grove*, 1988) created a category of "voice" to describe the theme of deflected women in academics.

In the following excerpt from a whole-class discussion, Anna earns her community membership by adding her point of view, by drawing on her own experiences. Here Donna's class is discussing the symbolic meaning of Eiseley's childhood tree in his essay "The Brown Wasps." Donna, as usual, opens with a question:

DONNA: Do things change or do we just change?

ALLIE AND OTHERS: Both.

DONNA: I mean Eiseley's tree is obviously gone. There's a change there.

RANDY: I think we change because things change.

MARY: Or vice versa. Things change because we change.

RANDY: I still think we change.

LINDA: Like you've grown up since you've been to high school and you go back and see it in a totally different way.

DONNA: Your attitude toward the soccer team has changed.

ANNA: I was just thinking that he has this tree in his memory and it was a comforting thing to think back to the tree when the present got harder. I found that when I'm really stressed out, I have memories to think back to or places that I think about where I want to— . . .

DONNA: To hold on to?

ANNA: Or just to comfort me.

TINA: You have a memory of a time and place when everything was all right and it wasn't so stressful.

DONNA: Maybe that's what meditation is all about. They say you go back to a place in your mind.

While there's nothing particularly remarkable about this discussion, it's a representative slice of Anna's talk in Prose Writing class. In her nervous and quick manner of speaking, she engages in the ongoing talk, drawing on her own knowledge and feelings: "I found that when I'm really stressed out, I have memories to think back to or places that I think about. . . ." She does not remain silent.

Her ability to speak out in Prose Writing can be explained by understanding such class discussions as ongoing conversations, rather than debates. Anna describes this collaborative talk: "There are some times in class when I really want to say something because I *agree* or I might find something that I feel is interesting to *add*. I get anxious to say it. . . . If I say something, I want it to mean something." Anna is not intimidated in this course because she sees herself as able to contribute. Whereas Randy wants to state his point of view and win ("I still think we change"), Anna's more interested in participation.

In a journal entry on the class, Anna further describes her need to   10
be engaged in talk, writing of how conversation supports her thinking process and gives her confidence:

> When I discover concerns of my own, they usually come from dia-
> logue with other people. . . . I really value discussions and bouncing
> ideas off people and getting responses. Maybe I'm insecure about

developing or accepting an opinion that is fresh to me without first conferring with a better informed friend.

It is interesting that Anna feels there's something almost wrong with validating her ideas with someone else, since talking with colleagues is, in fact, how most academic ideas are generated.

In our conversations together, Anna often berates herself for not knowing enough, for not having "expertise," comparing herself to her Northern Renaissance art history professor whose "mind is like some safe filled with all the myths of the world. . . . She knows so many different theories." The process of how thinking develops is missing from Anna's image of the hermetically sealed mind that stores its valuables in a safe. Nondisclosure of how scholars acquire their knowledge inadvertently misrepresents the nature of collaboration and interaction in higher education. Lack of modeling robs students of insights about the incubation process and denies them access to the messy rough-draft thinking involved in making meaning—from ideas, from texts, from colleagues.

Anna as Reader: Intimacy and Response

Anna's conversation in small reading groups reveals an even more intimate style than in the whole-class discussions. In these small peer groups, narrative, spontaneous talk dominates. In many of the reading-group transcripts for this class, the reading serves primarily as a stimulus for students to reread their own lives, rather than as a context devoted solely to deconstruction of the author's intentions.

The following reading-group episode I call "The Banking Concept of Love" because it reveals some of students' culturally acquired attitudes about love, particularly Nick's concept of love as an "investment." In the transcript as a whole, Anna has a difficult time wresting the conversational floor from Nick and Carlos who take over at many points, leaving Anna and Mary as spectators in the friendly male wrangle. For women, gaining access to the dominant discourse is often problematic, particularly in public settings. In the entire transcript from which this excerpt is taken, Nick has ninety-five conversational turns to Anna's twenty-five, so that she claims the floor 76 percent less of the time than he does. These small reading groups offer women an opportunity to work within a communal circle that is familiar and appropriate for members who belong to what anthropologists Edwin Ardner and Shirley Ardner[2] and, later, feminist literary critic Elaine Showalter (1981) call the

---

2. The Ardners' anthropological work is cited in the introduction to *Language, Gender, and Professional Writing: Theoretical Approaches and Guidelines for Nonsexist Usage*, edited by F. W. Frank and P. Treichler (1989).

"muted discourse group." The muted group belongs to, but is not always allowed, full participation in the talk of the dominant group. Ardner developed this idea to describe research claims he felt were being made about particular cultures or tribes based only on interviews with the men. Women, he said, were left out of the generation of meaning within these groups. Showalter, picking up on his metaphor, applies it to women and speech: "Thus muted groups must mediate their beliefs through the allowable forms of dominant structures. Another way of putting this would be to say that all language is the language of the dominant order, and women, if they speak at all, must speak through it" (1981, 200).

In the following frame we see that Anna *does* manage to bring in some personal responses to the group talk about Carver's story "What We Talk About When We Talk About Love." Nick is the designated leader of this group of Anna, Carlos, and Mary because he had selected the story for the group to discuss.

ANNA: That's a point in the essay too. People have a need for love.

MARY: Different kinds of love.

NICK: When you invest in a relationship, you invest a part of yourself so you necessarily are giving part of yourself up. You become half a person.

CARLOS: Do you think people can have a relationship without giving themselves up?

ANNA: I think you are fooling yourself if you're in a relationship and don't put anything in.

NICK: Yes. You're not committed.

MARY: You have to give up certain beliefs, certain prejudices. I know —my boyfriend—I've always been the type of person who says no drugs, no this, no that. He smokes pot. I say, "You shouldn't be doing that; it's wrong." He says, "I know it's wrong."

ANNA: If you can accept that, that's good.

MARY: You have to accept it—you give up a lot of your own moral values, not necessarily giving them up but accepting the ones that you know are wrong. Not that you are going to go out and do them but accepting the fact that you can't always change them.

ANNA: Someone I know, someone who's married and his wife doesn't let him smoke in the house, and when he's at work, he smokes like a madman. His wife, if she smells beer on his breath, makes him sleep on the couch. It's ridiculous stuff. She's not accepting him as a whole person.

MARY: If you love someone you have to accept them the way they are because you can't change them. You're not really loving them.

NICK: You also need their *investment*. You need to know that they're committed. You need to know that they have *taken a piece of themselves and given it to you.*

While the women in this group explore the interpersonal aspects of forming a relationship—of accepting new values, of welcoming the whole person—the males (mainly represented by Nick here) discuss commitment as an object—an emotional investment, as an actual piece of the self. From this short snip of conversation we learn that in intimate relationships, Nick draws boundaries: half of me for you and half for me. And Nick expects his part back.

Anna later reflects on this group discussion in her journal, which   15
represents an ongoing dialogue since she knows that Donna will respond. Donna underlines the following parts of Anna's entry as being interesting:

> Then he [Nick] went on to say that after he had broken up with his girlfriend, he was left with this refound half and didn't know what to do with it. Instead of putting it into another relationship, he had to sort through it. But I'm finding that *I gave or put more than half of myself into a relationship* and I need some of it back for me to become complete.

Anna's entry indicates that while women place fewer boundaries on relationships, they also make a larger capital investment ("more than half of myself"). Anna uses her journal to work out personal responses to ideas and readings that have been discussed in small peer groups. In her last journal entry for Prose Writing, Anna returns to the issue of love and relationships, showing that she is very much tuned into these concerns. She writes: "I think about love, I know I spend an incredible amount of time trying to figure out my love, his different channels, and where I can find myself in relation to these channels."

RESPONSE FORUMS: PEER AND PRIVATE

For Anna, the reading groups and teacher-student journals turned out to be her most effective learning and feedback forums in Prose Writing class. Her oral and written responses to members of her reading groups show her to be a generous reader who always offered extended comments. In an in-class essay, Anna writes that reading groups felt more like casual conversation to her, the kind of discussions she holds with friends:

> Tad and I have intensely intellectual conversations in which we talk about things disturbing us in the order of the world. We sort through relationships and individual growth. Though we don't talk often, when we do, we pick up on themes and discuss how our feelings and opinions have changed . . . Neither of us record these conversations. We apply them to our lives.

Anna apparently learns to apply what she reads to her life as well. When asked how she improved as a reader in Prose Writing, Anna writes: "I have become a better *connector*. A better reader for coherent ideas. A better rereader. I see things differently, pick up on ideas that I missed." One of the ways that Anna grew as a reader, she said, was through Donna's questions and responses to what was written in the journal, weaving a connective tissue between teacher and student. Connected knowing, as explained in *Women's Ways of Knowing*, may begin with understanding people but end as a procedure for understanding paintings or books as well: "Connected knowing involves feelings, because it is rooted in relationships: but it also involves thought. . . . Connected knowing is just as procedural as separate knowing, although its procedures have not been as elaborately codified" (Belenky et al. 1986, 121).

In this course, reading groups and journal writing both afford a way for students to relate personally to texts as well as provide a means for making the private act of reading communal. Unlike so much college work that's based on solitary reading without any modeling or feedback, Prose Writing offers a rich web of response forums. For the female student who may not feel able or confident to speak up in a large group discussion, these classroom literacy structures allow ways of keeping women involved in the academic conversation.

The journal response in particular invites women students to draw on a whole heritage of diary and journal keeping that has historically included women. Cinthia Gannett, tracing the gender differences in the journal tradition, suggests that for women writers the journal has often afforded a voice when otherwise women might have been, indeed often were, denied voice. Gannett suggests that the journal tradition has kept women engaged in a private discourse when their voices in the arena of public discourse may have been muted: "Simply put, since women have always had fewer ways to act on, to inscribe themselves on the world at large, they found ways to inscribe themselves, to make their own unique imprint, in texts" (Gannett 1987, 161). The use of the journal in higher education, Gannett asserts, helps women "work through their public voices and gain confidence as writers" (183–84). Although not a private journal keeper herself, Anna liked the kinds of comments Donna wrote on her journal entries, liked the dialogue that it afforded about her reading and thinking, liked being connected.

BIBLIOGRAPHY

Aisenberg, N., and M. Harrington. 1988. *Women of academe: Outsiders in the sacred grove.* Amherst: University of Massachusetts Press.

Atwell, N. 1985. Writing and reading from the inside out. In *Breaking ground: Teachers relate reading and writing in the elementary school,* ed. J. Hansen, T. Newkirk, and D. Graves. Portsmouth, N.H.: Heinemann.

Belenky, M., B. Clinchy, N. Goldberger, and J. Tarule. 1986. *Women's ways of knowing: The development of self, voice and mind.* New York: Basic Books.

Elbow, P. 1973. *Writing without teachers.* London: Oxford.

Emig, J. 1977. Writing as a way of learning. *College Composition and Communication, 28:* 122–128.

Frank, F.W., and P. Treichler, eds. 1989. *Language, gender and professional writing: Theoretical approaches and guidelines for nonsexist usage.* New York: Modern Language Association.

Gannett, C. 1992. *Gender and journals: Diaries and academic discourse.* Albany: SUNY Press.

Gilligan, C. 1982. *In a different voice: Psychological theory and women's development.* Cambridge, Mass.: Harvard University Press.

Olsen, T. 1978. *Silences.* New York: Delacorte Press.

Rich, A. 1979. When we dead awaken. In *Lies, secrets and silence.* New York: W. W. Norton.

Showalter, E. 1981. "Feminist criticism in the wilderness." In *Critical Inquiry,* Winter: 179–205.

Vygotsky, L.S. 1978. *Mind in society: The development of higher psychological processes.* Cambridge, Mass.: Harvard University Press.

Reading the Text

1. Explain in your own words what "transactional learning" is.
2. What are the differences between composition classes and other courses, in Chiseri-Strater's view?
3. What, according to Chiseri-Strater, are male learning styles?
4. Why are journals particularly valuable tools for women learners?

Reading the Signs

1. In your journal, reflect on your own style as a learner. When do you feel comfortable participating in class, and why? How does your behavior in small groups compare with that during whole-class discussion? How important are conversations with others to your intellectual growth? Do you fit the gender patterns that Chiseri-Strater describes?
2. To what extent do the classroom conversations in "Anna" demonstrate the characteristics of women's language described by Robin Tolmach Lakoff ("Women's Language," p. 624)?
3. Compare and contrast Anna and Nick as learners. What features of their learning styles do you think are gender-marked, and which may relate to their individual personalities?
4. Compare and contrast Anna's and Fan Shen's experiences in their composition classes ("The Classroom and the Wider Culture," p. 485). Be sure to take into account how gender and ethnicity may both have affected their experiences.
5. What learning and teaching styles do you observe in the classes you are taking this term, including your writing class? Note patterns of behavior during class: Who talks, and when? What sort of activities occur in class—

lectures? Group work? How do students respond to each others' contributions? Do you notice any patterns that are gender-marked? To interpret your observations, you may want to consult Holly Devor, "Gender Role Behaviors and Attitudes," p. 603, and Robin Tolmach Lakoff, "Women's Language," p. 624.

R I C H A R D   K.   H E R R E L L

The Symbolic Strategies of Chicago's Gay and Lesbian Pride Day Parade

Americans love a parade, and parades have long been a way for the many different cultures and ethnicities in this country to express themselves and their sense of identity. In the early 1970s, American gays and lesbians adopted the parade model to let America know that they, too, formed a community and were proud of who they were. But as Richard K. Herrell (b. 1950) points out in this semiotic analysis of Chicago's Gay and Lesbian Pride Day Parades, what gays and lesbians have communicated through their parades has changed over the years. From parades designed "to overcome invisibility" through the flaunting of drag and leather, to the AIDS-era parades that present the gay community "as composed of families, of churches, of sports leagues, of clubs and professional organizations," Chicago's annual festivals chart the direction of gay identification and politics throughout the country. Richard K. Herrell is completing work on his Ph.D. at the University of Chicago and is currently researching the conflict in America between being gay and being a good citizen.

The *Chicago* magazine listings of things to do for June 1988 contained the following item: "Neighborhood Festivals: Chicago is a city of neighborhoods, and these local festivals are a reflection of that ethnic diversity. All during the summer you can eat brats, tacos, pierogis, krumkake, and other ethnic foods, and then dance it off doing the marengue or the polka. For specifics call the Mayor's Office of Special Events."[1] This advertising copy is a sunny paraphrase of Chicago's rhetoric about itself, a city richly provided with colorful, tuneful, tasty differences. As for the

---

1. *Chicago,* June 1988, p. 38.

inequalities, racism, and constant political warfare that deeply divide the city, well, that doesn't make for good rhetoric or ad copy.

In the last ten years, as the number of Chicago's parades and neighborhood festivals has grown dramatically, the Gay and Lesbian Pride Week activities, including the Pride Day Parade, are now routinely listed in city publications and newspapers. A few years ago, former mayor Jane Byrne, out of office and in her endless search to get back in, popped up out of a black Mustang convertible during the parade line-up and coyly announced to reporters that she was there that day because "this is one of our summer neighborhood festivals."

This essay examines Chicago's Gay and Lesbian Pride Day Parade specifically in the context of Chicago's parades and festivals; an analysis of the gay and lesbian parades in New York, San Francisco, Los Angeles, or Europe might be quite different. The gay and lesbian parade in Chicago has adopted and transformed the parades of "ethnic groups"— the city's Irish, Polish, Mexicans, Italians, and so forth. "Ethnicity" has become a model for gays and lesbians, who now think of their community as one like other communities in Chicago, like them in having a space and a special parade to claim that space symbolically one day each summer, to express their relative cultural autonomy in the city, and to speak as a community with interests to legislators and other policymakers, but critically different from them in their historical exclusion from normative society.

Chicago's Gay and Lesbian Pride Day Parades

Chicago's Gay and Lesbian Pride Day Parade is one of several held annually on the last Sunday in June across the United States to commemorate the Stonewall Rebellion—the spontaneous, violent reaction by gay men and lesbians in New York City in 1969 to one of the arbitrary bar raids common at that time. These riots mark the emblematic beginning of the contemporary gay and lesbian rights movement, and those who came of age during the 1970s in its wake are sometimes called the "Stonewall generation." The parades have been held every year (with slightly different names in different cities) through the heady years of the birth and maturation of the gay liberation movement into the current full realization of the AIDS crisis.

Chicago's Gay and Lesbian Pride Day Parade and rally are planned and coordinated every year by the Pride Week Committee. On the day of the parade, participants assemble during the two hours beforehand along a three-quarter-mile stretch of Halsted Street while parade watchers gather along the parade route. Virtually an event in itself, the line-up takes on a party atmosphere as public address systems on floats and in apartment windows blare dance music and Sousa marches. After the step off, the parade moves south down Broadway, a narrow, two-lane business street, for about a mile. After the parade, a rally in Lincoln Park features speeches, presentation of awards for best floats and contingents, and music performed by the gay and lesbian choruses and guest performers.

Although attendance has grown substantially in recent years, participants who have seen the huge parades in New York and San Francisco find Chicago's event a small-town affair. The parade proceeds through Newtown—the social, organizational, entertainment, and residential focus of the city's gay scene—not down State Street or North Michigan Avenue, as though New York's and San Francisco's Gay and Lesbian parades were held in the gay neighborhoods there, on Christopher Street in the Village instead of Fifth Avenue or on Castro Street instead of Market Street.

As a gay neighborhood, Newtown had been established as a residential and to a lesser extent as an entertainment area by the early 1970s, but few of the organizations, bars, and businesses that anchor the community today date back to that time. Located along Chicago's north side lakefront, Newtown consists of three or four north-south corridors separated and crosscut by business streets, bounded roughly by Diversey in the south, Irving Park in the north, Sheffield in the west, and Lake Michigan in the east. It encompasses several entertainment strips, including a three-quarter-mile stretch along one of the thoroughfares in which there are fourteen gay bars. Residential properties near the lake and to the south are expensive, and rents are high. The population is largely white, single (gay and straight), and professional. To the north and west, the neighborhood abuts Uptown, whose population is generally poorer and more working class. The demographics of streets and blocks change rapidly as real estate developers rehabilitate old properties, driving less affluent residents of all races and sexual orientations away to less expensive neighborhoods.

Newtown is also the center of the gay community's social and community life, centering on the gay and lesbian community center and on the many gay and lesbian organizations headquartered in the neighborhood that meet in rental space provided by the center or in several small churches (mainline Protestant and one Catholic).

The neighborhood itself has become a complex symbol of the gay community—its place in the city and in the life of Chicago's gay men and lesbians. When I interviewed gay men and lesbians about Newtown, they typically called it the gay "turf" or "territory." They defined the neighborhood in terms both of a space bounded by certain streets and Lake Michigan and of anchors, important places—such as bars, organizations, buildings, etc.—that focus the community's life there.

In my interviewing, I asked what makes Newtown a gay neighbor- 10 hood. A long-time resident thought for a moment and said, "What makes that neighborhood gay for me is just that gay people live there. The Jewel is gay and the Dominick's is gay and the Treasure Island is gay [large neighborhood supermarkets] because gay people shop there."

More generally, most of the men and women I interviewed (residents of this neighborhood as well as others) see Newtown as a "place to be gay"—not to engage in homosexual acts (in fact, most of the establishments offering easily accessible sexual contacts are elsewhere) but to be safe from abuse, meet with other gay friends, attend meetings of gay organizations, patronize gay-owned businesses, and meet new friends. For most, Newtown is simply the place where they can be with other gays and lesbians: "It is where I feel most comfortable walking down the street. Like I belong. Most of the people I see are just like I am."

In the 1970s, the parade aimed to establish the presence of gay people, to try to overcome invisibility. "We are everywhere!" became one of the movement's most common slogans, and the parade visually emphasized two of the gay world's most notorious indexes: drag and leather. These two controversial images of male homosexuality—dangerous hypermasculinity and abandonment of manhood altogether—became the two visible and visually aggressive ways for gay men to assert themselves as gay in public, to be not invisible.

In 1979, the color guard was led by three leathermen. Although in the minority, leather and drag and beefcake were everywhere. "We *are* different from you," the parade said. "We have sex with each other. Kinky sex, too." The parade deliberately called attention to the elaborate sexual semiotica of the leather world. Keys, bandannas, and pieces of leather worn by men and also some women—many more than the leather crowd itself at that time—publicly announced and advertised for the kinds of sex acts the wearer sought. Drag queens, female impersonators, and the guerilla theater of "gender fuck" seemed to say, "Yes, we dress up as women, and we're going to rub your noses in it." Less flamboyantly—one could say antiflamboyantly—lesbians refused to "dress up like ladies," as one woman put it. Men displayed the sexual polarity of their stereotypic representations, while women deemphasized presenting themselves with gender-specific expectations at all.

The strategy of the early gay liberation movement was a confrontation, its issue visibility, and its means for demonstrating difference drag, leather, and "zaps" (street demonstrations, sit-ins, guerrilla theater, etc.). The Stonewall uprising became a creation myth of the new gay community, of a new way to be gay. Sex *was* the revolution. The private was aggressively identified as public, and the parade celebrated precisely the sexual difference between gay and nongay.

By 1987, the parade exhibited the changed context of a Chicago that had elected its first woman and first black mayors, encouraging all minorities to renew demands for a progressive agenda at city hall. For the third time, the mayor proclaimed the week Gay and Lesbian Pride

15

Week and June 28 the Gay and Lesbian Pride Parade Day in Chicago. In the 1987 parade, there were 126 entries, including bars, social service and community organizations, political organizations, beer distributors, gay and lesbian religious congregations, several aldermen and other local political figures, professional associations, service providers for people with AIDS, sports leagues, student and academic associations, and performing arts organizations. Thirty of the entries—nearly a fourth—were not self-identified as lesbian or gay. Estimates of the parade participants, including spectators, ranged up to eighty thousand.

As in the last several years, the color guard of the 1987 Chicago parade was led by the gay and lesbian social service organization's youth group for gay and lesbian teenagers. While the parade seemed no less celebratory than earlier ones (although some observers claimed it was more somber), there was much less drag and leather. But, more important, what was being said by the parade and rally had changed. Gay politics has become mainstream, and so have the messages of the parade. Civil rights legislation is advocated so that "we can be just like the rest of you, because we are just like the rest of you." Not zaps but lobbying is the tactic of choice. As AIDS has come to dominate all gay politics, activists argue that AIDS is not a "gay disease"—it affects everyone. The goals are not confrontation but assimilation. Today, the parade aims to establish that "gay"—the community of gay men and lesbians—is *not* simply "homosexuality," sex acts performed by two people of the same sex. It is all the things gay people are and have done. It is the gay and lesbian community itself. Said one participant of the first time she saw the parade, "What I took pride in at the first one was all the gay churches, all the gay organizations and businesses, because I was unaware of it. It was a real enlightening experience for me."

The parade was not less "party" and more "political," but what is being said and what semiotic means are employed have changed. In 1987, the parade specifically challenged the ways homosexuals have been defined as sinners, sick people, and criminals. Gay politics (along with American politics generally since the 1960s) has changed. Confrontation has given way to assimilationist discourse.

Although the official theme of the parade was "Proud, Strong, United," during the line-up, members of a political organization passed out signs that read, simply, "Veto Senate Bill 651 House Bill 2682." The signs were added to every float, contingent, car, and motorcycle. Unlike their usual focus on the flamboyant, the media in Chicago noticed that every entry carried signs urging Illinois's governor James Thompson to veto these bills on his desk that would establish the tracing of sexual contacts for people who are infected with HIV, institute mandatory testing, and allow quarantine of those infected. The *Chicago Tribune* reported the parade as "subdued in comparison to years past. The few drag queens and skimpily clad young men were outnumbered by sedate marchers representing various church groups, singing ensembles and associations somehow connected with AIDS."[2]

Whereas in the 1960s and 1970s sex itself was foregrounded as the revolutionary act (and indeed the gay liberation movement was part of the political and sexual revolution of the 1960s), sex and "gendered" aspects of representing gay men are now left in the background rhetorically. At the rally following the parade in 1987, the crowd responded with thunderous applause as the major speaker called out, "Make our opponents talk about our love, not our sex. Our love is the same as theirs." Presenting the gay community as composed of families, of churches and sports leagues, of clubs and professional associations, of everything about normative society except simply sexual behavior, has become the new strategy. The political agenda as frequently calls for the right to a conventional family life as for sexual freedom. In the era of AIDS, the personal script and collective myth for "coming out" (i.e., "coming out of the closet," telling others that one is gay) is based no longer on the sexual revolution of Stonewall but on a community of individuals and organizations involved in fund-raising for research, taking care of people with AIDS, offering networks of support, and defending the rights of the infected: in short, not on acts of sex but on acts of love. As the politics has become less radical and more assimilationist, participation in the parade has steadily increased.

Parades in Chicago

Chicago's gay and lesbian parade takes place in a city of parades. In   20 the early 1950s, Mayor Richard J. Daley brought the St. Patrick's Day Parade downtown from the Irish neighborhoods and made it a public demonstration of his constituency and his coalition. The Chicago Irish had created the Democratic machine in the early decades of the twentieth century, when they were the abused and despised working and under class of Chicago. Moving the St. Patrick's Day Parade downtown signaled the arrival of Irish influence at City Hall.[3] Under Daley, the Irish, Polish, and other "white ethnics" (as they are now known) ran Chicago's political machine. As black Chicagoans, including Harold Washington, were brought (in a highly qualified role) into the system, they learned the business of city government. Chicago's black leadership used their new-found knowledge to gain power under Washington's leadership.

Neighborhood events—and especially neighborhood events that move downtown—are a correlate to ethnic identity and political ma-

---

2. *Chicago Tribune,* 29 June 1987, sec. 2, p. 3.
3. On the history of the Irish in Chicago, see Lawrence McCaffrey, ed., *The Irish in Chicago* (Urbana: University of Illinois Press, 1987).

turity in Chicago. The "neighborhood" is the home turf of the "ethnic community" in Chicago's political lexicon. Virtually every neighborhood has a summer street festival of some sort, featuring a parade or procession, entertainment, and food from the local eateries, as an expression of its cultural and neighborhood autonomy, typically celebrating an immigrant identity and "cultural awareness." Having a parade for one's neighborhood, community, or ethnic group is critical for having a political presence in the social consciousness of the city.

The summer calendar for these events is extensive; there are as many as three and four a weekend. The *Chicago Tribune* listed ninety-six festivals and parades for the 1988 season, including a series of "Ethnic Festivals" held at Navy Pier downtown: the Festival Polonaise, the Irish Festival, the Pan American Festival, the Festa Italiana, and the Rhythm and Blues Festival. Many other festivals in Chicago are modest neighborhood events, organized by and for local merchants as a venue for their food and wares. Others among Chicago's ethnic minorities—which are usually not called "ethnics"—also have fairs and festivals: the Chinatown Moon Festival, the Fiesta Del Sol (Mexican) in Pilsen, and the Bud Billiken Day Parade (African American) on the South Side.

Ward organizations, neighborhood events, and the relation between neighborhoods and downtown are all imbued with the "ethnic algebra" of Chicago politics. Being "ethnic" and having an "ethnic identity" is a critical part of Chicago's political map and idiom. "Ethnic communities" are seen to have interests as such and are expected to demand representation. These parades and festivals have become tightly linked with influence real and perceived: Who comes? Who speaks? Who marches? Harold Washington was the first mayor who spoke at a Gay and Lesbian Pride Day rally. After his appearance, mass media reports for the first time treated the parade as something other than flamboyantly dressed homosexuals having a party in the street. After Washington's death, the articles reporting the 1988 parade in the gay and lesbian newspapers focused on who among the candidates for mayor attended or failed to attend the rally and parade: the acting mayor, Eugene Sawyer, failed to appear for a scheduled speech at the rally, while his archrival, Alderman Tim Evans, alone among the mayoral candidates (all of whom supported passage of the pending "gay rights" ordinance) made a surprise showing, riding in a convertible with a fellow alderman.

Reading the Text

1. What is the significance of the Stonewall Rebellion to gay culture?
2. How has Newtown become a symbol of the gay community in Chicago, according to Herrell?
3. How has the AIDS epidemic affected the Gay and Lesbian Pride Day Parade in Chicago?

Reading the Signs

1. In your journal, explore Herrell's claim that "ethnicity has become a model for gays and lesbians." How are homosexuals an oppressed group in America, as are many ethnic minorities? What differences are there between gays and ethnic groups?
2. Write an interpretive essay explaining how the gay pride parade works as a sign of gay identity and community. What messages are the participants sending through parade banners and themes, to both the gay and the heterosexual communities?
3. How has the meaning of the gay pride parade changed from the 1970s through the 1980s? How do you account for the symbolic changes that occurred over the years?
4. How does the Gay and Lesbian Pride Day Parade illustrate the notion of "camp," as discussed by Andy Medhurst ("Batman, Deviance, and Camp," p. 323)?
5. What sort of symbols might Douglas Crimp and Adam Rolston ("The Semiotics of AIDS Activism," p. 708) suggest for next year's Gay and Lesbian Pride Day Parade? Sketch some banners or placards, and share them with your class.

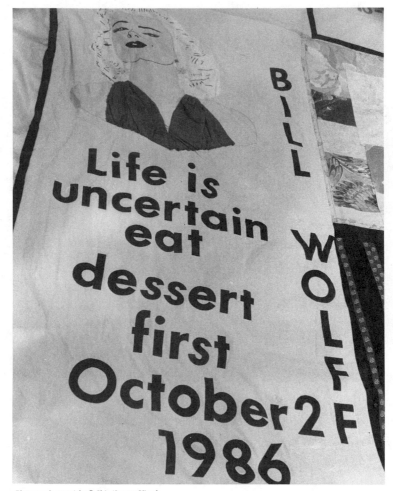

Life is
uncertain
eat
dessert
first
October 2
1986

BILL
WOLFF

Photograph copyright © Shia / Impact Visuals.

CHAPTER TEN

JOURNALS OF THE PLAGUE YEARS

The Social Mythology of AIDS

The topic of this chapter might puzzle you. AIDS, after all, is a disease; what could it possibly have to do with culture? Shouldn't we leave this one to physicians and public health workers and stick to more obvious cultural issues like race and gender? We could, but then we'd be ignoring one of the most significant cultural issues in our lives today. If AIDS doesn't look like an issue to you, think about the concrete ways it has shaped your own life and behavior. What difference has AIDS made to you, even if neither you nor anyone you know actually has it?

Thinking about AIDS for a moment reveals how it is much more than a disease and how it has become a major, if bleak, force in our culture. Consider the effect of AIDS on American sexuality. Before AIDS, America's sexual mythology had been evolving toward a more open system than our culture has ever had. But AIDS has changed that. How does our society view sexual activity now? And how are those views reflected in popular culture—say, in the way Hollywood has increasingly equated sex with violence or death in film after film during the 1990s?

The profound impact of AIDS on the psyche of young America makes it an essential topic for semiotic analysis. You can begin that analysis by exploring what AIDS means to you in your day-to-day behavior. How does it affect your dating habits? Do you take precautions? Do you resent the fact that you have to take precautions? Are you nostalgic for the era before AIDS?

But AIDS has a number of semiotic dimensions. Remember the semiotic precept that social reality is what we make of it, and that "nature" is often politics in disguise. The AIDS epidemic, now in its second decade, is an especially powerful illustration of this fundamental principle, for few recent diseases have been so susceptible to symbolism and politicization. We do not mean to imply that the disease, or, more precisely, the syndrome, is merely a sign, but it is also more than a medical condition. For while AIDS denotes the devastation wrought upon the human body by a complex set of highly unstable viruses, it also connotes a vast range of political meanings: Indeed, AIDS is part of a system of social constructions that have transformed the biologically based syndrome into an ideologically charged mythology.

To see how AIDS exists as a sign as well as a syndrome, look at the cover of the August 3, 1992, issue of *Time* reprinted on page 660. Our reproduction is in black and white, but the original featured a stark red border framing a black background, with "AIDS" printed in red block letters. The main headline, "LOSING THE BATTLE," appeared in white block letters that sharply contrasted with the sinister blackness of the page, as did the three subheads: "MYSTERIOUS NON-HIV CASES EMERGE," "THE SEARCH FOR A CURE STALLS," and "INFECTION AMONG WOMEN GROWS."

Now interpret this *Time* cover as a sign. Start with the colors. What do the colors red, black, and white suggest to you? What difference would other colors such as green and yellow, make? Consider the headlines. What is their emphasis? Does the fact that the feature article inside the magazine was itself headlined in bold red letters reading INVINCIBLE AIDS help you to determine what view of the disease *Time* was presenting? How, in short, has the story of AIDS been packaged?

You may think, "but AIDS *is* invincible, the search for a cure *has* stalled, and its infection *has* grown among women. What's so political about this cover?" Well, for one thing, the article was not as apocalyptic as its cover. Written in response to the Eighth International Conference on AIDS (where, it must be said, researchers certainly delivered a lot of bad news), the article actually was filled with evidence of all the work being done to stop the disease. In fact, we hear the head of the Walter Reed Army Institute of Research expressing optimism at the conference. At the same time, the announcement that "Mysterious Non-HIV Cases Emerge" among heterosexuals has turned out to be premature. A handful of such cases was immediately publicized in a way that the first appearances of AIDS among gay men was not. So the question is: Why are the headlines designed the way they are? Why the color scheme? Why are we being told about AIDS this way rather than another? As usual, our semiotic question is, "What is really going on here?"

To help you answer this question, consider the presence of another article in the same issue of *Time*. It was a feature about the gay com-

---

Exploring the Signs of AIDS

What difference has the AIDS epidemic made to you? In your journal, explore the personal consequences of this disease. Have you made adjustments in personal habits or sexual behavior? Did controversies related to AIDS, such as the distribution of condoms, arise in your high school? How did you feel about them? What do you think your response would be if a close friend or relative contracted the disease? If you don't feel you've been at all affected by the AIDS epidemic, why do you think that's the case?

---

munity called "An Identity Forged in Flames." At the time this article appeared, the rate of AIDS infection among American homosexuals was dramatically declining, while its rate among black and Hispanic heterosexuals was exploding. Finally it had become medically clear that AIDS was dangerous to everyone, and yet there is that article on gay America set next to the article on AIDS. What is the effect of that juxtaposition? How does it reinforce the image that AIDS still holds in America? How does our attitude toward AIDS reflect our attitudes toward sexual orientation? Do you view some AIDS victims as "innocent" and others as "guilty"? If you do, why? In short, what is the social image of AIDS, and how are your own opinions shaped by that image?

The Medium Is the Message

The construction of AIDS as a sign began with the first reports on the mysterious new illness. Here the media played a crucial, and perhaps even culpable, role, as the initial images of AIDS came to dominate how it was received and understood. We can recall our own introduction to AIDS as a lesson not only in recent medical history but also in the sexual behavior of the gay community. It was during a broadcast of National Public Radio's *All Things Considered* one evening in 1981 that we first learned of the as-yet-unnamed epidemic. The report seemed routine enough at first. A mysterious new disease, apparently afflicting only young homosexual men, had suddenly appeared. But the story was not limited to medical reportage. Much of it detailed the sexual practices of gay men in San Francisco and New York, and it elaborated on the speculated link between the disease and the use of "poppers," stimulants used for gay sex. And it was this focus on, even obsession with, a certain life-style that set AIDS off from other illnesses from the very beginning.

When a mysterious fatal illness broke out amidst a convention of American Legionnaires in 1976, for example, the media said nothing about its victims' social habits. But in NPR's report on AIDS, as in most other media reports, a presumably heterosexual audience not simply was informed about a medical phenomenon but was regaled with the details of the sexual habits of the first people with AIDS—even though it was not at all clear at the time that AIDS was a sexually transmitted disease. An indelible link between the disease and the sexual habits of its victims was established.

Ever since these first reports, AIDS has borne the dual stigmata of difference and disease. Had AIDS been presented only as an illness, albeit a fatally infectious one, do you think that it would have incurred the burden of shame that it now carries? After all, cancer and heart disease, which also lack reassuring preventative vaccinations and reliable cures, claim many more lives than AIDS has claimed. But it is AIDS that has been cast as a disease of the irredeemably different. Like Hester Prynne's scarlet letter "A," "AIDS" is the sign of the outcast. Even in the 1990s, AIDS remains such an unspeakable affliction that the obituaries of prominent young men who have succumbed to the syndrome often avoid mentioning the causes of their deaths, instead making oblique references to pneumonia or septic shock. And when the world-famous ballet star Rudolph Nureyev died in 1992, he not only told no one that he had AIDS but ordered his doctor to conceal his affliction. AIDS is still a disease of whispers.

The Language of AIDS

Behind the whispers exists a set of metaphors that have been decisive in shaping the social image of AIDS. One of the first metaphors used for AIDS—by historians, physicians, the gay community, and the public alike—was that of the Plague, the Black Death that devastated Europe in the fourteenth century. This is understandable, for humans understand new experiences in terms of the experiences they have already had. With terrible infectious diseases such as smallpox, tuberculosis, diphtheria, and polio under control in the modern era, the appearance of a hitherto unknown infectious killer was almost instantly associated with the greatest medical catastrophe of European history. For like that disastrous visitation of the Middle Ages, the modern "plague" too seemed to sweep from out of nowhere. And also like that earlier cataclysm, the ferocity of the disease seemed to suggest something more than mere medical mayhem let loose in the world. To some, it had all the appearance of a divine punishment.

That is what made the inaugural metaphor so powerful and political. The illness was soon dubbed the "gay plague," and this association with the medieval disease turned AIDS into a sign of divine wrath against those who were America's first victims. Indeed, the religious right cast

AIDS as an instrument of retribution against sexual wickedness. Had AIDS first appeared among Middle-American heterosexuals, do you think that its social construction would have been the same? The fact that there was an outbreak of sexually transmitted herpes among American heterosexuals in the 1970s that attracted immediate medical attention but no metaphors of divine retribution can help you see just how influential those first metaphors of the AIDS epidemic have been.

Race, Class, and AIDS

As with so much else in American culture, class and race also play an important role in the social construction of AIDS. For the most part, the AIDS story thus far underplays both the heterosexual pandemic in Africa and Asia and the spread of the disease among minority IV drug users in America. There are a few nonpolitical reasons for this apparent neglect, of course. American IV drug users began to become infected with AIDS later than did gay men, so one would expect less writing about them at this date. But still, there are political and cultural explanations for the kind of writing that has dominated the scene so far. The first people with the disease in America, though often condemned for their sexual orientation, nonetheless tended to hail from the middle and upper-middle classes. They were often white professionals, and many were artists and writers who were already in the public eye or who could pen their own account of the disease. Heterosexual victims from racially oppressed groups, as well as IV-infected patients, have not had this kind of access. So the story of AIDS does not simply reflect cultural attitudes toward sexuality: class and race enter the equation too.

Consider the case of the Haitians. Early in the epidemic, the Centers for Disease Control published a list of those most at risk for contracting the disease. This list included gay men, IV drug users, and—in a peculiar inclusion of an entire nationality—Haitians. The fact that Haitians are black added a racial slant to the social codification of AIDS, one that was based on a misunderstanding of the nature of the epidemic as it spread through Haiti. For what the CDC didn't know was that different social mores prevented the compiling of accurate demographic statistics. Many of the Haitian patients were bisexual men exposed to HIV through homosexual contacts, but given a different cultural understanding of sexual identity, few considered themselves to be "homosexual," and so did not identify themselves as such in the surveys. As a result, Haiti initially was considered a heterosexual anomaly in the New World picture of AIDS, and the entire nation was cast as a special case, a risk group all its own.

Even as the medical realities of the disease become more and more apparent, the mythology remains stubbornly intact. AIDS today bears

Discussing the Signs of AIDS

One controversy surrounding the AIDS epidemic involves the cost of medicines, particularly drugs such as AZT, which can run into many thousands of dollars annually. One result of the high cost is that many people with AIDS cannot afford medication for their symptoms. In class, debate this controversy. Should such drugs be available to AIDS patients at a subsidy provided by the government or by the drug companies themselves? Or should the free market prevail, with pharmaceutical companies recouping research costs by charging whatever the market will bear?

much the same social stigma it bore from the beginning. It is still perceived as a disease of the "other," as a National Research Council report released in 1993 demonstrates. The epidemic will eventually "disappear," the *Los Angeles Times* cited in the report's conclusions, "because those who continue to be affected by it are socially invisible, beyond the sight and attention of the majority population"—that is, those whose race and class differ from that of the majority population.

Speaking of AIDS

The population first afflicted by AIDS in America constructed its own code as well, a code that Randy Shilts calls AIDSpeak. This language sprang up to make sure that no one's feelings were hurt in speaking of this most politically sensitive of diseases. "Under the rules of AIDSpeak," Shilts writes, "AIDS victims could not be called victims. Instead, they were to be called People With AIDS, or PWAs, as if contracting this uniquely brutal disease was not a victimizing experience. 'Promiscuous' became 'sexually active,' because gay politicians declared 'promiscuous' to be 'judgmental,' a major cuss word in AIDSpeak. The most-used circumlocution in AIDSpeak was 'bodily fluids,' an expression that avoided troublesome words like 'semen.'"

Shilts's observations point out that what we call something may not be merely a matter of harmless semantics. For the generalized term "bodily fluids" caused real panic in the mid-1980s. Saliva, after all, is a bodily fluid. "Can you get AIDS from kissing?" people asked. Or sweat? Or sneezing?

Even the acronym "AIDS" reflects the political dimensions of the syndrome. Originally called GRID (or Gay-Related Immune Deficiency), the illness was initially identified with sexual preference, pure and simple. Soon, it was renamed both to avoid the explicit finger-pointing indicated by the telltale "G" and to reflect the medical realization that AIDS is an equal-opportunity killer. But even the apparently neutral "AIDS" bears a hidden judgment. Consider the moral connotation of that scarlet letter "A." While it signifies "acquired" to distinguish this sort of immune deficiency disorder from the congenital kind, the letter is not so innocent as it appears. It also suggests that you have to do something to get AIDS, you have to act to "acquire" it, and in so doing incur a burden of moral responsibility in a climate in which it is mostly the "passive" victims of disease who receive the sympathy of their unstricken neighbors. It is instructive to note that when in 1992 the creator of the cartoon strip "Rex Morgan, MD" chose to run a series involving AIDS, he cast a young female physician as the patient, a surgeon whose exposure to HIV resulted from her professional duties in an urban trauma center. Try to imagine a popular cartoon featuring a gay man with the disease.

To appreciate the moral and political overtones of the acronym, the way it differentiates people with AIDS from the victims of such mortal ailments as cancer and heart disease, consider how you would react if the disease were called "Montagnier's syndrome," after the French researcher whose laboratory first isolated the HIV virus. This, after all, is how leprosy lost its age-old stigma, by being renamed "Hansen's disease" after the nineteenth-century biologist who discovered its causative bacterium. Or what if AIDS were called "Rock Hudson's disease" or "Magic Johnson's disease," after its most famous patients, just as Lou Gehrig lent his name to the rare ailment (ALS) that broke his consecutive game string?

It may be too late for that now, however. The word "AIDS" probably will never lose its moral burden. Though the French were puzzled from the start by America's obsession with the homosexual side to the epidemic (in France, AIDS, or SIDA, is regarded as a largely African contagion), the hidden "G" continues to dominate its semiotic horizon. Indeed, AIDS has been so associated with homosexuality that hemophiliac children with AIDS have been hounded out of their schools and homes, while at first some physicians denied that "innocent" children could contract it from their mothers or that transfusion recipients could be infected by tainted blood. And an occasional doctor still won't think of testing female patients for HIV, believing that they are "too nice to have AIDS." For many Americans, AIDS remains more a behavioral disorder than a viral condition, something you get as punishment for having a socially "unacceptable" sexual orientation.

The Readings

We begin this chapter with Paul Monette's personal story of the death of Roger Horvitz, a testimony that puts a human face on the often dehumanized image of AIDS in America. Susan Sontag then analyzes the particular metaphors and analogies that first shaped the imagery of AIDS, arguing that the way AIDS was initially defined and conceived was crucial in its political construction. Michael Quam extends Sontag's analysis, showing how AIDS, like syphilis in the past, is a sign, or *stigma,* of social marginalization, while Kate Scannell, a physician from San Francisco, presents a personal testimony to what AIDS means to a doctor who has had to redefine her understanding of the role of healer. Evelynn Hammonds analyzes the way AIDS has become a disease of the racially and sexually marginalized in America, while Randy Shilts critiques the use of AIDSpeak. We conclude with Douglas Crimp and Adam Rolston's interpretation of the "silence = death" symbol, a potent response to both the disease and its social construction.

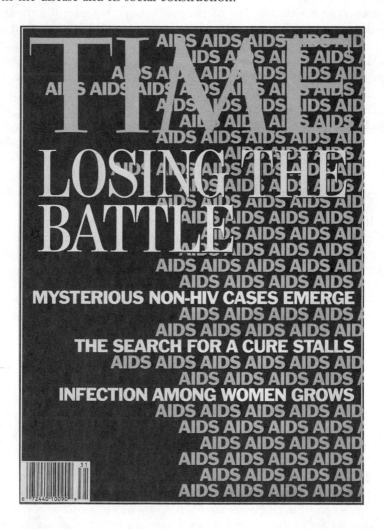

Borrowed Time: An AIDS Memoir

||||||||||||||||||||||||||||||||||||||||||||||||||||||||

In the beginning, before it had a name, AIDS appeared to be a rare form of cancer afflicting only those gay men who engaged in particularly risky sexual practices. But as Paul Monette writes in this excerpt from Borrowed Time: An AIDS Memoir *(1988), AIDS soon appeared among the kind of men Monette and his companion Roger Horvitz felt themselves to be: successful, upper-middle-class professionals living together in stable relationships. Finding that he and his friends were not immune from the "gay plague" that began its sweep through America in 1981, Monette began living, in his own phrase, "on the moon": that is, in a nightmare world of disease and death that separated him forever from the world of ordinary life. Writing from the moon, Monette here tells his story of love and death in the face of a relentless enemy, all the while preparing for death himself. The winner of the National Book Award for Non-Fiction in 1993 for his autobiography* Becoming a Man: Half a Life Story, *Paul Monette continues to live and write in Los Angeles, in the same house he shared with Roger Horvitz.*

I don't know if I will live to finish this. Doubtless there's a streak of self-importance in such an assertion, but who's counting? Maybe it's just that I've watched too many sicken in a month and die by Christmas, so that a fatal sort of realism comforts me more than magic. All I know is this: The virus ticks in me. And it doesn't care a whit about our categories—when is full-blown, what's AIDS-related, what is just sick and tired? No one has solved the puzzle of its timing. I take my drug from Tijuana twice a day. The very friends who tell me how vigorous I look, how well I seem, are the first to assure me of the imminent medical breakthrough. What they don't seem to understand is, I used up all my optimism keeping my friend alive. Now that he's gone, the cup of my own health is neither half full nor half empty. Just half.

Equally difficult, of course, is knowing where to start. The world around me is defined now by its endings and its closures—the date on the grave that follows the hyphen. Roger Horwitz, my beloved friend, died of complications of AIDS on October 22, 1986, nineteen months and ten days after his diagnosis. That is the only real date anymore, casting its ice shadow over all the secular holidays lovers mark their calendars by. Until that long night in October, it didn't seem possible that any day could supplant the brute equinox of March 12—the day of Roger's diagnosis in 1985, the day we began to live on the moon.

The fact is, no one knows where to start with AIDS. Now, in the seventh year of the calamity, my friends in L.A. can hardly recall what it felt like any longer, the time before the sickness. Yet we all watched the toll mount in New York, then in San Francisco, for years before it ever touched us here. It comes like a slowly dawning horror. At first you are equipped with a hundred different amulets to keep it far away. Then someone you know goes into the hospital, and suddenly you are at high noon in full battle gear. They have neglected to tell you that you will be issued no weapons of any sort. So you cobble together a weapon out of anything that lies at hand, like a prisoner honing a spoon handle into a stiletto. You fight tough, you fight dirty, but you cannot fight dirtier than it.

I remember a Saturday in February 1982, driving Route 10 to Palm Springs with Roger to visit his parents for the weekend. While Roger drove, I read aloud an article from *The Advocate:* "Is Sex Making Us Sick?" There was the slightest edge of irony in the query, an urban cool that seems almost bucolic now in its innocence. But the article didn't mince words. It was the first in-depth reporting I'd read that laid out the shadowy nonfacts of what till then had been the most fragmented of rumors. The first cases were reported to the Centers for Disease Control (CDC) only six months before, but they weren't in the newspapers, not in L.A. I note in my diary in December 1981 ambiguous reports of a "gay cancer," but I know I didn't have the slightest picture of the thing. Cancer of the *what*? I would have asked, if anyone had known anything.

I remember exactly what was going through my mind while I was reading, though I can't now recall the details of the piece. I was thinking: How is this not me? Trying to find a pattern I was exempt from. It was a brand of denial I would watch grow exponentially during the next few years, but at the time I was simply relieved. Because the article appeared to be saying that there was a grim progression toward this undefined catastrophe, a set of preconditions—chronic hepatitis, repeated bouts of syphilis, exotic parasites. No wonder my first baseline response was to feel safe. It was *them*—by which I meant the fast-lane Fire Island crowd, the Sutro Baths, the world of High Eros.

Not us.

I grabbed for that relief because we'd been through a rough patch the previous autumn. Till then Roger had always enjoyed a sort of no-nonsense good health: not an abuser of anything, with a constitutional aversion to hypochondria, and not wed to his mirror save for a minor alarm as to the growing dimensions of his bald spot. In the seven years we'd been together I scarcely remember him having a cold or taking an aspirin. Yet in October 1981 he had struggled with a peculiar bout of intestinal flu. Nothing special showed up in any of the blood tests, but over a period of weeks he experienced persistent symptoms that didn't neatly connect: pains in his legs, diarrhea, general malaise. I hadn't been feeling notably bad myself, but on the other hand I was a textbook hypochondriac, and I figured if Rog was harboring some kind of bug, so was I.

The two of us finally went to a gay doctor in the Valley for a further set of blood tests. It's a curious phenomenon among gay middle-class men that anything faintly venereal had better be taken to a doctor who's "on the bus." Is it a sense of fellow feeling perhaps, or a way of avoiding embarrassment? Do we really believe that only a doctor who's *our* kind can heal us of the afflictions that attach somehow to our secret hearts? There is so much magic to medicine. Of course we didn't know then that those few physicians with a large gay clientele were about to be swamped beyond all capacity to cope.

The tests came back positive for amoebiasis. Roger and I began the highly toxic treatment to kill the amoeba, involving two separate drugs and what seems in memory thirty pills a day for six weeks, till the middle of January. It was the first time I'd ever experienced the phenomenon of the cure making you sicker. By the end of treatment we were both weak and had lost weight, and for a couple of months afterward were susceptible to colds and minor infections.

It was only after the treatment was over that a friend of ours, diag- 10
nosed with amoebas by the same doctor, took his slide to the lab at UCLA for a second opinion. And that was my first encounter with lab error. The doctor at UCLA explained that the slide had been misread; the squiggles that looked like amoebas were in fact benign. The doctor shook his head and grumbled about "these guys who do their own lab work." Roger then retrieved his slide, took it over to UCLA and was told the same: no amoebas. We had just spent six weeks methodically ingesting poison for no reason at all.

So it wasn't the *Advocate* story that sent up the red flag for us. We'd been shaken by the amoeba business, and from that point on we operated at a new level of sexual caution. What is now called safe sex did not use to be so clearly defined. The concept didn't exist. But it was quickly becoming apparent, even then, that we couldn't wait for somebody else to define the parameters. Thus every gay man I know has had to come to a point of personal definition by way of avoiding the chaos of sexually transmitted diseases, or STD as we call them in the trade. There was obviously no one moment of conscious decision, a bolt of clarity on the shimmering freeway west of San Bernardino, but I think of that day when I think of the sea change. The party was going to have to stop. The evidence was too ominous: *We were making ourselves sick.*

Not that Roger and I were the life of the party. Roger especially didn't march to the different drum of *so many men, so little time,* the motto and anthem of the sunstruck summers of the mid-to-late seventies. He'd managed not to carry away from his adolescence the mark of too much repression, or indeed the yearning to make up for lost time. In ten years he had perhaps half a dozen contacts outside the main frame of our relationship, mostly when he was out of town on business. He was comfortable with relative monogamy, even at a time when certain quarters of the gay world found the whole idea trivial and bourgeois. I realize that in the world of the heterosexual there is a generalized lip service paid to exclusive monogamy, a notion most vividly honored in the breach. I leave the matter of morality to those with the gift of tongues; it was difficult enough for us to fashion a sexual ethics just for us. In any case, I was the one in the relationship who suffered from lost time. I was the one who would go after a sexual encounter as if it were an ice cream cone—casual, quick, good-by.

But as I say, who's counting? I only want to make it plain to start with that we got very alert and very careful as far back as the winter of 1982. That gut need for safety took hold and lingered, even as we got better again and strong. Thus I'm not entirely sure what I thought on another afternoon a year and a half later, when a friend of ours back from New York reported a conversation he'd had with a research man from Sloan-Kettering.

"He thinks all it takes is one exposure," Charlie said, this after months of articles about the significance of repeated exposure. More tenaciously than ever, we all wanted to believe the whole deepening tragedy was centered on those at the sexual frontiers who were fucking their brains out. The rest of us were fashioning our own little Puritan forts, as we struggled to convince ourselves that a clean slate would hold the nightmare at bay.

Yet with caution as our watchword starting in February of 1982, Roger was diagnosed with AIDS three years later. So the turning over of new leaves was not to be on everybody's side. A lot of us were already ticking and didn't even know. The magic circle my generation is trying to stay within the borders of is only as real as the random past. Perhaps the young can live in the magic circle, but only if those of us who are ticking will tell our story. Otherwise it goes on being *us* and *them* forever, built like a wall higher and higher, till you no longer think to wonder if you are walling it out or in.

For us the knowing began in earnest on the first of September, 1983. I'd had a call a couple of days before from my closest friend, Cesar Albini, who'd just returned to San Francisco after a summer touring Europe with a group of students. He said he'd been having trouble walking because of a swollen gland in his groin, and he was going to the hospital to have it biopsied. He reassured me he was feeling fine and wasn't expecting anything ominous, but figured he'd check it out before school started again. AIDS didn't even cross my mind, though cancer did. Half joking, Cesar wondered aloud if he dared disturb our happy friendship with bad news.

"If it's bad," I said, "we'll handle it, okay?"

But I really didn't clutch with fear, or it was only a brief stab of the hypochondriacal sort. Roger and I were busy getting ready for a four-day trip to Big Sur, something we'd done almost yearly since moving to California in 1977. We were putting the blizzard of daily life on hold, looking forward to a dose of raw sublime that coincided with our anniversary—September 3, the day we met.

Cesar was forty-three, only ten months older than Roger. Born in Uruguay, possessed of a great heart and inexhaustible energy, he had studied in Europe and traveled all over, once spending four months going overland from Paris to China at a total cost of five hundred dollars. He was the first Uruguayan ever to enter Afghanistan through the mountains—on a camel, if I remember right. He spoke French, Italian, Spanish and English with equal fluency, and he tended to be the whole language department of a school. We'd both been teaching at secondary schools in Massachusetts when we met, and we goaded one another to make the move west that had always been our shared dream. Thus Cesar had relocated to San Francisco in July of 1976, and Roger and I landed in L.A. four days after Thanksgiving the following year.

Cesar wasn't lucky in matters of the heart. He was still in the closet   20 during his years back East, and the move to San Francisco was an extraordinary rite of passage for him. He always wanted a great love, but the couple of relationships he'd been involved in scarcely left the station. Still, he was very proud and indulged in no self-pity. He learned to accept the limited terms of the once-a-week relations he found in San Francisco, and broke through to the freedom of his own manhood without the mythic partner. The open sexual exultation that marked San Francisco in those days was something he rejoiced in.

Yet even though he went to the baths a couple of times a week, Cesar wasn't into anything *weird*—or that's how I might have put it at that stage of my own denial. No hepatitis, no history of VD, built tall and fierce—of course he was safe. The profile of AIDS continued to be mostly a matter of shadows. The L.A. *Times* wasn't covering it, though by then I had come to learn how embattled things had grown in New York. The Gay Men's Health Crisis was up to its ears in clients; Larry Kramer was screaming at the mayor; and the body count was appearing weekly in the *Native*. A writer I knew slightly was walking around with Kaposi's sarcoma. A young composer kept getting sicker and sicker, though he stubbornly didn't fit the CDC's hopelessly narrow categories, so that case was still officially a toss-up. And again, we're talking New York.

I came home at six on the evening of the first, and Roger met me gravely at the door. "There's a message from Cesar," he said. "It's not good."

Numbly I played back the answering machine, where so much appalling misery would be left on tape over the years to come, as if a

record were crying out to be kept. "I have a little bit of bad news."
Cesar's voice sounded strained, almost embarrassed. He left no details. I
called and called him throughout the evening, convinced I was about to
hear cancer news. The lymph nodes, of course—a hypochondriac knows
all there is to know about the sites of malignancy. Already I was figuring
what the treatments might be; no question in my mind but that it was
treatable. I had Cesar practically cured by the time I reached Tom, a
friend and former student of his. But as usual with me in crisis, I was
jabbering and wouldn't let Tom get a word in. Finally he broke through:
"He's got it."

"Got what?"

It's not till you first hear it attached to someone you love that you   25
realize how little you know about it. My mind went utterly blank. The
carefully constructed wall collapsed as if a 7.5 quake had rumbled under
it. At that point I didn't even know the difference between KS and the
opportunistic infections. I kept picturing that swollen gland in his groin,
thinking: What's *that* got to do with AIDS? And a parallel track in my
mind began careening with another thought: the swollen glands in my
own groin, always dismissed by my straight doctor as herpes-related and
"not a significant sign."

"We're not going to die young," Cesar used to say with a wag of his
finger, his black Latin eyes dancing. "We won't get out of it *that* easily!"
Then he would laugh and clap his hands, downing the coffee he always
took with cream and four sugars. It looked like pudding.

I reached him very late that night and mouthed again the same
words I'd said so bravely two days before: We'll deal with it. There is
no end to the litany of reassurance that springs to your lips to ward away
the specter. They've caught it early; you're fine; there's got to be some
kind of treatment. That old chestnut, the imminent breakthrough. You
fling these phrases instinctively, like pennies down a well. Cesar and I
bent backward to calm each other. It was just a couple of lesions in the
groin; you could hardly see them. And the reason everything was going
to be all right was really very simple: We would fight this thing like
demons.

But the hollowness and disbelief pursued Roger and me all the way
up the gold coast. Big Sur was towering and bracing as ever—exalted as
Homer's Ithaca, as Robinson Jeffers described it. We were staying at
Ventana, the lavish inn high in the hills above the canyon of the Big Sur
River. We used the inn as a base camp for our day-long hikes, returning
in the evening to posh amenities worthy of an Edwardian big-game
hunt. On the second morning we walked out to Andrew Molera Beach,
where the Big Sur empties into the Pacific. Molera stretches unblemished
for five miles down the coast, curving like a crescent moon, with weathered headlands clean as Scotland. It was a kind of holy place for Roger
and me, like the yearly end of a quest.

"What if we got it?" I said, staring out at the otters belly up in the kelp beds, taking the sun.

I don't remember how we answered that, because of course there 30 wasn't any answer. Merely to pose the question was by way of another shot at magic. Mention the unmentionable and it will go away, like shining a light around a child's bedroom to shoo the monster. The great ache we were feeling at that moment was for our stricken friend, and we were too ignorant still to envision the medieval tortures that might await him.

But I know that the roll of pictures I took that day was my first conscious memorializing of Roger and me, as if I could hold the present as security on the future. There's one of me on the beach, then a mirror image of him as we traded off the camera, both of us squinting in the clear autumn light with the river mouth behind. Back at the inn, I took a picture of Rog in a rope hammock, his blue eyes resting on me as if the camera weren't even there, in total equilibrium, nine years to the day since our paths crossed on Revere Street. His lips are barely curved in a quarter-smile, his hands at rest in his lap as the last wave of the westering sun washes his left side through the diamond weave of the rope.

Reading the Text

1. Why does Monette say that the AIDS epidemic prompted him to look at other gays as "us" and "them"?
2. What does Monette mean by "the turning over of new leaves was not to be on everybody's side"?
3. How did Monette respond to the illness of his friend Cesar?

Reading the Signs

1. Write an essay analyzing why Monette responded both to the general AIDS epidemic and to his and Roger's illness with denial. How did Monette distinguish himself from other gay men? What social-class issues may have affected his perception of this disease?
2. Read or review Michael Quam's "Stigma" (p. 679). How might the notion of a stigma explain Monette's response to the AIDS epidemic?
3. Monette's "Borrowed Time" is an autobiographical narrative, not an analytical essay. In class, "translate" Monette's selection into a one-page essay, working individually or in groups, then read the essays aloud. Discuss what different effects the storytelling and analytic modes have on you as the audience. (You may want to consult Leslie Marmon Silko's "Language and Literature from a Pueblo Indian Perspective," p. 495, for her comments on the value of storytelling.)

4. In your journal, explore the significance of Monette's title, "Borrowed Time."
5. Rent a videotape of the film *Longtime Companion,* a chronicle of a group of friends coping with the AIDS epidemic. Show the film in class, and discuss how the characters depicted in the film respond to the illness. How does their response compare with Monette's?

SUSAN SONTAG
AIDS and Its Metaphors

tttttttttttttttttttttttttttttttttttttttttttttttttt

When Susan Sontag (b. 1933) was diagnosed with cancer in the 1970s, she not only set out, successfully, to fight the disease, she began an exploration of the social construction of illness throughout history. The result of her study, Illness as Metaphor *(1978), became the basis for her more recent book,* AIDS and Its Metaphors *(1989), from which this selection has been taken. Like any illness, Sontag argues, AIDS is a sign as well as a medical phenomenon. Constructing AIDS as a "plague" especially predisposes us to regard it according to a religious mythology that isolates its victims, Sontag suggests. Even the way AIDS is medically defined has social implications, especially the term "full-blown" AIDS, which can imply that HIV infection itself is already AIDS, albeit not yet developed. Having herself felt the isolating effects of cancer, Sontag argues against the use of metaphors that dehumanize people with AIDS. The author of numerous books, essays, stories, and screenplays, Sontag has most recently published a novel,* The Volcano Lover *(1992).*

Just as one might predict for a disease that is not yet fully understood as well as extremely recalcitrant to treatment, the advent of this terrifying new disease, new at least in its epidemic form, has provided a large-scale occasion for the metaphorizing of illness.

Strictly speaking, AIDS—acquired immune deficiency syndrome— is not the name of an illness at all. It is the name of a medical condition, whose consequences are a spectrum of illnesses. In contrast to syphilis and cancer, which provide prototypes for most of the images and metaphors attached to AIDS, the very definition of AIDS requires the presence of other illnesses, so-called opportunistic infections and malignancies. But though not in *that* sense a single disease, AIDS lends itself to being regarded as one—in part because, unlike cancer and like syphilis, it is thought to have a single cause.

AIDS has a dual metaphoric genealogy. As a microprocess, it is described as cancer is: an invasion. When the focus is transmission of the disease, an older metaphor, reminiscent of syphilis, is invoked: pollution. (One gets it from the blood or sexual fluids of infected people or from contaminated blood products.) But the military metaphors used to describe AIDS have a somewhat different focus from those used in describing cancer. With cancer, the metaphor scants the issue of causality (still a murky topic in cancer research) and picks up at the point at which rogue cells inside the body mutate, eventually moving out from an original site or organ to overrun other organs or systems—a domestic subversion. In the description of AIDS the enemy is what causes the disease, an infectious agent that comes from the outside:

> The invader is tiny, about one sixteen-thousandth the size of the head of a pin. . . . Scouts of the body's immune system, large cells called macrophages, sense the presence of the diminutive foreigner and promptly alert the immune system. It begins to mobilize an array of cells that, among other things, produce antibodies to deal with the threat. Single-mindedly, the AIDS virus ignores many of the blood cells in its path, evades the rapidly advancing defenders and homes in on the master coordinator of the immune system, a helper T cell. . . .

This is the language of political paranoia, with its characteristic distrust of a pluralistic world. A defense system consisting of cells "that, among other things, produce antibodies to deal with the threat" is, predictably, no match for an invader who advances "single-mindedly." And the science-fiction flavor, already present in cancer talk, is even more pungent in accounts of AIDS—this one comes from *Time* magazine in late 1986—with infection described like the high-tech warfare for which we are being prepared (and inured) by the fantasies of our leaders and by video entertainments. In the era of Star Wars and Space Invaders, AIDS has proved an ideally comprehensible illness:

> On the surface of that cell, it finds a receptor into which one of its envelope proteins fits perfectly, like a key into a lock. Docking with the cell, the virus penetrates the cell membrane and is stripped of its protective shell in the process. . . .

Next the invader takes up permanent residence, by a form of alien takeover familiar in science-fiction narratives. The body's own cells *become* the invader. With the help of an enzyme the virus carries with it,

> the naked AIDS virus converts its RNA into . . . DNA, the master molecule of life. The molecule then penetrates the cell nucleus, inserts itself into a chromosome and takes over part of the cellular machinery, directing it to produce more AIDS viruses. Eventually, overcome by

its alien product, the cell swells and dies, releasing a flood of new viruses to attack other cells. . . .

As viruses attack other cells, runs the metaphor, so "a host of opportunistic diseases, normally warded off by a healthy immune system, attacks the body," whose integrity and vigor have been sapped by the sheer replication of "alien product" that follows the collapse of its immunological defenses. "Gradually weakened by the onslaught, the AIDS victim dies, sometimes in months, but almost always within a few years of the first symptoms." Those who have not already succumbed are described as "under assault, showing the telltale symptoms of the disease," while millions of others "harbor the virus, vulnerable at any time to a final, all-out attack."

Cancer makes cells proliferate; in AIDS, cells die. Even as this original model of AIDS (the mirror image of leukemia) has been altered, descriptions of how the virus does its work continue to echo the way the illness is perceived as infiltrating the society. "AIDS Virus Found to Hide in Cells, Eluding Detection by Normal Tests" was the headline of a recent front-page story in the *New York Times* announcing the discovery that the virus can "lurk" for years in the macrophages—disrupting their disease-fighting function without killing them, "even when the macrophages are filled almost to bursting with virus," and without producing antibodies, the chemicals the body makes in response to "invading agents" and whose presence has been regarded as an infallible marker of the syndrome.[1] That the virus isn't lethal for *all* the cells where it takes up residence, as is now thought, only increases the illness-foe's reputation for wiliness and invincibility.

What makes the viral assault so terrifying is that contamination, and therefore vulnerability, is understood as permanent. Even if someone infected were never to develop any symptoms—that is, the infection remained, or could by medical intervention be rendered, inactive—the viral enemy would be forever within. In fact, so it is believed, it is just a matter of time before something awakens ("triggers") it, before the appearance of "the telltale symptoms." Like syphilis, known to genera-   5

---

1. The larger role assigned to the macrophages—"to serve as a reservoir for the AIDS virus because the virus multiplies in them but does not kill them, as it kills T-4 cells"—is said to explain the not uncommon difficulty of finding infected T-4 lymphocytes in patients who have antibodies to the virus and symptoms of AIDS. (It is still assumed that antibodies will develop once the virus spreads to these "key target" cells.) Evidence of presently infected populations of cells has been as puzzlingly limited or uneven as the evidence of infection in the populations of human societies—puzzling, because of the conviction that the disease is everywhere, and must spread. "Doctors have estimated that as few as one in a million T-4 cells are infected, which led some to ask where the virus hides. . . ." Another resonant speculation, reported in the same article (the *New York Times,* June 7, 1988): "Infected macrophages can transmit the virus to other cells, possibly by touching the cells."

tions of doctors as "the great masquerader," AIDS is a clinical construction, an inference. It takes its identity from the presence of *some* among a long, and lengthening, roster of symptoms (no one has everything that AIDS could be), symptoms which "mean" that what the patient has is this illness. The construction of the illness rests on the invention not only of AIDS as a clinical entity but of a kind of junior AIDS, called AIDS-related complex (ARC), to which people are assigned if they show "early" and often intermittent symptoms of immunological deficit such as fevers, weight loss, fungal infections, and swollen lymph glands. AIDS is progressive, a disease of time. Once a certain density of symptoms is attained, the course of the illness can be swift, and brings atrocious suffering. Besides the commonest "presenting" illnesses (some hitherto unusual, at least in a fatal form, such as a rare skin cancer and a rare form of pneumonia), a plethora of disabling, disfiguring, and humiliating symptoms make the AIDS patient steadily more infirm, helpless, and unable to control or take care of basic functions and needs.

The sense in which AIDS is a slow disease makes it more like syphilis, which is characterized in terms of "stages," than like cancer. Thinking in terms of "stages" is essential to discourse about AIDS. Syphilis in its most dreaded form is "tertiary syphilis," syphilis in its third stage. What is called AIDS is generally understood as the last of three stages—the first of which is infection with a human immunodeficiency virus (HIV) and early evidence of inroads on the immune system—with a long latency period between infection and the onset of the "telltale" symptoms. (Apparently not as long as syphilis, in which the latency period between secondary and tertiary illness might be decades. But it is worth noting that when syphilis first appeared in epidemic form in Europe at the end of the fifteenth century, it was a rapid disease, of an unexplained virulence that is unknown today, in which death often occurred in the second stage, sometimes within months or a few years.) Cancer *grows* slowly: It is not thought to be, for a long time, latent. (A convincing account of a process in terms of "stages" seems invariably to include the notion of a normative delay or halt in the process, such as is supplied by the notion of latency.) True, a cancer is "staged." This is a principal tool of diagnosis, which means classifying it according to its gravity, determining how "advanced" it is. But it is mostly a spatial notion: that the cancer advances through the body, traveling or migrating along predictable routes. Cancer is first of all a disease of the body's geography, in contrast to syphilis and AIDS, whose definition depends on constructing a temporal sequence of stages.

Syphilis is an affliction that didn't have to run its ghastly full course, to paresis (as it did for Baudelaire and Maupassant and Jules de Goncourt), and could and often did remain at the stage of nuisance, indignity (as it did for Flaubert). The scourge was also a cliché, as Flaubert himself observed. "SYPHILIS. Everybody has it, more or less" reads one entry in the *Dictionary of Accepted Opinions,* his treasury of mid-nineteenth-century platitudes. And syphilis did manage to acquire a darkly positive association in late-nineteenth- and early-twentieth-century Europe, when a link was made between syphilis and heightened ("feverish") mental activity that parallels the connection made since the era of the Romantic writers between pulmonary tuberculosis and heightened emotional activity. As if in honor of all the notable writers and artists who ended their lives in syphilitic witlessness, it came to be believed that the brain lesions of neurosyphilis might actually inspire original thought or art. Thomas Mann, whose fiction is a storehouse of early-twentieth-century disease myths, makes this notion of syphilis as muse central to his *Doctor Faustus,* with its protagonist a great composer whose voluntarily contracted syphilis—the Devil guarantees that the infection will be limited to the central nervous system—confers on him twenty-four years of incandescent creativity. E. M. Cioran recalls how, in Romania in the late 1920s, syphilis-envy figured in his adolescent expectations of literary glory: He would discover that he had contracted syphilis, be rewarded with several hyperproductive years of genius, then collapse into madness. This romanticizing of the dementia characteristic of neurosyphilis was the forerunner of the much more persistent fantasy in this century about mental illness as a source of artistic creativity or spiritual originality. But with AIDS—though dementia is also a common, late symptom—no compensatory mythology has arisen, or seems likely to arise. AIDS, like cancer, does not allow romanticizing or sentimentalizing, perhaps because its association with death is too powerful. In Krzysztof Zanussi's film *Spiral* (1978), the most truthful account I know of anger at dying, the protagonist's illness is never specified; therefore, it *has* to be cancer. For several generations now, the generic idea of death has been a death from cancer, and a cancer death is experienced as a generic defeat. Now the generic rebuke to life and to hope is AIDS.

"Plague" is the principal metaphor by which the AIDS epidemic is understood. And because of AIDS, the popular misidentification of cancer as an epidemic, even as a plague, seems to be receding: AIDS has banalized cancer.

Plague, from the Latin *plaga* (stroke, wound), has long been used metaphorically as the highest standard of collective calamity, evil, scourge—Procopius, in his masterpiece of calumny, *The Secret History,* called the Emperor Justinian worse than the plague ("fewer escaped")— as well as being a general name for many frightening diseases. Although the disease to which the word is permanently affixed produced the most lethal of recorded epidemics, being experienced as a pitiless slayer is not necessary for a disease to be regarded as plague-like. Leprosy, very rarely fatal now, was not much more so when at its greatest epidemic strength, between about 1050 and 1350. And syphilis has been regarded as a plague—Blake speaks of "the youthful Harlot's curse" that "blights with plagues the Marriage hearse"—not because it killed often, but because it was disgracing, disempowering, disgusting.

It is usually epidemics that are thought of as plagues. And these mass incidences of illness are understood as inflicted, not just endured. Considering illness as a punishment is the oldest idea of what causes illness, and an idea opposed by all attention to the ill that deserves the noble name of medicine. Hippocrates, who wrote several treatises on epidemics, specifically ruled out "the wrath of God" as a cause of bubonic plague. But the illnesses interpreted in antiquity as punishments, like the plague in *Oedipus,* were not thought to be shameful, as leprosy and subsequently syphilis were to be. Diseases, insofar as they acquired meaning, were collective calamities, and judgments on a community. Only injuries and disabilities, not diseases, were thought of as individually merited. For an analogy in the literature of antiquity to the modern sense of a shaming, isolating disease, one would have to turn to Philoctetes and his stinking wound.

The most feared diseases, those that are not simply fatal but transform the body into something alienating, like leprosy and syphilis and cholera and (in the imagination of many) cancer, are the ones that seem particularly susceptible to promotion to "plague." Leprosy and syphilis were the first illnesses to be consistently described as repulsive. It was syphilis that, in the earliest descriptions by doctors at the end of the fifteenth century, generated a version of the metaphors that flourish around AIDS: of a disease that was not only repulsive and retributive but collectively invasive. Although Erasmus, the most influential European pedagogue of the early sixteenth century, described syphilis as "nothing but a kind of leprosy" (by 1529 he called it "something worse than leprosy"), it had already been understood as something different, because sexually transmitted. Paracelsus speaks (in Donne's paraphrase) of "that foule contagious disease which then had invaded mankind in a few places, and since overflowes in all, that for punishment of general licentiousnes God first inflicted that disease." Thinking of syphilis as a punishment for an individual's transgression was for a long time, virtually until the disease became easily curable, not really distinct from regarding it as retribution for the licentiousness of a community—as with AIDS now, in the rich industrial countries. In contrast to cancer, understood in a modern way as a disease incurred by (and revealing of) individuals, AIDS is understood in a premodern way, as a disease incurred by people both as individuals and as members of a "risk group"—that neutral-sounding, bureaucratic category which also revives the archaic idea of a tainted community that illness has judged.

Not every account of plague or plaguelike diseases, of course, is a vehicle for lurid stereotypes about illness and the ill. The effort to think critically, historically, about illness (about disaster generally) was attempted throughout the eighteenth century: say, from Defoe's *A Journal of the Plague Year* (1722) to Alessandro Manzoni's *The Betrothed* (1827). Defoe's historical fiction, purporting to be an eyewitness account of bubonic plague in London in 1665, does not further any understanding of the plague as punishment or, a later part of the script, as a transforming experience. And Manzoni, in his lengthy account of the passage of plague through the duchy of Milan in 1630, is avowedly committed to presenting a more accurate, less reductive view than his historical sources. But even these two complex narratives reinforce some of the perennial, simplifying ideas about plague.

One feature of the usual script for plague: The disease invariably comes from somewhere else. The names for syphilis, when it began its epidemic sweep through Europe in the last decade of the fifteenth century, are an exemplary illustration of the need to make a dreaded disease foreign.[2] It was the "French pox" to the English, *morbus Germanicus* to the Parisians, the Naples sickness to the Florentines, the Chinese disease to the Japanese. But what may seem like a joke about the inevitability of chauvinism reveals a more important truth: that there is a link between imagining disease and imagining foreignness. It lies perhaps in the very concept of wrong, which is archaically identical with the non-us, the alien. A polluting person is always wrong, as Mary Douglas has observed. The inverse is also true: A person judged to be wrong is regarded as, at least potentially, a source of pollution.

The foreign place of origin of important illnesses, as of drastic changes in the weather, may be no more remote than a neighboring country. Illness is a species of invasion, and indeed is often carried by

---

2. As noted in the first accounts of the disease: "This malady received from different peoples whom it affected different names," writes Giovanni di Vigo in 1514. Like earlier treatises on syphilis, written in Latin—by Nicolo Leoniceno (1497) and by Juan Almenar (1502)—the one by di Vigo calls it *morbus Gallicus,* the French disease. (Excerpts from this and other accounts of the period, including *Syphilis; Or a Poetical History of the French Disease* [1530] by Girolamo Fracastoro, who coined the name that prevailed, are in *Classic Descriptions of Disease,* edited by Ralph H. Major [1932].) Moralistic explanations abounded from the beginning. In 1495, a year after the epidemic started, the Emperor Maximilian issued an edict declaring syphilis to be an affliction from God for the sins of men.

The theory that syphilis came from even farther than a neighboring country, that it was an entirely new disease in Europe, a disease of the New World brought back to the Old by sailors of Columbus who had contracted it in America, became the accepted explanation of the origin of syphilis in the sixteenth century and is still widely credited. It is worth noting that the earliest medical writers on syphilis did not accept the dubious theory. Leoniceno's *Libellus de Epidemia, quam vulgo morbum Gallicum vocant* starts by taking up the question of whether "the French disease under another name was common to the ancients," and says he believes firmly that it was.

soldiers. Manzoni's account of the plague of 1630 (chapters 31 to 37) begins:

> The plague which the Tribunal of Health had feared might enter the Milanese provinces with the German troops had in fact entered, as is well known; and it is also well known that it did not stop there, but went on to invade and depopulate a large part of Italy.

Defoe's chronicle of the plague of 1665 begins similarly, with a flurry of ostentatiously scrupulous speculation about its foreign origin:

> It was about the beginning of September, 1664, that I, among the rest of my neighbours, heard in ordinary discourse that the plague was returned again in Holland; for it had been very violent there, and particularly at Amsterdam and Rotterdam, in the year 1663, whither, they say, it was brought, some said from Italy, others from the Levant, among some goods which were brought home by their Turkey fleet; others said it was brought from Candia; others from Cyprus. It mattered not from whence it came; but all agreed it was come into Holland again.

The bubonic plague that reappeared in London in the 1720s had arrived from Marseilles, which was where plague in the eighteenth century was usually thought to enter Western Europe: brought by seamen, then transported by soldiers and merchants. By the nineteenth century the foreign origin was usually more exotic, the means of transport less specifically imagined, and the illness itself had become phantasmagorical, symbolic.

At the end of *Crime and Punishment* Raskolnikov dreams of plague: 15 "He dreamt that the whole world was condemned to a terrible new strange plague that had come to Europe from the depths of Asia." At the beginning of the sentence it is "the whole world," which turns out by the end of the sentence to be "Europe," afflicted by a lethal visitation from Asia. Dostoevsky's model is undoubtedly cholera, called Asiatic cholera, long endemic in Bengal, which had rapidly become and remained through most of the nineteenth century a worldwide epidemic disease. Part of the centuries-old conception of Europe as a privileged cultural entity is that it is a place which is colonized by lethal diseases coming from elsewhere. Europe is assumed to be by rights free of disease. (And Europeans have been astoundingly callous about the far more devastating extent to which they—as invaders, as colonists—have introduced *their* lethal diseases to the exotic, "primitive" world: Think of the ravages of smallpox, influenza, and cholera on the aboriginal populations of the Americas and Australia.) The tenacity of the connection of exotic origin with dreaded disease is one reason why cholera, of which there were four great outbreaks in Europe in the nineteenth century, each with a lower death toll than the preceding one, has continued to be more memorable than smallpox, whose ravages increased as the century went on (half a million died in the European smallpox pandemic of the early 1870s) but which could not be construed as, plaguelike, a disease with a non-European origin.

Plagues are no longer "sent," as in Biblical and Greek antiquity, for the question of agency has blurred. Instead, peoples are "visited" by plagues. And the visitations recur, as is taken for granted in the subtitle of Defoe's narrative, which explains that it is about that "which happened in London during the Last Great Visitation in 1665." Even for non-Europeans, lethal disease may be called a visitation. But a visitation on "them" is invariably described as different from one on "us." "I believe that about one half of the whole people was carried off by this visitation," wrote the English traveler Alexander Kinglake, reaching Cairo at a time of the bubonic plague (sometimes called "oriental plague"). "The Orientals, however, have more quiet fortitude than Europeans under afflictions of this sort." Kinglake's influential book *Eothen* (1844)—suggestively subtitled "Traces of Travel Brought Home from the East"—illustrates many of the enduring Eurocentric presumptions about others, starting from the fantasy that peoples with little reason to expect exemption from misfortune have a lessened capacity to *feel* misfortune. Thus it is believed that Asians (or the poor, or blacks, or Africans, or Muslims) don't suffer or don't grieve as Europeans (or whites) do. The fact that illness is associated with the poor—who are, from the perspective of the privileged, aliens in one's midst—reinforces the association of illness with the foreign: with an exotic, often primitive place.

Thus, illustrating the classic script for plague, AIDS is thought to have started in the "dark continent," then spread to Haiti, then to the United States and to Europe, then . . . It is understood as a tropical disease: another infestation from the so-called Third World, which is after all where most people in the world live, as well as a scourge of the *tristes tropiques*.[3] Africans who detect racist stereotypes in much of the speculation about the geographical origin of AIDS are not wrong. (Nor are they wrong in thinking that depictions of Africa as the cradle of AIDS must feed anti-African prejudices in Europe and Asia.) The subliminal connection made to notions about a primitive past and the many hypotheses that have been fielded about possible transmission from animals (a disease of green monkeys? African swine fever?) cannot help but activate a familiar set of stereotypes about animality, sexual license, and blacks. In Zaire and other countries in Central Africa where AIDS is killing tens of thousands, the counterreaction has begun. Many doctors, academics, journalists, government officials, and other educated people believe that the virus was sent to Africa from the United States, an act of bacteriological warfare (whose aim was to decrease the African birth

---

3. *tristes tropiques*   French, the sad tropics.—EDS.

rate) which got out of hand and has returned to afflict its perpetrators. A common African version of this belief about the disease's provenance has the virus fabricated in a CIA–Army laboratory in Maryland, sent from there to Africa, and brought back to its country of origin by American homosexual missionaries returning from Africa to Maryland.[4]

At first it was assumed that AIDS must become widespread elsewhere in the same catastrophic form in which it has emerged in Africa, and those who still think this will eventually happen invariably invoke the Black Death. The plague metaphor is an essential vehicle of the most pessimistic reading of the epidemiological prospects. From classic fiction to the latest journalism, the standard plague story is of inexorability, inescapability. The unprepared are taken by surprise; those observing the recommended precautions are struck down as well. *All* succumb when the story is told by an omniscient narrator, as in Poe's parable "The Masque of the Red Death" (1842), inspired by an account of a ball held in Paris during the cholera epidemic of 1832. Almost all—if the story is told from the point of view of a traumatized witness, who will be a benumbed survivor, as in Jean Giono's Stendhalian novel *Horseman on the Roof* (1951), in which a young Italian nobleman in exile wanders through cholera-stricken southern France in the 1830s.

Reading the Text

1. Why does Sontag assert that AIDS "is not the name of an illness at all"?
2. What metaphors have shaped our understanding of AIDS, according to Sontag?

---

4. The rumor may not have originated as a KGB-sponsored "disinformation" campaign, but it received a crucial push from Soviet propaganda specialists. In October 1985 the Soviet weekly *Literaturnaya Gazeta* published an article alleging that the AIDS virus had been engineered by the U.S. government during biological-warfare research at Fort Detrick, Maryland, and was being spread abroad by U.S. servicemen who had been used as guinea pigs. The source cited was an article in the Indian newspaper *Patriot*. Repeated on Moscow's "Radio Peace and Progress" in English, the story was taken up by newspapers and magazines throughout the world. A year later it was featured on the front page of London's conservative, mass-circulation *Sunday Express*. ("The killer AIDS virus was artificially created by American scientists during laboratory experiments which went disastrously wrong—and a massive cover-up has kept the secret from the world until today.") Though ignored by most American newspapers, the *Sunday Express* story was recycled in virtually every other country. As recently as the summer of 1987, it appeared in newspapers in Kenya, Peru, Sudan, Nigeria, Senegal, and Mexico. Gorbachev-era policies have since produced an official denial of the allegations by two eminent members of the Soviet Academy of Sciences, which was published in *Izvestia* in late October 1987. But the story is still being repeated—from Mexico to Zaire, from Australia to Greece.

3. Why does Sontag feel that syphilis is a closer analogy to AIDS than is cancer?
4. Why does Sontag believe that the metaphors by which we understand a disease are so important?

Reading the Signs

1. In your journal, freewrite on your understanding of AIDS. How do you view the disease? Has your thinking about the disease evolved since you first learned about it? Then, with Sontag's essay in mind, reflect on your freewriting. What myths and metaphors have guided your own thinking about AIDS?
2. Compare and contrast AIDS and the bubonic plague. In what ways are the diseases' biological effects on the human body similar and different? How do people's responses to the diseases compare? What is the metaphoric history of each disease? To develop your essay, you might also consult Evelynn Hammonds, "Race, Sex, AIDS: The Construction of 'Other,'" p. 692.
3. Visit your library and locate a human physiology or medical textbook (alternatively, you might visit your campus health center and pick up brochures on AIDS). Write an essay in which you analyze the discussion of AIDS. What language is used to describe the disease? Does it use any of the metaphors or images that Sontag discusses? If so, what impact do they have on your understanding of the disease?
4. How would Sontag explain Paul Monette's ("Borrowed Time," p. 661) response to AIDS in the early years of the epidemic? How did the metaphors and images of AIDS either facilitate or impede his understanding of the disease?
5. Sontag's *AIDS and Its Metaphors,* from which this selection was taken, was controversial because of Sontag's claims about the progress of the disease. Research the current medical wisdom about AIDS, perhaps by reading about the most recent international AIDS conference. Then write an essay in which you show the extent to which Sontag's assumptions about the medical progress of AIDS are considered valid today.

MICHAEL D. QUAM
Stigma

IIIIIIIIIIIIIIIIIIIIIIIIIIIIIIIIIIIIIIIIIIIIIIIIIIIIIIIIIIIIII

*Of all the diseases that afflict us, sexually transmitted ones bear the
most severe social stigmas. In this analysis of the especially harsh stigma
associated with AIDS, Michael D. Quam (b. 1939) shows its relation
to such historically stigmatized illnesses as syphilis, which has also been
a source of social ostracization as well as physical suffering for its victims.
The AIDS patient is seen not only as someone with an illness but as
someone bearing a sign of his own "pollution," a sign like the mark put
upon Cain in the Bible. Michael Quam, a professor of anthropology
and public health at Sangamon State University, specializes in the
biocultural aspects of health, sexuality, AIDS, and public health policy.
He is the author of numerous papers on AIDS and its national and
international impact.*

In his critique of Parsons, Freidson (1970:235–40) explores the phenomenon of stigma as a dynamic element in the way we respond to
certain illnesses.

> For "normal" illness, many normal obligations are suspended; only the
> obligation to seek help is incurred. But in the case of the stigmatized,
> a complex variety of new obligations is incurred. Whereas in the
> former instance the burden of adjustment (through permissiveness and
> support) lies on the "normals" around the sick person, the burden in
> the latter lies on the stigmatized person when he is around "normals."
> (ibid.:236)

According to Goffman (1963:11), in the original Greek meaning of the
term, *stigma* referred to "bodily signs designed to expose something
unusual and bad about the moral status of the signifier," although today
stigma "is applied more to the disgrace itself than to the bodily evidence
of it." In either case—and both are applicable to AIDS—the individual
is marked by a trait that is "discredited" or, if hidden, is "discreditable"
(ibid.:14). When personal responsibility for the stigma can be imputed
to the individual, the severity of stigmatization increases (Jones 1984:58–
60).

Several studies (cited in Jones 1984) have established fear as a highly
salient feature of stigma. In an example directly relevant to the case of
AIDS, Bobys and Laner (1979) found "ex-homosexuals"[1] were stigma-

---

1. The term "ex-homosexual" may strike some readers as rather odd. Bobys and

tized primarily because they were perceived as "dangerous." Goffman (1963:15) is even more direct when he says, "By definition, of course, we believe the person with a stigma is not quite human." The possibility of contagion seems to be the basis for some of this fear. Goffman (ibid.:43, 64, 147) alludes to the tendency of stigma to spread from the stigmatized to close associates, ironically labelling this phenomenon "courtesy stigma." Of course, people with communicable diseases are at least temporarily avoided because of the real danger of contagion, but this social reaction may also extend to care-givers and close associates. When it takes on the form of stigma, the avoidance becomes shunning and is much more widespread. Remarkably, the stigma of danger from communicable diseases extends even to noncommunicable diseases and disabilities (Jones 1984:69–71). And the phenomenon of "courtesy stigma" is based on ideas of at least symbolic contagion.

The ascription of stigma to any condition arises out of the symbol system within a culture, and, like other symbolic acts, follows a logic within which relationships are more emotional than rational. Not too long ago in a hospital in rural Illinois, an elderly woman patient adamantly refused a medically necessary blood transfusion because, she said, she feared she might become a "homosexual." Her confusion regarding cause and effect is better understood as illuminating some of her culture's deepest fears regarding the disease and stigmatization of AIDS. Because of its associations with nonmonogamous, and especially homosexual, sex and with intravenous drug use, activities that are considered immoral by some and in some venues even illegal, any contact with the symbolic or real bearers of this disease must be avoided. Persons who are known to be infected have been shunned by their closest friends and family members, have been evicted from their dwellings, and have been dismissed from their employment. The extreme stigmatization of AIDS derives in part from its associations with deviant behaviors but has also, as a sort of added "courtesy stigma," increased the rejection of those who are thought to be "at risk" of being infected. The "danger" they pose has given rise to an increase in acts of interpersonal violence against gay men and lesbians (Meislin 1986). In response, health professionals trying to stem the tide of disease through the usual practices of disease control and health care have found it necessary to impose airtight measures of confidentiality in their contacts with infected persons.

Fear and stigma have also charged the political atmosphere surrounding governmental efforts to address this epidemic (Shilts 1987). During the first five years of the epidemic while thousands of cases were ap-

---

Laner (1979) are referring to men who formerly were exclusively or primarily homosexual in their sexual behavior but who have subsequently become exclusively heterosexual in their sexual behavior.

pearing, the president of the United States did not publicly mention the name of this dreaded disease. The federal health bureaucracy was forced to make internal reallocations for AIDS programs because it was politically impossible to secure adequate funding for the research and prevention programs they knew were needed. Seven years into the epidemic, the chairperson of the Presidential Commission on the HIV Epidemic admitted that "there has not been a national strategy" to combat the disease (Boffey 1988).

The barrier to action seems to be the inevitable association with stigmatized behavior that health education and risk reduction activities entails. Those who would limit such efforts to simple messages of moral condemnation and exhortation have the cultural imprimatur of stigma avoidance as their foundation. Teaching people in plain and common terms how to avoid infection, for example, use condoms and disinfect needles, seems implicitly to condone the stigmatized "life-styles" that involve high-risk behavior. And because the stigma itself is contagious, the logic of symbolic associations dictates that the behaviors themselves must also be contagious. Americans have used the term "epidemic" to characterize the growth of the drug use problem, and even before AIDS, gays were thought to be dangerous and were often forbidden to be school teachers, as it was feared a gay teacher would corrupt the youngsters in his charge. Gays are still excluded from the ranks of the military.

But how and why would such corruption occur? Apparently, in most people's minds these forbidden activities, namely homosexuality and drug use, must be pleasurable (albeit, "perversely" so), and therefore one could be seduced into them. The symbolic connection between sex and drugs is borne out in the testimony of intravenous drug users themselves. They describe their first experience as similar to their initiation into sex, and needle-sharing partners are also frequently sexual partners (Des Jarlais, Friedman, and Strug 1986). Furthermore, in the popular image, one shot of heroin is enough to make one an addict. As with drugs, so with sex. Even if actual addiction is not the result, and even if the person abandons those deviant activities, the stigma of the behavior becomes a permanent part of the person's identity (Freidson 1970:236), staining one's character forever.

Among some Christian sects, AIDS is seen as another example of the biblical admonition that "the wages of sin is death." For many Americans such an idea has meaning derived from messages they internalized during their childhood. Their parents and other parental authorities warned them that if they succumbed to the "appetites of the flesh," they would suffer dire consequences. Now AIDS has appeared to fulfill such prophecies. And even if liberal tolerance dictates acceptance of "alternative life-styles," the fearsome fact of death remains. Many people have seen or read descriptions of persons with AIDS. The body is wasting away, the person disintegrating, losing mental abilities, losing physical powers, losing any reason or ability to go on. That this terrible death has befallen a person in the prime of life (most persons with AIDS are under 50) makes it even more threatening. Death at an early age is itself stigmatized, for the dying person reminds the witnesses of their own vulnerability (Jones 1984:66–67).

The AIDS stigma of deviance and death has influenced the delivery of health care services to persons who are infected (Quam 1986). At the local level many physicians refuse to have their names placed on a referral list for patients with HIV-related disease. The issue was brought into the national limelight when a prominent surgeon in Milwaukee refused to operate on an HIV-infected patient and counseled other physicians to exercise the same judgment (Heart Surgeon 1987). The debate over this kind of discriminatory behavior has continued inside the American Medical Association (Pear 1987). The dentistry profession is even more intransigent. Despite the professional rhetoric of commitment to service, in many communities it is nearly impossible to find a dentist who will serve a patient known to be infected (Quam 1986). Dentists argue that they will lose their technical staff and their other patients if it is suspected that they are working with infected persons. Some dentists and physicians who avoid contact with infected persons claim the dangers involved are not acceptable to their family members.

Nurses have reported the subtle distinctions drawn in hospital care between AIDS patients who are "innocent victims," infants who were infected by their mothers and adults who were infected through transfusions, and those who are by implication guilty, those who became infected through sexual or drug use activities. The amount of "sentimental work" done (Strauss et al. 1985),[2] the quickness of response to patient requests for assistance, the interaction with the patient's family and friends can all be affected by this moral evaluation.

It should be noted, however, that the fear element in AIDS stigma can override any moral discrimination, as evidenced by the rejection of school children who are infected through the use of blood products to control another disease, hemophilia. Some parents and school officials have proposed testing all children with hemophilia for HIV infection or simply banning them from school. In a nationally publicized case in Florida, the family of two such children was forced to leave town after threats of violence and an arson fire in their home (Family in AIDS Case 1987). This attack was a shocking indication of the emotional depths

2. Strauss et al. (1985), describe "sentimental work" within health care as interaction with the patient as a person, including knowledge and sensitivity to the patient's relationships with family members and other loved ones, awareness of fears and anxieties, and so forth.

touched by the fear of AIDS. To understand these extreme reactions, we need to add some depth to our conceptual framework.

Pollution

As one who has suffered the disease and stigma of cancer, Susan Sontag writes with great passion and insight about the way Americans symbolically construct and respond to disease. "Any disease that is treated as a mystery and acutely enough feared will be felt to be morally, if not literally, contagious. . . . Contact with someone afflicted with a disease regarded as a mysterious malevolency inevitably feels like a trespass; worse, like a violation of a taboo" (Sontag 1978:5–6). AIDS is universally characterized as both mysterious and malevolent. One of the most common phrases one hears regarding AIDS, even from medical scientists, is "we know so little about it." And infection with the virus that causes AIDS is felt to be a defilement, a violation of the person, even an assault (in several legal jurisdictions people have been charged with assault because it was believed they exposed someone to infection [Deadly Weapon 1987; Boorstin 1987; Johnson 1987]).

These intense feelings bring to mind the kind of fear associated with beliefs regarding pollution. As Mary Douglas (1966), our leading contemporary theorist on this subject, has pointed out, pollution is fundamentally the result of contact with "dirt." Contemporary European and North American ideas of defilement by dirt seem to focus on aesthetics and hygiene: "Our idea of dirt is dominated by the knowledge of pathogenic organisms" (Douglas 1966:35). In the case of AIDS, the orifices of the body where the virus enters, at least when it is sexually transmitted, are symbolically considered "dirty": the anus because of feces, the vagina where menstrual blood flows, and the penis because of urination, ejaculation, and penetration of the "dirty" vagina or anus. But feelings regarding this kind of dirt run even deeper. The multivocal and dialectical nature of symbolic realities is evident in American thinking about AIDS. The fact that two primary vital elements, semen and blood, should be the carriers of pollution and death increases the sense of the polluting power of AIDS and the fear of the disease.

At a more basic level, dirt is "matter out of place, . . . the by-product of a systematic ordering and classification of matter, in so far as ordering involves rejecting inappropriate elements" (Douglas 1966:39). Something that does not fit in the classification system is anomalous, and one of the ways of dealing with anomalous events or elements is to label them dangerous. So dirt is disorder that is dangerous. As Douglas (1966:113) puts it, "A polluting person is always in the wrong. He has developed some wrong condition or simply crossed some line which should not have been crossed and this displacement unleashes danger for someone." Furthermore, danger beliefs are used in order to enforce the moral code:

> The laws of nature are dragged in to sanction the moral code: this kind of disease is caused by adultery, that by incest . . . certain moral beliefs are upheld and certain social rules defined by beliefs in danger- ous contagion, as when the glance or touch of an adulterer is held to bring illness to his neighbors or his children. (Douglas 1966:3)

Within American culture and society, gays and intravenous drug users are anomalous, they do not fit "normal" social categories. Such persons have crossed some line, some boundary of "nature" that makes them less than human and essentially dangerous. Now, with the advent of AIDS, gays and intravenous drug users are epidemiologically labeled the "high risk groups." Through a linguistic double entendre, unintended by the epidemiologists, the culturally defined danger these groups pose for the "normals" seems to be medically confirmed.

Speaking more concretely, how is this pollution danger experienced? Let us once again draw an analogy with cancer. Sontag (1978:5, 8, 13) says cancer is "an illness experienced as a ruthless, secret invasion." The cancer patient is invaded by "alien cells," and the disease "works slowly and insidiously." Furthermore, cancer is "obscene," that is, "ill-omened, abominable, repugnant to the senses." An obvious biomedical connection exists between cancer and AIDS. One of the most common opportunis- tic diseases associated with AIDS is Kaposi's sarcoma, a tissue cancer that is manifest in spots and lesions, literally marking its sufferers and thus being repugnant and stigmatizing. And, of course, AIDS also works slowly and insidiously.

Parsons (1951), in his analysis of the American medical system, dis- cusses the inviolability of the body as an important emotionally loaded value in American culture, noting how people are squeamish about needles even when used for medically necessary injections. By symbolic analogy, the virus that causes AIDS infects a person by penetrating the body somehow, and that biological fact is felt as an invasion and violation of the body. Epidemiologically, the principal identified modes of HIV transmission are, in fact, acts of penetration; culturally, they are acts of violation. Penile penetration of the rectum is considered "abnormal" within the dominant culture, even "unnatural" (albeit that it is not uncommon in heterosexual intercourse), and thus it is violating. This notion is reinforced by popular tales of violent homosexual rape in prisons and by medical explanations of why rectal intercourse is especially risky for viral transmission, the rectum is not built for this kind of use and the walls are traumatized/ruptured/torn by this unusual friction. Injecting illegal drugs that alter the person's thinking and feeling is also

15

seen as a violation of the person. Even though this violation is self-generated, the loss of self-control through addiction is frightening and is often characterized as suicidal. For those who do not knowingly put themselves at risk through these particular acts, the fear that they might still somehow become infected by polluting contact is a fear of violating bodily penetration: symbolically, a fear of rape.

Both concretely and metaphorically, the body is often the locus of pollution. Douglas (1966:115–21) states this point very clearly.

> The body is a model which can stand for any bounded system. Its boundaries can represent any boundaries which are threatened or precarious. . . . [We can] see in the body a symbol of society, and . . . see the powers and dangers credited to social structure reproduced in small on the human body. . . . Why should body margins be thought to be specially invested with power and danger? . . . [A]ll margins are dangerous. If they are pulled this way or that the shape of fundamental experience is altered. Any structure of ideas is vulnerable at its margins. We should expect the orifices of the body to symbolize its specially vulnerable points. Matter issuing from them is marginal stuff of the most obvious kind. Spittle, blood, milk, urine, faeces or tears by simply issuing forth have traversed the boundary of the body.

To understand what precarious social or cultural margins are being mirrored in pollution beliefs regarding the body, Douglas advises, we must "try to argue back from the known dangers of society to the known selection of bodily themes and try to recognize what appositeness is there" (1966:121). As an exercise in such analysis, let us consider the body pollution of AIDS.

What vulnerable social boundaries are being symbolically evoked by the threat of AIDS? The first that immediately comes to mind is personal safety. With rising rates of street crime and home invasion—armed robbery, assault, rape, and murder—Americans have come to fear the dangerous stranger. This pervasive sense of physical insecurity is the result of the failure of social community to provide some kind of embracing protection, and the failure of the police powers to protect the vulnerable individual from increasing risk of violent attack. With a growing awareness of domestic violence comes the fear of the dangerous intimate. People sense a failure in the institutions of courtship, marriage, and the family to protect the individual from harm by someone with whom they have been intimate, that is, let down their self-protective guard and become vulnerable.

The social apparatus of science and technology in which Americans have invested so much faith is also now suspect. The failure of the technological experts to protect people from the experiment, procedure, or complex machine that goes wrong and unleashes an uncontrollable life-threatening danger is the theme of many popular novels, movies, and television dramas. A recent paperback thriller, *June Mail* (Warmbold 1986), is based on the premise that AIDS is the result of a U.S. biological warfare experiment, a conspiracy theory that has enjoyed wide circulation in the Third World and in some U.S. circles. Attempts by public health officials to argue against such speculation are undermined by an erosion of confidence in the competence and integrity of the people who control advanced technology. Recent disasters in nuclear power (Three Mile Island and Chernobyl), the space program (the explosion of *Challenger*), and toxic chemical production (Union Carbide in Bhopal and in West Virginia) belie the experts' soothing assurances of safety.

A second set of social and cultural margins is also precarious. Ambiguities and contradictions have developed in the moral code, especially reflected in the conflict between the Protestant ethic of self-denial and the impulsiveness of hedonism. Americans envy those who have led a hedonistic life, not followed the rules of good citizenship and instead crossed some boundaries for the sake of self-gratification (witness the national fascination with the indiscretions of celebrities). But they find their own repressed desires very frightening, because if they were to act on such impulses, the resulting disruption would threaten their social security and personal identity. For most Americans, to work hard and be law-abiding is to be a good person in the eyes of others and in one's own eyes, but it is also to be a drone, to deny oneself the life of glamour, adventure, and danger that is held up for admiration and envy in images that bombard the public daily from television, movies, magazines, even from the evening news. In talking with Americans about AIDS, one is frequently struck by a tone of satisfaction underlying the expressions of fear. They seem to be saying that finally something undeniably awful has occurred that makes clear the dangers of self-indulgence.

AIDS is a nearly perfect metaphor for all of these insecurities and   20
ambivalences. Both social and personal control seem to be breaking down. In Yeats's (1956:184–85) famous lines,

> Turning and turning in the widening gyre
> The falcon cannot hear the falconer;
> Things fall apart; the centre cannot hold;
> Mere anarchy is loosed upon the world,
> The blood-dimmed tide is loosed, and everywhere
> The ceremony of innocence is drowned;
> The best lack all conviction, while the worst
> Are full of passionate intensity.

And through it all the person has been left defenseless. Now Americans are plagued by a disease that attacks the very defense system of the body, is borne by bodily fluids, is inflicted through the violation of the body, and destroys the person. Small wonder that such a threat gives rise to feelings of pollution and to demands for pollution control.

REFERENCES

Bobys, R. S., and M. R. Laner. 1979. On the Stability of Stigmatization: The Case of Ex-homosexual Males. *Archives of Sexual Behavior* 8:247–61.

Boffey, P. M. 1988. Panel on AIDS Urges Growth in Health Care. *New York Times,* Feb. 25:Y1.

Boorstin, R. O. 1987. AIDS Spread Brings Action in the Courts. *New York Times,* June 19:Y1.

Deadly Weapon in AIDS Verdict Is Inmate's Teeth. 1987. *New York Times,* June 25:Y11.

Des Jarlais, D. C.; S. R. Friedman; and D. Strug. 1986. AIDS and Needle-sharing within the IV-drug Use Subculture. In *Social Dimensions of AIDS: Method and Theory,* pp. 111–25. D. A. Feldman and T. M. Johnson, eds. New York: Praeger.

Douglas, M. 1966. *Purity and Danger: An Analysis of the Concepts of Pollution and Taboo.* London: Routledge and Kegan Paul.

Family in AIDS Case Quits Florida Town after House Burns. 1987. *New York Times,* August 30:Y1.

Freidson, E. 1970. *Profession of Medicine: A Study of the Sociology of Applied Knowledge.* New York: Harper and Row.

Goffman, E. 1963. *Stigma: Notes on the Management of Spoiled Identity.* Harmondsworth, England: Penguin.

Heart Surgeon Won't Operate on Victims of AIDS. 1987. *New York Times,* March 13:Y11.

Johnson, K. 1987. New York Police Say Suspect Bit Officer and Claimed to Have AIDS. *New York Times,* June 10:Y16.

Jones, E. E., et al. 1984. *Social Stigma: The Psychology of Marked Relationships.* New York: W. H. Freeman.

Meislin, R. J. 1986. AIDS Fears Said to Increase Prejudice Against Homosexuals. *New York Times,* Jan. 21:Y10.

Parsons, T. 1951. *The Social System.* New York: The Free Press.

Pear, R. 1987. A.M.A. Rules that Doctors Are Obligated to Treat AIDS. *New York Times,* Nov. 13:Y10.

Quam, M.D. 1986. Community Preparation for AIDS. Paper presented at the American Anthropological Association Annual Meeting, Philadelphia, PA.

Shilts, R. 1987. *And the Band Played On: Politics, People, and the AIDS Epidemic.* New York: St. Martin's.

Sontag, S. 1978. *Illness as Metaphor.* New York: Vintage.

Strauss, A., et al. 1985. *Social Organization of Medical Work.* Chicago: University of Chicago Press.

Warmbold, J. 1986. *June Mail.* Sag Harbor, N.Y.: The Permanent Press.

Yeats, W. B. 1956. *The Collected Poems of W. B. Yeats.* New York: Macmillan.

Reading the Text

1. Explain in your own words what Quam means by "stigma."
2. In what ways are stigmas "signs"?
3. How has the stigma of AIDS affected the political response to the disease in America, according to Quam?
4. How is the notion of "pollution" related to Americans' understanding of AIDS?

Reading the Signs

1. In groups, brainstorm other stigmas (whether medical or social) in America. Then pick one, and discuss the cultural assumptions that have led to this stigmatized status.
2. Use the *Readers' Guide to Periodical Literature* to locate five articles about AIDS in popular magazines, preferably from different years (say, 1984, 1989, and 1994). To what extent do they portray the disease as carrying a stigma? How might you account for any differences in the portrayal of AIDS?
3. If one of the articles you collected for the previous question stigmatizes AIDS, try rewriting it with the goal of removing the sense of stigma attached to the disease and those who have contracted it. Share your rewritten article with your class.
4. Quam links the fear of AIDS to Americans' growing concerns for personal safety, suspicion of science and technology, and envy of a "hedonistic" life-style. Do you find his argument persuasive? Write an essay in which you support, challenge, or elaborate on the connections Quam makes between our society's response to AIDS and these other insecurities of American life.
5. Quam points out that, in American culture, gays are "anomalous, they do not fit 'normal' social categories." Read or review Richard Herrell's "The Symbolic Strategies of Chicago's Gay and Lesbian Pride Day Parade" (p. 643), and write an essay in which you explore how the parade is a response to the status of being an anomalous group. What strategies are used in the parade to combat stigmatization?

KATE SCANNELL
Skills and Pills

||||||||||||||||||||||||||||||||||||||||||||||||||

Doctors are trained to heal people, but what can a doctor do when there is no cure and the patient's illness is fatal? In this personal testimony, Kate Scannell (b. 1953) describes her own "retraining" in the wake of the AIDS epidemic. Learning that sometimes the Hippocratic oath has to be adjusted in the face of suffering for which there is no release but in death, Scannell shares the private thoughts of a physician fighting against a vicious killer in a battle in which she has been given no effective weapons save compassion. Kate Scannell is a clinical immunologist who has practiced at San Francisco General Hospital and taught medicine at the University of California, San Francisco.

When I originally set foot in this Bay Area county hospital, I had no intention to work primarily with AIDS patients. Fresh out of university-based medical practice as an internal medicine resident, rheumatology fellow, and bench researcher, I had decided to forgo academic medicine and practice community-based general medicine in my favorite setting, a county hospital. By now, I have been working for more than two years in this county hospital's AIDS ward.

Shortly after my arrival in the hospital, I discovered that a number of beds were taken by AIDS patients. Most of them were about my age, and many were dying. Several of them had arrived in the county health care system through tragic personal circumstances attending their AIDS diagnosis, which had cost them their jobs and sometimes their health insurance. I was overwhelmed by their illness, their very complex medical problems, their awesome psychological and emotional needs, and their dying. I was frightened by the desperation of many who wanted to be made well again or to survive that which could not be survived.

I felt all I really had to offer these patients were the tools in my doctor's bag and this head stuffed with information. So it became imperative that this small offering from me be the best and biggest it could.

During the first few months of my work, I began my hospital rounds with the non-AIDS patients because so much time was involved in the AIDS ward routine. I stayed late hours without meals nearly every day so I could figure out the fever sources, treat the pneumonias, push the chemotherapy, perform the lumbar punctures, and counsel the lovers and families. Like a very weary but ever-ready gunfighter, I stalked the hallways ready for surprise developments and acute medical problems to present themselves; I would shoot them down with my skills and pills. The diseases that would not respond favorably to my treatments and the patients who would die were all my failures, fought to the end. No patient who wanted treatment died because they did not receive aggressive full-service care from me. I became such a sharpshooter for AIDS-related medical problems that the patients with AIDS were soon gravitating to my medical service.

Some patients were so emaciated by profound wasting that I could   5
not shake disquieting memories of photographs I had seen as a little girl which depicted Auschwitz and Buchenwald prisoners. There were young men on the ward who were grossly disfigured by masses of purple skin tumors. One of these men, who had one eye bulging forward and the other closed tight because of his tumors, caused me to have a recurring nightmare about the Hunchback of Notre Dame.

There were so many sad stories and unhappy events on the ward. I barely spoke of these to my closest friends, and I avoided telling them how I was being personally affected by all the tragedy and death. I was hesitant to be so serious with my friends, and I really didn't even know how to verbalize what it was I was seeing, hearing, and experiencing in the first place.

Months elapsed in this way. One day Raphael, a twenty-two-year-old man, was admitted to the ward. He was a large, bloated, purple, knobby mass with eyes so swollen shut that he could not see. His dense, purple tumors had insinuated themselves into multiple lymph nodes and into the roof of his mouth. One imposing tender tumor mass extended from the bottom of his right foot so that he could not walk. His breathing was made difficult by the massive amount of fluid surrounding and compressing his lungs. Tears literally squeezed out from the cracks between his eyelids. He asked me to help him. I heard the voices of my old teachers who prodded me through my years of medical training—I heard them telling me to fix this man's breathing disfunction, instructing me how to decipher and treat his anemia, reviewing with me how to relieve his body swelling with medications while correcting his electrolyte disturbances. I heard these voices reviewing with me the latest therapies for Kaposi's sarcoma. Raphael asked me to help him. I stuck needles into his veins and arteries to get more information about him. I stuck an intravenous line into one of the few spots on his arm that wasn't thickened by firm swelling or hard purple tumors.

He asked for more help. I stuck a plastic cannula into his nose to give him more oxygen. I gave him potassium in his IV line. I told him his problems were being corrected and we could discuss chemotherapy options in the morning. After I left the hospital that night, feeling exhausted but confident I'd given "my all," another physician on duty was called to see my patient. Raphael asked the physician to help him. The physician stopped the intravenous fluid and potassium, cancelled the blood testing and the transfusion, and simply gave Raphael some morphine. I was told Raphael smiled and thanked the doctor for helping him, and then expired later that evening.

I think of Raphael often now and I ask him for his forgiveness during my frequent meditations. I also tell him that I have never practiced medicine the same way since his death; that my eyes focus differently now, and that my ears hear more clearly the speaker behind the words. Like the vision of Raphael's spirit rising free from his disease-racked corpse in death, the clothing fashioned for me by years of traditional Western medical training fell off me like tattered rags. I began to hear my own voices and compassionate sensibilities once again, louder and clearer than the chorus of voices of my old mentors. Nowadays, as in an archaeological expedition, I sometimes try to uncover how I had become so lost in the first place. I envision that I got crushed under mounds of rubble that collected over the years of my intense and all-consuming medical training, during which I strove so hard, twenty-four hours a day, to become a physician in the mode of traditional Western medicine. Some of the rubble I can identify as parts of this structure: the trend towards increasing technological interventions; the overriding philosophy that competent physicians save lives, not "lose" them; the blatant chastisement of physicians who use their "sensors" and intuitive insights when interacting with patients; the taboo against using compassion as a diagnostic and therapeutic medical skill.

Shortly after Raphael's death, I assumed the position of clinical   10
director of AIDS services at this county hospital. Subsequently, the targets for my diagnostic sharpshooting abilities became fewer and smaller. I am no longer frightened by this awesome disease and I no longer have nightmares. I cry often and stand the bedside deathwatch frequently. I have been able to communicate with patients now, when I know that I am hearing and seeing them with tremendous clarity, and when I am able to speak clearly to them with the truths I know in my heart as well as my mind. I have substituted ice cream or local bakery products as primary or sole therapy for some AIDS patients with "complex medical disease." I have officially prescribed sunshine, a trip to Macy's, and massages for some patients who had no need for my traditional skills and pills.

On daily rounds, I have visited a demented AIDS patient whose intermittent cerebral flailings sometimes made him think he was back on his Texas ranch tending the pigs and chickens. For days we had discussed the problems a few of the pigs were posing and the most lucrative way to sell eggs; once we made plans to invite the neighbors (other patients on the ward) over for a farm-style breakfast. He never saw my stethoscope or a needle in his arms; I believe he was peaceful and pain-free when he died. As each AIDS patient experiences stages of understanding and accepting of his own disease and death in the Kübler-Ross scheme, I feel I have passed through similar stages as a physician in response to the entire specter of AIDS.

I am currently waddling between grief and acceptance of this disease. I am learning how to temper hope with reality. Through a long period of unhappiness responding to all the death I was seeing, I have been able to find some peace, walking comfortably, day to day, alongside the promise of my own death. And I am grateful to hear my own voices and feel the strength of my compassionate sensibilities once again. I think of Raphael often.

Reading the Text

1. What was Scannell's initial response to AIDS patients?
2. How did Scannell's response to AIDS evolve as she spent more time treating patients with the disease?
3. Why did Raphael have such an impact on Scannell?

Reading the Signs

1. Discuss in class how Scannell's attitudes toward her chosen profession, medicine, have changed because of AIDS.
2. Compare and contrast the evolution of Scannell's understanding of AIDS with that of Paul Monette ("Borrowed Time," p. 661). What difference does it make that one writer is a physician treating people with AIDS, while the other is himself a person with AIDS who has watched his loved ones die from the disease?
3. Outline the many metaphors Scannell uses as she describes her psychological evolution as a physician treating patients with AIDS. Then, using Susan Sontag's "AIDS and Its Metaphors" (p. 668) as your critical framework, analyze the progression of Scannell's metaphors. How do the different metaphors reflect a different view of the disease?
4. Scannell decries the absolute reliance on "traditional Western medicine" in treating AIDS symptoms. Research how alternative medical practices, such as acupuncture, have been used to treat the symptoms of AIDS. How do they differ from Western approaches?
5. Interview a doctor or nurse who treats AIDS patients, asking your interviewee how the disease has affected his or her attitudes toward the medical profession. Then write an essay in which you compare your interviewee's response to Kate Scannell's.

EVELYNN HAMMONDS

Race, Sex, AIDS: The Construction of "Other"

||||||||||||||||||||||||||||||||||||||||||||||||||||||

Like all highly stigmatized diseases, AIDS turns the world into "us" and "them." "They"—those with AIDS—are perceived as different and alien by those who do not have it. In this essay, Evelynn Hammonds analyzes the role that difference plays in the AIDS epidemic, especially racial and sexual difference, and how those differences have contributed to the social marginalization of people with AIDS. Would AIDS have been neglected as long as it was if its first victims were Boy Scouts, or any other group considered part of mainstream society? Or did the fact that the first people with AIDS hailed from the gay community and the black underclass contribute to a national policy of indifference? Hammonds, who writes on the intersection of science, medicine, and feminism, is currently assistant professor of the history of science at Massachusetts Institute for Technology.

In March of this year [1987] when Richard Goldstein's article, "AIDS and Race—the Hidden Epidemic" appeared in the *Village Voice,* the following statement in the lead paragraph jumped out at me: "a black woman is thirteen times more likely than a white woman to contract AIDS, says the Centers for Disease Control; a Hispanic woman is at eleven times the risk. Ninety-one percent of infants with AIDS are non-white." My first reaction was shock. I was stunned to discover the extent and rate of spread of AIDS in the black community, especially given the lack of public mobilization either inside or outside the community. My second reaction was anger. AIDS is a disease that for the time being signals a death notice. I am angry because too many people have died and are going to die of this disease. The gay male community over these last several years has been transformed and mobilized to halt transmission and gay men (at least white gay men) with AIDS have been able to live and die with some dignity and self-esteem. People of color need the opportunity to establish programs and interventions to provide education so that the spread of this disease in our communities can be halted, and to provide care so that people of color with AIDS will not live and die as pariahs.

My final reaction was despair. Of course I *knew* why information about AIDS and the black community had been buried—by both the black and white media. The white media, like the dominant power structure, have moved into their phase of "color-blindness" as a mark of progress. This ideology buries racism along with race. In the case of AIDS and race, the problem with "color-blindness" becomes clear. Race remains a reality in this society, including a reality about how perception is structured. On the one hand, race blindness means a failure to develop educational programs and materials that speak in the language of our communities and recognize the position of people of color in relation to the dominant institutions of society: medical, legal, etc. Additionally, we must ask why the vast disproportion of people of color in the AIDS statistics hasn't been seen as a remarkable fact, or as worthy of comment. By their silence, the white media fail to challenge the age-old American myth of blacks as carriers of disease, especially sexually transmitted disease. This association has quietly become incorporated into the image of AIDS.

The black community's relative silence about AIDS is in part also a response to this historical association of blacks, disease, and deviance in American society. Revealing that AIDS is prevalent in the black community raises the spectre of blacks being associated with two kinds of deviance: sexually transmitted disease and homosexuality.

As I began to make connections between AIDS and race I slowly began to pull together pieces of information and images of AIDS that I had seen in the media. Immediately I began to think about the forty-year-long Tuskegee syphilis experiment on black men. I thought about the innuendoes in media reports about AIDS in Africa and Haiti that hinted at bizarre sexual practices among black people in those countries; I remembered how a black gay man had been portrayed as sexually irresponsible in a PBS documentary on AIDS; I thought about how little I had seen in the black press about AIDS and black gay men; I began to notice the thinly veiled hostility toward the increasing number of IV drug users with AIDS. Goldstein's article revealed dramatically, the deafening silence about who was now actually contracting and dying from AIDS—gay/bisexual black and Hispanic men (now about 50% of black and Hispanic men with AIDS); many black and Hispanic IV drug users; black and Hispanic women, and black and Hispanic babies born to these women.

In this culture, how we think about disease determines who lives   5
and who dies. The history of black people in this country is riddled with episodes displaying how concepts of sickness, disease, health, behavior and sexuality, and race have been entwined in the definition of normalcy and deviance. The power to define disease and normality makes AIDS a political issue.

The average black person on the street may not know the specifics of concepts of disease and race but our legacy as victims of this construction means that we know what it means to have a disease cast as the result of the immoral behavior of a group of people. Black people and other people of color notice, pay attention to what diseases are cast upon us and why. As the saying goes—"when white people get a cold, black people get pneumonia."

In this article I want to address the issues raised by the white media's silence on the connections between AIDS and race; the black media's silence on the connections between AIDS and sexuality/sexual politics, the failure of white gay men's AIDS organizations to reach the communities of people of color, and finally the implications for gay activists, progressives, and feminists.

It is very important to outline the historical context in which the AIDS epidemic occurs in regards to race. The dominant media portrayals of AIDS and scientists' assertions about its origins and modes of transmission have everything to do with the history of racial groups and sexually transmitted diseases.

The Social Construction of Disease

A standard feature of the vast majority of medical articles on the health of blacks was a sociomedical profile of a race whose members were rapidly becoming diseased, debilitated, and debauched and had only themselves to blame.[1]

---

1. James H. Jones, *Bad Blood: The Tuskegee Syphilis Experiment* (New York: Free Press, 1981), p. 21.

One of the first things that white southern doctors noted about blacks imported from Africa as slaves was that they seemed to respond differently than whites to certain diseases. Primarily they observed that some of the diseases that were epidemic in the South seemed to affect blacks less severely than whites—specifically, fevers (e.g., yellow fever). Since in the eighteenth and nineteenth centuries there was little agreement about the nature of various illnesses and the causes of many common diseases were unknown, physicians tended to attribute the differences they noted simply to race.

In the nineteenth century when challenges were made to the insti-   10
tution of slavery, white southern physicians were all too willing to provide medical evidence to justify slavery.

> They justified slavery and, after its abolition, second-class citizenship, by insisting that blacks were incapable of assuming any higher station in life. . . . Thus, medical discourses on the peculiarities of blacks offered, among other things, a pseudoscientific rationale for keeping blacks in their places.[2]

If as these physicians maintained, blacks were less susceptible to fevers than whites, then it seemed fitting that they and not whites should provide most of the labor in the hot, swampy lowlands where southern agriculture was centered. Southern physicians marshalled other "scientific" evidence, such as measurement of brain sizes and other body organs to prove that blacks constituted an inferior race. For many whites these arguments were persuasive because "objective" science offered validity to their personal "observations," prejudices, and fears.

The history of sexually transmitted diseases, in particular syphilis, indicates the pervasiveness of racial/sexual stereotyping. The history of syphilis in America is complex, as Allan Brandt discloses in his book *No Magic Bullet.* According to Brandt, "venereal disease has historically been assumed to be the disease of the 'other.'" Obviously the complicated interaction of sexuality and disease has deep implications for the current portrayal of AIDS.

Like AIDS, the prevailing nineteenth century view of syphilis was characterized early on in moral terms—and when it became apparent that a high rate of syphilis occurred among blacks in the South, the morality issue heightened considerably. Diseases that are acquired through immoral behavior were considered in many parts of the culture as punishment from God, the wages of sin. Anyone with such a disease was stigmatized. A white person could avoid this sin by a change in behavior. But for blacks it was different. It was noted that one of the primary differences that separated the races was that blacks were more

---

2. *Ibid.,* p. 17.

flagrant and loose in their sexual behavior—behaviors they could not control.

> Moreover, personal restraints on self-indulgence did not exist, physicians insisted, because the smaller brain of the Negro had failed to develop a center for inhibiting sexual behavior.[3]

Therefore blacks deserved to have syphilis, since they couldn't control their behavior . . . the Tuskegee experiment carried that logic to [the] extreme—blacks also deserved to die from syphilis.

> [B]lacks suffered from venereal diseases because they would not, or could not, refrain from sexual promiscuity. Social hygiene for whites rested on the assumption that attitudinal changes could produce behavioral changes. A single standard of high moral behavior could be produced by molding sexual attitudes through moral education. For blacks, however, a change in their very *nature* seemed to be required.[4]

If in the above quotation, you change blacks to homosexuals and whites to heterosexuals then the parallel to the media portrayal of people with AIDS is obvious.

The black community's response to the historical construction of sexually transmitted diseases as the result of bad, inherently uncontrollable behavior of blacks—is sexual conservatism. To avoid the stigma of being cast with diseases of the "other," the black media, as well as other institutions in the community, avoid public discussion of sexual behavior and other "deviant" behavior like drug use. The white media on the other hand is often quick to cast blacks and people of color as "other" either overtly or covertly.

Black Community Response to AIDS

Of 38,435 diagnosed cases of AIDS as of July 20, 1987, black and Hispanic people make up 39% of all cases even though they account for only 17 percent of the adult population.[5] Eighty percent of the pediatric cases are black and Hispanic. The average life expectancy after diagnosis of a white person with AIDS in the United States is two years; of a person of color, nineteen weeks.[6]

The leading magazines in the black community, *Ebony* and *Essence,* carried no articles on AIDS until the spring of this year. The journal of the National Medical Association, the professional organization of black

15

---

3. *Ibid.,* p. 23.
4. *Ibid.,* p. 48.
5. "High AIDS Rate Spurring Efforts for Minorities," *New York Times,* Sunday, August 2, 1987.
6. *Mother Jones,* Vol. 12, May 1987.

physicians, carried a short guest editorial article in late 1986 and to date
has not published any extensive article on AIDS. The official magazines
of the NAACP and the National Urban League make no mention of
AIDS throughout 1986 nor to date this year. Only the Atlanta-based
SCLC (Southern Christian Leadership Conference) has established an
ongoing educational program to address AIDS in the black community.

When I examined the few articles that have been written about
AIDS in the national black press, several themes emerged. Almost all the
articles I saw tried to indicate that the black people are at risk while
simultaneously trying to avoid any implication that AIDS is a "black"
disease. The black media has underemphasized, though recognized, that
there are significant socioeconomic cofactors in terms of the impact of
AIDS in the black community. The high rate of drug use and abuse in
the black community is in part a result of many other social factors—
high unemployment, poor schools, inadequate housing, and limited access to health care, all factors in the spread of AIDS. These affect specifically the fact that people of color with AIDS are diagnosed at more
advanced stages of the disease and are dying faster. The national black
media have so far also failed to deal with any larger public policy issue
that the AIDS crisis will precipitate for the community; and most importantly homosexuality and bisexuality were dealt with in a very conservative and problematic fashion.

Testing

In terms of testing *Ebony* encourages more opportunity for people
to be tested anonymously; *Essence* recommends testing for women thinking of getting pregnant. Both articles mention that exposure of test results
could result in discrimination in housing and employment but neither
publication discusses the issue at any length. There is no mention of
testing that is going on in the military and how those results are being
used nor is there mention of testing in prison. It is clear from the sketchy
discussion of testing that the political issues around testing are not being
faced.

Sexuality

The most disappointing aspect of these articles is that by focusing
on individual behavior as the cause of AIDS and by setting up bisexuals,
homosexuals, and drug users as "other" in the black community, and as
"bad," the national black media falls into the trap of reproducing exactly
how white society has defined the issue. But unlike the situation for
whites, what happens to these groups within the black community will
affect the community as a whole. Repressive practices around AIDS in

prisons will affect all black men in prison with or without AIDS and their families outside and any other black person facing the criminal justice system; the identification of significant numbers of people of color in the military with AIDS will affect all people of color in the military. Quarantine, suspension of civil liberties for drug users in the black community with AIDS, will affect everyone in the community. Health care and housing access will be restricted for all of us. If people with AIDS are set off as "bad" or "other," no change in individual behavior in relation to them will save any of us. There can be no "us" or "them" in our communities.

The *Ebony* article entitled "The Truth about AIDS: Dread Disease   20 Is Spreading Rapidly through Heterosexual Population," while highlighting the increase of AIDS among heterosexuals in the black community, makes several comments about black homosexuals. The author notes that there is generally a negative attitude toward homosexuals in the community and quotes several physicians who emphasize that the reticence on this issue is a hindrance to AIDS education efforts in the community. It does not emphasize that, because of this "reticence," only now as AIDS is being recognized as striking heterosexuals, is it beginning to be talked about in the black community.

> One of the greatest problems in the black community, other than ignorance about the disease, is the large number of black men who engage in sex acts with other men but who don't consider themselves homosexuals.[7]

The point is then that since AIDS was initially characterized as a "gay disease" and many black men don't consider themselves gay in spite of their sexual practices, the black community did not acknowledge the presence of AIDS.

The association of AIDS with "bad" behavior is prominent in this article. Homosexuals and drug users are described as a "physiologically and economically depressed subgroup of the black community."[8]

The message is that to deal with this disease the individual behavior of a deviant subgroup must be changed. Additionally, the recommendation to heterosexuals is to "not have sex" with bisexuals and drug users. There are no recommendations about how the community can find a way to deal with the silence around the issues of homosexuality/ bisexuality, sexual practices in general, and drug use. The article fails to say what the implications of the sexual practices of black men are for the community.

---

7. *Ebony,* April, 1987, p. 128, quoting a Los Angeles AIDS expert.
8. *Ibid.,* p. 130.

The *Essence* article, entitled *Nobody's Safe,* avoids the issue as well.[9] The authors describe a scenario of a thirty-eight-year-old middle-class professional woman who is suddenly found to have AIDS. Her husband had died two years earlier due to a rare form of pneumonia. After testing positive for AIDS she is told by one of her husband's relatives that he had been bisexual. The text following this scenario goes on to describe how most women contract AIDS; it gives a general sketch of the origins of the disease and discusses the latency period and defines asymptomatic carriers of the virus. There is no mention of bisexuality or homosexuality. The implication is again—just don't have sex with those people if you want to avoid AIDS. It avoids discussion of the prevalence of bisexuality among black men, and consequently the way that AIDS will ultimately change sexual relationships in the black community.

The Mainstream (White) Press

In general the mainstream media have been silent on the rise of AIDS in the black and Hispanic communities. Until very recently, with the exception of a few special reports, such as a quite excellent one on the PBS *MacNeil-Lehrer Report,* most media reports on AIDS continue to speak of the disease without mention of its effects on people of color. In recent months specific attention has been paid to the "new" phenomenon of heterosexuals with AIDS or "heterosexual AIDS." This terminology is used without the slightest mention that among Haitians and extensively in Africa, AIDS was never a disease confined to homosexuals.

The assumption in reports about the spread of AIDS to heterosexuals   25 is that these heterosexuals are white—read that as white, middle-class, non-drug-using, sexually active people. The facts are that there are very few cases of AIDS among this group. As many as 90 percent of the cases of AIDS among heterosexuals are black and Hispanic. In many media reports blacks and Hispanics with AIDS are lumped in the IV drug users group. What the media has picked up on is that heterosexual transmission in the United States now endangers middle-class whites.

A good example of the mainstream media approach is an article by Kate Leishman in the February 1987 issue of *Atlantic Monthly.* She writes that most Americans, even liberals, have the attitude that AIDS is the result of immoral behavior. Leishman lists the statistics on heterosexual transmission of AIDS at the beginning of her article. Fifteen pages later the following information appears:

---

9. *Essence,* June 1987.

> In the case of sexually active gay men [AIDS] is a tragedy—as it is for poor black and Hispanic youths, among whom there is a nationwide epidemic of venereal disease, which is a certain cofactor in facilitating transmission of HIV. This combination with the pervasive use of drugs among blacks and Hispanics ensures that the epidemic will hit them hardest next.[10]

Her first explicit mention of people of color describes them as a group that uses drugs extensively, and as also riddled with venereal disease (a fact she does not support with any data). The image is one of the "unregenerate young street tough" that causes all the trouble in our cities, in short the conventional racist stereotype of black and Hispanic youth displayed in the press almost every day. Her use of the word "tragedy" because of the risk to blacks, Hispanics, and gays is gratuitous at best. The main focus of the article is the risk of AIDS to white heterosexuals and the need for them to face their fears of AIDS so they can effectively change their behavior.

In a passage reminiscent of nineteenth-century physicians' moral advice she notes the problems associated with changing people's behavior and promoting safe sex, and wonders if one can draw any lessons for heterosexual behavior from the gay male experience.

> Many people believe that the intensity or quality of homosexual drives is unique, while others argue that the ability to control sexual impulses varies extraordinarily within groups of any sexual preference.[11]

What I find striking in this passage is that there is still debate over whether certain "groups" of people have the same ability to exercise control over their sexual behavior and drives as "normal" white heterosexuals do. The passage also suggests that white heterosexuals are still the only group who have the strength, the moral fortitude, the inherent ability if educated, to control their sexual and other behavior. After all, this is a disease about behavior and not viruses, right? Leishman doesn't interview any blacks or Hispanics about their fears of AIDS, or how they want to deal with it with respect to sexual practice or other behavior.

Two months later in May several letters to the editors of *Atlantic Monthly* appeared in response to Leishman's article. In particular one reader observed her omission of statistics about the risk of AIDS to blacks and Hispanics. She responded in a fairly defensive manner:

> My article and many others have commented on the high risk of exposure to AIDS among blacks and Hispanics. Mr. Patrick's observations that blacks and Hispanics already account for ninety percent of

---

10. *Atlantic Monthly*, February 1987, p. 54.
11. *Ibid.*, p. 40.

the case load seems oddly to suggest that AIDS is on its way to becoming a disease of minorities. But the Centers for Disease Control has stressed that the overrepresentation of blacks and Hispanics in AIDS statistics is related not to race per se but to underlying risk factors.[12]

The risk factor she mentions is intravenous drug use. Leishman fails to deal with the "overrepresentation" of blacks and Hispanics in AIDS statistics. To mention our higher risk only implies that AIDS is a disease of minorities if you believe minorities are inherently different or behave differently in the face of the disease or if you believe that the disease will be confined to the minority community.

So pervasive is the association of race and IV drug use that the fact   30 that a majority of black and Hispanic men who have AIDS are gay or bisexual, and *non*-IV drug users, has remained buried in statistics.[13] In the face of the statistics, the *New York Times* continues to identify IV drug use as the distinguishing mode of transmission among black and Hispanic men, by focusing not on the percentage of black and Hispanic AIDS cases that are drug related, but on the percentage of drug-related AIDS cases that are black or Hispanic, which is 94%. This framework, besides blocking information that the black and Hispanic communities need, also functions to keep the white community's image "clean."

Conclusion

As this article goes to press, media coverage of the extent of AIDS in the black and Hispanic communities is increasing daily. These latest articles are covering the efforts in the black and Hispanic communities both to raise consciousness in these communities with respect to AIDS and to increase government funding to support culturally specific educational programs. Within the black community, the traditional source of leadership, black ministers, are now publicly expressing the reasons for their previous reluctance to speak out about AIDS. The reasons expressed tend to fall into the areas I have tried to discuss in this article, as indicated by the following comments that recently appeared in the *Boston Globe:*

> Although some black ministers described gays as the children of God and AIDS as just another virus, many more talked about homosexuality as sinful, including some who referred to AIDS as a God-sent plague to punish the sexually deviant.[14]

---

12. *Atlantic Monthly,* May 1987, p. 13.
13. *New York Times,* Sunday, August 2, 1987.
14. *Boston Globe,* Sunday, August 9, 1987, p. 1.

> There's a lot of fear of stigmatization when you stand up. . . .
> How does this label your church or the people who go to your church?
> said Rev. Bruce Wall, assistant pastor of Twelfth Baptist Church in
> Roxbury. Rev. Wall said ministers may also fear that an activist role
> on AIDS could prompt another question: "Maybe that pastor is gay."[15]

The arguments I have made as to the background of these kinds of
comments continue to come out in the public discourse on AIDS and
race in the national media. As the public discussion and press coverage
have increased, one shift is apparent. The media is now focussing on
why the black and Hispanic communities have not responded to AIDS
before as a "problem" specific to these communities, while there is no
acknowledgment that part of the problem is the way the media, the
CDC, and the Public Health Service prevented race-specific information
about AIDS from being widely disseminated. Or, to say it differently,
there is no recognition of how the medical and media construction of
AIDS as a "gay disease" or a disease of Haitians has affected the black
and Hispanic communities.

Finally, as the black and Hispanic communities mobilize against
AIDS, coalitions with established gay groups will be critical. To date,
some in the black community have noted the lack of culturally specific
educational material produced by these groups. Some gay groups are
responding to that criticism. For progressives, feminists and gay activists,
the AIDS crisis represents a crucial time when the work we have done
on sexuality and sexual politics will be most needed to frame the fight
against AIDS in political terms that move the politics of sexuality out of
the background and challenge the repressive policies and morality that
threaten not only the people with this disease but all of us.

Reading the Text

1. Why does Hammonds consider the ideology of "color-blindness" in the
   media to be a problem?
2. Why, according to Hammonds, has the black community remained silent
   about the AIDS epidemic?
3. What relationship does Hammonds see between syphilis and other sexually
   transmitted diseases and the stereotyping of blacks?
4. What is Hammonds's explanation for the relative lack of media coverage
   of the AIDS epidemic in the black and Hispanic communities?

---

15. *Ibid.,* p. 12.

Reading the Signs

1. Compare and contrast the coverage of AIDS in the black press and in the white, or mainstream, press. To develop your essay, both refer to Hammonds's evidence and generate your own by analyzing current coverage of AIDS in popular magazines.
2. Using Michael D. Quam's "Stigma" (p. 679) as your critical framework, write an essay in which you explain the extent to which fear of being stigmatized may account for the black community's response to AIDS.
3. Go to the library and research the Tuskegee syphilis experiment that Hammonds describes, and then write an essay in which you explore her claim that "'objective' science" has been used to support racist stereotypes.
4. Both Hammonds and Susan Sontag ("AIDS and Its Metaphors," p. 668) focus on the images and metaphors by which we understand the disease. Compare and contrast their analyses of this issue. Which author do you find more persuasive? How do differences in ethnicity affect the tone and purpose of their essays?
5. How might Sam Fulwood III ("The Rage of the Black Middle Class," p. 462) and bell hooks ("Madonna: Plantation Mistress or Soul Sister?" p. 190) respond to Hammonds's argument? Role-play a discussion among Fulwood, hooks, and Hammonds in class, being sure to note issues on which they are likely to differ as well as agree.

RANDY SHILTS
AIDSpeak Spoken Here

||||||||||||||||||||||||||||||||||||||||||||||||||||||||||||||||||||||||

The author of the authoritative history of the early years of the AIDS epidemic And the Band Played On *(1987), from which this selection is excerpted, Randy Shilts has distinguished himself not only for the thoroughness of his reportage but for his independence of thought as well. In this selection, Shilts takes on the discourse of the AIDS community, dubbing it the language of AIDSpeak. For Shilts, the euphemisms of AIDSpeak are not harmless gestures of political correctness: They actively contributed to the early misunderstanding of AIDS, as when the euphemistic "bodily fluids" got Americans thinking that AIDS could be spread through sneezing. The national correspondent for the* San Francisco Chronicle, *Randy Shilts was the first reporter in America assigned full-time to cover the AIDS epidemic. Shilts's most recent book is* Conduct Unbecoming: Gays & Lesbians in the U.S. Military *(1993).*

In San Francisco, plague met politics. Instead of being confronted by a united authority with intelligent plans for defense, it found divided forces among which the question of its presence became the subject of factional dispute. There was open popular hostility to the work of the sanitarians, and war among the City, State and Federal Health authorities . . . For a while the people were in the gravest danger and it seemed impossible to convey any adequate warnings to them.

– Eradicating Bubonic Plague from San Francisco, 1907,
THE REPORT OF THE CITIZENS' HEALTH COMMITTEE

JUNE 2, 1983
SAN FRANCISCO DEPARTMENT OF
PUBLIC HEALTH

"Dr. Silverman, this poster says people should have fewer sexual partners. Does that mean that if somebody had ten sexual partners a week last year that they can cut down to five sexual partners a week now and they won't get AIDS?"

Merv Silverman looked uncomfortable. He had taken Barbara Taylor, a no-nonsense reporter for the all-news KCBS radio, and a *Chronicle* newsman to proudly unveil the health department's AIDS poster, the one everybody was talking about.

"We're trying to give a message that people will pay attention to," said Silverman.

For five years Merv Silverman had served as a popular public health director. The media loved him; the gay community adored him. He wasn't accustomed to such sharp questioning. Barbara Taylor, who had spent the last seven years listening to politicians, pressed on.

"Dr. Silverman, it says on this poster that people should limit their   5
use of recreational drugs. Does that mean that if somebody was shooting up, say, three times a week, that they'd be safe from AIDS if they shot up just once a month? You're not saying not to use recreational drugs; you say limit your use of drugs."

"We're trying not to lecture people," answered Silverman. "It doesn't do any good if you give people a message they don't listen to."

"I thought we were trying to tell people how not to get AIDS," said Taylor. "Why aren't we telling them that?"

Merv Silverman thought Barbara Taylor was taking an old-fashioned, textbook kind of approach to public health. The health director understood this approach; after all, his master's in public health came from Harvard. The silver-haired forty-five-year-old had spent his life in the field. But AIDS was not a classical public health problem. It was sensitive. It required messages that were . . . appropriate.

Taylor thought the poster was a lot of bullshit and that Silverman was soft-peddling AIDS prevention so he wouldn't have a lot of angry gay activists yelling at him for being homophobic. There'd been a lot of that in the past few days.

The reality was a mix of both Silverman's good intentions and   10
Taylor's more cynical political analysis. The result was the first major public demonstration of AIDSpeak, a new language forged by public health officials, anxious gay politicians, and the burgeoning ranks of "AIDS activists." The linguistic roots of AIDspeak sprouted not so much from the truth as from what was politically facile and psychologically reassuring. Semantics was the major denominator of AIDSpeak jargon, because the language went to great lengths never to offend.

A new lexicon was evolving. Under the rules of AIDSpeak, for example, AIDS victims could not be called victims. Instead, they were to be called People With AIDS, or PWAs, as if contracting this uniquely brutal disease was not a victimizing experience. "Promiscuous" became "sexually active," because gay politicians declared "promiscuous" to be "judgmental," a major cuss word in AIDSpeak. The most-used circumlocution in AIDSpeak was "bodily fluids," an expression that avoided troublesome words like "semen."

Most importantly, however, the new syntax allowed gay political leaders to address and largely determine public health policy in the coming years, because public health officials quickly mastered AIDSpeak, and it was fundamentally a political tongue. With politicians talking like public health officials, and public health officials behaving like politicians, the new vernacular allowed virtually everyone to avoid challenging the encroaching epidemic in medical terms.

Thus, the verbiage tended toward the intransitive. AIDSpeak was rarely employed to motivate action; rather, it was most articulately pronounced when justifying inertia. Nobody meant any harm by this; quite to the contrary, AIDSpeak was the tongue designed to make everyone content. AIDSpeak was the language of good intentions in the AIDS epidemic; AIDSpeak was a language of death.

As public health director for the only city in the United States that was paying much attention to the epidemic, Mervyn Silverman became the chief translator of AIDSpeak for the general population. The former Peace Corps administrator was well qualified for the role since he was a virtual warehouse of good intentions for the gay community. The past few days had demonstrated this amply.

The brouhaha had started on page two of the *Chronicle* a few days   15
before in a story concerning the lack of any AIDS information in the city's bathhouses and sex emporiums. At least 200,000 gay tourists were about to descend on the city for the Gay Freedom Day Parade, the story noted. Many gay men came, in part, to make use of San Francisco's

fabled sex emporiums; most still regarded AIDS as strange media hype. The scenario was one in which epidemics thrived.

Bill Kraus had quietly leaked an account of the ill-fated meeting with bathhouse owners. A public health official, who was not Mervyn Silverman but who asked not to be identified, told the paper about how it would be best to close the joints down; but barring that, they should be required to post some kind of warning.

"I don't have the power to force the bathhouses to post anything," Silverman initially told an inquiring reporter.

Technically, he was telling the truth. The only power Silverman had was to use his broad authority to close anything that was a threat to public health. He wasn't about to do that. In a letter to a citizen in May, Silverman had denied even having this power, saying it would be "illegal for me to close down all bathhouses and other such places that are used for anonymous and multiple sex contacts. It is my belief that we would insult the intelligence of many of our citizens and it would be an invasion of privacy to take such an action."

Silverman also was not inclined to force the gay businesses to alert customers about the death potential inherent in the use of their facilities. "The government can only play a certain role in this," he said. "The real validity comes with information from peers. The information that will get across will come from the gay community itself."

Like all AIDSpeak, the explanation sounded sensible, although it 20
evaded the question of why public health officials exist. If preventing disease in a community was best done by the community itself, why bother to have a public health department?

Dr. Silverman was well tutored by gay political leaders on the question of why the bathhouses shouldn't be shut down. "If you close the bathhouses, people will simply go elsewhere to have unsafe sex," he said.

For the past decade, spokespeople of the gay rights movement had held endless press conferences to argue against the stereotype that gay men were sex fiends wholly preoccupied with getting their rocks off. With AIDSpeak, however, many of these same spokespeople were now arguing that bathhouses must stay open because gay men were such sex fiends that they would be screwing behind every bush if they didn't have their sex clubs.

After the initial *Chronicle* story on the sex managers' refusal to post warnings, Mayor Dianne Feinstein inveighed: "Within the language of the health code, I think Dr. Silverman can write to them and tell them to post whatever warnings are necessary. I do think it is advisable." A majority of the board of supervisors also said that the public health director should order the obdurate bathhouse owners to post warnings. A day later, Dr. Silverman announced he would require warnings in the bathhouses. If the proprietors didn't cooperate, he would shut them down. "We would have done this anyway," he said.

By Thursday morning, June 2, Silverman was meeting with the bathhouse owners who suddenly said they were "looking forward" to putting up the posters. The public health director pledged the most "intensive" public health education campaign in city history. After that press conference, Silverman showed Barbara Taylor the AIDS poster. It gave four pieces of advice: "use condoms," "avoid any exchange of bodily fluids," "limit your use of recreational drugs," and "enjoy more time with fewer partners." The poster did inform gay men that there was a nasty disease out there that could kill you; but in saying to only "reduce" the number of partners and "limit" drugs, it did not get to the blunt fact that just one partner or bad needle could bring death.

Reading the Text

1. Explain in your own words what Shilts means by "AIDSpeak."
2. Why did Merv Silverman believe that "AIDS was not a classical public health problem"?
3. How, according to Shilts, was AIDSpeak useful to politicians?

Reading the Signs

1. Visit your school's student health center (or a community health center), and pick up brochures on AIDS or safe sex. Bring the brochures to class, and in small groups, analyze the language. To what extent are the brochures written in AIDSpeak? Do you think AIDSpeak would be appropriate for the audiences for whom the brochures are intended?
2. Shilts implies that AIDSpeak can do more harm than good. Write an argumentative essay in which you support, challenge, or modify his position.
3. Rent a videotape of the Magic Johnson AIDS video, *Time Out,* and show it in class. Analyze semiotically the video's depiction of the disease. What images does the video use, and what is their social significance? To what extent does the video use AIDSpeak? What might Evelynn Hammonds ("Race, Sex, AIDS: The Construction of 'Other,'" p. 692) say about the role of ethnicity in the video?
4. What parallels do you see between AIDSpeak as Randy Shilts explains it and the "political correctness" movement on college campuses? To develop your essay, consult Nat Hentoff's "'Speech Codes' on the Campus and Problems of Free Speech," p. 385.
5. Shilts's selection opens by referring to a public health campaign AIDS poster. In teams, create your own public information poster about AIDS, and design it for a particular audience (students, say, or gay men). Then present the poster to the entire class, explaining your choice of language and image.

DOUGLAS CRIMP AND
ADAM ROLSTON

The Semiotics of AIDS Activism

||||||||||||||||||||||||||||||||||||||||||||||||||

Almost from the beginning, the AIDS epidemic was charged with a political dimension. In response to the Reagan administration's silence about the disease in the early 1980s, many activist groups formed to press for increased research funds and improved health care for people with AIDS. One of the most energetic of such groups is ACT UP, an organization that promotes community action and political response by disrupting the public's sense of complacency about AIDS. In the following selection from AIDS Demographics *(1990), Douglas Crimp and Adam Rolston describe the crucial role that images can play in the fight against this killer. Douglas Crimp (b. 1944), a professor of visual studies at the University of Rochester, is editor of* AIDS: Cultural Analysis/Cultural Activism *and coeditor of* How Do I Look? Queer Film and Video. *A conceptual artist and free-lance architect, Adam Rolston (b. 1962) obtained a degree in architecture from Syracuse University; his areas of interest include the demographics of AIDS and popular culture.*

Although our struggles are most often waged at the local level, the AIDS epidemic and the activist movement dedicated to ending it is national—and international—in scope, and the U.S. government is a major culprit in the problems we face and a central target of our anger. ACT NOW, the AIDS Coalition to Network, Organize, and Win—a national coalition of AIDS activist groups—has coordinated actions of national reach, most notably against the Food and Drug Administration (FDA) in October 1988. Health care is a national scandal in the United States; the FDA, the Centers for Disease Control (CDC), and the National Institutes of Health (NIH) are all critical to our surviving the epidemic, and we have monitored, lobbied, and fought them all. We have also taken our demands beyond U.S. borders. The Fifth International AIDS Conference in Montreal in June 1989 was *our* conference, the first of these annual, previously largely scientific and policy-making AIDS roundups to have its business-as-usual disrupted by the combative presence of an international coalition of AIDS activists. We took the stage—literally—during the opening ceremonies, and we never relinquished it. One measure of our success was that by the end of the conference perhaps one-third of the more than 12,000 people attending were wearing SILENCE = DEATH buttons.

That simple graphic emblem—SILENCE = DEATH printed in white Gill sanserif type underneath a pink triangle on a black ground—has come to signify AIDS activism to an entire community of people confronting the epidemic. This in itself tells us something about the styles and tragedies of the movement's graphics. For SILENCE = DEATH does its work with a metaphorical subtlety that is unique, among political symbols and slogans, to AIDS activism. Our emblem's significance depends on foreknowledge of the use of the pink triangle as the marker of gay men in Nazi concentration camps, its appropriation by the gay movement to remember a suppressed history of our oppression, and, now, an inversion of its positioning (men in the death camps wore triangles that pointed down; SILENCE = DEATH's points up). SILENCE = DEATH declares that silence about the oppression and annihilation of gay people, *then and now,* must be broken as a matter of our survival. As historically problematic as an analogy of AIDS and the death camps is, it is also deeply resonant for gay men and lesbians, especially insofar as the analogy is already mediated by the gay movement's adoption of the pink triangle. But it is not merely what SILENCE = DEATH says, but also how it looks, that gives it its particular force. The power of this equation under a triangle is the compression of its connotation into a logo, a logo so striking that you ultimately *have* to ask, if you don't already know, "What does that mean?" And it is the answers we are constantly called upon to give to others—small, everyday direct actions—that make SILENCE = DEATH signify beyond a community of lesbian and gay cognoscenti.

Reading the Text

1. Summarize in your own words the significance of the "silence = death" symbol.
2. Why is a simple symbol so important to AIDS activists?
3. What do the authors mean by a "community of lesbian and gay cognoscenti"?

Reading the Signs

1. In class, discuss the symbolic significance of another AIDS-related sign: the red ribbon. Have you seen people wearing red ribbons? What message does the ribbon send? How does the ribbon relate to other similar signs, such as a black armband?
2. Visit a local activist organization, such as ACT UP, and collect some current AIDS-related pamphlets and literature. What other symbols and images are being used today in the fight against AIDS, and what messages do they send? Who is the audience for these signs?
3. In class, brainstorm other political symbols and slogans, particularly those related to historically oppressed groups. Then write an essay in which you support, disprove, or modify Crimp and Rolston's claim that AIDS activists use graphics "with a metaphorical subtlety that is unique."
4. Using Crimp and Rolston's explanation of the silence = death emblem as your model, write an analysis of the significance of the "X" symbol popularized since the release of *Malcom X*.
5. Create your own symbol or image for a political issue in which you believe strongly. Share your symbol with the class, explaining its semiotic significance.

GLOSSARY

Archetype (n.) A character type, symbol, or pattern that is repeated in different stories or narratives. Moby Dick and Jonah's whale are sea monster archetypes.

Canon (n.) A group of books or works that are considered essential to a literary tradition. The plays of Shakespeare are part of the canon of English literature.

Class (n.) A group of related objects or people. Those who share the same economic status in a society are said to be of the same social class: for example, working class, middle class, upper class. Members of a class tend to share the same social interests and political viewpoints.

Code (n.) A system of signs or values that assigns meanings to the elements that belong to it. Thus, a traffic code defines a red light as a "stop" signal and a green light as a "go," whereas a fashion code determines whether an article of clothing is stylish. To **decode** a system is to figure out its meanings, as when one discovers what an unlaced basketball sneaker means in the code of teen fashion.

Connotation (n.) The meaning emotively suggested by a word, as opposed to its objective reference, or **denotation**. Thus, the word "flag" might connote (or suggest) feelings of patriotism, while it literally denotes (or refers to) a pennantlike object.

Consumption (n.) The use of products and services, as opposed to their production. A **consumer culture** is one that consumes more

than it produces. As a consuming culture, for example, America uses
more consumer goods such as TV sets and stereos than it manufactures, which results in a trade deficit with producer cultures (such as
Japan) with which America trades.

Context (n.)   The environment in which a sign can be interpreted. In
the context of a Grateful Dead concert, for example, tie-dyes and
beads can mean that one is part of the group. Wearing the same
outfit in the context of a job interview at IBM would be interpreted
as meaning that you don't really want the job.

Culture (n.)   The overall system of values and traditions shared by a
group of people. Not exactly synonymous with a "society"; a society
can include numerous cultures within its boundaries. A culture
encompasses the worldviews of those who belong to it. Thus,
America, which is a **multicultural** society, includes the differing
worldviews of people of African, Asian, Native American, and European descent.

Denotation (n.)   The particular object or group of objects to which a
word refers; compare with **connotation**.

Discourse (n.)   The system of words and concepts that constitutes the
knowledge and understanding of a particular community, often academic or professional. In the discourse of modern medicine, for
example, it is presumed that illness is caused by material causes—
e.g., chemical problems or invasive agents—rather than by spiritual
causes.

Dominant culture (n.)   The group within a multicultural society
whose traditions, values, and beliefs are held to be normative. The
European culture is dominant in the United States.

Eurocentric (adj.)   Related to a worldview based on the traditions and
history of European culture, usually at the expense of non-European
cultures.

Function (n.)   The utility of an object, as opposed to its cultural meaning. Spandex or Lycra shorts, for example, are valued for their function by cyclists because they're lightweight and aerodynamic. On
the other hand, such shorts have become a general fashion item for
both men and women because of their cultural meaning, not their
function. Many non-cyclists wear Spandex to project an image of
hard-bodied fitness, sexiness, or plain trendiness, for example.

Gender (n.)   One's sexual identity and the roles that follow from it, as
determined by the norms of one's culture rather than by biology or
genetics. The assumption that women should be foremost in the
nurturing of children is a gender norm; the fact that women alone
can give birth is a biological phenomenon.

Icon (n.) (adj. **iconic**)   In semiotics, a sign that visibly resembles its
referent, as a photograph looks like the thing it represents. More

broadly, an icon is someone (often a celebrity) who enjoys a commanding or representative place in popular culture. Michael Jackson
and Madonna are music video icons.

Ideology (n.)   A set of beliefs, interests, and values that determines
one's interpretations or judgments. For example, in the ideology of
modern business, it is the purpose of a business to produce profits,
not jobs or social benefits.

Image (n.)   Literally, a pictorial representation; more generally, the
identity that one projects to others through such things as clothing,
grooming, speech, and behavior. Andre Agassi, for example, has
made a commercial career out of his image as a tennis outlaw, a
rock-'n'-roll court demon.

Multiculturalism (n.)   In American education, the movement to incorporate the traditions, history, and beliefs of America's non-European cultures into a traditionally **monocultural** (or single-culture)
curriculum dominated by European thought and history.

Mythology (n.)   The overall framework of values and beliefs incorporated in a given cultural system or worldview. Any given belief
in such a structure—such as the belief that "a woman's place is in
the home"—is called a **myth**.

Politics (n.)   Essentially, the practice of promoting one's interests in a
competitive social environment. It is not restricted to electioneering;
there are office politics, classroom politics, academic politics, and
sexual politics.

Popular culture (n.)   The segment of a culture devoted to phenomena
with mass appeal, such as entertainment and consumer goods.

Postmodernism (n.)   The worldview behind much of contemporary
literature, art, music, architecture, and philosophy, which rejects
traditional attempts to make meaning out of human history and
experience. For the **postmodern** (adj.) artist, art should not attempt
to create new explanatory myths or symbols but should rather re-
codify, recycle, or repeat existing images, as in the art of Andy
Warhol.

Semiotics (n.)   In short, the study of signs. Synonymous with **semiology**, semiotics is concerned with both the theory and practice
of interpreting linguistic, cultural, and behavioral sign systems. One
who practices semiotic analysis is called a **semiotician** or **semiologist**.

Sign (n.)   Anything that bears a meaning. Words, objects, images and
forms of behavior are all signs whose meanings are determined by
the particular codes, or systems, in which they appear. See also **code**
and **system**.

Symbolic sign (n.)   A sign, according to semiotician C. S. Peirce,
whose significance is arbitrary. The meaning of the word "bear," for

example, is arbitrarily determined by those who use it. Contrast with
iconic sign.

System (n.)   The code, or network, within which a sign functions,
and so achieves its meaning. The English language is a sign system,
as is a fashion code.

Text (n.)   A complex of signs, which may be linguistic, imagistic, behavioral, or musical, that can be read or interpreted.

Acknowledgments (Continued from page iv)

Gloria Anzaldúa, "How to Tame a Wild Tongue" from *Borderlands / La Frontera: The New Mestiza* by Gloria Anzaldúa. Copyright © 1987 by Gloria Anzaldúa. Reprinted with permission from Aunt Lute Books, (415) 558-8116.

Diane Barthel, "A Gentleman and a Consumer" from *Putting on Appearances* by Diane Barthel. Copyright © 1988 by Temple University. Reprinted by permission of Temple University Press.

Roland Barthes, "Toys" from *Mythologies* by Roland Barthes, trans. Annette Lavers. Copyright © 1972 by Annette Lavers. Reprinted with permission of Hill & Wang, a division of Farrar, Straus and Giroux.

Léon Bing, "Faro," originally titled "South Central," from *Do or Die* by Léon Bing. Copyright © 1991 by Léon Bing. Reprinted with permission of HarperCollins Publishers.

Robert Bly, "Men's Initiation Rites," from the April–May 1986 issue of *The Utne Reader*. Copyright © 1986 by Robert Bly. Reprinted with permission from Robert Bly.

Valerie Boyd, "The Word on 'Malcom X,'" originally titled "Points of View: The Word on 'Malcolm X,'" edited by Valerie Boyd. Appeared in the November 18, 1992, edition of *The Atlanta Journal*. Copyright © 1992 by *The Atlantic Journal*. Reprinted with permission from *The Atlantic Journal* and *The Atlantic Constitution*.

Holly Brubach, "Rock-and-Roll Vaudeville," by Holly Brubach. First appeared in *Atlantic Monthly*, 1984. Copyright © 1984 by Holly Brubach. Reprinted with permission from *Atlantic Monthly*.

Anne Campbell, "The Praised and the Damned" and "A Day with Connie" from *The Girls in the Gang* by Anne Campbell. Copyright © 1984, 1991 by Anne Campbell. Reprinted with permission of Basil Blackwell, Ltd.

Jane Caputi, "Seeing Elephants: The Myths of Phallotechnology" by Jane Caputi. Copyright © 1988 by Jane Caputi. Reprinted by permission of Feminist Studies and the author.

Elizabeth Chiseri-Strater, from "Anna in Prose Writing: A Member of the Troupe," from *Academic Literacies: The Public and Private Discourse of University Students* (Boynton/Cook Publishers, Inc., Portsmouth, NH, 1991). Reprinted with permission of the author.

Wanda Coleman, "Say It Ain't Cool, Joe" by Wanda Coleman. First appeared in the October 18, 1992, edition of *The Los Angeles Times Magazine*. Copyright © 1992 by Wanda Coleman. Reprinted with permission from the author.

James Crawford, from "Guardians of English" and "Democracy and Language," from *Hold Your Tongue: Bilingualism and the Politics of English Only* (pp. 3–5, 257–60, 277) by James Crawford. Copyright © 1992 by James Crawford. Reprinted with permission of Addison-Wesley Publishing Company, Inc.

Douglas Crimp and Adam Rolston, from "AIDS Activist Graphics: A Demonstration" from *AIDS Demographics* by Douglas Crimp and Adam Rolston. Copyright © 1990 by Douglas Crimp and Adam Rolston. Reprinted with permission from Bay Press.

e. e. cummings, from "she being Brand" from *is: 5 poems* by e. e. cummings, edited by George James Firmage. Copyright © 1985 by e. e. cummings Trust. Copyright 1926 by Horace Liveright. Copyright © 1954 by e. e. cummings. Copyright © 1985 by George James Firmage. Reprinted with permission of Liveright Publishing Corporation.

Holly B. Devor, "Gender Role Behaviors and Attitudes" from *Gender Blending*. Copyright © 1989 by Indiana University Press. Reprinted by permission of Indiana University Press.

Umberto Eco, "*Casablanca,* or, the Clichés Are Having a Ball" by Umberto Eco. Copyright © 1984 by Umberto Eco. Reprinted by permission of Umberto Eco.

715

Barbara Ehrenreich, "Ice-T: Is the Issue Creative Freedom?" originally titled ". . . Or Is It Creative Freedom?" First appeared in the June 20, 1992, issue of *Time* magazine. Copyright © 1992 by Time Inc. Reprinted with permission.

Gary Engle, "What Makes Superman So Darned American?" from *Superman at Fifty!* by Gary Engle. Copyright © 1987 by Octavia Press. Reprinted with permission from Octavia Press.

Stuart Ewen, from "Form Follows Power," from *All Consuming Images* by Stuart Ewen. Copyright © 1988 by Basic Books, Inc. Reprinted with permission from Basic Books, a division of HarperCollins Publishers, Inc.

Susan Faludi, "Teen Angels and Tart-Tongued Witches," originally titled "Teen Angels and Unwed Witches: The Backlash on TV," from *Backlash: The Undeclared War Against American Women* by Susan Faludi. Copyright © 1991 by Susan Faludi. Reprinted by permission from Crown Publishers, Inc.

"Four minimum-wage jobs" reprinted with courtesy of Duck Head Apparel.

Sam Fulwood III, "The Rage of the Black Middle Class," originally appeared in the November 3, 1991, edition of *The Los Angeles Times Magazine*. Copyright © 1992 by Sam Fulwood III. Reprinted by permission of Sam Fulwood III.

Peter Gibian, "The Art of Being Off-Center: Shopping Spaces and Spectacles" by Peter Gibian. Originally appeared in Tabloid #5 (1981). Copyright 1981 by Peter Gibian. Reprinted with permission of the author.

Todd Gitlin, "On the Virtues of a Loose Canon," from the Summer 1991 edition of *New Perspectives Quarterly*. Copyright © 1991 by *New Perspectives Quarterly*. Reprinted with permission of *New Perspectives Quarterly*.

Richard Goldstein, "Hate Speech, Free Speech, and the Unspoken" was originally published in *Tikkun*. Reprinted from *Tikkun* magazine, a bi-monthly Jewish critique of politics, culture, and society. Subscriptions are $31.00 per year from *Tikkun*, 251 West 100th Street, 5th floor, New York, NY 10025.

Thomas C. Grey, "Responding to Abusive Speech on Campus: A Model Statute" by Thomas C. Grey. Originally appeared in the Winter 1990 edition of *Reconstruction*. Copyright © 1990 by Thomas C. Grey. Reprinted with permission from *Reconstruction* and the author.

Guess? advertisement is reprinted with permission of Guess?, Inc.

Evelynn Hammonds, "Race, Sex, AIDS: The Construction of "Other" by Evelynn Hammonds. Originally appeared in *Radical America*, vol. 20. Copyright © 1987 by Evelynn Hammonds. Reprinted with permission of the author.

Nat Hentoff, "'Speech Codes' on the Campus and the Problems of Free Speech," from the Fall 1991 issue of *Dissent*. Copyright © 1991 by Nat Hentoff. Reprinted with the permission of the author.

Richard K. Herrell, "The Symbolic Strategies of Chicago's Gay and Lesbian Pride Day Parade," from *Gay Culture in America*, edited by Gilbert Herdt. Copyright © 1992 by Beacon Press. Reprinted with permission of Beacon Press.

bell hooks, "Madonna: Plantation Mistress or Soul Sister?" from *Black Looks: Race and Representation* by bell hooks. Copyright © 1992 by bell hooks. Reprinted with the permission of South End Press.

Minabere Ibelema, "Identity Crisis: The African Connection in African American Sitcom Characters" from *Sexual Politics and Popular Culture*, edited by Diane Raymond. Copyright © 1990 by The Popular Press of Bowling Green State University. Reprinted by permission of The Popular Press of Bowling Green State University.

Leslie Marmon Silko, "Language and Literature from a Pueblo Indian Perspective," from *English Literature: Opening Up the Canon,* edited by Leslie A. Fiedler and Houston A. Baker, Jr. Copyright © 1979 by The Johns Hopkins University Press. Reprinted with permission from The Johns Hopkins University Press.

Susan Sontag, from *AIDS and Its Metaphors* by Susan Sontag. Copyright © 1989 by Susan Sontag. Reprinted with permission of Hill & Wang, a division of Farrar, Straus & Giroux.

Shelby Steele, "Malcolm Little" Copyright © 1993 by The New Republic, Inc. Reprinted by permission of *The New Republic.*

Gloria Steinem, from "Sex, Lies, and Advertising" by Gloria Steinem. Originally published in *Ms.* magazine. Copyright © 1990 by Gloria Steinem. Reprinted by permission of the author.

Deborah Tannen, "Wears Jump Suit. Sensible Shoes. Uses Husband's Last Name." Originally appeared in the June 20, 1993 issue of the *New York Times Magazine.* Copyright © 1993 by Deborah Tannen. Reprinted with permission of the author.

Teen Angels Magazine, "Summertime" art. Originally appeared in *Teen Angels* Magazine, no. 114. Reprinted by permission of *Teen Angels* Magazine.

Studs Terkel, "Peter Soderstrom," "Ron Maydon," and "Margaret Welch" from *Race: How Blacks and Whites Think About the American Obsession* by Studs Terkel. Copyright © 1992 by Studs Terkel. Reprinted with permission of The New Press.

James Diego Vigil, "Gang Styles: Cholo Dress and Body Adornment" from *Barrio Gangs: Street Life and Identity in Southern California* by James Diego Vigil. Copyright © 1988 by James Diego Vigil. Reprinted by permission of the author and the University of Texas Press.

"Weld a Peace Sign to the Hood" reprinted courtesy of Subaru of America.

Andrew Wernick, from "Vehicles for Myth: The Shifting Image of the Modern Car" from *Cultural Politics in Contemporary America,* edited by Ian Angus and Sut Jhally. Reprinted with permission of Sage Publications.

Cornel West, "Diverse New World" originally appeared in the July/August 1991 issue of *Democratic Left,* vol. XIX, No. 4. Copyright © 1991 by Cornel West. Reprinted with permission of the author.

"What Would You Do? Ask people to judge me by my ability, not my disability" reprinted courtesy of Esprit de Corp.

"Who Says Guys Are Afraid of Commitment?" reprinted courtesy of Eastpak.

Patricia J. Williams, from "Gilded Lilies and Liberal Guilt" and "A Word on Categories" from *The Alchemy of Race and Rights* by Patricia J. Williams. Copyright © 1991 by the President and Fellows of Harvard College. Reprinted with permission of Harvard University Press.

Elizabeth Wilson, "Oppositional Dress" from *Adorned in Dreams: Fashion and Modernity* by Elizabeth Wilson. Copyright © 1985 by Elizabeth Wilson. Reprinted by permission of The University of California Press and Virago.

Frontispiece Credits

Chapter One
Mall of America photograph appears courtesy of Steve Woit / NYT Pictures.

Chapter Two
Eveready Bunny appears courtesy of Eveready Battery Company, Inc.

INDEX OF
AUTHORS AND
TITLES

Adams, McCrea, *Advertising Characters: The Pantheon of Consumerism,* 359

Advertising Characters: The Pantheon of Consumerism (Adams), 359

AIDS and Its Metaphors (Sontag), 668

AIDSpeak Spoken Here (Shilts), 703

Anna (Chiseri-Strater), 635

Antihero Worship (Rainer), 318

Anzaldúa, Gloria, *How to Tame a Wild Tongue,* 431

Art of Being Off-Center, The: Shopping Center Spaces and Spectacles (Gibian), 32

Barthel, Diane, *A Gentleman and a Consumer,* 128

Barthes, Roland, *Toys,* 95

Batman, Deviance, and Camp (Medhurst), 323

B-Boys (Poulson-Bryant), 56

Bing, Léon, *Faro,* 540

Bly, Robert, *Men's Initiation Rites,* 617

Borrowed Time: An AIDS Memoir (Monette), 661

Boyd, Valerie, *The Word on Malcolm X,* 296

Brubach, Holly, *Rock-and-Roll Vaudeville,* 175

Bruce, Tammy. *See* Lafferty and Bruce, 422

Campbell, Anne, *The Praised and the Damned,* 544

Caputi, Jane, *IBM's Charlie Chaplin: A Case Study,* 117

Casablanca, or the Clichés Are Having a Ball (Eco), 260

Children in Gangs (Rogers), 535

Chiseri-Strater, Elizabeth, *Anna,* 635

Class and Virtue (Parenti), 283

Classroom and the Wider Culture, The: Identity as a Key to Learning English Composition (Shen), 485

Coleman, Wanda, *Say It Ain't Cool, Joe,* 356

721

Cool Pose: The Proud Signature of Black Survival (Majors), 471

Crawford, James, *Hold Your Tongue: The Question of Linguistic Self-Determination,* 424

Creating the Myth (Seger), 250

Crimp, Douglas, and Rolston, Adam, *The Semiotics of AIDS Activism,* 708

Dead White Male Heterosexual Poets Society (Modleski), 278

Devor, Holly, *Gender Role Behaviors and Attitudes,* 603

Diverse New World (West), 400

Doomed by Deconstructo (Jones, Randall, and Elliott), 370

Eco, Umberto, Casablanca, *or, the Clichés Are Having a Ball,* 260

Ehrenreich, Barbara, *Ice-T: Is the Issue Creative Freedom?,* 418

Elliott, Randy. *See* Jones, Randall, and Elliott

Engle, Gary, *What Makes Superman So Damned American?,* 309

Ewen, Stuart, *Hard Bodies,* 60

Faludi, Susan, *Teen Angels and Tart-Tongued Witches,* 219

Faro (Bing), 540

Fiction of Truth in Advertising, The (Williams), 122

Fraternal Bond as a Joking Relationship, The (Lyman), 609

From Common Dullness to Fleeting Wonder: The Manipulation of Cultural Meaning in the Teenage Mutant Ninja Turtles Saga (Lewis, G.), 340

Fulwood, Sam, III, *The Rage of the Black Middle Class,* 462

Gang Styles: Cholo Dress and Body Adornment (Vigil), 570

Gender Role Behaviors and Attitudes (Devor), 603

Gentleman and a Consumer, A (Barthel), 128

Gibian, Peter, *The Art of Being Off-Center: Shopping Center Spaces and Spectacles,* 32

Gitlin, Todd, *On the Virtues of a Loose Canon,* 405

Goldstein, Richard, *Hate Speech, Free Speech, and the Unspoken,* 411

Grey, Thomas C., *Responding to Abusive Speech on Campus: A Model Statute,* 392

Hammonds, Evelynn, *Race, Sex, AIDS: The Construction of "Other",* 692

Hard Bodies (Ewen), 60

Hate Speech, Free Speech, and the Unspoken (Goldstein), 411

Hentoff, Nat, *"Speech Codes" on the Campus and Problems of Free Speech,* 385

Herrell, Richard K., *The Symbolic Strategies of Chicago's Gay and Lesbian Pride Day Parade,* 643

Hispanic in America: Starting Points (Isasi-Diaz), 503

Hold Your Tongue: The Question of Linguistic Self-Determination (Crawford), 424

hooks, bell, *Madonna: Plantation Mistress or Soul Sister?,* 190

How to Tame a Wild Tongue (Anzaldúa), 431

Ibelema, Minabere, *Identity Crisis: The African Connection in African American Sitcom Characters,* 198

IBM's Charlie Chaplin: A Case Study (Caputi), 117

Ice-T: Is the Issue Creative Freedom?
(Ehrenreich), 418
*Identity Crisis: The African Connection
in African American Sitcom
Characters* (Minabere), 198
*In Living Color: Race and American
Culture* (Omi), 449
Isasi-Diaz, Ada María, *Hispanic in
America: Starting Points,* 503

Jones, Gerard; Randall, Ron; and
Elliott, Randy, *Doomed by
Deconstructo,* 370

Kirn, Walter, *Twentysomethings,* 229
Kondo, Dorinne K., *On Being a
Conceptual Anomaly,* 477
Kron, Joan, *The Semiotics of Home
Decor,* 66

Lafferty, Elaine, and Bruce, Tammy,
Suddenly, They Hear the Words,
422
Lakoff, Robin Tolmach, *Women's
Language,* 624
*Language and Literature from a Pueblo
Indian Perspective* (Silko), 495
Lewis, George H., *From Common
Dullness to Fleeting Wonder: The
Manipulation of Cultural Meaning
in the Teenage Mutant Ninja
Turtles Saga,* 340
Lewis, Lisa A., *Male-Address Video,* 182
Lyman, Peter, *The Fraternal Bond as a
Joking Relationship,* 609

Maasik, Sonia, and Solomon, Jack,
Signs of the Street: A Conversation,
560
*Madonna: Plantation Mistress or Soul
Sister?* (hooks), 190
Majors, Richard, *Cool Pose: The Proud
Signature of Black Survival,* 471

"Malcolm X" (Steele), 287
Male-Address Video (Lewis, L.), 182
Marchand, Roland, *The Parable of the
Democracy of Goods,* 109
Medhurst, Andy, *Batman, Deviance,
and Camp,* 323
Men's Initiation Rites (Bly), 617
Modleski, Tania, *Dead White Male
Heterosexual Poets Society,* 278
Monette, Paul, *Borrowed Time: An
AIDS Memoir,* 661
More Factor, The (Shames), 25
Mydans, Seth, *Not Just the Inner City:
Well-to-Do Join Gangs,* 587

Not as Tough as It Looks (Raymond),
264
*Not Just the Inner City: Well-to-Do Join
Gangs* (Mydans), 587

Omi, Michael, *In Living Color: Race
and American Culture,* 449
On Being a Conceptual Anomaly
(Kondo), 477
On the Virtues of a Loose Canon
(Gitlin), 405
Oppositional Dress (Wilson), 45
Our Barbies, Ourselves (Prager), 353
Ozersky, Josh, *TV's Anti-Families:
Married . . . with Malaise,* 209

Parable of the Democracy of Goods, The
(Marchand), 109
Parenti, Michael, *Class and Virtue,*
283
Portfolio of Advertisements, 156
Poulson-Bryant, Scott, *B-Boys,* 56
Prager, Emily, *Our Barbies, Ourselves,*
353
Praised and the Damned, The
(Campbell), 544

Quam, Michael D., *Stigma,* 679

Race, Sex, AIDS: The Construction of "Other" (Hammonds), 692

Rage of the Black Middle Class, The (Fulwood), 462

Rainer, Peter, *Antihero Worship,* 318

Randall, Ron. *See* Jones, Randall, and Elliott, 370

Ray, Robert B., *The Thematic Paradigm,* 241

Raymond, Diane, *Not as Tough as It Looks,* 264

Responding to Abusive Speech on Campus: A Model Statute (Grey), 392

Rock-and-Roll Vaudeville (Brubach), 175

Rogers, Carl, *Children in Gangs,* 535

Rolston, Adam. *See* Crimp and Rolston, 708

Say *It Ain't Cool, Joe* (Coleman), 356

Scannell, Kate, *Skills and Pills,* 688

Seger, Linda, *Creating the Myth,* 250

Semiotics of AIDS Activism, The (Crimp and Rolston), 708

Semiotics of Home Decor, The (Kron), 66

Sex, Lies, and Advertising (Steinem), 139

Shames, Laurence, *The More Factor,* 25

Shen, Fan, *The Classroom and the Wider Culture: Identity as a Key to Learning English Composition,* 485

Shilts, Randy, *AIDSpeak Spoken Here,* 703

Signs of the Street: A Conversation (Maasik and Solomon), 560

Silko, Leslie Marmon, *Language and Literature from a Pueblo Indian Perspective,* 495

Skills and Pills (Scannell), 688

Solomon, Jack. *See* Maasik and Solomon, 560

Sontag, Susan, *AIDS and Its Metaphors,* 668

Speaking About Race (Terkel), 508

"Speech Codes" on the Campus and Problems of Free Speech (Hentoff), 385

Steele, Shelby, "Malcolm X", 287

Steinem, Gloria, *Sex, Lies, and Advertising,* 139

Stigma (Quam), 679

Suddenly, They Hear the Words (Lafferty and Bruce), 422

"Summer Time": An Illustration from Teen Angels Magazine, 592–93

Symbolic Strategies of Chicago's Gay and Lesbian Pride Day Parade, The (Herrell), 643

Tannen, Deborah, *Wears Jump Suit. Sensible Shoes. Uses Husband's Last Name,* 629

Teen Angels and Tart-Tongued Witches (Faludi), 219

Terkel, Studs, *Speaking About Race,* 508

Thematic Paradigm, The (Ray), 241

Toys (Barthes), 95

TV's Anti-Families: Married . . . with Malaise (Ozersky), 209

Twentysomethings (Kirn), 229

Vehicles for Myth: The Shifting Image of the Modern Car (Wernick), 78

Vigil, James Diego, *Gang Styles: Cholo Dress and Body Adornment,* 570

Wears Jump Suit. Sensible Shoes. Uses Husband's Last Name (Tannen), 629

Wernick, Andrew, *Vehicles for Myth: The Shifting Image of the Modern Car,* 78

West, Cornel, *Diverse New World,* 400

What Makes Superman So Darned American? (Engle), 309

Williams, Patricia J., *The Fiction of Truth in Advertising,* 122

Wilson, Elizabeth, *Oppositional Dress,* 45

Women's Language (Lakoff), 624

Word on Malcolm X, *The* (Boyd), 296

To the Student

We regularly revise the books we publish to make them better. To do this well we need to know what instructors and students think of the previous edition. At some point your instructor will be asked to comment on *Signs of Life in the U.S.A.*; now we would like to hear from you.

Please take a few minutes to rate the selections and complete this questionnaire. Send it to Bedford Books of St. Martin's Press, 29 Winchester Street, Boston, Massachusetts, 02116. We promise to listen to what you have to say. Thanks.

School _____

School location (city, state) _____

Course title _____

Instructor's name _____

	Liked a lot	Okay	Didn't like	Didn't read
1. Consuming Passions				
Shames, *The More Factor*	____	____	____	____
Gibian, *The Art of Being Off-Center*	____	____	____	____
Wilson, *Oppositional Dress*	____	____	____	____
Poulson-Bryant, *B-Boys*	____	____	____	____
Ewen, *Hard Bodies*	____	____	____	____
Kron, *The Semiotics of Home Decor*	____	____	____	____
Wernick, *Vehicles for Myth*	____	____	____	____
Barthes, *Toys*	____	____	____	____
2. Brought to You B(u)y				
Marchand, *The Parable of the Democracy of Goods*	____	____	____	____
Caputi, *IBM's Charlie Chaplin*	____	____	____	____
Williams, *The Fiction of Truth in Advertising*	____	____	____	____
Barthel, *A Gentleman and a Consumer*	____	____	____	____
Steinem, *Sex, Lies, and Advertising*	____	____	____	____
Portfolio of Advertisements	____	____	____	____

	Liked a lot	Okay	Didn't like	Didn't read

3. M(ore) TV

	Liked a lot	Okay	Didn't like	Didn't read
Brubach, *Rock-and-Roll Vaudeville*	____	____	____	____
Lewis, *Male-Address Video*	____	____	____	____
hooks, *Madonna: Plantation Mistress or Soul Sister?*	____	____	____	____
Ibelema, *Identity Crisis*	____	____	____	____
Ozersky, *TV's Anti-Families*	____	____	____	____
Faludi, *Teen Angels and Tart-Tongued Witches*	____	____	____	____
Kirn, *Twentysomethings*	____	____	____	____

4. The Hollywood Sign

	Liked a lot	Okay	Didn't like	Didn't read
Ray, *The Thematic Paradigm*	____	____	____	____
Seger, *Creating the Myth*	____	____	____	____
Eco, Casablanca, *or, the Clichés Are Having a Ball*	____	____	____	____
Raymond, *Not As Tough As it Looks*	____	____	____	____
Modleski, *Dead White Male Heterosexual Poets Society*	____	____	____	____
Parenti, *Class and Virtue*	____	____	____	____
Steele, *Malcolm X*	____	____	____	____
Boyd, *The Word on* Malcolm X	____	____	____	____

5. Larger Than Life

	Liked a lot	Okay	Didn't like	Didn't read
Engle, *What Makes Superman So Darned American?*	____	____	____	____
Rainer, *Antihero Worship*	____	____	____	____
Medhurst, *Batman, Deviance, and Camp*	____	____	____	____
Lewis, *From Common Dullness to Fleeting Wonder*	____	____	____	____
Prager, *Our Barbies, Ourselves*	____	____	____	____
Coleman, *Say It Ain't Cool, Joe*	____	____	____	____
Adams, *Advertising Characters*	____	____	____	____

	Liked a lot	Okay	Didn't like	Didn't read
Jones, Ron Randall, Randy Elliott, *Doomed by Deconstructo*	___	___	___	___

6. Speak No Evil

Hentoff, *'Speech Codes' on the Campus and Problems of Free Speech*	___	___	___	___
Grey, *Responding to Abusive Speech on Campus*	___	___	___	___
West, *Diverse New World*	___	___	___	___
Gitlin, *On the Virtues of a Loose Canon*	___	___	___	___
Goldstein, *Hate Speech, Free Speech, and the Unspoken*	___	___	___	___
Ehrenreich, *Ice-T*	___	___	___	___
Lafferty and Bruce, *Suddenly, They Hear the Words*	___	___	___	___
Crawford, *Hold Your Tongue*	___	___	___	___
Anzaldúa, *How to Tame a Wild Tongue*	___	___	___	___

7. A Gathering of Tribes

Omi, *In Living Color*	___	___	___	___
Fulwood III, *The Rage of the Black Middle Class*	___	___	___	___
Majors, *Cool Pose*	___	___	___	___
Kondo, *On Being a Conceptual Anomaly*	___	___	___	___
Shen, *The Classroom and the Wider Culture*	___	___	___	___
Silko, *Language and Literature from a Pueblo Indian Perspective*	___	___	___	___
Isasi-Diaz, *Hispanic in America*	___	___	___	___
Terkel, *Speaking About Race*	___	___	___	___

8. Street Signs

Rogers, *Children in Gangs*	___	___	___	___
Bing, *Faro*	___	___	___	___
Campbell, *The Praised and the Damned*	___	___	___	___

	Liked a lot	Okay	Didn't like	Didn't read
Maasik and Solomon, *Signs of the Street*	___	___	___	___
Vigil, *Gang Styles*	___	___	___	___
Mydans, *Not Just the Inner City*	___	___	___	___
"Summer Time": An Illustration from *Teen Angels* Magazine	___	___	___	___

9. You've Come a Long Way, Maybe

	Liked a lot	Okay	Didn't like	Didn't read
Devor, *Gender Role Behaviors and Attitudes*	___	___	___	___
Lyman, *The Fraternal Bond as a Joking Relationship*	___	___	___	___
Bly, *Men's Initiation Rites*	___	___	___	___
Lakoff, *Women's Language*	___	___	___	___
Tannen, *Wears Jump Suit. Sensible Shoes. Uses Husband's Last Name.*	___	___	___	___
Chiseri-Strater, *Anna*	___	___	___	___
Herrell, *The Symbolic Strategies of Chicago's Gay and Lesbian Pride Day Parade*	___	___	___	___

10. Journals of the Plague Years

	Liked a lot	Okay	Didn't like	Didn't read
Monette, *Borrowed Time*	___	___	___	___
Sontag, *AIDS and Its Metaphors*	___	___	___	___
Quam, *Stigma*	___	___	___	___
Scannell, *Skills and Pills*	___	___	___	___
Hammonds, *Race, Sex, AIDS*	___	___	___	___
Shilts, *AIDSpeak Spoken Here*	___	___	___	___
Crimp and Rolston, *The Semiotics of AIDS Activism*	___	___	___	___